the
world
beyond
the
hill

Books by Alexei Panshin:

Heinlein in Dimension (1968)
Rite of Passage (1968)
Star Well (1968)
The Thurb Revolution (1968)
Masque World (1969)
Farewell to Yesterday's Tomorrow (1975)
Transmutations (1982)

Books by Alexei and Cory Panshin:

SF in Dimension (1976)
Mondi Interiori (1978)
Earth Magic (1978)

the world beyond the hill

SCIENCE FICTION AND THE QUEST FOR TRANSCENDENCE

Alexei and Cory Panshin

JEREMY P. TARCHER, INC.
Los Angeles

Library of Congress Cataloging in Publication Data

Panshin, Alexei
    The world beyond the hill : science fiction and the quest for trans-
cendence / Alexei and Cory Panshin.
        p.   cm.
    Includes index.
    1. Science fiction–History and criticism.   I. Panshin, Cory.   II. Title.
PN3433.5.P26   1989   89-35626
809.3'8762–dc20   CIP

0-87477-436-5

Jeremy P. Tarcher, Inc.
9110 Sunset Blvd.
Los Angeles, CA 90069

Design by Rosa Schuth

Typesetting by Elephant Books
RD 1, Box 168
Riegelsville, Pennsylvania 18077

Manufactured in the United States of America

10   9   8   7   6   5   4   3   2   1

This book is dedicated to

John W. Campbell
Edmond Hamilton
E. E. "Doc" Smith
and
Jack Williamson

CONTENTS

The intermediary between the world of Mystery and the world of visibility can only be the Imagination...

—IBN ARABI

For as long as we humans have existed in our present intermediate state as creatures more than merely animal but also less human than we can be and will be, there have been mythic storytellers. These are men and women who have taken the best knowledge of their time and place and combined it with a sense of the incompleteness of mankind and the fundamental mystery of existence, and then told stories of higher possibility: Stories of fear and wonder. Stories of quest into unknown lands and return with magical gifts which transform the world. Stories of the beginning and the end of all things.

The myths that we learn as we are growing up provide us with guidance in life. In their conservative aspect, myths confirm us in our localness. They teach us how to be a citizen of Rome, a Huichol Indian, or a contemporary American. But far more important is that in their radical aspect, myths alert us to the limitations of how we presently live and who we take ourselves to be, and lead us on toward what we are not yet.

By the manner in which we conduct ourselves and the goals for which we strive, we attempt to make our myths come true in the world. The efforts we make change the world and alter our knowledge. Then new myths become necessary.

The myth of the modern Western world has been science fiction. The ability of this literature to guide our efforts and set our goals can be seen all around us.

The submarine that first traveled to the North Pole—the first nuclear-powered ship—was named the *Nautilus* after the super-scientific submarine of Jules Verne's Captain Nemo. And its commander would later say that he had been inspired to become a submariner by reading *20,000 Leagues Under the Sea* as a youngster.

The idea that an atomic bomb might actually be made first came to a physicist who had originally encountered the concept of atomic weapons in a story by H.G. Wells.

An orbital shuttle—an almost-spaceship—has been named the *Enterprise* after the galaxy-exploring spaceship imagined in the television series *Star Trek.*

The world that we live in has been formed in the image of the myth of science fiction. Anything we use today may have been made by a robot. Children play interactive games with household computers, and thinking machines play championship-level chess. Men in rockets have traveled to the moon, and we have even sent off greetings to the stars.

The story of the complete life cycle of this myth is presented in this book, beginning with the first faint glimmerings that "science" might be a new name for higher possibility, and ending with modern mythmakers able to imagine that mankind might assume control of its own destiny, establish a galaxy-wide stellar empire, and evolve into a higher order of being.

For those who are interested in the dynamics of myth, this book tells how a new myth comes into being, how the makers of myth conceive and produce their stories, how myth both responds to worldly change and anticipates it, and how one myth at the conclusion of its usefulness may evolve into another.

For those who have love for the myth of science fiction, this book shows where its central ideas and images came from and how they developed, from a time prior to the point when this literature even had a name up until the moment of crisis and opportunity when mythmakers came to the realization that their sense of higher human potential could no longer be contained by the name "science" and began to use another.

And for those with dreams of a sounder, more holistic, more human way of life beyond the fragmentation and purposelessness which presently dominate our society, this book indicates not only how our myths change us, but how we change our myths. It shows how the storytellers of SF, having come to recognize the limitations of a world built upon scientific materialism, altered their myth and laid down the basis for a new age of higher consciousness.

The Mystery of
Science Fiction

Science fiction is a literature of the mythic imagination. In science fiction stories, spaceships and time machines carry us outside ourselves, outside our world, outside everything we know, to distant realms that none of us has ever seen—to the future and outer space. In science fiction, we encounter unknown powers, alien beings, and worlds of wonder where things become possible that are presently impossible to us.

These marvels, these symbols of transcendent possibility, are the very essence of science fiction. They are the source of science fiction's fascination and appeal. Without them, science fiction would be just like everything else—normal, known, ordinary, and commonplace. As it is, science fiction is irrational, extraordinary, elusive, wonderful, never completely to be known.

The acknowledgment of transcendence was present from the moment that science fiction existed as a distinct literary form.

It was the conscious hope of Hugo Gernsback, the immigrant technocrat who named the genre, that science fiction should be fiction about science. It was Gernsback's aim to publish a literature that would foresee the possibilities of science-to-come, stories of imaginary technology, stories that would be extravagant fiction today, but cold fact tomorrow.

To this end, in 1924, Gernsback sent out a circular to 25,000 people announcing a new magazine. It was to be called *Scientifiction*. This was a portmanteau word of Gernsback's own devising, meaning "scientific fiction." But the response to Gernsback's circular was so poor that he abandoned his idea for two years.

Then, in March 1926, Gernsback took a gamble. Without any prior announcement, he issued the first number of a new magazine which he described as "a magazine of scientifiction." But this magazine was called *Amazing Stories*.

In an editorial in an early issue, Gernsback attempted to justify what he had done. He wrote:

We really need not make any excuse for *Amazing Stories*, because the title represents exactly what the stories really are. There is a standing rule in our editorial offices that unless the story is *amazing*, it should not be published in the magazine. To be sure, the amazing quality is only *one* requisite, because the story must contain science in *every* case.

Gernsback was able to fulfill his true desire to the extent that it was he who selected the name by which this new literature would present itself to the world-at-large: First "scientifiction," and then later the name that would stick—"science fiction."

But when Gernsback chose a title to attract an audience to the magazine he published, he had to put transcendence—"the amazing quality"—ahead of science.

And so it would be, again and again. The transcendence at the heart of science fiction can be seen revealed in the meanings of a whole constellation of words used as the titles of one science fiction magazine or another. These words have been the promise of the genre for those who have loved it: *amazing, astonishing, astounding, fantastic, marvel, miracle, startling, thrilling wonder, unknown, worlds beyond.*

These evocative words are related to each other. Many of them share common roots. To look up the meaning of one in the dictionary is inevitably to be referred to another:

To *astound* is to bewilder with sudden surprise, to amaze.

To *amaze* is to fill with great surprise or sudden wonder, to astonish.

To *astonish* is to fill with sudden wonder or surprise.

To *wonder* is to be seized or filled with amazement, to marvel.

To *marvel* is to become full of wonder, be astonished or surprised.

Around and around these words chase each other, all the while pointing to something unexpected, mysterious and impressive. The deeper we look into these words—and into the older words in other languages from which they sprang—the more we can see that taken together, they indicate a unique extra-dimensional presence.

What characteristics are to be discerned of this elephant in the dark?

It is baffling to the rational mind, as bewildering as a blow on the head. It is sudden or shocking. Its appearance is strange or weird. It is piercing, like being struck by a bolt of lightning. It causes shivers of excitement. It arouses feelings of admiration and awe. It apparently contradicts known scientific laws. It has a connection with the faculty of the imagination. It "seizes," it "fills," it "shows," it "makes visible." It is of a higher reality. It is the measure of things.

That is what these potent words have meant during their long history. They are the indications of transcendence: of unknown things, higher possibilities, and human becoming.

We are all familiar with the transcendent symbols of ancient myth. Even though they are no longer *believed in* by modern Western culture, these symbols have been preserved into the present in religious texts and fairytales and echoed in contemporary fantasy stories.

As examples, there are the marvelous old magical powers: wishing rings, enchanted swords, draughts of immortality, caps of invisibility, seven-league boots, ever-filled purses, wells of wisdom, runes, spells, curses and prophecies. There are the ancient mythic beings: gods and ghosts, witches and wizards, brownies and elves, ogres and angels, cyclopses and centaurs, giants and jinns. And in ancient myth, there are places of wonder, countries where anything might happen to us, mysterious realms with names like Eden and Arcadia, the Forest Primeval, Valhalla, the Isles of the Blessed, and East of the Sun and West of the Moon.

Science fiction has been different from this. Like ancient myth, science fiction has presented transcendent powers, beings and realms, but they have had very different names and been conceived of in different ways than the wonders and marvels of previous myth:

The transcendent powers of science fiction have been "scientific" rather than "magical" in nature.

The transcendent beings of science fiction have not been demons and spirits, but rather mechanical robots, mutated humans, and alien creatures from other planets.

The transcendent realms of science fiction have not been located in the heavens or the underworld of ancient religious conception. Instead, these marvelous countries have been placed in the outer space of astronomical study, or in the parallel worlds theoretically posited by our mathematics, or in the future.

From its beginnings, science fiction has been the mythic vehicle of one particular culture, the rational, materialistic, weigh-and-measure, science-and-technology minded culture that has arisen in Europe and America since the Renaissance—so-called modern Western civilization. As a myth, science fiction speaks in their own language to those persons who "think Western," those people who are the product of the logic of Descartes, the physics of Newton, the encyclopedism of Diderot, the skepticism of Voltaire, the practical experimentation of Franklin, the biology of Darwin, the inventions of Edison, and the revised relativistic physics of Einstein.

This is our culture's best knowledge. And active myth always presents the transcendent in terms which reflect current best knowledge and then reach beyond its bounds.

It is no accident that Hugo Gernsback declared that fiction in *Amazing Stories* had to be scientific—true to best knowledge—as well as transcendent. This is the recipe for myth in every culture and at every time.

We seek that which is beyond the bounds of our best knowledge. And when we find it, we bring it home and add it to our store. This is how human beings learn, and how cultures change and develop.

Fantasy stories are not fully mythic because they cling to ancient images of transcendent possibility which no longer appear plausible. Although these may inspire us with reminders of the mysteriousness of transcendence, they are inconsistent with our best knowledge and so cannot guide us to action.

Mundane fiction is also incompletely mythic because the only things it sees as possible are those which exist or which have existed. As strongly as it may reinforce our sense of plausible possibility, at best it can only present larger-than-life characters and situations that remind us of the existence of transcendence without actually daring to be transcendent.

Science fiction has been effective myth for our time because it respects both the actual and the transcendent. It takes account of what we know and what we don't and then looks beyond the here-and-now to thrill and inspire us with dreams of what might be.

This is the story of the dreams that have been presented by the modern myth of science fiction—and of the consequences when they began to come true.

PART 1

BEFORE
SCIENCE FICTION

*The end of our Foundation is the knowledge of Causes,
the secret motions of things; and the enlarging of the bounds
of Human Empire, to the effecting of all things possible.*

—*FRANCIS BACON*

2

A Mythic Fall

In founding *Amazing Stories* in 1926, Hugo Gernsback recognized science fiction as the special mythic vehicle of modern Western scientific culture. He gave the genre a name and a home of its own.

But science fiction was not Hugo Gernsback's private invention. SF had a long and slow proto-development before the days of Gernsback, before it was a named and recognized form.

Gernsback was aware of himself as working in a tradition that *Amazing Stories* was intended to extend. In his very first editorial in *Amazing*, Gernsback attempted to define and justify his "new" literary form by pointing to the work of three writers of the previous hundred years: "By 'scientifiction' I mean the Jules Verne, H.G. Wells, and Edgar Allan Poe type of story—a charming romance intermingled with scientific fact and prophetic vision."

But the true roots of that SF development which Gernsback consolidated under the name "science fiction" can be traced even earlier than the work of Edgar Allan Poe.

It would be fair to say that as soon as there was a special and distinctive modern Western mode of thought, there was a need and a potential for SF as a special and distinctive form of myth. And all of that which has happened up to Gernsback's time and since has been the gradual unfolding and fulfillment of that potential and that need.

The new myth of SF became necessary when a new worldview was adopted by the West during the Seventeenth Century. This worldview rejected the very basis of traditional conceptions of transcendence.

The transcendent symbols of ancient myth were all grounded in a fundamental belief in the existence of *spirit*, as distinct from *matter*. It was the given opinion of all traditional thought that there was a realm of spirit as well as a realm of matter with connections between the two. But it was spirit that was the more powerful and enduring, and closer to the true origin of things.

During the Seventeenth Century in the West, there was a great revolution of thought, a rebellion against *spirit* and the worldly order of kings and prelates that justified itself by appeal to the invisible. Men of a new scientific cast of mind appeared, concerned with objective examination of the world around them, men like Francis Bacon and Johannes Kepler, Galileo and Descartes. As the result of their writings and investigations, a new philosophy of rational materialism came to be adopted. In the view of this new Western philosophy, all that could not be proved, measured, or logically argued from material principles was subject to doubt.

The new scientific philosophy did not make its way easily or lightly. In 1600, the Italian philosopher Giordano Bruno was burned by the Inquisition for asserting, among other things, the existence of a multiplicity of worlds beyond our Earth. Other adherents of the new mode of thought were silenced, like Galileo, or imprisoned for years, like Tommaso Campanella. Nonetheless, through the Seventeenth Century, the attention of the West moved gradually but inexorably away from the invisible world of spirit and toward the study and manipulation of matter.

The concept of spirit was not immediately and totally discarded, but a sharp separation was made between spirit and matter. Two elements of spirit were still conceded, even by the most radical thinkers—God and the human soul. God was a cosmic clockmaker who, some long whiles past, had set the great machinery of the universe in motion, withdrawing discreetly to let it tick and whir its way to eternity. As for the human soul—one brave and tattered shred of spirit in a universe otherwise made of dead matter—why, that was the hope and promise of human specialness and purpose, and could not easily be surrendered. But the new prevailing materialistic philosophy of the West would not allow that God or the soul had any direct influence on the everyday cause-and-effect world.

An appropriate date to mark the emergence of scientific rationalism as the leading mode of Western thought and culture is the year 1685. It is possible to argue that the old worldview still prevailed prior to that time. But after that year, we can say that the balance of opinion in Western society was in favor of rational materialism.

We can see our point illustrated in two facts. The year 1685 was when the last execution for witchcraft in England took place. Also in England in 1685, Isaac Newton arrived at the Universal Law of Gravitation. In both cases, the passing of the old belief in the realm of spirit is indicated. After this, spirit-based witchcraft, for centuries the bugaboo of Western man, would no longer be given serious credence by leaders of opinion—the men who make and enforce the law. At the same time, a new rule of rational physics had proclaimed the high heavens—formerly considered to be a part of the spirit realm—to be subject to the same mechanisms that govern the motion of bodies on Earth.

The shift from one worldview to the other is visible in the imaginative literature of the Seventeenth Century. In the early years of the Seventeenth Century, in *Macbeth, Hamlet* and *The Tempest*, Shakespeare might write of witches, ghosts and magic. Even as late as the 1660s and 1670s, in *Paradise Lost* and *The Pilgrim's Progress*, John Milton and John Bunyan could still write with the old seriousness of Hell and Heaven. By the 1690s, this was no longer possible. The transcendent symbols of traditional mythic literature could no longer be considered plausible. As things of the spirit, they had no part in a material world.

By the turn of the century, the old wonders and marvels could only appear as the stuff of simple entertainments, such as the literary fairytales like "Cinderella" and "Beauty and the Beast" that were the delight of the French court during the Age of Reason. One of these, "Princess Rosette" by Madame d'Aulnoy, who died in 1705, may serve as an example of the degree to which even fairytales were affected by the change in worldview. The one fantastic element in this story is the troop of fairies who come to the princess's christening. But these once clearly transcendent beings apparently live in the vicinity of the court rather than in their own spirit realm of Faerie. And instead of giving the child traditional magical gifts—we are told "they had left their book of magic at home"—their role is reduced to giving well-intentioned but incomplete and misleading advice.

The new scientific doubt of the Seventeenth Century was a powerful weapon, a glittering inevitable razor. One slash—and all that was not subject to measurement, to proof or to rational argument was cut away!

A great simplification was undergone in the West. Long-standing political arrangements, the power of religion, the social order itself—all these were eventually to be altered by the change in belief. Much was gained and much was lost in the shift of worldview.

On the one hand, in the West, the great static accumulated weight of the invisible spirit realm was shrugged off. Popular revolutions of a kind previously unthinkable took place in England in 1642 and 1688 and in France in 1789. Kings with a right to rule that had been given to them by God were turned into mere mortal men who might be executed or sent into exile. The Roman Catholic church, which had held the power and dignity of a state for more than a thousand years, was reduced to wielding a merely theoretical authority.

The superstitions of the ages were discarded overnight. There was a great release of pent-up energy. Everything was open to examination; nothing was free from doubt. Armed with his newly invented weapons and machines, his science and skepticism, Western man set off to conquer the whole world.

On the other hand, what was sacrificed was also great: all traditional wisdom, morality, and knowledge based in spirit. Western man, as he launched himself into the world-at-large, was a brainy toolmaker with no morals, out for the main chance, practical, powerful and unscrupulous.

There have always been those in the West who have regretted the choice that was made. For as long as the new ways have been adopted, there have been nostalgists who have longed for the secure order of the old ways, who have wished again for the comfort of mother church and the natural order of feudal society.

But, of course, there is no going back. We are now three hundred years down this particular road. The existential decision to abandon the old given spiritual authority has been made, and it is compelling. Whether we like it or not, we in the West are condemned to examine everything for ourselves and to accept responsibility for the decisions that we make. We were set on this road long ago and we cannot resist it now. We can only follow it out to the end and see where it leads, remembering as we do that what far too often has been taken by Western man as a right to license in the absence of moral rule, first began as the existential moral decision to subject all aspects of life to scientific scrutiny.

Among that which was discarded when Western man set out on his special path was traditional myth with its spirit-based transcendent symbology. The appearance and development of SF can be understood as the gradual re-establishment of myth in the Western world, starting from first principles, and phrasing itself in a new, deliberately "non-spiritual" symbolic vocabulary. From 1685 until the time of Gernsback and his consolidation of the genre, SF developed almost subliminally, slowly working out those basic arguments that would permit transcendent powers, beings and realms to be considered plausible within the special terms and standards of Western rationality and materialism.

But the very first step that was taken by SF—the new myth—was a fall. *Hamlet* and *Paradise Lost*, which might be named as final works written within the old imaginative order, are high literature. The Age of Reason can boast no imaginative work of comparable stature.

The early Eighteenth Century is a mythic desert. There is very little imaginative literature of any kind from this period, as though without recourse to the traditional symbols, the mythic faculty was stunned into silence.

What little imaginative work there was, like *Gulliver's Travels*, can boast only such limited wonders as dwarfs and giants and talking horses employed for purposes of satire. Next to examples of the old myth like *The Odyssey* or *Beowulf*, *The Divine Comedy* or *Doctor Faustus*, a story like *Gulliver's Travels* must seem an imaginative, moral and mythic reduction.

The nearest thing to a new contemporary myth that the period could offer was the utopian story. Though a form of fiction, utopian stories primarily consisted of static and didactic descriptions of the workings of the Perfected Society. This superior mode of living, conceived as the outward expression of man's God-given rational soul, was the only transcendence this form of imaginative literature had to offer.

In the absence of high mythic literature—epic, romance and tragedy—the new major literary form of the Eighteenth Century was the mimetic novel of social and sexual intrigue, the reflection of the mundane, materialistic middle-class world that was beginning to emerge. One reason that SF developed in comparative obscurity from the beginning of the Age of Reason and Enlightenment to Gernsback's time was that imaginative literature in general was completely overshadowed by the successes of the mimetic novel as exemplified by Fielding and Austen, Dickens and Dostoevsky, Tolstoy and Twain. Beside fictions about the real factual world of materiality, the new SF seemed frivolous stuff, merely fanciful.

And SF was also overshadowed by the imaginative literature of former times, which was still held in high regard, even though it was no longer believed in. Next to ancient myth—or even next to comparatively graceless contemporary imitations or retellings of ancient myth—the new SF seemed trivial.

Trivial and frivolous—those were the beginnings from which science fiction grew. SF before Gernsback, and even since, has very often been trivial and frivolous—that is, apparently playful and unserious. Deliberately courting these qualities has been a survival strategy for SF in its times of unpopularity, a way of attracting an audience craving to be entertained, and even a deliberate artistic method. But underneath this protective disguise of playful unserious-ness, throughout its history SF has been continuously engaged in the very serious business of reestablishing transcendence in all its guises, and the reinvention of high myth.

The state of the invisible and nonexistent SF of the Eighteenth

Century—its uncertainty, its limitation, its special problems and the first tentative steps toward their solution—is best illustrated by one novel published nearly eighty years into the rational era: *The Castle of Otranto* (1764), by Sir Horace Walpole. What is significant about *The Castle of Otranto* insofar as SF is concerned is that it was the first attempt to reshape traditional mythic material into a form acceptable to the modern Western sensibility.

The author of *The Castle of Otranto*, Sir Horace Walpole, was the youngest child of a British prime minister. Walpole was himself a member of Parliament, an extreme political liberal, but is better remembered as a writer of letters and as an eccentric. Walpole was a nostalgist, an antiquarian, one of those who long for the bygone days and ways. In 1753, he began the physical conversion of his country villa, Strawberry Hill, into a little Gothic castle, with details copied out of one book and another. The haunted medieval castle described in *The Castle of Otranto* is Strawberry Hill combined with Trinity College, Cambridge, and written large.

The Castle of Otranto is Walpole's only novel, although he wrote one play and a number of other books, including a defense of Richard III. Like various SF stories in other eras, *The Castle of Otranto* came to its author in a dream, and then gripped him utterly. In 1765, the year after it was written, Walpole described its genesis in a letter to a friend:

> I waked one morning in the beginning of last June from a dream, of which all I could recover was, that I had thought myself in an ancient castle (a very natural dream for a head filled like mine with Gothic story) and that on the uppermost bannister of a great staircase I saw a gigantic hand in armour. In the evening I sat down and began to write, without knowing in the least what I intended to say or relate. The work grew on my hands, and I grew fond of it—add that I was very glad to think of anything rather than politics. In short I was so engrossed with my tale, which I completed in less than two months, that one evening I wrote from the time I had drunk my tea, about six o'clock, till half an hour after one in the morning, when my hands and fingers were so weary, that I could not hold the pen to finish the sentence, but left Matilda and Isabella talking, in the middle of a paragraph.

To another of his correspondents, Walpole wrote:

> I gave reign to my imagination; visions and passions choked me. I wrote it in spite of rules, critics, and philosophers; it seems to me the better for that. I am even persuaded that in the future, when taste will be restored to the place now occupied by philosophy, my poor *Castle* will find admirers.

The Castle of Otranto tells the story of the overthrow of a tyrant prince in an Italian state during the time of the Crusades, and the restoration of the rightful line in the person of a seeming peasant boy of noble bearing. The instrument of this turnabout is the vengeful ghost of the boy's ancestor, Alfonso, poisoned in the Holy Land.

At the outset of the story, the ghost appears as "an enormous helmet, an hundred times more large than any casque ever made for human being, and shaded with a proportionate quantity of black feathers," and dashes the son of the tyrant prince to bits. At the end, he appears again, after various hauntings, after melodrama and murder, and identifies the rightful heir:

> A clap of thunder at that instant shook the castle to its foundations; the earth rocked, and the clank of more than mortal armour was heard behind. ... The walls of the castle behind Manfred were thrown down with a mighty force, and the form of Alfonso, dilated to an immense magnitude, appeared in the centre of the ruins. Behold in Theodore, the true heir of Alfonso! said the vision: and having pronounced these words, accompanied by a clap of thunder, it ascended solemnly towards heaven, where the clouds parting asunder, the form of saint Nicholas was seen; and receiving Alfonso's shade, they were soon wrapt from mortal eyes in a blaze of glory.

In today's terms, we might call *The Castle of Otranto* a fantasy in a historical setting. The most obvious model for this novel is the plays of Shakespeare, particularly *Macbeth* and *Hamlet*. But Walpole, writing his Gothic fantasy in an era of rules, critics, and philosophers, "which wants only *cold reason*," was not at all certain beforehand what reception his strange dream-begotten story would arouse in a skeptical modern public. He was so uncertain that he took great pains to hide his identity and the true time and place of the book's origin.

He hid himself, and then hid himself again. The title page of the first edition of *The Castle of Otranto* declared that it was translated by William Marshal, Gentleman, from the original Italian of Onuphrio Muralto, Canon of the Church of St. Nicholas at Otranto.

Walpole did his best to further muddy the waters in a preface written in his persona of Marshal-the-translator. He began by claiming, "The following work was found in the library of an ancient catholic family in the north of England. It was printed at Naples, in the black letter, in the year 1529."

Walpole went on to suggest that the story might have been written at the time it was supposed to happen—that is, at some time roughly between 1095 and 1243. But then again, from the names of the servants, perhaps it was written rather nearer in time and place to its original appearance in print. And as for the good Canon Onuphrio Muralto—not mentioned by name in the preface—"Marshal" describes him conjecturally as someone who might have been "an artful priest" who used his abilities as an author to enslave vulgar minds and confirm the populace in their ancient errors and superstitions.

But it was not enough that Walpole attempted to slide his story off on an irresponsible person in some former time and place. As Marshal, he went on in his preface to apologize at length for the marvels in his story:

> The solution of the author's motives is however offered as a mere conjecture. Whatever his motives were, or whatever effects the execution of them might have, his work can only be laid before the public at present as a matter of entertainment. Even as such, some apology for it is necessary. Miracles, visions, necromancy, dreams, and other preternatural events, are exploded now even from romances. That was not the case when our author wrote; much less when the story itself is supposed to have happened. Belief in every kind of prodigy was so established in those dark ages, that an author would not be faithful to the *manners* of the times who should omit all mention of them. He is not bound to believe them himself, but must represent his actors as believing them.
>
> If this *air* of the *miraculous* is excused, the reader will find nothing else unworthy of his perusal. Allow the possibilities of the facts, and all the actors comport themselves as persons would do in their situation.

What? Excuse the miraculous, the very inspiration and fabric of his story, as "unworthy"? Plead verisimilitude and plausibility? Here the mask of the weird priest Muralto slips aside and we see the author of the preface for a moment revealing himself as the author of the story, a modern attempting to conjure up the miraculous again in a bygone setting for a modern audience that could not accept the miraculous as a fact in its own daily life.

So—hiding behind a false title page, hiding behind a misleading and apologetic preface, hiding behind two different false beards—Walpole gave his story of the miraculous to the Eighteenth Century British public...and a miracle occurred! Walpole's dream-begotten fancy was enthusiastically received.

The 500-copy first edition of *The Castle of Otranto*, published in December 1764, quickly sold out. When a second edition was published in April 1765, Walpole's initials were on the title page, a clear indication of his identity to the reading public of the time. In a new preface, Walpole explained his intentions more honestly and directly, this time writing not as an uncertain miracle-monger attempting to slip one over on the public, but as a successful artist, hailed as a breath of fresh air, who is explaining how his special trick is performed:

> It was an attempt to blend the two kinds of romance, the ancient and the modern. In the former all was imagination and improbability: in the latter, nature is always intended to be, and sometimes has been, copied with success. Invention has not been wanting; but the great resources of fancy have been dammed up, by a strict adherence to common life. But if in the latter species Nature has cramped imagination, she did but take her revenge, having been totally excluded from old romances. The actions, sentiments, conversations, of the heroes and heroines of ancient days were as unnatural as the machines employed to put them in motion.
>
> The author of the following pages thought it possible to reconcile the two kinds. Desirous of leaving the powers of fancy at liberty to expatiate through the boundless realms of invention, and thence of creating more interesting situations, he wished to conduct the mortal agents in his drama according to the rules of probability; in short, to make them think, speak and act, as it might be supposed mere men and women would do in extraordinary positions.

This is what Walpole, under his masks, had been saying and not-saying in his original preface: his aim, as a modern, was to combine the transcendent *mystery* of ancient romance with the *plausible* characters of the contemporary novel. The rest of the preface is devoted to a defense of Shakespeare as a model of this kind of mixture.

And, clearly, *The Castle of Otranto* is, on one level, warmed-over ersatz Shakespeare. On another level, however, taken in the context of its own time as an experiment in the novel—and as a unique synthesis of mystery and plausibility—it is revolutionary. *The Castle of Otranto* is given credit by the *Encyclopaedia Britannica* for sparking the Romantic Revival, the great wave of artistic longing for the bygone spiritual ways that seized the West during the following three-quarters of a century.

But the influence that *The Castle of Otranto* has had can be traced even further. Walpole's novel is in some degree the ancestor of at least six separate literary forms of the present day: the mimetic historical novel, the Gothic romance, the supernatural horror story, the mystery story, heroic fantasy in the Tolkien style, and modern science fiction.

Of these, the connection to science fiction may be the least obvious—but still it is present and present again. *The Castle of*

Otranto, inasmuch as it initiated the Romantic Revival, which influenced, nurtured and shaped Nineteenth Century SF, is an indirect ancestor of science fiction. However, more directly, *The Castle of Otranto* was the forefather of Mary Shelley's *Frankenstein,* which was both in the Gothic tradition and a crucial reaction against it. And finally, still more directly, *The Castle of Otranto* is the ancestor of the new SF because of its concern for both mystery and plausibility, or, in Walpole's words, "the great resources of fancy" and "the rules of probability."

Walpole managed to blend the two, more or less, but his synthesis was both unique and incomplete. It was unique because no later storyteller of the Eighteenth Century, neither Walpole nor anyone else, was able to successfully blend mystery and plausibility again in this same manner. It was incomplete because it was only the human characters, "the mortal agents," that Walpole aimed to make plausible. The ghost of Alfonso, the central transcendent symbol of *The Castle of Otranto,* remained as implausible, as not-to-be-believed, as unacceptably *spiritual,* as ever—the one note in his story that Walpole must hang his head over and call "unworthy."

It is as though by some accident of timing, of special interest, and of passion, Walpole had delivered himself of a prodigy—a blend of the two kinds of romance, the ancient and the modern. As a prodigy, a unique event, *The Castle of Otranto* could be accepted, but it could not be exactly copied.

Walpole's earliest would-be imitator was Clara Reeve, author of a historical study of the romance as well as one novel, *The Champion of Virtue, a Gothic Story* (1777), which is better known as *The Old English Baron.* As in her model, Reeve's Gothic story was set in an earlier time, the Fifteenth Century, and involved a ghost-haunted castle. But the marvelous element was clearly a problem for her, and she aimed to keep it "within the utmost *verge* of probability."

Reeve's ghost is confined to a cupboard, where he is given liberty to do no more than groan occasionally. Eventually someone looks within the cupboard and discovers, not the ghost, but his skeleton, evidence of his murder. Here we have, not the actual marvels and unreined imagination of *The Castle of Otranto,* but only that *"air* of the *miraculous"* of which Walpole spoke in his first preface.

Reeve's narrowness was the natural result of the confinement of her story to familiar historical settings. Transcendence that appears within the context of the everyday world—which we may call the Village—has to be tightly limited in expression and effect, or appear implausible.

The proper home of transcendence lies beyond the boundaries of the Village, in what we will call the World Beyond the Hill.

Here marvelous power displays itself everywhere, there are superior beings to be encountered, and we may undergo experiences that Village knowledge cannot encompass.

In order to enter the World Beyond the Hill, it is necessary to travel to the edge of the Village and then press on. In distant places where things are no longer the things we know, higher states than ours may plausibly exist. Distance and difference are the first indications of the World Beyond the Hill.

But the true test and proof of the World Beyond the Hill is its ability to generate transcendence. The World Beyond the Hill is the wellspring of transcendence, and any country where transcendence burgeons must be the World Beyond the Hill.

Transcendence discovered within the Village may at most be conceived as intruding there briefly from the World Beyond the Hill in order to carry out certain limited purposes and then departing.

In Walpole's novel, the ghost of Alfonso is just such an intruder—and at the end of the story he is received back into the World Beyond the Hill.

But Clara Reeve could not accept anything as blatantly spiritual as a heavenly realm in her tale. As a result, her ghost is earthbound and unrooted. He comes from nowhere, he vanishes into nothingness, and he accomplishes very little in between.

In Walpole's next imitator, Mrs. Ann Radcliffe, who wrote a handful of novels in the early 1790s, the seeming mystery would be even more rationalized. Mrs. Radcliffe's gambit was to suggest the supernatural—and then to explain it away as the result of human agency and natural coincidences.

In Mrs. Radcliffe's best-remembered novel, *The Mysteries of Udolpho* (1794), which we may take as our example, there is once more the historical setting, this time closer yet to the present—the end of the Sixteenth Century. There is the castle and the haunt. But this time the haunter is no ghost at all, but Montoni, lord of the castle of Udolpho and chief of a local robber band, and the hints of the supernatural are all a plot to intimidate an heiress.

Here is a balance of mystery and plausibility more in keeping with the temperament of the time, and hereafter the model of the Gothic story would be Radcliffe rather than Walpole. Beyond Radcliffe, we can see the Gothic romance, with its old manses, frightened heroines and Byronic heroes; we can see the rational detective story; and we can see the unsupernatural historical romances of Sir Walter Scott, who in 1824 wrote an appreciation of Mrs. Radcliffe's work for a new edition.

If these lines of literary descent from Walpole through Ann Radcliffe came to abandon transcendence entirely, except for that faintest *air of the miraculous* still present only to be dispelled by rationality, there were other stories written after the manner of Walpole in the late Eighteenth and early Nineteenth Centuries in which undispelled mystery continued to figure, but at the opposite price, the abandonment of plausibility. The most extreme example may be *The Monk* (1796), by Matthew Lewis, which compounds a fantastic stew of dead babies, matricide, incestuous rape, torture by the Spanish Inquisition, ghosts, devils, and the Wandering Jew. Stories of this sort aimed to entertain and titillate, to shock and unnerve, but not to persuade.

Horace Walpole's concern in *The Castle of Otranto* had been truly mythic to the extent that he aimed to combine mystery and plausibility. The crucial imperfection of *The Castle of Otranto* was the fundamental implausibility—in modern Western terms of thought—of the central transcendence.

Certain lines of literary descent from Walpole—the Gothic romance, the rational detective story, the historical novel—could not tolerate the implausible and so abandoned transcendence in favor of a strict adherence to "the facts"—the facts of history, the facts of society, the facts of love and marriage, the facts of life and death. And, to the extent to which they favored *what is* over *what might be*, these lines became mythically sterile.

Other forms that owe something to Walpole, like heroic fantasy and the supernatural horror story, could not give up the old spirit-based transcendence. But they were not effective myth, either. They were conservative. They looked backward. They ignored "the facts." And so they have been reckoned implausible escapist fantasy without relevance to the ordinary conduct of daily life.

SF is that line of descent through Walpole which has sought to find new grounds of plausibility for transcendence that a modern Western audience could relate to and accept. In this book, we are going to follow the line of development that has aimed to extend both the plausibility and the mysteriousness of transcendence. While other Western literary forms have favored either mystery or plausibility, SF is the line that has striven to be complete myth.

The New Prometheus

The first writer after Walpole concerned to find a point of balance between mystery and plausibility was Mary Shelley. She was able to solve the problem that Walpole had not solved, nor any other writer of the Eighteenth Century. In her story *Frankenstein, or the Modern Prometheus* (1818), begun when she was not yet nineteen years old, Mary Shelley presented an argument that rendered transcendent power plausible in contemporary Western terms.

The argument that Mary Shelley discovered was an argument for the potential transcendence of creative science. Walpole could not have thought of it—but more than fifty years had passed since *The Castle of Otranto*. The times had changed. The quality of life had changed. In this altered atmosphere, new arguments were possible.

It takes time for new beliefs to be accepted, and even more time for changes in belief to be translated into changes in life. The roots of modern Western scientific thought can be traced at least as far back as the Thirteenth Century, when the English Franciscan friar-philosopher Roger Bacon taught the tools of mathematics and deductive scientific reasoning, and for this and other reasons, such as denying the truth of unexamined authority, was perceived as dangerous by the superiors of his order and placed in confinement. It took no less than four hundred years after this, as we have seen, until the late Seventeenth Century, for the philosophy of scientific rationalism to wrest the leadership of society from the traditional spiritual philosophy.

Even then, the argument between materialism and spiritualism was not settled. Through the Eighteenth and Nineteenth Centuries, the representatives of spirit were a great conservative force in society. Spirit had vast inherited material wealth and position. It had prominent spokesmen. It had great capacity for resistance to the pace and direction of scientific progress. Even as late as 1860, it was possible for a bishop and a biologist to debate in public the propriety of the scientific theory of evolution. It was only in the 1920s—the era of Gernsback and the founding of *Amazing Stories*—that scientific materialism finally broke the last grip of traditional thought on the reins of Western society.

For the first hundred years of the modern period, well into the Eighteenth Century, it was possible for most people in the West to live as though nothing had changed, as though the old traditional beliefs were still the rule of society. The scientific doubt of Descartes and the scientific theory of Newton might convince a reasonable man, but for all that, life was still much the same. There was a great deal of radical thought, but very little radical action. Kings and nobles were still kings and nobles, priests were still priests, merchants still merchants, peasants still peasants. Whatever ideas for new parts and for independent action might be in their heads, the actors in the social drama still fit their traditional roles.

The perfect example is Horace Walpole. Just as *The Castle of Otranto* combined the ancient and the modern with no apparent sense of the fundamental contradiction in terms that defeated all imitators, so was Walpole's personal life also a contradiction in terms. In politics, as a member of Parliament, Walpole was a liberal -- a modern man. In private lifestyle, Walpole was a conservative. He was a member of the British ruling class, in the last years of his life inheriting the noble title Earl of Orford. He had traditional tastes. He lived a traditional life of high privilege. Life and thought were two different matters to him.

At the end of the Eighteenth Century, when Walpole was an old man, the social stasis was shattered. The American Revolution of 1776 and, even more, the French Revolution of 1789 were profound social events. The American Revolution was an assertion of political independence of thought. The French Revolution was a radical overturning of traditional society in the very heartland of the Western world. People at last had begun to act in accordance with their private thoughts. During the 1790s, the structure of traditional society began to break down.

At this very same time, the new Western material science finally overcame its inertia and moved beyond the stages of criticism and theory, beginning to demonstrate its practical power to transform the world. In the latter part of the Eighteenth Century, the Industrial Revolution began. The steam engine was perfected. The power loom was invented, and the modern factory system emerged. Canals were dug to facilitate commerce. Balloons were flown, demonstrating scientific mastery of the skies. With the Nineteenth Century, the pace of change began to accelerate. In the fifteen years that followed Horace Walpole's death in 1797, the gaslight, the steamboat and the locomotive were all invented.

Mary Wollstonecraft Shelley was born in the year that Horace Walpole died. The world that she grew up in was very different from his. It was a world with reason to believe in change, a world that was beginning to associate change with the creative powers of science.

At the turn of the Nineteenth Century, the balance between the old views and the new was still precarious. There was profound ambivalence about the new modern world that was being ushered into being. Great enthusiasm alternated with great fear and reluctance, sometimes within the same person. Often within the same person. The new moderns of the Nineteenth Century dared to do what had not been done before, and were frightened at their own audacity.

Mary Shelley was an archetypical young modern of the early Nineteenth Century—a second-generation modern. Her parents had been among the first during the 1790s to advocate new ways contrary to tradition and attempt to live them. Mary's mother, Mary Wollstonecraft, author of *A Vindication of the Rights of Women*, had lived with a married man and borne a child out of wedlock. Mary's father, William Godwin, to whom *Frankenstein* is dedicated, was a minister turned freethinker, the author of *Political Justice*, a radical critique of society, and the pioneer social novel, *Caleb Williams.*

When the young poet Percy Bysshe Shelley was dismissed from Oxford in 1811 for authoring a pamphlet entitled "The Necessity of Atheism," it was only natural that he would seek out the acquaintance of the foremost freethinker of the day, William Godwin. In 1814, he met young Mary Godwin in her father's home, and with the aid and company of Mary's stepsister, Claire Clairmont, eloped with her. Mary was sixteen, Shelley five years older. Shelley was already married and a father, with another child on the way, but no matter. In terms of traditional society, Percy Shelley's and Mary Godwin's conduct might be scandalous, but they were only acting out of principle. The willful new ideas of the times were in their heads and they could not bear not to live as they believed.

In the summer of 1816, when she began *Frankenstein*, Mary and Shelley were living with Claire near Geneva, Switzerland. Much had happened to Mary in two years. She had borne Shelley two children, one of whom had died when only two months old. She and Shelley would not be married until the end of December, three weeks after the discovery of the suicide of Shelley's wife, Harriet, who drowned herself in the Serpentine.

Their party in Geneva was joined by George Gordon Byron, with whom Claire had begun an affair, and by whom she would have a daughter in 1817. In an age when poets were pop stars, Byron was a poet and rebellious spirit even more notorious than Shelley, singing sympathy to the devil. He was rumored to have an incestuous relationship with his half-sister. Crippled and handsome, the bearer of a noble title, a rakehell and a revolutionary, Byron was the living embodiment of the contradictions of the time. He and Shelley hit it off well together, each influencing the other.

It was a rainy May and they were forced to spend time indoors. For amusement, they turned to reading supernatural horror stories, stories that from Mary Shelley's description sound closely related to *The Castle of Otranto*:

> Some volumes of ghost stories, translated from the German into French, fell into our hands. There was the History of the Inconstant Lover who, when he thought to clasp the bride to whom he had pledged his vows, found himself in the arms of the pale ghost of her whom he had deserted. There was the tale of the sinful founder of his race, whose miserable doom it was to bestow the kiss of death on all the younger sons of his fated house, just when they reached the age of promise. ... I have not seen these stories since then; but their incidents are as fresh in my mind as if I had read them yesterday.

It was Lord Byron who proposed to the party that each of them should write a ghost story. Byron and Shelley both set to the job confidently, though neither of them did more than turn out fragments. Byron's physician, Dr. John Polidori, also set out to write a story, and in fact did complete one. It was entitled *The Vampyre* and was published in 1819 with a preface and afterword by Byron.

Mary included herself in the competition. Shelley had been pressuring Mary to follow the example of her parents and write, and she had spent her childhood in composing fanciful stories for her own amusement. She volunteered that she, too, would write a story. At first, however, she could not think of one. As she remembered in 1831:

> I busied myself *to think of a story*—a story to rival those which had excited us to this task. One which would speak to the mysterious fears of our nature, and awaken thrilling horror—one to make the reader dread to look round, to curdle the blood, and quicken the beatings of the heart. If I did not accomplish these things, my ghost story would be unworthy of its name. I thought and pondered—vainly. ... *Have you thought of a story?* I was asked each morning, and each morning I was forced to reply with a mortifying negative.

What was the problem? If the problem was merely *to think of a story* and no more, then Mary Shelley might have whipped together some trifle about ghosts and kisses of death, and then either finished it like Dr. Polidori or set it aside like the others. The problem was to write a story that could be believed in. That was what baffled Byron and Shelley and what stymied Mary. How could these people, with their histories and their beliefs, write of inconstant lovers wrapped in the arms of the ghosts of the women they had deserted? That might be well enough for Polidori—"poor Polidori" as Mary calls him, shaking her head over his story—but it would not do for a young modern.

Mary only found the key to her story at last as a result of listening to a conversation between Byron and Shelley:

> Many and long were the conversations between Lord Byron and Shelley, to which I was a devout but nearly silent listener. During one of these, various philosophical doctrines were discussed, and among others the nature of the principle of life, and whether there was any probability of its ever being discovered and communicated. They talked of the experiments of Dr. Darwin, (I speak not of what the Doctor really did, or said that he did, but, as more to my purpose, of what was then spoken of as having been done by him,) who preserved a piece of vermicelli in a glass case, till by some extraordinary means it began to move with voluntary motion. Not thus, after all, would life be given. Perhaps a corpse would be reanimated; galvanism had given token of such things: perhaps the component parts of a creature might be manufactured, brought together, and endued with vital warmth.

What a typically blasphemous conversation! Here these young mods of the early Nineteenth Century were, titillating each other by separating the power of life from God and speculating about spaghetti coming to life like a pair of giggling eight-year-olds. The Darwin they mentioned was Erasmus Darwin, the grandfather of Charles, who in the years around 1790 wrote poems about science and evolution. The scientific experiments they discussed were the experiments of Luigi Galvani, who had made the muscles in the legs of dead frogs move through the application of electricity, the newest discovery of science.

After this conversation, Mary went to bed, but lay awake in a twilight state, her mind racing with visions:

> When I placed my head on my pillow, I did not sleep, nor could I be said to think. My imagination, unbidden, possessed and guided me, gifting the successive images that arose in my mind with a vividness far beyond

the usual bounds of reverie. I saw—with shut eyes, but acute mental vision—I saw the pale student of unhallowed arts kneeling beside the thing he had put together. I saw the hideous phantasm of a man stretched out, and then, on the working of some powerful engine; show signs of life, and stir with an uneasy, half vital motion. Frightful must it be; for supremely frightful would be the effect of any human endeavour to mock the stupendous mechanism of the Creator of the world. His success would terrify the artist; he would rush away from his odious handiwork, horror-stricken. He would hope that, left to itself, the slight spark of life which he had communicated would fade; that this thing, which had received such imperfect animation, would subside into dead matter; and he might sleep in the belief that the silence of the grave would quench for ever the transient existence of the hideous corpse which he had looked upon as the cradle of life. He sleeps; but he is awakened; he opens his eyes; behold the horrid thing stands at his bedside, opening his curtains, and looking on him with yellow, watery, but speculative eyes.

Once again, at a crucial point in the development of SF, we have vital conception taking place within a nonordinary mental state. Mary's creative imagination had accomplished what all her vain "thought and pondering" could not:

Swift as light and as cheering was the idea that broke in upon me. "I have found it! What terrified me will terrify others; and I need only describe the spectre which had haunted my midnight pillow." On the morrow I announced that I had *thought of a story*. I began that day with the words, *It was on a dreary night of November*, making only a transcript of the grim terrors of my waking dream.

Like lightning, the solution to the problem of plausible transcendence had broken in upon Mary. It was the power of science that would bring horror to life. She hardly says more than this in her story, but it is enough.

We all know some version of Mary's story from the many *Frankenstein* movies, which are the offspring of Nineteenth Century stage plays. But all these *Frankensteins* were revised and refined, altered for dramatic effect, updated for the sake of plausibility. They are not Mary's story as she wrote it. Her *Frankenstein* was an early Nineteenth Century story, written in the context of the times.

Inasmuch as it is removed into the past and evokes horror, Mary Shelley's *Frankenstein* is in the Gothic tradition. But it is far less Gothic than its popular adaptations. In the original story there is no castle, no baron, no hunchbacked assistant, no dungeons, no chains, and no peasants with torches and pitchforks.

Mary Shelley's *Frankenstein* is set in modern times, during the Eighteenth Century, in Walpole's lifetime when science was making its first great impact on the world. Her central character is no nobleman with a private electrical generator and basement laboratory. Her Victor Frankenstein is merely a student of chemistry in nearby Geneva with great aptitude and strange ambitions.

Through diligent study, Victor has learned the secrets of life. As in Byron's and Shelley's conversation, his impulse is to gather the component parts of a creature and endue them with vital warmth. He collects bones from the charnel house and animates them.

We hardly see how the trick is performed. There is none of the "powerful engine" that Mary, in 1831, reported herself as having seen in her dream. The crucial scene that Mary wrote on the morning after her inspiration, the scene of the animation of the monster that begins Chapter 5, is very spare:

> It was on a dreary night of November that I beheld the accomplishment of my toils. With an anxiety that almost amounted to agony, I collected the instruments of life around me, that I might infuse a spark of being into the lifeless thing that lay at my feet. It was already one in the morning; the rain pattered dismally against the panes, and my candle was nearly burnt out, when, by the glimmer of the half-extinguished light, I saw the dull yellow eye of the creature open; it breathed hard, and a convulsive motion agitated its limbs.

This is all we get of the mechanics. As in her dream, Mary's protagonist is immediately horrified at what he has done and runs away. He will tell us no more:

> I see by your eagerness, and the wonder and hope which your eyes express, my friend, that you expect to be informed of the secret with which I am acquainted; that cannot be; listen patiently until the end of my story, and you will easily perceive why I am reserved upon that subject.

Here in *Frankenstein* is evidence that exact detail, however useful to plausibility, is not itself necessary for plausibility to be achieved. The plausibility—the potential possibility—of the transcendent science that animates Victor Frankenstein's creature is established through a dramatic argument. We are prepared for the monster's animation by this argument, which is presented in the form of the story of Victor Frankenstein's education.

Mary Shelley's argument for new plausible transcendence is designed to encapsulate the experience of the early Nineteenth Century, still tied to the past, but a witness to change:

At the age of thirteen, Victor Frankenstein stumbles across the alchemical works of Cornelius Agrippa, Albertus Magnus and Paracelsus, the representatives of the old spiritual science, and is struck by their mystery and power. Stimulated by these marvels, he seeks to find the elixir of life and attempts to raise ghosts and devils. But he fails. Victor is a modern, and this ancient spirit-based science will not work for him.

Then Victor becomes acquainted with more contemporary science. Its overwhelming power of doubt ends his attempts to operate the old transcendent science. But it also makes him bitter:

> I had a contempt for the uses of modern natural philosophy. It was very different when the masters of the science sought immortality and power; such views, although futile, were grand: but now the scene was changed. The ambition of the inquirer seemed to limit itself to the annihilation of those visions on which my interest in science was chiefly founded. I was required to exchange chimeras of boundless grandeur for realities of little worth.

However, when Victor goes off to the university, his outlook on science is changed. A lecturer in chemistry speaks to his class about ancient science and modern science—and lays the groundwork of plausibility for the marvel of transcendent science that will ensue:

> "The ancient teachers of this science," said he, "promised impossibilities, and performed nothing. The modern masters promise very little; they know that metals cannot be transmuted, and that the elixir of life is a chimera. But these philosophers, whose hands seem only made to dabble in dirt, and their eyes to pore over the microscope or crucible, have indeed performed miracles. They penetrate into the recesses of nature, and show how she works in her hiding places. They ascend into the heavens: they have discovered how the blood circulates, and the nature of the air we breathe. They have acquired new and almost unlimited powers; they can command the thunders of heaven, mimic the earthquake, and even mock the invisible world with its own shadows."

If science can do so much, how much more is there that it may yet do?

What a powerful and subtle argument this is, as Mary presents it. It notes the demonstrable historical continuity between alchemy and modern chemistry, and calls them both "science." It steals the fire from the old transcendence at the same time that it dismisses it and alleges the superior power of modern science.

This powerful new science is not science as it may be now, but science-as-an-ideal, science as a potential higher state. This is mythic science, transcendent science, science-beyond-science. It is plausible inasmuch as it is an extension of existing science, and it is mysterious in that it is science that does not yet exist. All that we must do is acknowledge that there are miraculous powers, like the power of life, which modern science may yet discover—and the creature is ready to stir. Transcendence is ready to be born again.

It is not Victor Frankenstein, with his vague "instruments of life," who is the true "modern Prometheus," bringer of fire down from heaven, darer of divine wrath. Behind Victor stands his creator. It was she who truly dared the wrath of heaven, who in fear and trembling reanimated the corpse of transcendence. She gave it a shot of super-science, these bones she had reassembled, and watched in horrified fascination as they began to move. Such is the power of super-science.

Mary and Percy Shelley had some sense of the potential inherent in their argument. *Frankenstein* was published anonymously in 1818. In a preface—written, as Mary later recalled, by Percy—a claim is made. The claim is made in as roundabout and self-denying a fashion as the claim of Walpole in the "William Marshal" preface of *The Castle of Otranto*, but nonetheless, a claim is made:

> The event on which this fiction is founded has been supposed, by Dr. Darwin, and some of the physiological writers of Germany, as not of impossible occurrence. I shall not be supposed as according the remotest degree of serious faith to such an imagination; yet in assuming it as the basis of a work of fancy, I have not considered myself as merely weaving a series of supernatural terrors. The event on which the interest of the story depends is exempt from the disadvantages of a mere tale of spectres or enchantments. It was recommended by the novelty of the situations which it develops; and however impossible as a physical fact, affords a point of view to the imagination for the delineating of human passions more comprehensive and commanding than any which the ordinary relations of existing events can yield.

What is said here so languidly and elliptically is that *Frankenstein* is based on a scientific speculation which the author considers an impossibility. Nonetheless, this scientific transcendence is superior to spectres, enchantments and supernatural terrors. It is exempt from their disadvantages, the author of the preface says, without spelling out the disadvantages. He suggests merely that science-beyond-science permits novel situations and points of view.

In fact, there are great limitations to what Mary Shelley was able to accomplish. What she argued for was transcendent power, and no more. Not transcendent aliens or realms.

Frankenstein's creature, although brought to life in a miraculous manner by the transcendent power of science-beyond-science, and endowed with strength and endurance greater than that of an ordinary human being, has no miraculous powers of its own. It is the product of super-science, but it is not itself the master of higher powers. It is not a higher alien.

Oh, there are some moments when the creature does seem to take on the appearance of a possibly superior being...as it lurks in the background, climbs nearly perpendicular ascents during savage lightning storms, and follows poor Victor all over Europe, ruthlessly murdering his bride and his brother while remaining unseen by anyone but Victor.

However, when he is finally observed at close range, the creature does not retain his mystery. The instant he opens his mouth to speak and give an account of himself, the creature reveals himself to be just one more Romantic, pained and wounded by the world. He wonders why men are not more rational, and strikes out wildly in fits of passion and revenge. Another young modern.

No, of the three forms of transcendence, it was transcendent power alone that Mary Shelley was able to reawaken. The simplest transcendence—the power of creation and destruction. As presented in *Frankenstein*, this was superior power without a proper home, or source, or realm of being. It was superior power without superior beings to operate it. It was live, raw, untamed power, standing alone.

A further limitation of *Frankenstein* was that its transcendence was made after the model of the spirit-based transcendence of former times. Mary Shelley was attempting to write a story—in more contemporary terms—that would be the functional equivalent of *The Castle of Otranto*. The embodiment of her new transcendent science-beyond-science was set to do the work of an old-fashioned ghost— to haunt poor Victor, *clank, clank, rattle, rattle*—as though science-beyond-science didn't have any better work to do than that.

Mary Shelley should suffer no blame for this. She had, after all, set forth with the intention of writing a ghost story in the first place. She was making up her argument for the first time, and because it was the model of transcendence available to her—and the appropriate model to offer to the state of understanding of her audience—her new transcendent science-beyond-science necessarily looked very much like old-fashioned spirit-based necromancy in its effect. Even so, this cutting of science-beyond-science to the shape and size of spiritual conjuring was a limitation.

A third limitation in *Frankenstein* was the attitude of horror taken toward the new transcendence. Within the story, it is precisely because of this attitude that everything goes wrong for Victor Frankenstein. If he had only been able to master his ambivalent passions and sit down and have a chat with his creature, he would have found that they had much in common and a great deal of useful information to exchange. Instead, the instant the creature is born, Victor gets a rising gorge and runs and hides under the bedcovers, and it is this act of rejection that turns his creature against him.

Again, this is not so much a fault as it is a sign of the state of mind of the early Nineteenth Century: They were launched into the new worldview. Science and the general mood of inquiry were having effects on life. People didn't know how they felt about it.

Mary was looking to speak to the mysterious fears of our nature and to curdle the blood. She needed something she genuinely felt ambivalent about. She found that in the speculative conversation between Byron and Shelley. It was well enough to be a freethinker, a challenger of convention, but here was the promise of material science to usurp the power of the Creator and awaken life, even in a corpse. She didn't know how she felt about that. It seemed like a step too far. To write her story was to deal with her anxiety.

But this kind of anxious horror, however necessary a stage, was an impediment. As long as this stage persisted, it effectively prevented any development of the possibilities of science-beyond-science.

Frankenstein was the model of SF for the following forty years, until the 1860s and the stories of Jules Verne. It was not quite as singular and inimitable a model work as *The Castle of Otranto*— but neither was there any clear advance or development of the insights of *Frankenstein*. With its awakening of life in a creature that almost might be a devil, *Frankenstein* was the very limit of dareable speculation. The work that followed it was written well within its shadow.

We should understand that SF at this point had no name and was not a genre. It was not even so much as a story type. It consisted of no more than an argument—the argument for transcendent science-beyond-science. And that argument itself was not taken seriously, so that even Percy Shelley in the original preface to *Frankenstein* could state on Mary's behalf, "I shall not be supposed as according the remotest degree of serious faith to such an imagination...."

Before Mary Shelley, during the Age of Reason of the Seventeenth and Eighteenth Centuries, there had been no possibility at all of SF literature. This was a time of reaction against the old spirit realm and all its creatures. In a period of "rules, critics, and philosophers" all athirst for rationality, mysterious unknown things were generally not given leave to exist.

Science itself was not then considered to be mysterious. Rather, it was taken to be the rational process of consideration of phenomena that were known but not yet understood. Science was undertaken by gentlemen amateurs. It had a distinctly practical and material nature. It was only at the end of the Age of Reason, with the isolation of the unknown gas oxygen in 1774, the discovery of the unknown planet Uranus in 1781, the launching of the first balloon in 1783, and similar scientific news, that it became just barely possible to perceive science as mysterious.

But who was mentally prepared to make this perception?

During the succeeding Western phase—the Romantic Period of the late Eighteenth and Nineteenth Centuries—the spirit of SF was able to descend only now and then, when conditions were just right, to light a fire in the brain of the some dreaming or drugged-out writer. The stories that resulted were rare and occasional and uncertain. From time to time, one writer or another would pick up the argument for transcendent science-beyond-science for one story or two—at the utmost half-a-dozen in a lifetime's work—and produce a tale about some weird scientist toying with the forbidden and paying the necessary penalty.

It is this period that is the source of the cliché of the mad scientist studying knowledge that man was not meant to know. In these stories, transcendent science-beyond-science always looks very much like old-fashioned spirit-based transcendence and is used to evoke horror.

Notice how isolated all this is. We have an occasional argument for the power of super-science, mainly employed after 1835, and used for its horror and novelty and not for any more serious purpose. It is the rare writer who writes this stuff, and he writes it only now and again. And in these stories that followed the line of *Frankenstein*, the scientists, like Victor Frankenstein, are lonely figures—like alchemists or wizards in their private towers—operating "science" known only to themselves.

At the conclusion of *Frankenstein*, the creature, having killed Victor and delivered his last lament, departs for the North Pole—"the most northern extremity of the globe"—there to immolate himself on a solitary funeral pyre. In the stories that followed *Frankenstein*, there was a continuing presumption that transcendent science was somehow unnatural and that after it had turned on its discoverer it would dispose of itself conveniently or gutter out.

No one who wrote of transcendent science had the knowledge or the nerve to push the imagined accomplishments of science beyond the present actual state of science in a mood of calm inquiry, just to see what might be discovered. These Romantic lovers and fearers of transcendence always struck a spark of creative power, and then ran and hid under the bedclothes.

There was no foundation yet for more than this. The new times of the Nineteenth Century were just beginning to reveal a few isolated instances of the power of actual science. It would only be after years of living with the gaslight, the steamboat and the locomotive and their effects that it would become plausible to think of science linking up with science, science altering science, change compounding change.

The mentation of the early Nineteenth Century was not yet prepared to accept more. It needed to assimilate the horror and hubris of daring to usurp the powers of Nature, of daring change at all.

Frankenstein was the most extreme speculation of the period, the only one that must actually be hidden from. The SF stories that followed it only pretended to the horrible and terrifying. In effect, they lit wastebasket fires just to see the flame, and then instead of running and hiding, they threw water on them. In this way, the curiosity of the Romantics mastered their hysteria.

An indication of the narrowness of the SF which followed *Frankenstein* may be seen in its degree of restriction to familiar settings. Romantic SF was confined to the Village. It did not freely enter the World Beyond the Hill in the manner of ancient myth or of modern science fiction.

It was not yet prepared to explore the World Beyond the Hill and encounter transcendence there. The very thought was unsettling.

Writers of Romantic SF might half-glimpse the possibility of transcendent aliens. They might toy with the thought of passing beyond the bounds of the Village and entering the World Beyond the Hill. They might hint at these possibilities. They might even intimate them in stories that were cast as jokes or pipe dreams. But they could not and did not present dramatic encounters with fully transcendent aliens or realms. Stories that set out to do these things ended abruptly, half-finished, or blew themselves out in storms of conventional hysteria.

One writer of mid-century who made gestures in the direction of transcendent aliens was Fitz-James O'Brien, a literary Bohemian who came to New York City from Ireland in the 1850s. O'Brien was a writer of plays and stories who acted out the by-then well-worn Romantic charades of rebellion and excess and died in the American Civil War, age 34.

O'Brien was neither a writer of Mary Shelley's startling originality nor a literary master of the stature of those other sometime creators of Romantic SF, Nathaniel Hawthorne and Edgar Allan Poe. However, in two short stories written at the end of the Fifties, O'Brien presented a beauty and a monster discovered in the crannies of the Village, exotic beings who might, just might, be transcendent. In these two stories, O'Brien came as close as it was possible to come to writing of transcendent aliens in the mid-Nineteenth Century.

In "The Diamond Lens" (1858), the narrator, employing a superscientific microscope, the heart of which is a lens he has obtained through murder, peers into a drop of water and there spies a girl whom he names Animula. This typical madman of science tells us: "It was a female human shape. When I say 'human,' I mean it possessed the outlines of humanity—but there the analogy ends. Its adorable beauty lifted it illimitable heights beyond the loveliest daughter of Adam."

Wow! A girl who might be more than human within a drop of water! But is this a truly superior creature, a transcendent being, or are we merely listening to the normal hyperbole of the lovestruck?

There is no way to be sure. The drop of water evaporates and Animula dies. The presumptuous wretch of a narrator faints in a conventional fit of hysteria and comes up muttering, "They say now that I am mad; but they are mistaken."

Sixty years later, in a story such as Ray Cummings' "The Girl in the Golden Atom" (1919), it would be possible to dream of more than merely seeing an Animula, isolated and alone, inside an atom. In Cummings' story—taken as highly original in its own day—it would be possible to imagine penetrating an atom and finding a world, a girl, and adventure there. Not yet, however.

In O'Brien's "What Was It? A Mystery" (1859), we are presented with a second creature who might be a transcendent alien. This being, mysterious and invisible, drops down onto the narrator from the vicinity of the ceiling one night when our man has been lying awake after hitting the opium pipe too hard. After a furious struggle, the creature is subdued. But even after capture it remains resolutely silent and invisible until at last it starves to death.

Is this a transcendent alien? Or is it perhaps only a lonely superscientist who has discovered the secret of invisibility, and who will not speak lest his Romantic excuses for himself give the game away? We don't know. It is all a mystery, and remains one.

Of all the writers of Romantic SF, it was Edgar Allan Poe who made the bravest and best attempts to break loose from the confines of the Village. Poe, born in 1809, was a classic Romantic misfit, a threadbare Byron hooked on opium and death. He was the offspring of frail turn-of-the-century Romantic spirits. His father had thrown away a law career to go on the stage. He married Poe's mother, a young actress, and then abandoned her. Before he was three, Poe was an orphan, both of his parents dead. He was taken in and raised as a Virginia gentleman, a style of life he had no way of maintaining as an adult.

Poe worked as an editor and as a writer of poems, tales, reviews and random essays. But because of his temperament and style, he was unable to sustain relationships or hold jobs. He alternated alcohol with his opium, though he lacked all tolerance for liquor. Before his collapse in a Baltimore saloon and death at 40, Poe had taken to muttering to himself in the streets and breaking down in public.

Poe's stories are all attempts to dislocate perception, using a wide variety of methods. They are japes and satires, and tales of the bizarre, mysterious and horrible. If there is a strange fact or a grotesque imagining, Poe will employ it in his attempts to convince us that the familiar world is not as it seems.

Of the writers who came after Mary Shelley, it was Poe who wrote most often and most brilliantly of transcendent science-beyond-science. On at least two occasions, Poe made gestures in the direction of the World Beyond the Hill, but then could not follow through. He was not able to pass beyond the limits of the age to actually show us a world of transcendence.

In "The Unparalleled Adventure of One Hans Pfaall" (1835), a strange dwarf appears in the skies over Holland in a balloon. He drops a manuscript containing a narrative by one Hans Pfaall, a disappeared bellows-maker, telling of his trip to the Moon in a balloon of his own manufacture. The story proper is Pfaall's narrative.

Poe is very exact in his details of the mechanics of the journey, in as sustained a passage of elaborated science-beyond-science as the Romantic Period has to offer. The trip itself becomes possible by the assumption of a continuous atmosphere from the Earth to the Moon and the discovery of a mysterious gas whose "density is about 37.4 times *less than that of hydrogen.*"

In a note appended to the story, Poe reviews previous utopian stories of ventures to the Moon and claims that his is superior on account of its greater plausibility—using that very word, even italicizing it. He concludes this note by saying: "In 'Hans Pfaall' the design is original, inasmuch as regards an attempt at *verisimilitude,* in the application of scientific principles (so far as the whimsical nature of the subject would permit), to the actual passage between the earth and the moon."

As much as any other thing, it is Poe's tone of exactness and certainty of detail that would affect later SF and give Hugo Gernsback reason to list Poe among the progenitors of scientifiction. In the next generation after Poe, a young Jules Verne would read "Hans Pfaall" and be deeply impressed by it. In Verne's own *From the Earth to the Moon* (1865), a character describes Poe as "'a strange, moody genius'" and recalls the gas thirty-seven times lighter than hydrogen, and all the members of the Baltimore Gun Club whom Verne has gathered together stand and cry, "'Hurray for Edgar Poe.'"

In the narrative of Hans Pfaall, the balloon venturer arrives at a moon-city, and there follows a two-page catalog of hinted lunar wonders. There is, for instance, "the incomprehensible connection between each particular individual in the moon with some particular individual on earth." Even more promisingly, there are "those dark and hideous mysteries which lie in the outer regions of the moon,—regions which, owing to the almost miraculous accordance of the satellite's rotation on its own axis with its sidereal rotation about the earth, have never yet been turned, and by God's mercy, never shall be turned, to the scrutiny of the telescopes of man."

Dark and hideous mysteries? Well, that is the times and that is Poe—the atheist who invokes God's mercy, the believer in mystery and the fearer of mystery.

Here we are, plausibly transported from our familiar Village Earth into the World Beyond the Hill, arrived in a place where things promise to be endlessly mysterious. But what kind of a world of wonder—or death—is this? Is it a transcendent realm?

It could be. It should be. But it isn't.

"Hans Pfaall" does not maintain itself as a story. All the plausible reasoning and hinted mystery have not been for the purpose of establishing a realm of transcendence. Instead, we have been set up to have the rug pulled out from under our feet:

The mystery, we are told, is not real. The narrative has all been a hoax. Hans Pfaall has been playing a trick on the burgomasters and astronomers of Rotterdam.

Dutchmen were the Nineteenth Century's comic dumbheads. Only characters with names like von Underduk and Rubadub could have been taken in for a moment by a dwarf in a balloon "manufactured entirely of dirty newspapers" who is passing as an inhabitant of the Moon. Only they could have been stupid enough to have taken seriously a narrative of a fantastic journey that begins on the first of April. Only they would swallow an invented gas that is described as "tasteless but not odorless" but also as "instantaneously fatal to animal life." It is all a hoax on gullible Dutchmen—and a joke by Poe on us.

How strange and typical of Poe that immediately after a conclusion that turns all that has gone before into a jape at our expense, he should proclaim the superior plausibility of his method. If the Moon is not the world of wonder and mystery that Poe first suggests, but only a joke, then the superior plausibility of his method can have no point.

Was his plausibility serious, or was it a joke? Poe will have it both ways, and must have it both ways. As far as his immediate audience is concerned, it's a joke. Neither he nor they dare to brave the World Beyond the Hill long enough to encounter its transcendence. But, inasmuch as Poe is talking to later writers of SF like Jules Verne, he is completely serious. His appendix is an arrow pointing to the most innovative aspect of "Hans Pfaall"—plausible argument that can carry us to a transcendent realm—even though he himself isn't up to facing that mystery. But then, it has not been unusual in the development of SF for serious methods and arguments to be embodied in very unserious vehicles.

In his longest work, the novel *The Narrative of Arthur Gordon Pym* (1837), Poe made another essay at a trip to a transcendent realm, and again broke off short, unable to nerve himself to enter and stay. Some three-quarters of the novel is taken up with mundane bizarreness: mutiny, shipwreck and cannibalism. Only eventually do we travel sufficient distance to find those signs of radical difference that are the heralds of the World Beyond the Hill. The expedition that has rescued Pym sails unexpectedly into ice-free waters near the South Pole and finds islands there with unknown animals, purple water of strange consistency, and a race of savages with a terror of the color white. Poe even has Pym write: "Many unusual phenomena now indicated that we were entering upon a region of novelty and wonder."

In the last chapter, Pym, a companion, and a dying native are in a canoe that is being carried dreamily over the waters toward an impossible cataract from the heavens. The story concludes:

And now we rushed into the embraces of the cataract, where a chasm threw itself open to receive us. But there arose in our pathway a shrouded human figure, very far larger in its proportions than any dweller among men. And the hue of the skin of the figure was of the perfect whiteness of the snow.

With this glimpse of transcendent promise—or, again, of death—the story ends. A note apologizes for the loss of the remaining few chapters at the time of Pym's "sudden and distressing death," the facts of which, we are told, the public is well acquainted with through the medium of the daily press.

But, of course, we don't know the facts and there were no further chapters, not ever, even though Poe lived another twelve years. *Pym* was simply another story that Poe couldn't press through to a conclusion. So—he twists our noses, and quits.

From his interests, we may guess that Poe may have had in mind an entry into the hollow interior of the Earth through a hole at the Pole. This was a theory of the time that intrigued him. But Poe's imagination, the wildest of his era, simply balked when it came to passing that spectral guardian and entering the true region of novelty and wonder waiting at the bottom of the chasm. To speak of additional chapters and then not supply them was Poe's way of admitting that more was required in his story than he could bring himself to write.

The transcendent aliens and realms that were impossible for Fitz-James O'Brien and Edgar Allan Poe to imaginatively sustain in the first part of the Nineteenth Century would become readily possible by century's end when Charles Darwin's arguments for evolution, published in 1859, had been absorbed and assimilated. In the meantime, however, SF had another necessary stage of development to pass through, a stage in which SF grew accustomed to the rarefied air of the World Beyond the Hill. In these stories, hysteria was quelled, the nature and uses of super-science were investigated, and transcendent realms were entered at last.

4

Into the Unknown

After Mary Shelley's *Frankenstein* and the suggestive but incomplete stories of Edgar Allan Poe, the next great contribution to the development of SF was made in half-a-dozen books written during the 1860s by a Frenchman, Jules Verne. In these stories, nominally written for boys, Verne was able to do what the Romantics had not done. He treated science-beyond-science calmly and seriously, not as a joke or as an object of fear. He brought transcendent science out of the closet and into the world-at-large and allowed it to have influence on the policies of nations. And in a series of imaginary thrusts into the unknown, Verne was able to pass beyond those mental barriers which had baffled Poe, Verne's master and model, and prevented him from entering the true region of novelty and wonder.

The great difference between Verne and the writers who came before him was that he trusted and believed in transcendent science in a way they did not. The artistic priority of the Romantic movement of the early Nineteenth Century had been the recovery of spirit, or something very much like it. To the extent that science-beyond-science was invoked at all by the Romantics, it was as an argument of convenience, a quick assurance that seemingly supernatural events did have some justification. It was a thin wash of plausibility over a central mystery.

For the Romantics, mystery—the demonstration that rational materialism was not all—was primary. It is a common concern with the assertion of states other than the ordinary which binds a New England Transcendentalist like Emerson, a mystic like Blake, and an opium-taking poet like Coleridge. Likewise, the dreams, drugs, hoaxes, ciphers, and jokes that are found throughout Poe are all intended to be jolts to conventional thought, varying expressions of a single artistic strategy: hang the explanations, take them by the scruff of the neck and show them something *different*.

Plausibility was a matter of relative indifference to the Romantics, and the specific means by which plausibility might be achieved even more so. Inevitably, in this atmosphere, the argument for science-beyond-science was only one among many for the evocation of mystery, and not at all the most important, ranking far behind opium and mysticism. In order for the special significance of transcendent science to be perceived, changes in attitude and changes in the world were necessary.

As the Romantic Period drew to a close, changes of precisely this sort were taking place. Science was no longer a hobby, as it had been in the Eighteenth Century, but a daily activity, even a profession. The word *scientist* was coined in 1840. And, as more and more such men appeared, and more and more scientific knowledge was accumulated and integrated, the very concept of scientific practice began to alter. In the Age of Reason, science had chiefly consisted of the observation and classification of facts. In this new day, there was an increasing tendency to perceive science as the elaboration of general laws and the discovery of new truths.

At the same time, it was becoming easier to perceive the practical power of science. The application of scientific knowledge to the daily affairs of men, the increasing dependence of society on scientific advance, made scientific mystery a more and more plausible concept. Indeed, it was near the end of the Romantic Period, in 1859, that the word *technology* first began to be used to describe the new products of applied science. This new daily world of "scientists" and "technology" was the world in which Verne would grow up.

Jules Verne was born at the height of the Romantic Period, in 1828, in the inland port city of Nantes—the very place where the inventor of the mysterious gas in Poe's "Hans Pfaall" was said to live. As a boy, Verne once stowed away aboard a ship, but he was pursued and caught before it reached the sea. He was whipped by his father and, so he later recalled, made to promise his mother, "From now on, I will travel only in my imagination."

At the age of 20, Verne was sent to study law in Paris. He arrived in the aftermath of the popular Revolution of 1848, which Verne had longed to take part in. The Romantic Era was in decline. Verne found himself in a position to absorb the fruits of Romanticism without being overwhelmed by them.

While a student living on the Left Bank, Verne fell into the orbit of Alexandre Dumas, author of *The Three Musketeers* and *The Count of Monte Cristo*. Dumas accepted a one-act farce by Verne for production in his theater in 1850, and its moderate success confirmed Verne in his desire for a literary career. When he finished his law studies in 1851, he declined to return to Nantes and join his father's law practice as he was expected to do.

In the most respectful manner, this young Romantic rebelled against parental authority. He wrote to his father:

> The only career for which I am really suited is the one I am already pursuing: literature. I am deeply moved by your suggestions, but surely I must trust my own judgement in this matter. If I took it on, your practice would only wither away. Please forgive your respectful and loving son.

Verne was not simply a Romantic young boulevardier, a writer of light comedies and operettas. He had a continuing interest in geography, and a taste for science. He was a fan of science, reading regularly in the subject at the Bibliothèque Nationale.

At mid-century, the popular attitude toward science was beginning to shift. At the outset of the Nineteenth Century, Erasmus Darwin's poetic celebrations of the powers of science were so unusual as to make him a figure of fun, the butt of mad-scientist jokes like the one about Darwin and the vermicelli. By mid-century, the hysterical and ambivalent Romantic view of science was giving way before the everyday reality of a new world made by technology. An enthusiasm for science, if by no means a universal, was no longer a rarity. It was possible that your neighbor might share the same passion, or perhaps his bright young son.

The year of Verne's declaration of independence, 1851, might serve as a key year to illustrate the change in progress. Mary Shelley, the representative of the old Romantic attitude who had argued for science-beyond-science but feared it, died in 1851.

This was also the year of the Great Exhibition, the first great international science and trade exposition. It was housed in Hyde Park in London within a splendid building of glass and iron enclosing twenty acres—the Crystal Palace—specially erected for the occasion as a boast of the new powers of modern technology. The Great Exhibition was a wondrous fair in which the bounties of Western science, technology and commerce were displayed. In the five and a half months that it was open, six million visitors trooped through, discovering the new world-to-come of this century of invention. International expositions became a fad of the Fifties. In 1855, one was held in Verne's own city of Paris.

Recently, what may prove to have been the first use of the term *science fiction* has been traced to our same representative year of change. In 1851, in the course of setting down somewhat commonplace reflections on the subject of poetry, a writer named

William Wilson made the suggestion of a new form of literature which he called "Science-Fiction." In almost Gernsbackian phrases, Wilson wrote: "the revealed truths of Science may be given, interwoven with a pleasing story which may itself be poetical and *true*— thus circulating a knowledge of the Poetry of Science, clothed in a garb of the Poetry of Life."

As far as anyone has discovered, Wilson's suggestion had no influence on the actual course of development of SF. He made only passing mention of the potential powers of science and technology. His argument was chiefly for the celebration of actual present science.

But if Wilson's term was not adopted until the time of Gernsback, and then was used somewhat differently, to refer to stories with "prophetic vision" and "the amazing quality," the seeming parallel of thought between Wilson and Gernsback is no illusion. Wilson and Gernsback are united by their uncritical enthusiasm for science. They represent the beginning and the end of a common attitude. Even though it didn't bear the name during the period, it is precisely during the seventy-five years from 1851 to 1926 that SF might most deservedly have been known as "science fiction."

Jules Verne, who would have the actual impact on the development of SF that William Wilson did not have, was open to the same insights that swept over Wilson in 1851. In that year, Verne conceived the notion of writing romances of science that would be the equivalent of the historical romances of his mentor, Dumas. He criticized himself in a letter to his parents for "lingering on well-trodden paths, when science is performing miracles and thrusting into the unknown." Here in a phrase are the materials of the fruitful SF stories that Verne would write in the 1860s.

In 1851, Verne published his first short story, "A Balloon Journey," in which he not only symbolized the transition from Romantic to Victorian attitudes toward science, but clearly foreshadowed his own later work. Like so much of Verne, "A Balloon Journey" was influenced by Edgar Allan Poe, then two years dead.

In "A Balloon Journey," a balloonist discovers a stowaway aboard his balloon car—"a pale and excited young man" who tells him, "'I have studied aerostatics thoroughly. It has affected my brain.'" The young man claims that he knows the only way to steer a balloon. He wishes to plunge higher and higher into the celestial depths. "'We shall land on the sun!'" he cries. The balloonist and the madman wrestle for control of the ship. The Romantic falls to his death. The technologist survives and rides a leaky gas bag back to earth.

Here, in this one early short story, is the very substance of later Verne. In Verne during the Sixties, there is the extension of fact beyond fact, as in the experimental balloon of this story. There are the great visions of impossible possibility, like the madman's dream of landing on the sun. Finally, there is the split between the dreamer and the man of fact, the man of fact's fear of reaching too high and falling, and a wrestle between the two for control.

Before these intimations of 1851 bore fruit, more time had to pass. Verne was not yet ready to write his significant stories. He did not yet recognize his materials or know how to express them. Before he would discover his form and his audience, he would spend more than ten years as an unsuccessful playwright, the victim of a catalog of psychosomatic disorders, a man forced to earn a living as a stockbroker.

By the early 1860s, Verne was in a state of desperation, the literary success he had hoped to attain by the age of 35 still eluding him. He had written a long essay on Edgar Allan Poe, but had been unable to sell it to his usual essay market. A book-length manuscript on the history of ballooning, including speculation on the use of balloons in African exploration, had met with rejection. Verne even threw the manuscript into the fire, from which his wife rescued it.

In the fall of 1862, Verne's friend, the balloonist and pioneer photographer Nadar, whom Verne had met at the new club, Le Cercle de la Presse Scientifique, and from whom he had derived many of his ideas on the future of ballooning, directed Jules to Pierre Hetzel. Hetzel was a publisher of George Sand and of Balzac whose new specialty line of books for children had been so successful that he was entertaining plans for a children's magazine. He was looking for writers.

Hetzel declined to publish Verne's book in its original form. He suggested that it might be rewritten as a story for boys presenting all the factual matter Verne had gathered, but focusing on the possibilities of exploration of Africa by balloon. Verne had written no fiction since 1855, only essays and plays. Here, however, suddenly, was a possibility that resonated with that idea Verne had once entertained of writing a romance of science like the historical romances of his friend Dumas. But not a romance . . . a strange journey, a thrust into the unknown using the powers of advanced science.

Verne rushed home and began to write furiously. In a matter of two weeks, so great was the power of the spell that gripped him, he produced a novel, *Five Weeks in a Balloon*, which Hetzel published as a book the day before Christmas, 1862.

Verne's story concerns the crossing of the continent of Africa from east to west by a party of Englishmen in a balloon named the *Victoria*. *Five Weeks in a Balloon* obviously owes something in

inspiration to Poe's "A Balloon Hoax" (1844), in which a party
of Englishmen is said to have crossed the Atlantic Ocean from
east to west in a balloon also named the *Victoria*.

Just like the actual European explorers of Africa of the time,
Verne's travelers hope to spy that once nearly mystical goal, the
sources of the Nile. Verne writes: "Formerly, to seek the sources of
the Nile was regarded as the act of a madman; a wild dream, in fact."

The *Victoria* is a minimally transcendent super-scientific balloon.
It was based on the new experimental design of Verne's friend Nadar,
then in the planning stage, with the addition of a furnace to heat
hydrogen so that the balloon might rise and fall in search of favorable air currents without the use of ballast or the loss of gas. This
science-beyond-science may seem questionable today—to heat
hydrogen in this manner would surely risk an explosion—but Verne
made it appear thoroughly plausible to the audience he was addressing by the confident citing of "fact."

Within the story, so effective is Verne's imaginary science that
the *Victoria* successfully negotiates its passage across Africa, whereas,
by contrast, the nonfictional (and non-steerable) balloon constructed
by Nadar crashed after a flight in Europe of only four hundred miles
in October 1863. Verne's balloon crosses portions of Africa that
were then unexplored. However, nothing more fundamentally
mysterious than the sources of the Nile is spied. The Nile is confirmed to have its rise in Lake Victoria, as the English explorer
John Speke had suggested in 1858, and the characters congratulate
themselves that their "discoveries are entirely in accord with the
forecastings of science."

In the France of 1863, *Five Weeks in a Balloon* was exactly the
right book at the right moment. The use of domesticated science-
beyond-science to influence the present-day world was something
new in fiction. Verne's story was an imagination, to be sure, but
so spare and in command of fact was it, so confident and plausible
in presentation, that it almost might be tomorrow's headline.

And it was. Not only was the construction and launching of
Nadar's actual balloon widely discussed in the press in 1863, but, in
a masterpiece of timing, just after *Five Weeks in a Balloon* was published, John Speke emerged again from the jungle to say that he had
found the source of the Nile in Lake Victoria the previous July—
just one month after Verne's fictional balloon was supposed to have
made its passage. To use imaginary science to steal a march on the
contemporary explorers of Africa, and be proven correct—how
audacious! *Five Weeks in a Balloon* was a great popular success,
not just with those boys born since mid-century who were its intended audience, but with adults as well.

Here, at last, was the literary career that Verne had always desired. He bade farewell to his friends at the stock exchange—according to one of them, in these words:

I am leaving ycu. I have had an idea, the sort of idea that, according to Girardin, ought to come to every man once a day, but has come to me only once in my life, the sort of idea that should make a man's fortune. I have just written a novel in a new form, one that is entirely my own. If it succeeds, I shall have stumbled upon a gold mine. In that case, I shall go on writing and writing without pause, while the rest of you will go on buying shares the day before they drop, and selling them the day before they rise. I am leaving the Bourse. Good evening, my friends.

What was this once-in-a-lifetime idea that had descended upon Verne and kissed him on the brow so tenderly? Lacking direct testimony from Verne of the kind that we have had from our earlier writers, it is difficult to say how he might have phrased his intentions in 1863—or how he did actually phrase them. Verne had such an intense sense of personal privacy that in 1898, seven years before he died, he burned his early unpublished manuscripts, his letters and private papers. His thinking is veiled from us.

However, one bit of evidence about his idea is to be found in the public phrase that Verne chose to characterize this new novel form of his—*voyages extraordinaires.* Extraordinary voyages. This is the outwardness, the common frame within which sixty-five books by Verne would be made. In this concept is Verne's abiding love of geography and imaginary travel.

As for the content of his voyages, that was foretold by Verne in that long-ago letter to his parents in which he spoke of science "performing miracles and thrusting into the unknown." Verne had faith in science. Science—performing miracles and thrusting into the unknown—was Verne's chosen guide and companion on his extraordinary voyages.

Whatever conscious thoughts of geography and science Verne may have had in mind, however, there is another element in Verne's formula for the extraordinary voyage that cannot be overlooked. It may be the most important: Edgar Allan Poe. In the same way that Mary Shelley's original intent in conceiving *Frankenstein* was no more than to write a ghost story *right*, at its most essential and immediate, Verne's gold mine of an idea might well have been as simple as this—to write Edgar Poe *right*.

Verne the late Romantic admired Poe deeply. He liked Poe's cryptograms, puzzles and strange facts. He was fascinated by Poe's fevered characters. He loved Poe's occasional use of scientific materials, and his sense of mystery, his ability to dislocate vision.

But Verne the scientific Victorian was bothered by Poe's incomplete trust in science and his general lack of concern for plausibility. In spite of the note at the end of "Hans Pfaall," it was clear to Verne that Poe didn't really care a great deal about plausibility. In his essay on Poe, Verne specifically criticized "Hans Pfaall" for its abandonment of scientific principle in the matter of that thin atmosphere extending from the Earth to the Moon that permits the balloon to make its passage.

Verne wrote: "The most elementary laws of physics and mechanics are boldly transgressed. This has always seemed astonishing to me as coming from Poe, who, by a few inventions, could have made his story more plausible." That was where Poe could be improved upon.

All of the early extraordinary voyages might be described as Jules Verne's attempt to write Edgar Allan Poe more plausibly. At the outset of the series, an alternative description of Verne's stories was offered by his publisher: *Voyages dans les mondes connus et inconnus.* Journeys to worlds known and unknown. By enlisting the protective power of science and placing all his trust in it, Verne aimed to go into the unknown in confidence where Poe had gone doubtfully and pulled up short.

This may have been Verne's aim, but it was one that he was only able to carry out in part. He was able to set off into the unknown bravely enough, even to enter the region of novelty and wonder that Poe evoked but avoided. But Verne wasn't able to remain very long in the heady atmosphere of the World Beyond the Hill.

Just as in his first story of 1851, "A Balloon Journey," Verne's wild Romantic heart and his sober Victorian head still remained in conflict. Again and again in his early stories, Verne would wrap himself in super-science and launch himself into the unknown. All would go well enough for a time, but at last, in each case, the mystery would become too much for him, the threat of transcendence too overwhelming. Verne's nerve would break and he would retreat to the safety of the Village.

Verne was a Nineteenth Century man. He identified with the powers of science and technology and the changes in life they had brought. Science-beyond-science, so alien and dangerous to Mary Shelley and her fellow Romantics, was a form of transcendence Verne could face without fear. He'd grown up with it. It seemed almost natural to him.

In Verne's stories, transcendent power was presented as familiar and plausible. It was identified with contemporary scientific knowledge and practice. Its mysterious effects were limited to the powering of super-scientific means of travel and exploration, vehicles and devices similar to actual inventions of the day but in advance of them, like the balloon *Victoria* in *Five Weeks in a Balloon*. This domesticated science-beyond-science was one of Jules Verne's two major contributions to the development of SF.

The other and greater was his penetration into unknown places in the World Beyond the Hill, one of them at least an undeniably transcendent realm. This was difficult for Verne. Domesticating science-beyond-science was a plausible and rational thing to do. But to leap with this science-beyond-science into the World Beyond the Hill was not rational. In the World Beyond the Hill, far beyond the reach of Village society and law, untamed undomesticated mystery is to be found. For Verne, this was almost as frightening and unbearable a prospect as it had been for Poe.

To Poe, the unknown region of novelty and wonder wore the aspect of Death. It was guarded by awesome spectral figures. It was filled with dark and hideous mysteries.

For Verne, the World Beyond the Hill was not quite as deadly as it was for Poe. For Verne, the unknown World Beyond the Hill was identified with sex and irrationality. He pictured it again and again as the Abyss, alluring and dangerous, a yawning chasm gaping wide into which rationality dare not take a header. To his great credit, however, once or twice Verne took the plunge.

Verne's formula of imaginary science, travel and Edgar Allan Poe, and his yearnings and limitations, can all be seen displayed in his second extraordinary voyage. *The Adventures of Captain Hatteras* was serialized in 1864, initiating Hetzel's new juvenile magazine, the *Magasin d'éducation et de récréation*, of which Verne had been made a co-editor.

In *The Adventures of Captain Hatteras* the aim of travel is the North Pole. Like the goal in *Five Weeks in a Balloon*, this was a unique spot on the Earth that contemporary explorers strained to reach, a place with mystical overtones. The Poles were still a great unknown in the Nineteenth Century. As in Poe's *A. Gordon Pym* or Mary Shelley's *Frankenstein*, they might be treated as a region of novelty and wonder.

We may remember that at the end of *Frankenstein* the creature intends to make his way to the North Pole and there immolate himself. Even more interestingly, at the outset of *Frankenstein* the polar explorer who receives Victor Frankenstein's story and the last confessions of his creature writes in anticipation to his sister:

"I try in vain to be persuaded that the pole is the seat of frost and desolation; it ever presents itself to my imagination as the region of beauty and delight. ... There snow and frost are banished;

and sailing over a calm sea, we may be wafted to a land surpassing in wonders and beauty every region hitherto discovered on the habitable globe."

But if a transcendent land with the familiar wonders of the old spirit realm does not reveal itself to this explorer at the Pole, he expects that he may at the least discover there a wonder of a new kind—the secret of the compass. That is, if not old-fashioned transcendence, then science-beyond-science.

For his part, Edgar Allan Poe was fascinated by the theory of one John Cleves Symmes that great holes exist at the Poles which lead to another world at the interior of the Earth. Poe suggested this theory a number of times in his stories without ever quite daring to propound it directly. We may remember the great chasm at the South Pole at the conclusion of *A. Gordon Pym*. Beyond this, in Poe's very first story, "MS. Found in a Bottle" (1833), there is a gigantic whirlpool at the South Pole which swallows the narrator's ship. And in "Hans Pfaall," as the balloon rises above the North Pole toward the Moon, a sharply defined circular depression is seen in the ice "whose dusky hue, varying in intensity, was, at all times, darker than any other spot upon the visible hemisphere, and occasionally deepened into the most absolute blackness."

Verne's party to the North Pole in *Captain Hatteras* consists of an American arctic explorer, a ship's doctor, two sailors, and their leader, the Romantic English multimillionaire, Captain Hatteras, who is bent on being the first man to set foot on the North Pole. This central character is the impediment to Verne's success. Although Verne cites many scientific facts as his party suffers through great realistic arctic hardships, his main character is not devoted to science. Rather, Captain Hatteras is a madman with an obsession akin to the mania of the stowaway in "A Balloon Journey."

Just as Poe's Pym had found those strange open waters that were previously expected by Mary Shelley's captain in the vicinity of the Pole, so do Verne's explorers, who launch a small sloop they have brought with them by dogsled. Verne, no less than Poe, was fascinated by the Symmes Hole theory. His man of fact, the ship's doctor, observes: "In recent times it has even been suggested that there are great chasms at the Poles; it is through these that there emerges the light which forms the Aurora, and you can get down through them into the interior of the earth."

However, here, as in subsequent Verne novels, the high Romantic expectations of his characters outstrip the actualties they are permitted to discover. This possibility of a Symmes hole is too wild and dangerous a mystery for Verne to contend with. Instead, like Poe, he shies away from it, and makes a non-transcendent substitution.

In the middle of the eerie northern sea, Verne's party comes upon a small island. On this island is a flaming volcano. It is the volcano that is the location of the North Pole.

Captain Hatteras the Romantic will not be kept from his goal. Like his predecessor in "A Balloon Journey," he is drawn to the fire. He rushes up to the lip of the volcano and is about to throw himself into the abyss when the American pulls him back to safety. Hatteras faints. When he returns to consciousness, he is hopelessly insane.

And so the story concludes, as an old-fashioned Romantic cliché. This is certainly no improvement on Poe.

Hatteras the Romantic destabilizes Verne's story. With him running things, Verne is unbalanced from the beginning. No more than he will land on the sun will Verne enter a Symmes Hole or leap into a living volcano and then imagine what comes next. And certainly not with a madman like Hatteras at the center of his story.

In his next novel, the third extraordinary voyage, however, Verne took the substance of *Captain Hatteras* and recast it. *Journey to the Centre of the Earth*, also first published in 1864, is the most imaginative SF story that Jules Verne ever wrote. In this story, in the course of pursuing fact down a rabbit hole into the earth, almost without realizing it, Verne's travelers penetrate into what is undeniably the World Beyond the Hill.

One vital recasting that Verne made in *Journey to the Centre of the Earth* was to make the leader of his expedition a dedicated man of science rather than a Romantic. Professor Lidenbrock the German geologist may have his little obsessions and rigidities, but he is no egocentric madman. Verne can trust his stability as he could not trust the unscientific judgment of Captain Hatteras. The Romantic in *Journey to the Centre of the Earth* is the narrator, Professor Lidenbrock's ineffectual nephew Axel, who is much given to fainting.

Once again, there is a volcano, but this time an extinct one located in the wastes of Iceland rather than at the emotionally charged North Pole. The story begins when Professor Lidenbrock and Axel discover and decipher a coded message from a heretical Sixteenth Century Icelandic alchemist which has fallen out of an old manuscript.

The message reads: "Descend into the crater of Sneffells Yokul, over which the shadow of Scartaris falls before the kalends of July, bold traveller, and you will reach the centre of the earth. I have done this. Arne Saknussemm."

The dispassionate man of reason and fact, Professor Lidenbrock, has no doubt at all about what he will do. He and Axel are off to Iceland instantly, and down they go into Sneffells Yokul. This volcanic mount has two peaks and a crater containing three chimneys, the middle one of which is a hundred feet in diameter and leads into the unknown. In a passing moment that is a defused replay of the climax of *Captain Hatteras*, as they start downward Axel the Romantic is overcome by an attack of vertigo on the edge of the abyss and must be pulled back to safety.

Professor Lidenbrock, Axel and an Icelandic guide named Hans descend into the darkness armed with two of the recently invented Ruhmkorff coils, arc lamps which provide them with electric light. Like Verne's steerable balloon *Victoria*, this was a transformation of contemporary science into super-science. With less than a wave of the hand from Verne, clumsy experimental lights are altered into reliable and efficient devices capable of continuing to work for as long as the party remains underground.

And it is no mere afternoon outing they are bound upon. The party spends weeks hiking through underground caverns where successive strata of perfectly preserved fossils serve to dramatize the latest ideas about prehistory, and to give us a clue that we have left the Village and entered the World Beyond the Hill.

What the party has found is not a Symmes Hole leading directly to an interior world with its own suns. In fact, they are nowhere near the center of the Earth, the destination promised in the book's title. More plausibly, Verne says that they are in caverns eighty-eight miles below the surface of the Earth. Yet this is enough. We may not be in a Symmes Hole. We may never reach the center of the Earth. But this maze of underground caves and passages does lead to a transcendent realm, a place of inexhaustible mystery.

Native transcendence first appears when Axel becomes lost in the dark and breaks his arc light. In the attempt to rejoin his companions, he knocks himself unconscious. He awakens on the shores of a mysterious underground ocean. Everywhere there is light:

> It was not the light of the sun with its dazzling shafts of brilliance and the splendours of its rays; nor was it the pale vague glow of the moon, which is just a cold reflection. No, the power of this light, its tremulous diffusion, its clear bright whiteness, its coolness, and its superiority as a source of illumination to moonlight, clearly indicated an electrical origin. It was like an aurora borealis, a continuous cosmic phenomenon, filling a cavern big enough to contain an ocean.

Imaginative Axel, dumbfounded by the immensity of this cavern with its mysterious illumination, wonders briefly if Symmes's theory of an interior world with its own suns might not be true. But even if it isn't—which we never find out, since the possibility of a Symmes Hole is thereafter dropped uninvestigated—these wonders in themselves are enough to tell us and Axel where we are. As Axel puts it:

I gazed at these marvels in silence, unable to find words to express my feelings. I felt as if I were on some distant planet, Uranus or Neptune, witnessing phenomena quite foreign to my "terrestrial" nature. New words were required for new sensations, and my imagination failed to supply them. I gazed, I thought, I admired, with a stupefaction not unmixed with fear.

It is clear to Axel, at least, in his stupefaction and fear, that they are in an alien realm, even if he cannot articulate his perception. After this recognition by Axel, in the previously desolate underground region they have entered prehistoric living things begin to spring into existence, fossils taking on life. The travelers encounter ancient plants—tree-ferns and gigantic mushrooms. Then they build themselves a raft and set sail on the underground ocean, where extinct fishes and saurians swim.

As they travel this immense ocean, as great in extent as the Mediterranean, Axel falls into a "prehistoric daydream" which may be the most imaginative passage that Verne ever wrote. Back through time Axel passes, witnessing the earlier stages of life. The dream climaxes:

The whole of this fossil world came to life again in my imagination. I went back to the scriptural periods of creation, long before the birth of man, when the unfinished world was not yet ready for him. Then my dream took me even farther back into the ages before the appearance of living creatures. The mammals disappeared, then the birds, then the reptiles of the Secondary Period, and finally the fishes, crustaceans, molluscs, and articulated creatures. The zoophytes of the transitional period returned to nothingness in their turn. The whole of life was concentrated in me, and my heart was the only one beating in that depopulated world. ...

Centuries passed by like days. I went back through the long series of terrestrial changes. The plants disappeared; the granite rocks softened; solid matter turned to liquid under the action of intense heat; water covered the surface of the globe, boiling and volatilizing; steam enveloped the earth, which gradually turned into a gaseous mass, white-hot, as big and bright as the sun.

In the centre of this nebula, which was fourteen hundred thousand times as large as the globe it would one day form, I was carried through infinite space. My body was volatilized in its turn and mingled like an imponderable atom with these vast vapours tracing their flaming orbits through infinity.

Heavy stuff! Axel wakes from this vision of imaginative possibility—this "brief hallucination" as he calls it—by nearly throwing himself off the raft into the ocean under the dream's influence, and being pulled back to safety from the infinite sea by Hans the Icelander.

Thus far the perception of transcendence has been limited to Axel. Where he discerns marvels, the unflappable Professor Lidenbrock sees only confirmations of the theories of science. When Axel cries, "That's wonderful!" the professor overrules him with, "No, it's perfectly natural." It is only by the constant maintenance of this double vision that Verne is able to penetrate so deeply into the World Beyond the Hill without losing his head.

This is not to last, however. On the farther shore of the underground ocean, the party comes across a vast plain entirely covered with heaps of fossil bones. Among these, they find a perfectly preserved human skull, and then the mummified fossil of an ancient man. When they travel a little further, they encounter a Tertiary Period forest and a living herd of mastodons ripping away tree branches and eating them.

Here the unresolved conflict between Axel's dreams and intimations of mystery and Lidenbrock's plausible scientific explanations comes to a head. Axel is the first to come to the realization that dream and fact are one. He thinks:

"So that dream in which I had had a vision of the prehistoric world, of the Tertiary and Quaternary Periods, was finally coming true. And there we were, alone in the bowels of the earth, at the mercy of its fierce inhabitants!"

But Professor Lidenbrock is not yet convinced. In spite of Axel's protests, he wishes to have a closer look. Then, however, they see the shepherd of these mastodons. It is a shaggy human figure over twelve feet tall—twice the size of the fossil man they have found.

This is more than heavy stuff—it is freaky. In 1864, the existence of earlier forms of man, differing from present humankind, had not yet been conclusively demonstrated. To meet a prehistoric man, a giant, in this underground region is a strangeness that not even a Professor Lidenbrock can reduce to lecture-room rationality.

Axel flees in terror. And he pulls his uncle along behind him, "who for the first time in his life allowed himself to be persuaded."

The moment of integrated vision ends. From the safe vantage of retrospection, Axel-the-narrator interjects a denial of what we have just seen:

Now that I can think about it unemotionally, now that I am quite calm, now that months have gone by since that strange, extraordinary encounter, what am I to think, what am I to believe? Was it a man we saw? No, that is impossible! Our senses were deceived, our eyes did not

see what we thought they saw. No human being could exist in that sub-
terranean world; no generation of men could live in those deep caverns
of the globe, caring nothing about the inhabitants of the surface and
having no communication with them. The very idea is insane! ...It must
have been a monkey, however improbable that may seem. The idea that
a man, a living man, and with him a whole generation, should be buried
down there in the bowels of the earth is unacceptable.

As though the thought of a twelve-foot monkey herding mastodons in an electrically lit underground wonderland would be any
more inherently plausible. No, it is ultimately Verne himself for
whom the shaggy man has been too much. It is Verne who finds
his own imagination unacceptable and rejects it. Verne can no
longer go on splitting his vote between Axel and Lidenbrock, mystery and plausibility, dream and fact. He is in a transcendent realm
within the World Beyond the Hill and the strangeness of it is more
than he can bear.

Immediately after refusing to confront this fearsome alien creature,
the travelers find their path downward blocked. When they attempt
to blast it open with guncotton, the earth splits apart and their raft
is swept into the abyss by the waters of the ocean.

For hour after hour they fall—and then they begin to rise again,
carried upward on a magic cushion of boiling water and red-hot
lava, an experience they find trying but not threatening. Axel once
more loses consciousness. When he awakens, he is on the slopes of
the newly erupted volcano Stromboli, near Sicily, safe and sound
with his companions in the familiar world of everyday. Back in the
Village again, and without a single burn to show for having been
spewed out of a volcano.

The twelve-foot shaggy man has frightened Verne into retreating,
as though it were Frankenstein's monster returned, and he Victor
Frankenstein. He has had to bail out of his story any way that he
can, and hang the implausibility of the device. No matter that the
volcanic fire that he could not face with Hatteras is given as the
safe and easy means of return with Lidenbrock. In their relief to
be home, Verne, Axel and the reader will all agree not to question
this mystery.

But in spite of this abrupt ending, what Verne had accomplished
in *Journey to the Centre of the Earth* was the beginning of a new
step in the development of SF. Sleepwalking, splitting his awareness,
pretending to himself all the while that he knew not what he was
doing, Verne had penetrated into the World Beyond the Hill with
the aid of super-science and found transcendence there. It is of no
importance that Verne thereafter lost his head and ran away from

what he had found. The entire history of SF, one step at a time, has been made by people who were out of their heads or beyond their depth.

What is of importance is that Verne had connected the World Beyond the Hill and the Village. The return passage from the realm of wonder into the world of known things at the end of *Journey to the Centre of the Earth* may have been mysterious; the journey outbound from the familiar into the unknown was a thoroughly plausible step-by-step slog. After this story, a roadway existed from the Nineteenth Century Village into the World Beyond the Hill.

Journey to the Centre of the Earth was the most forthright penetration of the World Beyond the Hill that Verne ever made. It was the only one that took him into territory that was not merely unknown but completely imaginary, and therefore free to display any imaginative possibility that Verne might conceive of. In no other book by Verne was the subtle balance between the Romantic dreamer and the Victorian man of science maintained so successfully.

However, in further extraordinary voyages written during the 1860s, Verne did nerve himself sufficiently to return twice more to the World Beyond the Hill—in each case seeking undomesticated transcendence, but in each case avoiding a confrontation with it. In both stories he protected his characters from mystery by encasing them in tightly closed super-scientific exploratory vehicles and filling their heads with litanies of scientific fact to chant in self-defense.

The fourth extraordinary voyage was Verne's attempt to improve on "Hans Pfaall," which he had criticized so specifically for implausibility in his essay on Edgar Poe, finally published in 1864. *From the Earth to the Moon* (1865) was the most technically detailed SF story written to this point. In constructing it, Verne not only enlisted the aid of his cousin, a mathematician, but claimed to have consulted five hundred reference works.

In Verne's story, the American Civil War is over and the artillerymen who make up the Baltimore Gun Club are restive. They decide to shoot a projectile from a giant cannon and strike the Moon. While their 900-foot-long gun is building, a French adventurer, Ardan, modeled on Verne's friend Nadar, arrives and alters the thrust of the project. When the gun is fired, he wishes to be inside the cannonball. His enthusiasm is so compelling that eventually a party of three—Ardan and two scientists—decides to go on this one-way trip to the Moon.

Verne's space-gun was no more realizable science than the hydrogen-heating furnace described in *Five Weeks in a Balloon*. Firing this giant cannon would instantly kill all within the projectile. So great would air resistance within the barrel be that the aluminum bullet would not even reach the mouth of the gun. *From the Earth to the Moon* is a convincing demonstration that plausibility in SF is far more a matter of effective arguments aimed at the state of knowledge of a particular audience than an absolute condition of accuracy to literal fact. Verne's wealth of fact and figure, his calculations and arguments were all more than sufficient to establish the literary plausibility of his super-scientific space-cannon.

But the story is only half a story. *From the Earth to the Moon* ends abruptly with the firing of the cannon and the announcement from Cambridge Observatory that the projectile has not struck the Moon as it was aimed to, but rather has gone into orbit around it. How strange! How mysterious!

Once again, Verne proved himself capable of entering the celestial abyss by super-scientific means. But no more than Poe was he prepared to explore the Moon and face what he might find there. He has had to stop his story in the middle, put it in a state of suspension, and leave his readers dangling.

It took Verne four years to complete his story. In *Around the Moon*, serialized in 1869, it is explained that a meteor whizzing unexpectedly out of space had deflected the course of the space-bullet.

Verne cannot allow his party's expressed intention of landing on the Moon and introducing itself to the inhabitants to be fulfilled. His travelers only approach the Moon closely enough to make observations that confirm the plausible speculations of contemporary science, but not closely enough to see anything radically unexpected. In this manner, Verne shields his characters—and himself—from intolerable levels of mystery.

In *Around the Moon*, the viewpoint shifts from Earth to the three men aboard the space-bullet, off in the World Beyond the Hill. And what a strange dissociated trip it is! In his striving for plausibility, Verne has overburdened us with fact. He has placed us safely (good heavens!) inside a cannonball and shot us into space. With a cosmic hand, he has altered the course of the voyage. And all the while, he keeps the attention of his characters firmly fixed on detail so that they won't *notice* what is happening to them: "Instead of asking where they were going, they passed their time making experiments, as if they had been quietly installed in their own study."

Verne keeps his characters as distanced from the mystery of the Moon as he can. The bullet swings around to the far side of the Moon, where Poe had placed those dark and hideous mysteries he prayed we might never have to witness, but the passage is made during that region's nighttime. Darkness conceals whatever may lie below. Only for one brief moment, by the light of another convenient cosmic fireball rushing by in space, do Verne's voyagers get a glimpse of what may be traces of atmosphere and water. And later, the French adventurer Ardan conceives the Romantic possibility that certain formations below might be ruined buildings.

But this is as much of a hint of lunar mystery as Verne can permit himself. That the Moon might be an active, present transcendent realm is a possibility that Verne won't allow into his story. Never again! Verne draws the line there.

His characters will not be granted the opportunity to encounter the lunar equivalent of that alien shaggy man in the underground wonderland of *Journey to the Centre of the Earth.* They will not be given the chance that Axel had to perceive that the material of scientific theory and the archetypal symbols of dreams and madness may be the same.

No, Verne draws his limits exactly. When his voyagers fire their tiny guidance rockets with the renewed intention of landing on the Moon, Verne summarily overrules them. Far from landing on the Moon, quite unexpectedly, as though the laws of physics had temporarily been suspended, they find themselves headed back home to Earth again.

With Verne's heavy auctorial hand nudging the space-bullet this way and that, first parking it in orbit at a discreet distance from the Moon, then directing it back home contrary to the intent of his voyagers, the most that his characters can do is speculate. They can conclude that if the Moon ever did support life and civilization, these must now be long extinct. And then his travelers can subside back into Village normality.

In a return that is reminiscent of the end of *Journey to the Centre of the Earth* in its convenience, the space-bullet comes to a safe splashdown in the Pacific. When rescuers arrive, they find the voyagers calmly playing cards, just as though nothing at all had happened to them.

Verne's last great work of SF was *20,000 Leagues Under the Sea* (1869-70). The novel opens with a reminder to the reader of the mysterious sea-thing that was disturbing the nations of the world by ramming ships in the year 1866. This thing is the *Nautilus,* a super-scientific submarine under the command of Verne's most interesting and powerful character, the anonymous Captain Nemo. Nemo is a nationless outlaw with a hatred of tyranny. He is an idealist who has seemingly been embittered by the betrayal of the popular revolutions of 1848 which had shaped the political thought of the young Jules Verne.

Here we have a dangerous and exciting departure for Verne:

a story in which a Romantic is the master of science-beyond-science. We might say that Nemo represents Verne's final attempt to regain the imaginative balance displayed in *Journey to the Centre of the Earth*, his last attempt to give the two sides of his nature an integrated expression.

But this attempt is only partially successful. The narrator of *20,000 Leagues Under the Sea* is Pierre Arronax, a more conventional scientist than Nemo, who has set out to investigate the great mystery and, in company with his servant and a harpooner, has fallen into the hands of Captain Nemo. We are never allowed to witness Nemo's thought directly. He is an aloof and enigmatic personage, his true motives revealed to us only in occasional outbursts of passion.

Arronax and his companions are not sufficiently Romantic themselves to fully appreciate the wild and nearly transcendent nature of Nemo and his undersea realm. The only transcendence that Arronax is capable of apprehending is the super-scientific submarine. Arronax is astonished by the *Nautilus*, and well he might be. It is Verne's most evolved vehicle of super-science, capable of going anywhere under the ocean.

The *Nautilus* is Verne's best-remembered imaginary invention, cited as an example of accurate prediction by those like Hugo Gernsback who have most forcefully presented the idea that science fiction is fiction about science. In his editorial in the first issue of *Amazing Stories*, Gernsback would write: "Take the fantastic submarine of Jules Verne's most famous story, 'Twenty Thousand Leagues Under the Sea' for instance. He predicted the present day submarine almost down to the last bolt!"

In fact, however, as a true vehicle of transcendence, the *Nautilus* is capable of being interpreted as both plausible and mysterious. In the last years before he died, Verne gave several interviews to British journalists in which he made revealing remarks on the nature of the *Nautilus* which have it both ways.

In the first interview, in 1903, he came down on the side of the mystery of the submarine. He said:

> The Italians had invented submarine boats sixty years before I created Nemo and his boat. There is no connection between my boat and those now existing. These latter are worked by mechanical means. My hero, Nemo, being a misanthropist, and wishing to have nothing to do with the land, gets his motive force, electricity, from the sea. There is scientific basis for that, for the sea contains stores of electric force, just as the earth does. But how to get at this force has never been discovered, and so I have invented nothing.

Here Verne gives credit for the bolts of his submarine to the Italians. He takes credit only for imagining (in a properly scientific manner) that the sea is a great electric battery from which the *Nautilus* draws power. Since no one has discovered how to do this, he, Verne, is an imaginist and not an inventor.

In the second interview, given in 1904, Verne placed his weight on the other foot. In the course of trying to distinguish his work from that of H.G. Wells, Verne spoke again of the *Nautilus*, by way of example, and this time emphasized its plausibility rather than its mystery:

> Take, for instance, the case of the *Nautilus*. This, when carefully considered, is a submarine mechanism about which there is nothing extraordinary, nor beyond the bounds of actual scientific knowledge. It rises or sinks by perfectly feasible and well-known processes, the details of its guidance and propulsion are perfectly rational and comprehensible. Its motive force is no secret: the only point at which I have called in the aid of the imagination is in the application of this force, and here I have purposely left a blank for the reader to form his own conclusions, a mere technical hiatus, as it were, quite capable of being filled in by a highly-trained and thoroughly practical mind.

That is transcendence for you—an attainable leap that remains unattained, a goal for highly trained and thoroughly practical minds to strain after vainly.

In fact, the power source of the *Nautilus*, as the actual pages of the story make clear, is transcendent power passing under the plausible name of "electricity," as so much transcendence did during the Nineteenth Century. The unveiling of the motive power of the submarine in *20,000 Leagues Under the Sea* is a model presentation of domesticated science-beyond-science:

> "Before going any further, Professor, I must explain a few things," said Captain Nemo. "So please listen."
>
> After a few minutes of silence, he said: "There is one source of power which is obedient and rapid, easy and pliable, and which reigns supreme aboard my ship. It does everything. It gives me light, heat and is the soul of all my machinery. This source is electricity."
>
> "Electricity!" I cried, somewhat surprised.
>
> "Yes, Monsieur."
>
> "But Captain, the great speed with which your ship can move would seem to have little to do with electric power. Until now, its dynamic force has remained very limited and able to produce no more than a very small amount of energy!"

"Professor," answered Captain Nemo, "my electricity is not the usual kind, but I hope you will permit me not to go into it further."

And there you are. First, a promise of complete explanation. A trumpet blast, then the pronouncement: "Electricity!" followed by the proviso (not of the usual kind)—and a quick duck behind "I hope you will permit me not to go into it further."
Arronax can't help wondering:

There was a mystery behind all this, but I did not want to ask too many questions. How could electricity be made to produce such power? Where did this almost limitless force originate? Was it in some high tension developed by a new kind of coil? Was there something about its transmission that an unknown system of levers could increase infinitely?

But there is no way of knowing exactly, nor any assurance that we ever shall:

"Captain," I said, "I can only admire what you've done. You have obviously discovered something which other men will one day find out: the true dynamic force of electricity."
"I'm not so sure they will find it," Captain Nemo answered coldly.

In *20,000 Leagues Under the Sea*, the undersea realm is the World Beyond the Hill. It is not only a source of electrical power, it is Nemo's garden, providing him with every necessity of life. One last time, Verne probed into the World Beyond the Hill, hoping still (and fearing) to confront the mysteries of the Abyss.
The first suggestions of mystery that they encounter are muted. Together, Arronax and Nemo brood for an hour over the ruins of Atlantis—which, like those hypothetical ruins sighted on the Moon in *Around the Moon*, are unthreatening because they are safely dead. The *Nautilus* dives under the great ice barrier that guards the South Pole—but this time what is discovered is neither a Symmes Hole nor a volcano crater, living or dead, but merely a stark peak of volcanic rock.
Although his companions are anxious to escape, Arronax is fascinated by the adventure. He distracts himself from the strangeness and peril of his situation in the typical Verneian manner— by constantly enumerating the species of fish that can be seen from the windows of the *Nautilus* as they travel from ocean to ocean.
At last, however, Nemo can no longer keep his passionate Romantic nature contained. He sinks a warship and heads north at an

enormous rate of speed. It is only then that Arronax finally admits the region of novelty and wonder that he finds himself in:

> It seemed as if night and day, as happens in polar regions, no longer followed each other in their normal order. I felt myself entering a strange world in which Edgar Allan Poe would have felt at home. Any moment I expected to see, like the fabulous Gordon Pym, "a shrouded human figure, very far larger in its proportions than any dweller among men, lying athwart a cataract which bars all access to the North Pole."

The last phrase in this quotation, of course, is an interpolation by Verne. But this is not the last evocation of Poe in *20,000 Leagues Under the Sea*. Nemo's destination is the Maelstrom near the Lofoten Islands off Norway, a great sea whirlpool which was the subject of an 1841 Poe story, "A Descent into the Maelstrom," in which one brother is driven mad and sucked to the bottom of the Abyss, while the other is spit out with whitened hair to tell the tale. Nemo means to dive his submarine into this "Navel of the Ocean."

One last time, this is too much for Verne and he must retreat. As Nemo aims the *Nautilus* into the maw of the Maelstrom, Arronax and his companions attempt a desperate escape. Arronax hits his head on an iron rib and loses consciousness. End of chapter. The final chapter begins:

> Thus ended this voyage beneath the seas. What happened that night, how the dinghy escaped the powerful currents of the Maelstrom, and how Ned Land, Conseil and I came out of that chasm alive, I cannot say. But when I regained consciousness, I was lying in a fisherman's cottage on one of the Lofoten Islands.

Once more, Verne, unable to steel himself to a dive with a madman to the bottom of the Abyss, has had to retreat from the World Beyond the Hill by whatever unlikely means. And this time, for all essential purposes, was the last time.

Verne was the most lively, learned, able and imaginative SF writer of the first ninety-five years of the Nineteenth Century, unrivaled for fully thirty years after his first extraordinary voyage. By aiming his work at a whole new reading audience of literate juveniles, Verne became the first writer of SF to make a living from his writing. During his period of maximum imaginativeness, from 1862 to 1870, Verne made two great contributions to the development of SF: the domestication of science-beyond-science, and the penetration of the World Beyond the Hill.

After 1870, perhaps in reaction to France's humiliating defeat in the Franco-Prussian War and to growing doubts about science in the hands of fallible men, Verne made an imaginative retreat. At the very age at which Poe had died, Verne dropped the element of Poeian mystery from his extraordinary voyages. The science-beyond-science that Verne wrote of became more constrained in effect. Verne continued to write SF stories to the end of his career, but most of the later extraordinary voyages were ordinary mimetic adventure stories, journeys to known worlds.

We might compare Verne's fruitful period from 1862 to 1870 with Walpole's production of *The Castle of Otranto*. Verne, like Walpole, was a man standing between two generations with vastly different states of mind, not fully at home with either but able to serve as a mediator between them. Walpole was neither an ancient nor a modern, but in his one fantastic novel, an idiosyncratic synthesis that no one else could manage to repeat, he attempted to make these two head-states compatible.

The practical result was to reintroduce mystery into the materialistic modern Western world. The Romantics who succeeded Walpole, rather than exactly repeating Walpole's synthesis, found themselves wrestling with the problem of mystery that he had given to them, dealing with it in various ways, as we've seen.

Similarly, Verne was a man who was neither a wild Romantic nor a sober Victorian. He was something of both, but never fully at ease as either. The psychosomatic illnesses that had plagued the young Verne continued to afflict him in his years of success. Even as a Victorian patriarch, honored and respected, Verne was driven for years to travel almost incessantly, like one of his own characters, without fixed destination, aim or rest.

Verne's formula, like Walpole's, was a unique synthesis of old and new that managed to work only within a limited span of time. Throughout the 1860s, as long as his nerve lasted, Verne kept attempting stubbornly to make this personal concoction of imaginary travel, science-beyond-science and Edgar Allan Poe do what he wanted it to do.

Again and again he tried his formula, altering the balance of elements from story to story. And he never quite managed to do what he had originally set out to do: write Poe *right*. No more than Mary Shelley had successfully written a ghost story, or Walpole had written Shakespeare, try as they might. Rather, almost as a by-product, Verne had produced two new developments in SF for his successors to wrestle with.

The writers who joined Verne the Victorian after 1870 and worked beside him during the next twenty-five years radically extended the scope and power of domesticated science-beyond-science.

They far outstripped Verne in inventing a wide range of plausible new super-scientific devices and phenomena and in imagining the effects that transcendent science might have on the contemporary world and the near future.

These same writers followed the paths that Verne had blazed into the World Beyond the Hill. But what they found under the ground or beneath the sea or on other planets was not the untamed mystery-upon-mystery encountered by Axel and Hans and Professor Liden-brock in *Journey to the Centre of the Earth*. Instead, again and again they were to discover advanced human societies, masters of domesticated super-science.

If Verne, even in his years of imaginative retreat after 1870, remained the premier SF writer of the generation, the model, the standard, it was because his fellow Victorians were less daring in their imagination than the half-Romantic Verne of the 1860s had been. They had a resource unacceptable to Verne—a new attitude toward science—and this permitted their advances in domesticated science-beyond-science. Nonetheless, even with this resource they could not press beyond Verne. They were working within his imaginative territory.

Not until H.G. Wells produced *The Time Machine* in 1895 would another writer find the nerve to take up the challenge of Verne at his most imaginative and pass again into a fully transcendent realm. Verne's daring accomplishment in *Journey to the Centre of the Earth* of "thrusting into the unknown" would remain a solitary imaginative event for fully thirty years.

To properly appreciate Verne, we might say that, like Walpole, he had a visionary glimpse of the unknown. In Walpole's case, the glimpse was of mystery. In Verne's, it was of a transcendent realm. Pushing themselves to their limits, finding special points of balance, both Walpole and Verne were able to express these visions once.

Only once. The visions could not be recaptured. Just as Clara Reeve could not duplicate the mystery of *The Castle of Otranto*, the Jules Verne of *20,000 Leagues Under the Sea* could not write of a transcendent realm as the Jules Verne of *Journey to the Centre of the Earth* had done.

In order to fulfill the mystery of *The Castle of Otranto*, a new generation of Mary Shelleys and Edgar Allan Poes with new arguments was necessary. And they did offhandedly what Walpole had done only in one special fevered moment.

In the same way, in order to fulfill the promise of the transcendent realm encountered in *Journey to the Centre of the Earth*, it was necessary for a new generation with new arguments to arise. H.G. Wells, Edgar Rice Burroughs and A. Merritt would go lightly and easily into those transcendent places that Poe intuited and did not dare to brave and that Verne only once surprised himself into finding in a fit of somnambulism.

PART

2

SCIENCE FICTION
EMERGES

The past is but the beginning of a beginning, and all that is and has been is but the twilight of the dawn.... A day will come when beings who are now latent in our thoughts and hidden in our loins shall stand upon this earth as one stands on a footstool, and shall laugh and reach out their hands amid the stars.

—H. G. WELLS

5

The Higher Powers
of Science

For the first two hundred years of the modern era—from the accession to the leadership of Western society by the philosophy of rational materialism in the late Seventeenth Century to the appearance of techno-warfare in the Franco-Prussian War of 1870-71—there was no such thing as science fiction literature. Through all this time, writers had no conscious awareness of working in a connected and cumulative SF tradition. Such a thing as science fiction was unthinkable, unimaginable. It didn't exist.

How very different the situation is today! In the late Twentieth Century, nobody at all would think to doubt that there is such a thing as science fiction. Paperback racks are filled with books labeled "SF." There is a great visible science fiction industry: writers, editors, critics, magazines, books, films, fans, clubs, conventions, awards, and much much more.

The difference between the situation prior to 1870, when SF could not be said to exist, and the situation we are heir to today, is the general acceptance by the Western world of the plausibility of scientific mystery. This acceptance, this new faith, began to take hold right around 1870.

As we have suggested, in order for myth to be an effective indicator of yet-unrealized possibility, there must be some basis for a belief in transcendence. We must think that there could be mysterious higher states of being and awareness, and we must be able to believe that we might plausibly attain those higher states.

In ancient myth, *spirit* provided such a groundwork for belief in plausible mystery. After 1870, *science* became sufficiently developed as a concept and a practice to serve as a new foundation for belief.

But this was not so prior to 1870, which is why we can say that during the first two hundred years of modern Western society, SF literature did not exist. It is only retrospective wisdom that allows us to peer into the past and single out a literary possibility here, a dynamic metaphor there, a subtle argument or an imaginary exploration, and identify these highly separated moments of special creativity as a connected series of advances necessary for the coming into being of SF literature.

It is our awareness of the nature of later science fiction—and our appreciation of the invisible working of the transcendent spirit of SF—that allows us to perceive what these varying bits and pieces had in common: All were attempts at the presentation of plausible scientific mystery.

But SF literature still did not exist as late as the advent of Verne in the 1860s. He was not working in an active tradition, a contemporary literary form. Rather, he was recognized as a marvel, a writer with his own unique product. It was as though Verne were a last solitary Romantic wizard with a formula all his own—like Captain Nemo, that master of his own special brand of electricity.

After 1870, however, in the very moment of Jules Verne's imaginative retreat, modern Western civilization entered a new phase, the Age of Technology. And immediately, science fiction was born.

The new era was the result of a change in the attitude of society toward science. The consequence of the change was that after 1870 it was possible to set out consciously to write science fiction. No longer was SF a feat that a rare Romantic wildman, lit by inspiration while in some unique state of acute mental receptivity, might aim at once in a lifetime. Science fiction became a form that almost anyone could write, and after 1870 there would always be a number of writers at work producing SF.

The shift in attitude that made the Age of Technology and SF literature possible might be called the final fruit of the Romantic Period. The change was, in effect, the solution to the major problems that the whole Romantic Period had been attempting to solve.

One of these problems was the lack of plausible mystery in the world. Without transcendence, the Romantics felt like orphan children. They mooned after the old spiritual mystery that the Age of Reason had rejected. And they hunted vainly for new mystery everywhere in the hopes of finding it somewhere—and didn't necessarily recognize it when they had it.

Another problem was the science and applied science that the Romantic Period had inherited from the Age of Reason. This rational activity was beginning to alter life, and the Romantics didn't know how they felt about that. The Romantic Period looked upon monster science with the same ambivalence and apprehension that Victor Frankenstein felt for his creature.

It was the change in the practice of science during the Nineteenth Century that we have described that finally made it possible for the Romantics to see that one of their problems was the answer to the other. Through the course of two phases in Western society—the Age of Reason and the Romantic Period—the "practice of science" had meant the careful observation of the material world, the gathering and classification of fact. But in the later years of the Romantic Period, this familiar definition was strained beyond its limits.

First to appear were radical new mathematical systems like non-Euclidean geometry and symbolic logic. These systems were self-consistent but, by ordinary standards, irrational. They seemed to apply to something more or something other than the ordinary earthly realm.

These new forms of systematic thinking were followed in the 1860s by strange new scientific theories, all of which pointed beyond the known into the unknown.

There was Darwin's theory of evolution. This suggested—from current scientific evidence—that both man and nature had once been something different than they now were. And further, that they might alter again in the future.

There was Pasteur's germ theory of disease. This pointed beyond the new infinitesimal lifeforms that science had discovered to claim that similar living motes that were unknown might have crucial influence on our health and well-being.

There were Maxwell's equations. These took the apparently separate electrical and magnetic phenomena of longtime scientific study and established them at last as part of a single continuous spectrum which even included visible light. And further predicted the existence of forms of energy then unknown.

There was Mendeleev's periodic table of the elements. Once again a generalization unified an ill-understood chaos of information, and then went beyond the known to suggest the unknown, in this case the existence of hitherto undiscovered forms of matter.

Wow! New powerful forms of life. New energy, new matter, new levels of being. Most important of all, a mutable mankind risen from lower forms and with a destiny that was unknown, instead of the old familiar conception of a fixed mankind specially created and loved by God.

Shifts in attitude had to take place. From being in the background of awareness, one element of society among many, scientific study and its technological application were now recognized as the most superior and advanced aspect of Western society. The leading edge, like it or not.

And science itself was no longer understood to be the practice of looking at familiar material things and taking their measurements. Rather, it was redefined. "Science" was now taken to be the sum total of that which is known and that which might be known. Anything that man might someday measure or bring under the rule of a scientific generalization, any knowledge that man might master, any possibility he might attain—*that* was the sphere claimed as its own by "science."

This new science was no longer just the occasional discoverer of minor unknowns. The new science was mysterious by definition. It was the wisdom of a universe that was more unknown than known.

Oh my! A universe that was *more* unknown than known. That was a radical new concept indeed.

It was this new valuation of science and understanding of its nature that brought the Age of Technology into being and made a literature of scientific transcendence possible. Science fiction in full flower was the post-1870 myth of the limitless unknown powers of science.

As we shall see, this new literature changed and developed all through the Age of Technology, which lasted from 1870 until the onset of World War II—and then transcended itself in the succeeding Atomic Age.

At the beginning of the Age of Technology, SF didn't even have a name. And even very late in the day, in Hugo Gernsback's time, it would pass under a multitude of different names. But from 1870 or thereabouts, it is at last possible to say that a literature that we can recognize as science fiction was visible and acknowledged.

After the beginning of the Age of Technology, when an SF novel was published, it would not be looked upon as a unique prodigy. Instead, reviewers might compare it to some earlier story. Writers would consciously answer each other and extend each other's notions. A literary tradition existed.

Jules Verne, caught between generations, only partly made the transition to the new Age of Technology. He accepted the idea that science and technology were the leading edge of Western civilization—though in time a certain doubt about that began to creep into his stories. But his real sticking point was the new image of science as the wellspring of unknown things.

That was more than Verne could handle. In *Journey to the Centre of the Earth*, he had glimpsed the wonder inherent in evolutionary theory and presented it in the form of Axel's overwhelming vision and the subsequent encounter with the giant herder of mammoths. But then he had panicked and run away, calling these intuitions of mystery "insane" and "unacceptable."

In preference to the new ideas of science as a discoverer of the unknown, Verne continued to cling to the old idea of science as an extender of the known. And, along with him, there were other SF writers in the new Technological Age who continued to hold to this old-fashioned image of science.

The product of these writers was simple invention stories, which might be called the fictional equivalent of the work of Thomas Alva Edison. Edison, the greatest inventor of the Age of Technology, was the creator of the light bulb, the phonograph and motion pictures. He was not an explorer of the unknown reaches of higher science, but rather a new type of man—the master of applied science. Edison was an entrepreneur of inventions, as much businessman as scientist.

Most common among the Edisonian invention stories that held to the idea of science as an extension of known things were SF dime novels. These stories were melodramas of technology written for young boys, the new children of the Technological Age.

SF stories were only one type of dime novel, an American publishing format that was both the product and the reflection of the age. Dime novels were cheap paperbacks with lurid covers. These crude action-adventure stories were run off by the million on the new modern presses of the late Nineteenth Century to catch the nickels and dimes of the young reading audience which sprang up with the spread of literacy and basic education.

The first dime novel SF story was written by Edward S. Ellis, a man who was the supreme master of early dime novel hack writing. *The Steam Man of the Prairies* (1868), Ellis's only invention story, became the prototype of the form. In this story, a ten-foot-tall steam-powered automaton is invented by a fifteen-year-old boy and used to look for gold and to chase buffalo out West.

The degree of mystery in this imaginary technological achievement was extremely limited. Ellis's steam man is most mysterious in the opening paragraphs of the story. It is first spied at a distance of two miles and described as "looking like some Titan as it took its giant strides over the prairie." A comic Irishman even mistakes it for "'the ould divil.'"

And, we are told: "No wonder that something like superstitious awe filled the breasts of the two men who had ceased hunting for gold, for a few minutes, to view the singular apparition; for such a thing had scarcely been dreamed of at that day, by the most imaginative philosophers...."

But thereafter throughout the story, the steam man is described in thoroughly plausible terms as a mobile steam boiler with a quasi-human form. Even howling savages can see through it: "...their previous acquaintance with the apparatus had robbed it of all its supernatural attributes...."

Now, the steam man *might* have been a creature with at least the danger, uncertainty and power of Victor Frankenstein's monster. Only it isn't. It has no intelligence or volition of its own. It moves only where it is pointed. Eventually it is pointed at attacking Indians, the boiler is deliberately overloaded, and the steam machine explodes.

The only real mystery is the means of the machine's movement. This is how Ellis describes the crucial step before the automaton is animated and runs into its first wall:

> It required two weeks before Johnny Brainerd succeeded. But it all came clear and unmistakable at last, and in this simple manner:—
>
> (Ah! but we cannot be so unjust to the plodding genius as to divulge his secret. Our readers must be content to await the time when the young man sees fit to reveal it himself.)

This is the old I-can-tell-you-but-I-won't trick that we have met before. We can hear echoes of Mary Shelley's presentation in *Frankenstein*. But Victor Frankenstein wouldn't tell us the details of his knowledge of the secrets of life in order to protect us readers from suffering a fate like his. In the case of *The Steam Man of the Prairies*, it is the poor bright young inventor Johnny Brainerd, dwarfish and hunchbacked, who is to be protected until he has the chance to patent and publish his work, and make a buck out of it.

This is typical. In the words that Jules Verne used in 1904 to describe the mysterious motive power of his submarine the *Nautilus*—imagined at almost the same moment as Ellis's story—the mystery of the steam man could fairly be said to amount to no more than "a mere technical hiatus, as it were, quite capable of being filled in by a highly-trained and thoroughly practical mind."

So it would be with later SF dime novels. Almost invariably, they involved devices powered by steam or electricity, usually vehicles of some sort—cars, submarines or aircraft. Not very different from Verne's steerable balloon *Victoria*. Always their inventors were teenage boys who employed these marvels of technology for purposes of adventure.

The dime novel invention story was established as a genre in 1876, following the third printing of *The Steam Man of the Prairies*, when a second SF dime novel written in close imitation of Ellis appeared. Thereafter, as long as dime novels were published—essentially to the end of the century—invention stories were issued in large numbers.

Of the many such stories published during the 1880s and 1890s, it has been estimated that 75% were the work of one man, Luis Philip Senarens, most frequently writing under the pseudonym Noname. In a lifetime production of fifteen hundred stories under twenty-seven different names, Senarens wrote several hundred of these minimally transcendent technological stories.

In 1880, when he was at the very outset of his SF writing career—and still a teenager—Noname received a letter of praise from an admirer of his dime novel invention stories, none other than Jules Verne. And, in time, as the Age of Technology continued, Jules Verne's own later stories would come to seem like dime novel SF—better written, perhaps, but of much the same kind.

But these conservative stories of the lower reaches of possible science were not the leading edge of the new SF literature. During the twenty-five years between Verne's imaginative retreat and the rise of H.G. Wells, the first great master SF writer of the Age of Technology, many stories were written that tested the potentialities of that higher science which Verne had dreamed of in *Journey to the Centre of the Earth* but then found too overwhelming.

A convenient date to mark the birth of science fiction might be the month of May 1871. In that month, three highly significant SF stories were published, two of them by the very same publisher on the very same day. The three stories were "The Case of Summerfield" by William Henry Rhodes, "The Battle of Dorking" by Lt. Col. George Chesney, and *The Coming Race* by Edward Bulwer-Lytton. They might be thought of both as epitomes of Romantic proto-SF and as first examples of the new science fiction literature of the Age of Technology.

"The Case of Summerfield" was published in a newspaper, *The Sacramento Daily Union*, on Saturday, the 13th of May, 1871. Even more than the fiction of Jules Verne, this story might be said to be the completion or the fulfillment of Edgar Allan Poe.

William Henry Rhodes was a San Francisco lawyer, a frequent contributor of poems, essays and letters to local newspapers under the pseudonym Caxton. "The Case of Summerfield," however, appeared as a page one newspaper story, purportedly reprinted from the *Auburn Messenger* of November 1870. It was, of course, an example of that familiar Romantic literary form, the newspaper hoax. And it worked pretty well in catching the gullible citizens of California and stirring up a public hubbub.

What remains interesting about this long-forgotten jape is the sheer audacity of the science-beyond-science that it presents, token of the new understanding of the meaning of the word *science* in the Age of Technology. In "The Case of Summerfield," a mad scientist demonstrates to a lawyer that he has the power to make water burn. He threatens to start an unquenchable fire in the Pacific Ocean that will destroy the entire world unless he is paid off.

Like Verne's balloon and Moon-cannon, like the steam man of

the prairies, this is science-beyond-science brought out of the closet and allowed to have public effect in the world. But the nature of this science-beyond-science is of a new and different order. It can't be passed off as a mere "technical hiatus."

The "science" of "The Case of Summerfield" is not just an extension of what we know about the world. It is a reversal of our every normal expectation: no less than the assertion that science can find the means to make water burn, and not only burn, but burn so fiercely and unstoppably that the whole world might be consumed.

And people were ready to find this plausible. No wonder, then, that the day of SF literature was at hand.

Through the 1870s and 1880s, many stories comparable to "The Case of Summerfield" were published. Often they were cast as hoaxes. Many were published anonymously in newspapers. These stories were often of types established during the Romantic Period—tales of novel inventions, of bizarre medical experiments, or of natural or scientifically induced disasters. But the most original and daring of these otherwise old-fashioned tales, like "The Case of Summerfield," did introduce new examples of radical science-beyond-science: anti-gravity, invisibility, matter transmitters, the fourth dimension, time travel.

Because H. G. Wells made these devices his own, in our day they are generally credited to him. No, indeed. They were pioneered in often trivial and old-fashioned, but radically speculative stories written during the first two decades of the Age of Technology, the years when Wells was a boy, a student, and a young teacher.

Our second story of May 1871, "The Battle of Dorking" by Lt. Col. George Chesney, was more serious in intent than "The Case of Summerfield" and is better remembered, not because of any particular merit it may have as fiction, but because it was the first in a special genre of SF war stories.

Chesney was a member of a brilliant British military family, the most notable of whom was his elder brother Charles, an army engineer and military historian said to have "held at the time of his death a unique position in the army, altogether apart and above his actual place in it." Charles Chesney was the author of an analysis of the Battle of Waterloo that spared neither Napoleon nor Wellington, and a commentator on the American Civil War. At the conclusion of the Franco-Prussian War early in 1871, Charles was sent on a special military fact-finding mission to France and to the newly created country of Germany to report on the lessons of the war.

George Chesney had a more public career than his brother. He, too, was a military engineer. He fought in the Indian Mutiny, was wounded and promoted. He wrote textbooks for the administration of the colonial Indian government and founded an engineering college. He became a ranking general, was knighted, and finished his career as a member of Parliament. Along the way, he wrote novels and contributed to the periodical magazines.

By 1871, the familiar character of war had altered, as both the American Civil War and the Franco-Prussian War had demonstrated, and the point was not lost on George Chesney. He knew that he was no longer living in the Romantic Period, but rather in a new Age of Technology. In an attempt to alert a drowsy public to previously unconsidered dangers, he published an anonymous novelet, "The Battle of Dorking," in *Blackwood's Magazine*.

Chesney's story peered into the near future and envisioned an invasion of Britain by a Germany using new and advanced weapons. This view of future possibility stirred up great controversy. It was reprinted as a slim book, published in all of the English-speaking nations, and translated into seven European languages, including German. It prompted many imitations, answers and variants that continued to be published until the eve of World War I. The genre might even be taken as being in some sense a pre-vision of World War I.

In its science-beyond-science, "The Battle of Dorking" was not much more imaginative than a Verne story or a dime novel. Its special importance to SF literature is that it opened up a new imaginary locale—the Future—that had been all but completely outside the sphere of Romantic proto-SF.

What's this? Was there a time when the Future was not at the very center of SF? Didn't old Hugo Gernsback himself once say, "Science fiction—under *any* term or name—must, in my opinion, deal first and foremost in futures. It must, in story form, forecast *the wonders of man's progress to come*"?

It is true that the imagined future has been the primary locus of the World Beyond the Hill in science fiction, but Romantic proto-SF was never a futuristic literature. It was set in the present or in the recent past. "The Future" was a concept that belonged to a very different form of imaginative literature, the utopian story.

If science fiction has been the mythic expression of post-1870 materialistic Western techno-culture, then utopian literature could be said to have been the mythos of the immediately preceding stage in Western civilization—the period in which the modern Western world was conceived and brought into being. Instead of being a myth of science and the vast unknown, utopian literature was a myth of rationality and the Perfected Society.

Utopian literature was not fully materialistic, as science fiction has been. But neither was it an expression of the old spirit realm of ancient mythology. Rather it reflected that in-between period and state of mind in which man was assumed to have been specially created by a benevolent Deity and to be connected to Him still by the faculty of the rational soul.

In utopian literature, it was presumed that man might rise to God by creating the perfect rational society here in the material world. Utopian society was transcendent because it was superior to any now existing—the living fulfillment and expression of the God-given soul. And it was plausible inasmuch as it was considered to be an extension of the actual rationalization and modernization of Western civilization then taking place.

The model story for all subsequent utopian literature, which lent its name to the genre, was Sir Thomas More's *Utopia* (1516). "Utopia" is a Greek pun which can mean either "no place" or "the good place." More's story would set forth the limits of transcendence observed by all subsequent utopian fiction.

More—who was a humanist, a lord chancellor of England, and a martyred Catholic saint—begins the narrative by informing us that he was in the city of Antwerp while serving as an ambassador in Flanders for Henry the Eighth, when a friend introduced him to a voyager named Raphael Hythloday, who then relates his story. This man avers that he traveled to the New World with Amerigo Vespucci, and then continued on from there around the world— a feat that would not be accomplished in reality until the expedition of Magellan in 1519-22.

The traveler Hythloday is questioned closely by More and his friend:

> But what he told us that he saw in every country where he came, it were very long to declare; neither is it my purpose at this time to make rehearsal thereof. But peradventure in another place I will speak of it, chiefly such things as shall be profitable to be known, as in special be those decrees and ordinances, that he marked to be well and wittily provided and enacted among such peoples, as do live together in a civil policy and good order. For of such things did we busily inquire and demand of him, and he likewise very willingly told us of the same. But as for monsters, because they be no news, of them we were nothing inquisitive. For nothing is more easily to be found, then be barking Scyllas, ravening Celenos, and Loestrygonians devourers of people, and such like great and incredible monsters. But to find citizens ruled by good and wholesome laws, that is an exceeding rare, and hard thing.

This rings more humorously to us than it did to its original readers. In its own time, this was radical stuff! It says that the old mythic monsters might be found anywhere, but good, just and wholesome societies were so rare that you might have to travel to the far ends of the Earth—to a wholly unknown country—to find one.

In stories by the writers who followed More, it was always a new social order that was sought rather than ravening Celenos and Loestrygonians devourers of people. The Perfected Society might be located in some distant corner of the world, on the Moon or another planet, or under the ground. But always it was a human society (or some satirical distortion of human society with horses or sentient vegetables playing the human part) that was discovered.

Francis Bacon, Johannes Kepler and Tommaso Campanella were all writers of works in the utopian tradition as well as being pioneers of the new scientific thought. The improved societies espoused in these stories were a minimal sort of transcendence carefully couched in terms that would be no threat to the still-overwhelming spiritual forms of transcendence. But to argue mythically for change in the social order at all was phenomenally challenging to the rigidity and backward-gazing of the men and institutions that derived their worldly authority from spirit, which is why so many of the utopian mythmakers were executed or thrown into jail.

It could be said that Western man took up rational thought in order to free himself from the accumulated weight of the past and the breathless grip of the *ancien régime.* The final step in this process was the introduction of the concept of *progress*—the last rational idea necessary in order to make conceptually possible the revolutions and overturnings of traditional society that would soon be taking place. This came in the reading of a paper to the Sorbonne by a brilliant young theological student, Anne Robert Jacques Turgot, in 1750. The paper was entitled *A Philosophical Review of the Successive Advances of the Human Mind.*

The concept of progress suggested that the modern man of today was superior to the unwashed barbarian of yesterday. And the man of tomorrow might be the citizen of the Perfected Society.

In short, the utopian society need not be located off on the Moon or in "no place." The good society might be the familiar countries of Western Europe at some time in the Future.

The first significant utopian story to be set in the Future appeared in 1771, Louis Sebastien Mercier's *Memoirs of the Year 2440.* In this story, the Future is reached in a dream. There has been a great rationalization of clothing, education and government. The wig, for instance, is no longer worn.

This book was a heavy political document. Like "The Battle of Dorking" a hundred years later, it went through many printings and translations. The King of Spain was one of those who recognized its true implications; he banned it in 1778 as blasphemous and anarchic. In later times, Sebastien Mercier himself was ready to claim credit for having anticipated the French Revolution.

After *Memoirs of the Year 2440*, most utopias were set by convention in the Future. The Future became the locus of the rational perfection that would be. And precisely for that reason, it was no home for proto-SF.

The Romantic wildmen who first developed the materials of science-fiction-literature-to-come were rebels against the Age of Reason. They doubted social progress, rejected perfection, and assiduously sought the irrational. The utopian Future—the heartland of rational perfection—was the last place they would find what they were looking for.

There is one Romantic document that is sometimes offered as a proto-SF story with a setting in the Future—Edgar Allan Poe's sketch "Mellonta Tauta" (1849). The story takes the form of a letter supposedly written on board the balloon *Skylark* on April 1, 2848, while the balloon is crossing the Atlantic.

But this story is quite different from Poe's more obvious proto-SF. It is, in fact, an anti-utopian satire. Its title is another Greek pun— a retort to More's *Utopia* and to all the contemporary futuristic utopian stories of Poe's day. "Mellonta Tauta" means either "things to come" or "more of the same."

Greater numbers of utopian stories were published in the Nineteenth Century than in the previous three hundred years put together. Many of these were trivial, no more than light romances set in an advanced future society. Some were stories of future war or future catastrophe. But always the perfection of society remained the focal point of this literature, its central transcendence.

There were many instances of advanced science in these utopias: cures for disease, electric-powered cities, mobile homes, weather control, and new power sources superior to steam. It would be fair to say that almost every one of Verne's imaginary scientific devices had been anticipated at some previous time in a utopian story.

But this advanced imaginary science was not itself transcendent. Transcendence in a story is singular, irreducible, dominating mystery. Any lesser mystery that is displayed in the progress of a story will eventually be recognized as an aspect or an effect of that central transcendence.

In the utopian story, the central transcendence was the perfect rational society. And advanced science of the kind we have cited was only a by-product of that rational perfection. It wasn't independently transcendent, ready to go its own way and possibly even alter or destroy the society which created it. In just the same way that the steam man of the prairies, which at first glance appears to be an independent superior being, a Titan or devil, is then revealed to be a marvelous artifact created by a young master of transcendent science, so the advanced science of the utopian story was always explained to be the consequence and docile tool of rational social improvement.

It is on this ground that "The Battle of Dorking," which otherwise might be taken as a futuristic utopian war story, can be seen to be actually an example of the new, pushy SF story intruding into the imaginative territory of utopian literature. In "The Battle of Dorking," social advance is not the highest value. Rather, social change—the collapse of Britain's commerce and the loss of her colonies—is seen to result from technological advance. This is a reversal of all previous utopian value—the tail, science, wagging the dog of society.

Like "The Case of Summerfield," Chesney's "The Battle of Dorking" is further evidence of the shift in values that in 1871 was bringing the Age of Technology into being. In a test of strength between the powers of the rational spirit and technological might, the vote of "The Battle of Dorking" is for the newer and more powerful transcendence—science-beyond-science.

For the first time, the higher potentials of material science were assumed to be more powerful than the last remnant of spirit, man's God-given soul. In "The Battle of Dorking," science trumps utopia in utopia's own heartland, the Future.

In an 1871 retort to Chesney, Charles Stone's anonymous "What Happened After the Battle of Dorking, or the Victory of Tunbridge Wells," the conclusions of the original story were disputed. It was Stone's contention that no mere superiority of arms or preparation by the Germans could outweigh the indomitable *spirit* of the British people.

But the times were on Chesney's side. And during the twenty-five years between Verne's heyday and the fiction of H.G. Wells, one story after another would follow Chesney in pressing the claims of the new transcendent science. Like barbarians storming the walls of Rome, SF stories would wander the streets of the fallen city Utopia and usurp whatever they pleased to of what had once been the special materials of the utopian story, and convert them to their own purposes.

Another example of this process is to be seen in our third SF story of May 1871, *The Coming Race*, which is the best remembered of the three and the only one still read. Like our other two examples—and like so many of the proto-SF stories we have looked in upon—*The Coming Race* was published anonymously, issued by the Scottish publisher Blackwood on May 1st, the same day as the *Blackwood's Magazine* containing "The Battle of Dorking."

The author of *The Coming Race* was Edward Bulwer-Lytton, 1st Baron Lytton. Bulwer-Lytton was of the same high Romantic generation as Mary Shelley and Edgar Allan Poe. As a young dandy, Edward Bulwer—as he was then—had been among the last to seek wisdom at the feet of William Godwin. However, rather than dying young like a proper Romantic, the ambitious Bulwer had made good in life. He became a highly successful popular novelist and playwright, author of *The Last Days of Pompeii* (1834) and other Romantic fictions. Bulwer-Lytton had a long and active parallel political career, serving in Parliament first for ten years as a liberal advocate of the views of the utilitarian philosopher Jeremy Bentham, and fourteen more years as a conservative. He was created a baronet in 1838, and in 1866 was elevated to the peerage.

The Coming Race was Bulwer-Lytton's first work of fiction in many years. And such a splash did this anonymous work make that it was even ripped off for commercial purposes. It is the super-scientific force *vril* in *The Coming Race* that is the source of the name of the popular British beef tea, Bovril. At the time of his death in 1873, however, *The Coming Race* was still publicly unacknowledged by Bulwer-Lytton.

The Coming Race was one of three final works—the last still in serialization when Bulwer-Lytton died—that his son, the poet Owen Meredith, said had been intended "to exhibit the influence of modern ideas upon character and conduct." The modern idea at the heart of *The Coming Race*, of course, was the new concept of science as constituting the entire sphere of knowledge potentially attainable by man.

The Coming Race is yet another singular book, in this case a unique combination of the matter of utopian literature, science-beyond-science, and occultism. Its form, like those of "The Case of Summerfield" and "The Battle of Dorking," is old-fashioned. In appearance, it seems to be just another conventional utopian story—static, didactic, and only minimally marvelous.

In *The Coming Race*, a young man exploring the farther reaches of a mine discovers deep underground a strange civilization populated by giant human beings. The details of this superior civilization are then unfolded to him.

This is much the same pattern as any number of previous utopian stories. It was no rare thing for utopia to be found in a tucked-away underground world. Justifications for such an unlikely situation were not a primary concern of these stories. What was centrally important to utopian literature was the description of the laws and constitution of the Perfected Society.

But we might take note that the situation presented in *The Coming Race* was precisely the same as that which Jules Verne, attempting to write scientifically, had found too overwhelming to be contemplated in *Journey to the Centre of the Earth*, published only six years earlier. That is, giant human beings living underground.

We may recall Verne, in the person of Axel, writing: "The idea that a man, a living man, and with him a whole generation, should be buried down there in the bowels of the earth is unacceptable."

But in *The Coming Race* just such a generation of giant men does live in deep caverns, "caring nothing about the inhabitants of the surface and having no communication with them." This idea, which was too intense to be borne by a Verne thinking primarily of scientific mystery, is rendered almost homey by Bulwer-Lytton, writing within the tamer tradition of the utopian story.

But, no, he isn't! He is writing a story that *looks* utopian. But in spite of its conventionally didactic surface and its typically superior society, *The Coming Race* is not a utopian story. It is SF.

It is not the superior society itself that is transcendent in *The Coming Race*. Rather, the advanced society that Bulwer-Lytton's narrator discovers is supported and maintained by the super-scientific power, vril. Vril is the very basis of civilization:

> So important a bond between these several communities was the knowledge of vril and the practice of its agencies, that the word A-Vril was synonymous with civilisation and Vril-ya signifying "The Civilised Nations," was the common name by which the communities employing the uses of vril distinguished themselves from such of the Ana as were yet in a state of barbarism.

Like the utopian story, *The Coming Race* admits the notion of progress, but this progress is specifically given as *scientific* progress. It is the scientific power vril that is the measure of difference between barbarism and civilization. Here is the description of vril:

> I should call it electricity, except that it comprehends in its manifold branches other forms of nature, to which, in our scientific nomenclature, differing names are assigned, such as magnetism, galvanism, etc. ... These subterranean philosophers assert that, by one operation of vril, which Faraday would perhaps call "atmospheric magnetism," they can influence the variations of temperature—in plain words, the weather; that by other operations, akin to those ascribed to mesmerism, electro-biology, odic forces, etc., but applied scientifically through vril conductors, they can exercise influence over mind, and bodies animal and vegetable, to an extent not surpassed in the romances of our mystics.

Now, truly this is a most impressive and powerful form of science-beyond-science. It unifies physical, mental, and electromagnetic forces. It lights the underground world. It is even used by children of the Vril-ya to dispose of those monsters that lurk in the dimmer and further caverns—those ravening Celenos and Loestrygonians with which purist utopian fiction was always unconcerned.

Vril is presented to the reader as being somehow connected to the familiar scientific practice of the Nineteenth Century, but also as immensely superior to it. This is spelled out to the narrator during a visit to a museum:

> In another department there were models of vehicles and vessels worked by steam and of a balloon which might have been constructed by Montgolfier. "Such," said Zee, with an air of meditative wisdom, "such were the feeble triflings with nature of our savage forefathers ere they had even a glimmering perception of the properties of vril!"

Bulwer-Lytton had even higher game in mind than the mere presentation of super-science, as the title of his book makes apparent. In *The Coming Race*, Bulwer-Lytton was trying to depict transcendent beings—creatures of a higher order than man. This was a feat that no writer of Romantic proto-SF had been able to bring off.

In a letter to a friend, Bulwer-Lytton explained that *The Coming Race* depended "on the Darwinian proposition that a coming race is destined to supplant our races, that such a race would be very gradually formed and be indeed a new species developing itself out of our old one, and that this process would be invisible to our eyes, and therefore in some region unknown to us."

And, in fact, when they are first introduced to us, the gigantic human beings of the underground world are presented in terms similar to the initial description of the steam man of the prairies of beloved memory. But these terms are far more extravagantly phrased and much more seriously intended:

> And now there came out of this building a form—human; was it human? ...It came within a few yards of me, and at the sight and presence of it an indescribable awe and tremor seized me, rooting my feet to the ground. It reminded me of symbolical images of Genius or Demon that are seen on Etruscan vases or limned on the walls of Eastern sepulchres—images that borrow the outlines of men, and are yet of another race. ...I felt that this manlike image was endowed with forces inimical to man. As it drew near, a cold shudder came over me. I fell on my knees and covered my face with my hands.

But that is just an initial impression. The more we see of the Vril-ya, the less transcendent they seem. Like the Indians getting over their immediate awe of the steam man of the prairies, Bulwer-Lytton's narrator, too, soon gets over his indescribable awe. Eventually he, and we, must take the Vril-ya as more powerful than ordinary men by virtue of their employment of vril, but not as a new and superior order of being.

In large part, this occurs because Bulwer-Lytton's intention of presenting superior beings comes into conflict with his more immediate and practical aim of reconciling the rational ideals of the utopian story with the new modern idea of unknown science. The more the Vril-ya are made to look like the rational-minded human citizens of utopia (with a basis in science that looks exactly the same as the old basis of the soul), the less they can look like transcendent "images that borrow the outlines of men, and are yet of another race."

In *The Coming Race*, Bulwer-Lytton is attempting to hold onto the high and noble values of utopian literature, the values that had brought modern Western civilization into being. Beliefs such as justice, morality, and the higher connection to God.

At the same time, Bulwer-Lytton is trying to take full account of the most advanced product of Western civilization, rational society's monster child, science. Bulwer-Lytton is trying to say that the new science of Michael Faraday—the predecessor of James Maxwell who first suggested the unity of magnetic and electrical phenomena—and of Charles Darwin, the chief exponent of the theory of evolution, is *not different* from the old values.

The reconciliation of soul and science is Bulwer-Lytton's true game. *The Coming Race* can be seen as trying to ease the transition from the Romantic Era into the Age of Technology, to bridge the apparent gap between the old order of value and the new. Bulwer-Lytton's means of reconciliation were occultist arguments.

Occultism is the mystical doctrine which says that the visible structure of religion—any religion—is a sham, a fraud, a ruin. But that occulted—hidden—in this ruin, hidden here, hidden there, is a secret treasure, an inner core of Higher Truth.

Before the modern Western world came into being, Renaissance occultists like Paracelsus and the authors of the original Rosicrucian documents helped to stimulate the appetite for change by proclaiming the existence of a Higher Truth beyond the bounds of accepted wisdom and authority and identifying this with the study of nature and the moral reform of society and man.

With the security of a belief in occultism, the philosophers and critics of the Age of Reason could perceive their idea of a perfectible

rational soul as that hidden kernel of Higher Truth that was waiting
to be revealed, and feel free to attack the old order as no better than
a hollow facade. Occult societies like the Masons would play an
active role in the American and French Revolutions and be feared for
this throughout the Western world.

Occultism had its appeal for the wildmen of the next era, too. The
Romantics dyed their skins brown and sneaked into Mecca. They
sought hidden mysteries in the literature of Egypt, Persia, India, and
Tibet. The central argument of Mary Shelley's *Frankenstein* which
equated the ancient secret arts of alchemy and necromancy with
the wild life-awakening science of young Victor Frankenstein was
an occultist argument.

However, the peak of occultist belief and practice may have come
during the Age of Technology. Just as much as it was a period of
scientific law and life-altering inventions, it was also an era of séances
and Ouija boards, of Theosophists and Anthroposophists, of Atlantis
cultists and would-be black magicians.

To people in a later day, all this flurry of activity would look like
so much superstitious nonsense. By the mid-Twentieth Century,
occultist would be a dirty word—and so would *utopian*.

In reality, however, something very serious and consequential was
taking place. Occultism was a means of mediating the transition from
the phase of Western civilization that believed in the soul to a new
phase of strict materialism. Occultism was used in at least three
different ways.

It was a conservative position. It was a ground of argument on
which a belief in God and the soul could be maintained despite every
reductionist argument offered in the name of modern science. In
effect: "No matter what you say, I still believe in an irreducible
inner kernel of Higher Truth."

It was a radical position. Just as the revolutionaries of the Age
of Reason had identified occult inner truth with whatever they
liked of traditional society and discarded the rest, so the young
radicals of the Age of Technology could use occultist arguments
to redefine alchemy and magic and call them lost science.

But occultism could also be a position beyond the merely radical
or merely conservative. At its highest, occultism was the recognition
that "the rational soul" and "science" might be just as much facades
as "religion"—and that hidden within all three might be a common
kernel of Higher Truth wearing different names in different eras.

It is in this last sense that *The Coming Race* is occultist. *Vril* is a
term that refers to a force that is at one and the same time spiritual,
rational, scientific, and more.

If *The Coming Race* is still kept in print these days, it is not as a work of science fiction, and not as a utopian story. It is occult publishers who continue to reissue the book. In a recent edition of *The Coming Race* from one of these, vril is identified in a foreword variously as "God's Will," "Will," and "Divine Law." It is possible to see these terms as bows to the spiritual, to the rational, and to the scientific interpretations of Higher Truth.

In its way, *The Coming Race* was almost as special and pivotal a book as Horace Walpole's *The Castle of Otranto*. Both were transitional works popping up in the crack between radically different head-states, bridging the two without being ultimately committed to either. This served an immediate function for an audience that was surrendering an old mode of thought for a new one. Beyond this, while neither book could be called great literature, both had within them secret treasures with consequences for a later time.

In the case of *The Castle of Otranto*, the treasure was the principle of irreducible transcendence, simultaneously mysterious and plausible. That insight was of the greatest relevance to the science fiction literature born one hundred years later.

In the case of *The Coming Race*, the treasure was the recognition of the relativity and inadequacy of any and every term by which transcendent Truth might be represented for a time. As we will see, by the end of the Age of Technology, the concept of "science" would start wearing thin as a name for the fundamentally mysterious, and begin to be superseded by transcendence phrased in terms of "consciousness." When we witness this happening, we would do well to remember that the mysterious *something* which Bulwer-Lytton called "vril" was simultaneously spiritual, rational, physical and mental.

The Coming Race was a work with great influence in the late Nineteenth and early Twentieth Centuries. It was the model for a whole new form of utopian/occultist SF—the lost race story.

The locations featured in this genre were freely borrowed from the utopian story—an isolated island, or a blank spot on the map, or the planet Mars. But the strange people discovered in these places wouldn't be utopians devoted to showing visitors their decrees, ordinances, and good and wholesome laws.

Instead, they would turn out to be people with a relationship to the familiar Village world, but radically out of place. They might, for instance, be the descendants of shipwrecked pirates. But more often they would have ancient or legendary antecedents. They would be survivors of sunken Atlantis, or some long-forgotten outpost of the Roman Empire.

People hidden away from the world-at-large who have exalted origins and are the custodians of secret knowledge—this would be the occult aspect of the lost race story.

However, the knowledge that the lost race possesses in these stories would most usually be scientific knowledge. At first, it might well look like the magic and miracles of myth and legend, especially if the lost people were of a lineage associated with such things. In time, however, these powers would be revealed to actually be ancient science of a kind still unknown to the outside world. In other cases, the special advanced knowledge might appear in a form more familiar to the Age of Technology—like the Sacred Locomotive which is venerated by an underground culture in one story of the 1890s.

Lost race stories... future war stories... dime novel invention stories... tales of advanced science-beyond-science... As soon as science fiction began to exist, it did so in a multitude of forms.

These initial forms were somewhat makeshift—crude and even a bit old-fashioned in appearance. In a sense, they were old bottles containing new wine. But what all of them had in common—what made them ultimately one thing—was that every one of them bowed to transcendent mystery wearing the guise of presently unknown higher powers of science.

A Universe Grown Alien

Although science fiction existed in a variety of forms as early as the 1870s, it would be more than a further fifty years before SF was named and defined as a literature in the pages of *Amazing Stories*. And when it was, we may remember, editor Hugo Gernsback would identify the new "scientifiction" he proposed to publish in terms of the works of three writers—Edgar Allan Poe, Jules Verne, and H.G. Wells.

Of these three seminal writers, it was Wells who was the most significant in the early development of SF. In practice, Gernsback would reprint only half-a-dozen stories each by Poe and Verne, but he would showcase an SF story by Wells in every single issue of *Amazing* for as long as he published the magazine. It was Wells who was the very model of a modern scientifiction writer.

The reason for this is that while all three of Gernsback's exemplary writers produced charming romances in which scientific fact was intermingled, a crucial difference separated the work of Wells from that of Poe and Verne. Wells presented a wholly new concept of the universe in his stories, and it was the Wellsian universe within which subsequent science fiction would be written.

The universe as imagined by the Age of Reason, and the Romantic Period as well, was human-centered, comfortable and cozy. This universe was all too narrow, safe and regular for the wild Romantics, who aimed to reach beyond its limits and find mystery.

Poe and Verne, Romantics both, had tested the boundaries of this constricting imagined universe, aiming to break loose from it. Traveling to the edges of the familiar Village and beyond, they had caught sight of the transcendent beings and transcendent realms of the World Beyond the Hill.

But these glimpses of mystery had proved too much for them. Poe and Verne—each in turn was overwhelmed by what he saw.

They saw strange realms and alien beings, but they identified this transcendence as Madness and Death and hastily retreated from it back into the safe confines of the Village.

Wells went far beyond Poe and Verne. He shattered the boundaries altogether that divided the Village from the World Beyond the Hill. He destroyed the comfy, cozy human-centered universe of the rational utopians forever.

In a brilliant series of scientific romances written during the 1890s—including such books as *The Time Machine* (1895) and *The War of the Worlds* (1898)—Wells set forth the parameters of a radical new conceptual universe. This universe was derived from the cool-minded reasonings of science rather than from inherited religious assurances of God's special concern for man and man's privileged place in the world.

The dimensions of this new scientific universe are reflected in the title of an early Wells story collection—*Tales of Space and Time* (1899). H.G. Wells might be called the first master of space and time.

The Wellsian universe was vast and merciless, chilly and uncaring. It owed not a thing to mankind. It might even prove to be hostile to all of man's ethics, all of man's aspirations. But, almost magically, within the yawning reaches of this new universe it was possible to discover all of the transcendence that Poe and Verne had intuited but could not accept. Wells made it possible to imaginatively sustain the beings and realms that his Romantic predecessors had denied and rejected.

Here, in the opening paragraph of *The War of the Worlds*, Wells specifically contrasts the attitudes of the narrow universe that was passing with the disquieting facts of the new universe of science:

No one would have believed in the last years of the nineteenth century that this world was being watched keenly and closely by intelligences greater than man's and yet as mortal as his own; that as men busied themselves about their various concerns they were scrutinised and studied, perhaps almost as narrowly as a man with a microscope might scrutinise the transient creatures that swarm and multiply in a drop of water. With infinite complacency men went to and fro over this globe about their little affairs, serene in their assurance of their empire over matter. It is possible that the infusoria under the microscope do the same. No one gave a thought to the older worlds of space as sources of human danger, or thought of them only to dismiss the idea of life upon them as impossible or improbable. It is curious to recall some of the mental habits of those departed days. At most terrestrial men fancied there might be other men upon Mars, perhaps inferior to themselves and ready to welcome a missionary enterprise. Yet across the gulf of space, minds that are to our minds as ours are to those of the beasts that perish, intellects vast and cool and unsympathetic, regarded this earth with envious eyes, and slowly and surely drew their plans against us. And early in the twentieth century came the great disillusionment.

How fresh and powerful this writing is! And how completely different it is in style and tone from anything that we have seen before. Even as we are threatened with annihilation, our jaded spirit is restored. This brisk exact narration in itself speaks of new possibilities of thought and action.

Science in Wells is no longer just a tool, a talisman, a convenient argument, a means to get from one place to another. No, science is *everything* here. It provides the frame of reference—the new universe of space and time. It is the model for Wells's detached and analytical mode of thought. ("It is curious to recall some of the mental habits of those departed days.") It even supplies Wells with his metaphoric microscope and his microbes.

Most remarkable of all, how simultaneously lyrical and ghastly does Wells's new vision contrive to be! As the infusoria—a word which means either a class of protozoans or the products of decay—under the microscope are to us, so may we be to greater intelligences than ourselves, intellects vast and cool and unsympathetic. (Again and again Wells would be driven to use that word "vast.") These beings—these alien Martians—may be as mortal as we are, but they are an older and more powerful race, evolved far beyond us. They lurk across the gulf of space, studying our weaknesses and limitations. Soon they will strike.

Beware! says Wells. Tremble! The universe is not what you think it is, little man.

It is nothing less than a "great disillusionment" that Wells is after. He means to bring the walls of the tidy Village world crashing down with a personally wielded power that is no less shattering in its effect than the destructive force of his invading Martians striding over the fallen ruins of familiar London.

Wells means to reveal to a complacent mankind bent on its own little affairs the true nature of its relationship to the universe. Yet even so, while the initial impact may be one of disillusionment, we need to be aware that this disillusionment comes as the result of the unveiling of an awesome mystery—a new wider universe!

Through the remainder of the Age of Technology, and even after, H.G. Wells would cast an immense shadow. The universe that was portrayed by Wells would be the universe in which SF stories would be set. And it would be the dangers and possibilities which Wells

delineated in his stories of the Nineties that would be the central
issues of science fiction.

Herbert George Wells was born just prior to the dawning of the
Age of Technology, on the 21st of September, 1866. That, we may
remember, was the same year in which the late Romantic, Captain
Nemo, was said to have been prowling the seas and sinking ships in
his super-scientific submarine, the *Nautilus*. Wells was born in a
suburb of London that was later to be engulfed by the city. His
parents were former servants turned shopkeepers.

And this marks a turn in our story. The makers of proto-SF, from
Walpole to Bulwer-Lytton, were all lords, lesser nobility, aristocrats
and gentlefolk. Bertie Wells was anything but that. He was from the
upper fringes of the lower class, one small but significant step from
being a peasant or laborer, a jumped-up Cockney determined
enough and lucky enough to escape from the drapery shops that
swallowed his two older brothers. It would be from common clay
like Bertie Wells, persons on whom the impact of the Age of Technology was most marked, that the makers of Twentieth Century
science fiction would come.

It was a world in turmoil that Wells opened his eyes upon. At the
beginning of the Nineteenth Century, despite all the revaluations of
the Age of Reason, despite the upset of the French Revolution,
something like traditional society still held sway in most places.
There were still kings and nobles and peasants, just as there had
always been. But by the beginning of the Age of Technology, after
a century of revolutions and the construction of new nation states,
the familiar and comfortable old remnant feudal structure of society
had been broken like Humpty Dumpty.

The very nature and character of society had been altered. Society
was now remaking itself into the image of giant engines run by
masters of machinery, the Bosses.

The new superior class was not an aristocracy of blood and breeding, as before, but capitalists, plutocrats, men whose only recommendation was that they controlled money. New gigantic businesses
were ruled by corporate overlords, captains of industry. There were
steel barons, rail barons, oil barons, coal barons, wheat barons, even
sleeping car barons—autocrats to rule over every aspect of commerce
and industry. It was the era of the sweatshop and of machine politics.

The underclass of society was now no longer the rural peasant,
but rather urban industrial laborers—proletarians. These were
people who had been forced off the land and set to work in the
mills, factories and foundries. There they were used up, worn out,
and then discarded. In the late Nineteenth Century, these proles
rocked society by rebelling against their lot, by striking, by struggling

to organize themselves into great powerful machines of their own, the labor unions.

The Western nations acted no differently. They set up the machinery of empire and made themselves the bosses of the world. During the 1880s and 1890s, in exactly the same manner that the new giant corporations banded together in trusts and cartels in an attempt to lessen competition, divide territories, monopolize markets and maximize profits, so did the countries of Europe. They dismembered the continent of Africa. They divided the whole world up into spheres of influence.

It was a ruthless time. If the machine was the model for society, the justification for the moral style of the Technological Age was adapted from Charles Darwin's theory of evolution, the deepest and most complete explanation of the meaning of existence that the new religion of science had to offer. Social Darwinism was the philosophy of the day, and the message that was drawn from Darwin by the Age of Technology was this: "Struggle to exist. If you are fit, you may survive."

No wonder then that the most prominent citizens of the advanced Western nations should feel *obliged* to consolidate all the wealth and power they could, to seek personal advantage wherever it could be found, and to deliver a ruthless justice to the poor, the weak and the backward. They couldn't help themselves. That was what the struggle for existence was all about. To think otherwise and to act otherwise would be foolhardy.

Like everyone else, Bertie Wells had to struggle to exist. However, he wasn't fit by any standard. He was a small and sickly child. But, strangely enough, he managed to negotiate the minefield of late Nineteenth Century society by failing his way to success. One illness, accident and disaster after another honed and turned and shaped Wells just so, to make him that one person in the Nineties prepared to recognize the new insecure universe of space and time and man's precarious place within it.

Wells's parents kept a china and glass shop, but sold little ware. His father was a well-known local cricket player, and sold bats and balls in the shop. Otherwise he was a dreamer. Wells's mother, a conventionally pious former lady's maid, had all the family ambition. Her idea of success was a good steady position in a cloth shop, and she apprenticed all three of her sons to drapers.

When he was seven, Bertie was tossed into the air by an older boy and accidentally dropped. His leg was broken. And this was his first stroke of good fortune. During his enforced confinement, the boy became a compulsive reader.

When Wells was eleven, there was a second broken leg, this time his father's. Joseph Wells fell off a ladder while trimming a grapevine and fractured his thigh. His cricket-playing career was brought to an end, and the dusty china shop became insufficient to support the family. Wells's mother, Sarah, went back into domestic service, becoming the housekeeper of Up Park, the country estate of her former mistress, Miss Fetherstonhaugh (pronounced Fanshaw).

And this was another blessing in disguise. Bertie, at the times he was living with his mother, was given the run of the library at Up Park. Here he encountered Shelley and Voltaire, read the unexpurgated *Gulliver's Travels*, and discovered the first account of a model society, Plato's *Republic.*

This paradise was never to last. Bertie was apprenticed no less than three times, twice to drapers and once to a pharmacist. Each time he contrived to fail. He was dismissed as incompetent, he argued his way free, or he simply walked away. Each time he returned to Up Park and the library.

What Wells really wanted was education, and in between his failed apprenticeships he was sent to one minimal school after another. Eventually he was offered a position as student assistant at Midhurst Grammar School, the first of a number of teaching jobs that he would hold in secondary schools and cram colleges, the new hastily established educational institutions of the late Nineteenth Century.

England had found the advanced European technology displayed at the Crystal Palace Exhibition of 1851 profoundly disturbing. An Education Act had been passed in 1871 as a reaction to the Franco-Prussian War, that even more unsettling display of European technology. In later life, Wells would speak regretfully of his lack of genuine education when he was young, but at least the Education Act of 1871 provided him with a certain space for self-education within the shelter of one half-established or fraudulent school after another.

The nearest that Wells came to any proper education at all was the three years from 1884 to 1887 that he spent at the Normal School of Science, a college for teachers of science in South Kensington, London. Wells arrived at the Normal School by passing a number of exams for his own reasons and winning an unanticipated scholarship.

And for a time he was in his element. Bertie was the prime mover in the establishment of a school magazine, the *Science Schools Journal.* He edited the magazine and contributed a wide variety of material to it. And he took an active part in the Debating Society, experimenting with the utterance of unthinkable ideas.

The best part of his formal education at the Normal School was the first year spent studying biology and zoology under Thomas

Huxley, whom Wells admired vastly. Huxley, known as "Darwin's Bulldog," had become famous as a champion of the theory of evolution. In an 1860 debate that had insured the acceptability of evolution—if not won its immediate acceptance—Huxley had made a monkey out of his opponent, Bishop "Soapy Sam" Wilberforce. Huxley was the era's chief spokesman for the scientific point of view.

Huxley's influence on Wells was brief but it was crucial. Early in the year, Huxley became ill and soon had to withdraw. It was to be his last year of teaching.

In Wells's second year, his attention began to turn to his extracurricular activities and his grades slipped badly. In the third year of his three-year course he did so disastrously that his scholarship was withdrawn and he had to drop out of college. Not finishing at the Normal School meant that Wells had unfitted himself for a successful career as a teacher or scientist. To all appearances, he had placed himself on an evolutionary sidetrack.

But appearances—and his own later opinions—to the contrary, in terms of what he would come to make of himself, Wells's incomplete and one-sided education was exactly the education he needed. The only formal study that made any impression on him at all was the time spent with Huxley—"beyond all question, the most educational year of my life." He revered Huxley as an intellectual giant of the same stature as Plato and Galileo, and he listened enraptured to Huxley's ideas of evolution. That was the nucleus around which he came to form himself.

Otherwise, Wells was self-taught. Where others had to deal with the burden of a good traditional education, Bertie's ideas were his own. This gave him a tremendous advantage in comprehending and dealing with the new realities of the Age of Technology.

The change from the Romantic Period to the Technological Age was a very difficult transition for society to negotiate. The Age of Technology was not accepted easily or gladly by most people. In many ways, it was a very bitter pill to swallow.

It was a time of widespread disillusion. Behind the late Victorian world lay all those centuries of thought and toil by Western man in the name of the rational soul and the reformation of society. But what had been the actual worldly result of all that utopian striving? Brutish, boss-ridden, late-Victorian machine civilization.

Was *this* rationality? Was *this* society Utopia?

There was a great revulsion against the artificiality of civilization. Artists and philosophers began to doubt the validity of everything they had been taught about the world, a radical skepticism far beyond any doubts or reservations held by the Romantics. Men could not help but wonder whether the whole impulse toward rationality had not been a delusion.

In this moment of radical doubt, only the new science spoke with certainty. It increasingly seemed that everything that existed had a scientific explanation, a mechanistic cause. But science had nothing to say about morality, justice or higher purpose. Did such things exist? They were not visible in nature. You couldn't detect the soul with a microscope.

So, at the same time that rationality was doubted, there was great reluctance even among the most radical to abandon the soul and rush to embrace the new science. All of man's hopes for a more-than-animal existence had been identified with the rational soul for so long. Without that last bit of spirit, the promise of man's self-transcendence, life could seem to be without purpose or meaning.

Was Western man to be condemned to live out his years in a technological hell with only soulless science to give him comfort? Or was there some vital principle, inaccessible to scientific explanation—a principle which might or might not be called "the soul"—underlying the phenomena of life and consciousness?

In the last quarter of the Nineteenth Century there was a ferocious war between science and the last bastions of rationalized religion. Could the two be reconciled? Must science carry the day? Often this war was fought in public, but the chief battleground was the individual human heart.

Some, like H. G. Wells's own mother, could simply not accept the new ideas. These people turned off their minds and determined to continue to believe the old beliefs. The end of the Nineteenth Century was a period that saw an outpouring of fervent Christian Fundamentalism. It was an era of evangelists and revival meetings and claims of the literal truth of the Bible.

Other Victorians, like Bulwer-Lytton in *The Coming Race*, attempted to find some ground for the reconciliation of science and spirit, some point of compromise. These men had been raised on the Latin and Greek classics and the Bible. This traditional wisdom was not to be lightly discarded. And so they did their best to accommodate their educations and values to the new facts of science. But this became increasingly difficult to do as the conclusions of science varied more and more from the premises of received religion.

The attachment to morality and the soul was not surrendered easily. The conflict and ambivalence of the moment can be seen written large in the imaginative fiction of Edward Page Mitchell. Mitchell was an American newspaperman who published many anonymous stories in newspaper syndication between 1874 and 1886. Some of Mitchell's stories were SF and some were not, but most of them were caught up in the debate between spirit and matter.

On the side of spirit, Mitchell wrote stories of séances, the mysterious affinity of twins, and the swapping of souls. On the side of strict materialism, he wrote of matter transmission, of drugs as a source of religious belief, and of an idiot's brain replaced by a logic machine, "an artificial intellect that operates with the certainty of universal law."

In Mitchell's materialistic mood, the thrust of his argument is that man is nothing but matter. The mind is a machine, human personality can be altered by drugs or operations, and the vitality of the body does not depend on a soul or even a brain. The seemingly supernatural can be achieved mechanically. But Mitchell in his stories clearly abhores this materialist philosophy. He is against the mad scientists who propound it.

At the same time, Mitchell had a great interest in the spiritual and occult. He tried over and over again in his fiction to find some loophole in science that would allow room for spirit, some undeniable but anomalous phenomenon that would admit of no material explanation. But the majority of these occult stories end as hoaxes or delusions.

There is a great internal struggle going on in Mitchell. Altogether, he gives the impression of one longing to hold onto spirit but being moved toward the materialist position quite against his will.

The ambivalence of the period can be seen in even so strong a champion of science as Thomas Huxley. Huxley, born in 1825, was raised with conventional religious views which he gradually shed bit by bit in favor of the conclusions of material science. But even he could be sufficiently dismayed by the vision of the universe revealed by science that he could seek to keep a hold on the lifeline of religious morality. Morality without the religious part. Morality standing alone.

Huxley's scientific convictions forced him to see Evolution as a merciless cosmic process that would eventually doom man to extinction. Morality was man's one wan hope. In "Evolution and Ethics," the epitomal Romanes Lecture that Huxley delivered at Oxford in 1893, two years before he died, he said, "Social progress means a checking of the cosmic process at every step and the substitution for it of another, which may be called the ethical process." And he said, "Let us understand, once for all, that the ethical progress of society depends, not on imitating the cosmic process, still less in running away from it, but in combating it." In Huxley's grim view, human ethics was the only countermeasure to Evolutionary Doom.

What a tangle this question of science and human moral purpose was. It took a man like H.G. Wells to cut through the Gordian knot.

Bertie Wells lacked all attachment to traditional society, traditional education and traditional values. His initial assumptions were Thomas Huxley's reluctant conclusions. It was simple to him:

If this was the universe that science said it was, and there was a conflict between the chilly prospect of human decline and extinction and the old sentimental illusion of human morality and progress, why then, *kill illusion*. Have done with all superstitious nonsense, however comforting. Doubt God. Discard the soul. Face the facts. Look the universe in the eye.

The struggle between science and traditional religion in the last half of the Nineteenth Century was like an arm-wrestling match, with religion on the defensive and science the aggressor with the advantage, piling on the pressure, piling on the pressure. A point came in the late 1880s when religion gave way and science, love it or not, was the clear victor.

Science was bound to prevail. It was the new religion of the day and all the miracles were on its side: high-speed printing, photography, the steamship, the railroad, the telephone, the phonograph, the electric light, the dynamo, the bicycle, the motor-cycle, the automobile.

All of these wondrous things had been invented by 1887, a year that we can use as a handy reference point. It was 1887 when Bertie Wells dropped out of Normal School. And by 1887, Edward Page Mitchell had ceased to write his ambivalent imaginative stories, as though the question he had been trying to resolve had been answered for him and there was no need to continue. But more significant of change was a crucial scientific experiment that took place in 1887.

Ever since the time of Newton and the beginnings of Western rational culture, it had been assumed by physics that there was an invisible solid medium through which light waves were transmitted— the "luminiferous ether." Ether was the fabric of space. Nineteenth Century interpretations of Newton's laws of motion assumed this fabric as the reference point against which absolute motion was to be calculated.

In 1887, two American scientists, Albert Michelson and Edward Morley, attempted to determine the Earth's motion in relation to the ether. But no matter in what direction they turned their subtle scientific instrument—an interferometer—they found no invisible underlying fixed medium. No ether.

No ether? The fabric of space, the soul-stuff of the universe, the cosmic glue, was instantly dissolved. Western man was thrown into the physical universe that he has inhabited since: relative rather than absolute, irrational, moving in many directions at the same time, particulate, held together by nothing. It is this alien, etherless universe without a soul that Wells would present in *The War of the Worlds*.

The shift in balance in the direction of science that occurred in the late 1880s was reflected in a new confidence on the part of SF literature, and in a new receptivity to SF among the reading public. In the late Nineteenth Century, SF was more generally published and read by a broader public than it would be at any time in the next hundred years. Anyone who read at all might read an occasional SF story. There was a great surge in the number of SF stories written, and far more of them than ever before were novels. Perhaps most indicative of the gain in confidence is the fact that more and more of these new stories were published under their authors' own names, rather than anonymously as had so often been the case in the past.

At the same time that they were becoming more popular, SF stories were also growing far more imaginative and broader in scope. It was as though there was no imaginative possibility too fantastic to suggest as long as it was attributed to the powers of science.

Writers were emboldened to envision more exotic worlds. An increasing number of stories concerned the discovery of strange creatures—prehistoric beasts, or giant spiders, or unknown human species. And, in the name of science, writers were able to posit radical disruptions in the existing state of things. There were stories of catastrophe, and of human collapse into barbarism, even stories of the end of the world.

As a student at the Normal School of Science—later to be called the Royal College of Science, and still later the Imperial College of Science and Technology—young Bertie Wells was as sensitive to the new powers of science as anyone. And he was one of those who aimed to join in the writing of the bold new science fiction.

As he left the Normal School in 1887, Wells contributed a slight sketch to the *Science Schools Journal* entitled "A Tale of the Twentieth Century." And in 1888—when he was no longer associated with the college—the *Science Schools Journal* still published his incomplete serial story, *The Chronic Argonauts*, Wells's first attempt at what would eventually become, after seven years and many rewritings, his first great success, *The Time Machine*.

SF was burgeoning, but Wells was not yet ready to be part of the process. He was not yet ready to become a successful SF writer.

Before that could happen, it was necessary for three things to occur. Society had to fall into a still more unsettled, intense and questioning state of mind—receptive to Wells's extreme ideas of the lessons of science. The publishing industry had to alter, and new markets in chronic need of material had to become established. Finally, Wells himself had to mature. His writing abilities needed time to ripen, and he had to grow more desperate.

In the meantime, the new SF literary tradition continued to expand itself and its sense of its own powers. Just as Wells was readying himself to become a unique new SF writer, so was a readership being prepared to accept and appreciate a writer like Wells when he was finally ready to step on stage.

Perhaps the most significant element in this expansion, the harbinger of the new universe, was a sudden broadening in the time scale of SF. Previously, science fiction had been a literature of the present, the era of modern science. During the late Eighties and early Nineties, this changed radically. SF followed up the lesson of "The Battle of Dorking" by invading the Future, the territory of the utopian story, and taking it over. In the same way, it moved into the past, the land of ancient myth and legend, and tossed fantasy out.

There was a final flowering of the utopian story at the end of the Nineteenth Century, so that between 1888 and 1895 as many utopias were published as in all the previous part of the century. But most of this work was intended to either support or refute one book, Edward Bellamy's *Looking Backward, 2000-1887* (1888). The particular importance of this novel is that it marks the capitulation by the utopian story to the forces of science.

To all obvious surface appearance, *Looking Backward* is another typical utopian story. The main character is hypnotized because of a sleeping problem, falls into a slumber in 1887 and makes the conventional transition to the Future. There, as usual, he is cosseted and made much of, lectured at length, and shown the wonders of the Perfected Society.

What is different is that the central transcendence of this Perfected Society is technological industry, and not the rational soul. The ingenious argument of *Looking Backward* is that machine society, hideous in Bellamy's time and apparently growing ever more so, would one day complete itself, cast off its disguise and reveal itself as true utopia:

> The movement toward the conduct of business by larger and larger aggregations of capital, the tendency toward monopolies, which had been so desperately and vainly resisted, was recognized at last, in its true significance, as a process which only needed to complete its logical evolution to open a golden future to humanity. Early in the last century [i.e., the Twentieth] the evolution was completed by the final consolidation of the entire capital of the nation. The industry and commerce of the

country, ceasing to be conducted by a set of irresponsible corporations and syndicates of private persons at their caprice and for their profit, were entrusted to a single syndicate representing the people, to be conducted in the common interest for the common profit.

It would happen as simply as this: First the government would nationalize all business and industry. Then everybody in society in a condition to serve would be drafted into the industrial army.

Everyone is content in Bellamy's utopia. Life is simple. Life is fair. And there is only the least hint of coercion:

"...To speak of service being compulsory would be a weak way to state its absolute inevitableness. Our entire social order is so wholly based upon and deduced from it that if it were conceivable that a man could escape it, he would be left with no possible way to provide for his existence. He would have excluded himself from the world, cut himself off from his kind, in a word, committed suicide."

This has a somewhat awful ring to our ears. From our later perspective we can recognize Bellamy's society in *Looking Backward* as the Twentieth Century totalitarian state, the industrial dictatorship, only defined as benevolent and altruistic and painted with a smiling face. But even if we are able to resist its charms, we still must recognize what a powerful and overwhelming vision this was in its own time.

Looking Backward was a radical and shocking new point of view, both enthusiastically accepted and desperately resisted. The story was controversial because it symbolized the shift from a faith in rational quasi-materialism and the soul to a belief in scientific materialism and the powers of technology.

The reactions to Bellamy were immediate. The American politician and writer Ignatius Donnelly, for instance, doubted the sudden overnight capitulation by the bosses of society and the subsequent transformation into an egalitarian society in which all would be equally draftable. In his novel *Caesar's Column* (1890), published under the pseudonym Edmund Boisgilbert, Donnelly foresaw a technological future completely dominated by the trusts, with society divided between the wealthy few and the oppressed masses. A revolt against this tyranny is unsuccessful, hundreds of thousands of people are killed, and the hero and his friends must flee to another continent to make a stab at starting civilization afresh.

For his part, William Morris, the British painter, designer, poet and fine printer, called *Looking Backward* "a Cockney paradise"— a vulgar vision of the triumph of machine culture. In answer to it, he wrote *News from Nowhere* (1890), in which a dreamer departs from the blighted England of the late Nineteenth Century and finds himself in a transformed world, peaceful and green and devoted to handicrafts. It is essentially the medieval world, but sanitized of religion and ignorance.

But there is a crucial difference between Morris's *News from Nowhere* and Bellamy's *Looking Backward* which shows where the true power of active conviction lay. In *Looking Backward*—in keeping with the new doctrine of scientific materialism—it is the narrator's *body* that travels forward in time to the year 2000. When, near the end of the story, he briefly believes himself back in 1887, that proves to be only a nightmare from which he awakens.

In Morris's book, however, the sleeper travels to the new society not in body, but as a dreamer in spirit. It is not a specific future year that he travels to, but "nowhere," a land without a location. And when the book is over, the dream is ending. This sleeper will awake to find himself back amidst the horrors of 1890.

Looking Backward is a serious attempt at prophecy. *News from Nowhere* is only a vote of no confidence in the present.

In spite of protests like *Caesar's Column* and attempted exceptions like *News from Nowhere*, after *Looking Backward* it became clear that technology had taken over the future of the utopian story. The barbarians now ruled Rome.

Henceforth, to the extent that utopias would continue to be imagined, they would be imagined as technologically perfected societies. Protests against industrial utopia became centered in the dystopian story, which conceded that metal-and-glass technoparadise would be the society of tomorrow, but reserved the right to complain about it. It seemed that either you liked this world-to-come or you didn't, but either way, scientific utopia was the only Perfected Society that could be.

At precisely the same time that science overthrew the utopian future and placed itself in charge, it also made a move on the more-or-less historical territory of legendary fantasy. The most striking example of this process is to be found in Mark Twain's *A Connecticut Yankee in King Arthur's Court* (1889), in which a practical and unsentimental American machinist and superintendent of labor is struck a blow on the head which returns him to the days of Camelot. Twain's character dubs himself "The Boss" and sets out to take over this medieval world and industrialize it, pitting guns and railroads against knights in armor and the magic of Merlin.

And time and time again in this story, it is technology that triumphs: "Somehow, every time the magic of fol-de-rol tried conclusions with the magic of science, the magic of fol-de-rol got left."

In effect, *A Connecticut Yankee in King Arthur's Court* is the new voice of scientific materialism informing legendary fantasy that it must pack its bags and quit history. No more stories would be allowed like *The Castle of Otranto*, set in the Twelfth Century and featuring ghosts in conformity with the fantastic beliefs of the period. Like the future, the past was now the province of science. Magic and superstition must vacate.

This eviction from familiar imaginative quarters can most easily be traced in the sonorous romances that William Morris, the author of *News from Nowhere*, wrote during the later years of his life. The first ones that he produced, such as *The House of the Wolfings* (1889), were legendary tales set in remote historical times in Northern Europe. The last few, like *The Wood Beyond the World* (1894) and *The Well at the World's End*, published posthumously in 1896, were more frankly magical. But as their titles suggest, they were set outside history and geography in some imaginary region whose relationship to our ordinary world was not plausibly fixed. Full-blown magic was now permitted to exist only in such nonce worlds.

The Victorians were as fascinated by ancient civilizations and prehistory, lately uncovered by science, as the Romantics had been by the Middle Ages. As magic and legend were nudged and shoved and pushed out of history, stories invoking technology rushed in to replace them. In H. Rider Haggard's classic lost race novel *She* (1887), for instance, a goddess-like woman surviving from ancient times is discovered ruling a native tribe in present-day Africa. But those powers that have sustained her so long, at first seeming to be magic and sorcery, are ultimately revealed instead to be a kind of science:

"I started back aghast, and cried out that it was magic....

"'Nay, nay, O Holly,' she answered, 'it is no magic; that is a fiction of ignorance. There is no such thing as magic, though there is such a thing as knowledge of the secrets of Nature.'"

The prehistoric past of dinosaur bones, Neanderthal skeletons and stone axes was, of course, the natural property of science, which had discovered them. The first stories set in the Stone Age appeared at just this same time, Andrew Lang's "The Romance of the First Radical" in 1886, and Henry Curwen's *Zit and Xoe* in 1887. The invariable subject of stories like these was the invention of civilization and material culture.

This great broadening of the SF canvas, this extension into the past and into the future, made a true master of space and time like Wells possible. It was a writer writing with a conscious knowledge of what he was about who would produce in 1897 novelets with the parallel titles "A Story of the Days to Come" and "A Story of the Stone Age." Not at all by accident, "A Story of the Days to Come" concerns a failed attempt to escape from the grip of metal-and-glass techno-utopia. And "A Story of the Stone Age" is about the invention of the first stone club by a brainy caveman of fifty thousand years ago, out to increase his power to survive through technological innovation.

But those stories were the work of the mature Wells, the one man who could look at the new scientific universe without blinking. That Wells would be the first writer since Jules Verne in *Journey to the Centre of the Earth* to penetrate into an undoubtable transcendent realm. That Wells would be the envisioner of powerful and dangerous alien creatures. But before Bertie, the young would-be SF writer, could become that Wells, it was necessary for him to suffer and fail some more, to suffer and fail until he had nothing at all to lose.

When Wells left Normal School in 1887, he returned to teaching as the most obvious way of making a living. But a crushed kidney from a kick received on the soccer field plus signs of tuberculosis soon sent him back to Up Park for an extended period of recuperation.

There he attempted a social novel called *Lady Frankland's Companion* and managed to write some 35,000 words before it got set aside incomplete. He sponged off friends, and earned small money writing and answering science questions for boys' papers.

After more than a year of illness and indecision, Wells found another teaching position. Teaching science would be his main occupation for the following four and a half years.

In all this period of six years after leaving school, Wells's one writing success would be a speculative essay, "The Rediscovery of the Unique," written at Christmastime 1890 at Up Park, two months after Wells finally got his degree in zoology from London University through examination. "The Rediscovery of the Unique" was bought by the legendary editor Frank Harris and published in the *Fortnightly Review* in July 1891. What is most interesting about this essay is that in it "science" stands both for the knowledge of man and for the great unknowns lying beyond him. The essay concludes:

> Science is a match that man has just got alight. He thought he was in a room—in moments of devotion, a temple—and that his light would be reflected from and display walls inscribed with wonderful secrets and pillars carved with philosophical systems wrought into harmony. It is a curious sensation, now that the preliminary splutter is over and the flame burns up clear, to see his hands lit and just a glimpse of himself and the patch he stands on visible, and around him, in place of all that human comfort and beauty he anticipated—darkness still.

In 1893, two years after this solitary essay was published—six full years after he had dropped out of Normal School—Wells's situation was considerably more desperate than it had ever been before. He had not sold any further writing, though not from want of trying. And his personal life was suddenly extremely burdensome.

Wells had married his cousin Isabel in 1891 out of need and frustration. But the marriage had not proven satisfying to him. Isabel was unresponsive both sexually and intellectually. Wells had now fallen in love with one of the new forthright young women of the Nineties, Amy Catherine Robbins, one of his cram college students.

In early 1893, Wells's mother lost her position as housekeeper at Up Park. And his older brother Fred was fired from his job in a drapery shop in order to make way for his employer's son. Suddenly, Bertie Wells, not yet 27, was the sole financial support for his entire family.

It was too much for him. In May 1893, Wells collapsed again, coughing blood. It became clear to Bertie that he would have to give up teaching.

It was in this moment of awfulness and desperate need that things finally began to fall into place for H. G. Wells. It was as though it were necessary for him to be shaken violently, spun out of his course, flogged within an inch of his life, and then stopped dead in his tracks, in order for him to *perceive* what it was that he really needed to do.

What he did immediately after his collapse was to travel to the seashore to recover. While he was there, Wells picked up a lending library copy of *When a Man's Single*, a novel by J. M. Barrie, later to write *Peter Pan*.

In this book, one character explains to another in passing how it is possible to write saleable sketches out of the commonest elements of everyday experience. A light dawned. Wells set the book down and straight away on the back of an envelope wrote the first draft of an article entitled "On the Art of Staying at the Seashore."

And Barrie's advice proved accurate. This facetious little trifle sold immediately to the *Pall Mall Gazette*, a newspaper.

Wells had been aiming his work at the literary magazines and failing. Now he began to write humorous trifles for newspapers and popular magazines. And he found his work instantly in demand. Before the end of 1893, he had sold more than thirty chatty articles.

The newspapers and magazines for which Wells had begun to write were a new publishing phenomenon of the Nineties, a second-order result of the same Age of Technology that had produced Wells himself. It was as simple as this: In order to manufacture and maintain the complex new machinery of the day—such as high-speed presses—

it was necessary to educate the poor and ignorant. It was as part of this upgrading process that Wells had received his own education.

Wells says, "The Education Act of 1871 had not only enlarged the reading public very greatly but it had stimulated the middle class by a sense of possible competition from below." A new and broader reading audience had now graduated from boys' papers and penny dreadfuls—the British equivalent of the dime novel. It was seeking more meaty fare. Suddenly, then, there were new publications everywhere, and new forms of publication including the all-story pulp magazine and the middle-class popular magazine.

Wells hit this new expanded marketplace just at the moment that it first came into being: "New books were being demanded and fresh authors were in request. Below and above alike there was opportunity, more public, more publicity, more publishers and more patronage."

Bertie was the rare writer jumped up out of the narrow twilight area between the working class and the new expanded middle class and able to speak to both. A man like Wells was actively *needed* by the new publications, who were ready to swallow almost any piece of work that he could hand them. And there is no doubt that if Wells had cared to stick at this point he could have had a fine extended career as a light humorist.

As it was, Wells became freed to make his own life. At the end of 1893, he walked away from a situation he didn't like one last time. He separated from his wife Isabel and moved in with his former student Amy Catherine Robbins. As Wells himself noted, it was an act that had more than a touch of Percy Shelley eloping with Mary Godwin about it, as though what had once been the behavior of the radical aristocracy had over the course of eighty years come trickling down to the lower classes. Even so, it was still a chancy and disgraceful act, all the more so because Shelley had not had to earn a living, while Wells did.

Wells continued to beaver away industriously. He had all the ready markets available to him that poor Edgar Allan Poe had lacked. In the course of 1894, he sold at least seventy-five articles. He wrote about anything and everything: colds, swearing, his father as a cricket player, his uncle the one-armed con man. And everything that he turned out was snatched right up. In his autobiography, Wells says, "I was doing my best to write as other writers wrote, and it was long before I realized that my exceptional origins and training gave me an almost unavoidable freshness of approach...."

Some of what he wrote was more seriously intended, in much the same vein as his first essay, "The Rediscovery of the Unique." These speculative pieces were often based on pet ideas that Wells had dreamed up in some form in the *Science Schools Journal* or tried out before the Debating Society.

In 1893, there was "The Man of the Year Million." In this essay, published in the *Pall Mall Budget*, there is a disquieting vision of mankind in the far future:

> There grows upon the impatient imagination a building, a dome of crystal, across the translucent surface of which flushes of the most glorious and pure prismatic colours pass and fade and change. In the centre of this transparent chameleon-tinted dome is a circular white marble basin filled with some clear, mobile, amber liquid, and in this plunge and float strange beings. Are they birds?
>
> They are the descendants of man—at dinner. Watch them as they hop on their hands...about the pure white marble floor. Great hands they have, enormous brains, soft, liquid, soulful eyes. Their whole muscular system, their legs, their abdomens, are shrivelled to nothing, a dangling, degraded pendant to their minds.

This was the first appearance of the Big Brain theme, which would haunt science fiction for the next fifty years. What an awful and gleeful suggestion for Wells to make: that our children might not be the clean-cut citizens of the Perfected Society at all, but instead might evolve into revolting creatures with no resemblance at all to present humanity, great thoughtful sacs of brain matter hopping about on their hands.

Not at all the sort of material one would guess as having wide popular appeal. But this was no ordinary time. This was the *fin de siècle*.

This phrase of the day means no more than "the end of the century," but it was pronounced, understood and felt as though it meant the end of the world. There was a great weariness to be felt in society. Victoria had been queen of England for more than fifty years...it seemed forever. Everything was infinitely old and tired and decadent. This was the period of Aubrey Beardsley and Oscar Wilde, strange twisted neo-Romantics who appeared, blossomed briefly like pale lilies of the night, and died.

The very same decade was also called the Gay Nineties, as though the only reasonable thing to do in view of all that tosh about the end of the world was to sing, dance, make merry and hail the birth of the new. It was an era of radical, forward-looking men, the decade of the rise of George Bernard Shaw and the Fabian Socialists. There was a great receptivity to news of science and to speculation about the future.

Bertie Wells was a man made for this moment. Such was the

darkness, the confusion and the fever of the Nineties that it was
not always possible to tell at the time what was decadent and what
was farseeing. The two seemed almost the same—intertwined, intermingled, impossible to clearly distinguish.

Which was Wells, a decadent or a prophet? He was neither, he was
either, he was both. He couldn't know.

He'd been held down, held back all his life, and he was filled with
a towering rage. He was a sick man, a tubercular case living with
another tubercular case. A man uncertain even of seeing the dawn
of the new century. He might well be another decadent, another
strange twisted harbinger of doom.

But at the same time, he was a man newly set free. A man with a
head full of the *damndest* notions, ideas that he had been carrying
around for years and incubating with no one to hear them. And
now people were ready to hear them. He would live forever!

And so you have an article like "The Man of the Year Million,"
simultaneously serious and humorous, promising and horrifying,
decadent and prophetic. The perfect expression of Bertie Wells—
and a mirror for the *fin de siècle*.

In 1894, Wells published many articles of a similar sort. Among
them was an alternative view of mankind's fate. In "The Extinction
of Man," instead of seeing Big Brain as man's future, Wells suggested
that we might be overtaken and replaced altogether by crustaceans,
cephalopods, ants, or bacilli:

> We think, because things have been easy for mankind as a whole for a
> generation or so, we are going on to perfect comfort and security in the
> future. We think that we shall always go to work at ten and leave off at
> four and have dinner at seven forever and ever. ... Even now, for all we
> can tell, the coming terror may be crouching for its spring and the fall
> of humanity be at hand. In the case of every predominant animal the
> world has seen, I repeat, the hour of its complete ascendance has been
> the eve of its entire overthrow.

Also in 1894, there were two essays on alternatives to our familiar
carbon-based form of life—"The Living Things That May Be" on
silicon-based life, and "Another Basis for Life" on inorganic quasi-
living systems. In that year, Wells even dug up his old school masterpiece, *The Chronic Argonauts*, and rewrote it for the fifth time.
It was published as a series of seven unsigned articles on the theme
of time travel.

In these early essays, from "The Rediscovery of the Unique" in
1891 to the variously titled pieces on time travel in 1894, Wells set
down all of the major questions and themes that he would explore

in his scientific romances: "Science" both as the limited state of man's knowledge and as the larger questions posed for man by nature; the vast, promising and threatening new universe of time and space; alternative forms of life; possible successors to man; most important of all, the future prospects of mankind, either extinction by some more ruthless race of being or an ending as the alien and inhuman Big Brain.

And it was while he was in this acute state of readiness and rehearsal that Wells at last was solicited to write science fiction stories by two different editors. First, Lewis Hind—who later said, "I touched the button only"—commissioned Wells to write short stories with scientific themes for the *Pall Mall Budget*. Wells began with a story entitled "The Stolen Bacillus," and sold no less than five SF stories in 1894. When the *Budget* soon failed, it was no matter. There were other and better-paying markets ready to buy this kind of work.

Far more important, W.E. Henley, the editor at *The National Observer* who had published Wells's time travel articles, wrote to him to say that he was starting a new magazine. He proposed to Wells that he rewrite his articles as a serial story for this magazine, *The New Review*, and offered him the tempting sum of 100 pounds to do it.

The effect was something like the effect on Jules Verne when Pierre Hetzel suggested that he take his history of ballooning manuscript and turn it into a balloon adventure story. In a period comparable to the few weeks of fevered writing that it took Jules Verne to produce *Five Weeks in a Balloon*, Wells went off on vacation and in two weeks wrote *The Time Machine*—a story to which all previous SF was but a predicate.

As a serial story, *The Time Machine* attracted all the attention that Henley could have wished. As a book—one of four that Wells published in 1895, including *The Stolen Bacillus and Other Incidents*—*The Time Machine* made a name for Wells. If he had died then and there, instead of continuing to write for another fifty years, Wells would still be remembered for *The Time Machine*. It is an amazingly original story.

It begins with two framing chapters. But even here we are dealing with something strange and new.

The story opens: "The Time Traveller (for so it will be convenient to speak of him) was expounding a recondite matter to us." We are in the middle of an intellectual discussion after a dinner party. And already, by beginning the story at all, we have accepted that there is a man who can travel in time.

Very shortly, he is informing the party of the nature of the universe they live in: "'There are really four dimensions, three which we call the three planes of Space, and a fourth, Time.'"

And before the first chapter is done, he has brought out a model time machine. The toy is "a glittering metallic framework, scarcely larger than a small clock, and very delicately made. There was ivory in it, and some transparent crystalline substance." A crucial lever is pressed by one of his guests, the toy becomes indistinct, and then disappears.

The guests are then shown the not-quite-complete Time Machine itself. This is a classic bit of science-beyond-science. The Time Machine is described in terms that are simultaneously vague and concrete. There is a saddle to sit upon and levers to push. It is like the toy, but larger:

> Parts were of nickel, parts of ivory, parts had certainly been filed or sawed out of rock crystal. The thing was generally complete, but the twisted crystalline bars lay unfinished upon the bench beside some sheets of drawings, and I took one up for a better look at it. Quartz it seemed to be.

On any level of exact description, this is so vague as to amount to hocus-pocus. Quite exasperating, if you care about specificity and fact. But not important if what you really care about is traveling in time.

Late in life, in 1903, Jules Verne allowed himself to be drawn out on the subject of Wells, and a measure of exasperation did escape from him as he commented on *The First Men in the Moon* (1901), misremembered in the heat of the moment as a story about Mars:

> I do not see the possibility of comparison between his work and mine. ... I make use of physics. He invents. I go to the moon in a cannon ball, discharged from a cannon. He goes to Mars in an airship, which he constructs of a metal which does away with the law of gravitation. *Ca, c'est tres joli*, but show me this metal. Let him produce it.

But this was not completely appropriate or just. If we were to place Wells's Cavorite, the anti-gravity metal, beside Captain Nemo's special private brand of electricity which no one else will ever discover, which of the two would we choose? Is Verne's Moon-Cannon to be preferred to Wells's Time Machine? All of this various science-beyond-science is imaginary. All of it is presented in terms that are somewhere crucially vague.

Once again, we should remind ourselves that fact and plausibility are not the same. And if we are to take *The Time Machine* as our example of Wells's methods, in the first chapter he has more than established plausibility. He has presented us with an introduction to a time traveler. He has given us a philosophical rationale, shown us a scale model, tested the model's powers, permitted us to clamber about on an almost-complete machine, and even shown us a brief glimpse of the blueprints. In terms of plausible demonstration, as opposed to exact description, Wells could hardly have given us more. If we are disposed to believe him, we will surely believe.

In a second interview, given in 1904, Verne volunteered additional comment on Wells, this time not only more admiringly—"There is an author whose work has appealed to me from an imaginative stand-point, and whose books I have followed with considerable interest"—but also more acutely. This time Verne said:

> I have always made a point in my romances of basing my so-called inventions upon a groundwork of actual fact, and of using in their construction methods and materials which are not entirely without the pale of contemporary engineering skill and knowledge. ... The creations of Mr. Wells, on the other hand, belong unreservedly to an age and a degree of scientific knowledge far removed from the present, though I will not say entirely beyond the limits of the possible. Not only does he evolve his constructions entirely from the realm of the imagination, but he also evolves the materials of which he builds them.

This is much closer to the mark. Part of what separates Verne and Wells is the generational difference between the two in their understanding of the meaning of the word *science*. To Verne, it was still known things and their extension. To Wells, science was the vast unknown.

In the second chapter of *The Time Machine*, a week has passed and another dinner party assembles. The host, the Time Traveller, is missing, however. And then he staggers in, dirty, rumpled and haggard. After a drink, a change of clothing, and dinner, he shares his story, the central narrative.

And this is where the true difference between Verne and Wells becomes unmistakably apparent. Verne, at his most adventurous, used super-scientific vehicles to cruise the fringes of the World Beyond the Hill, spy out transcendence, and then retreat. Wells is out to use the Time Machine as a device of convenience to take us into a realm of wonder like nothing we have ever seen before, a truly alien realm.

The first, and major, stop that the Time Traveller makes is in the year 802,701 A.D. And this in itself is a sign of Wells's power and confidence. He has leaped completely out of the religious frame of time that presented the world as having been created only 4000 years before Christ. He has stridden far into the future, well beyond the seven-hundred-year utopian projections of *Memoirs of the Year 2440* and the one-hundred-year projections of *Looking Backward*. In one giant step, he has moved fully eight hundred thousand years beyond the present moment into territory never previously imagined.

On the one hand, the Time Traveller carries with him his utopian expectations of "great and splendid architecture" and "a profoundly grave and intellectual posterity." On the other hand, he brings his *fin de siècle* fears with him: "What might not have happened to men? What if cruelty had grown into a common passion? What if in this interval the race had lost its manliness, and had developed into something inhuman, unsympathetic, and overwhelmingly powerful?"

When the machine finally stops, the first thing the Time Traveller sees is a statue of a White Sphinx. Like the sphinx of ancient mythology, this statue has been set here to ask us to ponder on the riddle of the nature of man.

All around is a pastoral landscape to all appearances not unlike the best hopes of a William Morris: "The air was free from gnats, the earth from weeds or fungi; everywhere were fruits and sweet and delightful flowers; brilliant butterflies flew hither and thither."

The inhabitants of this green and pleasant land are the Eloi. These are little people, beautiful, charming, delicate and graceful. But they have no more intellect than a five-year-old child, and they are completely lacking in creativity. They are content to romp and play, and to live in the ruins of colossal buildings.

What has happened? The Time Traveller's first theory (soon discarded) is that he is in the decayed remains of Utopia. Nature has been completely conquered, but through lack of the grindstone of pain and necessity to keep it keen, mankind has grown dull.

Then the Time Machine is stolen, dragged by someone within paneled doors in the pedestal of the statue of the Sphinx. At first, the Time Traveller is thrown into total panic, fearing that he may be stranded in this beautiful but alien world. But then he calms himself. He counsels himself to be patient: "Face this world. Learn its ways, watch it, be careful of too hasty guesses at its meaning. In the end you will find clues to it all."

What bravery! What courage! What a change from the Romantic hysteria of Jules Verne's Axel or Mary Shelley's Victor Frankenstein. This is a completely new human temperament revealing itself.

What the Time Traveller soon learns is that the Eloi are not the only inhabitants of this future world. Living underground are dull-white ape-like creatures which remind him of human spiders:

Gradually, the truth dawned on me: that Man had not remained one species, but had differentiated into two distinct animals: that my graceful children of the Upper World were not the sole descendants of our generation, but that this bleached, obscene, nocturnal Thing, which had flashed before me, was also heir to all the ages.

And so we have a dual human future—child man or monster man. Again we must ask, what has happened in the gap of eight hundred thousand years to produce this strange situation?

The Time Traveller arrives at a new theory, which he says specifically he has never seen in any utopian book—though we have seen something like it in the novel *Caesar's Column.* He guesses that the contemporary struggle between Capital and Labor has continued through the ages. The rich got richer. The poor were shoved underground to tend the machinery of society:

"So, in the end, above ground you must have the Haves, pursuing pleasure and comfort and beauty, and below ground the Havenots; the Workers getting continually adapted to the conditions of their labour."

The Eloi, the children of the idle rich, have grown soft and stupid. The descendants of the proletariat, the monstrous Morlocks, have retained some bestial vigor. But neither is quite human any more, neither the "frail creatures who had forgotten their high ancestry" nor "the white Things of which I went in terror."

Then the Time Traveller discovers a grim fact. The Morlocks are meat eaters, and the meat they eat is the Eloi. Are the Eloi, the more attractive remnant of man, nothing but cattle? And the Morlocks, are they cannibals?

It is the Time Traveller's final theory that he is present at the sad conclusion of the brief dream of human intellect, one part of man degenerated into feeble prettiness, the other into bestiality. But he concedes that even this theory may be wrong.

The ultimate effect of all this theorizing is to leave us uncertain of anything. We do not know what has happened. We cannot know. The eight hundred thousand years between now and then is a great mystery.

All we can be certain of here is our experience. We have had revealed to us a world constantly alien, constantly strange. A world that no expectation is equal to.

This is that place of dark and hideous mysteries on the outer reaches of the Moon where Poe never permitted himself to arrive. This is the underground wonderland that Verne entered once, but then found too overwhelming. This, beyond doubt, is the World Beyond the Hill, the place where anything can happen.

The Time Traveller seizes an opportunity to recover his machine. Beating off Morlocks, he pushes at the levers of his vehicle and presses on into the Future.

On and on he goes into remote time, finally stopping at a moment when the Earth has become tidally locked and the sun hangs permanently red and sullen in the sky. There is lichen growing, and the Traveller sees a huge white butterfly and monstrous crabs on the shore of an oily sea.

Once more he pushes on into time, stopping thirty million years from now. The Earth is closer to the sun now, and the sun is a larger and duller red. An eclipse is beginning. The wind is bitter cold. The Time Traveller sees green slime and a tentacled thing flopping in the blood-red water. Then dread overtakes him at last and he returns to tell the tale to his dinner guests in our own time.

And what is the nature of the tale we have been told? It is an evolutionary nightmare. It is nothing less than the same dream that Axel had while sailing the underground sea in Verne's *Journey to the Centre of the Earth*—that strange overpowering "prehistoric daydream."

Axel saw himself as slipping backwards in time and witnessing the creation of things as though it were a disappearance: the mammals gone, then the crustaceans, then the zoophytes, finally the granite rocks melting and the Earth itself being volatilized. *The Time Machine* presents the same materials as Axel's dream, but not as a wrong-way vision of the past—as a picture of the coming devolution of things: mammals gone, monster crabs gone, finally the green slime will go, too, and the ultimate fate of the Earth will be to fall into the sun and be consumed.

But in *The Time Machine*, these events are not merely the stuff of passing reverie. They are witnessed. They are experienced. Such is the unprecedented power to *do* of the super-scientific ivory-and-nickel machine that we were allowed to examine from so many different angles in the first chapter!

The day after the Time Traveller unfolds his tale, he disappears again into the vast reaches of time. Nothing further is heard from him. The narrator of the framing story is left to wonder about the Traveller's fate—and ours:

> Did he go forward, into one of the nearer ages, in which men are still men, but with the riddles of our own time answered and its wearisome problems solved? Into the manhood of the race: for I, for my own part, cannot think that these latter days of weak experiment, fragmentary theory and mutual discord are indeed man's culminating time! I say, for my own part. He, I know—for the question had been discussed among

us long before the Time Machine was made—thought but cheerlessly of
the Advancement of Mankind, and saw in the growing pile of civilization
only a foolish heaping that must inevitably fall back upon and destroy
its makers in the end. If that is so, it remains for us to live as though
it were not so. But to me the future is still black and blank—is a vast
ignorance lit at a few casual places by the memory of his story.

And so, in a flurry of final questions, mixed emotions, and
ambiguities, *The Time Machine*—this deep and subtle story—comes
to an end. Leaving us to ponder:

Is frankly hideous Victorian machine-civilization the peak and glory
of mankind's achievement? Or is there to be some more worthwhile
future for mankind in that "vast ignorance" that extends between
now and the year 802,701, some better time in which Victorian
riddles have been answered and wearisome Victorian problems
solved? Is it to such a place that the Time Traveller has aimed his
machine?

Probably not—if what the narrator of the framing story says in
this final paragraph is true. If the Time Traveller indeed "thought
but cheerlessly of the Advancement of Mankind" even before his
adventures began, then he is unlikely to have sought out some more
perfect society in which to end his days. Indeed, it would seem that
we have been misled throughout the story by the Time Traveller's
talk of utopian expectations.

We have to ask why the Time Traveller built his machine in the
first place. How did he *conceive* of it? What did he expect to prove
by it?

And the answer we are forced to give is that he built the Time
Machine, a scientific device, in *order* to travel outside utopian time—
historical time—into the vast unexplored expanses of scientific time.
The Time Traveller set out in the first place to discover not-utopia,
and he succeeded.

The deliberate result of the adventures of the Time Traveller has
been to trash all of the things that earlier generations had come
to think they knew about the Future. From being a place of
rational perfection, the Future has been turned into a blackness and
a blankness lit only in a few casual places. We are reminded of the
match that is struck at the conclusion of "The Rediscovery of the
Unique" only to reveal a greater darkness looming all around us.

Wherever we may have thought ourselves to be when the Time
Machine first picked us up, it has set us down in the new stark and
beautiful scientific universe of space and time. How frightening!
Because if there is one thing that the Time Machine has demonstrated to us that is beyond doubt, it is that this new scientific

universe of millions of years of time-to-come is a transcendent realm of wonder.

All of the marvels that we have seen, it can generate. And more.

Our ultimate conclusion must be that the Time Traveller has conceived and built his machine and traveled astraddle it into the Future because he is a scientific mystic. The hypothetical advancement of mankind—in which he does not believe—means nothing at all to him beside the mysteries of unknown time and space. He is willing to sacrifice the stale promise of a safe, easy and happy rational future for mankind for the wonderful and dreadful uncertainties of alien future time—the Future conceived as the World Beyond the Hill.

Here we have a step in the history of SF comparable to Mary Shelley's quickening of the dead with the power of science-beyond-science. A story character has scouted far ahead into the Future on a super-scientific vehicle and found there neither God nor perfected man, but destruction, devolution and doom—and the promise of wonder.

But where Victor Frankenstein struck his spark of life and then ran away and hid under the bedclothes from what he had done, the Time Traveller is prepared to accept the consequences of his actions, no matter how dread. Like some sterner-nerved Axel, he is willing to cast himself into the volcano, return to tell us the tale—and then throw himself back in again.

The presentation by Wells of an alien realm in *The Time Machine* was not the only contribution to science fiction that he would make. During the last half-decade of the Nineteenth Century, in a brief period of intense creativity, Wells wrote several dozen SF short stories and six book-length romances, the most conscious, controlled, concentrated and complete SF expression that any writer had yet produced. Not just one powerful dream-generated story like Walpole or Mary Shelley, nor a half-dozen hoaxes and incomplete gestures like Poe, nor even a series of stories cut to a patented pattern like Jules Verne—but a coherent body of work, a brilliant and varied presentation of the mythic implications of the new scientific universe of time and space.

These stories of Wells may be seen as a summation and re-expression of all the SF that had come before him. He took up themes from Mary Shelley, from Poe, from Verne, and even from contemporary work, and made them his own by converting them into terms of purest scientific materialism.

Other writers of imaginative literature in the late Nineteenth Century, like Edward Page Mitchell or the French astronomer Camille Flammarion, might waver between appeals to science and arguments based on spirit. Even writers of the Twentieth Century, men who followed Wells by fully fifteen or twenty years, like Edgar Rice Burroughs and H.P. Lovecraft, might cheerfully intermix scientific and occultist elements in their stories.

But not Wells. In the more than sixty years that separate the early Verne from the founding of *Amazing Stories*, it is Wells who stands head and shoulders above all other writers for the purity and totality of his commitment to science.

Spirit simply had no place at all in Wells's work. Neither traditional religion nor the rational soul meant anything to him. If he wrote occasional fantasy stories, they were material fantasies like his satiric story of an angel shot out of the sky by a vicar with a shotgun. If he took up themes or ideas that were conventionally associated with the spiritual or occult, he found a way to convert them into terms of unequivocal scientific materialism. The Time Machine is a ready example—a scientific and material equivalent to the out-of-body time-traveling dreams of the utopians.

Wells took on all of the major themes current in the imaginative fiction of his day that could be treated in purely scientific terms, and he added a number of new ones. He wrote of strange inventions and horrifying experiments, scientists both mad and sane, cosmic catastrophe, prehistoric man, scientific dystopia, weird creatures, future war, space travel and alien invasion. The only story forms that Wells did not take up were those in which the scientific and the occult were inextricably interwoven, like the lost race story.

Along with all else that he managed to accomplish during his reign as the *enfant terrible* of the *fin de siècle* imagination, the gleeful disturber of late Victorian peace of mind, Wells wrote a number of times of transcendent aliens. As we have seen, the depiction of transcendent aliens had been a continuing problem for Nineteenth Century SF. Fitz-James O'Brien had half-shown aliens, but without real conviction. Edward Bulwer-Lytton had intended to show a superior race of beings, but then emphasized vril power instead. Finally, during the expansive Eighties, there had been a couple of even nearer tries at presenting superior aliens.

One of these was by Edward Page Mitchell. "The Balloon Tree" (1883) presented a sentient flying cactus plant with the psychic presence of "a beautiful and gentle woman." This "Migratory Tree" rescues the dying protagonist, carrying him through the air on a fantastic night journey over a hundred miles to safety. But then, at the conclusion of the narrative, our license to believe is suddenly withdrawn. There is a reversal, and we are told that what we have heard is no more than a stretcher, a tall tale, a well-rehearsed club story.

A more self-convinced attempt at the presentation of alien beings is
to be found in the first short story of the French writer J. H. Rosny
aîné. In "Les Xipéhuz"—published in the significant year of 1887—
hostile crystalline beings that alter in color and shape appear in
ancient Mesopotamia a thousand years before civilization. They
threaten to increase in number, expand their circle of influence,
and take over the world. One man—a rationalist and monotheist
ahead of his time whose doctrine is "that men should really believe
only in those things tested by measurement"—carefully observes
these beings. He defeats the aliens by noting a point of vulnerability
and then overwhelming them with sheer weight of numbers, sacri-
ficing ten human lives for each Xipéhuz slain.

With Wells, there were no hoaxes, no dream fog, no removal to
prehistoric times, no occultism, and, most important, no assurances
of the superiority of human reason. Wells, typically, went straight
to the heart of the matter. He had no difficulty in imagining that
the scientific universe of time and space might produce creatures
whose powers exceed our own.

The first major example of Wellsian aliens is the invading Martians
of *The War of the Worlds*, published in 1898, three years after *The
Time Machine*. These vast, cool and unsympathetic intelligences are
masters of advanced science, able to shoot themselves in cannon
across the gulf of space from Mars, to stride over the countryside
in great glittering tripods, and to fire deadly heat rays. They are
superior to us by our own scale of valuation. But at the same time,
these beings are blood-sucking monsters, ravenous and unfathomable.
Here is the first description of a Martian:

> Those who have never seen a living Martian can scarcely imagine the
> strange horror of its appearance. The peculiar V-shaped mouth with its
> pointed upper lip, the absence of brow ridges, the absence of a chin
> beneath the wedge-like lower lip, the incessant quivering of this mouth,
> the Gorgon groups of tentacles, the tumultuous breathing of the lungs
> in a strange atmosphere, the evident heaviness and painfulness of move-
> ment due to the greater gravitational energy of the earth—above all, the
> extraordinary intensity of the immense eyes—were at once vital, intense,
> inhuman, crippled and monstrous. There was something fungoid in the
> oily brown skin, something in the clumsy deliberation of the tedious
> movements unspeakably nasty. Even at this first encounter, this first
> glimpse, I was overcome with disgust and dread.

Except in its horror, disgust and dread, this description is not
altogether unlike our first view of the Time Machine—simultaneously vague and highly specific. And the invocation of "the greater

gravitational energy of the earth" is the perfect scientific materialist touch.

Best of all, however, the ambiguity and alienness of the Martians never grow less as the story proceeds. We are not being presented with beings that impress us first as Titans but then prove to be no more than mobile steam engines. Unlike the Vril-ya of *The Coming Race*, the Martians are stranger than the super-science they command.

Indeed, by describing them in various ways throughout the story, Wells contrives to compound and increase our sense of the radical differentness of the Martians. For instance, at one point a soldier calls them "octopuses"—and we must be reminded that cephalopods were one of Wells's nominations for a possible successor to mankind in his article "The Extinction of Man." Then at a later point in the story, the narrator gets a longer, more sober look at the invaders and describes them as "huge round bodies—or, rather, heads— about four feet in diameter" and identifies their tentacles as "hands." These beings are also Big Brain, and after a page or two Wells's narrator spells this out for us by citing and discussing Wells's 1893 article, "The Man of the Year Million."

So there the Martians are—scientists, monsters, cephalopods and Big Brains all at the same time. Like the Future presented in constantly shifting guise in *The Time Machine*, the Martians are a shimmering ambiguity, simultaneously weird, wonderful, awful and impossible to put your finger on.

These are transcendent beings, both plausible and mysterious. But they are also mortal beings, as we may remember Wells pointing out in the very first sentence of *The War of the Worlds*. The Martians have a weakness, also glancingly referred to in the first paragraph of the story: the infusoria under the microscope.

Having "eliminated them ages ago," the Martians have no defense against microorganisms. And so, at the very hour of their complete ascendance, the Martians are overthrown. They fall down and die, "slain by the putrefactive and disease bacteria against which their systems were unprotected."

But even with the passing of these Martian invaders, there can be no grounds for human beings to rest easy. It was not the intelligence and power of man that defeated the Martians, but rather humble bacteria. If the Martians should remember the trick of how to eliminate microorganisms, they might yet return, this time better prepared for an assault on Earth. But even if they don't, there is still no comfort. We can only recall that in "The Extinction of Man," along with cephalopods, Wells also named crustaceans, ants and microbes among our potential successors.

Who is to say that what the infusoria did to the Martians, they might not do to us? Who can predict from what direction the next blow of the universe will come?

Expectably, *The War of the Worlds* culminates in one more antinomy. In one breath, Wells delivered himself of as grand a vision of human possibility as he ever allowed himself to express in any of his scientific romances, immediately followed by one more reiteration of cosmic doubt:

> Dim and wonderful is the vision I have conjured up in my mind of life spreading slowly from this little seed-bed of the solar system throughout the inanimate vastness of sidereal space. But that is a remote dream. It may be, on the other hand, that the destruction of the Martians is only a reprieve. To them, and not to us, perhaps, is the future ordained.

In his short career as a creative mythmaker, H.G. Wells did more to advance SF than any previous writer. He opened the door to a wonderful and terrible transcendent realm, a place where anything might happen if given sufficient time and space. And he introduced us to alien beings—like so many mirrors of our own nature, our limitations and our potential.

Set aside all else. Set aside Wells's fecundity, his range, his useful metaphors and arguments, his pure commitment to material science. Beyond all those things, this was Wells's contribution to the development of science fiction:

SF, when Wells took it up, was like a small child raised inside a closed house, daring occasional peeks through the curtain, but always turning back to the familiar world within. H.G. Wells, in the period in which there was nothing he didn't dare to imagine, took science fiction by the hand and led it outdoors, saying, *This wider world is the real universe, marvelous and deadly. You cannot ignore it. There are other beings out here like no one you have ever seen. Some of them are older and more powerful, and may mean you harm. You have no choice in the matter. Survive if you can.*

And that is the state in which Wells left SF—like a child abandoned in the cold, barren front yard of the vast universe of space and time, gazing around in fear and anticipation.

7

The Relativity of Man

In the Western world, the most dynamic and powerful social fact of the Nineteenth Century was the growth that took place in the influence of science and technology. At the beginning of the century, the practical influence of technology was slight. By the end of the century, the dynamos of science were about to become the central power source of Western society.

In company with this great change of outward circumstance, and helping to mediate it, there occurred a parallel radical increase in the effect, the power and the scope of the metaphorical science imagined in Western fiction. One step at a time, and with much reluctance and drawing back, the writers of SF re-created the powers, places and beings of the World Beyond the Hill in the new terms of science.

With H.G. Wells, this process of reinvention became complete. Wells was the first SF writer to fully accept the apparently limitless powers of unknown science, the vast new universe of space and time, and the potential of evolutionary forces to transform or destroy all that appears fixed and stable. As a result, the entire universe beyond Earth in the present moment became for him the World Beyond the Hill, filled with transcendent marvels.

However, with the onset of the Twentieth Century, Wells—just like the two earlier innovators, Mary Shelley and Jules Verne—found his sticking point, backed off from his great vision and pursued its implications no further. Wells would continue to write SF books to the end of his long career, as well as stacks of writing of other kinds, but after *The First Men in the Moon*, he ceased to be the central innovator of SF that he had been. Of the twenty-six novels and stories by Wells that Hugo Gernsback would come to reprint in his early science fiction magazines of the Twenties as examples of the literature he wished to publish, the vast majority were the product of the Nineties. A mere four were originally published between 1901 and 1905, and none later than that.

Wells left SF with a great deal to get used to. It would be more than a full generation after the early Wells before writers accustomed themselves to the vast distances and cold stillness of the universe of space and time. That same new lot of writers in the Thirties would also learn to tolerate dealings with domesticated aliens—beings imagined as fashioned differently than we, but not clearly our betters.

Still, the question remains—why did Wells need to retreat? Was it that the receptivity of his audience had changed, or was it that Wells had simply grown chubby and content? Was he frightened by the aliens that he imagined? Or did he just turn his attention to more practical work a little nearer home than the ends of the universe?

The best answer may be yes—all of these possibilities were true at one and the same time.

The temper of the times definitely altered at the turn of the century. The *fin de siècle* was over and the world had not ended. A new untouched century lay waiting. And in January 1901, just three weeks into the first year of the new century, Victoria, queen of England since 1837, finally died. What a relief! Freed at last from the eternal, smothering, oppressive bosom of Mama the Empress!

The new Edwardians drew in great gulps of fresh air and gazed around them at the nascent century. In this bright new morn, it was clear that the time for philosophizing was past. There was business to be attended to.

Nightmares emphasizing mankind's precarious existence in a hostile and rapacious universe were passing out of fashion, at least for the time being. There was a new and more confident mood stirring. For this reason alone, Wells may have felt the need to shift ground.

But it is also undeniable that he had changed personally. He was no longer a nonentity, an invisible man with nothing to lose by telling society the grimmest and nastiest cosmic howlers that he could imagine. He was financially successful, he was admired by the likes of Henry James and Joseph Conrad, and he was no longer a dying man. With a brand-new century opening wide, for the first time H.G. Wells had a future of his own to look forward to and plan for.

Yes, he did get fat. After the opening of the Twentieth Century, he changed in form from the gaunt-ribbed mustachioed mutt of the Nineties into the plump bristling terrier we remember as H.G. Wells.

Did this more attached, more connected Wells shrink back before the prospect of the aliens of his imagination? It is possible that he did. Certainly, his last great scientific romance, *The First Men in the Moon*, in serialization at the turn of the century, is a curious, ambivalent and broken-backed book. It ends once with an apparent minor success, then starts itself up again and concludes in what looks like disaster. And it is superior aliens who are the stumbling block.

In this novel, the scientist Cavor and the narrator Bedford, a failed business speculator turned would-be playwright, travel together to the Moon in a sphere treated with Cavorite, a substance "opaque to gravitation." It is Bedford's hope to make himself rich from the commercial exploitation of Cavorite.

The Moon proves to be a wondrous realm that springs to life when the sun shines. And in caverns below the surface of the Moon, by the shores of an underground sea, live intelligent beings, the antlike Selenites, who wear garments and tend machines and use gold as casually as we use iron.

Cavor and Bedford are taken captive by the Selenites. At this low moment Bedford is driven to make a passionate outburst against science:

"It's this accursed Science," I cried. "It's the very Devil. The medieval priests and prosecutors were right, and the Moderns are all wrong. You tamper with it and it offers you gifts. And directly you take them it knocks you to pieces in some unexpected way. Old passions and new weapons—now it upsets your religion, now it upsets your social ideas, now it whirls you off to desolation and misery!"

More optimistically, however, Cavor maintains that it may be possible to communicate with these Selenites. But Bedford believes that the gap between the Selenites and humanity is "insurmountable." In a fit of passion, Bedford strikes out and smashes a Selenite—the first of many he will kill—and the two humans escape.

When the two separate to search for their vehicle, Cavor is recaptured, leaving only an incomplete and blood-stained note for Bedford to find. Bedford then returns to Earth in the sphere with several bars of Moon gold—precisely the riches he hoped to realize from Cavorite.

The anti-gravity sphere is lost almost immediately through the meddling of a boy. The adventure is apparently over—a successful smash-and-grab expedition into the World Beyond the Hill.

But then there is a strange coda, seemingly written while the story was in serialization, as though Wells realized that something about his story was insufficient. But what he provides does not really make the story more satisfactory:

Radio messages—radio was newly invented then—have been received from Cavor on the Moon. It would seem that more of this story remains to be told that Bedford, because of his limitations, could not tell—Bedford being that fragment of Wells who could not handle the thought of Selenites, creatures different from us if not superior to us. Like Axel and his party in *Journey to the Centre of the Earth*, he has had to be sent home from his story early.

Cavor describes the Selenite civilization as a scientific dystopia, an anthill society in which different varieties of Selenite are shaped to different specialized purposes. Eventually, after his language has been learned, Cavor is taken to meet the Grand Lunar, the great dominating creature who rules the Moon. The Grand Lunar is a featureless brain-case many yards in diameter. Under interrogation, Cavor tells this being about human disunity and belligerence—and then fears he has said too much. The book ends with a disruption of Cavor's messages, and Bedford's image of an embattled Cavor overwhelmed (yet again!) by Selenites.

What has really happened on the Moon? Despite Bedford's dire suspicions, we cannot know—and lacking his anti-gravity sphere, neither can Bedford. It is all left a mystery. But we are entitled to feel that one interview with the likes of the Grand Lunar has been more than enough for Wells. He dares imagine no more and must abandon poor Cavor to his fate, whatever it may be.

It is apparent that Wells went through some sort of major crisis of faith around the turn of the century. Just what was his relationship to be with a Science that he found both promising and threatening?

Modern science, we may recall, grew out of the Seventeenth Century decision to investigate the world of matter and set the spiritual realm aside. And, for all the increase in its scope and power, the science of the late Nineteenth Century still resolutely held itself apart from those values considered to belong to the domain of spirit—love, honor, idealism, and morality.

There was no problem with this arrangement for as long as science continued to recognize that religion had its own right and truth. But as science and religion began to draw apart, science became increasingly committed to a narrow and mechanistic philosophy which perceived the universe as a great machine and man, at best, as an animal. It was these images of meaninglessness and amorality that troubled Wells.

As we have seen, real doubt about the effects of science is expressed in *The First Men in the Moon*. Moreover, the scientific civilization of the Selenites, with its extremes of overspecialization and personal limitation, is regarded with considerable uneasiness.

Most of all, it is by no accident that the Grand Lunar—like Wells's other superior aliens, the Martian invaders—should appear in the guise of our hypothetical descendant, Big Brain. Seemingly, Wells thought that man might survive in a hostile universe by becoming scientific, but feared that this might come at the cost of turning into some repulsive, inhuman, unsympathetic and overwhelmingly powerful creature before whom Wells could not even justify present humanity.

Wells resolved his crisis by giving up his extremes of philosophical question and doubt, and by reaffirming the power of science as the immediate practical method to be pursued in the name of survival. Pursue science and don't think too much about the more distant mysteries. That was a decision completely in keeping with the new practical human-centered Edwardian spirit.

During the Edwardian decade, Wells turned his considerable energies to the criticism and reform of society along more scientific lines. He wrote futurological forecasts; his first great success of the Twentieth Century was a pioneer work of prediction entitled *Anticipations of the Reaction of Mechanical and Scientific Progress Upon Human Life and Thought* (1901), which earned him an invitation to join the radical Fabian Society. He wrote comic social novels in which society was taken to task for wasting the potential of people who looked like alternate versions of the younger H. G. Wells. He wrote serious social novels in which society was taken to task for not cooperating with the desires of the present H. G. Wells. And he wrote inspirational utopian novels in which the limitations of present human nature and the benightedness of present human society were overleaped completely. Wells even tried and failed to take over the Fabian Society and turn it from vain theorizing to practical action.

In his autobiography, Wells makes a comment on the universe of space and time revealed by modern physics. It seems to capture the thinking behind his decision at the turn of the century to abandon scientific wonder stories in favor of social reform:

> In brief I realize that Being is surrounded east, south, north and west, above and below, by wonder. Within that frame, like a little house in strange, cold, vast and beautiful scenery, is life upon this planet, of which life I am a temporary spark and impression. There is interest beyond measure within that house; use for my utmost. Nevertheless at times one finds an urgency to go out and gaze at those enigmatical immensities. But for such a thing as I am, there is nothing conceivable to be done out there. Ultimately, those remote metaphysical appearances may mean everything, but so far as my present will and activities go they mean

nothing. The science of physics shrinks to the infinitesimal in a little sparkling flicker in a glass bulb or whirls away vastly with the extragalactic nebulae into the deeps of space, and after a time I stop both speck-gazing and star-gazing and return indoors.

During the Nineties, H.G. Wells felt an urgent need to go out and gaze at the enigmatical immensities. But at the beginning of the Twentieth Century, he ceased speck-gazing and star-gazing and returned indoors to work. It would be others than Wells who would conceive what was to be done by men out there in the larger world.

The most urgent problem presented to the heirs and successors of Wells was that of adjusting to the new universe of space and time. Scientific materialism might be acknowledged as the new order of the day, but still that took a considerable amount of getting used to—like a swimmer acclimating himself to the chill and power of the ocean by degrees.

There were two aspects to this problem. One was the vast indifferent power of the great cosmic ocean. How large, remote, awful and uncaring the great meat-grinding universe of space and time appeared! Wonderful the enigmatical immensities might be, but what did they have to offer to humanity except the certainty of disaster and doom? It was this humanly irrelevant universe that H.G. Wells had turned back from.

The other and reciprocal aspect of the problem was the denial of innate human specialness and superiority. How insignificant man seemed when measured beside the immensity of space and time! And this huge, overwhelming universe, so far beyond mankind, seemed to demand animal behavior from humanity. Its highest values were not love and morality, but survival by any means and at any cost. How humiliating to man's pretensions!

Both aspects of the problem—the chilly remoteness of the universe, and mankind's limited nature—can be seen in a highly influential essay by Bertrand Russell published just after the turn of the century. "A Free Man's Worship" (1903) may be taken as a credo of the new faith of scientific materialism.

The essay opens with a parable, a first attempt at an expression of man's true cosmic position. It is a cruel little fable of limitation and futility supposedly told by Mephistopheles to Faust as a history of creation.

It begins with a bored God, weary of worship by the angels to whom he has given endless joy. Ah, but then this God has a thought: "Would it not be more amusing to obtain undeserved praise, to be worshipped by beings whom he tortured?"

And so he creates a mad, monstrous world full of creatures breeding, fighting, devouring, and passing away, a world whose ultimate product is Man, touched with the power of thought and "the cruel thirst for worship."

The fable ends:

> And God smiled; and when he saw that Man had become perfect in renunciation and worship, he sent another sun through the sky, which crashed into Man's sun; and all returned again to nebula.
>
> "Yes," he murmured, "it was a good play; I will have it performed again."

But even this nihilistic little fantasy of human torture, humiliation and destruction allows humanity some purpose. It capitalizes the name of Man. It puts him at the center of the play. God may be shallow, stupid and sadistic, but mankind still has some importance to him, some amusement value that at least ensures that the play will be performed again.

This parable is at best a first approximation for Russell. It captures something of the Edwardian attitude. But it doesn't fully express the true situation as Russell understands it, so immediately on concluding his little fantasy, he discards it in favor of another vision which he suggests is like it, but is both more awful and more accurate. After the God of Mephistopheles murmurs his intent to repeat his comedy, Russell says:

> Such, in outline, but even more purposeless, more void of meaning, is the world which Science presents for our belief. Amid such a world, if anywhere, our ideals henceforward must find a home. That Man is the product of causes which had no prevision of the end they were achieving; that his origin, his growth, his hopes and fears, his loves and his beliefs, are but the outcome of accidental collocations of atoms; that no fire, no heroism, no intensity of thought and feeling, can preserve an individual life beyond the grave; that all the labours of the ages, all the devotion, all the inspiration, all the noonday brightness of human genius, are destined to extinction in the vast death of the solar system, and that the whole temple of Man's achievement must inevitably be buried beneath the debris of a universe in ruins—all these things, if not quite beyond dispute, are yet so nearly certain, that no philosophy which rejects them can hope to stand. Only within the scaffolding of these truths, only on the firm foundation of unyielding despair, can the soul's habitation henceforth be safely built.

Wow! With this as the new standard of belief, it is no wonder that acclimatization was necessary. Russell's image of meaningless-ness could haunt a science fiction writer born a generation after his essay was first published, and still seem a thorny problem to an adolescent born two generations later.

And yet, even in as bleak and awful a statement of the human situation as Russell's, there is still some mitigation. The name of Man is still capitalized. And the remainder of the essay is a call in the style of Thomas Huxley for mankind to resist the hostile universe and continue to assert human moral values. The essay concludes:

> Brief and powerless is Man's life; on him and all his race the slow, sure doom falls pitiless and dark. Blind to good and evil, reckless of destruction, omnipotent matter rolls on its relentless way; for Man, condemned to-day to lose his dearest, to-morrow himself to pass through the gates of dark-ness, it remains only to cherish, ere yet the blow falls, the lofty thoughts that ennoble his little day; disdaining the coward terrors of the slave of Fate, to worship at the shrine that his own hands have built; undismayed by the empire of chance, to preserve a mind free from the wanton tyranny that rules his outward life; proudly defiant of the irresistible forces that tolerate, for a moment, his knowledge and his condemnation, to sustain alone, a weary but unyielding Atlas, the world that his own ideals have fashioned despite the trampling march of unconscious power.

In the Edwardian decade there was a strange confidence in the powers of humanity, that weary but unyielding Atlas, a sense that even though the solar system might die and all of Man's achievement be buried beneath the debris of a universe in ruins, still there was a proudly defiant element in Man that was superior to this rude treatment and would prevail. This unreasonable confidence was shared by nearly everyone, regardless of their other beliefs. It might be called a common denominator of the period.

The given bases for Man's presumed superiority to the rest of material creation varied widely. The basis might be found, for instance, in a reaffirmation of traditional religion. In an SF story, a scientific probe might be imagined as peering two thousand years into the past and confirming the existence and miraculous nature of Jesus. Or occultists might write of scientific demonstrations of the existence of the soul. Humanists might assert the special worthi-ness of human morality, while pure materialists might suggest that the difference that made humanity superior was based in human intelligence. But all Edwardians were agreed that *something* about Man justified giving him that capital letter and setting him apart and above the rest of creation.

Edwardian SF stories say, yes...but. Yes, the cosmic night is dark...but *still* somehow Man will prevail, even though the universe grinds his bones.

Edwardian SF stories are like the endings of Wells's great scientific romances of the Nineties. Time and again, Wells would present the darkest visionary implications of the new universe—but then draw back, soften them, even contradict them. In *The Time Machine*, a sweep of time-to-come is revealed that is so vast that it makes man's civilization seem nothing more than a foolish heaping. But the narrator concludes: "If that is so, it remains for us to live as though it were not so." In *The War of the Worlds*, the technologically advanced Martians may yet return and wipe us out. But there is the counterweight of that dim and wonderful vision of mankind "spreading slowly from this little seed-bed of the solar system throughout the inanimate vastness of sidereal space." And in *The Island of Dr. Moreau* (1896), the entire novel is a demonstration to the narrator that he and his fellowmen are nothing better than poor tortured half-human animals. But still he says, "It must be, I think, in the vast and eternal laws of matter, and not in the daily cares and sins and troubles of men, that whatever is more than animal within us must find its solace and its hope. I hope or I could not live."

Similarly, Edwardian SF might admit—or half-admit—that time would bury all human accomplishment, that humanity might well be in jeopardy from cosmic indifference or cosmic hostility, and that mankind was only an animal. And still, Edwardian SF would cross its fingers, close its eyes, and hope. Somehow, human specialness would justify itself and win through.

The one clear exception to this Edwardian sentimentalization of Man was the tales of an Irish nobleman, Edward John Moreton Drax Plunkett, Lord Dunsany. This was one writer who would not deny the true relativity of man. Was the human situation awful, grotesque, and richly humorous—no better than a cosmic joke? This young soldier, at least, this veteran of the Boer War with its concentration camps and other harbingers of atrocity to come, was one person able to stand up and state the facts.

Dunsany was a strange fringe writer. He was an aristocratic debunker of aristocratic pretensions writing during the last happy decade that aristocratic ideals were to know. But even as his stories took Man down a peg, they themselves were a very special and superior kind of writing—glittering, colorful, cynical little fantasies set off in a special secondary universe, a nonce world like the settings of William Morris's last stories. The location of Dunsany's tales is sometimes given as "the little kingdoms at the Edge of the World," sometimes as "the Third Hemisphere."

What makes Dunsany special—one of the very few Edwardians to have an influence on the later development of SF—is that while there is no apparent modern human science in his fantasy stories, nonetheless they are steeped in the new scientific philosophy. More than any other imaginative fiction of their time, they are built on the firm foundation of unyielding despair.

Indeed, Dunsany's stories resemble nothing else so much as that first approximation of the human situation, that opening parable of human futility, torture and doom by Bertrand Russell in "A Free Man's Worship." The similarity between Dunsany and Mephistopheles' fable of human creation and human fate can be seen in this passage from a typical early Dunsany story:

"'Once I found out the secret of the universe. I have forgotten what it was, but I know the Creator does not take Creation seriously, for I remember that He sat in Space with all His work in front of Him and laughed.'"

Everywhere in Dunsany there is a seeking after gods. But the gods that are found are invariably cruel, or trivial, or false, and have nothing to offer to their human worshipers except suffering, disillusionment and death.

The title of Dunsany's collection *Time and the Gods* (1906) tells the true story. "Time" is one of the names of the vast and chilly god of science. So great is the power of the new science that even in the alternate universes of fantasy, time still holds sway. Time turns lesser gods into monkeys and mankind into an insect.

Dunsany was a mocker of idols—and the Edwardian exaltation of Man was an idol. Holding onto the belief in the innate specialness and superiority of humanity was a form of self-flattery, an easy way out of the dilemmas posed by the new scientific universe. Pretending that humanity was already Man was a way of avoiding the true hard facts of the matter.

Dunsany saw through that. His stories were specifically aimed to kill illusion. Would you put your faith in gods? After reading Dunsany, you must spit on all monkey gods. Would you take comfort in mankind's special superiority? After reading Dunsany, you must know man for what he really is, a pretentious, self-deluded piss-ant.

Lord Dunsany was not a highly popular writer. His unique combination of elitist artistry and mockery of the pretensions of Man made him a special taste. It seems no wonder that he had to pay for the publication of his first book.

If Dunsany had an effect on later writers and has continued to be read, it is largely because the history of the Twentieth Century has been a confirmation of Dunsany's criticism of human pretension.

The idea of innate human specialness and superiority—usually expressed and understood as the supposed superiority of some class or race or nation—would receive a terrible put-down in the Great War. It would be further humiliated in the Great Depression and be definitively discredited in World War II.

It was bound to happen. There was a fundamental incompatibility between the new scientific universe of space and time and outworn elitist principles ultimately based in the old idea of the rational human soul, that last wispy remnant of the long-rejected spirit realm.

During the Edwardian decade, the first expressions of a new idea of the nature of man more in keeping with the dictates of science began to be put forward. This line of thinking suggested that rather than stoically and futilely maintaining Man's moral superiority while the universe heaps rocks on our grave, perhaps humanity might get farther with the cosmos if we simply admitted and accepted our animal nature.

If the universe cared nothing for human moralizing, but did value survival, who were we to argue with that?

Human civilization seemed an ugliness that separated mankind from nature. On the one hand, it twisted and deformed humanity. On the other, it made man too soft to survive.

Of what value was civilization? Was it possible that the way to survive in the cosmos was to reject civilization altogether and become a wild animal?

One writer torn to pieces by these questions was the American, Jack London. London was born illegitimate in San Francisco in 1876. He suffered a rough and precarious upbringing. In his teens and early twenties, he was an oyster pirate, a sailor on a sealing ship, briefly a student, and then a tramp. Finally, he joined the Alaska Gold Rush of 1897 and prospected without success in the Klondike. After contracting scurvy, he retreated to California—and there began to write stories reflecting his experiences in the Far North.

These stories made London immediately and hugely popular, but popularity set up a tremendous conflict within him. Civilization had treated London badly, even brutally, torturing and repressing him. To escape civilization, he had run off to the purity of the wilderness. But the wild life had been more than he could handle. Still, he was able to celebrate it, and to throw it into the teeth of civilization. And only *then* was society ready to embrace and accept him.

It was a mind-bending paradox. London was more than a little bit like H. G. Wells—an outcast of society winning the acceptance of society by speaking against society. At what price this kind of success?

London loved and hated civilization, loved and despised his own popularity, loved and loathed himself. His writing was all an attempt to untangle the conundrum of his own life, to resolve the nature of man, and to reorder society on some saner basis. He wrote stories of powerful and violent men living brutish lives on the edge of society. He wrote socialist tracts and novels of the class struggle. And throughout his career, he wrote SF stories.

London's ambivalence can be seen very clearly in two of his early novels which disguise the question of human nature and civilization by seeming to ask it about domesticated animals. *The Call of the Wild* (1903) and *White Fang* (1906) are apparently naturalistic animal stories, a type of fiction that became highly popular in the early Twentieth Century. But the books are obviously more than that. They are a first, and more than a little tentative, inquiry into the possibility and desirability of embracing our own animal nature.

In *The Call of the Wild*, a powerful California dog named Buck is stolen and shipped to the Klondike. He becomes the lead dog of a sledge team. However, when his master is murdered, he runs off into the wilderness and establishes himself as the leader of a pack of wild wolves. Whether this should be taken as awful or as a triumph is not made explicit—but it must be guessed that most readers took the ending as a moment of liberation.

In the companion book, *White Fang*, the exact opposite story is presented, as though London were working through both sides in some formal debate. White Fang is a wolf-dog in the Yukon, another pack leader. But Indians brutalize him, and a white man, Beauty Smith, makes him into a killer dog. Finally, a nobler white man rescues him, recognizes his superior intelligence, and tames him with kindness. White Fang is then taken off to California, where he is so thoroughly domesticated that he nearly dies protecting his owner's home and family from an escaped convict.

Is this a triumph? Perhaps all that should be said is that the earlier parts of the book where White Fang is wild and free feel more convincing than the sentimental ending with a recovering White Fang surrounded by his puppies.

London felt the impulse to embrace wildness and animality, but he could never accept them wholeheartedly. And the reason was his inability to let loose of the idea of the soul. The evidence is to be seen in London's autobiographical novel *Martin Eden* (1909), the story of a popular writer who feels demeaned by the nature of his own success and ultimately commits suicide. Attached to the novel as an epigraph are these lines:

> Let me live out my years in heat of blood!
> Let me lie drunken with the dreamer's wine!
> Let me not see this soul-house built of mud
> Go toppling to the dust a vacant shrine!

London felt a need for civilization, that temple of the rational soul. And he hated it. He loved the purely animalistic, and he feared it. All these impulses can be seen working at once in one of London's SF stories, the novelet "The Scarlet Plague" (1912).

In this story, a global epidemic in 2013 is imagined as wiping out most of mankind. The civilization that is destroyed is a cruel and repressive plutocracy not unlike that in Ignatius Donnelly's *Caesar's Column*. But the alternative that follows is a nearly subhuman savagery. The survivors of the plague instantly revert to barbarism and ignorance. Tame animals go wild and prey on one another. Rank weeds crowd out the "soft and tender" domesticated vegetation.

After scene upon scene of brutality and degradation, the last old man who remembers the previous state of things—a former University of California English professor—muses on the blessings of the civilized state and the possibility of its return:

> The gunpowder will come. Nothing can stop it—the same old story over and over. Man will increase, and men will fight. The gunpowder will enable men to kill millions of men, and in this way only, by fire and blood, will a new civilization, in some remote day, be evolved. And of what profit will it be? Just as the old civilization passsed, so will the new. It may take fifty thousand years to build, but nevertheless it will pass.
>
> All things pass. Only remain cosmic force and matter, ever in flux.... Some will fight, some will rule, some will pray; and all the rest will toil and suffer sore while on their bleeding carcasses is reared again and yet again, without end, the amazing beauty and surpassing wonder of the civilized state.
>
> It were just as well that I destroyed those cave-stored books—whether they remain or perish, all their old truths will be discovered, their old lies lived and handed down. What is the profit—

London was never able to decide whether civilization was a surpassing wonder worth the price of fire and blood and fifty thousand years of effort, or whether it was a profitless futility. Was man better off without civilization? Should man surrender his soul and be an animal?

Because the problem of man, civilization, and the universe was so agonizing for him, London was able to present it with extraordinary clarity and passion. But he was helpless to resolve it. It was a knot that he couldn't unravel. To give up being civilized in order to run with the wild wolf pack seemed both frightening and desirable. But to abandon civilization was to deny the soul—and London was not capable of doing that. The soul was too dear to him. It was his ace in the hole, his assurance of his own special superiority.

Ultimately, London was torn apart by his unanswerable questions.

He became an alcoholic, and drug dependent. At last, in 1916, already a ruin of a man at the age of 40, he died of kidney failure. Or he committed suicide like his alter ego Martin Eden. The matter remains in question.

Even before he died, however, a new writer from Chicago had appeared on the scene who was heavily influenced by London, and whose stories held answers for London's questions. This writer was Edgar Rice Burroughs, the first great SF innovator of the Twentieth Century.

Burroughs was born in late 1875, just four months before Jack London, but his writing career only began in the days of London's decline. Burroughs' first two stories, *Under the Moons of Mars* and *Tarzan of the Apes*, both appeared in 1912 in the pages of *All-Story*, a pulp magazine.

Burroughs was a writer it was possible to overlook. His stories were juvenile and implausible wish-fulfillments published in cheap magazines aimed at the new unsophisticated mass audience. He was an entertainer, a not altogether serious person. In those first two stories, however, Burroughs presented a new style of hero, a new attitude toward the universe, and a solution to the problem of man and civilization. He could not have done that if he hadn't been writing for cheap sensationalistic magazines willing to accept almost any measure of implausibility in the name of novelty and entertainment.

In every way the two writers of the same age, London and Burroughs, make a striking contrast to each other. London, that elite writer, was a bastard child of the streets who desperately wanted to believe that he was special and different, that he had the soul of a prince. Burroughs, the pulp hack, was a pampered child of privilege who wanted just as much to be the kind of ordinary person for whom life was an adventure.

In fact, what Burroughs truly craved was a life like the one that London had been born to—but without its pains and frustrations. Burroughs had a restless, impulsive and enthusiastic nature, but he tended to drag his feet and then quit when faced with the prospect of hard and steady effort without reward.

Burroughs was the fourth son and youngest surviving child of a Union officer in the Civil War who had become a prosperous Chicago businessman. Two of Ed's older brothers were graduates of Yale. Ed himself was sent to the elite prep school Andover and was briefly president of his class until he contrived to flunk out.

It was a continuing source of embarrassment to Burroughs that he had studied Latin and Greek in one school after another, but never been set to the study of ordinary English.

He finished his formal education in a boys' military school in

Michigan. The one thing that he learned there was to become an expert horseman.

After school, Burroughs made a number of gestures toward locating the romantic adventure he craved. He volunteered for the toughest post in the cavalry, but found life as a trooper in peacetime so unpleasant and unrewarding that he had to beg his father to pull strings and get him released from the army. For a time, he was a cowboy in Idaho, but the days of the frontier were over. He joined his brothers in a gold-mining scheme, but the business went broke. During the Spanish-American War, he attempted to volunteer for the Rough Riders, but Teddy Roosevelt turned him down, writing Burroughs that it was too far to bring him from Idaho.

At a time when Jack London had gone to Alaska and returned to make a name for himself in serious literary magazines, Burroughs was no more than a boy-man vainly mooning after dreams of high adventure. As late as 1906, when he was past 30, he was still making futile attempts to get taken on as a cavalry instructor in China.

Even after he got married, Burroughs was still unable to settle down. He bounced from job to job. He dropped out more often than H.G. Wells.

He worked for his father. He worked for his brothers. He was a railroad policeman, a timekeeper, a salesman, an accountant, an office manager, and over and over again an unsuccessful would-be businessman. He aimed for competence and efficiency, but he wasn't competent or efficient. He aimed for quick riches, but he never made more than minimal money. He aimed to be a shrewd businessman, but his business schemes were always castles in air.

The best thing that can be said about the young Edgar Rice Burroughs was that he never lacked the courage to dump one line of pursuit and go off looking somewhere else for what he was missing in life.

In the summer of 1911, at the age of 35—when London was already a fading alcoholic pouring the unhappy profits of his success into boats that wouldn't sail and houses that burned—Burroughs was a never-was, a self-made failure, a man who had never stuck at anything long enough to make his mark at it. He was a dreamer pretending to be a practical man.

But Burroughs did have a number of well-formed attitudes that were unusual for a romantic dreamer. He was a Darwinian. He had bought a copy of Darwin's *The Descent of Man* in 1899 and kept it all his life. He did not merely bow to the concept of the survival of the fittest—he actively embraced it. He disliked civilization and idolized nature. Animals to him seemed nobler than humans.

Above all, he was a complete materialist. The soul was just another religious superstition to him, one more lie imposed on man to keep him in bondage.

That summer in 1911, sitting in the empty office of his latest venture, a failing pencil-sharpener business, Burroughs began to scratch a story in longhand on the back of old stationery. It was a wild romantic fantasy, a tale of an American soldier of fortune suddenly transported to another planet where he finds adventure and the love of a Martian princess.

What a strange and desperate flier that was for Burroughs to take! With children to feed and bills to pay and another business disaster on his hands, writing a fairytale such as this one was a ridiculous escape for him to indulge in. And Burroughs himself was none too confident of what he was doing. He attached the pseudonym Normal Bean to his manuscript to indicate that he was really a sound and sober citizen and not a mad dreamer.

He sent the manuscript to *All-Story*, a pulp magazine published by Frank A. Munsey. The pulps, which flourished from just before the turn of the century until after the end of World War II, were story magazines with garish covers, printed on the cheapest grade of paper that would take ink. They were a form of popular entertainment, acceptable but not quite respectable. The pulps had something of the same reputation for thrills and violence enjoyed by the earlier dime novel, which they largely replaced.

All-Story was far from the best-paying or the largest in circulation of the pre-World War I pulp magazines. But it was the target that Burroughs was aiming for, and he hit it. *All-Story* took his Martian yarn and serialized it from February to July 1912. It appeared as *Under the Moons of Mars*, the work of someone named Norman Bean.

So much for his pseudonym, which Burroughs thereafter dropped.

Under the Moons of Mars—better known by its 1917 book title, *A Princess of Mars*—was a success with the readers of *All-Story*. It was the work of a brand-new writer, learning as he went, with no time to polish or revise. It was sometimes clumsy. And at times the language was formal and wooden, at variance with the action of the story. None of that really mattered, however. Burroughs' story got a unique grip on the reader from the very outset and held onto his attention.

In part, this was a result of Burroughs' hero, Captain John Carter of Virginia. After a brief preface in which Burroughs introduces his "Uncle Jack," author of the manuscript, Carter's own narrative of his adventures begins. His initial self-description is thoroughly mysterious. He says:

I am a very old man; how old I do not know. Possibly I am a hundred, possibly more; but I cannot tell because I have never aged as other men, nor do I remember any childhood. So far as I can recollect I have always been a man, a man of about thirty. I appear today as I did forty years and more ago, and yet I feel that I cannot go on living forever; that some day I shall die the real death from which there is no resurrection.

How intriguing!

However, both the plausible introduction of Carter by Burroughs-the-narrator—who "remembers" a visit by John Carter to Burroughs' father's home in Virginia before the Civil War (!)—and Carter's own mysterious self-presentation remain undeveloped beyond their initial statement. We know nothing specific of Carter beyond the bare facts that he is "a typical southern gentleman of the highest type" and a soldier whose sword has been red in the service of three republics, an emperor, and several kings. We learn nothing that ties him more closely to his relatives in Virginia or to any particular government, country, war, cause or specific experience. Neither do we learn anything more about his strange lack of a childhood or his amazing failure to age. Neither Carter's lightly sketched background nor his unique nature has any direct part to play in the plot of A Princess of Mars.

They do, however, serve to set up a most unusual character. What we are ultimately left with is a human figure whom we may take to be heroic, but who carries no freight of past history, earthly ties, or ideology. John Carter is all potential. He is a blank slate. He is a person who may do or become anything.

John Carter's true essential nature is that he is a neotenic anomaly. This goes beyond his outward appearance. Physically he may be a perpetual mature young man at the height of his powers, but mentally John Carter is even younger, a perpetual kid, with all of an adolescent's flexibility and unfixedness. He says of himself: "I could pass anywhere for twenty-five to thirty years of age, and to be a great uncle always seemed the height of incongruity, for my thoughts and feelings were those of a boy."

In 1912, this was a radically new set of characteristics for a hero, charming for its newness. It was a pure pleasure to follow a John Carter just to see what unexpected things he might do next.

But there is another fuzzy element in A Princess of Mars, ultimately as completely unexplained as Carter's nonspecific being. This is the means of John Carter's sudden transference to Mars.

John Carter tells us that after the American Civil War, he was prospecting for gold in Arizona. He took refuge from Apache attack in a convenient cave. An eerie moaning sound was heard, which frightened the Indians away. Then Carter suddenly found himself standing naked beside his own apparently lifeless body. Outside the cave, his attention was drawn to the red planet Mars near the horizon:

> As I gazed at it on that far-gone night it seemed to call across the unthinkable void, to lure me to it, to draw me as the lodestone attracts a particle of iron. My longing was beyond the power of opposition; I closed my eyes, stretched out my arms toward the god of my vocation and felt myself drawn with the suddenness of thought through the trackless immensity of space. There was an instant of extreme cold and utter darkness.

When John Carter opens his eyes again, he is lying naked in the midst of a strange landscape. He knows himself to be on the planet Mars. And immediately his adventures in this land of wonder begin. He experiments with the effects of the lower gravitation of this smaller planet. He discovers a Martian egg hatchery. And before the chapter is out, he is taken prisoner by savage white-tusked four-armed Martian warriors standing fifteen feet high.

What a peculiar headlong transition into the World Beyond the Hill this is! Earlier writers like Verne might delicately probe at the boundaries of the World Beyond the Hill with the aid of some super-scientific vehicle, and then hastily retreat at the first evidence of wonder. Burroughs makes no attempt at all to present a plausible means of travel to Mars. He simply picks his character up by the scruff of the neck and sets him down naked in a transcendent realm.

Is the transition to Mars a dream? Burroughs tells us immediately that it is not: "I was not asleep, no need for pinching here; my inner consciousness told me as plainly that I was upon Mars as your conscious mind tells you that you are upon Earth. You do not question the fact; neither did I."

Has Carter's soul left his body behind in that Arizona cave and gone off on its own to do some astral traveling? This seems possible, especially since Carter wakes at the end of the story to find himself back in that same cave. But there is this objection—while John Carter is on Mars, he is no spirit. He has his normal physical body, and when he is in danger he seems to stand every risk of dying the real death from which there is no resurrection.

When Carter comes to himself again in the Arizona cave at the conclusion, he discovers the remains of a mummified old woman crouched over a brazier containing some green powder, while behind her, hanging from rawhide thongs, is a row of skeletons. But we have no easy connection that we can draw between this Indian witch—if that is what she is—and Carter's adventures on Mars.

So how did John Carter get to Mars? The best answer we can give is that Edgar Rice Burroughs wanted this particular representative of humanity there, and put him there.

The real question is why the readers of *All-Story* were willing to accept such bare-faced implausibilities as the special nature of John Carter and his sudden and miraculous removal to Mars. The answer would seem to be that the readers of *All-Story* were as curious as Edgar Rice Burroughs to discover what a lone human being might accomplish if set down naked in an alien world where the struggle for existence was even fiercer than on Earth. Burroughs' Mars was a fascinating experimental test case of the strengths and limitations of civilization, of the acceptance of animal nature, and most of all, of human encounter with the mysterious scientific universe of space and time. Readers were willing to accept almost any initial improbability in the setting up of cases in order to see this particular thought experiment played through.

Mars—known as Barsoom to its inhabitants—is a dying world whose original high civilization collapsed 100,000 years ago when the Martian oceans dried up. After a prolonged period of barbarism, civilization has been restored by red-skinned Martians who are a mixture of the yellow, black and white races of olden times. These red-skinned Martians lay eggs, but otherwise appear normally human.

In many ways, the civilization of the red-skinned Martians resembles a typical Victorian technological utopia. It possesses mechanical wonders far in advance of contemporary Earth technology. There are automated restaurants, elevator houses that rise into the air at night, and super-telescopes that can see everything that passes on Earth. Above all, the red-skinned Martians command the powers of the mysterious eighth and ninth rays of the solar spectrum.

This new Martian civilization may now be the match of the old civilization that fell. Its knowledge may equal the old knowledge that was lost. John Carter tells us:

> During the ages of hardships and incessant warring between their own various races, as well as with the green men, and before they had fitted themselves to the changed conditions, much of the high civilization and many of the arts of the fair-haired Martians had become lost; but the red race of today has reached a point where it feels that it has made up in new discoveries and a more practical civilization for all that lies irretrievably buried with the ancient Barsoomians, beneath the countless intervening ages.

At the same time, the eternal struggle to exist goes on here in this harsh world. The cities of the red Martians continue to contend with each other for scarce resources, and must also beat off the attacks of the savage green Martian hordes that roam the dead ocean bottoms.

The red Martians have not left all of their barbarism behind them in the long ages of recovery. When they are not traveling by airships powered by the eighth ray, they are jouncing around on the backs of horselike thoats. When they are not firing radium rifles that can shoot projectiles two hundred miles, they are engaging in hand-to-hand combat with long swords.

This is a very strange mixture of incongruous elements. It might almost seem that Burroughs, faced with the immense challenge of imagining the details of an alien planet, had responded by tossing anything and everything that occurred to him into the pot and stirring. Here a bit of occultism, like the transfer of John Carter to Mars. There a dash of utopianism, like the red Martian civilization. A dollop of lost race elements like the vanished ancient Barsoomian high civilization. And some choice scientific ingredients like the concern with the lesser Martian gravitation, and the central Darwinian struggle for existence.

But Burroughs is not merely messing around. He means something by all this. However clumsy the attempt, Burroughs is aiming to reconcile the best of civilization and the best of savagery, two states formerly thought to be totally incompatible.

There are times when he is not completely successful. When Burroughs juxtaposes his radium rifles that can shoot for miles and intimate combat with edged weapons, the effect is brash and colorful—perhaps acceptable as a novel notion, but otherwise more than a little bit silly. The two forms of fighting do not exist comfortably in the same frame of reference.

In one detail, however, the blending of utopianism and barbarism is perfectly achieved. This is the nakedness of the characters. It is not only John Carter who encounters Mars naked. Except for a few decorative trappings of leather, metal and feathers, the red Martians habitually go naked. So do the green ones. Here—in 1912!—is our first glimpse of Dejah Thoris, Martian princess:

"She was as destitute of clothes as the green Martians who accompanied her; indeed, save for her highly wrought ornaments she was entirely naked, nor could any apparel have enhanced the beauty of her perfect and symmetrical figure."

This nakedness may be taken as utopian. It is the ultimate end point in that rationalization of clothing that we can see beginning with the discarding of wigs in Louis Sebastien Mercier's *Memoirs of the Year 2440*.

But nakedness is also barbaric. The pervasive nudity in *A Princess of Mars* may be taken as an expression of a new mood that began to surface in the Teens—a positive eagerness to shed Victorian constraint and acknowledge humanity's animal nature.

During the Teens, people were beginning to try to get in touch with their bodies. The new popular music of the day was ragtime and jazz—racy music, improvised music, Negro music, body music. It was now okay to eat new foods like hamburgers and ice cream cones right out of hand, just as though civilized eating utensils had never been invented. And the Teens were the decade in which women shucked their corsets, and it first became possible to talk of sex, the forbidden Victorian topic.

The pulp magazines were part of this unloosening process. And so, in particular, were the early stories of Edgar Rice Burroughs.

John Carter is equal to the challenge of the red Martians. For all their nakedness, they are a somewhat repressed lot, bound by rigid convention. John Carter is quicker on his feet than they and does not share their fixed prejudices. In Burroughs' second Martian story—*The Gods of Mars*, serialized in *All-Story* in 1913—Carter exposes the exploitative religion of Mars with its false priests, false gods, and false hereafter. In the third story—*The Warlord of Mars*, which had its serialization in *All-Story* in late 1913 and early 1914— Carter conquers virtually the entire planet.

If the half-super-civilized, half-barbaric red Martians are one standard of measure by which John Carter is tested, the green four-armed Martian savages are another. These gigantic beings are embodiments of pure animal ruthlessness. Every green Martian is in constant direct competition with every other green Martian. The higher sentiments of love, mercy and compassion are all but unknown among them—regarded as dangerous atavisms. They laugh at the death of their companions and derive their greatest amusement from the torture of their enemies.

John Carter wins the initial respect of these creatures by beating them on their own terms. When a green Martian abuses him, he lashes out with his tremendously powerful Earth-bred muscles: "As he banged me down upon my feet his face was bent close to mine and I did the only thing a gentleman might do under the circumstances of brutality, boorishness, and lack of consideration for a stranger's rights; I swung my fist squarely to his jaw and he went down like a felled ox."

But John Carter is superior to the green Martians on other grounds than mere might. When brutal and decisive action is not called for, he is capable of love, friendship, loyalty and compassion. He can convert a savage Martian watchbeast into a friendly pooch. He is even able to command the personal friendship of one superior green Martian, Tars Tarkas, Jeddak of Thark.

Ultimately, the most successful blending of civilized enlightenment and barbaric vitality in *A Princess of Mars* is John Carter himself. As his princess, Dejah Thoris, says to him early in their acquaintance: "'You are a queer mixture of child and man, of brute and noble.'"

It is Carter's openness and personal flexibility that enable him to arrive naked in an alien world of wonder, meet it without prejudice or fear, and battle his way to the top. If we must struggle to exist within the scientific universe of space and time, Edgar Rice Burroughs' recommendation is that we be done with all our reluctant hanging-back. We should embrace the fact with the receptivity and eagerness of a John Carter.

Much of Burroughs' charm and freshness derive from the new attitude that he displays toward the universe. He does not perceive the scientific universe as an inexorable grinding-on of immutable cosmic laws certain to reduce all human effort to rubble. Rather, he sees the universe of space and time as an endless source of unfamiliar conditions which may try us, but which we may respond to. It is this attitude that permits Burroughs to imagine Barsoom as a transcendent realm throwing forth one marvelous challenge after another.

In this new attitude toward the universe and in his neotenic hero, Burroughs is offering the materials of an answer to the tangled problem of man, civilization, and nature. If the universe is not a meat grinder, then there is no need for us to make a choice between a high culture sure to grow effete and destroy itself and a wild and brutal savagery that trades morality for momentary survival. Rather, it is in adaptation to circumstances that the answer lies.

It is an answer for society. Do we need to fear that the fall of civilization will be the end of man? No. When the Martian oceans dried up and the ancient Barsoomian civilization fell, the Martians survived, and after "readjustment to new conditions" erected civilization anew.

Adaptation is also an answer for man. John Carter is a living example of adaptability. Among Southern gentlemen, he is a Southern gentleman. With children, he laughs and plays like a child. And when he is amongst the civilized red Martians, he is a natural red Martian prince.

John Carter is an early version of the Twentieth Century existential man who finds his meaning in encounter, not in affiliation. And in whatever circumstances he finds himself, Carter trusts to his intuition and always acts with instantaneous rightness, even when faced with death:

> ...In all of the hundreds of instances that my voluntary acts have placed me face to face with death, I cannot recall a single one where any alternative step to that I took occurred to me until many hours later. My mind is evidently so constituted that I am subconsciously forced into the path of duty without recourse to tiresome mental processes.

Here, then, in the implausible pulp romance *A Princess of Mars*—published the very same year as Jack London's "The Scarlet Plague"—was the answer to all of London's questions, a reconciliation of *The Call of the Wild* and *White Fang*. The answer was: Adapt. Do what is appropriate. When it is time to be Buck and lead the wild wolves, be Buck. When it is time to be White Fang and defend civilization, be White Fang. But don't make the mistake of identifying man's true flexible nature exclusively with either civilization or savagery.

Even as *A Princess of Mars* was in serialization, Burroughs was at work writing another novel that presented these same new ideas in other clothing. This novel—*Tarzan of the Apes*, published complete in the October 1912 *All-Story*—would make Burroughs famous.

Tarzan of the Apes is the story of an orphan child, an English lord born in the African jungle and raised by intelligent apes. Though it holds lost cities, odd beasts and strange peoples, the Africa of Burroughs' imagination is not as weird and marvelous as his Mars. But Tarzan is John Carter—the flexible man who combines the best of civilization and savagery—more effectively realized.

The similarity of the two characters is overwhelming. Tarzan's true name is John Clayton, Lord Greystoke. Not only are their names almost identical, but the two Johns, Clayton and Carter, are physical doubles as well. Both of them are tall, lithe and powerful fighting men with black hair and gray eyes.

If Tarzan is the more persuasive portrait of this person, it is because the background of John Carter of Mars is an enigma. We don't know what made him the strange new kind of person he is. But we see Tarzan grow into being from babyhood. We see his savage environment forcing him to be strong. We see his inherited intelligence asserting itself as he teaches himself to read. We see him encountering both the jungle and modern society, not quite a part of either, but superior to both.

Endless adaptability was Burroughs' strength and his limitation as a writer. He turned out one careless, colorful and imaginative story after another for the pulps, seldom deep, but within his formulas tirelessly inventive. Before his death in 1950, he wrote more than sixty books, of which twenty-six were Tarzan stories and eleven were stories of Mars.

Burroughs was the first great SF writer of the Twentieth Century. He did not have H.G. Wells's acute intelligence, his scientific knowledge, nor his breadth of vision. But he was able to do something new that Wells had not been able to do.

Wells had set forth the outlines of the new universe of space and time. But when it came to the difficult task of filling in those outlines with detail and action, Wells had not been able to do it. He was not able to imagine what a being like himself could find to do amongst the engimatical immensities.

But Edgar Rice Burroughs was able to manage that trick. He was not frightened by the universe of space and time. Nor was he daunted by the prospect of having to struggle and change to get ahead in this world. Burroughs was able to imagine a person much like himself living, loving, fighting, adventuring, and winning through on an alien world that was simultaneously scientific and a realm of the World Beyond the Hill. It was to characters like John Carter that the future of science fiction would belong.

8

The Death of the Soul

Edgar Rice Burroughs' two great stories of 1912—*Under the Moons of Mars* and *Tarzan of the Apes*—and the whole body of work that he produced before World War I, may be taken as a culmination of Edwardian SF and a foretaste of vigorous American science fiction to come. By sloughing off certain Edwardian values—by discarding the soul and primary dependence on civilization—Burroughs was able to imagine a new exemplar of human possibility, the adaptable existential man of action, who was the fulfillment of the irrational Edwardian confidence in Man.

But that Edwardian confidence in Man was to suffer a great shock with the coming of World War I, a horrible conflict in which all civilized restraint was cast aside and barbarity reigned. World War I—known in its own time as the Great War and the War to End All Wars—was a bloody animal struggle among the European nations to discover which was fittest and which had the right to survive.

This Great War, which lasted from 1914 to 1918, was that scientific war-of-the-future that had been under rehearsal in SF stories ever since George Chesney's "The Battle of Dorking" in 1871. The war was an awful international exhibition of marvelous weaponry and technological innovation, with rank upon rank of men sacrificed to prove the power of poison gas, machine guns and barbed wire. Great armored tanks, submarine boats and flying machines clashed together like a return of the Age of Reptiles in mechanical form.

In the face of the evidence offered by World War I, it was very difficult to continue to believe in the simple rational advance of mankind. If this war was civilized behavior, who needed civilization? With the brutal slaughter of ten million young men, how was it possible to maintain claims of the superiority of human morality?

During the war years, there was a great dieback of SF. Most affected was utopianoid SF—the oldest, most serious, most literary, and best respected element of this still-emerging literature. The largest part. There was a sudden disappearance of future war stories, techno-utopian schemes for the betterment of humanity, stories of natural catastrophe, and accounts of the fall of civilization.

What remained of SF was its most mysterious, transcendent, romantic and imaginative materials—along with its uneasy faith in super-science and the unknown scientific universe. What survived, in sum, was the most questionable, frightening and disreputable portion of SF.

SF did not have an excess of credit that it could afford to lose. Even in the days when it was widely published, it had always been a minority taste, always a bit suspect.

For an example of the questionable esteem in which SF was held during the Age of Technology, even in its best days, it is only necessary to look at the career of H.G. Wells. When Wells turned from writing his innovative scientific horror stories of the Nineties to writing more conventional Dickensian social comedies in the Edwardian decade, there was almost a sense of relief. The judgment of contemporary society was that this change demonstrated "a great advance in artistic power" on Wells's part, and both his book sales and his literary repute leaped.

World War I drove a wedge between SF and all hope of respectability. With the failure of utopianism, SF lost its one strong tie to high culture. At the same time, SF's central mystery—soulless science—became abhorrent and horrifying to genteel society.

SF, already wounded, was rejected and shunned by high culture. It was no longer acceptable in polite company. From the Teens on, SF had to make its way chiefly in the pulp magazines as a low form of popular literature that was considered both more than a bit dangerous and more than a bit crazy.

Both the shock to utopianism and the social fall of SF may have contributed to SF's great failure in Europe during World War I. Prior to the war, the development of SF had always been an enterprise swapped back and forth by British writers, Americans, and Europeans, in particular the French. There was a flowering of imaginative and explorative French SF as late as the end of the Edwardian decade. During the Great War, however, European SF ceased to be published, as though no one could bear to think about such things. When European SF resumed after the war, it never fully regained its former vitality.

Neither American self-esteem nor American confidence in science were shaken as they were in Europe by the events of World War I. America only entered the war at the last minute, in 1917. No grinding battles were fought on American soil, and the United States did not suffer the same harrowing casualties as the other participants. It was even possible for Americans to believe that they were responsible for winning the war.

All during the war years and immediately after, when utopian SF failed and European SF disappeared, a gaudy and romantic line of story much influenced by Burroughs did continue to be published in the American general fiction pulp magazines, particularly *All-Story* under the editorship of Robert H. Davis, and secondarily its sister magazine, *Argosy*. With the stories of Edgar Rice Burroughs and the new pulp writers who followed him, the leadership in the development of SF passed into American hands. It was only Americans, among all the people of the West, who retained enough confidence in man and in science to continue with the unsettling and dangerous business of imagining the new SF mythos.

With utopian plausibility denied to it, this American pulp SF of the Teens became highly imaginative. It was both escapist and exploratory. Sometimes these two aspects were difficult to distinguish.

During the Teens, there was a last great appearance of lost race stories. These were radically different from the original lost race narratives of the late Nineteenth Century. No longer was it merely remnants of known civilizations like Rome or Phoenicia that were discovered, or simple enclaves of technological utopians. In these Twentieth Century pulp magazine lost race stories, there was a new time scale reaching back into the forgotten past, back to Atlantis and before that to completely unknown civilizations fully as old as the ancient Barsoomian high civilization on Mars. And the populations of these places were now given as masters of ancient mystic wisdom, usually identified with science-beyond-science.

In Perley Poore Sheehan's *The Abyss of Wonders* (*Argosy*, January 1915), for example, his American venturer travels to a marvelous lost city surviving in the midst of the Gobi Desert, and there falls in love with a mysterious maiden. But the gift of insight that he brings back from his encounter with mystic wisdom is not ancient in form, but rather modern and technological:

"Hello," said the foreman. "Did you get as far as Omaha?"

"I guess so," Shan answered. Then he continued. "While I was knocking about I thought of that improvement you said was needed in the reversing-plate on the big lathe."

He borrowed a stub of a pencil from the foreman and drew a plan on the white-washed wall.

"You've got it," said the foreman. "Gee, that ought to make your fortune!"

Other American pulp SF stories of the Teens did not look for their inspiration to ancient occult wisdom, but instead headed off into the new worlds of space and time or into other dimensions to find their adventures. These stories of alien exploration invariably followed the same plan as their models—Wells's *The Time Machine* and Burroughs' *A Princess of Mars* and its sequels. Over and over, a contemporary Western person would pass into a strange other realm, be beguiled and threatened, retreat to the Village to tell his tale to some friend or relative, and then disappear into the World Beyond the Hill again.

Perhaps the most popular of these stories was "The Girl in the Golden Atom" (*All-Story*, March 15, 1919), by Ray Cummings, a writer and editor in the employ of Thomas Edison. This story was the fulfillment of Fitz-James O'Brien's "The Diamond Lens" (1858), the tale of a scientific madman's thwarted passion for Animula, the beautiful girl he sees within the confines of a drop of water. Like O'Brien's character, the protagonist of Cummings' story has a super-scientific microscope, peers into the infinitesimal world, and falls in love with a wondrously beautiful maiden he spies there—in this case, within an atom of his mother's golden wedding ring.

Fitz-James O'Brien's story, written before SF explorers had blazed the first trails into the World Beyond the Hill, had ended tragically. To O'Brien, the radically tiny world of Animula had seemed hopelessly inaccessible. And even so recent a writer as H. G. Wells, pioneer explorer of alien realms, had envisioned the microcosm as wonderful, but no place for a being such as himself.

Ray Cummings, however, was able to imagine bridging the gap between our world and the world of the very small. His character—named "the Chemist" after the example of Wells's "the Time Traveller"—synthesizes a new drug to reduce himself in size, and penetrates the atomic dimension in pursuit of love.

It was not particularly important that the adventures discovered in the world of the Golden Atom were ordinary and banal. What was thrilling to the audience of *All-Story* was that imaginary science had burst through another barrier and brought yet another dimension within its reach.

Of all the new writers who appeared in the American pulps during the World War I years and immediately after, the most significant and influential was A. Merritt, a newspaperman who took up story-telling in 1917 at the age of 33.

Abraham Grace Merritt was born in Beverly, New Jersey, north of Philadelphia on the Delaware River, on January 20, 1884. His father was a lapsed Quaker, an architect and builder. On his mother's side, Merritt was a great-great-grandnephew of James Fenimore Cooper.

Merritt's first aim was to be a lawyer, but when his father died when he was eighteen, lack of money forced Merritt to drop out of college and become a reporter. Writing fiction was never other than a hobby for Merritt, a sideline from his highly paid job as an editor for the Hearst newspapers' Sunday magazine, *The American Weekly*, of which he would eventually become editor-in-chief.

A. Merritt was not as innovative an SF writer as H.G. Wells, nor as inventive as Edgar Rice Burroughs, nor even as eager an explorer of new dimensions as any number of his pulp contemporaries. Neither was he particularly prolific. During an active writing career of seventeen years, Merritt wrote just eight novels and a handful of shorter stories, by no means all of which were scientific fiction.

Nonetheless, Merritt played a pivotal role in the development of SF. He unified and consolidated SF through his ability to see that one imaginative formulation might be essentially equivalent to another that was radically dissimilar in appearance.

Before Merritt wrote, modern imaginative fiction existed, but only as a variety of seemingly separate story types, not as a single coherent literature. Merritt observed none of the conventional boundaries. He switched effortlessly from the alien exploration story to lost race fiction, from otherworld fantasy to the occult horror story, mixing the symbols of one with the symbols of the next as though there was no essential difference between them.

His special power was his sense of universal mystery. Like some Romantic of a hundred years previous, a Blake or a Poe, Merritt perceived the ordinary appearance of things as a mere facade. It is of the essence of Merritt that Dr. Goodwin, the rational scientist who narrates his first novel, *The Moon Pool* (1919), is ultimately forced by his strange experiences to conclude, "our world *whatever* it is, is certainly *not* the world as we see it!"

This was a view to which the mood of the time was unusually receptive. World War I finally ground its way to an exhausted conclusion in November 1918. As everyone took note, with a sigh of wonder and relief, the armistice was signed in the eleventh hour of the eleventh day of the eleventh month. And, indeed, it did feel as though the end had come just in time, at the very last possible moment before the midnight hour in which the West would totally destroy itself.

In the entire course of this harrowing four-year war, no decisive battles were ever fought.

As much as by anything, the Great War was brought to a halt by the worldwide flu epidemic of 1918—which killed a further twenty million people beyond the casualties of the war.

In the moment of stunned silence that attended the end of the war, it seemed to many in the West that the world was a place of complete insanity. There was a positive eagerness to believe that somewhere else there might be a truer reality than this one. There was a willingness to consider any possible alternative. Writers of imaginative fiction cultivated hallucinatory and dreamlike prose styles. Interest in drug-taking, occultism and mysticism rose to a peak.

Among the SF writers of the day, it was Merritt who was most open to alternatives. Other writers might catch a fleeting glimpse of transcendent mystery through the prism of one particular belief or another—science, society, survival, the soul. But Merritt saw mystery as the fundamental fact, and only then tried on various means of expressing this vision.

Merritt's most powerful evocation of pure mystery appears in the opening paragraphs of his second and most speculative novel, *The Metal Monster* (1920). Like *The Moon Pool*, this novel, too, is narrated by botanist Walter T. Goodwin. But in this story, he is a much-changed man. He is no longer the scientific rationalist he used to be, but is now a scientific mystic, and he begins his new tale with a direct testimonial to the ubiquity of mystery:

> In this great crucible of life we call the world—in the vaster one we call the universe—the mysteries lie close packed, uncountable as grains of sand on ocean's shores. They thread, gigantic, the star-flung spaces; they creep, atomic, beneath the microscope's peering eye. They walk beside us, unseen and unheard, calling out to us, asking why we are deaf to their crying, blind to their wonder.
>
> Sometimes the veils drop from a man's eyes, and he sees—and speaks of his vision. Then those who have not seen pass him by with the lifted brows of disbelief, or they mock him, or if his vision has been great enough they fall upon and destroy him.

In the fact-minded Twentieth Century, such a total conviction of mystery has been no common thing. And professional newspapermen have more often been known as mockers and skeptics than as mystics. We may ask then just how it was that A. Merritt came to believe that mystery was not merely a fact, but *the* fundamental fact. How was he so prepared to take advantage of this moment of relative openness and receptivity? What caused the veils to drop from Merritt's eyes?

As with many among the original Romantics, the answer would seem to lie in a sensitivity to the anomalies of life, exposure to the alternative viewpoint offered by a foreign culture, and experimentation with mind-altering drugs.

In the days when Merritt was a young college dropout haunting the hospitals of Philadelphia looking for newspaper stories, he was taken in hand by two elderly doctors. One, Silas Weir Mitchell, was a specialist in nervous disorders. The other, Charles Eucharist de Medicis Sajous, was a pioneer endocrinologist. Between them, they gave Merritt what he would come to consider the equivalent of a four-year college course—packed into a year and a half—in conventional science and in less orthodox belief and practice.

S. Weir Mitchell, who would die in 1914 at the age of 85, was particularly influential on Merritt. In addition to being a medical researcher of considerable prominence, he was a well-known late-Nineteenth Century novelist and an investigator of strange phenomena.

Dr. Mitchell turned Merritt's attention toward the existence of mystery. He set him to reading books on medical anomalies, on surviving folk beliefs, on magical practices, and on the paranormal—all that in former times would have been considered "supernatural." Merritt would later repay Mitchell for his kindness by reporting to him his own personal observations of Pennsylvania Dutch witchcraft and animal sacrifice.

In 1903, Merritt's eccentric education was abruptly cut short when he became an inconvenient witness to a matter of political delicacy. He was hustled out of Philadelphia for a year, all expenses paid.

Merritt went south looking for exotic adventure, and found it. He hunted for treasure in Central America. He explored the ruins of the Mayan city of Chichen Itza. And he was initiated into the mysteries of an Indian tribe in Miraflores, Mexico.

Merritt says of himself that he "gained a curious knowledge of Indian customs and religious ceremonies that would have stood his Quaker ancestors' hair on end." At the impressionable age of 20, for a significant moment, young Abe Merritt stood outside the bounds of ordinary Western culture.

Merritt would have been content to go on living wild and free forever in Central America, but in time his supply of money came to an end. He was obliged to return to Philadelphia to take up a thereafter uninterrupted career as a newspaper reporter and editor.

After his return from his foreign adventure, Merritt continued to read widely, now centering his interests in archaeology, myth and comparative religion. He began to collect books on the outré. Eventually he would devote the entire third floor of his large home on Long Island to his library of the fantastic.

If his experience in Mexico did not include the use of peyote or psychedelic mushrooms—as is suggested by the vibrant colors that from the first would mark Merritt's most imaginative fictional passages—he would find some other route to experimentation with hallucinogenic plants. In later years, Merritt not only maintained several experimental farms in Florida, but kept what he would call a "garden of poisonous plants." Here he raised precisely those psychoactive plants, Old World and New, whose use is traditionally associated with witches and shamans—ultimately as many as sixty-seven of them, including mandrake, datura, marijuana and peyote.

Merritt lived two highly separate lives. On the job, he was a shrewd and knowledgeable editor, a pipe-smoking, tobacco-spitting news-paperman, as drunk and skeptical as could be asked for. But in his private life he was quite a different person. Working very slowly, basing what he wrote on his queer reading and his sense of mystery, and aiming only to please himself, Merritt became a scientific fantasist of unique power.

Something of this Merritt and his methods and values can be glimpsed in an account he would give a correspondent of the genesis of one short story. Merritt dreamed most of it in his sleep, but then half-awoke with the story unconcluded. Lying there, Merritt thought of an abrupt and violent ending for the story that would undercut and deny its fantastic element, and then fell back to sleep. But sleeping again, he dreamed a second ending that didn't undercut the fantasy—and that was the one he used. In his letter, Merritt would ask:

> Which was right—the ending of the half-awakening which brought in the conscious mind, and that part of my mind is very cynical, or the other which is in control largely when I write, and which is not? I do not know. It is a curious thing that just above I first wrote "right" for write—and then struck it out when I noticed it. Perhaps that was an answer to my question. I wonder. Certainly I never spelled "write" that way before.
>
> I sincerely hope it was a flash from Truth and that "right" was right. But—I do not know.

If we are disposed to view Merritt-the-storyteller as an intuition-led, mystery-sensitive Romantic out of time, however, he was a Romantic writing with every new imaginative resource that had been developed by the Victorians. He was an Edgar Allan Poe able to draw upon the differing formulations and arguments of Jules Verne, H. Rider Haggard, H. G. Wells and Lord Dunsany—and to make them all one through the unifying power of his sense of tran-scendent mystery.

The merging together of what had formerly been taken as separate is visible from Merritt's very first story. In "Through the Dragon Glass" (*All-Story*, November 24, 1917), an American venturer is drawn by a beguiling maid into the twilight world that lurks within an artifact which he has looted from the Forbidden City in China during the Boxer Rebellion. He is then wounded and chased from this place by the local demi-god who rules this realm. At the conclusion, having told his story to a friend in the usual way, the adventurer is headed back into the World Beyond the Hill, this time armed with an elephant gun.

This was a relatively minor story, but it yielded a major implication. It suggested that the nonce worlds of Dunsanian fantasy and the strange new realms lately reached by the alien explorers of scientific fiction might not be different and distinct, but the very same places.

There were even more important symbolic mergings in Merritt's first great popular successes, the 1918 *All-Story* novelet and the 1919 serial that together went to make up the novel *The Moon Pool*. In these stories, his characters encounter apparently supernatural beings in an underground realm beneath the Pacific Ocean, first the monstrous Dweller in the Moon Pool and then the godlike *Taithu*.

One character—the young Irish airman, Larry O'Keefe—takes the Dweller for a banshee and identifies the *Taithu* with the Tuatha Dé Danann of Irish legend. But, alternatively, Dr. Goodwin, the botanist narrator, theorizes that the Dweller is the product of lost race super-science and that the *Taithu* are a natural result of the processes of evolution:

"'I think,' I said cautiously, 'that we face an evolution of highly intelligent beings from ancestral sources radically removed from those through which mankind ascended.'"

He then goes on to take his argument for the existence of such evolutionarily superior creatures from H. G. Wells's *The War of the Worlds*:

"The Englishman, Wells, wrote an imaginative and very entertaining book concerning an invasion of earth by Martians, and he made his Martians enormously specialized cuttlefish. There was nothing inherently improbable in Wells's choice. Man is the ruling animal of earth today solely by reason of a series of accidents; under another series spiders or ants, or even elephants, could have become the dominant race."

So which are the *Taithu* really? Are they Irish gods from the Land Under the Wave, or are they some variation of Wells's evolutionarily advanced Big Brains? We can't be sure, and since we can't be sure, we must take them as both, or as either.

The Moon Pool forces us to ask ourselves whether there is any meaningful difference between the transcendent beings of traditional fantasy and the new transcendent beings imagined in scientific fiction—or whether the two in essence might not be the same.

But Merritt went even further than this in *The Moon Pool* toward reconciling old-fashioned supernatural mystery with science. In his stories, Wells had relied heavily for his effects on metaphor, analogy, and appeals to the limitless extent of the new scientific unknown. Burroughs had tossed in magical rays and new words like "radium" without much concern for their actual scientific meaning. But Merritt did genuine scientific homework. In *The Moon Pool*, he pioneered in the practice of sprinkling his pages with frequent scientific footnotes which speculated on the true nature of the marvels to be found in the underground realm and related them to actual contemporary science.

Most significantly, when Dr. Goodwin is forced by his experiences to admit that the-world-that-really-is is not the same as the world we perceive, he immediately refers the reader to a discourse on Einstein's Theory of General Relativity that had been delivered by the British physicist A.S. Eddington the previous year. This was a remarkable anticipation by Merritt. At the time that he wrote *The Moon Pool*, the work of Albert Einstein was still generally unknown and its implications unappreciated.

In 1919—after the serial version of the novel had appeared—a British expedition headed by Eddington would travel to the Atlantic to observe stars near the sun during an eclipse, and confirm a prediction by Einstein that light would be bent by the power of the sun's gravity. And Einstein's name would become an instant household word as the man who had altered the nature of space.

But this public recognition would only come at the end of the year, at almost the same moment as the book publication of *The Moon Pool*. Merritt's prescient reference to the new irrational theoretical physics of Einstein was an early recognition that Twentieth Century science might prove to be the source of mysteries fully as deep and strange and unfathomable as any that had ever been born of spirit.

During the little *All-Story* renaissance of the late Teens, A. Merritt went far toward drawing the various pieces of SF literature together. He made fantasy more plausible and the new scientific fiction more fantastic. Merritt's personal imaginative synthesis was an anticipation of that general consolidation of SF which would be achieved by Hugo Gernsback in *Amazing Stories* in 1926, and may have had a great deal to do with making it conceptually possible.

The farthest reaches of Merritt's vision of mystery simultaneously scientific and spiritual are to be found in *The Metal Monster*. This story was serialized in *Argosy All-Story Weekly* in 1920 soon after the two formerly separate general fiction pulp magazines were merged.

Like *The Moon Pool*, at its outset *The Metal Monster* has the appearance of a lost race novel. However, it, too, soon develops into a story of the discovery of alien beings—in this case creatures of crystalline metal in various geometric forms, very much like the strange Shapes in J.H. Rosny aîné's "Les Xipéhuz" (1887).

The prospect of living and thinking metal beings terrifies the explorers and fills them with dread. Dr. Goodwin is forced to arrive at an incredible conclusion—that consciousness, far from being a solely biological phenomenon, must be innate in the very basis of the material universe. He asks himself:

> Consciousness itself—after all what is it? A secretion of the brain? The cumulative expression, wholly chemical, of the multitudes of cells that form us? The inexplicable governor of the city of the body of which these myriads of cells are the citizens—and created by them out of themselves to rule?
>
> Is it what many call the soul? Or is it a finer form of matter, a self-realizing force, which uses the body as its vehicle just as other forces use for their vestments other machines? After all, I thought, what is this conscious self of ours, the ego, but a spark of realization running continuously along the path of time within the mechanism we call the brain; making contact along that path as the electric spark at the end of a wire?
>
> Is there a sea of this conscious force which laps the shores of the farthest-flung stars; that finds expression in everything—man and rock, metal and flower, jewel and cloud? Limited in its expression only by the limitations of that which it animates, and in essence the same in all. If so, then this problem of the Metal People ceased to be a problem; was answered!

This is a magnificent vision! It reconciles the new materialistic science with the old spirit-based mystery in terms of consciousness—the universal consciousness of all existence.

The sheer breadth encompassed by Merritt is immense. He was a Romantic, a lover of mystery. He was one of the last writers of SF to treat the metaphor of *the soul* with seriousness. He was the culmination of Nineteenth Century SF. He was a consolidator and integrator of the new scientifiction, one of the first writers to mark his text with scientific footnotes. During the hyper-materialistic era that followed his own, Merritt's great visions—of omnipresent mystery, of unfathomable transcendence, and of universal consciousness—would serve as a continuing challenge, stimulus and reminder of unfulfilled possibility. Merritt's work even reaches across the years to writers of the present with their radical crossbreedings of fantasy and science fiction and their explicit concern with states of consciousness.

But even A. Merritt's creative insight had its limits. Like the great

SF writers who came before him, Merritt, too, came to a sticking point and could go no further. Or, perhaps it might be more accurate to say, eventually the times put too great a strain on Merritt's fragile attempt to reconcile science and spirit, and it shattered in his hands.

It is in the midst of *The Metal Monster* that the bubble bursts. Merritt was able to present a vision of universal consciousness, but he was not able to sustain it. Fear and negativity overwhelm his story and change its focus from the conscious force that finds its expression in everything to the lesser question of which mode of consciousness may be fittest to survive.

When perceived with the eyes of fear, Merritt's Metal People begin to seem as implacably alien and relentlessly hostile as Wells's Martians. They are revolted by our organic nature, which appears messy and unnatural to them. No real communication with these Shapes is possible, only a desperate struggle for survival.

In this contest between metal life and human life, the Metal People have the advantage. They have the mathematical certitude and inexorability of cosmic law. They have direct awareness and command of energies both known to us and unknown.

As in *The War of the Worlds*, humanity is saved from annihilation, but not through the power of its own efforts. Instead, the metal creatures self-destruct in a kind of civil war. There is the implication that the fragmentation of the Metal People's formerly unified consciousness comes as a result of contamination by human anger, pride and sexual antagonism.

The novel concludes with a re-evocation of the sense of cosmic mystery that opens the book—but now tainted with menace:

> For in that vast crucible of life of which we are so small a part, what other Shapes may even now be rising to submerge us?
>
> In that vast reservoir of force that is the mystery-filled infinite through which we roll, what other shadows may be speeding upon us?
>
> Who knows?

These were dark times. The doubt and fear that mark the ending of *The Metal Monster* were a reflection of the unhappiness, despair and loss of confidence that gripped the Western world in the aftermath of the Great War.

In the half-dozen years that followed World War I, the world was stricken with epidemics, revolutions, massacres, starvation, economic turmoil, anarchy and subversion. It was a time of unsettlement and horror for many, a great psychic crashout.

Even in the United States, so much less severely affected by the war than Europe or Britain, and so much less shaken by the war's aftermath, there was a conviction that things were profoundly wrong, and a desperate search for scapegoats. There were political witchhunts and racial lynchings, labor violence, literary censorship, and laws passed against the teaching of evolution in schools.

It was as though genteel society hoped that if only the right people could be stuffed back into their proper places—Communists, Negroes, anarchists, unionists, freethinkers, free-speakers, and scientists—then perhaps the world might be set right again. At the same time, there was profound disillusionment, bitterness and cynicism, and the numb suspicion that no matter what was done, things could never be set right.

It seemed that the lost race mythos—like the future war story before it—had proven to be true. The Edwardian years before the war were looked back upon as some Golden Age of peace and ease whose like would never be seen again. Now civilization had fallen. Nothing was left but barbarity.

This was a wild time and a very sad time. It was not by chance that the wounded youngsters who survived the war called themselves the Lost Generation. Their youth and innocence were gone, and civilization was dead. They were poor lost souls adrift and wandering through the cold material universe.

Poor lost souls... If the Great War spelled the end to mighty Nineteenth Century civilization—the old order—it also made it impossible to go on any longer believing in the rational soul. The personal spiritual connection to God which had given life its meaning and purpose for so long now seemed implausible, a mere figment of religious wishful thinking.

If men did have a higher nature, would they have fought this awful war? If God did exist, could he have allowed men with souls to create a hell on earth like this one?

World War I and its bitter aftermath made Western people unbelievers. Certainly a great number of people did continue to consider themselves Christians, but after the Great War, Western society was clearly post-Christian, run with less and less regard for established religious notions of propriety.

But if the soul was no longer credible and Christianity no longer a guide, how were people to know how to proceed? Many did not.

This was a moment both of excess and of disgust with excess. Sex and drugs, which in the Teens had seemed to be modes of liberation, now took on overtones of decadent self-indulgence. Hollywood, the new sin and glamour capital of the West, was rocked by a string of scandals involving rape, murder and drug addiction, and the careers of a number of well-known movie stars were ruined.

In its sense of revulsion at human grossness and animality, Merritt's

The Metal Monster was very much of this moment. In this climate, it was possible for organic existence to be perceived as inherently flawed, rotten and foul. A mistake. An aberrancy.

The reciprocal of this disgust with the flesh can also be seen in *The Metal Monster*—an implicit admiration of the purity and simplicity of the metal Shapes. These postwar years were the period of the emergence of Art Deco; during the Twenties, the clean lines and unadorned efficiency of the machine would become a model for architecture and design.

In the Twenties, more than at any moment before or since, the universe of space and time appeared to people in the guise of a perfect inexorable machine. Mankind—that soulless barbarian, that revolting cosmic error—seemed no better than some noxious fungus gumming up the works.

The postwar years were not an easy period for SF. All the conflict at large in the world and all the uncertainty in people's minds were reflected in SF literature. It was necessary for writers to decide what they really believed. They had to make the choice between science and superstition, between the God-given soul and a sterile universe without meaning.

Making this decision was most difficult and agonizing for those writers from the old aristocracy—Britons, Europeans, and one gentleman from Virginia—who returned to imaginative literature after the hiatus of the war to produce some of the most heartfelt and striking work of the period. The soul, that phantasm, was the source of their personal and class superiority, while the new universe of the machine barbarians seemed both trivial and repulsive.

It was only a very few among the established—scientific utopians like H.G. Wells, and lifelong scientific materialists like his elder French contemporary, J.H. Rosny aîné—who could muster the will, the nerve and the energy to make positive statements about science and the material universe. More typically, British and European writers of privilege looked upon the face of science and responded with cries of denial, disgust, abhorrence and fear.

Some writers attempted evasion. The nonce worlds of fantasy seemed to offer the hope of a possible place of retreat from the disastrous Twentieth Century. In these nobler and more romantic regions, perhaps, mystery might still be magical, the fact of the soul might still be beyond doubt, and men of chivalric sensibility might still pursue higher purpose.

But where were these fantasy worlds to be found?

In one aristocratic fantasy, *Jurgen* (1919), by the Virginia novelist James Branch Cabell, such a place is imagined by the expedient of wrenching apart space and time. In a blank spot on the map, an area of Europe overlooked by mapmakers and geographers, in a time that never was, the gap between the end of the Middle Ages and the beginning of the Renaissance, Cabell located his sometimes magical realm of Poictesme.

In another aristocratic fantasy of the period, *The Worm Ouroboros* (1922), by the British civil servant and student of Old Norse, E. R. Eddison, the nominal setting is a place distant in space, the surface of the planet Mercury. But this imagined Mercury is a fanciful and unscientific realm that is reached by means of a deliberate dream.

What fantasies such as these were attempting to flee was expressed by Cabell in one typically wry and ambivalent episode in *Jurgen* that combines a twitting of the titular character's overweening egotism and a very genuine dismay at the meaningless nature of the universe as it was then understood.

In an attempt to purge Jurgen of his illusions, the magician Merlin has sent Jurgen to visit a transcendent being—not named, but apparently the god Pan. This superior creature entertains Jurgen by revealing a vision of All to him. But the shadow show displayed to Jurgen is a depiction of the Twentieth Century Western worldview, and Jurgen will not and cannot accept that:

> "Fact! sanity! and reason!" Jurgen raged: "why, but what nonsense you are talking! Were there a bit of truth in your silly puppetry this world of time and space and consciousness would be a bubble, a bubble which contained the sun and moon and the high stars, and still was but a bubble in fermenting swill! I must go cleanse my mind of all this foulness. You would have me believe that men, that all men who have ever lived or shall ever live hereafter, that even I am of no importance! Why, there would be no justice in any such arrangement, no justice anywhere!"

But this denial cannot be convincing to us. As much as it is a protest, it is also an admission. Whether he likes it or not, Jurgen must grant that the fantasy realm of Poictesme is a part of "this world of time and space and consciousness." And it is time, space and consciousness that are the parameters of the modern scientific universe.

It would seem, then, that the fantasy worlds of Poictesme and Mercury are vulnerable to scientific criticism. Would the land of Poictesme wink out of existence if we were to insist on looking closely at our maps and reading our history books with care? And what would befall the fantastic Mercury of *The Worm Ouroboros*, land of humanlike Demons and Witches, if an astronomer should happen to point out the true feeble gravity, blazing temperatures, and absence of atmosphere on the planet Mercury?

Lord Dunsany's *Time and the Gods* and A. Merritt's "Through the Dragon Glass" had previously implied that the nonce worlds of fantasy were open to invasion by universal scientific law and to subjugation by the power of technology. But what are we to make of fantasy worlds where the likes of Merlin and Pan—creatures of magic—disavow magic to become advocates of Twentieth Century Realism?

What we can say of these particular fantasy realms is that they were compromised as soon as they were conceived. If they are magical places, it is only that they appear magical to us for as long as we are willing to make believe. The very instant science begins to inquire into them seriously, they must become anomalous and implausible.

Like Lord Dunsany, their primary model, Cabell and Eddison were aware that the old values expressed in fantasy had become unfounded, and that new values reigned. And persisted in writing fantasy anyway. But a fantasy tinged by irony and self-doubt.

It is not surprising that both *Jurgen* and *The Worm Ouroboros* should undercut their own ideals of magic, chivalry and romance even as they presented them. As much as these books were protests against the Twentieth Century, they were also typical expressions of the Twentieth Century, touched by the postwar blight at the very instant they cried out against it. Both of these books had moments when old-fashioned idealistic morality was replaced by the new cynical hard-boiled pragmatism. And there were other moments in each book when the contemporary mood broke in and cool rational calculation suddenly gave way to shudders of physical and sexual revulsion.

Ultimately, these postwar aristocratic fantasies were not at all successful in evading the modern scientific universe that they so despised. It is by no accident that both *Jurgen* and *The Worm Ouroboros* (a title that refers to the world-girdling serpent that bites its own tail) were circular in construction, ending just where they began, with nothing changed or accomplished by the passage of four hundred pages. These fantasies aimed to run away from the scientific universe, only to be thrown back into it by a kind of self-applied, self-defeating judo move.

With entirely appropriate irony, Cabell's *Jurgen* became a success through a great public scandal. This witty and elliptical expression of uneasiness at the nature of the modern world was condemned by the American Society for the Suppression of Vice as a work of obscenity and was banned from sale for twenty months during 1920 and 1921—which had the contrary result of making this elitist work a popular bestseller. And the biggest joke, of course, was on all of those readers who bought this fantasy expecting to find it pornographic.

There were other aristocratic SF books during this postwar period that did not attempt to take flight from the foul and unjust Twentieth Century scientific universe, that unavoidable fact, but instead—queasily, unhappily, even masochistically—submitted to its power. Two books by British writers may serve as examples of this disgusted acknowledgment of gross matter.

David Lindsay's *A Voyage to Arcturus* (1920) was a simultaneously brilliant and murky occult SF novel. It told the tale of a trip to the planet Tormance, a place where fears and desires are given form and body. The gnostic conclusion of this story was that all material existence is the creation of a demonic demiurge whose snares of pleasure entice Spirit and then entrap it into shameful, unbearable degradation by Matter.

The Amphibians (1924), by S. Fowler Wright, was a time travel story that made reference to H.G. Wells. In this novel, the superior beings of half-a-million years from now are a commentary on the limitations of our physical nature. They are asexual creatures, and are also exempt from our need for food and sleep. They are even able to shed their vestigial bodies and then reincarnate at will. These mental beings view their human visitor from our imperfect era with a horror that he compares to that aroused in him by the sight of a maggot-ridden sheep.

H.G. Wells himself was one of the very few writers of standing who were able to look upon science and its works without despair. For more than twenty years, Wells had been the Western world's primary advocate of scientific progress. Even in the aftermath of World War I, science still seemed to him to offer men their only hope of survival. Wells blamed human selfishness and limitation for the great disaster, not monster science.

In *Men Like Gods* (1923), his last radically innovative SF story, Wells presented one more version of scientific utopia, this time set on another Earth in a parallel universe. This other Earth is both a near analog of the contemporary early Twentieth Century world and also radically advanced beyond it. Wells's party of characters does not arrive in this place through its own choice. Instead, it is swept up in the net of a dimensional experiment conducted by two Utopians.

This has its own special importance. It is the first suggestion that our own little Village world might not be of primary importance, but might be subject to higher science being operated from the World Beyond the Hill.

Indeed, what was most original about this book—as well as most mysterious—was not its utopian proposals, largely familiar by now, but rather its radical new argument for the existence of a multiplicity of worlds. In the course of justifying his alternate world, his improved near-variant of our own Earth, Wells, with his immense gift for effective analogy, presented an imaginational theory that not only accounted for the existence of this one random world, but embraced all of the various alternative worlds and alien realms that fantasy stories and scientific fiction had of late been investigating:

> Serpentine proceeded to explain that just as it would be possible for any number of practically two-dimensional universes to lie side by side, like sheets of paper, in a three dimensional space, so in the many dimensional space about which the ill-equipped human mind is still slowly and painfully acquiring knowledge, it is possible for an innumerable quantity of practically three-dimensional universes to lie, as it were, side by side and to undergo a roughly parallel movement through time. The speculative work of Lonestone and Cephalus had long since given the soundest basis for the belief that there actually were a very great number of such space-and-time universes, parallel to one another and resembling each other, nearly but not actually, much as the leaves of a book might resemble one another. ...And those lying closest together would most nearly resemble each other.

Later SF writers would come to find this general theory of parallel universes of immense usefulness, particularly in the broader form in which it was restated by Wells near the end of *Men Like Gods*:

> And yet, as he had been told, it was but one of countless universes that move together in time, that lie against one another, endlessly like the leaves of a book. And all of them are as nothing in the endless multitudes of systems and dimensions that surround them. "Could I but rotate my arm out of the limits set to it," one of the Utopians had said to him; "I could thrust it into a thousand universes."

This version of the argument accommodates not only worlds that closely resemble our own, but places utterly fantastic and different as well. This was, in fact, no less than the first attempt by any writer of SF to encompass the true size, scope and multiform nature of the World Beyond the Hill.

What a truly strange moment this was!

In this hour, stories of magical fantasy no longer had the courage of their convictions. They had lost their faith in spiritual transcendence, which was now reduced to little more than a leftover literary convention. Almost inevitably, then, these stories fell into endorsement of all the most parochial and limiting beliefs current in the Twentieth Century Village—beliefs such as the universe being nothing but an inexorable machine and human existence being no more than a meaningless and circular futility.

But at exactly this same moment that spirit was finally dying, a story of soulless science was able to intimate the existence of an uncountable number of higher states, and to suggest that those who could enter into them and master them would be men like gods. And that is the sort of message that is traditionally delivered by living myth.

What we have here is a monumental shift in value caught in its very moment of occurrence. After the year 1920, the soul was no longer an effective metaphor of transcendence. The last of the true magic in *spirit* had flown. More and more it would come to seem that if there was anything at all to what had formerly passed under the name of spirit that was not to be dismissed as superstition, humbug, lunacy or poetic piffle, then that real *something* had to be some sort of science.

From this moment on, it would be science alone that could be taken as touched by the inner fire of transcendence—as being magical. Science offered the only viable route to higher realities. If mystery was to be found, it could only be found through science.

After the year 1920, there would no longer be any real question of reconciling spirit and science on even terms, as in Merritt's *The Moon Pool.* At best, there was only the possibility of salvaging some portion of spirit by subordinating it to science or redefining it as science.

It would, for instance, be possible to preserve the existence of fantasy worlds like Cabell's Poictesme and Eddison's Mercury—but only if they frankly admitted themselves to be ultimately scientific rather than spiritual in nature. In the new Wellsian World Beyond the Hill—that multiplex place comprised of endless systems and dimensions—it should be possible to locate any number of plausible venues for fantastic realms of all sorts without any need for reference to unlikely locations like the continent of Europe or the planet Mercury. And eventually, to save their worlds, both Cabell and Eddison would make the necessary capitulation to science and redefine their later fantasies as alternate history or parallel dimensions.

Science in its broadest interpretation was now the basis of a new Twentieth Century occultism that was generally unrecognized as being occultism, most particularly by the very persons who subscribed to it. Nonetheless, theirs was an occult creed. Just like all previous occultists, they were convinced that hidden in the ruins of former human belief was a secret kernel of Higher Truth. The only mark of difference about these latter-day unconscious mystics was that they believed that the one true name of the hidden treasure was *science.* And thought of themselves as rational and logical beings, as materialists and practical men.

It was, of course, only a select minority who were able to perceive all human meaning as encapsulated in science, and accept science as the one path to Truth. Far from recognizing science as the road to godhood, most people after World War I were only able to perceive science in its crudest and most obvious aspect.

Science was barbed wire, machine guns and poison gas. Science was the destroyer of the old order. Science was the knife that had severed the human connection to God. Soul-killer science.

Only the special minority who identified completely with science were prepared to recognize the beauty, mystery, and range of possibility inherent in H. G. Wells's argument for the existence of parallel worlds when *Men Like Gods* was published in 1923. Most readers perceived far less. What was apparent to them was only one more dubious iteration of the benefits of the scientifically perfected society.

Wells, the Twentieth Century's chief advocate of scientific progress, was a natural target for aristocrats, nostalgists and all the others who doubted the benefits of science. And *Men Like Gods* would be taken as a particular object of dissent and rebuttal. Often the alienated folk who replied to the utopian Wells, advocate of Demon Science, did so in terms that were derived from the younger H. G. Wells, the sometime dystopian writer of the Nineties. So great was Wells's breadth and so central was his position that even his opponents were Wellsians.

One such rebel child was the Russian engineer, writer and revolutionary, Yevgeny Zamiatin, who had lived in England during World War I and was the author of a book on the works of Wells. Zamiatin reacted both to Wells and to the betrayal of the promise of the Russian Revolution, which occurred in 1917, just in time to turn Russia into the first of the Twentieth Century machine dictatorships. In his dystopian novel *We*, written in Russia in 1920 but first published in New York in English translation in 1924, Zamiatin presented a portrait of the United State, a scientifically perfected society of metal and glass—like the Crystal Palace Exhibition extended a thousand years into the future and made into the entirety of society.

But no, not quite the entirety. The United State is surrounded by a great Green Wall, and outside the boundaries wild hairy people roam.

D-503, the narrator of *We*, is an elite mathematician, the builder of a spaceship for the state. But he gets into trouble when he falls under the influence of a strange woman with contacts outside the Green Wall, and atavistically develops a soul. That is only the beginning of an epidemic of soul development.

There is no help for this condition but surgery, and at the end of the novel a soul-ectomy is performed upon him. The "center for fancy" is removed, and D-503 is restored to a proper condition of reason and obedience in which the torture of his lover means nothing to him:

> I am smiling; I cannot help smiling; a splinter has been taken out of my head, and I feel so light, so empty! To be more exact, not empty, but there is nothing foreign, nothing that prevents me from smiling. (Smiling is the normal state for a normal human being.)

Another Eastern European writer who juxtaposed advanced science and the death of the soul was the Czech playwright and satirist Karel Capek. In the play *R. U. R.* (1921), a physiologist named Rossum, whose "'sole purpose was nothing more or less than to prove that God was no longer necessary,'" and his son, an engineer, have produced organic beings, artificial humanlike creatures called "Robots," to perform industrial tasks—like so many Frankenstein monsters harnessed to useful purpose.

Later SF would adopt Capek's word *robot*, but apply it only to mechanical devices in quasi-human form. Living creatures like Rossum's Robots would more commonly be known as *androids*.

The current General Manager of the Rossum Universal Robot factory offers an account of their design and nature to Helena Glory, daughter of the country's president:

> "A gasoline motor must not have tassels or ornaments, Miss Glory. And to manufacture artificial workers is the same thing as the manufacture of a gasoline motor. The process must be the simplest, and the product the best from a practical point of view. What sort of worker do you think is the *best* from a practical point of view?"

Miss Glory answers him in old-fashioned terms: "'Oh! Perhaps the one who is most honest and hard-working.'"
But the manager says:

> "No. The one that is the *cheapest*. The one whose requirements are the *smallest*. Young Rossum invented a worker with the minimum amount of requirements. He had to simplify him. He rejected everything that did not contribute directly to the progress of work. Everything that makes man more expensive. In fact he *rejected man* and made the *Robot*. My dear Miss Glory, the Robots are not people. Mechanically they are more *perfect* than we are; they have an enormously developed intelligence, but they have no soul."

It is a major fear of the period that is represented in both *We* and *R. U. R.*—that rather than increasing the capacity of man and making men like gods, the effect of science might instead be to simplify and reduce mankind's humanity. It seemed that scientific civilization could produce beings of highly developed intelligence, but without any souls—creatures in human form who were no longer *people*.

In *R. U. R.*, just as in *We*, those who lack souls overwhelm those who have them. The Robots rise in revolt and exterminate their makers. All humanity is destroyed. The one hope that is offered by the conclusion of the play is that the Robots may now be in the process of developing souls of their own.

It was not only British and European elitist SF that was touched by negativity and confusion. American SF, too, felt the loss of the soul and the crushing weight of the material universe. During the great emotional crashout of the early Twenties, even American pulp SF, so expansive during the Teens, suffered from existential nausea.

There was a psychic retrenchment. Instead of exploring lost cities in pursuit of ancient knowledge or probing into alien realms in search of love and adventure, American SF stories of the early Twenties were much more likely to concern themselves with the horrors of the machine universe, competition from insect societies, and the threat of cosmic hostility. They were defensive rather than exploratory.

One writer particularly affected was A. Merritt. As we have already seen, the failure of spirit and the retreat from transcendence twisted and deformed the ending of *The Metal Monster*, his most imaginative work. During the Twenties, Merritt was no longer able to maintain his former unified vision of mystery. He fell into fragments. Sometimes, as in "The Face in the Abyss" (1923), Merritt was science-minded but cynical. Sometimes, as in *The Ship of Ishtar* (1924), he was vague and otherworldly. And at still other times, as in *Seven Footprints to Satan* (1927), he might write of phenomena that at first appearance seemed to be mysterious, but ultimately proved to be non-transcendent.

In the Twenties, even Edgar Rice Burroughs retreated. His best imaginative stories of the period—*Tarzan and the Ant Men* (1924) and *The Moon Maid*, a book composed of three novelets published between 1923 and 1925—were more society-minded and satirical than inventive and exploratory. After 1925, Burroughs would fall into copying and repeating himself and cease to be an innovative force in SF.

One important factor in the retreat of American pulp SF was the failure of *All-Story*, the home base of Burroughs and Merritt, and the chief center of imaginative exploration throughout the Teens.

After World War I, the newsstands began to be flooded with a new style of pulp magazine. The original prewar pulps—modeling themselves on the first pulp, *Argosy*—had published a wide variety of fiction. They had aimed to have stories to appeal to every member of the family in each issue.

But the new pulp magazines were specialized. Each concentrated on printing one and only one kind of fiction. There were detective magazines, love magazines, sports story magazines, Western magazines, air adventure magazines. A separate magazine for every taste.

In the competition for readership, the old general fiction pulp magazines were the losers. The new specialized magazines could survive with small but relatively secure audiences. And meanwhile, the once-large general audience for magazines like *Argosy* was being lured away, broken up, picked to pieces.

Suddenly, the position of *All-Story* was changed. Instead of being a lively companion to *Argosy*, a reinforcement of its promise of fiction that would please the whole family, *All-Story* was a competitor with *Argosy* for a declining share of the reading public. To ensure the continuation of *Argosy*, his oldest and most prestigious pulp magazine, publisher Munsey sacrificed his second-line general fiction title, *All-Story*.

In July 1920, the two magazines were merged together as *Argosy All-Story Weekly*. But it was essentially *Argosy* that continued, with the addition of a few star writers picked up from *All-Story*. Burroughs and Merritt would still be accepted—most of the time—but the new *Argosy All-Story* would not be nearly as receptive to imaginative fiction as the old *All-Story* had been.

What hurt was not merely that the market for SF stories was suddenly smaller. Or that the new *Argosy All-Story* might not quite dare to take a really far-out yarn that the old *All-Story* would have snatched right up. What was truly painful was that the imaginative center of things was gone, and no other pulp magazine was prepared to take up the role that *All-Story* had performed in the Teens.

SF was sufficiently peripheral, sufficiently unpopular, sufficiently frightening—and yes, still sufficiently unconceived as a unified category of fiction—that it would be almost ten full years after the merger of *Argosy* and *All-Story* before the first specialized pulp SF magazine would see publication. That magazine would be *Astounding Stories of Super-Science*, first published in December 1929.

The first new specialized pulp magazine that would regularly include SF stories among its contents was *Weird Tales*, founded in 1923. In addition to scientific fiction—never its chief stock in trade—*Weird Tales* published non-transcendent stories of the strange, bizarre and gruesome, Gothic fantasies of ghosts, vampires and werewolves, and tales of black magic and occult horror. The unifying element that held all this variety together was fear of the unknown.

The inspiration for *Weird Tales* came to its publisher, J.C. Henneberger, from a poem by Edgar Allan Poe entitled "Dreamland"—a Poeian invocation of the World Beyond the Hill typically filled with images of dread and death. These lines triggered Henneberger's imagination:

> From a wild weird clime that lieth, sublime
> Out of Space—out of Time.

It may be a sufficient indication of the nature of this moment to take note that the word that Henneberger chose to pluck from these lines to serve as the title of his magazine was *weird*. It was a sense of weirdness, a conviction of the fundamental fearsome black queerness of things, that was held in common by Poe the Romantic and the disoriented young materialists of the Lost Generation.

Weird Tales may be perceived as a kind of last after-shudder, the final dying tremor of the Romantic Movement. In its pages were to be found the last degenerate versions of all those Gothic stories of the past century and a half that had aimed to speak to the mysterious fears of our nature, awaken thrilling horror, and make the reader dread to look around.

At the same time, however, *Weird Tales* can be seen as a vehicle of transformation, a means for easing the cruel transition from the universe of God and the soul to the new universe of scientific materialism. In *Weird Tales*, spooks and spirits were tamed by the rule of law—scientized, regularized and dehorrified. The most prolific and popular author in *Weird Tales* was Seabury Quinn, at one time an editor of a trade journal for undertakers, who contributed more than ninety stories of the exploits of Jules de Grandin, an occult detective.

But by far the most significant writer for *Weird Tales* was H.P. Lovecraft, who himself was the living embodiment of the same contradictions of mind embraced by the magazine. Lovecraft was a reclusive nocturnal gentleman from Providence, Rhode Island, who combined old-fashioned aristocratic sentiments with a philosophy of complete scientific materialism.

More than any other writer, Lovecraft in his stories expressed the essence of the lines from Poe that first inspired *Weird Tales*. Fear and loathing in his fiction were attached not to the supernatural, in which

Lovecraft did not believe, but to the new unknown scientific universe, so vastly beyond man's powers of comprehension. Lovecraft's stories are an ultimate expression of horror at that greater darkness that surrounds the flare of man's little match flame in every direction.

Howard Phillips Lovecraft was born in 1890 to a family of privilege that was in the process of losing its money and position. When Lovecraft was a small boy, his father went violently insane and then died in a mental institution. Howard was a mama's boy, dressed like a girl by his mother. At the same time, she constantly told him that he was hideously ugly and refused to touch him. She would eventually die in the same mental institution as his father.

Lovecraft grew up with a highly developed sense of the weirdness of things. His lifelong favorite author, whom he discovered at the age of eight, was Edgar Allan Poe.

Lovecraft was essentially self-educated. His schooling was erratic and he never finished high school. For ten years after he dropped out, Lovecraft lounged around the house, lost in a state of complete lethargy. He and the two aunts he lived with scraped by on a small inheritance.

Even though he was penniless, Lovecraft was constitutionally incapable of even considering the possibility of holding a job. It was his conviction that a gentleman did not work for a living.

It was during this period that Lovecraft began to produce articles and then stories for his own amateur journal and the magazines of a few like-minded friends of superior taste. The chief influence on these early attempts was Poe.

Lovecraft was relatively late in finding his second great passion, Lord Dunsany, coming upon his work in 1919. But in November of that year—a mere two months after he first read *Time and the Gods*—Lovecraft learned that Dunsany was to deliver a lecture in Boston. The news was enough to cause Lovecraft to venture forth from Providence for the first time in three years.

The experience of seeing and hearing Dunsany had a vitalizing effect on Lovecraft, and he was inspired to dash off one story after another. During the next few years, he wrote his first effective fiction, his first stories that were not merely static black fragments. Many of these Dunsany-influenced visions of strange twilight landscapes, first published in the amateur journals, would be reprinted in early issues of *Weird Tales*.

In these stories of his late apprenticeship, Lovecraft evolved an appreciation of total mystery comparable to that expressed by Dr. Walter Goodwin at the outset of Merritt's *The Metal Monster*, together with a theory of accessible multiple worlds not unlike the one held by Wells's experiment-minded Utopians in *Men Like Gods*.

Here is how it is expressed by one character in Lovecraft's otherwise minor 1920 story, "From Beyond":

> "What do we know," he had said, "of the world and the universe about us? Our means of receiving impressions are absurdly few, and our notions of surrounding objects infinitely narrow. We see things only as we are constructed to see them, and can gain no idea of their absolute nature. With five feeble senses we pretend to comprehend the boundlessly complex cosmos, yet other beings with a wider, stronger, or different range of senses might not only see very differently the things we see, but might see and study whole worlds of matter, energy, and life which lie close at hand yet can never be detected with the senses we have. I have always believed that such strange, inaccessible worlds exist at our very elbows, *and now I believe I have found a way to break down the barriers.*"

After Lovecraft had finally found a professional place of publication for his work in the pages of *Weird Tales*, he began to move beyond the Dunsanian influence into new territory that was all his own. Increasingly, in his stories of the Cthulhu Mythos—his own special brand of horrified science fiction—Lovecraft speculated about the intolerable knowledge and insupportable alienness that might flood in upon the psychic venturer when the barriers between worlds were finally breached.

Here is the opening paragraph of the pivotal story, "The Call of Cthulhu," conceived in 1925, written in 1926, and finally published in *Weird Tales* in 1928:

> The most merciful thing in the world, I think, is the inability of the human mind to correlate all its contents. We live on a placid island of ignorance in the midst of black seas of infinity, and it was not meant that we should voyage far. The sciences, each straining in its own direction, have hitherto harmed us little; but some day the piecing together of dissociated knowledge will open up such terrifying vistas of reality, and of our frightful position therein, that we shall either go mad from the revelation or flee from the deadly light into the peace and safety of a new dark age.

Perhaps more than any other author, the obscure H.P. Lovecraft, writing in the marginal pulp magazine *Weird Tales*, most nearly caught the essence of the post-World War I moment of transition. The barriers of Western perception had broken down, and now one intolerable realization after another was flooding in:

No longer would one enlightened and superior class set an example for the rest of laggard mankind to measure up to. The gradual rational perfection of society that had brought Western civilization into being was now at an end. Catastrophe had occurred. Civilization was fallen, and the soul was dead.

In the new fragmented reality of the machine barbarians, anything at all was possible. All that was required was the scientific know-how and the will.

How exhilarating! And how horrifying!

If all the old rules were off, what would become of humanity? Would mankind degenerate, or would it transcend? Would we become robots without souls, or men like gods? Or would scientific revelation of the true terrifying vistas of reality and our frightful position therein overwhelm us and drive us mad?

Other writers might express one aspect or another of this state of postwar apprehension. But H.P. Lovecraft alone was able to encompass both the promise and the terror of this special moment of the triumph of science.

It was in 1926, in the midst of this postwar period of breakdown and reorientation, that the first magazine specifically devoted to SF was born. It was neither a general fiction pulp magazine like *Argosy*, nor one of the new specialized pulps like *Weird Tales*. *Amazing Stories*—"The Magazine of Scientifiction"—was not a pulp at all. It was something completely new, different in appearance, format and subject from every other magazine on the newsstand.

Evolution or Extinction

Just like so many of the other significant occurrences in the story of science fiction, the publication of the first issue of *Amazing Stories* in March 1926 was a Janus-faced event, looking simultaneously back into the past and forward into the future. The advent of this self-described "new sort of magazine" was an indication that one major phase in the development of SF was drawing to a close and another stage about to begin.

In the Age of Technology which started around 1870, as we've been able to see, it became possible for the first time to frankly assert that science was transcendence in new guise. In pursuit of scientific mystery, SF in its various forms laid claim to the future and to the past, traveled to the farthest reaches of time-to-come, journeyed to other planets, ventured into the microcosm, discovered alternate worlds, and postulated a further endless multitude of systems and dimensions.

This extravagant and dubious literature-in-becoming even had the nerve to tackle the most basic questions facing contemporary Western civilization—the true nature of the relationships between man and society and between man and the universe—and to offer wholly new answers to them. But there weren't a whole lot of people who were prepared to admire SF for this. The answers that it proposed were altogether too cold, too distant, and too disquieting.

The great disaster which was World War I made SF even less appealing to the general reading public. The Great War demonstrated that technology was now the dominant fact of Western society. But the brutality and excesses of the war were enough to scare and sicken anyone who held doubts about the value, truth and practical consequences of modern science.

Adding to the general revulsion against SF after the war was a shift that took place in the literature itself. Prior to this moment (with the stories of H.G. Wells as one notable exception), SF had always had a lingering quasi-spiritual aspect. But during the Twenties, as the representatives of spirit finally lost the power they had held over society and science stepped forward to assume control of all aspects of Western life, scientific fiction felt it only appropriate to cast off its cloak of spirit and stand revealed for what it really was— a Godless, soulless literature of complete materialism.

For those few who cherished SF, that might even be a cause for pride. But for those who didn't it was this uncompromising unbelief which made science fiction seem truly abhorrent.

By the early Twenties, SF had become so frightening and unpopular that when a new author, a food chemist named E.E. Smith, submitted a unique novel of interstellar exploration entitled *The Skylark of Space* to *Argosy*—*All-Story* no longer being available as a separate place of publication—the great former editor of *All-Story*, Bob Davis, didn't hesitate to reject it as too far-out for his readers, even though he personally found the story enjoyable and wrote Smith a three-page letter to say so. There was no book publisher who would touch *The Skylark of Space*, either. All told, Smith's story would be rejected more than fifty times by markets high and low.

Nor was it only newcomers who were having trouble selling SF. *Argosy* was Edgar Rice Burroughs' accustomed magazine market, and he ranked among its top authors. Yet in 1925, an assistant editor saw fit to reject his sixth Martian story, *A Weird Adventure on Mars*—a tale featuring brain transplants and jeers at organized religion. At this very moment, the editors of another pulp magazine were doing their best to persuade Burroughs to write stories for them so he sent the novel on to them. However, they hastily rejected it, too, saying that it was "extremely easy to read" but declaring it "too bizarre and shocking" to be acceptable.

So it was that as late as the end of the first quarter of the Twentieth Century, with the Age of Technology headed toward a climax, SF literature was neither respectable nor popular. Science might well be in the driver's seat of Western civilization now, but science fiction was generally disliked and unwelcome.

Even at this late date, SF was still more of a collection of loosely associated story types which shared a common regard for the higher powers of science than it was a unified, self-aware literature. It still had no generally recognized name or identity. It had no reliable audience. It could hardly get itself published at all.

And no wonder. All its other dubious qualities aside, it seemed that the SF stories which were being written and published at this time were lost in visions of human insignificance before the awesome uncaring power of the great cosmic machine.

By the mid-Twenties, the scattershot SF of the Age of Technology was all but completely untenable. It had to change or it would surely disappear.

Evolution or extinction...that was the choice.

It was at this moment that Hugo Gernsback's *Amazing Stories* made its appearance. *Amazing Stories* was an odd, limited and marginal publication that offered very little in the way of fiction which was truly new or different. There can be no question, however, that *Amazing Stories* was a major turning point in the development of science fiction.

In the pages of *Amazing*, SF literature at last became identified by a single name—"scientifiction." It was provided with a history. It was defined and demonstrated. It was consolidated and unified. In *Amazing*, SF became conscious of itself.

The imaginative formula "scientifiction" which produced *Amazing Stories* was narrowly conceived and highly personal. We might even say that in a real sense it was the private dream of *Amazing*'s editor and publisher, Hugo Gernsback.

We may recall that in the first issue of *Amazing*, Gernsback defined "scientifiction" as "the Jules Verne, H.G. Wells, and Edgar Allan Poe type of story—a charming romance intermingled with scientific fact and prophetic vision." And, in another early editorial, he would add: "If we may voice our own opinion we should say that the ideal proportion of a scientifiction story should be seventy-five per cent literature interwoven with twenty-five per cent science."

Strange and wonderful indeed that an explicit formulation of SF as limited and externalistic as this one by Gernsback could manage to serve as an effective summarizing principle for all the different kinds of Technological Age SF story. Yet it did.

By being concentrated in a single center like *Amazing Stories*, stories of scientific transcendence could at last be addressed to a restricted but enthusiastic group of readers rather than being thrown away upon a general reading audience indifferent to SF or even actively put off by it. The advent of *Amazing Stories*—the self-aware magazine of scientifiction—was the beginning of the segregation of SF from other kinds of story.

From this moment on—and for at least the next quarter of a century—science fiction would be published separately, written separately, and read separately from all other kinds of fiction. It would exist in a world all its own, insignificant to the outside eye, but to itself an immense self-sufficient universe.

It was as though in 1926, all of the variously limited story types that were the SF literature of the Age of Technology had gathered together, joined their individual strengths, and then out of the most unlikely materials—the man Hugo Gernsback, the name "scienti-fiction," and the vehicle of *Amazing Stories*—made a new home for themselves, a universe that stretched to the last moment of time and to the farthest star, but was contained in a tiny dust mote.

Anyone could find SF now, in its state of special apartness. As a specialized magazine literature, it would be easier to locate and more identifiable than it had ever been before.

At the same time, magazine SF would be difficult to penetrate. The face that it showed the world would be simultaneously pretentious and childish. The great boast of science fiction was that it was concerned with serious matters of science. Yet what it chose to display on its covers was adolescent fantasy—alien monsters, women in metal breastplates, robots, rayguns and rocket ships.

To any observer who lacked the necessary empathy to get past these barriers, the science fiction magazines could only appear unrevealing or actively off-putting. If you weren't either a devotee of science or an eager kid—a big-dome or a fruitcake—then science fiction would shut its door and warn you away.

The chosen audience of science fiction was bright teenagers, engineers and scientists, and no one else. Only these few would be invited inside to partake of its marvels. All others were barred.

American magazine science fiction would be a world entirely apart, with its own history, politics, language, ideals and standards. And the ur-event of this special world was the coming of the Gernsback *Amazing.*

So central and crucial a happening was the founding of *Amazing* presumed to be that future generations of SF readers would come to reckon the very creation of science fiction from April 1926, the cover date of the first issue. They would either forget or never even know that *Amazing Stories* itself was a summation—the completion and integration of a long slow gradual course of development—and take it for the absolute beginning of all things.

Amazing, of course, was nothing like the absolute beginning of all things science-fictional, but it would be easy for that mistake to be made. Generally speaking, the science fiction that was able to join in the course of special development initiated by *Amazing Stories*—pretentious, childish American magazine science fiction—was the SF that would survive. In its state of privacy and isolation, it would grow, alter and evolve. Just as generally speaking, the SF that did not follow this path would die.

The special appeals of ghetto science fiction to brains and to immaturity were present from the first issue of *Amazing.* They were expressed by the very size, shape and appearance of the magazine.

All of the many ordinary pulp story magazines on the newsstand were cut to standard dimensions—7 by 10 inches, or "pulp size." Though *Amazing*, too, was printed most of the time on pulp paper, it was fully one-third larger than other story magazines—8½ by 11 inches, or "bedsheet size."

This significant difference in dimension was intended to set *Amazing Stories* apart. It emphasized that even though *Amazing* might have to resort to the expedient of cheap paper, it was no mere ordinary pulp magazine peddling common stories of love and adventure. Rather, *Amazing Stories* was sister publication to the serious popular science magazines *Science and Invention* and *Radio News.*

The aim of *Amazing* was always to be scientific, educational and prophetic. Hugo Gernsback put it like this in his first editorial:

> Not only do these amazing tales make tremendously interesting reading—they are also always instructive. They supply knowledge that we might not otherwise obtain—and they supply it in a very palatable form. For the best of these modern writers of scientifiction have the knack of imparting knowledge, and even inspiration, without once making us aware that we are being taught.
>
> And not only that! Poe, Verne, Wells, Bellamy, and many others have proved themselves real prophets. Prophesies made in many of their most amazing stories are being realized—and have been realized. Take the fantastic submarine of Jules Verne's most famous story, "Twenty Thousand Leagues Under the Sea" for instance. He predicted the present day submarine almost down to the last bolt! New inventions pictured for us in the scientifiction of today are not at all impossible of realization tomorrow. Many great science stories destined to be of an historical interest are still to be written, and *Amazing Stories* magazine will be the medium through which such stories will come to you. Posterity will point to them as having blazed a new trail, not only in literature and fiction, but in progress as well.

With these claims to scientific seriousness and importance established, however, there was almost no compromise that Hugo Gernsback would not make nor tactic that he would not try, to hook a susceptible audience and sell them scientifiction.

The first such adjustment that he made was in the name of his magazine—not *Scientifiction*, but *Amazing Stories.* In an early issue of *Amazing*, Gernsback wrote quite frankly:

> The plain truth is that the word "Scientifiction" while admittedly a good one, scares off many people who would otherwise read the magazine. ...After mature thought, the publishers decided that the

name which is now used was after all the best one to influence the masses, because anything that smacks of science seems to be too "deep" for the average type of reader.

In a time when science seemed both deep and scary to the average type of reader, Gernsback had to convince fifty thousand or a hundred thousand readers to buy his magazine of scientific fiction from the newsstands each month. So he groped for a title that would not frighten simple folk away, but might lure them closer.

Gernsback identified the aspect of science fiction that most thrilled and delighted him—"the amazing quality"—and splashed it across the oversized cover of his magazine in two bright colors: AMAZING STORIES. The initial "A" loomed fully 4½ inches high. The rest of the title, in increasingly reduced capital letters, stretched off toward infinity.

The pictures on the covers of *Amazing* were also designed to grab attention. The cover paintings were all the work of Frank R. Paul, an Austrian immigrant with architectural training. Paul was more adept at rendering imaginary buildings or machines, or even alien beings, than at drawing people. But he was a brilliant colorist and his stiffly posed visions of cosmic menace were presented with a certain undeniable charm and power.

Paul's paintings might show humans reacting to giant flies or beetles, a submarine attacked by flying and swimming reptiles, a disembodied head speaking in a laboratory, Martian machines laying waste to the countryside, or New York City being swept aside by a glacier. These strange scenes would be set against backgrounds of a single intense color—deep blue, or pink, or orange, or violet, or some other unlikely but eye-catching hue.

The only appeal that Gernsback would not make on the often garish billboard-sized covers of *Amazing* was to sex. In the attempt to draw impressionable readers close and capture their attention, any other tactic was fair. As Gernsback wrote: "We knew that once we could make a new reader pick up *Amazing Stories* and read only one story, the cause was won with that reader...."

If Gernsback compromised just a little with the hard facts of commercial necessity in designing the exterior of *Amazing*, other kinds of compromise were at work within the covers of the magazine. Gernsback might talk as though his magazine had infinite resources, but in actuality *Amazing* was run on a shoestring. It paid very little for the fiction it printed, it paid very late, and then only with the greatest reluctance. Under these circumstances, it is understandable that the best work published in *Amazing* consisted of classic old stories that could be had for pennies or for nothing.

The spirit of the times—and Gernsback's tight purse—ensured that most of the original work printed in *Amazing* was nothing much to brag about. These new stories were mainly typical Twenties-style SF horror fiction—tales of hostile machines, threatening insect societies, emotionless Big Brains, and disintegrating technological futures.

This is not exactly the sort of material one would readily expect to captivate and inspire the new reader who might casually pick up a copy of *Amazing* and sample the pleasures of a single story. Yet Hugo Gernsback expected no less than that.

It was somehow as though Gernsback did not *notice* the deficiencies of his beloved magazine—that it was awkward, juvenile, overstated, pretentious and vulgar, filled with moldly old stories and grimly negative new ones. However anyone else might see it, Hugo Gernsback, at least, was positive that scientifiction was wonderful, inspiring, uplifting, educational, prophetic and clean. He said so over and over again, in editorials, in story blurbs, in letter columns, in quizzes and contests, and in countless schemes and promotional ploys.

The purity, strength and power of Gernsback's faith was so great that almost in spite of itself *Amazing Stories* became something of what he said it was. Hugo Gernsback's True Belief in science held *Amazing* together and welded it into a unity that no number of little compromises or deficiencies could alter.

Hugo Gernsback saw wonder in all science—even in hostile machines, threatening insects, or the prospects of human decline. And he expected others to see it, too, if only they would just once put aside their fears and limitations and *look* at the truth and beauty that was before them.

Hugo Gernsback, inventor and prophet of science, was the ultimate example of the all-unwitting Twentieth Century scientific occultist—possessed by the profoundly irrational conviction that there is no Truth other than scientific truth and that nothing lies beyond the reach of science. If only the magical word *science* was invoked, Gernsback could convince himself that anything at all was possible, or even any number of mutually incompatible things.

Here is one phrasing of Gernsback's hopes for science—as usual, presented as though it were not his own special viewpoint, but rather was the natural and inevitable opinion of every man:

> The man in the street no longer recognizes in science the word impossible; "What man wills, man can do," is his belief.
>
> Interplanetarian trips, space flyers, talking to Mars, transplanting heads of humans, death-rays, gravity-nullifiers, transmutation of elements— why not? If not to-day, well then, to-morrow. Are they surprises? Not to him; the modern man expects them.

Gernsback perceived SF in a highly special way. He saw scienti-fiction as a kind of invention, a machine of the imagination, a device for anticipating and stimulating scientific wonders-to-come. He felt that since even the most fantastic fiction at some time or other must inevitably come true, then the real role of SF writers was to be prophets—like him.

For Gernsback, aspects of SF like plot, character and emotion were purely secondary values, no more than so much sugar-coating for the essential scientific pill. It was not fictional values that Gerns-back expected to make an impact upon the reader, but prophetic vision. By presenting dramatized visions of the scientific wonders of tomorrow right now, he meant to educate and inspire the youngsters who would be tomorrow's scientists into bringing those wonders and others into being. He meant to generate both scientists and new science.

As the official slogan of *Amazing Stories* had it: "Extravagant Fiction Today—Cold Fact Tomorrow." That was Gernsback's dream of scientifiction.

It was not unnatural of Gernsback to perceive SF in this mechan-istic way. It was his habitual mode of thought. And it is quite possible that only such a narrow, intense, obsessive man as Hugo Gernsback could have conceived of scientifiction, determined to start a magazine like *Amazing Stories* in a moment like 1926, and brought the job off.

Hugo Gernsback was born in the Grand Duchy of Luxembourg in 1884. He grew up in the fevered heyday of the Age of Technology, when one marvelous invention after another was pouring forth from the laboratories and workshops of Europe and America.

Gernsback was inspired by science. His aim was to become an inventor, too, and help to create the new wonders of the Twentieth Century. In 1904, with an invention under his arm—a battery of his own design—he set off to seek his fortune in America, the native country of the world's greatest inventor, Thomas A. Edison.

The Edwardian decade, a moment of maximum scientific optimism, was the perfect hour for Gernsback to arrive in the United States. He was quick to make his mark in this land of golden opportunity.

Hugo Gernsback became a pioneer of radio—an inventor, a businessman, a broadcaster and a self-appointed educator. As early as 1906, he was marketing his own inexpensive home radio sets. In 1908, Gernsback's radio supply catalog metamorphosed into his first popular science magazine, *Modern Electrics*. In 1909, in a prophetic article, he coined the word *television*. And in the Twenties, Gernsback would become an actual early experimenter in television broadcast.

And yet, despite these accomplishments and his genuine contributions to scientific and technological progress—for which, in time, he would receive due recognition and honor—Gernsback wasn't above attempting to impress a naive young audience by laying claim to greater distinction as a scientist than he would ever actually enjoy. On the masthead of the first few issues of *Amazing Stories*, and in one early editorial, he would list himself as "F.R.S." The obvious implication was that Gernsback was a Fellow of the Royal Society, the most prestigious of Western scientific bodies—but at best this was wishful thinking.

From the very outset of his career as a publisher, Gernsback had the notion of using SF stories for purposes of education and prophecy. He included scientific fiction in the contents of each of his popular science magazines. *Modern Electrics* might be succeeded by *Electrical Experimenter* in 1913, and *Electrical Experimenter* might then be altered into *Science and Invention* in 1920, but this one continuing element in Gernsback's scientific publishing formula would remain the same.

Gernsback contributed SF stories of his own to his various magazines—like so many later editors, setting a personal example for others of the fiction he wanted to print. For *Modern Electrics*, he wrote *Ralph 124C 41+* (1911-12), a thoroughly clumsy story but a brilliant job of predicting science-to-come. Gernsback's second serial story, *Baron Munchausen's Scientific Adventures*, was first published in his *Electrical Experimenter* in 1915-16.

Just as he had coined the word *television*, so in 1915 did Gernsback, that born promoter, invent the word *scientifiction*. His private hope was that one day it might be included in standard dictionaries.

In 1923, Gernsback went so far as to devote the entire August issue of *Science and Invention* to scientific fiction. And the following year, he sent out his circular letter announcing the magazine *Scientifiction*, which would never be published due to the lack of favorable response.

In short, when *Amazing Stories* finally did appear in 1926, it was as the result of nearly twenty years of thought, preparation, experiment and rehearsal on Gernsback's part. It was not a fluke or aberration. Gernsback had been working up to this move for a long time.

The great strength of *Amazing Stories* was the flexibility and scope of Hugo Gernsback's conception of science. There was almost no story that he could not see fit to print, no matter how fantastic it was, if it but somewhere muttered its allegiance to science.

There were, however, certain aspects of SF as it had been that were excluded outright from *Amazing*. Gernsback believed in technological advancement, but he had no faith in human social perfection, so old-fashioned social utopianism had no place in his magazine. Gernsback did not believe in the supernatural, so stories of spiritualism, black magic and occult wisdom were also left out.

But still, what breadth of material Gernsback did manage to present!

For the first two years of its existence, *Amazing Stories* was dominated by a wide range of stories resurrected from the past, a recapitulation of the development of SF during the previous century. Gernsback reprinted Edgar Allan Poe's "A Balloon Hoax" and Fitz-James O'Brien's "The Diamond Lens." He unearthed Jules Verne's very first story, "A Balloon Journey," and reprinted it as "A Drama in the Air," and he serialized no less than five novels by Verne. He republished all of H. G. Wells's classic scientific romances from *The Time Machine* to *The First Men in the Moon,* as well as many of Wells's shorter stories.

Gernsback cast his net widely. He republished stories that had originally appeared in his own *Electrical Experimenter* and *Science and Invention.* He reprinted much fiction from the pulps, chiefly from *All-Story* and *Argosy.* He published *The Moon Pool* and several other stories by A. Merritt. From *Blue Book Magazine* he picked up Edgar Rice Burroughs' 1918 novel *The Land That Time Forgot.* He even published stories in translation from French and German.

Eventually, Gernsback found new writers with new stories. For the most part, these were eager, clumsy amateurs. Nonetheless, among the new work that he managed to arrange to publish were original stories by Ray Cummings and H.P. Lovecraft. He even solicited new fiction from Edgar Rice Burroughs, and was offered *A Weird Adventure on Mars.* Gernsback published it as *The Master Mind of Mars* in *Amazing Stories Annual* (1927), a one-shot magazine, and praised Burroughs' story for its "excellent science."

Within the context of the Age of Technology, Hugo Gernsback was a man of considerable vision, the one appropriate person able to serve as an instrument by which far-flung SF might be pulled together, given a single name, and made aware of itself. The pragmatism and elasticity of Gernsback's synthesis of science made possible the wide-reaching synthesis of SF that was presented in the pages of *Amazing Stories.* And it was this summarization of all that SF had previously been that was the true glory of the early *Amazing,* more than compensating for any little awkwardness or pretension that the magazine might chance to display.

But it should be remembered that the Age of Technology was drawing to a close, and when viewed from the perspective of the emerging era, Hugo Gernsback was not a man of vision and flexibility at all, but rather a highly limited individual with bad habits and firmly fixed ideas. And very shortly, Gernsback's flaws of character and vision would cause him to be left behind while the literature he believed he had invented continued to alter and evolve.

The first of Gernsback's great limitations was his fundamentally utilitarian attitude toward SF. He did not value it for itself, but only as one more tool of his own making that he was entitled to use in any way that seemed appropriate, whether it be to produce future science or to generate immediate cash.

Even in the boom times of the mid-Twenties, Gernsback had a great need for cash. He knew how to live well. He required money for his experiments. He had all sorts of ongoing businesses and projects, and by no means all of these were financially productive. His radio station and television broadcasts in particular were a heavy continuing financial drain.

Hugo Gernsback was an idealist—but he was always completely ready to be pragmatic. As much as he loved scientifiction and wished to promote it, he was prepared to squeeze *Amazing Stories* for every cent that it would produce. He saw it as a convenient personal pocket into which he could dip as he needed to.

It was authors who first suffered from Gernsback's pinchpenny tactics. At a time when a pulp magazine might pay as much as five cents a word for fiction, Gernsback was content to pay as little as one-fifth of a cent—if and when an author managed to catch up with him. On more than one occasion, Gernsback would have to be sued before he would pay up.

One experience with Gernsback's business methods proved to be more than enough for H.P. Lovecraft. He dubbed Gernsback "Hugo the rat" and retreated to the more honest environs of *Weird Tales*. But it wasn't only unknown authors who were abused by Gernsback. Edgar Rice Burroughs had such a time collecting payment for *The Master Mind of Mars* that thereafter he was careful to set his price, even for reprints, well beyond Gernsback's reach.

Gernsback's financial gamesmanship was not limited to his writers. As his radio station got into deeper and deeper trouble, he began to horse along all of his creditors as a matter of policy. It was a dangerous game that he was playing, and eventually Gernsback miscalculated. In February 1929, his printer and his paper supplier felt pushed too far, and sent Gernsback's publishing companies into bankruptcy.

Gernsback's scientifiction magazine, *Amazing Stories*, was considered a property valuable enough to keep alive. A new publishing company was organized by the receiver and creditors, and *Amazing Stories* continued regular publication without missing an issue. But Hugo Gernsback was out, severed from his invention.

Gernsback was nothing if not resilient. He was not ready to

abandon what he had come to consider his personal property. With an illicit copy of the *Amazing Stories* subscription list, unpublished manuscripts spirited away from the offices of *Amazing*, and financing from who-knows-where, Gernsback managed to have an entirely new SF magazine on the newsstands within two months of the time that he was thrown into bankruptcy.

His new magazine, *Science Wonder Stories*, was a close imitation of *Amazing*. It was of the same large bedsheet size. It had its cover by Frank R. Paul and its story by H. G. Wells. It had a quiz, a contest, and a standard Gernsback editorial. It offered a new brand name for SF—"science fiction"—a name that would soon be generally adopted and that eventually would appear in standard dictionaries while the original term "scientifiction" was all but forgotten.

Science Wonder Stories even sported its own special slogan that was almost identical in sense to the slogan of *Amazing*—"Prophetic Fiction is the Mother of Scientific Fact."

The following month, a second new Gernsback SF magazine appeared—*Air Wonder Stories*. Same size. Same Paul covers. Its slogan was "The Future of Aviation Springs from the Imagination."

A magazine devoted solely to flying stories of the future was a bit too specialized to be successful, even in this, the era of Charles Lindbergh. Within a year, *Air Wonder Stories* was merged into *Science Wonder Stories*. The result was a general SF magazine simply called *Wonder Stories*.

But *Wonder Stories* in any of its forms never really prospered. Even as it was born in 1929, the hard test of the Great Depression was just around the corner. And at this critical moment, Hugo Gernsback had not merely opened the door wide to competition. He had put himself in the peculiar position of attempting to imitate his own original creation, *Amazing Stories*.

Something priceless had been lightly thrown away and could not be recovered. Hugo Gernsback no longer had a monopoly of magazine science fiction. He was no longer the one person in a position to say what SF was really like and enforce his opinions by what he chose to print. This was a time when science was changing, and with it science fiction. And at just this moment, SF began to escape the grasp of Hugo Gernsback.

Amazing Stories should have been no real competition. The new editor of *Amazing* was T. O'Conor Sloane, Ph.D., a white-bearded old man who had formerly been Gernsback's chief subeditor. Sloane was an inventor whose son had married a daughter of Thomas Edison. When he became editor of *Amazing* in 1929, he was nearly 78 years old.

Sloane completely lacked Gernsback's vision and ambition. His ideas were narrow and fossilized. He did not believe in the possibility of space travel, for instance, and often said as much to his readers.

Even so, Gernsback's *Wonder Stories* never managed to overtake the Sloane *Amazing*. Part of the reason may have been that Sloane was not deterred from printing space travel stories simply because he did not believe in space travel. He was old-fashioned, but he was not doctrinaire. Another part of the reason may have been that writers who had tasted of Gernsback's generosity welcomed the opportunity to submit their work to someone else, anyone else other than Hugo the rat.

And then, suddenly, another order of competition made its appearance, a new magazine with a cover date of January 1930. It was a pulp magazine—the very first science fiction pulp—*Astounding Stories of Super-Science*.

On the face of it, *Astounding* was not to be taken seriously. It was not even a sister publication to respectable magazines of science like *Amazing Stories* or *Science Wonder*. It was only a casual experiment, created primarily as a means of reducing overhead for the Clayton chain of pulp magazines. A new magazine of some kind was called for. Almost by accident, it turned out to be *Astounding Stories of Super-Science*.

But, as a pulp, *Astounding* offered a direct and fundamental challenge to Hugo Gernsback's proprietorial dictate that the proper purpose of SF should be the creation of future science. The editor of *Astounding*, Harry Bates, had studied *Amazing Stories* on the newsstand. He had gone so far as to copy *Amazing*'s title. He had found something impressive about its covers. But he had been appalled by the magazine's contents:

"*Amazing Stories*! Once I had bought a copy. What awful stuff, I'd found it! Cluttered with trivia! Packed with puerilities! Written by unimaginables!"

It was Bates's strategy to outflank Gernsback. His aim was to produce a magazine that was more amusing and entertaining than *Amazing*—not more instructional, educational, scientific or prophetic. Instead of relying on bright-eyed amateurs of science for his stories, as Gernsback did, Bates called upon the professional pulp writers he was used to dealing with to supply his copy.

These professional storytellers did not produce much SF that could be called innovative. Most typically, the Bates *Astounding* published conventional stories of action-adventure with only the thinnest veneer of fantastic science, often added by the editor. Even so, its livelier, more open-minded approach to science fiction—and its much higher rate of payment—made *Astounding* an immediately powerful competitor for the bedsheet SF magazines, placing great strain on their resolve to be serious and superior.

Then, early in 1933, the chain which published *Astounding* abruptly collapsed when the publisher, William Clayton, attempted to buy out his partner and financial backer and failed. *Astounding* was purchased by another pulp chain, the doughty old firm of Street & Smith. After a hiatus of six months, the magazine made a reappearance with its October 1933 issue.

At precisely this same moment, the two SF magazines that Hugo Gernsback had founded were forced by the difficult circumstances of the Depression to reduce themselves in size and alter their approach. The Sloane *Amazing Stories* became a pulp magazine with its own October 1933 issue. The following month, Gernsback's *Wonder Stories*, which had found it necessary to pass as a pulp for twelve issues in 1930-31 before re-establishing itself in bedsheet size, capitulated too, and firmly and finally became a pulp magazine.

The commercial point was made—science fiction could not succeed by pretending to be educational literature. If it was to survive, it had to lower itself and fight to live as common pulp trash.

From the end of 1933, if not before that, *Astounding* was dominant among the American science fiction magazines. In some measure, this was a matter of highly fortuitous outward circumstances. With Street & Smith, *Astounding* was the newest link in what was perhaps the most stable and powerful of all pulp chains, while *Amazing* and *Wonder Stories* were both highly marginal publications—lone pulp titles issued by companies with no background or experience in pulp publishing. Quite simply, *Astounding* was assured far better newsstand distribution than its rivals. It was able to pay better money to contributors, and it paid much more reliably.

But the Clayton *Astounding* had offered similar advantages— including an even higher rate of payment—and still had not established such clear superiority to the other magazines. Far more central to the new dominance of *Astounding* was the greater vision of the editor Street & Smith put in charge of the magazine. F. Orlin Tremaine saw something in SF that Hugo Gernsback, T. O'Conor Sloane and Harry Bates had not perceived.

For Tremaine, science fiction was not fiction about science. Neither was it mere action-adventure fiction not essentially different from other kinds of pulp storytelling. Tremaine conceived of SF as a literature of thought.

Beginning with the December 1933 issue of *Astounding*, he announced a new editorial policy. In each issue, he meant to include at least one story that was a "thought variant." These stories would either present some fresh new concept, or at the least stand some tired old idea on its head. It was this deliberate policy that made the Tremaine *Astounding* so much more exciting and innovative a science fiction magazine than its two rivals, a true precursor of the "modern science fiction" so soon to come.

Hugo Gernsback, with his stodgy old utilitarian notions about SF, could not compete with F. Orlin Tremaine's thought experiments. He and his magazine were left behind, floundering, falling more and more out of touch with the changes that were going on in science fiction.

After it became a pulp, the heart went out of *Wonder Stories*. Gernsback's dream had never been to publish a common pulp magazine. He appointed a high school boy, Charles Hornig, to be editor. To win new readers, he printed stories that he was ashamed of—and then he begged his old loyal readers' pardon for having done it.

Of the three SF magazines, *Wonder Stories* was dead last. The circulation continued to fall. Distribution became erratic, even in New York City where it was published. And authors found it harder than ever to collect payment.

Finally, early in 1936, Gernsback gave up. He sold his failing magazine to the Thrilling Group of pulps and dropped out of the science fiction publishing business. The new owners renamed the magazine *Thrilling Wonder Stories* and did very well with it.

In 1938, a similarly faltering *Amazing Stories*—still under the editorship of 86-year-old T. O'Conor Sloane—would be sold to Ziff-Davis, another pulp chain. And once more a magazine that couldn't make its way was altered into a highly successful publication.

Science fiction suddenly became a very hot item in pulp publishing. In early 1939, each of the three pulp chains involved in science fiction added a second SF magazine. In January, *Startling Stories* was created as a companion to *Thrilling Wonder*. In March, Street & Smith added *Unknown* to *Astounding*. And in May, Ziff-Davis backed *Amazing Stories* with *Fantastic Adventures*. Other pulp chains hurried to jump on the bandwagon with their own SF magazines.

The lesson was unmistakable. During the course of the Thirties, Hugo Gernsback's functionalist concept of SF had been thoroughly tested in the public marketplace and decisively rejected. Gernsback's educational and prophetic scientifiction could not draw and hold an elite audience. Neither could it command a popular pulp magazine audience, the one audience that was prepared to pay attention to SF. Only when Gernsback and all that he stood for were swept out of the way did science fiction flourish. Thank you very much, Hugo.

However, even with science fiction firmly settled into its new role as a late and minor category of pulp publishing—the last distinct story type to emerge and establish itself in specialized magazines—

some part of the original Gernsbackian ideal would manage to continue to be preserved. The pulp SF magazines would all identify themselves by the Gernsback-devised label "science fiction." These magazines would pay their ritual respects to science, printing scientific news of interest and even speculative articles on borderline scientific subjects.

But if the Gernsbackian ideal continued to some extent, it was only through being shorn of Gernsback's limitations.

The first of these—the proprietary, functionalist, utilitarian attitude he adopted toward science fiction—was what had turned authors against him and then cost him ownership of *Amazing Stories*. It might even be said that it was this fixed viewpoint that rendered Gernsback so incapable of effective response to the less restrained approaches to SF adopted by the pulp science fiction publishers.

Gernsback's second and more significant failure of vision, however, was less a matter of personal character. This was the failure that would leave *Wonder Stories* floundering in the wake of the Tremaine *Astounding* during the Thirties. And it was this same blindness that would ultimately alienate Gernsback to the point that he could refuse to recognize science fiction stories that had been specifically singled out to be honored with an award named for him. He would say, "Either you have science fiction, with the emphasis on *science*, or you have fantasy. You cannot have both—the two genres bear no relation to each other."

The crucial limitation was this:

As much as any man of the Age of Technology, Hugo Gernsback was a lover of science. He believed that he knew science thoroughly and intimately. Science was the entirety of his life. But then, while Gernsback was preoccupied with the serious business of proclaiming science and promoting science and creating the science of tomorrow— and without his ever quite taking in that it was happening—science itself altered radically.

Advanced Twentieth Century science became something altogether different from the science that Hugo Gernsback's generation had known and loved, and Gernsback—together with a good many others—got left behind. Gernsback never really caught on to the new thing. Even after the Atomic Age had arrived, he remained what he was, a mental citizen of the Age of Technology.

One centrally important change was in scale. Between 1895 and the 1920s, the conceptions of science were radically extended in every dimension, so that a universe that was already disconcertingly vast and alien suddenly became incomprehensibly larger and more complex, as well as far older, than had previously been supposed.

With the discovery of radioactivity and the subatomic realm, the small became much smaller. With identification of the existence of other galaxies lying far beyond the boundaries of our own—and the subsequent conclusion that all these great stellar aggregations were rapidly moving away from each other as the cosmos expanded—the large became immensely larger. Geological and astrophysical evidence both suggested that the scale of time past had to be altered from mere millions of years to billions of years.

But even more disconcerting was a series of announcements from those physicists who had begun to probe into the microcosm and the macrocosm in search of the basic foundations of matter and energy. It was certainty and stability that they were seeking—the ultimate constituents of things. But what they managed to find instead was instability, uncertainty, ambiguity and paradox.

These scientists reported that it now appeared to be the case that where very large, very small, very fast and very prolonged processes were concerned, common sense and the familiar rules of classical physics did not necessarily apply. Time might vary. Space might be twisted or altogether abolished. Matter could be energy in another guise. And light was somehow both a particle and a wave—simultaneously matter and energy.

Most provocative of all was the suggestion from the new science of quantum mechanics—which leaped into being at precisely the same time that Hugo Gernsback was establishing *Amazing Stories*—that on the subatomic level events did not happen by cause-and-effect, but by probabilities. All of a sudden, seemingly solid matter was replaced by pure chance.

In short, at the very moment when material science had become the acknowledged leading edge of Western civilization, and society at large had followed science into finally rejecting the last remnant of insubstantial spirit, the most fundamental concepts of Western belief—time, space, matter, causality, even objective knowledge itself—were all being called into question. And by whom? By the masters of material science.

How utterly strange! Western scientists—the most devotedly materialistic of men—had spent two full centuries and more examining their precious matter with an ever finer scrutiny. And now, suddenly, in the early Twentieth Century, matter itself had lost its solidity and become insubstantial in their hands. Like the spirit-seeking Romantics of the previous era, sober scientists had come around to the belief that the true reality of the world was nothing at all like its appearance.

And so it was that you might now find a distinguished scientist like the British astrophysicist Sir James Jeans stepping forward to declare in his 1930 book, *The Mysterious Universe*:

"To-day there is a wide measure of agreement, which on the physical side of science approaches almost to unanimity, that the stream of knowledge is heading toward a non-mechanical reality; the universe begins to look more like a great thought than a great machine."

To Bertrand Russell in his seminal essay "A Free Man's Worship," written at the turn of the century, matter had appeared to be blind, reckless, relentless, irresistible and omnipotent. Now, however, as the Age of Technology was nearing its end, matter had lost its ruling power. Just at the time when SF writers—including many of those writing for Hugo Gernsback—were quailing before the horrible power of the great machine universe, here was science to say, well, no, maybe the universe was not like a great machine after all. Perhaps it was more like a great thought.

Hugo Gernsback was by no means the only person who was incapable of accepting and assimilating this new point of view. In spite of Sir James Jeans's claim that the new conclusions were almost unanimously accepted among physicists, the great Albert Einstein himself, responsible for so many of the most fruitful paradoxes of Twentieth Century physics, shied away from the prospect of the abolition of cause-and-effect. In a letter to Max Born, another grandfather of quantum physics, written in December 1926, he stated his profound reservation:

"Quantum mechanics is certainly imposing. But an inner voice tells me that it is not yet the real thing. The theory says a lot, but does not really bring us any closer to the secret of the Old One. I, at any rate, am convinced that He does not throw dice."

But Einstein was to be left isolated by his inability to accept the radical new physics—in just the same manner that Hugo Gernsback was to become alienated from the further development of science fiction. From the time that Einstein asserted that his God would never play dice with the world, and refused to consider altering his thinking, he lost his hitherto astonishing creative power. He made no more of the brilliant contributions to physics that had caused him to be popularly regarded as the supreme genius of the modern world.

There was a younger generation of scientists, however, that was willing to adopt the most far-out conclusions of its predecessor as its own premises, and press on with the business of science. Speaking for those who were prepared to accept the unfolding picture of existence revealed by advanced science no matter how odd it might turn out to be, the British biologist J.B.S. Haldane wrote in his 1927 book, *Possible Worlds*: "Now my suspicion is that the universe is not only queerer than we suppose, but queerer than we *can* suppose."

In 1931, this intimation of fundamental strangeness was to be given a theoretical underpinning by a highly important paper entitled "On Formally Undecidable Propositions" by the German—later American—mathematician Kurt Gödel. Specifically writing in answer to the *Principia Mathematica* (1910-13), a three-volume work by Bertrand Russell and Alfred North Whitehead that had attempted to reduce all mathematics to one grand logical system, Gödel demonstrated that within any system there must be statements that the system itself cannot prove or disprove.

The implication of Gödel's paper was that the universe must always exceed our logical understanding. There must always be more than we can consciously know. Relative to any particular system or frame of thought, transcendence must always exist.

Within all this new Twentieth Century scientific thought lurked highly important consequences for Western man's image of himself and the universe. The proudly defiant Man of the Edwardians, so special and so innately superior, who had been cast into discredit by World War I, was now completely dethroned.

Man could no longer be conceived to be the center of all existence. He was only a denizen of an insignificant planet circling around an average star on the fringes of a great galaxy containing stars to the number of a hundred billion or more. And that galaxy was only an average galaxy, one among many. What then was Man?

Man was puny, less than a flyspeck compared to a hundred billion suns. Man was peripheral, a galactic and universal side issue. He was problematical, a mere creature of chance. He was a formally undecidable proposition.

And simultaneously, the universe itself was altered into a realm of wonder. Mystery no longer had to be sought out there in the most distant places and farthest removed times. Mystery was now an innate part of the fabric of the universe. Glitches in reality could now open at any place, at any moment.

One positive consequence might be found in this radical disestablishment of humanity. Mankind was no longer caught in the hot spotlight of the great cosmic drama. Now man was no longer central enough or important enough to merit round upon round of gleeful torture from a God bent upon playing cat-and-mouse. Nor was he condemned to be a weary unyielding Atlas defiantly bearing the weight of the entire universe upon his frail shoulders.

But there was a price—at least from the point of view of the Age of Technology. And the price was that man was made more insignificant and random a being than he had ever been before.

Throughout the Technological Age, the central problem of the era had been how mankind was to cope with the vast size and the indifferent hostility of the universe revealed by science. It seemed that human civilizations might rise and human civilizations might fall, but that all human effort was eventually doomed to come to nothing. The human race might evolve, but only to decay again and be supplanted by some stronger, smarter or more rapacious form of Earthly life. Alternatively, mankind might fall victim to some random cosmic catastrophe. Or it might be overwhelmed by a savage alien onslaught from out of the depths of space.

And now here was Twentieth Century science ready to make a dire situation worse with the news that man's true position in the universe was even more peripheral and precarious than it had previously been imagined to be.

SF literature, already in the gravest difficulty in the Twenties, was challenged to take account of the threatening new cosmic situation revealed by modern science. And most SF did not respond well.

It was European SF that did the worst. During the Twenties and Thirties, even as a demoralized Europe, never fully recovered from the horrors of World War I and its aftermath, was falling into the iron grip of fascism, so was European SF finding it increasingly difficult to muster belief in anything at all. Not man. Not science. Not the universe.

During the Thirties, European SF turned sour, cynical, pessimistic and misanthropic. Again and again in the scattered European SF stories of the period, civilization collapses, man degenerates, the world ends—and it is all just as well that way.

In the course of the decade, European SF dwindled and then disappeared. It was formally banned by the Nazis in Germany as dirt and trash. In France, it simply ceased to be written and published.

Despite the willingness of British scientists like Jeans and Haldane to proclaim the new scientific view, British SF writers, too, were largely unable to accept the new science. In the early Thirties, three classic examples of SF were published in Britain—Olaf Stapledon's *Last and First Men* (1930), Aldous Huxley's *Brave New World* (1932), and James Hilton's *Lost Horizon* (1933). But of these three books, one was a cry of nostalgia for the soul, one was a rejection of modern technology, and one showed man defeated by the challenge of the great cosmic void.

The Thirties were a period when any number of the most prominent British writers publicly renounced the modern universe and attempted to find salvation through a return to traditional religion. In keeping with this, as the Great Depression wore on and then flared up into World War II, more and more the most notable British SF stories tended to be expressed in terms of nostalgic fantasy. These stories longed for the simpler and more comprehensible circumstances that existed—in the words of one of them,

J. R. R. Tolkien's *The Hobbit* (1937)—"one morning, long ago in the quiet of the world, when there was less noise and more green."

It was only rude crude American magazine science fiction—and by no means all of it, but only a small portion—that had the courage and insight necessary to take the bad news that had been delivered by science, face it squarely, and transmute it into something positive.

In the late Twenties in the Gernsback *Amazing*, and then more frequently within the more congenial context of *Astounding Stories*, a new kind of SF story began to appear. This fiction was written by men—and one woman—who were able to accept the immensity and instability of the physical universe, the disestablishment of man, and the radical uncertainty of existence.

In the last years of the Age of Technology, these writers—led by E. E. Smith, Edmond Hamilton, Jack Williamson, Stanley Weinbaum and John W. Campbell, Jr.—laid the basis for the new SF literature of the Atomic Age. In a period when even most Americans were writing of decay, defeat and devolution, these few writers demonstrated a positive eagerness to take on the challenge of the immense and random scientific universe. Employing the dismaying new insights of science as their own chief weapon, they aimed to tame the universe and turn it into a viable place for mankind.

SF would be altered by their experiments and explorations. Indeed, at the end of the Thirties, a whole new form of SF would make its appearance, erected on the foundation of this work. And in time the new SF of the Atomic Age would seem so strange and so different from the scientifiction from which it sprang that Hugo Gernsback could mistake it for fantasy.

The new SF would be known as *modern science fiction* in order to distinguish it from the old-fashioned Gernsbackian variety.

PART 3

MODERN
SCIENCE FICTION

There is no such thing as a destiny of the human race. There is a choice of destinies.

—*J.B.S. HALDANE*

Mastery of
Time and Space

The first steps toward "modern science fiction"—the re-emphasized, reformulated SF of the Atomic Age—were taken in three boldly imaginative American magazine stories of the late Twenties. Two of these significant stories—*The Skylark of Space* by E. E. Smith, and "Armageddon—2419 A. D." by Philip Nowlan—appeared in Hugo Gernsback's *Amazing Stories*. The third, "Crashing Suns" by Edmond Hamilton, was published in *Weird Tales*.

In another of the felicitous coincidences that have marked our narrative, all three of these stories saw original publication in the very same month, August 1928. Just as though some crucial line of demarcation had been passed, suddenly it became possible for a number of different writers to think and say what no writer had found it possible to think and say before this moment.

In these central stories—and in the sequels that followed each of them—a fundamental reorientation of vision was given its first expression. A stultifying perspective based on Earth in the here-and-now was swapped for a new viewpoint based on the future and outer space. The result was an exuberant new sense of power and freedom, the overwhelming impact of which we can only dimly appreciate today, so much have time, thought and SF changed since then. Even so, it is at least possible for us to catch fleeting echoes of that original feeling of wild exultation still ringing across the years in titles like "Crashing Suns" and *The Skylark of Space*.

The worldview that these liberating stories rejected had prevailed in the Western world for nearly sixty years—ever since the time of the Franco-Prussian War and the beginnings of the Age of Technology. We have seen one major aspect or another of this worldview reflected in the lost race story, in the scientific romances of H. G. Wells, in Jack London's "The Scarlet Plague" and in Edgar Rice Burroughs' *A Princess of Mars*.

This Technological Age worldview was a biologically based vision of eternal growth and decay. Its central image was of struggle to live, of flowering, and of inevitable decline.

According to this view—which we may take as a first crude attempt at evolutionary conceptualization—one great epoch was succeeded by another. Each distinct era was marked by its own brutal contest for survival. Each such period was bound to throw up a ruling species, or race, or civilization—which would enjoy its brief moment in the sun and then be doomed to fall like all the rest and pass from the scene.

But there were distinct limitations to this grand conception. For one thing, the Technological worldview was not so much truly evolutionary as it was an image of a succession of discrete episodes in which the same inevitable story was played through over and over again. For another, as broad as the sweep of these eternal cycles was, this great cosmo-historical pageant was perceived and interpreted from a fundamentally limited and egocentric viewpoint. A determinedly Village point of view.

Citizens of the Technological Era might be aware of the existence of immense expanses of space and time. They might have haunting suspicions of man's ultimate cosmic insignificance. And still somehow they were able to continue to presume that True Reality lay on this little planet Earth during this current phase of its existence. Indeed, to presume that the locus of True Reality was themselves.

They felt they needed to know no more than this: Western Scientific Man was in the saddle and riding high. He was boss of the whole world—exploring it, seizing it, taming it, ruling it, and turning it to his purposes. That in itself should serve as proof of his centrality and essential rightness.

The garnering of monopolies and the establishment of empires that so typified this period were justified by another major aspect of the worldview—the half-evolutionary credo of Social Darwinism. This popular philosophy suggested that we inhabit a dog-eat-dog world in which only the strong survive. Western man looked all around this world and congratulated himself on being topmost dog. And believed that he recognized the basic evolutionary necessity to do whatever was called for in order to stay that way.

Not altogether surprisingly, however, a great and growing nightmare troubled Western man's dominion over the Earth. This gnawing fear was that the rule of the West would prove to be as tenuous and temporary as that of *T. rex* or Alexander the Great.

Modern civilization, the white race, mankind as a species, the planet of man itself... it seemed that all of these were vulnerable. Just as the day of the dinosaurs had passed and the mighty ancient empires of Sumeria, Egypt and Rome had come to fall, so inevitably must Western man fall, too.

The only questions were when and how it would happen. But that it must inevitably happen, of this there seemed to be little doubt.

The fatal blow could come from almost any direction. Another race, perhaps—the dreaded Yellow Peril. Or armies of ants suddenly grown intelligent and invincible might sweep over us like a tide. A plague might bring civilization down. Alien invaders might land, or a cosmic fireball might strike from the heavens.

Contrariwise, the end might be spelled by human weakness and decadence, or by human pride. We might grow soft and lose our keen fighting edge. We might lose our sense of purpose. We might even become balloon-headed Big Brains and have nothing better to do than flop about passively thinking our deep thoughts until some larger, fiercer, more vital creature appeared out of the unlit darkness of space and time to destroy us utterly.

But whatever the particular details of our mode of passing might prove to be—whether it be later or whether it be sooner, whether at the hands of other creatures or by fiat of the universe—one thing at least was dead certain: In due time, our end must inevitably come. And then a new cycle would begin.

A relatively calm and dispassionate phrasing of the attitude of the Technological worldview toward humanity and its competitors and possible successors is to be found in a blurb that Hugo Gernsback attached to H.G. Wells's *The War of the Worlds* when he reprinted it in *Amazing* in 1927:

> Wells has often been condemned because of his pictured ruthlessness of Martians, but, after all, why should they not be ruthless? Are we not ourselves as ruthless when we dissect insects and low animals for our scientific investigations? If there were a superior intelligence, to which, by comparison ours was as inferior as that of a chicken compared to a man's, there would be no good reason why it should not be ruthless if it wanted to conquer the planet for its own designs. We humans ourselves would not hesitate to do the same thing if we sent an expedition, let us say, to the moon, if we found what we considered a low species there.

In a universe of ruthless struggle, all that appeared to count was coming out on top. And if humanity should reveal for a single moment that it was not smart enough or strong enough to maintain the upper hand, why, so much for mankind.

At the outset of the Age of Technology, ordinary Western man held faith in two forms of transcendence—the personal soul and modern science. At this point, the two were allies. The successes of science were taken to be the proof or demonstration of man's rational soul. But the soul was master and science was the servant.

By the beginning of the Twentieth Century, however, science and the soul had fallen into extreme conflict. As the last tattered remnant of that belief in *spirit* which now seemed so completely unfounded, the soul was highly vulnerable. An immense weight of scientific doubt was increasingly being brought to bear against the very idea of the existence of a personal human tie to God.

At the same moment that science was now prepared to dismiss the soul as a baseless superstition, unnecessary and unprovable, it was ready itself to unveil an awesome new transcendence all its own. This was the existence of a universe that was more immense than man had ever previously suspected, and that was possibly more alien than he was prepared to tolerate.

Science challenged man to rid himself of his illusions and face the true facts of existence...as science saw them. The soul of man was stripped away by science and discarded, and with it all of man's accustomed sense of worth and purpose. In its place, science offered man a new identity. Henceforth he was to be an orphan child in a universe vastly beyond his comprehension.

According to the scientific view—as we heard it from Bertrand Russell—man and all his works are nothing more than the result of accidental heapings of atoms. Man's devotion, his inspiration, his genius and his labors must ultimately count for nothing. All of these are doomed to total extinction in the vast death of the solar system. It is necessary for us to accept as inevitable that the sum of human achievement must eventually come to lie buried beneath the debris of a universe in ruins.

There was to be no safety for the soul in the spiritual connection to God. To the most informed and thoughtful people of the age— such as Bertrand Russell—it seemed that at best God must be a monstrous joker, if indeed he could be said to exist at all, a matter which seemed increasingly doubtful.

And there was no safety to be found for the soul in the material universe, either. The material universe was the domain of science, and modern science stood ready to say that the cosmos was a vast and alien place that held no special concern for mankind. Man was condemned to struggle to survive in this hostile world and do his utmost to rule—but he should bear in mind all the while that even if he should prove to be temporarily successful, his inevitable fate must still be disaster and death.

Man's noblest course was to lift his chin and laugh at the Great Cosmic Joke. To accept the immense weight of the universe on his puny shoulders and smile a resolute smile even as he was inexorably ground into dust.

The shift in belief from faith in God and the rational soul to a belief in material science left Twentieth Century Western man in a confused, vulnerable and highly dangerous state of mind. Not to have a personal relationship between the individual soul and God deprived Western man of his accustomed sense of direction and value, and set him adrift.

What should he do and why? He was no longer sure.

It was at exactly this moment in the early Twentieth Century that the old-fashioned social utopian story ceased to be written. Imagining and realizing the rationally perfected Godly state no longer seemed a viable goal.

More and more, Western society looked to science for guidance, but science did not offer much help. What science seemed to say was: "Survival is all that counts. So contend among yourselves. Fight it out. Attempt to prevail. But do remember that the wages of success are still death."

The loss of purpose, moral confusion, belligerence and despair so widespread in the West in the early Twentieth Century led almost inevitably to World War I. This war, so long rehearsed, had been imagined as a nice, clean, evolutionarily decisive struggle among nations to see which was fittest to survive and rule. In the event, however, the Great War proved to be a static, muddled, aimless, grinding conflict that nobody quite dared to win and that nobody was willing to lose.

Ever so cautiously, the war was conducted from the shelter of entrenched positions. Ever so recklessly, waves of men were sent forth from the trenches to be slaughtered in No Man's Land. The only recognized heroes of the war were the fighter pilots on both sides—men of technology who were somehow perceived as gallant knights of the air sailing high above the fog, barbed wire and confusion. It was these men whom H. G. Wells would come to nominate as the model of what men must be if mankind were to survive.

If it accomplished nothing else, the monstrous and irrational catastrophe of the war dealt belief in the rational soul a mortal blow, and forced the acceptance of the frightful new universe revealed by modern science.

The postwar state of mind was particularly glum and apprehensive. Western man had entered upon the Age of Technology still guided by the soul, and armed with a reckless new confidence in science and its powers. The world was a ripe plum there for the taking, and the West was only too eager to seize it. But then in the Great War, technology had turned upon man. All the familiar Western dreams of empire were suddenly shattered.

Thoughts of alienation, sterility and doom now bedeviled the West. The immediate era was drawing to a close. And not at all surprisingly—

given the set of beliefs that had dominated the Age of Technology—there were a good many people to whom it appeared that the long-prophesied last days of Western man were finally at hand.

These fears were lent a measure of intellectual credence with the publication of a major book by a German philosopher named Oswald Spengler. *The Decline of the West* (1918) was the ultimate scholarly expression of the nightmare of the age. It captured a large international audience by telling people what they were more than half-inclined to believe already.

Like some pulp storyteller, Spengler recounted the now wellworn tale of the life and death of cultures. He took the measure of Western civilization, and was prepared to say outright that it had passed its peak. He even was ready to nominate a successor. Like the editor of a common tabloid out to boost circulation, Spengler looked to the East and foresaw the rise to power of the yellow race.

It seemed that there was no way out. Every dog has its day, and the West had had its moment. Now it must be prepared to suffer the consequences.

In a succession of attempts to cope with the inevitable Fate it saw waiting, the early Twentieth Century Western world lurched from one state of bewilderment and overreaction to another. During the Teens, the West attempted to face the inexorable universe with nobility and stoic courage—and instead found itself fighting World War I, a war in which nobility and courage meant almost nothing. In the Twenties, the West did what it could to ignore the fearsome machine universe. If this was to be The End, well, what better way to go out than with one whale of a drunken party! But the world did not come to an end with the Twenties—and the wild whoopee concluded with a great economic crash.

Through the Thirties, the West sat lost in a puddle of depression, nursing its aching head. If the way to face the scientific universe and its threat was not nobility, and neither was it hedonism, then just what was the way?

Most of the West hadn't a clue. But in fact there was a solution to the Western dilemma—if only the courage and vision existed to perceive and pursue it.

The two most crippling limitations of the Technological worldview were its insistence on anticipating the dictates of Fate, and its resolutely Village-centered point of view. The Technological Age looked forth upon vast new sweeps of space and time—but from a standpoint that was firmly rooted on this planet during the brief current phase of its existence. Western man held up his brave little matchflame of quasi-ignorance and looked out into the greater darkness of unknown possibility that surrounded him—and quailed.

He could not help but feel small and helpless and overwhelmed as he awaited a doom that seemed both preordained and inescapable.

At the outset of the era, the West had been only too glad to accept the dictates of Fate. Late Nineteenth Century Technological man was taking over the world, seizing, ruling and making a profit everywhere. Fate was on his side, an easy justification for every act of force and greed. He was Fate's darling.

But the period had run its course only too quickly, and now, at the end of the Technological Era, certainty of success had given way to certainty of doom. Fate, once taken to be Western man's ally, was now cast as his executioner.

The ineffective behaviors of the early Twentieth Century—the stoic nobility and the outrageous hedonism—were both attempts to deal with implacable Fate. First the resolve to be brave and keep a stiff upper lip no matter what. Then the jaunty attempt to say what the hell, shrug, and blot the whole thing out with party noises and strong drink.

But fatalistic reactions such as these were surrenders. They offered no possibility of a way out of the Western dilemma. After the wars and parties were all over, the threat of the scientific universe was still there demanding to be dealt with. And the only way to deal with this threat with any hope of effectiveness was to abandon all illusions of certainty and predetermination. To take one's chances.

What? Take one's chances with the unknown? That was a very difficult proposition to entertain. The scientific universe was so very large and dark and intimidating. Who in all the world was prepared to imagine taking his chances with that?

Well—not H. G. Wells, for one.

Little Bertie Wells, the social outcast, had grown up to become H. G. Wells, the oracle of the age. As early as the beginning of the Twentieth Century, Wells had identified the problem of human fate and dedicated himself to doing what he could to solve it.

It was abundantly clear to Wells that if human decline and extinction were to be avoided, it would be necessary for mankind to change its nature, and he said so over and over again. If human beings were to survive, men would have to become scientific and assume control of their own destiny.

So far, so good. But Wells's advice was only a partial analysis of the problem and only a partial solution. His attachment to the conventional Earth-centered perspective of his time prevented Wells from perceiving that his cool and knowledgeable new scientific man—so urgently necessary in the face of the threat posed by the scientific universe—only made sense *within the context* of this larger unknown.

Wells could never completely accommodate himself to that larger universe. It is true that during his rebellious youth, when he had nothing to lose, Wells had been capable of imagining daring smash-and-grab excursions into the depths of time and space in stories like *The Time Machine* and *The First Men in the Moon.* But as an all-too-successful adult—with a heavy investment in his one-man program to make humanity scientific—Wells found the sheer immensity and incomprehensibility of the wider universe too much to contemplate, and had to turn away from it.

Wells's response was no more than the response of the era. Technological men might well feel an occasional urgency to go outside and look at the heavens for portents. But always after a short time they would begin to find the stark glitter of the enigmatical immensities too alien and chilling to be endured. And then they would turn away with a shudder and hastily return to their familiar business indoors.

The name of the urgency that first drove Techno-man outside to study the stars was Fate. It was Fate that frightened him. It was Fate that set him to meditating on the unknown possibilities of the world waiting beyond the limits of little Village Earth. Oh, but then the remote and forbidding appearance of the scientific universe would suddenly overwhelm him and send him scurrying once again pell-mell back indoors. Back into the waiting clutches of Fate.

That was the deadly circle of futility and fear that the Age of Technology could not see any way to break. We can view the dilemma of the era written large for us in the most grandly conceived and most noble-minded SF work of the entire Technological Age— *Last and First Men* (1930). The author of this sweeping book was Olaf Stapledon, a 44-year-old British philosopher who was influenced by Wells, but who aimed to see beyond him.

Last and First Men is a work of fiction, but it is not a story in any familiar sense. There is very little concern with the doings and fate of individuals. Instead, this book is a historical account of the future development of man. *Last and First Men* is an experiment in the recounting of future history.

Stapledon's scope is immense. He imagines the progress of mankind over the next two billion years. He sees man migrating from planet to planet of the Solar System, altering worlds, altering himself, passing through seventeen future forms.

Man's culmination is as winged beings, creatures of great aspiration, living on the planet Neptune. It is one of these Last Men, projecting his thoughts back to a person in our own time, who is given to be the ultimate source of our narrative:

A being whom you would call a future man has seized the docile but scarcely adequate brain of your contemporary, and is trying to direct its familiar processes for an alien purpose. Thus a future epoch makes contact with your age. Listen patiently; for we who are the Last Men earnestly desire to communicate with you, who are members of the First Human Species. We can help you, and we need your help.

What a wonderful promise is delivered here in *Last and First Men*— that humanity will not perish now, but will continue to survive for fully two billion years to come, growing and changing all the while. How far this book carries us beyond the temporary conditions and petty worries of the early Twentieth Century moment! What a sense of evolutionary possibility it displays!

And if we should pause for a moment and look back upon the first hesitant probings of time and space by SF at the beginning of the Age of Technology, and then compare these to *Last and First Men*, with its restructured human beings living on the farthest planet of the Solar System at an incredibly remote moment, we can only marvel. What a sweeping transformation of SF has occurred! What a lifting of horizons!

Ambitions previously unknown to SF were at work in the making of *Last and First Men*. In presenting his book to the reading public, Stapledon wrote:

Our aim is not merely to create aesthetically admirable fiction. We must achieve neither mere history, nor mere fiction, but myth. A true myth is one which, within the universe of a certain culture (living or dead), expresses richly, and often perhaps tragically, the highest admirations possible within that culture. A false myth is one which either violently transgresses the limits of credibility set by its own cultural matrix, or expresses admirations less developed than those of its culture's best vision. This book can no more claim to be true myth than true prophecy. But it is an essay in myth creation.

But for all its broad horizons and sense of evolutionary possibility, we must reckon *Last and First Men* at least a failed myth, if not a false one. And the reasons are not hard to find, even in Stapledon's own terms. Stapledon had too much affection for the tragic, he was too unwilling to chance transgressing the limits of his own cultural matrix, and he failed to take into account the newest admirations developed by his culture, the new scientific thinking of men like James Jeans and J.B.S. Haldane.

Or, as we might put it instead, *Last and First Men* founders as myth because Olaf Stapledon was unable to overcome the most typical and familiar limitations of mind of the Age of Technology. Like his fellow philosopher, Oswald Spengler, Stapledon fell victim to the early Twentieth Century dilemma. And the result was that *Last and First Men* is both Village-centered and Fate-ridden.

We never do directly experience the future that we are told about. Rather, we poor petty beings fixed in our own time are condemned to sit in a circle and listen to some inadequate contemporary as he cups his hand to his ear and relays the messages he says he is receiving from the ends of time. And what he tells us sounds remarkably like the most typical fears of the Western world in the 1920s—but imagined on a larger scale.

The Last Men are the Last Men because they are a dying breed. Fate has them by the throat. From somewhere in the outer darkness, strange intense "ethereal vibrations" have come to bombard and infect the sun. Now it is flaring up with a cosmic fever that will either completely consume it or reduce it to a cinder. Neptune is doomed, and with it, mankind.

Already the sickness of the sun has begun to affect men:

> Drenched for some thousands of years by the unique stellar radiation, we have gradually lost not only the ecstasy of dispassionate worship, but even the capacity for normal disinterested behavior. Every one is now liable to an irrational bias in favour of himself as a private person, as against his fellows. Personal envy, uncharitableness, even murder and gratuitous cruelty, formerly unknown amongst us, are now becoming common.

It is very difficult to avoid seeing the similarity between this situation and the mental state of the Western world in the early Twentieth Century. The sick sun and attendant "general spiritual degradation" of the Last Men sound remarkably parallel to the Technological Age's cretinous God and loss of belief in the soul.

We have heard the Last Man who is the narrator of the story tell us that the Eighteenth Men need our help. And were we capable of speaking to them, we might have help to give them.

The lesson that the Last Men have for us First Men would seem to be that there is a vast expansive future for mankind. We should not give up too soon.

The best help that we First Men could give to the Last Men would be exactly this same message: There is still a vast unknown future waiting. Do not give up.

Or, more specifically, we might say: If men in the past have moved from planet to planet of our solar system as it became necessary to do so, growing and changing all the while, well, why not do it once again? Why not leap boldly to the stars and become Nineteenth Man?

But, alas, the traffic on this particular phone line is all one-way. We can listen to the future, but we cannot reply.

And what we hear is that the Last Men—who would advise us poor pitiful First Men to give up our petty attachment to Village Earth—are themselves undetachably wedded to their limited Village Solar System. Listen—they are telling us that they tested the outer darkness once, and like characters out of Edgar Allan Poe or H.P. Lovecraft, the experience drove them mad:

> Recently an exploration ship returned from a voyage into the outer tracts. Half her crew had died. The survivors were emaciated, diseased, and mentally unbalanced. To a race that had thought itself so well established in sanity that nothing could disturb it, the spectacle of these unfortunates was instructive. Throughout the voyage, which was the longest ever attempted, they had encountered nothing whatever but two comets, and an occasional meteor. Some of the nearer constellations were seen with altered forms. One or two stars increased slightly in brightness; and the sun was reduced to being the most brilliant of stars. The aloof and changeless presence of the constellations seems to have crazed the voyagers. When at last the ship returned and berthed, there was a scene such as is seldom witnessed in our modern world. The crew flung open the ports and staggered blubbering into the arms of the crowd. It would never have been believed that members of our species could be so far reduced from the self-possession that is normal to us. Subsequently these poor human wrecks have shown an irrational phobia of the stars, and of all that is not human. They dare not go out at night.

Well, if this is the case, no wonder the Eighteenth Men are so resigned to their Fate. We really shouldn't expect them to dare the stars.

In the end, it would seem that what the Last Men really wish to have from us is not help at all, but appreciation of the artistry with which they are going forth to meet their fate. The book concludes:

> But one thing is certain. Man himself, at the very least, is music, a brave theme that makes music also of its vast accompaniment, its matrix of storms and stars. Man himself in his degree is eternally a beauty in the eternal form of things. It is very good to have been man. And so we may go forward together with laughter in our hearts, and peace, thankful for the past, and for our own courage. For we shall make after all a fair conclusion to this brief music that is man.

Thus, amidst forced laughter, self-congratulation, and whistling in the dark, exits Humanity stage left—pursued by a bear. We hear the muffled sounds of offstage carnage. How noble. How sad.

We might be forgiven for the thought that we have come altogether too far in time and space only to find ourselves at the end right back where we started from—face to face with the early Twentieth Century dilemma, and still unable to solve it. At the least, we must conclude that, grand myth though it may have aspired to be, *Last and First Men* was ultimately a prisoner of its own period.

What this moment called for was precisely what *Last and First Men* could not deliver—a radical realignment of thinking. Instead of constantly dodging and hiding from the universe, it was necessary to stand fast, to turn and face the new transcendent realm revealed by science, and then to imagine a place within it for men.

The adjustment of thinking that was called for was very closely parallel to the earlier reorientation of thought which had accompanied the transition from the Romantic Era to the Age of Technology. Just as late Nineteenth Century Western man had needed to quiet his fears of science-beyond-science and learn how to live with it and employ it, so was it essential now for the current generation to quiet its fears of the vast unknown universe that this higher science had come to reveal, and learn how to live and deal with that.

In order to enter the Technological Age, the Romantics had to come to the perception that their most frightening problem, the rise of soulless science, was in fact the answer to their greatest need, the rediscovery of mystery. Just so, in order to enter the coming Atomic Age, was it necessary for Techno-men to realize that what appeared to be their most terrifying problem—the vast new universe revealed by science—was in fact the answer to humanity's pressing need to escape execution by grim Fate.

The challenge of the moment was for men to give up their age-old dependency on the Village—a dependency that ultimately must doom them—and become mental citizens of the new wider universe. Men had to become at home in space and time.

Most people could not do this—they lacked the necessary orientation and values. But there were some who could.

Starting in the Twenties, a new breed of man began to appear in the West, especially in America. These were tough-minded men of fact who identified themselves totally with science. No doubts, no reservations.

As we have seen, a desperate struggle had been taking place throughout the Age of Technology. The old values of established society and traditional religion and the new values of material science had been at war with each other—most especially within the hearts and minds of individuals. But here in the person of the new man, the war was over, and it was science that was the victor.

Received values had no hold on this new Twentieth Century man of science. He was determined to set aside all dogma and preconception, to discover the true facts, and to judge matters as he found them.

One matter on which the new man of fact had a fresh perspective was the central fictive problem of the era and its worldly equivalent.

Over and over through the period, in one form or another, the same basic tale had been repeated—the story of the desperate contention of society and barbarism, and the flowering and death of civilizations. Whatever limitations and deficiencies it might have, this central story did encapsulate and express a very real truth. With the final rejection of *spirit*, a world was coming to an end. A grand old civilization did perish in the Great War, and there was no way to bring it back.

The new man was one who could observe this fact calmly and accept it without regret, just as he would any other fact. He was no poor little lamb who had gone astray, no member of the Lost Generation. He had no patience to spare for idle sentimentalizing.

The new Twentieth Century man of science was eager to look forward, not back. He might even be thought of as something of a barbarian—a barbarian with a slide rule dwelling in the ruins of a former high civilization, but completely indifferent to its fall because he had urgent new business to attend to. This new man was practical and filled with determination. He had utter confidence in his mastery of scientific power, and no fear at all of encounter with the unknown scientific universe.

Our three pivotal stories of August 1928—*The Skylark of Space*, "Armageddon—2419 A.D.", and "Crashing Suns"—were epitomal early expressions of this emerging state of mind.

The authors of these vital stories belonged to a new writing generation that had read and digested Burroughs and his fellows as youngsters back in the Teens. To turn away from the Void and surrender to Fate in the manner of *Last and First Men* was not for them. These brave visionaries of the late Technological Age were prepared to project their imaginations into the scientific unknown and to find answers there for every problem and every fear of their era.

Of these three central stories, by far the most fully imagined, the most innovative, and the most influential, was *The Skylark of Space*, a unique tale of interstellar exploration serialized in the August, September and October 1928 issues of *Amazing Stories*. This horizon-widening novel was written by Edward Elmer Smith in collaboration with Lee Hawkins Garby.

We may see in *The Skylark of Space* a story that serves as a link between the first brief flowering of tales of alien exploration in the American general-fiction pulps of the Teens, and the renewal of imagined venturings into the unknown that took place in the new SF magazines of the late Twenties.

The principal author of *The Skylark of Space* was E.E. Smith, a devoted reader of the SF published in *All-Story* and *Argosy*. When he conceived his story in the summer of 1915, he was an employee of the U.S. Bureau of Standards in Washington, D.C., and a graduate student of chemistry.

Lee Hawkins Garby was a neighbor, the wife of a friend and classmate. She encouraged Smith to set his story down on paper, and assisted him in writing the first third of it. Her specialty was the love element—which Smith did not feel competent to handle.

But Mrs. Garby's contribution to the story was distinctly limited, and except for giving this shy young scientist an initial nudge toward becoming a storyteller, she would have no further part to play in the creation of modern science fiction. She leaves our story even as she enters it.

On the other hand, "Doc" Smith—as he would come to be affectionately called by an SF magazine readership that valued the power and prestige of his advanced scientific degree in a time when such degrees were still a comparative rarity—was a writer who would have a tremendous impact on the development of science fiction.

Unlike so many of his Nineteenth Century predecessors—or even his coeval, that reclusive gentleman from Providence, H.P. Lovecraft—E.E. Smith was no smooth-palmed, high-born man of letters spinning out fantasies of the terrors of science. Smith was the forerunner of a wholly new kind of SF writer who would not become a commonplace for another quarter of a century—the practical man of technology who was prepared to perceive science as the means of fulfillment of all human aspiration.

Smith was an early example of the new Twentieth Century man of science. In his own person, he combined the open-minded flexibility of the Western frontiersman, a wide range of technical skills, an acute appreciation of the altered world that modern science and technology were creating, and a deep and abiding love of scientific mystery.

For a man like Smith, technology and applied science were fundamental tools. They were the natural means for an able boy of common name and common parentage to rise in an amazing new world in which technical competence counted for more than birth or position. E.E. Smith was the living embodiment of the new man for whom and by whom the Twentieth Century was made.

Edward Elmer Smith was born in Sheboygan, Wisconsin on May 2, 1890. His father was a one-time whaler become a sailor on the Great Lakes, and then turned carpenter. Soon after Edward was born, his family moved west, and he was raised on a homestead in the wilds of northern Idaho, where his father grew potatoes for the railroad.

If science appeared miraculous to Smith, it was in part because he grew up so far away from the centers of the Technological Age that the new inventions of the day were for him only a distant rumor to be encountered in the books he devoured in search of answers to his questions. And it meant that when he finally did experience the new age, it burst upon him as all the more marvelous.

During the Edwardian decade, the Age of Technology reached out to seize and enlist this backwoods boy. Smith became an active participant in the technological taming of the West. He worked as a logger and sawyer, a road paver, a railroad blazer, and a hardrock miner, as well as serving a spell as the conductor of a horse-drawn streetcar in Spokane, Washington.

Then young Smith—like H.G. Wells before him—suffered a fortuitous accident that changed his life. Fleeing from a boarding-house fire that he himself had inadvertently caused, Smith jumped through a fourth-floor window and broke five ribs, his leg, and his wrist, and became unable to work.

It seemed that the new possibility of the day—higher education— was the only answer for him. Smith's family drew together. An older brother offered the winnings from a marathon poker game. His two sisters also contributed money. Together, they sent young Edward off to study at the University of Idaho, an institution of learning that was barely older than he.

It was a timely moment to come out of the wilderness and settle to the study of science. This was the height of the pre-war period of technological optimism. And it was also the very hour when Edgar Rice Burroughs, that one-time Idahoan, was introducing his powerful and adaptable new characters, Tarzan of the Apes and John Carter of Mars, in the pages of *All-Story*.

Smith took a degree with honors in chemical engineering at the University of Idaho, but then did not stop with that. He won a government job through a civil service examination, and traveled east to work as a junior chemist at the U.S. Bureau of Standards in Washington, D.C. And while he held this job, he continued his scientific education.

In 1919, after brief non-combatant service in World War I, Smith would earn his doctorate in chemistry from George Washington University. He would then settle down as a food chemist, eventually specializing in the formulation of doughnut mixes.

The Skylark of Space, Smith's attempt at a scientific romance, remained unfinished at the time he received his Ph.D. He had set it aside in 1916, only one-third complete, when he was newly married to the sister of his college roommate, holding a full-time job, and also going to school.

Living and working in Hillsdale, Michigan in 1919, however, Smith found himself with time on his hands. He got out his old story and began to work on it again, this time without the aid of Mrs. Garby, and finished it at last early in 1920.

But times had changed by then. The postwar mood of despair had settled in. *All-Story* had been merged into *Argosy*. There was no longer the receptivity there had been during the Teens for stories of alien exploration.

For years on end, E.E. Smith sent his novel vainly from magazine to magazine, publisher to publisher. And it mattered to none of them that *The Skylark of Space* was an SF work of radical originality.

In his story, Smith introduced a new kind of character to science fiction—both a hero and a villain who were examples of the boldly effective new scientific man. Of even greater importance, however, was that Smith provided these characters with an appropriate context within which to show their stuff. He cut the leading strings of Mother Earth and set his brain children free within the immense new stellar universe that modern science had lately come to reveal. Smith imagined the stars as a playground, a place of human self-discovery.

In 1915, when Smith conceived his story, this was totally unheard-of stuff. And even in the Twenties, it remained too bizarre and frightening for the ordinary man to contemplate. How utterly frustrating it must have been for Smith to live with the knowledge that his vigorous and optimistic romance, rejected again and again as too far-out for readers to accept, was actually a far more accurate reflection of current scientific thinking than the narrow, fear-ridden SF stories that the publishers of the day were willing to accept and put in print.

Then, in the spring of 1927, Smith spied an issue of Hugo Gernsback's *Amazing Stories* on the newsstand. He got out his old manuscript and sent it off one more time. And at last it found acceptance from an editor who was not afraid to take a chance on a positive scientifiction story. And still, *The Skylark of Space* would be held for another year and a quarter before its appointed moment of publication finally arrived.

But so far ahead of his time was Smith as a scientific imaginist that even the passage of thirteen years did not adversely affect the impact of his story. When *The Skylark of Space* finally appeared in *Amazing* in 1928, Edward Elmer Smith was instantly recognized

as the premier writer of American magazine science fiction. And he
would remain that for fully a dozen years more with one expansive
serial novel after another.

The Skylark of Space begins abruptly with a powerful manifestation of super-science:

> Petrified with astonishment, Richard Seaton stared after the copper
> steam-bath upon which, a moment before, he had been electrolyzing his
> solution of "X," the unknown metal. As soon as he had removed the
> beaker with its precious contents the heavy bath had jumped endwise
> from under his hand as though it were alive. It had flown with terrific
> speed over the table, smashing a dozen reagent-bottles on its way, and
> straight on out through the open window. Hastily setting the beaker
> down, he seized his binoculars and focused them upon the flying bath,
> which now, to the unaided vision, was merely a speck in the distance.
> Through the glass he saw that it did not fall to the ground, but continued
> on in a straight line, its rapidly diminishing size alone showing the enor-
> mous velocity at which it was moving.

Richard Seaton, Smith's central character, is obviously modeled
upon the new human type introduced in the stories of Edgar Rice
Burroughs—the adaptable man strong in mind and body. Like Tarzan
and John Carter, Seaton is tall, dark-haired, gray-eyed, broad-shoul-
dered, narrow-waisted and physically powerful. He has both "the
wide brow of the thinker" and "the firm, square jaw of the born
fighter."

But in Richard Seaton, something new is added to the mix.
Seaton is also a brilliant scientist. Indeed, he might be described
as a John Carter equipped with the skills and background of E. E.
Smith. Like Smith, Seaton hails from the mountains of northern
Idaho. And like Smith, Seaton is a chemist employed in a govern-
ment lab in Washington, D.C.

Seaton is a casual but immensely able young fellow. He wears
flowered Hawaiian shirts and rides his motorcycle through the
streets of Washington. On the strength of his superior ability on
the tennis court, he has an egalitarian friendship with a young
millionaire, Martin Crane. And he is engaged to a beautiful Chevy
Chase socialite, Dorothy Vaneman.

When the copper steam-bath goes flying out of his laboratory
window, powered by a few droplets of X, the unknown metal,
Seaton realizes immediately what he has accidentally discovered—
a spaceship drive. He says to himself:

"'That bath is on its way to the moon right now, and there's no
reason I can't follow it. Martin's such a fanatic on exploration, he'll

fall all over himself to build us any kind of a craft we'll need—we'll explore the whole solar system. Great Cat, what a chance! A fool for luck is right!'"

When we recall that Smith's myth-attempting contemporary, Olaf Stapledon, had to imagine seventeen future forms of man in order to accomplish the exploration of the solar system, we may begin to understand why ordinary pulp magazine editors in the Twenties could have found Richard Seaton's offhandedly impetuous enthusiasm for space travel a trifle intimidating. Too far-out for them.

The story moves on at a headlong pace. In almost no time, Seaton and Crane have constructed a spaceship, which Dorothy Vaneman names *The Skylark*. Soon the two men take the ship out for a first after-dinner spin. This proves to be an instant recapitulation of Jules Verne, as Seaton makes evident to his fiancée and her father when the ship touches down again.

> "She flies!" he cried exultantly. "She flies, dearest, like a ray of light for speed and like a bit of thistledown for lightness. We've been around the moon!"
>
> "Around the moon!" cried the two amazed visitors. "So soon?" asked Vaneman. "When did you start?"
>
> "Almost an hour ago," replied Crane readily....

But Richard Seaton has an antagonist. He is Dr. Marc C. DuQuesne, a fellow scientist at the Bureau of Chemistry who is Seaton's physical and mental dark twin. As another co-worker says to DuQuesne early in the story: "'A fellow has to see your faces to tell you two apart.'"

Seaton and DuQuesne are both examples of the new scientific man, but there are significant differences between the two.

Seaton recognizes his own fundamental connection to the human race. For him, science is an extension of his humanity. It is a complement to his superior tennis game and his skills as an amateur magician. His personal relationships—particularly with Dorothy Vaneman, his fiancée, and Martin Crane, his friend and partner—are of the greatest importance to him. Crane touches upon the essence of the matter in Doc Smith's second novel, *Skylark Three*, serialized in *Amazing Stories* in 1930, when he remarks to Seaton: "'You are still the flashing genius and I am still your balance wheel.'"

"Blackie" DuQuesne, on the other hand, is the scientist as pure rationalizing intellect. He has neither friends nor a balance wheel. Humanity and human relationships are of no importance to him whatsoever. He cares about three things only—which may ultimately be one. DuQuesne values science, power, and truth to himself.

Very early in the game, DuQuesne figures out what Seaton and

Crane are up to, and in an attempt to thwart them and gain control of Seaton's discovery, he forges a black compact with the equally unscrupulous World Steel Corporation. This alliance of power-seekers— like the relationship between Seaton and Crane—is one more measure of the radical newness of *The Skylark of Space*. In former times, the mad scientists who experimented with science-beyond-science were gifted amateurs fooling around in private. Never previously were they imagined as professional chemists departing government service for greater opportunity as a consultant with the steel trust or an entrepreneurial partnership with an independent millionaire.

In their mad pursuit of power, DuQuesne and his allies will stop at nothing. They offhandedly commit burglary and murder. They steal some of the precious supply of X, the mysterious catalytic metal, and build a ship of their own. And they attempt to sabotage the construction of the *Skylark*.

But then the time comes when they overreach themselves. The day following Seaton and Crane's circumnavigation of the moon, DuQuesne swoops down in his spaceship. He leaps out, clad all in leather, and wearing an aviator's helmet with earflaps and amber goggles, and snatches up Dorothy Vaneman.

But Dorothy is a plucky girl. She kicks DuQuesne's henchman in the solar plexus and knocks him unconscious. The thug staggers against the control board, and the ship screams away toward the stars. Seaton and Crane set one of Seaton's inventions—"the object-compass"—on DuQuesne's ship, and follow in the *Skylark*.

Thus it is, through crime, an accident, and hot pursuit, that we arrive at the true business of *The Skylark of Space*. Not the exploration of the local solar system—but the exploration of the stars!

And we also have an answer to H.G. Wells's inability to imagine what an ordinary man might find to do out there amongst the enigmatical immensities. *The Skylark of Space* suggests that even if we had no other reason to travel to the stars, our own human conflicts, attitudes and aspirations might be enough in themselves to provide motive to go and reason to act once we arrived.

When Seaton and Crane finally catch up with DuQuesne's runaway ship, they find it in the gravitational grip of a dark star hundreds of light years from home and unable to free itself. The *Skylark* rescues DuQuesne, Dorothy Vaneman, and Margaret Spencer, another girl that World Steel had found inconvenient and intended to hide away on Mars.

Just how new and previously unimagined the territory is to which E.E. Smith has carried us is demonstrated by two of the major devices of the rescue. When the *Skylark* communicates with DuQuesne's ship, the means must be machine gun bullets fired against the side of the ship in Morse code for lack of a better method. And when DuQuesne and the two women transfer themselves from one ship to the other, the spacesuits they wear are made of fur.

By the time that Blackie DuQuesne has pledged his word to act as a member of the party and the *Skylark* has won free of the grip of the dark star, Seaton and his companions are fully five thousand light years from Earth. They lack the copper fuel to return home. And so they are almost obliged to explore the first planets they can locate.

If we were not previously convinced that the immense stellar universe that has been entered with the aid of super-science was a guise of the World Beyond the Hill, the first landing of the *Skylark* would end all doubt. The humans enter the system of a white sun and set down on one of its planets, touching down on an outcropping of rock that is guarded by a strange tree: "At one end of the ledge rose a giant tree, wonderfully symmetrical, but of a peculiar form, its branches being longer at the top than at the bottom and having broad, dark-green leaves, long thorns, and odd, flexible, shoot-like tendrils."

And, *mirabile dictu*, it seems that X has carried them home to X. The ledge they have landed upon is pure unknown metal.

But this is only the beginning. Hardly have they begun to explore when they are attacked by a giant carnivore, which DuQuesne shoots. This is the signal for an utterly bizarre explosion of violence:

> The scene, so quiet a few moments before, was horribly changed. The air seemed filled with hideous monsters. Winged lizards of prodigious size hurtled through the air to crash against the *Skylark's* armored hull. Flying monstrosities, with the fangs of tigers, attacked viciously. Dorothy screamed and started back as a scorpion-like thing ten feet in length leaped at the window in front of her, its terrible sting spraying the quartz with venom. As it fell to the ground a spider—if an eight-legged creature with spines instead of hair, faceted eyes, and a bloated globular body weighing hundreds of pounds may be called a spider—leaped upon it; and mighty mandibles against terrible sting, a furious battle raged. Twelve-foot cockroaches climbed nimbly across the fallen timber of the morass and began feeding voraciously on the carcass of the creature DuQuesne had killed. They were promptly driven away by another animal, a living nightmare of that reptilian age which apparently combined the nature and disposition of *tyrannosaurus rex* with a physical shape approximating that of the saber-tooth tiger. This newcomer towered fifteen feet high at the shoulders and had a mouth disproportionate even to his great size; a mouth armed with sharp fangs three feet in length. He had barely begun his meal, however, when he was challenged by another nightmare, a thing shaped more or less like a crocodile.

But then, with a decisive and unexpected act by the great guardian tree of the ledge, this superfluity of brute struggles concludes as abruptly as it began:

Suddenly the great tree bent over and lashed out against both animals. It transfixed them with its thorns, which the watchers now saw were both needle-pointed and barbed. It ripped at them with its long branches, which were in fact highly lethal spears. The broad leaves, equipped with sucking disks, wrapped themselves around the hopelessly impaled victims. The long, slender twigs or tendrils, each of which now had an eye at its extremity, waved about at a safe distance.

After absorbing all of the two gladiators that was absorbable, the tree resumed its former position, motionless in all its strange, outlandish beauty.

The second planetary stopover that the *Skylark* makes is also highly fantastic. Here they encounter a disembodied intelligence who appears in the likeness of first one and then another of the party.

This being sneers at their feebleness, calls them "nothings," and attempts to dematerialize them. But it is thwarted at last by the combined mental resistance of the five humans. The intelligence gives the most credit for its defeat to DuQuesne:

"Keep on going as you have been going, my potential kinsman; keep on studying under those eastern masters as you have been studying, and it is within the realm of possibility that, even in your short lifetime, you may become capable of withstanding the stresses concomitant with induction into our ranks."

And it withdraws. DuQuesne is left to say that he isn't sure which of the esoteric philosophies he has studied is the relevant one, but that he will try to find out because being a sexless, deathless, disembodied intelligence would be his idea of heaven.

On their third stop, Seaton and his companions discover a copper-bearing planet inhabited by humanlike aliens. This planet, Osnome—which may very well be a reference to the early Twentieth Century children's fantasies of the land of Oz by the American writer, L. Frank Baum—is caught in the grip of a 6000-year war between the opposing nations of Mardonale and Kondal. When they discover that the Mardonalians are a treacherous lot, completely lacking in any sense of honor or conscience, Seaton and Crane place their power at the service of Kondal and bring the war to a conclusion.

Richard Seaton and his Dorothy, Martin Crane and Margaret, are

married in a double ceremony on Osnome. The *Skylark* then follows
its object-compass back home to Earth, where DuQuesne escapes.
The story ends with a happy homecoming for the Seatons and
the Cranes.

Three crucial points separate *The Skylark of Space* from earlier
SF. All three of these points are confirmed and underlined in the
story's immediate sequel, *Skylark Three* (*Amazing*, Aug-Oct 1930).

The first significant difference is that Seaton and his friends are
neither daunted nor driven mad by the vast reaches of interstellar
space they have entered. Indeed, just before the first planetary
landing of the *Skylark*, Seaton speaks to his fiancée:

"'A strange world, Dorothy,' he said gravely. 'You are not afraid?'"
And she replies: "'I am only thrilled with wonder.'"

Seaton and his companions are natural citizens of the World Beyond the Hill, willing to accept whatever they find. In *The Skylark of
Space*, the new interstellar realm of wonder presents them with an
array of challenges: the power of dead matter in the form of the dark
star; the brute animal struggle for survival on the planet of the ledge;
the danger offered by a being of immensely superior intelligence; and
finally the great inexorable force of history on the planet Osnome.
And again and again, the party of humans manages to measure up.

Their fundamental reorientation from Village Earth to the greater
world of space is given explicit expression early in *Skylark Three*
when the Seatons and Cranes have taken off in their ship and left
Earth behind.

> Well clear of the Earth's influence, Seaton assured himself that every-
> thing was functioning properly, then stretched to his full height, writhed
> his arms over his head and heaved a deep sigh of relief.
>
> "Folks," he declared, "this is the first time I've felt right since we got
> out of this old bottle. Why, I feel so good a cat could walk up to me and
> scratch me right in the eye, and I wouldn't even scratch back. Yowp! I'm a
> wild Siberian catamount, and this is my night to howl. Whee-ee-yerow!"

Near the end of *Skylark Three*, Seaton and his friends pass entirely
outside of our home galaxy and look back upon it, one dim patch of
light among many. Dorothy declares that she is scared pea-green and
seeks comfort. And even Seaton admits, "'I'm scared purple myself.'"
But by the third story in the series, *Skylark of Valeron* (*Astounding*,
Aug 1934-Feb 1935), Seaton and his companions are able to leap
lightly from one galaxy to another without a qualm. There is nowhere
they cannot go and no challenge they cannot meet.

The second point of importance to be found in *The Skylark of
Space* is the rejection of ruthless self-interested rationalism, that road

of intellectuality that leads eventually to Big Brain, and perhaps beyond. In *The Skylark of Space*, this line of development is resisted in three different forms—first in the person of Dr. Marc "Blackie" DuQuesne; again in the aspect of the malevolent disembodied intelligence; and finally in the arrogant and untrustworthy Mardonalians of the planet Osnome.

In *Skylark Three*, the rejection of the rule of intellectual superiority alone is presented in the form of a war against a galaxy-threatening race of aliens, the Fenachrone. Early in *Skylark Three*, one of these announces to Seaton:

> "Know you, American, that we supermen of the Fenachrone are as far above any of the other and lesser breeds of beings who spawn in their millions in their countless myriads of races upon the numberless planets of the Universe as you are above the inert metal from which this your ship was built. The Universe is ours, and in due course we shall take it...."

Seaton and Crane counter the threat of the Fenachrone by gathering together the knowledge and power of a variety of beings, including the formerly warring Mardonalians and Kondalians.

This brings us to the third point of importance. What E. E. Smith sets in opposition to the road of hierarchic superiority is a kind of democratic pluralism that recognizes the validity of more modes of being than merely one.

We can see this illustrated in the various natures of the company of the *Skylark*. All are different, but somehow, united in their difference, all together they count for more than the purest of pure intelligences.

Margaret Crane is a sensitive moral being of vast insight. She is capable of seeing wonder in the most alien of races and something inherent in man as great as all they are encountering.

Dorothy Seaton is a cultured being. She is a Doctor of Music who can play the violin so beautifully that a staid old race is moved.

Richard Seaton is a refreshingly humble flashing genius—and also a bit of a goof, casual enough to hack around the universe in tennis sneakers.

Martin Crane is bright enough to follow Seaton into unknown realms of science, even though he lacks Seaton's originality. And he is also strong enough of character to serve as Seaton's balance wheel, his good common sense.

And there is even room in the mix for Blackie DuQuesne, a damned good man gone wrong—if only he will behave himself and act like a member of the party.

In *Skylark Three*, the danger of the Fenachrone is successfully met by the union of alien races organized by Seaton and Crane. One of these races, millions of years older than humanity, salutes Seaton for what may actually be the human party's one true mark of superiority—their larger frame of reference, their greater breadth of vision:

> "Doctor Seaton, I wish to apologize to you," the Dasorian said.... "Since you are evidently still land animals, I had supposed you of inferior intelligence. It is true that your younger civilization is deficient in certain aspects, but you have shown a depth of vision, a sheer power of imagination and grasp, that no member of our older civilization could approach."

It is not in inventions that human power ultimately lies—not in stardrives, spaceships and object-compasses—but rather in the ability to accept and unify vastly different beings and points of view. It is this combined power that ultimately defeats the Fenachrone, the would-be galactic master race.

In *The Skylark of Space* and its sequels, we are offered a solution to the Twentieth Century dilemma. Doc Smith's Skylark stories say that there is no necessary limit to human attainment. Mankind need not huddle in its stifling little Village, alternating between delusions of superiority and nightmares of cosmic doom. Rather, the way out of the problem of the age must lie in the abandonment of hierarchy and claims of special privilege, acceptance of the wider world of unknown possibility, and mastery of its perils through the unprejudiced cooperation of unlike persons and beings.

This democratic approach to the question of human survival was not just Doc Smith's alone, but was characteristically American. If the Europeans would very shortly come to the end of their ability to write creative SF, it was because they lacked the depth of vision and the sheer power of imagination necessary to alter their attitudes. The ultimate example of this rigidity must be Nazi Germany with its Aryan supermen, its attempts to eliminate the inferior and different, and its intent to rule Village Earth for a thousand years.

Significantly, the new attitudes on display in *The Skylark of Space* may be seen point for point in our other two crucial American magazine stories of August 1928.

In "Armageddon—2419 A.D." by Philip Francis Nowlan, published in *Amazing* alongside *The Skylark of Space*, we are presented with the narrative of Anthony Rogers, a veteran of the Great War. In a brief prologue, Rogers informs us that in the year 1927 he was exploring some abandoned coal mines in Pennsylvania on behalf of his employer, the American Radioactive Gas Corporation, when a cave-in trapped him in a pocket of gas. He was preserved in a state of suspended animation for nearly five hundred years, awaking in the year 2419.

Unlike a time machine, this mode of removal to the future allows Rogers no easy means of return to his own time. But no matter— Rogers does not tear his hair and bemoan his fate. He doesn't even think twice about the Village world left behind. He is as open-mindedly ready to become a citizen of the future as Richard Seaton and his friends are ready to become citizens of space.

The new world of wonder that Anthony Rogers discovers is a North America fallen from its former high state. The continent lies under the domination of the Hans, a race of arrogant and decadent Orientals ruling from the security of their great machine-cities.

The Hans are the living embodiment of the entire spectrum of early Twentieth Century fears: They are another would-be master race. They are the Yellow Peril. They are the eternal tyrant who rules for five hundred, a thousand, or even six thousand years. They are representatives of the grinding, inexorable and sterile machine universe.

In the sequel, "The Airlords of Han" (*Amazing*, Mar 1929), it is further suggested that the Hans are crossbreeds, a mixture of native Tibetans and "a genus of human-like creatures that may have arrived on this earth with a small planet (or a large meteor) which is known to have crashed in interior Asia late in the Twentieth Century, causing permanent changes in the earth's orbit and climate." Thus the Hans are also to be identified with racial mongrelization, cosmic catastrophe, and alien invasion.

Here in these stories of the adventures of Anthony Rogers in the Twenty-Fifth Century, we are offered one of the last literal presentations of the concept of the soul to be found in American science fiction: The Hans, we are told, are mentally superdeveloped, but they have "a vacuum in place of that intangible something we call a soul."

In opposition to the Hans, Rogers finds a wide variety of gangs and tribes, the remnants of the ordinary Americans of an earlier era. These are true scientific barbarians, living in the forested ruins of the civilization of our day like wild Indians, yet still tending the precious flame of science.

Here, in these stories, we may recognize the basis for the comic strip *Buck Rogers*, begun in 1929 and scripted by Phil Nowlan. We may take it as meaningful that in the initial episodes of the comic strip, which were based on the original *Amazing* novelets, a major new character is added to the story. This is an antagonist figure, the Blackie DuQuesne-like "Killer" Kane, an inventor, self-seeker, and rejected suitor of Buck Rogers' sweetheart, who is ready to betray his fellow Americans to the Mongol horde out of personal pique.

Ultimately, the scattered American gangs—one of them led by Anthony Rogers—defeat the Hans by joining their disparate forces together. A new age is inaugurated—"the most glorious and noble era of scientific civilization in the history of the American race."

In short, once again in the adventures of Anthony Rogers we find a ready acceptance of the World Beyond the Hill, a rejection of ruthless hyper-intellectual amorality, and the triumphant union of varying fragments working together synergetically to make a greater whole.

There can be no doubt that set beside the imaginative scope and detail of *The Skylark of Space*, Philip Nowlan's stories appear dull, clumsy and vague. But it is also clear that "Armageddon—2419 A.D." and "The Airlords of Han" are pointing in the same new direction as the Skylark stories.

Exactly the same thing is true of "Crashing Suns" by Edmond Hamilton, serialized in *Weird Tales* in August and September 1928. Compared to *The Skylark of Space*, this novelet and its sequels are simple-minded, dreamlike and repetitive. Even so, they also present the same new set of attitudes.

Edmond Hamilton was born in Ohio on October 21, 1904, and raised on a farm. He was the first major SF writer to be born in the Twentieth Century—fourteen years younger than Doc Smith and sixteen years younger than Philip Nowlan. But he was as impressed as they by the coming of the technological world. He once wrote:

"My formative first 7 years were spent on an Ohio farm so far back in that it must have had a time-lag of a decade. Horses reared up in buggy-shafts at sight of an automobile, and a steam-threshing-machine was a thing which frightened me horribly."

Hamilton was a precocious youngster. At the age of 14, he was a college freshman majoring in physics, he was eagerly reading *All-Story* and *Argosy*, and he was attempting to write his first SF stories.

His first published story was sold to *Weird Tales* in 1926, and Hamilton would soon become a regular contributor to the magazine. His science fiction stories were *Weird Tales'* answer to the challenge lately offered by *Amazing*.

Hamilton's crucial novelet, "Crashing Suns," is different in one important regard from the other two significant American SF stories of August 1928.

Doc Smith's Richard Seaton is a Twentieth Century person who makes the transition into the World Beyond the Hill, likes it, and stays to become a citizen of outer space. Philip Nowlan's Anthony Rogers is likewise a native of our Village who makes the transition from here and now, and then finds himself eager to become a citizen of the wild and marvelous land of the future.

But Edmond Hamilton's viewpoint character, Jan Tor, is a Captain in the Interplanetary Patrol one hundred thousand years in the future. "Crashing Suns" begins with his spaceship racing in toward Earth from the vicinity of Uranus, and coming to land beside "the gigantic white dome of the great Hall of Planets, permanent seat of the Supreme Council and the center of government of the Eight Worlds."

In this story, as in Stapledon's *Last and First Men*, the outermost planet is still Neptune, and men are confined to the solar system. And once again, as in *Last and First Men*, the life of the sun is threatened. This time, however, it is not mysterious ethereal vibrations that are the danger, but rather a dying sun that has mysteriously changed its course and one year hence is due to smash into our star, shattering forever the peace and harmony of the utopian Eight Worlds: "*'For the planets of our system will perish like flowers in a furnace, in that titanic holocaust of crashing suns!'*"

Boyish and naive as it undoubtedly was even in its own time, "Crashing Suns" nonetheless affords an effective yardstick by which to measure the limitations of *Last and First Men*. In Stapledon's would-be myth, the one human expedition ever to brave the outer tracts beyond the solar system returned mad. And throughout the final 20,000 years of human existence, as Eighteenth Man declines and society disintegrates, no party of Last Men ever sets off into the universe to pit itself against the source of the ethereal vibrations that are destroying one star after another.

On the other hand, Jan Tor strides into the Hall of Planets to hear the bad news of our sun's impending destruction, and is appointed captain of an expedition to investigate. He is told, "'If we can discover what phenomena are the causes of the star's deflection, there is a chance that we might be able to repeat or reverse those phenomena, to swerve the star again from the path it now follows, and so save our solar system, our universe.'"

Only minutes later, Jan Tor is in the conning tower of an experimental space cruiser—which incidentally uses "etheric vibrations," the great threat of *Last and First Men*, as its means of propulsion—and is taking off for the dying star. Within a matter of hours the ship is beyond the last frontier of the solar system, in regions previously unknown to man.

Stapledon's voyagers proceeded no farther than the point where the sun was reduced to being the most brilliant of stars, and found themselves crazed by the aloof and changeless presence of the constellations. By contrast, Hamilton's bold venturers travel past the point where the sun becomes just one speck of light among millions. And here they find that "even more than between the planets, the stars lay before us in their true glory." And they are clearly thrilled.

Quite interestingly, when Jan Tor's space cruiser reaches the dying red sun, the expedition discovers that it is not a cruel, uncaring cosmos that threatens humanity with destruction. Rather, it is an alien race who hope to catch a light by crashing their dying sun into ours. Our destruction will be their reinvigoration.

These aliens are described as Big Brain:

> They were globes, globes of pink, unhealthy-looking flesh more than a yard in diameter, each upheld by six slender, insectlike legs, not more than twelve inches long, and each possessing two similar short, thin limbs which served them as arms and which projected at opposite points from their pink, globular bodies.

But the humans are not afraid to take on these powerful aliens. The space cruiser of Jan Tor races back to spread the news and raise a mighty fleet of spaceships from the Eight Worlds. Battle is joined in space between human and alien. The day is ultimately won when Sarto Sen, the human scientist who designed the experimental cruiser, sacrifices his own life to split the invading sun in two.

The conclusion of "Crashing Suns" again stands in extreme contrast with *Last and First Men*. Olaf Stapledon's great vision of humanity's future metamorphoses ends with stoic acceptance of the passing of the brief music that is man. But "Crashing Suns," the crude American novelet, ends with this bold assertion of human possibility:

> "It was from this Earth that the first man went out, Jan Tor. Out to planet after planet, until a universe was theirs. And now that Sarto Sen has saved that universe, and has given us these cruisers, how far will man go, I wonder? Out—out—universe after universe, star after star, constellations, nebulae—out—out—out...."
>
> He paused, a dark, erect figure beside me there, his arm flung up in superb, defiant promise toward the brilliant thronging stars.

After his own fashion, Edmond Hamilton would do his best to fulfill this promise. He was perhaps the first writer to attempt to make a living primarily by writing for the American SF magazines. To survive, he had to turn out a lot of wordage, and he took no particular shame in endlessly repeating himself. Beginning with "The Star Stealers" (*Weird Tales*, Feb 1929), he produced one sequel to "Crashing Suns" after another. And each had exactly the same plot as the first story:

Again and again, a cosmic threat is detected and a party is sent out to investigate. The true source of trouble proves to be an alien race wielding super-science, who are then engaged in battle and destroyed.

Something does change from one story to the next—the scope is constantly broadened: Hundreds of thousands of years pass. The Interplanetary Patrol becomes the Interstellar Patrol. The Eight Worlds become the Federation of Stars and then the Council of Suns. By the third story, "Within the Nebula" (*Weird Tales*, May 1929), it is the entire Galaxy that is threatened, and the investigating party bearing the no-prejudice utopian names Ker Kal, Sar Than and Jor Dahat are a human, a tentacled Arcturan, and a Capellan plant-man.

Ultimately, these Interstellar Patrol stories by Edmond Hamilton amount to little more than a statement of faith and a rough sketching of possibility. But, taken in company with the other seminal stories of August 1928—Doc Smith's *The Skylark of Space* and Philip Nowlan's "Armageddon—2419 A.D."—they were an unmistakable indication that American magazine SF was ready now to alter its nature, to leave the close confines of Village Earth behind and seek new meaning and purpose for humanity in the wider world of time and space—The World Beyond the Hill.

The Laws of Chance

When viewed from a distance, the new American SF magazines that sprang into life in the last decade of the Age of Technology have the appearance of an unstable mishmash of fundamentally incompatible elements. These magazines were a place of summary, experiment, struggle and confusion as writers strove to find their way out of one mind-set that was no longer viable, and into a wholly new state of mind.

During the Thirties, all the forms of SF that had been current during the post-1870 era were given leave to exist at once in the pages of these marginal American pulp magazines. There was no kind of imaginative fiction—from stories of super-scientific experiment, to the lost race story, to stories of the exploration of alien realms, to stories of the supernatural—that could not find a home in one magazine or another.

Underneath all of this multiplicity and respect for the past, however, old familiar categories were breaking down. Story types that had once seemed clearly separate borrowed freely from each other, or casually crossbred. At the same time, whole new story formulations—like space opera and the time paradox—were finding their way into existence.

It is by no means always possible for us to be sure how the writers themselves felt about the materials they were presenting. The most extreme radical and conservative elements might be conjoined in the very same story:

The latest astronomical news might turn up in a story about cruelly indifferent higher beings who fly through the interplanetary ether on leathery wings. A bold spaceman on Mars might encounter an ancient mythological horror. The Earth might be presented as the egg of some immense and unknowable space creature, and all human history and purpose might be instantly shattered when the hour of its hatching finally arrives. Or the latest speculations of physics on the fundamental uncertainty of being might be presented in a mood of total despair—lightly covered over with breeziness, jokes and slang.

The Thirties were a period of general transition. Just as the social and economic spheres of life were caught up in change, so also were order and value within science fiction. In this agonizing extended moment of economic breakdown and cultural rearrangement, given attitudes and received truths of all kinds were subject to the most extreme question and doubt. Nothing was certain and anything might be possible.

Through this maze of ambivalence, breakdown and confusion, the thread for us to follow is the nature and direction of the changes going on in science fiction during the years of the Great Depression. Out of the apparent old-fashionedness, muddle and doubt, we will pick the writers, the stories and the special fictional moments that best illustrate the ongoing subliminal shift from the values and orientations of the Age of Technology to the new psychic state of the Atomic Age.

In particular, we will be looking at the work of two writers. One of these is John W. Campbell, Jr.—the writer of the period who was most consciously aware of the shift taking place, and who most directly occupied himself with the problem of reformulating science fiction.

Campbell was far from being the most popular or prominent science fiction writer of the decade, even though he did enjoy a certain measure of recognition as an SF writer, particularly in the first few years of his career when he seemed a bright young phenom. But during the Thirties, the special programmatic nature of Campbell's effort went generally unremarked, in part because the major portion of it was performed under cover of a pseudonym, and partly because another large segment was nonfiction.

As a result of this work, however, at the end of the decade John W. Campbell, Jr. would be precisely the right man in exactly the right place to effectively serve as the chief architect in the establishment of modern science fiction.

The other writer of major concern is E. E. Smith. Beyond any doubt, Doc Smith was the SF magazine writer who was most popular and prominent during the last decade of the Age of Technology. His unparalleled reach and grasp were recognized from the moment that his first story saw publication.

It would be difficult to overstate the impact that *The Skylark of Space* had upon American SF readers and writers. It turned heads. It blew minds. It seemed an ultimate example of what science fiction could be. Even before the serialization of Smith's first story was complete, *Amazing* was inundated by letters of praise for *The Skylark of Space*, and it was years before the murmurs finally died down.

But Smith didn't rest with *The Skylark of Space*. He treated it as an opening card rather than a final statement, and through the decade he wrote novel after novel of ever-increasing scope. And when he tried to restrict his canvas to the solar system, as he did in the novel *Spacehounds of IPC* (*Amazing*, July-Sept 1931), readers protested. They could get that from anyone, and they demanded more from Smith.

Smith's great power was his breadth of vision. Far more than any other writer of the Age of Technology, Doc Smith was able to appreciate the incredible scope of the new universe revealed by science—and then to offset this mere vastness by imagining higher reaches of human potential and command of science.

Smith's first rival, Edmond Hamilton, with his series of rewrites of a single story to larger and larger scale, was not a rival for long. In relatively short order, Doc Smith would adopt the most promising details of "Crashing Suns" and its sequels—the space patrol, battles in space, and domesticated aliens—and make them his own. Hamilton, by contrast, was completely unable to match either the scope or the complexity of Smith's great vision. Very shortly, he would give up trying and content himself with work of lesser ambition.

Then, in the early Thirties, a second rival to Smith made his appearance—the young John Campbell. But this rivalry, too, was largely an illusion of the moment. Smith was a true innovator. Campbell, twenty years his junior, was at best a Smith imitator, at least at the outset, as Campbell himself was well aware.

In 1928, John W. Campbell, Jr., as an 18-year-old freshman at M.I.T., was one of those readers bowled over by the serialization of *The Skylark of Space*. And even as much as thirty-five years later, Campbell, by then long recognized as science fiction's most distinguished editor, would still attest to E.E. Smith's continuing centrality—and deny his own—saying: *"The Skylark of Space* was written in *1918!* Since *1918* nobody has come up with a major breakthrough in science fiction!"

Under the overwhelming stimulus of his first encounter with *The Skylark of Space*, the young Campbell was inspired to sit down and attempt a science fiction story of his own, which he submitted to *Amazing*. And, lo and behold, "Invaders from the Infinite" was actually bought!

It was never published, however, In the period of upheaval when *Amazing* changed ownership for the first time, "Invaders from the

Infinite" turned up missing. Campbell had made the beginner's mistake of keeping no carbon copy, and his story was permanently lost.

The first of Campbell's stories actually to appear in print, "When the Atoms Failed," was published in *Amazing Stories* in January 1930—the very same month that saw the publication of the first issue of *Astounding*, the magazine with which Campbell would eventually come to be identified.

Very shortly, Campbell launched himself into the new science fiction of scope and power, attempting to top his master Smith with evocations of mighty science. But there was no real contest between them. Campbell was a boy still struggling to form his own concepts, while Doc Smith was a mature man enjoying his freedom to give expression at last to ideas he had been forced to keep under his hat for years. Campbell was able to match Smith only in terms of gross throw-weight of imaginary scientific zap, but not at all in terms of basic writing skill, storytelling ability, human sensitivity, or overall conception.

The epitome of the early John W. Campbell—powerful, crude and more than a little vague and incoherent—may be this world-busting passage from a second story entitled *Invaders from the Infinite*, a novel published in the Spring-Summer 1932 issue of *Amazing Stories Quarterly*:

> What use is there to attempt description of that scene as 2,500,000,000, 000,000,000,000,000 tons of rock and metal and matter crashed against a wall of energy, immovable and inconceivable. The planet crumpled, and split wide. A thousand pieces, and suddenly there was a further mistiness about it, and the whole enormous mass, seeming but a toy, as it was from this distance in space, and as it was in this ship, was enclosed in that same, immovable, unalterable wall of energy.

In truth, the closest that the young zero-gargling John Campbell came to achieving parity with his hero was that thrilling moment in late 1934 when the two had serials running concurrently in the pages of the Tremaine *Astounding*—Smith's third Skylark story, *Skylark of Valeron*, and Campbell's last attempt at the epic of super-science, *The Mightiest Machine*. But after this, Campbell, too, dropped away. Or, more precisely, turned his attention elsewhere.

In the last half of the Thirties, E. E. Smith stood alone, completely without peer. And, competing with himself, Smith still contrived to top Smith. He put the Skylark series aside and launched himself into a new super-story that he had been incubating for ten years, ever since the moment he had finally sold *The Skylark of Space* to *Amazing*.

The Lensman series—four novels serialized in *Astounding* from 1937 to 1947—was conceived on a scale that made even the Skylark stories seem limited and parochial. In this series, the entire galaxy is one ongoing multifaceted civilization, in which Earth—here often called "Tellus"—was an early leader, but is not set apart or specially privileged.

These stories, as nothing else, would reveal the true difference between Smith and his quasi-rivals, Hamilton and Campbell. In his Interstellar Patrol stories, Edmond Hamilton presented human beings lightly turning aside the threats offered by larger and larger increments of space and time. In his epics of super-science, John W. Campbell imagined ever-larger quantifications of the potential power of human thought. But underlying all of Smith's fiction was an altogether more subtle vision—the conviction of the existence of level upon level of potential being and becoming.

As early as *The Skylark of Space*, this conviction may be seen in the form of the disembodied intelligence who creates the illusion of a planet for the members of the Skylark party to land upon and toys with them for a brief hour before allowing them to depart. This being not only operates on another and higher level of existence, but also indicates to the Skylarkers that this other level may potentially be attained by human beings.

Richard Seaton himself is a leap-taker. The increases in power and scale from story to story in the Skylark series, until the dauntless companions are boldly jumping from galaxy to galaxy in mile-long spaceships, may be taken as exact reflections of Richard Seaton's increases in imaginative grasp, scientific command, and personal acceptance of responsibility.

But there were limitations to the possible scope of the Skylark stories inherent in their very structure. They were the personal adventures of one contemporary genius from Idaho and his best buddy and their wives, and no more.

So, in a switch that was in itself a conceptual leap—an example of the very idea he was attempting to express in the form of fiction— Smith dropped the Skylark stories and launched the Lensman series.

In these novels, there is a hierarchy of being and responsibility in the galaxy. Galactic Civilization respects all forms of intelligent life. And the very best beings of any kind may aspire to become Galactic Patrolmen and help to maintain the peace of Galactic Civilization.

The most advanced members of the Galactic Patrol wear the Lens. This individually tailored "lenticular jewel" is both a sign of their superior character and an instrument of overwhelming power. More than that, in a real sense it is the very basis on which Galactic Civilization is founded.

Early in the first story in the series, *Galactic Patrol* (*Astounding*, Sept 1937-Feb 1938), we are told:

"The Lens, which, being proof against counterfeiting or even imitation, makes identification of Lensmen automatic and positive, was what made our Patrol possible. Having the Lens, it was easy to weed out the few unfit. Standards of entrance were raised ever higher, and when it had been proved beyond question that every Lensman was in fact incorruptible, the Galactic Council was given more and more authority. More and ever more solar systems, having developed Lensmen of their own, voted to join Civilization and sought representation on the Galactic Council, even though such a course meant giving up much of their systemic sovereignty."

Only some of the Lensmen are human, of course. Most are not. But the very best of the Lensmen is Smith's protagonist, another John Carter figure, Kimball Kinnison, whose special talents and abilities increase from story to story as he and his Lens-wearing fellows are pitted against a succession of ever more powerful, repellent and dangerous antagonists, some human and some not.

But the obvious and apparent levels of galactic conflict in these stories ultimately prove not to be the most important level. Gradually, it would be revealed that behind the brave and able wearers of the Lens stand the beings who make the Lens—the good Arisians, a higher race who hide themselves from view lest the very fact of their immense superiority disturb and intimidate impressionable younger beings. And behind the layers of menace that the Galactic Patrolmen strip away, there is eventually to be found another superior race—the evil Eddorians, interlopers from another space/time continuum.

A desperate struggle between good and evil is going on in the universe at every level, led by Arisia and Eddore, and humanity has a significant role to play in the conflict. Once more it is possible for men to have something to say about the making of their own destiny rather than merely serving as a toy of Fate.

Smith's Skylark and Lensman stories presented a strikingly positive vision of human vigor, power and potential. At this moment, by contrast, even the best and noblest works of British SF were lost in uneasy dreams of human inability and senescence.

For example, in *Brave New World* (1932), a satire of Wellsian scientific utopia by Aldous Huxley—a grandson of Thomas Huxley, the great biologist and teacher of Wells—it is five hundred years After Ford. This future has no frontiers—space travel, for instance, is never mentioned—and no sense of human dignity and purpose. Humanity is genetically engineered to fit the needs of society. War and art have been eliminated, and men live solely for comfort and pleasure. At the conclusion of the novel, the one character who represents traditional human values—"the Savage"—must commit suicide in utter despair at this sterile existence and his own degradation.

In *Odd John* (1935), by Olaf Stapledon, a mental and moral superman sets up a colony of his own kind in the South Seas. But the jealousy and fear of ordinary humans will not tolerate its separate existence. The supermen are confronted by a combined fleet of ships from the governments of Britain, France, the United States, Holland, Japan and Russia. Finally, rather than fight—or make common cause with lesser beings—Odd John and his fellows elect to commit mass suicide:

> The supernormals might have chosen to end their career by simply falling dead, but seemingly they desired to destroy their handiwork along with themselves. They would not allow their home, and all the objects of beauty with which they had adorned it, to fall into subhuman clutches. Therefore they deliberately blew up their power-station, thereby destroying not only themselves but their whole settlement.

Finally, *Star Maker* (1937), also by Stapledon, presents a picture of the farther reaches of time and space in a book that is an extension of the visions of *Last and First Men*. The narrative begins with a contemporary human, lost in despair, desperately wishing for confirmation that humanity is not alone in the cosmos. This wish is given an answer through a kind of disembodied astral travel that allows the narrator's consciousness to eavesdrop on many different stellar worlds through coming time. The narrator observes race upon race of life forms—some lower than man, some higher—and is even permitted a glimpse of the Star Maker, a cruel, remote and chilly god not unlike those presented by Bertrand Russell and Lord Dunsany at the turn of the century.

But human beings have no direct part to play in this vast universe. In *Last and First Men*, the hand-wringing Eighteenth Men, themselves unable to brave the interstellar void, launch great sperm ships to scatter human seed among the stars. But this project has no consequence reported in *Star Maker*. It is only one more futile gesture. The conclusion of *Star Maker* brings the narrator full circle, back home to contemporary Earth, where he is left to look forward to imminent catastrophe, beyond that to the demise of the human race on Neptune, and beyond that to the complete physical quiescence of all existence.

By contrast, Doc Smith's Lensman stories incorporate many of the very same materials as these distinguished but despairing British books—the advanced scientific society, human eugenics, the emergent superman, higher races, and great sweeps of space and time—but to completely different effect:

The future painted by Aldous Huxley in *Brave New World* is a limited place without challenge or purpose. Human breeding can only lead to an obscene fragmentation and diminution of human nature. But Smith's future is a universe that is wide open, a world in which genetic selection is not an evolutionary dead end, but a way upward.

Olaf Stapledon's superman in *Odd John* is a murderer of ordinary humans as a child. And in the very first paragraph of the story we are told, "The word 'man' on John's lips was often equivalent to 'fool.'" But Smith's Lensmen are not so snotty and self-indulgent. As the best of their worlds, part of a continuum of capacity and responsibility, they have real work to perform serving as the guardians and protectors of their less advanced brothers and sisters.

Stapledon's vision of the wider universe in *Star Maker* is of a remote realm that has no viable place within it for mankind. At best, it may engage our aesthetic appreciation. We may applaud its brilliance (and our own) before we are permitted to die. But E.E. Smith's universe is a very different kind of place. It is made for intelligent creatures, including mankind, and offers itself to their mastery.

In the second story in the series, *Gray Lensman* (*Astounding*, Oct 1939-Jan 1940), there is a highly significant passage where, for a brief moment, while his ship is traveling through intergalactic space, Kimball Kinnison misplaces his usual sense of purpose and falls into self-doubt before the vastness of the universe. But then he remembers himself, and reasserts the power of man:

> Despite the fact that Kinnison had gone out there expecting to behold that very scene, he felt awed to insignificance by the overwhelming, the cosmic immensity of the spectacle. What business had he, a sub-electronic midge from an ultra-microscopic planet, venturing out into macro-cosmic space, a demesne comprehensible only to the omniscient and omnipotent Creator?
>
> He got up, shaking off the futile mood. This wouldn't get him to the first check-station, and he had a job to do. And after all, wasn't man as big as space? Could he have come out here, otherwise? He was. Yes, man was bigger even than space. Man, by his very envisionment of macro-cosmic space, had already mastered it.

Like the extraordinary voyages of Jules Verne in an earlier moment of transition, Smith's epics of super-science served as a bridge between eras. They were the culmination of one period and the foundation for another. Just as Verne's fiction, with its domestication of wild science and its probes into the unknown, summed up Romantic Era proto-SF and made possible the new scientific fiction of the Technological Age, so Smith's stories, with their mastery of the macrocosm and visions of higher levels of possible being, simultaneously served to sum up Age of Technology science fiction and laid the groundwork for the modern science fiction of the coming Atomic Age.

Smith's great sweeping science fiction stories made all things possible. During the Thirties, Doc Smith's confident and optimistic vision of the universe and man's place within it offered an imaginative basis for the most progressive experiments of American magazine science fiction.

Within the great imaginative domain encompassed by Smith, there was room aplenty for acclimatization to the future and outer space, and for new views of time and matter. Old story material might be cast in new guise. Old problems might be resolved, and old scores settled. Stories that otherwise might have seemed too muddled, tenuous or ambivalent to accept, stories that in many cases could never have been imagined at all without the scope and courage lent by his example, were protected and legitimized by Smith's work.

One instance of this was the fruitful revival of the alien exploration story. In the early Thirties, a number of writers produced stories that were modeled on the tales of transition into unknown realms they had once read and loved in the *All-Story* and *Argosy* of the Teens. But these new stories had significant differences from the old ones.

In the new story of alien exploration, as in the old, a character from our world would be transferred into another world—a different dimension, or the far future, the microscopic realm, or perhaps some world in space. But the means of transference would not usually be occult, as had so often been the case in the Teens. And the destination would not be a world of spirit, but rather some strange corner within the new scientific multiverse.

As an example of this form, we might take the first story of Clifford Simak, a midwestern newspaperman. Simak was another of the rural children born at the turn of the century who were struck by wonder at the sight of modern science and technology and grew up to write science fiction. Simak was born on August 3, 1904, and was raised in a log house on a farm in the woods of Wisconsin. He once commented, "I sometimes think that despite the fact my boyhood spanned part of the first and second decades of the Twentieth Century that I actually lived in what amounted to the tail end of pioneer days."

In Simak's novelet "The World of the Red Sun" (*Wonder Stories*,

Dec 1931), two contemporary explorers in a time machine gone
astray encounter a Big Brain named Golan-Kirt—"He-Who-Came-
Out-of-the-Cosmos"—ruling the Earth of five million years hence.
The American venturers laugh this tyrant invader down, and
then when he is helpless they pot him with their .45s. Ah, but
when they attempt to return home, they only find themselves
in an even-more-remote dying world where their deeds have become
the stuff of ancient broken statuary.

Many things about this story are typical of Thirties' alien exploration—from taking a wrong turning at the beginning to being stranded
at the end. Where E. E. Smith's confident Skylark voyagers paid
visits to a variety of stellar worlds in a spaceship that was both
completely substantial and deliberately directed, and might at
any time follow their object-compass back home to Earth, the
protagonists of stories of alien exploration tended to be flipped into
some particular alien world, usually when an experimental scientific
device began to operate in a manner wholly unexpected, and then
had no way to get back home again. No surprise, then, that stories
of this kind tended to be haunted and brooding and bittersweet.

In this, they bore a resemblance to British and European SF of the
day. And yet, there was an active and progressive quality to these
new stories of alien exploration that made them genuinely different
in kind. Despite all their regret and grief at the passing of old worlds,
stories of alien exploration were a means by which the unknown
universes of science were discovered, investigated and tamed.

In earlier SF, Village Earth was at the very center of things,
and all around was the impenetrable darkness of the cosmos. Stories
of the exploration of alien realms like Wells's *The Time Machine*
or Ray Cummings' "The Girl in the Golden Atom" would always
be relayed to us through some stay-at-home subnarrator, who
himself would have the tale from the lips of the actual venturer.
But now, in a story like "The World of the Red Sun," the narrative
would both begin and end in the World Beyond the Hill, with
present-day Earth serving only as an offstage possibility or memory.

And, however erratically and accidentally the protagonists of
the new alien exploration story might travel into the unknown,
they did go mentally prepared to do what was necessary to deal
with what they found. Unlike their predecessors of the Teens,
they did not have to retreat to Village Earth all maimed and
mangled in order to heal and properly arm themselves. They traveled
packing .45 automatics on their hips as potent symbols of human
scientific authority. And they were not loath to pull the trigger.

The violent rejection of Big Brain in "The World of the Red Sun"
was not an isolated incident, either, but a typical theme. In one alien

exploration story after another Big Brains alien and Big Brains human were shot, bludgeoned, or even stomped to death.

The most popular SF novelet of the Thirties was an alien exploration story that transcended the usual limits of the genre. "Colossus" (*Astounding*, Jan 1934), by Donald Wandrei, was the second story to be presented by new editor F. Orlin Tremaine as a special "thought-variant."

In "Colossus," a spaceship takes off from Earth, fleeing the devastation of a new world war, a war that has claimed the life of the hero's beloved fiancée Anne. Out into the cosmos the ship *White Bird* travels, past Saturn, Uranus, Neptune and Pluto, into a universe of "150,000,000 galaxies, each composed of millions of stars."

The farther and faster this ship travels, the larger it becomes. And, at last, it leaves our world entirely for another: *"He had burst through the atom that was his universe and had emerged on a planet of a greater universe, a superuniverse!"*

Here, the hero is examined by titanic beings, who inquire whether he can return to his own atom again. He replies:

> "I do not know where it is. I would not know how to find it. If I could find it, I would not be able to enter. Something happened, when I burst through. I am bigger than my whole universe was. I cannot shrink down. Besides, millions of years have passed back there since I departed. I do not even know whether Earth, my planet, still exists."

But this transference into a higher dimension is not just another stranding, but rather a redemption and a new beginning. On an idyllic planet to which he is directed by the Titans, the hero finds a girl who looks like his lost Anne, and the recognition is mutual: "Her lips parted and her eyes, showing neither the fear nor the mistrust that he might have expected, shone of something secret, as if to greet some dimly remembered and half-forgotten friend of long ago."

Also in the early Thirties, at precisely the same time that the new alien exploration story was being written, another livelier and generally more optimistic story form was making its appearance—space opera. The setting of space opera stories was the planets of our own Solar System, a frontier world of the relatively near future.

The early model of space opera was the series of Hawk Carse novelets published in the Clayton *Astounding* in 1931 and 1932 under the name Anthony Gilmore. The true authors of these stories were *Astounding*'s first editor, Harry Bates, and his assistant, Desmond Hall, who were attempting to provide an example to their writers of the kind of fiction they were seeking for publication.

The first paragraph of the first story in the series—"Hawk Carse" (*Astounding*, Nov 1931)—displays both the vigor and the simple-minded conventionality that typified space opera:

> Hawk Carse came to the frontiers of space when Saturn was the frontier planet, which was years before the swift Patrol ships brought Earth's law and order to those vast regions. A casual glance at his slender figure made it seem impossible that he was to rise to be the greatest adventurer in space, that his name was to carry such deadly connotation in later years. But on closer inspection, a number of little things became evident: the steadiness of his light gray eyes; the marvelous strong-fingered hands; the wiry build of his splendidly proportioned body. Summing these things up and adding the brilliant resourcefulness of the man, the complete ignorance of fear, one could perhaps understand why even his blood enemy, the impassive Ku Sui, a man otherwise devoid of every human trait, could not face Carse unmoved in his moments of cold fury.

In these few lines, we may catch the materials and postures of a thousand pulp stories of gunfighters and cavalrymen, soldiers of fortune and Oriental adventurers. And, beyond them, the echoes of a long tradition of heroic sagas and legends.

It was a hot news flash from science in 1930 that made possible the reconception of the staid old utopian Eight Worlds of the Solar System as a wild frontier: A new ninth planet had been observed!

The young man credited with the discovery of the planet Pluto was Clyde Tombaugh, an astronomy-loving farmboy from Illinois. On the strength of his enthusiasm, young Tombaugh had caught on as an assistant at the Lowell Observatory in Flagstaff, Arizona, and been set to the purely mechanical task of comparing photographs of small sections of the sky in search of evidence of planetary movement.

And in February 1930, he spotted a flicker of just the kind he had been set to look for. A new world! Tombaugh's reward for the successful outcome of his labor was to be sent off to college to receive formal instruction in the regular and proper study of astronomy.

The last planet previously identified had been Neptune back in 1846. And for all the SF writers of the Age of Technology—from Jules Verne at the beginning to Edmond Hamilton and Olaf Stapledon at the end—it had been a given fact that Neptune was the outermost world, the far boundary of the Village Solar System.

But now all that was changed. What had seemed fixed and eternal was now uncertain.

Almost inevitably, there were some SF writers who took the discovery of Pluto as a bad omen. In "The Whisperer in Darkness"

(*Weird Tales*, Aug 1931), H.P. Lovecraft—ever wary of the monstrous unknowns lurking just beyond the reach of perception—had his narrator write: "Sometimes I fear what the years will bring, since that new planet Pluto has been so curiously discovered."

But for other writers, the discovery of Pluto seemed a more positive portent, the opening wide of a door of possibility. In one instant, the perception of the Solar System as a shuttered Village was altered, and it was possible to see the Solar System as a new frontier land, a fitting replacement for the now-closed American frontier of E.E. Smith's and Clifford Simak's boyhood.

Space opera lifted characters and story elements from every kind of popular fiction and gave them leave to exist in the rough-and-ready new world. Sailors, slave traders, homesteaders, aborigines, beachcombers, foreign legionnaires, cops, colonists, crooks and cowboys were all transposed into outer space. In tough tent towns thrown up beside exotic dying cities on Mars, smugglers and space patrolmen rubbed shoulders with indentured Venusian stoop-laborers and beautiful winged princesses from Callisto. Meanwhile, out in the Asteroid Belt, beyond the reach of law, claim jumpers attacked honest prospectors and space pirates waylaid passenger liners on the Earth-Jove run.

Not even ancient creatures of mythology were barred from the worlds of space opera. In "Shambleau" (*Weird Tales*, Nov 1933), the first story of C.L. Moore, a 22-year-old female bank teller from Indianapolis, the mythic past of Earth was re-presented as the even more ancient and mysterious past of the Solar System. Northwest Smith, a space adventurer much like Hawk Carse, rescues a Shambleau from a bloodthirsty mob in a camp-town on Mars. Shambleaus are snake-haired psychic vampires—members of "an older race than man, spawned from ancient seed in times before ours, perhaps on planets that have gone to dust"—who are remembered on Earth as the Medusae. This one thanks Northwest Smith for his aid by mentally beguiling, seducing and degrading him, until at last she is shot by his Venusian friend Yarol.

In one sense, space opera was nothing more than borrowings. It was usually rote and easy and formulaic rather than innovative and imaginative. But as a device of transition, space opera did serve several highly useful purposes.

Speaking conservatively, it gathered and preserved stereotypical fictional materials—some of which might also be archetypal story materials as old as mankind. More creatively, space opera took the wider universe—the enigmatic immensity that H.G. Wells could not conceive as containing useful work for one such as himself—and filled the immediate neighborhood with a colorful array of human social activities and a variety of roles to play.

Space opera had an immediate early flowering in the years when its formulas were first falling into place. And space opera set within the Solar System would continue to be written through the Thirties, and even after—even though the genre was only rarely an object of admiration by SF readers hungry for stories that were like nothing they had ever seen before.

Nonetheless, as the first step toward more complex and sophisticated stories of space, the space opera form would prove to have continuing influence. Even Doc Smith would make his contributions to space opera in serials of the early Thirties like *Spacehounds of IPC* (*Amazing*, July-Sept 1931) and *Triplanetary* (*Astounding*, Jan-Apr 1934), and would employ incidental background material adapted from space opera throughout the Lensman series.

But the most important fact about space opera may be that it, like the epic of super-science and the new story of alien exploration, presented a reversal of figure-and-ground from previous Technological Age science fiction. In space opera, Village Earth was no longer the center of things, but was just another place, one world among a number. The basic field of play was now the wider universe.

This highly significant shift in perspective was explicitly expressed by Doc Smith in *Galactic Patrol*, the first of the Lensman stories. At one point, the young woman who will ultimately marry Kimball Kinnison and bear him super-children, Nurse Clarrissa MacDougall, has become impatient with the habitual abruptness of Kinnison's leave-takings. But a Port Admiral knows better. He realizes that Kinnison simply has more urgent and important business to attend to:

"He knew, as she would one day learn, that Kinnison was no longer of Earth. He was now only of the galaxy, not of any one tiny dust-grain of it."

But not every writer of the Thirties was satisfied with the new worlds presented in the alien exploration story or space opera. To some it seemed too simplistic to find Big Brain yet again, or beautiful alien princesses so physically compatible with men of Earth that romance might develop. The universe revealed by Twentieth Century science—the universe of Arthur Eddington, James Jeans and J.B.S. Haldane—was *queerer* than that.

One writer who picked up that sense of radical queerness from A. Merritt and attempted to express it in terms of the new scientific universe was Jack Williamson. Williamson, who began his career young, and who would still be writing SF more than sixty years later, was one of the earliest full-time professional writers of science fiction. Such was his adaptability, his enthusiasm, and his fertility of imagination that he became the one writer of the day who was acceptable to every SF magazine and every editor, selling as readily to *Weird Tales* as to Hugo Gernsback or the Tremaine *Astounding*.

Jack Williamson was the last of the turn-of-the-century backwoods children who became the pioneers of Twentieth Century science fiction. He was born in Bisbee, Arizona Territory, on April 29, 1908, and he spent his first years on the Bitch-Wolf Ranch in the mountains of Sonora, Mexico. He has said, "Life there was still nearly at a Stone Age level." At the age of seven, as a refugee from revolution in Mexico, Jack moved with his family from Texas to the sandhills of New Mexico, traveling in a covered wagon.

Williamson was a loner, a reader and dreamer who only discovered science fiction belatedly. After an acquaintance showed him the November 1926 issue of the Gernsback *Amazing*, he sent away for a free copy, answering a promotional ad in a farm paper.

The magazine that he would receive was the March 1927 *Amazing Stories*. It contained a treasure trove of reprints: the usual short story by H. G. Wells, a portion of *The Land That Time Forgot* by Edgar Rice Burroughs, and, best of all, A. Merritt's second story, "The People of the Pit."

Williamson was instantly hooked. And it was Merritt who most intrigued and impressed him, particularly with *The Moon Pool*, serialized in *Amazing* in the summer of 1927.

Very soon, Williamson would be led to try to write science fiction himself. Like many beginners, his first attempted steps were in other people's shoes. First, Williamson won a Gernsback editorial contest by successfully echoing Gernsback's own standard line. His guest editorial, "Scientifiction, Searchlight of Science," appeared in the Fall 1928 issue of *Amazing Stories Quarterly*. Then, a few months later, when Williamson was still just 20, his first story, "The Metal Man"—modeled on "The People of the Pit"—would be featured on the cover of the December 1928 *Amazing Stories*.

But Williamson was more than a mere parrot. In his guest editorial, he did manage to reach beyond the limitations of Hugo Gernsback toward a new kind of science fiction that did not yet exist, a science fiction that he himself would help to invent. He wrote:

> Here is the picture, if we can but see it. A universe ruled by the human mind. A new Golden Age of fair cities, of new laws and new machines, of human capabilities undreamed of, of a civilization that has conquered matter and Nature, distance and time, disease and death. A glorious picture of an empire that lies away past a million flaming suns until it reaches the black infinity of unknown space, and extends beyond.

In these words, we can hear a reiteration of old dreams of scientific utopia, and also perceive a foreshadowing of stories of galactic empire. Not to mention catch one more intimation of a mentalism that might be a replacement for *spirit*.

In 1930, after two years of study at West Texas State College, Williamson dropped out of school to write full time. With the aid of an older writer, Dr. Miles J. Breuer, whom he visited in Lincoln, Nebraska, he learned to discipline his Merritt-influenced purple prose and his somewhat slapdash imagination. And gradually, Williamson began to sound more original notes.

In the February 1932 *Wonder Stories*, he published "The Moon Era," an alien exploration story notable for its presentation of a thoroughly strange but warm and friendly alien being, "the Mother."

And it was Williamson who wrote "Born of the Sun," an audacious thought-variant story in the March 1934 issue of the Tremaine *Astounding* in which the Earth is a giant egg that hatches out into a luminescent, multicolored space-bird. Though most of mankind is killed in this great cosmic disaster, a few men are freed to roam and conquer space. At the conclusion, they look out their spaceship window at the stars and declare, "The new, free race will be greater than the old."

Jack Williamson was also the author of the single most popular SF novel serialized during the Thirties—*The Legion of Space* (*Astounding*, Aug-Sep 1934). In this bold synthesis of wildly disparate elements, young Williamson at last came close to his goal of not merely copying A. Merritt, but of matching Merritt's wide-ranging sense of fundamental mystery in the new emerging terms of science fiction.

In *The Legion of Space*, Earth in the Thirtieth Century has come under attack by an alien race called the Medusae, cold, emotionless intelligences "more like machines than men." With the aid of a human traitor, the aliens have kidnapped a human girl, Aladoree, the custodian of the mysterious power of AKKA, and carried her off to the stars. Four discredited but devoted Legionnaires of Space— patterned after the Three Musketeers and Falstaff—follow in the stolen ship *Purple Dream*. They hide their ship in the sea, slog through the jungles of an alien planet, enter the mysterious black metal city of the Medusae, and rescue Aladoree.

But as they escape in their spaceship, they are subjected to the terrible red gas that is the chief weapon of the Medusae. Aladoree turns green and falls into a coma, while John Star, leader of the party of Legionnaires, is thrown into a futile state of mind in which the meaningless death of mankind at the hands of the aliens seems truly funny: "What a cosmic joke!"

But, like a true hero of the new science fiction, John Star shakes off this state of doubt. And Aladoree, back home on Earth, responds

to John Star's loving pleas and comes back to consciousness in time
to turn the power of AKKA into a mighty weapon.

It does not look like much:

> Two little metal plates, perforated, so that one could sight through
> their centers. A wire helix between them, connecting them. And a little
> cylinder of iron. One of the plates and the little iron rod were set to
> slide in grooves, so that they could be adjusted with small screws. A
> rough key—perhaps to close a circuit through the rear plate, though
> there was no apparent source of current. That was all.

But this seeming child's toy is enough to utterly destroy the
Moon, and with it the invading force of Medusae.

In *The Legion of Space*, we can see a synthesis of ancient myth,
fairytales, romantic novels, stories of alien invasion, space opera,
the story of alien exploration, the lost race story and the epic of
super-science. And a wonderful proliferation of marvels.

H.G. Wells would not have approved. We may say this because
in 1934—the very year in which Williamson's story was serialized—
Wells published a highly revealing preface to *Seven Famous Novels*,
the American version of a collection of his great early scientific
romances. In all of the most innovative and exploratory pulp SF
stories of 1934—"Colossus," "Born of the Sun," *The Legion of
Space*, *Skylark of Valeron*, or *The Mightiest Machine*—wonder
may have been heaped upon wonder. But meantime, in his preface
to *Seven Famous Novels*, H.G. Wells was vainly protesting that the
number of marvels in any SF story should properly be limited to
one:

> Anyone can invent human beings inside out or worlds like dumbbells
> or gravitation that repels. The thing that makes such imaginations inter-
> esting is their translation into commonplace terms and a rigid exclusion
> of other marvels from the story. ... Nothing remains interesting where
> anything can happen. ... Any *extra* fantasy outside the cardinal assump-
> tion immediately gives a touch of irresponsible silliness to the invention.

Wells might have a point if SF were only stories of the manifestation of super-science within the confines of the Village. But he
must be wrong where stories of the World Beyond the Hill are
concerned. It is only by the multitude of wonders encountered that
we can ever know that we have entered a realm of transcendence.

What Wells says cannot even account for the underground wonderland of Verne's *Journey to the Centre of the Earth*, let alone for
The First Men in the Moon, with its anti-gravity metal, its marvelous

lunar landscape, its antlike lunar society, and its Big Brain lunar overlord. And it doesn't begin to come to terms with the burgeoning new science fiction of the American pulps.

It was not merely that the new epics of super-science, stories of alien exploration and space operas accepted the wider universe instead of fearing it. Nor that there had been a fundamental switch in primary point of view from the Village to the World Beyond the Hill. In the pulp science fiction stories of the Thirties, the wider universe itself underwent a *quickening* that can only be compared to the sudden increase in the power of super-science at the beginning of the Age of Technology. The wider universe was suddenly both more plausible *and* more mysterious than it had ever previously been imagined.

We can see both an increase in plausibility and a heightened strangeness on display in the best-loved SF short story of the Thirties, the highly influential "A Martian Odyssey" (*Wonder Stories*, July 1934), by Stanley Weinbaum.

Weinbaum, born in Louisville in 1902 and raised in Milwaukee, was the forerunner of a new breed of SF writer who would only become common in the Forties and Fifties—the slick, bright young urbanite. Clever as he was, however, Weinbaum was neither happy nor successful in life. He was a Jew in early Twentieth Century mid-America—in that time and place, a natural outsider—who was burdened with unfulfilled longings for social acceptance, glamour and fame.

Weinbaum was Hollywood-struck. The promises of Hollywood were the product of men not unlike Weinbaum—and Weinbaum desired all that was promised by Hollywood. He dreamed Hollywood dreams.

He earned a bachelor's degree in chemical engineering in 1922, but rather than working as a chemical engineer, Weinbaum spent the Twenties managing movie palaces. As his ticket to the big time, Weinbaum attempted to write popular fiction. But the best he was able to do was to place a society romance, *The Lady Dances*, in newspaper syndication under the pseudonym Marge Stanley.

Weinbaum was a longtime fan of SF. He had read Poe, Verne, Wells, Burroughs, and the utopian writers, and he had picked up *Amazing Stories* from the first issue. But his own attempted science fiction novels, *The Mad Brain* and *The New Adam*, were old-fashioned movie-minded variations on the Jekyll-and-Hyde theme, and went unpublished.

As he read the science fiction magazines of the early Thirties, Weinbaum must have felt provoked by the stupidity and simple-mindedness of stories about idyllic planets and fairytale space princesses who recognize the hero's valor and virtue at first glance. His scientific training told him that the universe was odder and less comprehensible than this. His own continuing lack of success in the pursuit of his dreams may have suggested that victories come as much through chance as from displays of right-minded effort. And his ego surely whispered to him that his own unpublished writings were far superior to tripe like this.

So science fiction readers wanted stories of Mars, did they? Very well, then, he would give them a Mars to remember.

The story that Weinbaum produced was "A Martian Odyssey"— the tale of the first human expedition to land on another planet. This thoroughly bizarre piece of fiction was unlike anything previously published in the SF magazines. It was at one and the same time a good-hearted spoof, a surreal movie cartoon, an expression of cynicism and dismay, and an exercise in personal wish-fulfillment.

One example of this wish-fulfillment at work is the main character of "A Martian Odyssey." Dick Jarvis is the professional chemist that Weinbaum might have been. And his girlfriend back home on Earth is the famous vision entertainer, Fancy Long.

At the outset of the story, Jarvis, who has been off on a lone scouting trip, has just been rescued after having been missing for ten days. His fellows are gathered close in the cabin of their spaceship, all eager to hear of his adventures.

This will turn out to be a very queer tale indeed, so to draw the reader in and gain his confidence, Weinbaum employs every device he knows to ensure that "A Martian Odyssey" appears plausible. One is this circle of attentive listeners. These are not skeptical folk back home in the tidy little Village who must be convinced, as in Wells's *The Time Machine*. These are Jarvis's companions in this strange world—ready to serve as confirming witnesses for portions of his story.

Weinbaum adds further immediate plausibility with a trick taken from the futuristic utopian story—the setting of his narrative in a historical context. It is a well-known past event that we are asked to contemplate:

> Dick Jarvis was chemist of the famous crew, the *Ares* expedition, first human beings to set foot on the mysterious neighbor of the earth, the planet Mars. This, of course, was in the old days, less than twenty years after the mad American Doheny perfected the atomic blast at the cost of his life, and only a decade after the equally mad Cardoza rode on it to the moon. They were true pioneers, these four of the *Ares*. Except for a half-dozen moon expeditions and the ill-fated de Lancey flight aimed at the seductive orb of Venus, they were the first men to feel other gravity than earth's....

What makes this buildup so effective is not just its historical certitude, but its tone of breezy familiarity. Who could possibly doubt it? And take notice that at the same moment we are accepting these offhand historical references, we are also accepting the impetuosity and imbalance of early space travelers and the mystery of Mars.

But there is more. In the opening pages of "A Martian Odyssey," Weinbaum deliberately deconstructs familiar romantic expectations of Mars derived from reading Edgar Rice Burroughs and space opera. The Mars he presents has no red-skinned, egg-laying Martian princesses or exotic dying cities. Instead it is given as a prosaic place—a gray plain, a flat and desolate landscape. The air here is thin and cold, and Jarvis has developed a badly frost-bitten nose from exposure.

And, in one last ploy adapted from the hoaxes of Edgar Allan Poe, Weinbaum fills the early pages of his story with fact. In particular, with calculation after calculation of distance and time and weight:

"'Weighed about two hundred and fifty pounds earth-weight, which is eighty-five here. Then, besides, my own personal two hundred and ten pounds is only seventy on Mars, so, tank and all, I grossed a hundred and fifty-five, or fifty-five pounds less than my everyday earth-weight.'"

Taken together, all of this amounts to a much heavier freighting of plausibility than pulp science fiction was used to carrying. And the result was that "A Martian Odyssey" appeared far more real to its readers than previous interplanetary SF.

At the same time, however, in the tradition of Poe, the narrative of "A Martian Odyssey" was jokey and quirky and not at all to be relied upon. Two of the crew members talk in music-hall foreign accents and comically misinterpret much of what is said. And one of them even bears the humorous name Putz—like Poe's Rubadub or Von Underduk.

And the account that Jarvis gives is nothing less than an old-time marvelous journey transplanted to Mars. A real whopper of a traveler's tale:

Jarvis says that while walking back from his crashed scoutship to rejoin the expedition, he came across an ostrich-like creature on the banks of a Martian canal, struggling to free itself from the grip of a black tentacled dream-beast, a projector of delusions. He shot the monster with his automatic, and he and the birdlike Martian became fast friends.

Tweel the Martian—admired by the likes of H.P. Lovecraft for being so strange yet sympathetic—is probably the best remembered element of "A Martian Odyssey." He thinks and acts in a manner totally peculiar. He travels by making prodigious leaps through the air and then landing on the point of his beak. But although Tweel is so different that he and Jarvis can hardly communicate, he is not hostile. The two have a natural affinity:

"'Our minds were alien to each other. And yet—we *liked* each other!'"

Traveling on together, these two unlikely companions encounter a series of mysteries. And all of them involve strange Martian creatures.

First, they stumble across an age-old exercise in futility. This is a half-million-year-long trail of larger and larger empty pyramids built by a creature that does nothing but shit bricks, erect structures around itself, and then move on. Jarvis says:

"That queer creature! Do you picture it? Blind, deaf, nerveless, brainless— just a mechanism, and yet—immortal! Bound to go on making bricks, building pyramids, as long as silicon and oxygen exist, and even afterwards it'll just stop. It won't be dead. If the accidents of a million years bring it its food again, there it'll be, ready to run again, while brains and civilizations are part of the past."

Then they have a second encounter with a dream-beast. This time it is Jarvis who is subjected to the power of one of the black tentacled monsters. He is dazzled by an alluring vision of Fancy Long, his video star girlfriend. And it is Tweel who saves him by shooting the dream-beast with a steam-powered glass pistol.

Finally, the two enter a mud-heap city that belongs to odd little barrel-shaped beasts who rush around shoving pushcarts full of rubbish and accomplishing nothing. At the heart of their anthill, there is a great machine. The barrel beasts empty their pushcarts here and then throw themselves under the wheel of the great machine to be ground to pieces.

On a pedestal that stands beside this strange machine, Jarvis finds a fluorescent crystal egg. This proves to have the property of destroying diseased tissue while leaving healthy tissue unharmed. It cures a wart on Jarvis's hand and soothes his frost-bitten nose.

Just then, however, the barrel beasts attack Tweel and Jarvis while chanting "'We are v-r-r-riends! Ouch!'" over and over. The two must make a run for it. In the nick of time, Putz the engineer comes along to rescue Jarvis and carry him back to the spaceship, while Tweel escapes, bounding away to safety on his beak.

As proof of this story, Jarvis displays to his friends the cause of the fight with the barrel beasts. It is the wonderful fluorescent crystal—which the captain of the *Ares* expedition has just suggested "'might be the cancer cure they've been hunting for a century and a half.'"

And this was another example of wish-fulfillment. Only eighteen months after the publication of "A Martian Odyssey," Stanley Weinbaum would be dead from throat cancer.

But the strangest thing of all is that "A Martian Odyssey" proved to be the great success that had always previously eluded Weinbaum. Whatever Weinbaum may have intended this surreal series of encounters with the alien, the delusory, the futile and the incomprehensible to mean, it was interpreted by the SF audience as a wonderful new sort of science fiction.

Readers delighted in its realism, its breezy charm and screwball humor, its glamour, and its bizarre creatures. Above all, they appreciated the eccentric but lovable Tweel. "A Martian Odyssey" was the best-liked piece of fiction ever published in *Wonder Stories.*

The underlying darkness of the story, its conservatism, and its futilitarian philosophy went completely unnoticed. All that the SF audience of the Thirties was prepared to see was that "A Martian Odyssey" was faster and funnier, more plausible and yet more mysterious than other science fiction.

"A Martian Odyssey" was immensely influential. Its virtues were copied over and over, and refined both by Weinbaum himself and by other writers, including E. E. Smith. This story would set new standards for both detail and inventiveness in fiction about other planets.

But it was not the dimension of space alone that took on heightened definition and greater mystery during the early Thirties—as in almost all of the stories we have been considering thus far. It was every dimension of the scientific multiverse.

Just as there was a quickening of space, so was there a parallel quickening of time. Formerly thought of as static and inert, time now began to pulse and shimmer and assume a dynamic quality it had never had before.

We can see this happening in the very first piece of fiction selected by F. Orlin Tremaine as a thought-variant, Nat Schachner's time travel story, "Ancestral Voices" (*Astounding*, Dec 1933). In earlier stories of travel through time, like Wells's *The Time Machine,* time was fixed. What had happened, would happen. The coming and going of the traveler had only obvious first-order consequences. But in Schachner's story, a time traveler to the year 452 A.D. kills a Hun in a fight—and the result is to cause his own disappearance plus the complete elimination of 50,000 more people from our time.

The dimension of time had now suddenly become fluid and subject to alteration. Messing with the past might change the present. Decisions made in the present might determine the nature of the future. Writers began to play around with the paradoxical possibilities inherent in interference with the course of time.

But also in the SF of the last decade of the Age of Technology, new definition and structure were projected onto time. A larger and more inclusive history was invented for mankind that carried men up from the caves and out to the stars. We can see this new consensus history in the making in Olaf Stapledon's *Last and First Men*, in Edmond Hamilton's Interstellar Patrol stories, and in E. E. Smith's Lensman series. But it is also visible in such things as the easy historical detailing thrown off in a short story like "A Martian Odyssey."

And there was enough disagreement among the historians and sufficient gaps in the account that almost anything might still be imagined to happen. Writers in *Weird Tales* even invented a new genre—sword-and-sorcery—that preserved magic, the occult, and the materials of the lost race story by removing them to remote moments in time. Clark Ashton Smith at times wrote of a magic-haunted dying Earth—a flat Earth—under the red sun of the far future. And, in his Conan stories (1932-36), Robert E. Howard, a Texan, recounted the adventures of a vigorous young barbarian in a world of black magic and sorcery located between the fall of Atlantis and the rise of known history.

Among the most intriguing and fruitful speculations on time published in the SF of the Thirties were the ideas presented by Jack Williamson in another romantic adventure, *The Legion of Time* (*Astounding*, May-July 1938). In this short novel, there are "two conflicting possible worlds of futurity"--the utopian city of Jonbar, which may lead to the further perfection and glory of man, and the black city of Gyronchi, which spells the way to man's dehumanization and extinction. Which of the two comes into permanent existence will ultimately depend on whether a 12-year-old Ozark country boy in 1921 pauses to pick up a rusty magnet or a stone.

The beautiful red-haired Lethonee, spokeswoman for Jonbar and for the even more glorious New Jonbar that lies beyond it, explains to Williamson's hero, Denny Lanning:

> "The world is a long corridor, from the beginning of existence to the end. Events are groups in a sculptured frieze that runs endlessly along the walls. And time is a lantern carried steadily through the hall, to illuminate the groups one by one. It is the light of awareness, the subjective reality of consciousness.
>
> "Again and again the corridor branches, for it is the museum of all that is possible. The bearer of the lantern may take one turning, or another. And always, many halls that might have been illuminated with reality are left forever in the dark."

It remains an open question whether Lethonee and Jonbar will prevail—or the blonde and malevolent Sorainya, ruler of the slave legions of the city of Gyronchi. But if one of these two comes into existence, the other will not.

The balance between these two possible futures has been disturbed by the temporal probings of Denny Lanning's one-time Harvard roommate, the mathematician and inventor Wil McLan. In his book *Probability and Determination*, McLan writes:

> "Probability, in the unfolding future, must be substituted for determination. The elementary particles of the old physics may be retained, in the new continuum of five dimensions. But any consideration of this hyper-space-time continuum must take note of a conflicting infinitude of possible worlds, only one of which, at the intersection of their geodesics with the advancing plane of the present, can ever claim physical reality."

After many adventures, much effort and suffering, Wil McLan, Denny Lanning, and the brave companions of the Legion of Time manage to retrieve the crucial rusty magnet from the possession of Sorainya, who has stolen it. They replace it in the path of John Barr, the Ozark country boy in 1921, and he picks it up.

But the result of all their interference with time is that it is neither Jonbar nor Gyronchi that comes into permanent existence, but rather a blending of the two. This state of neither utopia nor extinction is symbolized by Lanning receiving the love of a girl who is a fusion of Lethonee and Sorainya.

In pulp science fiction and fantasy stories of the Thirties, dimensionality itself became interconnected in wholly new ways. C. L. Moore wrote a series of stories in *Weird Tales* about Jirel of Joiry, a warrior maid in a medieval world that is not necessarily our own past, who has adventures in a number of different realms.

In the third of these stories, "Jirel Meets Magic" (*Weird Tales*, July 1935), Jirel finds herself in a hall belonging to the sorceress Jarisme. The hall is filled with doors. And each door opens into a different time or place. Jirel thinks:

> It must be from here that Jarisme by her magical knowledge journeyed into other lands and times and worlds through the doors that opened between her domain and those strange, outland places. Perhaps she had sorceror friends there, and paid them visits and brought back greater knowledge, stepping from world to world, from century to century, through her enchanted doorways.

In yet another story of the period, "Sidewise in Time" (*Astounding*, June 1934)—a thought-variant by old pro Murray Leinster, whose first SF story had appeared in *Argosy* in 1919—dimensionality comes all unhinged. In this novelet a professor of mathematics says:

> "We talk of three dimensions and one present and one future. There is a theoretic necessity—a mathematical necessity—for assuming more than one future. There are an indefinite number of possible futures, any one of which we would encounter if we took the proper 'forks' in time."

But it is not merely a number of possible futures that are given to exist in "Sidewise in Time," but any number of possible pasts and alternate presents. A variety of worlds of possibility exist, of which ours is only one. And in a cosmic disaster—a time-quake—a scrambling together of all these worlds takes place. Until things settle back down to something like normal, contemporary Virginians find themselves co-existing with Chinese colonists of America, Confederates, wild Indians, Roman legionaries, Vikings, and even dinosaurs.

In these American SF stories of the Thirties, former notions of stability and certainty were gradually abandoned in keeping with the new ideas of quantum physics. In Williamson's *The Legion of Time*, mathematician Wil McLan puts it like this:

> "Certainty is abolished. Let a man stand on a concrete floor. It is no longer certain that he will not fall through it. For he is sustained only by the continual reaction of atomic forces, and they are governed by probability alone.
>
> "It is merely a very excellent statistical probability that keeps the man from radiating heat until his body is frozen solid, or absorbing it until he bursts into flame, or flying upward into space in defiance of Newtonian gravitation, or dissolving into a cloud of molecular particles.
>
> "Mere probability is all we have left."

It is this replacement of certainty by probability that is the key to all of the burgeoning of dimension that occurred in the SF of the Thirties. There was no longer to be merely one single Future in which the inevitable decline and fall of man was absolutely mandated. Rather, humanity was now free to choose among a variety of possibilities.

This was a breathtaking and wonderful realization, but also a frightening and demoralizing responsibility. This is shown in another Stanley Weinbaum story, "The Lotus Eaters" (*Astounding*, Apr 1935).

In this story, Ham and Pat Hammond, two venturers on the dark side of Venus, encounter a mobile, warm-blooded sentient plant, whom they dub Oscar. Oscar is a deep philosophical thinker, an able extrapolator.

He says: "I start with one fact and I reason from it. I build a picture of the universe. I start with another fact. I reason from it. I find that the universe I picture is the same as the first. I know that the picture is true."

Oscar is a perfect informational mirror. He will answer any question for Ham and Pat—but only in the words they are able to provide him with. Pat asks:

"Oscar, I have the words time and space and matter and law and cause. Tell me the ultimate law of the universe?"

"It is the law of—" Silence.

"Conservation of energy or matter? Gravitation?"

"No."

"Of—life?"

"No. Life is of no importance."

"There's a chance," said Ham tensely, "that there is no word!"

"Yes," clicked Oscar. "It is the law of chance. These other words are different sides of the law of chance."

Oddly enough, however, in this universe that is ruled by chance, Oscar's own fate is still completely determined: Like the rest of his kind, he will be eaten in due course by a Venusian triops. Very soon, these philosophical plants will become extinct. And it really doesn't matter much to them.

Pat tells Ham that this is the difference between humanity and Oscar's kind: "An animal has will, a plant hasn't. Do you see now? Oscar has all the magnificent intelligence of a god, but he hasn't the will of a worm."

Without some exercise of *will*, a universe of chance must prove as inevitably deadly as the old absolutely determined universe. But to what end should human will be applied? It appeared that if mankind was not to succumb numbly to a storm of random buffets, like Oscar and his kind or the doomed Eighteenth Men of Neptune, then man must turn all of his science and power to the task of making himself master of the laws of chance.

The one writer of the Thirties to whom this was most evident was John W. Campbell, Jr. Campbell approached science fiction as though it were a form of theoretical science. During the decade, in stories that were deliberate thought experiments, he sought to work out answers to the continuing dilemmas of the Age of Technology— the threat of the vast unknown universe, the dangers offered by hostile superior aliens, and the prospect of inevitable human decline—

in terms suggested by the radical new science of the Twentieth Century and by the expansive new science fiction of Edmond Hamilton and E.E. Smith.

John Wood Campbell, Jr. was born in Newark, New Jersey on June 8, 1910. His father was a science-minded authoritarian. His mother was emotionally manipulative. Their influence bent John Campbell into a compulsive doubter and disputer, just the youngster to deliberately attempt to take apart the givens of Technological Age science fiction and then reassemble them in a new pattern.

Campbell's father, John, Sr., worked as an engineer for Bell Telephone. He was a Vermont Yankee, a Scot, a Victorian, and a Man of Science—a cool, remote man who prided himself on his complete objectivity in all matters as he laid down the law for his family.

Very early, young John lit upon science as an activity that his father would not disapprove of and reject. One of his continuing fascinations became the new physics and astronomy as expounded by Arthur Eddington and James Jeans. He turned into an able scientific tinkerer and experimenter—except for one occasion as a teenager when he blew up his basement chem lab.

Campbell also did his best to overset his father's rule by developing a superior command of fact and facility at argumentation. Campbell would become so successful at this by the time he reached his teens that all through the rest of his life, his major mode of relating to other people would be to attempt to draw them into argument.

It may be understandable that living in such a household, Campbell's mother should rely on playing upon the emotions that her husband habitually denied as her most effective means of getting her own way. But greatly complicating this tendency toward emotional gamesmanship was the fact that Dorothy Campbell was one of a set of identical twins so alike that not even her own family could tell them apart. And never would she be more sweet and affectionate to her son than in the presence of her childless twin—who retaliated by snubbing and rejecting the boy. When he approached what appeared to be his mother, young John could never be certain what his reception would be.

John W. Campbell, Jr. grew up a doubter of appearances and a rebel against orthodoxy, always ready to stand up in class and challenge the pronouncements of a teacher. Not surprisingly, his grades were erratic. He failed to graduate from the prep school he was sent to, and his lack of enthusiasm for the required study of German caused him to flunk out of M.I.T. in his junior year. He completed his degree at Duke University in North Carolina in 1932.

Campbell was a longtime reader of SF. As a boy in the Teens, he had delighted in the books of Edgar Rice Burroughs. He bought *Argosy* and *Weird Tales* for their science fiction stories, and he snatched up the very first issue of *Amazing Stories* when it appeared on the newsstand. The climax of his SF reading was that wonderful moment in 1928 that saw "Crashing Suns" and *The Skylark of Space* published just as Campbell was preparing to set off for college.

The element in Campbell that chafed against all limits and restrictions responded to these radical new stories. He instantly adopted their expansiveness and power as his own personal means of liberation. Thus it came to be that at the very same time that Campbell the college student was failing in German and only barely squeaking by in his English classes, John W. Campbell, Jr., the whiz-kid science fiction writer, was engaged in emulating his mentors Hamilton and Smith, mastering the universe of his imagination with epics of super-science like *The Black Star Passes* (*Amazing Stories Quarterly*, Fall 1930) and *Islands of Space* (*Amazing Stories Quarterly*, Spring 1931).

These early stories expressed Campbell's belief in the power of human-directed science. In his epics, men employing super-science were enabled to travel from star to star, galaxy to galaxy, and dimension to dimension. They turned aside the threat of ancient alien beings, dominated and directed lesser aliens, explored the cosmos, fought great battles in space, and exploded planets like rotten tomatoes.

By the conclusion of *Invaders from the Infinite* (*Amazing Stories Quarterly*, Spring-Summer 1932), Campbell's bold inventors had come to command the power of gods. As one of them says:

"'Man can do what was never before possible. From the nothingness of Space he can make anything. Man alone in this space is Creator and Destroyer.'"

But there was something more to Campbell's early super-scientific big bang stories than the mere display of overwhelming material power by men of overwhelming intellectual brawn. To a very real extent, his models, the expansive stories of Smith and Hamilton, were expressions of pure faith that did not deal with the limits of the Age of Technology so much as simply overleap them. John W. Campbell could not rest content with that. He had to test those limits for himself.

And so, even in a story like *The Black Star Passes*, there is the central suggestion that cultural decline need not be final and permanent. In this story, decadent aliens attempt to trade their dead star for ours, and are repulsed by Campbell's heroes. But their contact with humanity is still enough to rouse these beings from their ancient lethargy and give them the resolve to capture a new sun yet: "They had fought, and lost, but they had gained a spirit of adventure that had been dormant for millions of years."

In *Invaders from the Infinite*, there is the implication that science may not be the ultimate power. When Campbell's inventors name their mightiest spaceship, they do not call it *Science*. Rather, they dub it *Thought*:

> "The swiftest thing that ever was, *thought!* The most irresistible thing, *thought*, for nothing can stop its progress. The most destructive thing, *thought*. Thought, the greatest constructor, the greatest destroyer, the product of mind, and producer of powers, the greatest of powers. Thought is controlled by the mind. Let us call it *Thought*."

And in the last of Campbell's epics of super-science, *The Mightiest Machine* (*Astounding*, Dec 1934-Apr 1935), there is the contention that even though physical limits may exist, ways may also exist to bypass these limits:

> "Here's an illustration of the case. Take that piece of wire there—a piece of copper. I can truly and safely say that a wire as thin as the lead of a pencil can't be made the shaft of a machine carrying ten thousand horse power twenty miles. Impossible! But that doesn't mean that ten thousand electric horse power can't be conducted through it. As a driving shaft, as direct mechanical energy in other words, it would be impossible. As a conductor for a second-hand energy, it is possible."

During his college days, Campbell was exposed to several radical new lines of scientific inquiry that would become a central part of his thinking. As a student at M.I.T., he attracted the friendship of Professor Norbert Wiener, who would be the founder of the science of cybernetics, with whom he argued problems of intelligent machines. And while he was at Duke University, he became interested in the pioneering efforts of Dr. J.B. Rhine of Duke to place the study of parapsychological phenomena, formerly thought of as manifestations of spirit, on a firm scientific foundation—even serving as a subject in ESP experiments.

When Campbell graduated from college in the direst moment of the Great Depression, it soon became apparent that he could not make a living writing science fiction. So he took whatever jobs were available. He sold cars. He sold exhaust fans. He sold gas heaters. He worked in the research department of Mack Truck. He worked for an instrument manufacturer. And for six months he was a technical writer and editor for a New Jersey chemical company.

Meanwhile Campbell the science fiction writer had begun to try out a more thoughtful line of story than he had ever written previously—stories that directly addressed the most fundamental problems of Technological Age SF.

The first transitional example of this was "The Last Evolution" (*Amazing*, Aug 1932). This short story contained all the offhand invention of machines and weapons that Campbell's readers had come to expect from him—zap topping zap. But in its basic orientation, "The Last Evolution" was completely different from Campbell's usual thing. Rather than picturing mankind as the natural boss of the universe, master of Thought, and all-powerful Creator and Destroyer, this story envisioned the decline and extinction of humanity.

In "The Last Evolution," man in the year 2538 is imagined living in comfort on the labor of his machines. But then alien invaders—"the Outsiders"—swoop down from the stars. They lightly turn aside the defenses of Earth, and begin to scour the planet with a deadly green ray that annihilates all life.

It is too late for humanity. One of the two remaining human scientists speaks prophetically:

> "The end of man. ... But not the end of evolution. The children of man still live—the machines will go on. Not of man's flesh, but of a better flesh, a flesh that knows no sickness, and no decay, a flesh that spends no thousands of years in advancing a step in its full evolution, but overnight leaps ahead to new heights."

And new superior machines do appear in response to the attacks of the Outsiders. But when the power of the most advanced of these machines, F-2, still proves insufficient to defeat the invaders, an even higher evolution is demanded. F-2 produces an entity of "pure force and pure intelligence."

This glowing golden sphere still acknowledges itself an heir of man. It demonstrates its overwhelming superiority to the aliens by turning their flagship inside out and back again without harm. And it sends the Outsiders scooting back home, tails between their legs.

At the conclusion, the narrator of the story reveals himself to be none other than F-2. He is now the last surviving metal machine, living in a world populated by force-intelligences 125,000 years hence, and directing his story back through time for our edification.

Campbell elaborated upon this vision in two further experimental stories, "Twilight" and "Night," published under the pseudonym Don A. Stuart, a variation upon the maiden name of Campbell's wife, Doña. Taken together, "The Last Evolution," "Twilight,"

and "Night" may be seen as a kind of triptych, a three-part meditation on the destiny of man and the universe, a statement of the worst
possible case.

"Twilight," the first Don A. Stuart story, was written late in 1932.
It was not a conventional story of conflict and response like "The
Last Evolution." Rather, it was a deliberate mood-piece, a melancholy vision of the remote future not unlike the last sad probings
of distant time by Wells's Time Traveller.

The protagonist of "Twilight" is a mysterious hitchhiker picked
up along the roadside. This magnificent wide-browed man in soft
silver clothing identifies himself as a venturer who has traveled
from his own high scientific society of the year 3059 to a future
moment fully seven million years from now. On his return he has
overshot his mark by a trifling amount. In effect, he has made a
slight detour to December 1932 in order to tell his story to an
audience that will really appreciate it.

The venturer says that he found himself near a great city. The
sun seven million years hence is still yellow, not red. But the people
are gone from the city. And still it lives on, oiled and dusted and
kept in good running order by the faithful abandoned machines
of humanity.

In two other great cities, some humans do still survive, but these
are shrunken, lonely Big Brains: "They stand about, little misshapen
men with huge heads."

Once men lived on all the planets of the solar system. Now they
are in decline. They have few children, and they lack all curiosity or
will. Long ago, they committed the error of eradicating all other
earthly life except for a few decorative plants:

> And now this last dwindling group of men still in the system had no
> other life form to make its successor. Always before when one civiliza-
> tion toppled, on its ashes rose a new one. Now there was but one civil-
> ization, and all other races, even other species, were gone save in the
> plants. And man was too far along in his old age to bring intelligence
> and mobility from the plants. Perhaps he could have in his prime.

The venturer does what little he can. He learns the last mournful
and bewildered human songs. And he programs the machines of
man to develop the power of curiosity. Then, with a sigh, he sets
off again back through time.

When it was written, "Twilight" was altogether too strange and
plotless to be published. It was rejected by all the existing science
fiction magazines. Only after the death of the Clayton *Astounding*
and its resurrection by Street & Smith under the editorship of

F. Orlin Tremaine, was this highly different story accepted at last. It appeared in the November 1934 issue, one month before the beginning of the serialization of *The Mightiest Machine.*

Heretofore, Campbell had not been published in *Astounding.* But he was welcome there now. F. Orlin Tremaine perceived something extraordinary in this argument-prone young writer—another person besides himself who understood that science fiction could be an experimental mode of thought. Tremaine did his best to dissuade Campbell from writing further epics of super-science. Instead, he encouraged him to develop a new line of thoughtful and provocative stories for *Astounding* under the Stuart name.

This was an opportunity that Campbell the tester of limits could not resist. *The Mightiest Machine* would be the only story ever published in *Astounding* under Campbell's own name. But "Night" (*Astounding*, Oct 1935)—the last of Campbell's phrasings of the ultimate problem—would be the eighth Don A. Stuart story published in the space of one year.

"Night" was another mood-piece, an extension and completion of "Twilight" in something of the same manner that Olaf Stapledon's *Star Maker* would be an extension and completion of *Last and First Men.* In this story, our witness of things to come is a contemporary experimenter with anti-gravity who is suddenly hurled far into the future. Far, far into the future—120 billion years from now.

Man is gone. The faithful machines of Earth have finally sighed and died. The Sun is a great red cinder that gives no heat. The cosmos has fragmented into pieces and only a handful of stars are to be seen in the sky. The universe is a cooling corpse, and the traveler has been called to view the remains:

"The city had been dead a score of billions of years. The Sun was dead. The Earth was dead. The very atoms were dead. The universe had been dead a billion years. Time himself was dying now, dying with the city and the planet and the universe he had killed."

The traveler seeks some trace of humanity on Neptune, but all he finds are a last few highly evolved machines still carrying on. These glowing golden globes have power and curiosity, but they are lacking in purpose.

Final night is called "the one problem they do not want to solve— the problem they are sure they cannot solve." Long ago, the machines permitted a degenerating humanity to pass from the scene. Now they can see the end of things approaching for them, too, and they welcome surcease.

Even the traveler is ready to lie down and commit suicide... until suddenly he finds himself back in his own time again, being given oxygen by his friends.

"The Last Evolution," "Twilight," and "Night" are extreme
examples of the intermixing of radical and conservative elements
so typical of Thirties SF. In their depiction of the decline and
extinction of man, in their presentation of a fixed and unalterable
framework of time, and in their relentless Earth-centeredness,
these stories were highly old-fashioned. At the same time, however,
in their bold experimentalism as science fiction, in their vision of the
machine as man's favored child, and most of all, in their exponential
widening of scale from thousands to millions to billions of years,
these stories were distinctly new.

These three central stories, with their restatement and updating
of themes familiar from H.G. Wells, Bertrand Russell and Olaf
Stapledon, set forth the major problems that John W. Campbell
would attempt to resolve during the Thirties. His primary (though
by no means only) mode of attack would be under the guise of
Don A. Stuart.

Don A. Stuart was conceived as a professional questioner and
heretic. As Campbell would one day say in introducing a collection
of Stuart stories: "In many of the Don A. Stuart stories, there is the
element of a dirty, underhanded crack at the pretensions of science-
fiction—dressed in the most accepted terms of science-fiction."

As Don A. Stuart, Campbell would write stories about small
scientific observations and inventions that have major unforeseen
consequences, about the burdens of excessive knowledge and freedom,
and about scientists wasting their lives aiming for results they have
already unwittingly achieved. When challenged with the supposed
impossibility of such things, Campbell/Stuart would also attempt a
science fiction love story and a science fiction mystery. But of the
sum total of sixteen Don A. Stuart stories published between the
end of 1934 and the end of 1939, fully half would be concerned
with the interrelated problems of ending human overdependence on
the machine, fighting back from cultural stagnation, and throwing
off the tyranny imposed by superior invading aliens.

In the meantime, Campbell would be involved in two other
significant projects under his own name. By far the more important
of these was the assignment he accepted from F. Orlin Tremaine in
1936 to write a series of articles on the subject of the Solar System.
These appeared in eighteen consecutive issues of *Astounding* from
June 1936 to November 1937.

A Study of the Solar System would prove to have great continuing
influence. By setting forth the known facts about the planets in a
lively and dramatic fashion, Campbell presented science fiction
with a new and higher standard than it had previously felt the
need to observe.

Campbell's essays drew a line in the dirt: These were the true facts—and the facts *must* be respected. No longer would it be possible to write dumb-dumb space opera stories about slave traders trekking through the jungles of Saturn with the beat of native drums throbbing in their ears.

At the same time, however, the verve and fire of Campbell's writing suggested that nothing vital need be lost by this change. Fact, and speculation based on fact, could provide the subject matter for a thousand and one new and better stories.

The other of Campbell's projects under his own name was a first attempt to put this new standard into practice. In a series of five Weinbaum-influenced stories published in the post-Gernsback *Thrilling Wonder*, Campbell presented two human adventurers, Penton and Blake, encountering menacing life forms on different planets of the Solar System and overcoming them through a mastery of known scientific fact.

In actual practice, the Penton and Blake stories were relatively trivial. In the first of the series, "The Brain Stealers of Mars" (*Thrilling Wonder*, Dec 1936), for example, Penton and Blake have the problem of distinguishing each other from a host of Martian imitators. Penton picks the Blake who sneezes and kills all the rest, knowing that the coordination of no less than five hundred sets of muscles is necessary to produce a sneeze, and betting that the Martians can't mimic that. Fortunately, he is right. And Blake distinguishes amongst all the Pentons by challenging them to drink a concentrated dose of tetanus—which he knows the real Penton has been inoculated against.

There were large holes in this story. Why, for instance, would two adventurers on a jaunt to Mars "happen" to have tetanus toxin lying around their laboratory?

But trivial and contrived though it may have been, "The Brain Stealers of Mars" nonetheless did set forth a new and more exacting set of values that would prove central to the creation of modern science fiction. Campbell would demonstrate as much a year and a half later by taking the problem and solutions presented in "The Brain Stealers of Mars" and generalizing upon them. The Don A. Stuart story that resulted, "Who Goes There?" (*Astounding*, Aug 1938), would come to be recognized as a point of departure—the first story of modern science fiction.

Before that moment, however, one more highly significant Don A. Stuart story would see publication—"Forgetfulness" (*Astounding*, June 1937). In this story, Campbell would take the basic materials of "The Last Evolution" and "Twilight" and subject his own work and thought to the Don A. Stuart process. The result, if not exactly modern science fiction, would be a final classic statement of Techno-logical Age SF.

In "Forgetfulness," a colonizing expedition from another star has landed on Earth ten million years in the future. The space travelers discover magnificent crystalline cities and mighty machines beyond their understanding—but all long abandoned.

As in "Twilight," the human descendants of the city builders yet survive. They are not misshapen Big Brains, however, but a tall, lean telepathic folk who live pastoral lives in little domed houses among the trees. When asked about the scientific principles that underlie the cities and the machines, they can only smile apologetically and say that they have forgotten them.

The colonizers are shocked and saddened by this great degenera-tion. All the more so when they come to realize that the departed city builders of Earth were the golden gods of their own legends who long ago brought them the secrets of fire and the bow.

In true imperial style, the colonizers propose to confine the degenerate descendants of the city builders to reservations for their own protection. They themselves will occupy the crystalline cities and rediscover the ancient forgotten knowledge. Instead of this, however, they find themselves instantaneously transferred by the mental power of the Earth people back through space to their home planet—a journey that had taken their own ships six full years to accomplish.

Humanity, it seems, is not degenerate at all. It has simply passed beyond the need for cities and machines:

> "Seun is not a decadent son of the city builders. His people never forgot the dream that built the city. But it was a dream of childhood, and his people were children then. Like a child with his broomstick horse, the mind alone was not enough for thought; the city builders, just as ourselves, needed something of a solid metal and crystal, to make their dreams tangible."

"Forgetfulness" may be seen as a culminating synthesis. In this one story, Campbell interwove the three great problems of the age that he had set out to solve: the problem of human dependence on the machine; the problem of human degeneration; and the problem of alien invasion. And, without firing off a single colored ray or exploding a single planet, Campbell managed to satisfactorily answer all three problems at once.

The way past the traps of dependence, degeneration, and defeat, Campbell now perceived, lay in a grand leap to a higher state of being where such problems were no longer problems. Like his model,

E.E. Smith, Campbell had come to accept the necessity of higher levels of human being and becoming.

In "Forgetfulness," Campbell envisioned no less than four stages of human evolution: first, the step from less-than-man to man, as exemplified by the leap taken by the invaders in that long-ago moment when they were first stimulated with the gift of fire by the golden gods; then the further step from man to scientific man, who as master of the atom and space travel need no longer remember how to chip flint or scrape hides; and finally, the step from scientific man to mental man, who no longer need understand the workings of crystalline cities and mighty machines, but who can accomplish all things by the power of mind alone.

In "Forgetfulness," the chancy wider universe that had haunted the early Twentieth Century was perceived not as hostile and threatening, but as offering mankind every fair chance:

The chance not to degenerate into Big Brain, but to become a higher and finer kind of being—more human, not less.

The chance to use the machine for a time and then put it away. To face the threat of aliens and lightly turn their folly aside. To solve even ultimate problems, if not now, then eventually.

The chance to grow up.

What a promise! In the context of "Forgetfulness," all the overwhelming problems of Western scientific man and Village Earth in the early Twentieth Century suddenly shifted and became merely relative—the growing pains of human infancy.

Very shortly after he came to this new perspective on man's relationship to the universe, John W. Campbell, Jr. was offered his own opportunity for personal evolution.

In the summer of 1937, within a few months of the publication of "Forgetfulness," and with E.E. Smith's first Lensman novel, *Galactic Patrol*, on line and ready to begin serialization in *Astounding*, F. Orlin Tremaine received a promotion at Street & Smith. From being a magazine editor, he became an editor-in-chief, with the responsibility of supervising a number of different magazines. Suddenly, it was necessary to hire a new editor for *Astounding*. And not altogether surprisingly, the man Tremaine selected as his successor was his most reliable and thoughtful writer.

John W. Campbell, Jr. became the editor of *Astounding Stories* beginning with the October 1937 issue. And through changes of title and changes of publisher, he would remain editor of the magazine until his death in 1971.

Universal Principles
of Operation

When young John Campbell, Jr., recently turned 27 years old, was offered a job as a magazine editor late in the summer of 1937, it must have come as a great relief to him. An end, at last, to his state of continuing uncertainty.

Ever since his graduation from college, all through the long, hard, grinding Depression years, Campbell had had to thrash and struggle constantly to stay alive and produce his science-fictional visions and investigations. Living always on the thin edge of nothing, writing when and as he could, but by no means getting everything he wrote published, Campbell had dedicated himself to nothing less than the solution of the great outstanding problems of the age.

And now this was his reward for all his effort and sacrifice—to be offered the editorship of *Astounding Stories*. At last, a regular job that Campbell could stomach. What a splendid opportunity this was for one like him!

Nonetheless, the challenge that Campbell faced was formidable. Street & Smith was the pre-eminent pulp publisher of the period, and *Astounding Stories* was dominant amongst science fiction pulp magazines. The natural assumption of Campbell's new employers was that *Astounding* would remain successful, even in the face of competition in science fiction from other pulp chains who were now buying up the old Gernsback-originated magazines or starting new titles of their own.

But John Campbell's actual editorial experience was mighty slim. He really didn't know the first thing about how to produce a monthly pulp magazine. As of yet, he hadn't even learned how to type.

It was quite true, of course, that Campbell had been selected by F. Orlin Tremaine to be his successor for his questioning turn of mind, and not for his editorial expertise. But the first question that Tremaine's protégé chose to ask—as recalled by Campbell in later years—was nothing less than a revelation of his state of near-total ignorance:

"When I first came to Street & Smith—quite some years ago, now—I asked the editor-in-chief: 'What does an editor do when he doesn't get enough stories to fill the magazine?' He sort of looked at me and said: 'An *editor* does.'"

Campbell was quick to recognize that he had a great deal to master in order to become a man who could fill the pages of *Astounding* with stories each month. The very first thing he set out to do was to teach himself the fundamental mechanics of his new profession.

In these early days of his editorship, one of Campbell's regular visitors was Frederik Pohl, a 17-year-old high school dropout who was attempting to pass himself off as a literary agent, selling his own stories and the SF stories of his friends, mostly fellow young New York City science fiction fans. And Pohl remembers himself as a beneficiary of John Campbell's own learning process.

A visitor to *Astounding Stories* like Pohl would be directed by a secretary to walk through the Street & Smith printing plant, past great strong-scented rolls of pulp paper, through a maze of corridors back to the little office hidden behind more rolls of paper where the editor waited. And John Campbell, a large, sharp-featured man who looked like a bear with glasses, would swivel around in his chair, lean back, and fit a cigarette into his cigarette holder. Then he would toss out his latest provocative notion, or suggest a story idea, or simply begin to lecture.

Pohl remembers Campbell's good writing advice and Campbell's habit of sharpening his arguments on all visitors in advance of writing his monthly editorial. Pohl adds: "He was also a fount of information on the technological infrastructure of publishing: line engraving, halftones, four-color separation, binding machines. ... He was a great teacher. Later I figured out why. He was learning the same things, too, maybe forty-eight hours ahead of me on the track, rehearsing his own learning by teaching it to me."

Pohl attests to the great influence this personal instruction had upon him: "Every word he said I memorized. ... I had never known anyone else who knew about these things, and I learned from him as from Jesus on the Mount." Pohl was a particularly apt pupil, too. Just two years later, when he was still not yet twenty, Pohl would be hired as founding editor of two new SF pulps, *Astonishing Stories* and *Super Science Stories.*

How strange it seems that John Campbell, in these early days of his own ignorance and uncertainty, should spend so much care and attention on a boy like Pohl! Campbell would buy precious few stories from Pohl in his role as agent, and none from Pohl as a writer.

All that he accomplished was to train Pohl to be his own competitor. Why ever did he do that?

The least good answer—though it does have some small measure of truth to it—is that Campbell simply could not help himself. He was a compulsive argufier, and holding forth for an audience was his primary social mode. Even thirty years later, Campbell would still be attracting crowds of respectful teenage boys to listen to his latest heretical notion and chorus, "Whatever you say, Mr. Campbell."

A better answer might be that Campbell got back from Pohl just as much as he gave him. This sharp youngster offered Campbell a highly useful opportunity to practice his craft, to learn and experiment, test and suggest. As Pohl himself half-intimates, Campbell was making an editor out of himself even as he was making an editor out of Pohl.

But the answer that may be closest to the mark is that Campbell conceived of himself as a teacher of science-fictional thinking, taking on all comers and giving each one whatever clues he would accept. What he taught Pohl was what Pohl was ready to learn, which was editing. And it mattered not at all to Campbell that along the way he might be creating a competitor.

It says much about the two men and the nature of their relationship that some twenty-five years after they first met, Campbell was present to hear Pohl deliver a keynote address to the American Astronautical Society. Running into Pohl at the airport afterward, he patted him on the shoulder and said, "Fred, you did real good for science fiction." And Pohl could still blush with embarrassed pleasure at the unexpected compliment.

However, not only was Campbell as a new editor open enough to latent possibility to devote valuable working time to the nurture of bright kids come walking in off the street—Fred Pohl being by no means the only one—but he was ready to solicit advice on science fiction from any quarter in hopes that it might lend him light. Campbell's receptivity to every clue is apparent in the account given by Catherine Crook, a schoolteacher who would soon marry science fiction writer L. Sprague de Camp, of her first visit to Campbell's apartment in New Jersey in the spring of 1939:

> When I first met him, John was ensconced in a lounge-chair with his feet propped up on a hassock. He could not rise for introductions because his lap, the chair arms, and the floor around him were covered with manuscripts. He waved a manuscript at me and said: "Come right in. I want you to read this story and tell me what you think of it."
>
> I protested: "But I don't know anything about science fiction..."
>
> "Splendid," John replied. "That's exactly why I want your reaction."
>
> So I sat on a pale green sofa in a sea-green living room and read story

after story. Every so often, I would look up to see John studying my face. "What made you smile just then?" he would ask. Or: "You look puzzled. Why?"

Once, hoping my remarks would not blight the career of some budding writer, I remember saying: "Well, it took three pages to find out where I was and why I was there."

"Just what I thought myself," he replied. And back the story went for revision.

It would soon become clear, however, that John Campbell had much more in mind than just achieving a technical command of pulp publishing, or tutoring receptive youngsters, or learning to gauge the effect of a story on the ordinary unversed reader. From the very outset, he was determined to become a complete *editor*—not merely a filler of pages with stories, but a setter of new directions.

For a time, at least, F. Orlin Tremaine had been such an editor. But Campbell aimed to pick up the torch—just as he had been challenged to do. He would become a true *editor* and alter both *Astounding Stories* and the face of science fiction.

And so it was that Campbell embarked on a program of systematic change in the magazine. The very first thing that he did was to widen the scope of the letter column, which since the beginning of 1937 had been restricted to scientific discussions. He wanted feedback and reader participation in *Astounding*, and he specifically invited them.

Then Campbell asked for new writers to come forward and contribute. This was a theme he was to sound again and again in the coming months: there was an ongoing open contest at *Astounding*, all comers welcome, with payment and publication as the prize. Step forward and try your skill.

When Campbell did find a new writer, he would point the fact out. And when he could, he would have the new writer contribute stories under one or more pseudonyms as well, and then would proudly point to those "new writers," too.

As early as his fourth issue—the *Astounding* dated January 1938—Campbell began to draw attention to his policy of change. In his editorial, which was titled "Mutation," Campbell asked the question, "Does evolution apply to *Astounding Stories*?" And answered, "Certainly."

As evidence of this, Campbell instituted a new feature in this issue, a regular preview of upcoming things running under the title "In Times to Come." And in both the first installment of this column and in his editorial, Campbell made the promise of significant changes in *Astounding*. Beginning with February, there would be a series of "*Mutant* issues."

Campbell wrote: "In each of the *Mutant* issues that are to come during 1938, the change may seem small in itself, but it will be fundamental. It will help to determine the *direction* that the evolution of *Astounding Stories* and science fiction must take."

The very first such "genuine, fundamentally different and original" mutation that Campbell asked his audience to note was the cover of the February issue of *Astounding*. This was an astronomical painting—a view of the Sun as seen from Mercury—the visual equivalent of Campbell's now concluded series of articles on the Solar System.

Back in 1926, on the first cover of *Amazing Stories*, the beloved Frank R. Paul might include a view of Saturn as background for a picture illustrating Jules Verne's *Off on a Comet*. But that Saturn resembled nothing so much as a brightly striped toy gyroscope. And the foreground of the picture was a band of merry human ice skaters, their attention all on their fun—ignoring the lack of cometary gravity, ignoring the lack of atmosphere, ignoring their precarious cosmic situation.

This *Astounding* cover was different. It placed human figures— tiny and spacesuited—in intimate relationship to the true facts of the wider universe. The implication of this cover picture was that *Astounding* was not idle fancy, but about real human possibility. Here was a place that men might really go, and this is how things would appear to them.

In the course of 1938, Campbell would print no less than three of these cover pictures of men swarming abroad in the Solar System. The third of these—of Jupiter as seen from its moon Ganymede— had an error in it. Campbell did not just admit this—he proclaimed it. He made a game out of it, and challenged readers to imagine themselves in this perspective and catch the glitch.

The next month after the first astronomical painting, Campbell introduced yet another meaningful innovation. Throughout the Thirties, the title of the magazine had flip-flopped back and forth between *Astounding Stories of Super-Science* and plain *Astounding Stories*. Now Campbell altered the title to *Astounding Science-Fiction*. It was Campbell's intention to gradually shift the name of the magazine from *Astounding* (which he didn't much care for, perhaps thinking it imitative of *Amazing*—which, we may remember, it had been) to the generic *Science Fiction*. He would be forestalled when, early in 1939, one of the many new SF pulps then springing up was named *Science Fiction* first.

And still, Campbell had established a point. The first magazine to specifically present itself as *science fiction*—using those words as part of its title—was the Campbell *Astounding*.

Month after month, the changes continued. Another new department was added—"The An Lab"—with ever-more-exacting numerical analyses of reader reaction to the stories in each issue. There were increasingly speculative and far-ranging science articles. And, before the end of 1938, there was a redesign of the magazine's contents page and title.

But what was ultimately the most important change of all was one that was completely unforeseen. In May 1938, Campbell's supervisor, F. Orlin Tremaine, came to a parting of the ways with Street & Smith, leaving the company abruptly. From this moment on, John Campbell would be in complete editorial command of *Astounding* with no superior above him to question his understanding of science fiction or his choice of direction for the magazine.

For the next dozen years—until May of 1950—John W. Campbell, as editor of *Astounding*, would completely dominate American magazine science fiction. He would oversee and orchestrate the shift from science fiction as it had been since 1870 to the new modern science fiction of the Atomic Age. In Campbell's hands, the disparate pieces of Technological Age SF would be regularized and rationalized, unified and codified. Without losing its essential plausible yet mysterious character, science fiction would undergo an alteration. It would become a dynamic new literature with attitudes, ideas and style befitting a new age.

The crucial moment of society-wide transition to the Atomic Age occurred during exactly that period in 1938-39 when John Campbell was taking command of *Astounding* and launching his series of radical changes in the magazine. Just as the beginning of the Age of Technology may be conveniently linked to the Franco-Prussian War of 1870-71—which explicitly demonstrated the latent power of applied science—so the end of the Age of Technology and the inception of the Atomic Age may be effectively reckoned from the splitting of the uranium atom that was achieved by German scientists in 1938 and recognized by the international scientific community early in 1939.

During the coming era, the new irrational and immaterial Twentieth Century high science would pass from merely being speculative theory that might be conveniently ignored to being an undeniable world-altering everyday actuality. At the same time, there would be vast social change. After this pivotal moment of 1938-39, the balance of worldly power would shift ineluctably from the hands of those who were born superior to those clever and competent enough to master the laws of higher science.

Throughout the Age of Technology, Western society had been run for the benefit of a class of special privilege that varied somewhat from country to country, but still might be said to be defined by its money, position, race, religion and breeding. The social favoritism enjoyed by this class of privilege was ultimately rooted in inherited notions of innate superiority based upon gradations of refinement of soul.

Standing in opposition to this accepted scale of relative human value were all of those who believed that with skill, talent and will—and perhaps a necessary smidgen of educational opportunity—a man might make anything of himself. H. G. Wells was living testimony of the possibility of this kind of self-actualization. And when Wells joined the radical Fabian Society at the turn of the century and attempted to redirect its efforts from intellectual debate to social action, or when he wrote semi-autobiographical novels exposing the waste of the brains and talents of the disadvantaged class, or when he produced polemic after polemic to urge that the present incompetent directors of society be replaced by an able and dedicated scientific elite, it was the principle of innate social privilege that was his true object of attack.

After World War I, it seemed far less evident that one soul was born superior to another. In this new climate, the tendency was to justify the continued existence of special privilege by appeals to the survival of the fittest—those currently in power being presumed to be the fittest. But this was a thoroughly dangerous ground of argument, since it left the disadvantaged complete latitude to assert their own fitness by any and every means.

The tension between the advantaged and disadvantaged was only exacerbated by the coming of the Great Depression. Not only was immense pressure brought to bear on the stability and shape of the familiar social order, but the Depression also served to highlight all the continuing inequities, snobberies, barriers and exclusions of a socially stratified society. To many people during the Thirties, the Western world appeared to be hanging in the balance between violent revolt and massive repression.

Even in the United States of America, the most democratic Western nation and the least traumatized by World War I, there were those to whom a radical restructuring of society seemed the only answer. The attractions of this point of view at this particular moment were so great that a bright scuffling Brooklyn kid like Fred Pohl might very well find the Flatbush Young Communist League the natural place to look for music, girls and political direction.

In the event, however, no revolution would prove necessary to bring needed change to the United States. During the Thirties, without extremes of violence or repression, the American social contract was redrawn. And the chief architect of this change was President Franklin Delano Roosevelt, himself a member of the class of privilege.

Using the new medium of radio as his means of reaching out to the nation as a whole, and addressing his audience as "my friends," Roosevelt drew the United States together against the fearsome Depression monster by making a fundamental commitment to alter society so that no one would be left in want and every man would have his fair chance. Roosevelt promised America a social New Deal.

The European response to the economic, social and psychic trials of the Depression was not so inclusive or experimental. Rather than Europe moving on toward increased social equity, the tendency was to try to get back to where it once had been, to reaffirm all its old values and beliefs: racial superiority, national superiority, traditional religion, the old class structure, and the rule of the many by the few. One after another during the Thirties, postwar European experiments in democracy were subverted and overthrown.

The country that was most wedded to the age that was passing was Germany. It was Germany more than any other Western nation that had invented and believed in the top-dog-of-the-era, survival-of-the-fittest, cyclical history mythos of the Age of Technology and done its best to live by it. The beginning of this age of Western technological empire had been signaled by the Prussian victory over France and the foundation of the united German state in 1871. Germany had naturally presumed that it was destined to rule the era.

Instead, Fate had treated Germany unkindly. The Germans had lost their bid for supreme power in the Great War, and afterward they had been humiliated, forced to accept total blame for the disaster. Not only had onerous conditions been imposed upon them, but ever since the war Germany had been kept at a continuing economic, political and military disadvantage by countries that it still despised and believed were its natural inferiors.

Germany's fragile postwar democratic government was caught between extremes of right and left. At last, under the stress of the Depression, at the very time in 1933 that a democratically elected Franklin Roosevelt was taking office in the United States, forces of nationalist and racist reaction were allowed to seize control of Germany.

In January 1933, Adolf Hitler, the Austrian immigrant who headed the right-wing Nazi Party, was asked to serve as Chancellor. Within months of assuming office, by the judicious use of fraud and force, Hitler would make himself dictator of Germany.

Like Roosevelt, Hitler also employed radio as a major means of addressing his country. But where Roosevelt, the patrician turned democrat, opened his arms to all Americans, Hitler, the marginal German, raised his voice to reiterate the old disastrous dreams of innate German specialness. Rather than promises of greater fairness of opportunity, Hitler offered the completion of cyclical history:

If Germany had lost World War I, it was only because it had been betrayed by an international Jewish plot, a conspiracy of the inferior against the superior. But it was not too late—Germany might yet fulfill its appointed destiny.

Germany must purify itself. There must be a ruthless weeding out of the weak, the inferior and the degenerate. Then Germany would be fit to exact its due revenge. The German Master Race would rule the world for a thousand years. *Deutschland über alles!*

In our pivotal year of 1938, Hitler, at the head of a re-armed Germany, made his first warlike moves. In the spring he annexed his native Austria, and then in the fall he occupied a large part of Czechoslovakia—all in the name of the reunification of the German people. Though Britain and France temporized, unable then to nerve themselves to oppose Germany's aggressions, it was clear that another Great War was coming. The only question was when— and that would prove to be September 1939, after Hitler had first occupied the rest of Czechoslovakia and then invaded Poland.

This war that was on its way may be seen as a contest of force and will between the old Technological Age order of born superiority and the new democratic pluralism of the emerging Atomic Age.

The year 1938 was not merely a turning point in science and international power politics. It can also be seen to mark a significant shift in social mood in the United States.

In the breathing space of three years between the beginning of the Atomic Age and the moment in late 1941 when the United States finally became an active participant in the Second World War, a new societal consensus was reached. The confusion, doubt and amorality that had characterized the early Thirties were replaced by a clear-cut sense of direction and purpose. It seemed that the forces of oppression and tyranny were launching attacks everywhere upon tolerance and freedom. And it was imperative that these central values be maintained and defended no matter what the cost.

There was a great rallying around the idea of democratic pluralism— which in the early and middle Thirties had been doubted by both the left and the right. In this new period, it would seem more and more apparent that the true strength and value of American society was that it guaranteed the right of every man, however humble or different he might be, to stand up and demonstrate his own individual knowledge, skill and worth.

With the coming of this era of the ordinary Joe, the popular arts in America took on a legitimacy they had never had before. They concentrated and reflected the essence of this new hour. Suddenly, at the end of the Thirties, there was a creative Golden Age in one medium after another all across the spectrum of popular entertainment, from Hollywood movies and cartoons to swing music to comic books. And though science fiction was only relatively recently established as a form of popular art, it too took part in this creative flowering.

At the time when John Campbell became an editor in 1937, there were still only three SF magazines: *Astounding, Amazing* and *Thrilling Wonder*. But by 1941, no fewer than twenty-one different SF pulp magazines were being published. As never previously, these were boom times for science fiction.

Campbell's *Astounding* was a beneficiary of the boom. In March 1939, Street & Smith would even see fit to launch a companion magazine for *Astounding* under Campbell's editorship, a magazine at first called *Unknown*, and later retitled *Unknown Worlds*.

Judged strictly in terms of circulation figures, Campbell's *Astounding* and *Unknown* were not the most successful SF magazines of the boom period. Campbell did not print stories by the very biggest names of the Technological Age—no new fiction by Edgar Rice Burroughs or reprints of classic A. Merritt stories. And he never sold as many copies as the magazines that did.

But yet, within the microcosm of those concerned with the fortunes of science fiction—the writers and readers and fans—there was a universal recognition of the precedence of *Astounding* and *Unknown* among SF pulp magazines. Other editors were just doing a job as best they were able. John Campbell alone was in active public pursuit of the evolution of science fiction and his own magazine, and able to demonstrate over and over in action what this might mean. Campbell alone was seeking to remake SF in the image of the new can-do age.

So complete would Campbell's editorial dominance be during the early Atomic Age SF boom, and so lingering the effects of his editorial example, that afterward he would come to be commonly credited with complete responsiblity for the emergence of modern science fiction. Indeed, this period would be remembered specifically as the Golden Age of *Astounding*, or as the Campbell Golden Age.

Writer Isaac Asimov, who was another of the youngsters who found their way in to see Campbell and stayed to be instructed, once put it this way:

To many science fiction readers who are now in their middle years, there was a Golden Age of Science Fiction—in capital letters. That Golden Age began in 1938, when John Campbell became editor of *Astounding Stories* and remolded it, and the whole field, into something closer to his heart's desire. During the Golden Age, he and the magazine he edited so dominated science fiction that to read *Astounding* was to know the field entire.

Campbell's pre-eminence was not merely because he was quicker off the mark than other SF editors, or more committed than they to seeking the path of evolutionary change during this sudden new moment of social and psychic realignment. The fact of the matter is that Campbell was the possessor of a great secret and an even greater vision, and it was ultimately these that set him apart from all other editors and that gave meaning and direction to his resolve to pursue change.

John Campbell's great secret was the degree of his belief in the usefulness, power and truth of science fiction. For Campbell, science fiction was neither sugar-coated education nor mere popular entertainment. Science fiction had its own validity. It was the literary embodiment of science, man's most certain source of knowledge about the real universe. More than that—science fiction was a powerful tool of mind that could have actual effect on the world. Science fiction was dreams that might come true.

And Campbell had evidence to support this belief. For years, science fiction had imagined the possibility of liberating the power locked in the atom. Campbell himself, as Don A. Stuart, was the author of a story entitled "Atomic Power" (*Astounding*, Dec 1934). In June of 1938, Campbell even stuck his neck out and made the editorial prediction in *Astounding* that the discoverer of atomic power was a man then living and working.

And, almost instantly, this prophecy was fulfilled. In January 1939, certain puzzling experimental results obtained by German scientist Otto Hahn and his associates during the course of 1938 were finally recognized as evidence of the splitting of the uranium atom. The integrity of matter had been successfully challenged by material science! One element had been altered into two others, and in the process energy had been released. The foundation was now laid for the whole succeeding era of atomic bombs and nuclear power plants.

John Campbell, of course, recognized the significance of what had happened. Within two months of the announcement of the fission of uranium, he would have an *Astounding* on the newsstands with an editorial entitled "Jackpot!" And Campbell's jubilation was not just at the achievement of the first step toward nuclear power. It was also for the success of science-fictional prophetics—the new science of seeing ahead.

In this dawning moment of the Atomic Age, John Campbell was able to look around himself and recognize what no lesser editor was prepared even to consider: that the defining conditions of this new age had been conceived, directed, molded and made a bit at a time by the SF invention stories of the Age of Technology. From now on, Campbell realized, it was a science fiction world that people would be living in, filled with atomic power, rockets, thinking machines, helicopters, and television. All of the various gadgets, machines and inventions that had been imagined in the course of a thousand SF stories—but *all at once!*

The evidence for this was plain enough. It would be on public display in 1939 at the New York World's Fair, where souvenir buttons would even be given out attesting "I Have Seen the Future." And still no one but John Campbell was able to put the whole together and see that SF underlay the coming world. No one else quite tumbled to the immense power inherent in science fiction.

Though he would have been unlikely to use the term himself, John Campbell was the first to perceive science fiction as modern myth. For him, science fiction had the power of myth, the truth of myth, and the ability of myth to reshape the world. Accepting science fiction as myth, he had faith that there was no problem that it could not fruitfully address and resolve.

Some measure of the scope of science fiction as conceived by John Campbell—and also the reason that this conception was so much his own private belief—may be glimpsed in a highly revealing incident that happened shortly before Campbell's death in 1971. Writer Harry Harrison remembers it like this:

His sense of humor was of the roguish kind and many of his declarations and editorials were designed to provoke cries of rage from his readers. Characteristic is a statement he made just a few months before he died. There was a group of us and the talk came around to literature and the place of science fiction in the greater whole of English letters. It was pointed out that some enthusiastic aggrandizers of SF stand on the barricades and declare that someday, due to innate superiority, the short story and the novel will be engulfed by science fiction and become a part of it. Others, perhaps more realistically, say that SF is one specialized part of the whole of literature. But not John Campbell! With a sweep of one great hand he dismissed these feckless arguments, then spread his arms wide. "This is science fiction," he said, from open-armed fingertip to fingertip. "It takes in all time, from before the universe was born, through the formation of suns and planets, on through their destruction and forward to the heat death of the universe. And after." His hands came together so that his index fingers delimitated a very tiny measure of space. "This is English literature, the most microscopic fraction of the whole."

We have to take this statement seriously. For, even as Harrison suggests that Campbell must have been only foolin', he also off-handedly acknowledges that here in Campbell's assertion lies the essence of the Golden Age.

But what should be important for us to note is that as late as 1971, a crowd of science fiction writers—men who had grown up under the influence and direction of John Campbell, men who dealt with SF on a regular basis—could still choose to imagine that his personal concept of science fiction was just a joke, another of Campbell's typical roguish provocations. From this, we may judge just how truly far ahead of his time, how invisibly powerful, and how solitary was a John Campbell armed with these convictions in 1938, in the moment when he first set out to bring change to science fiction.

But yet, even more fundamental than Campbell's conception of the scope and role of science fiction was the vision of the unity and coherence of the universe that formed the foundation for this conception. We may see something of this vision peeking through in Campbell's assertion that science fiction takes in all time, from before the universe was born until its death—and then after.

It is not just that no one had previously thought about science fiction in this way. No one had previously thought about the *physical universe* in this way—as a discrete event with a limited life span, a before and an after, which humanity might be superior to.

All through the Technological Age, the material universe had presented a demonic appearance. It was the vast Unknown, remote, incomprehensible and terrifying. It was the great enemy of man, his ultimate executioner.

But then, in the last days of the Age of Technology there was a turn of the cosmic kaleidoscope, and all of a sudden science-minded visionaries throughout the Western world were permitted to view the universe in a completely new light. To John Campbell, to the inventor and futurist Buckminster Fuller, to the men who would conceive cybernetics and games theory and systems theory, and to a good many others to a greater or lesser degree, it suddenly came to seem apparent that the immensity and complexity displayed by the material universe must be only superficial appearance.

Beneath the surface of immaterial materiality, interconnecting it and holding it together, there must be a relatively small number of fundamental general principles. And everything in the universe—even life, even consciousness—was ultimately to be defined and controlled by these basic rules of nature.

We may understand this vision as the scientific and philosophic variant of the new understanding that was concurrently finding its social expression in the form of democratic pluralism: These universal principles were no respecters of person. They were not reserved for the private use of those born to privilege. They were radically democratic, applying to all and accessible to all.

It appeared that for anyone who was prepared to ask for them, these general principles of relationship and operation would not prove impossible to discover. John Campbell would express it this way in one of his early editorials: "I have heard it said that Nature will give a truthful answer to any intelligent question properly asked. ... The trick in getting the oracle of Nature to answer is to ask intelligent questions properly."

Or, as he would say elsewhere: "Nature is a blabbermouth."

The promise implicit in this new scientific vision was that if men would just get on with their proper business of achieving mastery over the fundamental laws of existence, then there was no limit to potential human power, and no need for mankind to fear the universe.

In Buckminster Fuller's case, this new vision had come upon him in 1927, in a moment when he was on the point of drowning himself in Lake Michigan. His beloved daughter had died on her fourth birthday, his business career was in shambles, and he was filled with despair at the meaninglessness of his existence. But then, in this totally hopeless moment, he was given a sudden glimmering of the order and beauty underlying incomprehensibility. Fuller immediately abandoned his attempt at suicide and dedicated himself to a new life work. As he would later put it: "I made a bargain with myself that I'd discover the principles operative in the universe and turn them over to my fellow men."

Even though John Campbell did not need to be pushed to the brink of suicide in order to arrive at his version of this vision, nonetheless, by his own route and in his own time, he had come to make a very similar compact with himself. Except that Campbell's particular dedication was to discover the operating principles of the universe—and then to turn them over to his fellow men in the form of science fiction stories.

It was Campbell's grasp of the new scientific vision and his personal dedication to seeing the vision fulfilled that account finally for his great edge as an editor. He was a man with a job to do, in precisely the right place at just the right moment to see it done.

To a degree that no other SF editor could possibly match, Campbell *knew* what his business was. And the series of changes that he made in *Astounding*, the writers he chose to favor, the scientific news and paradoxes and insights he stimulated them with, the content of the stories he picked to publish and the nature of the story revisions that he insisted upon—all of these are to be explained by John Campbell's determination to place human hands on the controls of the universe.

That was the real nature of his work. And his means of seeing the work accomplished was "modern science fiction," Campbellian science fiction, SF altered in such a way as to proclaim and to represent and to apply the new vision of underlying universal operating principles.

Modern science fiction was the answer that Campbell had so painstakingly worked out in the course of the Thirties to the early Twentieth Century dilemma—that unshakeable nightmare that said no matter what mankind might do or how far it might go, ultimately, inevitably, it must still be destroyed and eliminated by the universe. Campbell's "mutations" in *Astounding*, taken in sum, offered an alternate picture of man in the universe—a whole new scenario. The story they told was this:

Things hang together. The universe is not to be feared; it will respond if only it is asked the right questions. The facts are the key, but the facts must be determined. The future may be anticipated. Human evolution is possible. The way to proceed is through the acceptance of change. The method is science and engineering applied with reason and imagination. The ultimate end is human dominion over the universe.

To write modern science fiction for John Campbell, all that would be necessary would be to take one or more of these fundamental tenets and give them expression in story form.

But before any modern science fiction stories had actually been written, their outline was already visible in the form and fabric of the 1938 *Astounding*. In a very real sense, the first and best example of modern science fiction—the template, the basic model—would be the Campbell *Astounding* itself.

The new construction of reality was expressed in every possible way by the new *Astounding*. It was demonstrated, it was pictured, it was assumed, it was implied.

Campbell might say about the change in title design: "The new cover lettering...represents an effort to bring the style of type used, more into conformation with the type of material appearing in the magazine; a modern, simple type-face, clean-cut and definite."

And the implication was that Campbell wanted material that

was modern, simple, clean-cut and definite. And also that all parts and elements of *Astounding* were a reflection of the whole.

Campbell might even state some portion of his credo loud and plain, as when he declared editorially, "The old order not only does change, but *must* change," even as he was turning *Astounding* inside out.

But nowhere did Campbell state the whole of his vision as explicitly as we have just tried to do. That was because the closest thing to a complete statement of Campbell's new ordering of things was the magazine itself.

But that was part of the message, too. *Things hang together*, said *Astounding*.

Anywhere at all that you might look in the magazine would be some fragment or indication of the new whole: "The An Lab"— a new department of performance analysis. "In Times to Come"— a new department of prophecy. Cover paintings that portrayed man poking his nose into the far corners of the real Solar System. And—everywhere and always—change, change, change.

And even so, a leap of understanding would be required to grasp that what was being indicated was not just one thing and another, but different aspects of a new dynamic order.

Perhaps as close as Campbell came to stating the essence of his belief directly was in this comment in the March 1938 editorial that accompanied the change in title from *Astounding Stories* to *Astounding Science-Fiction*:

"We presuppose, in these stories, two things: that there is yet to be learned infinitely more than is now known, and that Man can learn it."

What a deceptively simple thing to say, now that it was said— that men can always learn whatever it is they need to know! But to be able to say this and believe it, it was necessary first to accept that the universe, however unknown it might be, is not alien, hostile and incomprehensible; that necessary information will always be there when needed; that learning and change are always a human possibility; and that things do hang together.

In the continuing Twentieth Century debate between the forecasters of human glory and the criers of human doom, this was the implicit answer of the optimistic H.G. Wells, Edgar Rice Burroughs, E.E. Smith and John Campbell—the lineage of emergent modern science fiction—to the pessimist Wells, Bertrand Russell, H.P. Lovecraft, Olaf Stapledon and the Europeans. But only now, at last, able to be given utterance.

Campbell's timing was just right. There proved to be a body of readers waiting who had enough sense of the new vision to be able to put together all the bits and pieces of his message, to make a whole of it, and to believe in it.

The readers of *Astounding* understood that *Astounding* was now a works project, an experimental laboratory, an open college dedicated to the creation of modern science fiction, and they leaped to support Campbell. They eagerly rated stories for him. They argued and debated his questions in the letter column. Above all, they applauded the changes he was making and yearned for more.

And all of this was before much in the way of actual modern science fiction even existed. It would not be too far off the mark to say that Campbell spent his first year as editor in preparing readers to understand and accept modern science fiction and in training writers to write it.

What is usually reckoned the essential early example of modern science fiction was not published until the August 1938 issue, almost a year after Campbell became editor of *Astounding*. This was a long novelet entitled "Who Goes There?" and its author was John Campbell's alter ego, Don A. Stuart.

This pivotal story was specifically directed to the question of whether men must fear the difference of the un-Earthly, or whether they might make the regularity and reliability of the universe their particular tool and ally.

In "Who Goes There?" an American polar expedition has discovered a spaceship and an alien being that have been frozen in the ice of Antarctica for twenty million years. The spaceship has been accidentally destroyed, but the scientists have carried the alien back to camp in a block of ice with the intention of examining it.

The very appearance of the alien is upsetting. It is a hideous Lovecraftian being, blue-skinned, red-eyed and obviously malevolent. Strong men retch and retreat at the sight of it, even entombed in a chunk of ice:

"Three mad, hate-filled eyes blazed up with a living fire, bright as fresh-spilled blood, from a face ringed with a writhing, loathsome nest of worms, blue, mobile worms that crawled where hair should grow—"

And its behavior is even more frightening. This nightmare-inducing creature does not merely thaw out and then begin to decay in the normal manner. Instead, after twenty million years in cold storage, it comes back to life! What is more, it proves to be a shape-changing, telepathic monster that can take over the protoplasm of any living creature—be it a dog, a cow, a bird or a man—and convert it into its own kind while still retaining the capabilities and appearance of the original.

In short, here, just as in Campbell's earlier story, "The Brain Stealers of Mars" (*Thrilling Wonder*, Dec 1936), human beings are confronted by the prospect of shape-shifting mind readers. But, what in the earlier story was only a half-comic question of distinguishing a pair of human originals from a host of Martian imitators, in "Who Goes There?" becomes the wholly urgent need to prevent a monstrous alien from escaping the Antarctic and taking over the world.

What a completely horrifying prospect!

And yet, the emphasis in "Who Goes There?" is not upon horror or excitement, as it is in the two Hollywood movies that would be made from Campbell's story—*The Thing* (1951) and *The Thing* (1982). If thrills had been Campbell's object, then almost certainly he would have chosen to start his story at an earlier moment than he does. Say—as a bronze ice ax chips into something and breaks off, and an American scientist suddenly finds himself staring into the three glowing red eyes of a frozen snake-haired alien. Or as a magnesium spaceship suddenly catches fire, and sparks and burns away to nothing beneath the polar ice.

But action and emotion are not the heart of "Who Goes There?" Horror and excitement in sufficient measure may be used to carry the story along, but they aren't what Campbell is after. In fact, in a very real sense, it is horror and excitement that the characters of the story are called upon to overcome if they are to perceive their situation clearly and deal with it effectively.

And so it is that "Who Goes There?" does not open with the high thrills of the discovery of the creature and the destruction of the alien spaceship. Rather, it opens back at base camp with all the members of the expedition gathering to hear a chalk talk summary of what has been found.

Indeed, the very first thing the story offers is a bracing whiff of the atmosphere of the camp:

"The place stank. A queer, mingled stench that only the ice-bound cabins of an Antarctic camp know, compounded of reeking human sweat, and the heavy fish-oil stench of melted seal blubber."

This is just the beginning. On the litany of reeks and stenches continues: liniment, wet furs, burnt cooking fat, dogs, machine oil, harness dressing—and the queer, neck-ruffling taint of thawing alien. (There it is in the background, underneath a tarp, dripping away.)

No place described in earlier science fiction ever stank like this! But it is precisely this overwhelming atmosphere of pervasive, inescapable specificity—of smelly feet and seal blubber—that establishes a context in which naked fact and universal principle may plausibly rule.

The true emphasis in "Who Goes There?"—like much of Camp-bellian science fiction—is on the definition and solution of a problem. And the problem set forth in this initial story of modern science fiction is a fundamental one:

The creature from another world is strange, terrifying, and immensely powerful. But is it different in essence from what we know, or is it only different in kind?

Here is the very significant reaction of the expedition's doctor when he is first told that the monster has come back to life and escaped:

"Copper stared blankly. 'It wasn't—Earthly,' he sighed suddenly. 'I—I guess Earthly laws don't apply.'"

With this response, Campbell precisely catches the basic elements of the "literature of cosmic fear" described by H.P. Lovecraft in his classic 1927 essay, *Supernatural Horror in Literature*:

> A certain atmosphere of breathless and unexplainable dread of outer, unknown forces must be present; and there must be a hint, expressed with a seriousness and portentousness becoming its subject, of that most terrible conception of the human brain—a malign and particular suspension or defeat of those fixed laws of Nature which are our only safeguard against the assaults of chaos and the daemons of unplumbed space.

This is the Techno Age attitude toward the wider universe at its most timorous—laid down as an aesthetic requirement!

But in "Who Goes There?" John Campbell has raised his demon of unplumbed space not to confirm us in our habitual cosmic fear, but rather with the intention of resolving the problem of this alien monster using the new general principles of relationship and operation. Not mere Earthly law—which perhaps might not apply to demonic creatures from another star—but Universal Law, which surely does.

As Blair, the biologist of the expedition, says, very shortly before he goes mad and has to be placed in isolation:

"'This isn't wildly beyond what we already know. It's just a modification we haven't seen before. It's as natural, as logical, as any other manifestation of life. It obeys exactly the same laws.'"

What a radical new idea this was—that the biology and behavior of even an alien might be governed by laws as simple and manipulable as those of classical physics! And yet, this becomes the premise that the members of the expedition proceed upon. They set out to test scientifically who is a monster and who is not.

What is more, in "Who Goes There?" it is assumed that all true human beings will naturally accept the appropriateness and efficacy of scientific testing. Indeed, the members of the human expedition are completely confident that those monsters masquerading as men will raise no objections to the principle of testing because anything less than complete assent to the power of science would be a dead giveaway of their non-humanity.

However, the first test that the American scientists devise is not a success. Like the tests in "The Brain Stealers of Mars"—which were the presumed inability of the Martians either to copy human muscles well enough to sneeze, or to duplicate an acquired human immunity to tetanus—it is an Earth-minded test. The scientists immunize one of their sled dogs with the blood from two men. Their expectation is that the blood from any monster pretending to be human will be revealed as something other-than-human under laboratory examination.

But the monster proves to have outmaneuvered them. The dog reacts to human blood—but also to monster blood. Not only is the test hopelessly compromised, but also it is certain that one of the two apparent humans who originally contributed blood must actually be an alien.

In this traumatic moment, some of the members of the party are driven over the edge into madness, religious hysteria and murder. But others keep their balance. They devise a new and more effective test—this time not a test of human genuineness, but rather a direct test of alien difference. It employs a universal principle—the law of self-preservation—in such a way as to make the monster's own superiority give it away:

Does each part of the monster have independent life and crave to preserve it? Then take a sample of blood from each man and touch it with a hot wire. If it screams and tries to escape, it must be monster blood.

This scientific trial-by-fire proves just the thing, and one by one, fifteen human-imitating monsters are duly identified and eliminated. And the last of these is Blair, the "mad" biologist. When he is discovered, it is with two homemade inventions—anti-gravity and atomic power.

If he had survived for only a few more minutes, the world would have been his for the taking. As it is, human beings have been left with a couple of neat bonuses.

There are a number of unexamined ambiguities within this pivotal story. Not the least of these is that Dr. Copper, who could only stare blankly and suggest the Lovecraftian otherness of the creature, is one of those who proves to be a genuine human being, while Blair the biologist, who first proposed that the alien must be a natural being subject to the same laws as any other manifestation of life, turns out to be a monster. How very odd it is that the creature should be the one to propose the basis for its own destruction!

In fact, the respect that the monsters volunteer for the new rule of scientific testing of universal principle is nothing short of remarkable. Despite their large numbers, common nature, and telepathic powers, the false humans completely eschew the possibility of joint resistance. They docilely take their turn in line to be tested and then electrocuted or ripped to shreds. We may be forgiven for concluding that if these malevolent monsters tamely bow down and worship the new vision of universal principle, it is because it is their vision, too.

"Who Goes There?" would prove to be the most influential SF story since Stanley Weinbaum's "A Martian Odyssey." In effect, it was a highly visible public demonstration, a sign to all who could see, that John Campbell was out to turn science fiction into something new.

But this electrifying story would be almost the last piece of fiction John Campbell would write. In the coming months, he would publish two more stories as John W. Campbell, Jr., and two as Don A. Stuart, but after the middle of 1939, when he wrote a Stuart short novel to fill a hole in *Unknown*, he would cease to produce fiction.

The explanation usually given for this is that Campbell was called in by his superiors at Street & Smith and flatly told to stop writing fiction and stick to his editing—and that Campbell valued his paycheck enough to obey.

But while there may be a degree of truth to this story, it doesn't sound very much like John Campbell, a man who was rarely one to do anything he didn't wish to do. If Campbell was prepared to give up his science fiction writing, it just may have been because he had finally figured out how to be an *editor* and get other people to do the writing for him. At least, Isaac Asimov tells us:

> I once asked him, years ago (with all the puzzlement of a compulsive writer who can imagine no other way of life), how he could possibly have borne to leave his writing career and become an editor. I had almost said *merely* an editor. He smiled (he knew me) and said, "Isaac, when I write, I write only my own stories. As editor, I write the stories that a hundred people write."

The problem in creating modern science fiction would be to find a hundred writers with some sense of the new vision, or a willingness and ability to pick it up, and to get rid of the rest. Along with the changes he made in the magazine, Campbell cleaned house at *Astounding* through 1938 and 1939. He swept out the debris of the

Technological Age. He got rid of stories of mushy occultism, unfounded fancy and cosmic fear. He picked and chose among the established writers of science fiction, discarding all those who could not play by the new rules.

E. E. Smith, of course, was one established writer acceptable to Campbell. His first Lensman novel, *Galactic Patrol*, had just begun serialization as Campbell became editor of *Astounding*. This was the most grandly scaled science fiction story yet, the climax of all Smith's efforts since *The Skylark of Space*, and its very presence in the pages of *Astounding* gave Campbell's editorial career the strongest possible initial boost.

Even though Doc Smith would never exactly be a writer of modern science fiction, Campbell would continue to publish Lensman novels through the next ten years. Once more, Smith would be something like Jules Verne—a founding father who continued to work on into an era that was not his own.

But even so, there would be good reasons aplenty for Campbell to give Smith's great epic houseroom in the pages of *Astounding*. There was a moral confidence and an imaginative breadth to the Lensman stories that modern science fiction—for all its many special qualities and virtues—would simply never be able to equal. And indeed, even though during the Forties the Lensman series might sometimes seem a side issue, a relic, a leftover from an earlier era of SF, it would eventuallly prove to be the conceptual foundation upon which the latter-day Campbellian science fiction of the Fifties and Sixties would come to be erected.

But Campbell's other early inspiration, Edmond Hamilton, would not fare so well with him. Hamilton would appear in the Campbell *Astounding* just once at the end of 1938, and then never again.

It happened this way: Campbell and Hamilton had been fellow members of a New York area SF writers circle. After he became editor, Campbell asked most of the writers he knew, including Hamilton, to contribute stories to his magazine. And Hamilton was glad to dash one off for him.

But then Campbell did the Campbellish thing. He pointed out flaws in the story and asked for a rewrite. Ed Hamilton was an old pro accustomed to turning out first-draft copy, to repeating his plots, and to selling everything he wrote. So he was quite taken aback by this request. He fixed the story, but he didn't send any more to Campbell.

In later years, Hamilton would say in explanation: "The trouble was that I was trying to make a living writing s-f. John had very meticulous standards, and I would not be able to sell him enough s-f to live on. I sometimes regret I didn't stay with John. With his help I could have become a lot better s-f writer."

By contrast, a writer who was not attempting to make a living from SF alone and who was able to make the stretch to meet Campbell's strictures might well perceive his appointment as editor as an unprecedented opportunity to do work of a kind and quality previously impossible. One such writer was newspaperman Clifford D. Simak. In the early Thirties, he had written "The World of the Red Sun" and several other science fiction stories, but after the failure of the Clayton *Astounding*, he had turned away from SF.

But when he learned that John Campbell had become editor of *Astounding*, his interest was revived. Simak told his wife that Campbell would want a new kind of SF, and that he was confident that he would be able to satisfy Campbell's requirements—both of which proved to be true. Writing science fiction strictly as a sideline, Simak would contribute stories to Campbell for the next twenty-five years.

But it was not sufficient for Campbell to simply sort through the established writers of science fiction in search of those capable of working with him. Too few of the established writers of science fiction were in tune with the new scientific vision, and even fewer were prepared to be taken over the jumps by young John Campbell.

To write his new science fiction, Campbell had to draft, discover and invent a whole new set of writers. Of all the many labors that he performed as he strove to bring modern science fiction into being, this gathering and training of new writers would be by far the most significant.

Campbell was at his very best in pursuit of these unknown persons capable of presenting the new vision for him. He was subtle, observant, patient, persistent, and infinitely resourceful. And even so, one of the first writers he found was initially forced upon him against his will.

At the very outset of Campbell's editing career, in that brief moment when he was still expressing a measure of uncertainty about filling the pages of a monthly magazine with new stories, his superiors at Street & Smith thought to provide him with an insurance policy. They called in a couple of top pulp adventure writers—reliable professional yarnspinners—and told Campbell to accept any work they cared to submit to him.

Campbell protested this vigorously. Science fiction was fundamentally different from other pulp literature. It wasn't just to be cranked out by the yard. What is more, to pay these guys his top rates for anything and everything they wrote would cut the heart right out of his budget. He didn't want to do it. But F. Orlin Tremaine was one person he would heed, and when Tremaine told him to do it, he did it.

Campbell was already familiar with one of the writers imposed upon him, Arthur J. Burks. Burks actually had some previous science fiction writing experience, including stories published in the Clayton *Astounding*. And one way or another, he and Campbell did accommodate themselves to each other to the tune of one so-so novel and a series of mild, rationalized space opera stories. But after only one year and half-a-dozen stories—and the departure of F. Orlin Tremaine from Street & Smith—Burks would be gone from the pages of *Astounding*, swept out in Campbell's great spring housecleaning.

But the other writer who had been forced on Campbell would serve as a longer-term asset—of a kind. This was L. Ron Hubbard, who is best known for his later career as the founder of the religion/mind-control system Scientology.

This big redheaded people-charmer was born in Tilden, Nebraska on March 13, 1911. Probably. Possibly. With Hubbard it is hard to know exactly where the real truth lies since his greatest continuing pleasure in life was in telling stretchers, striking poses, and seeing just how much falsity he could get other people to swallow. In a revealing moment, he once said:

> "Now you say you have to be absolutely truthful. Sincerity is the main thing, and truthfulness is the main thing and don't lie to anybody... and you'll get ahead. Brother you sure will. You'll get ahead right on that cycle of action, right toward zero! ... It's a trap not being able to prevaricate....
>
> "You say, 'You know, I was downtown the other day and there's this Yellow Taxi there, and I started to step into this Yellow Taxi, and I'll be a son of a gun if there wasn't a big ape sitting in the back smoking a cigar. And I closed the door and walked on down the street.'
>
> "This makes life more colorful."

Hubbard's usual public pretense at the time he and Campbell met was that he was a globe-trotting explorer who paused from time to time between adventures to catch his breath and turn out pulp stories. In this, he would be imitating earlier writers of pulp adventure who may or may not have had a better claim to the pose.

In fact, however, the only real accomplishment of this college dropout had been to sell his dreams of adventure to others in story form. And when he blew into town with his latest tale of being shipwrecked in the Aleutians and forced to survive on whale meat and seaweed, or whatever, the actual fact was that he was living in the state of Washington with a wife and son, either attempting to psych himself up to write or else pounding out stories at red-hot speed.

At the times when he was able to write, Hubbard would slap

first-draft copy onto a long roll of typing paper, not wishing to be slowed down or have his mood broken by having to remove one sheet of paper and replace it with another. And when his stories were finished, he would have his wife check them over and mail them out, but he wouldn't necessarily read them himself after they had passed through his typewriter.

The result of these habits was stories which moved along pell-mell, with a certain verve and charm and superficial plausibility, but which ultimately didn't add up to much. They were good enough to get by, but they weren't original or substantial work.

For the claim that Hubbard (and Burks) were initially forced upon Campbell over the editor's protest, we have only the word of this dedicated toyer with the truth. So take warning that the tale is not completely to be relied upon.

What makes it seem possible, however, is that Hubbard had no previous background at all in writing science fiction, or even in reading it. He was in no way a natural writer for John Campbell to pick out and cultivate on his own. Not only did Campbell take him on as a writer, however, but it is clear that at the outset the editor was bowled over by Hubbard's personal flash and dazzle. He went out of his way to find niches for this operator within his magazine and to work out grounds for him to write SF.

That took a certain amount of discussion and negotiation. The fact is that Hubbard had no more than a glancing acquaintance with most contemporary science. He'd lingered in engineering school only long enough to pick up the talk. He had read some fantasy—*The Arabian Nights* and Washington Irving's *Tales of the Alhambra*. He'd read quite a bit of occult literature. And he had an interest in the hidden powers of the mind.

That was where he and Campbell found their first common ground. Hubbard began writing for *Astounding* with rationalized stories of wild mental talents—a short story, "The Dangerous Dimension" (July 1938), followed by the serial novel, *The Tramp* (Sept-Nov 1938).

And the next year, when Campbell started *Unknown*, he would even set aside a special preserve for Hubbard—stories of contemporary men involved with alternate worlds based on *The Arabian Nights*. The editor would write to Hubbard:

> I'm damn glad you'll be with us on the Arabian Nights stuff—and you needn't worry about having it yours. I've been telling a few of the boys to read Washington Irving as an example of pure fantasy and complete acceptance of magic, enchantment, et cetera, and adding that they aren't to do Arabian Nights because the field is preempted by you. It's been held open for you.

By whatever means it was arranged, the open door for Hubbard's stories at *Astounding* and *Unknown* represented a considerable opportunity for him. For perhaps the only time in a life that was generally misspent, Hubbard's true nature, interests, knowledge and gifts coincided with the chance to do work with an aspect of genuine creativity, instead of his usual fakery.

Hubbard would never be one of John Campbell's special pupils or central innovators. But during the time before he entered the Navy during World War II, Hubbard would be involved enough and reliable enough to serve as a steady hack writer for Campbell. He would sell the editor eleven novels and twenty-two shorter stories, published under his own name and three pseudonyms.

This was good-bad work, turned out far too fast, often flat and untranscendent, usually a little rickety, but generally good enough to serve. And sometimes, in a few rare conceptions and occasional brilliant moments, it was more than that.

But L. Ron Hubbard was not at all the usual Campbell writer. Far more typically, the writers that Campbell enlisted to produce the stories he needed were amateurs with some background in science and a long history of reading SF.

Indeed, what is truly remarkable, considering that Campbell was no populist and no social wiz, is the sheer range of people that he attracted or convinced to write for him. The editor was one of those who followed H.G. Wells in believing that the old elite of birth should be replaced by a new and more effective elite—an elite of competence. For Campbell, the value of democratic pluralism was that it allowed competence the opportunity to display itself.

What it took to get along with Campbell was a display of the hallmarks of competence—an eagerness to work, a willingness to question, a determination to think and to learn. In his usual state of high editorial dedication, Campbell would never pause to worry about non-essentials like age or reputation or ethnic background. He would work with anyone in whom he spied even the faintest glimmering of real understanding.

This is all the more important to note because on the ordinary emotional level, Campbell was not completely free of the common prejudices of the period and class in which he was raised. He might, for instance, state flatly that it would be better for all concerned if the United States marched down to Latin America and took the place over. And—coming as he did from an earlier era in which SF writers were *always* named something like Wells, Burroughs, Merritt, Smith, Hamilton...or Campbell—he was even capable of suggesting to several of his more exotically named writers that they might consider the possibility of adopting Anglo-Saxon or Scottish pen names, since such names were bound to ring better in the reader's ear.

But that was as far as it went. As an editor, Campbell was usually able to keep his latent cultural prejudices from interfering with his higher aims. What truly mattered to him—far more than any White-Male-Scottish-American chauvinism—was that a writer be resilient enough, bright enough and capable enough to put up with his criticisms, his arguments and lectures, and his eternal testing and prodding—and then repay him for his trouble and effort by coming back to him with stories that were *new*.

If a writer could do that, Campbell didn't care what his origins might be. In his eyes, all true makers of science fiction were of one kind—above and beyond questions of mere ethnicity. And, in actual practice, the contents page of the Golden Age *Astounding* would display a flowering rainbow of unusual surnames, their sheer variety and their aura of differentness helping to contribute to the unique appeal of the magazine.

The ultimate example of Campbell's ability to exercise tolerance and patience in the name of science fiction with a person from a completely different background than himself may be seen in his treatment of one young would-be writer, an 18-year-old Jewish immigrant named Isaac Asimov.

In June 1938, Isaac Asimov made the trek from his father's little neighborhood candy store in Brooklyn to Campbell's office in lower Manhattan. He was wearing his second-best suit and carrying his first attempt at an SF story, a manuscript entitled "Cosmic Corkscrew." What a thoroughly unprepossessing character this Asimov was—a loud, bright, pimple-faced kid, particularly obnoxious when nervous, as he was at this moment of first encounter.

Asimov was born in Russia at the beginning of 1920, and then raised in the close confines of a series of Brooklyn candy stores. When he wasn't studying, eating or sleeping, he was working in the family store. It was there, at the age of nine, that he had discovered magazine science fiction. He was certainly precocious—at 18 already at the end of his junior year as a premed student at Columbia— but all he knew of the world was narrow little neighborhood candy stores, books, school, and science fiction.

Nonetheless, when Asimov showed up unannounced at Street & Smith, Campbell had the outer secretary send him back. Asimov was a science fiction fan, and Campbell recognized his name.

Altogether, Campbell devoted more than two hours of working time to the youngster. He soothed Asimov's jitters by showing him that he had a letter printed in each of the next two issues of *Astounding*. He told Asimov about the beginnings of his own writing career. He showed him "Who Goes There?" which was also about to see publication. And he promised the boy that he would give "Cosmic Corkscrew" prompt and complete attention.

And, in fact, he did. He read "Cosmic Corkscrew" overnight—and rejected it immediately. But not without a thoughtful two-page letter of comment.

By contrast, when Asimov read Campbell's story "Who Goes There?", it was with "delight mingled with despair." He recognized that the story presented a challenge to all would-be writers of science fiction.

But he was ready to accept that challenge. It didn't matter to him that his first story had been rejected. John Campbell had treated him and his writing with respect! More than that, Asimov had caught something crucial from Campbell—a spirit of enthusiasm and a sense of new possibility. Asimov desired no happier fate than to be allowed to write another science fiction story that John Campbell could see fit to publish.

Month after month, Asimov would journey to Campbell's office with a new story in hand, not yet sure precisely what was required, but always hoping that he might have come closer to the mark this time. And month after month, Campbell would interrupt his work to give Asimov personal attention, read his latest story, and then promptly reject it.

At last, however, there came the wonderful day when Campbell perceived a faint possibility buried in an Asimov manuscript—the suggestion of possible social resistance to space travel. He called Asimov back to his office only one week after his usual monthly visit and told him to rewrite this latest effort putting social reaction at the center. Asimov did, and Campbell bought it, publishing it under the title "Trends" in the July 1939 *Astounding*.

Asimov would soon find himself adopted as John Campbell's most favored pupil. And eventually, after two or three years of now-weekly visits, Asimov would justify Campbell's faith in him by assuming a place as one of his most central innovators.

But who except John Campbell would ever have thought to see a potential giant of science fiction in the strange and hapless adolescent who first entered Campbell's office clutching an unprintable story called "Cosmic Corkscrew"? Even Asimov himself couldn't help but wonder about this:

> Many years later I asked Campbell (with whom I had by then grown to be on the closest terms) why he had bothered with me at all, since that first story was surely utterly impossible.
>
> "It was," he said frankly, for he never flattered. "On the other hand, I saw something in *you*. You were eager and you listened and I knew you wouldn't quit no matter how many rejections I handed you. As long as you were willing to work hard at improving, I was willing to work with you."

That was John. I wasn't the only writer, whether newcomer or oldtimer, that he was to work with in this fashion. Patiently, and out of his own enormous vitality and talent, he built up a stable of the best s.f. writers the world had, till then, ever seen."

It was not merely that Campbell might groom and tutor and nudge a writer like Asimov until he was capable of producing the kind of work Campbell was seeking. When Campbell suggested to Asimov that as editor he wrote the stories that a hundred writers wrote, he wasn't altogether exaggerating the case. In countless instances, Campbell prompted his writers by providing them with the basic ideas for new stories.

Some measure of the continuing degree of involvement, both direct and indirect, that Campbell might have in a writer's fiction may be seen in his relationship with another early contributor, science fiction fan Lester del Rey.

Ramon Felipe Alvarez-del Rey (longer versions of his name have been offered) was a short, slight young man born in 1915, the largely self-educated son of a Minnesota tenant farmer. At the end of 1937, when he made his first story submission to Campbell, he was living in Washington, D.C., and falling in and out of different lines of work.

At first appearance, del Rey might not seem a prime candidate to write for Campbell. He was a feisty, opinionated little cuss, completely bent on living life according to his own lights. Far more important to him than the jobs he might hold was his pursuit of an ever-changing set of hobbies and interests, of which science fiction was just one.

But it happened that one day, as young Lester was reading the January 1938 issue of *Astounding*—the very issue in which John Campbell first announced his policy of change—he came to find a particular story intolerable rubbish, and hurled the magazine across the room in a sudden critical fit. His then-girlfriend wouldn't hold still for this. She challenged him to do as well himself.

Del Rey wasn't used to thinking of himself as a writer. But he knew that John Campbell was now editor of *Astounding*, and in the past he had written letters of comment to the SF magazines that had included words of praise for Campbell's stories. He thought there was a good chance that Campbell would remember his name and at least give him some minimal attention. So he asked the girl if she would be willing to settle for a personal note of rejection. And she agreed.

"The Faithful," the story that del Rey wrote in response to this challenge, was a nostalgic tale of loyal intelligent dogs as the heirs to a dying mankind. Del Rey thought of himself as writing a reply to the story he had so disliked—"Pithecanthropus Rejectus" by Manly Wade Wellman. But it is also possible that somewhere in the back of his mind were a few lines thrown out in the course of Don A. Stuart's "Twilight":

"Dogs. They must have been remarkable animals. Man was reaching his maturity then, and his animal friend, the friend who had followed him through a thousand millenniums to your day and mine, and another four thousand millenniums to the day of man's early maturity, had grown in intelligence."

But John Campbell didn't reject his story outright, as del Rey had prepared himself to expect. Rather, he bought "The Faithful" and published it immediately in the April 1938 *Astounding*.

Quite naturally, then, del Rey tried dashing off several more SF stories. But these Campbell did reject. And at this point, del Rey was ready to consider his story sale a lucky fluke and conclude that he wasn't really meant to be an SF writer. On to other things.

But Campbell wouldn't let go of him. He needed his new writers, and he wasn't about to let this del Rey slip away. What Campbell did was to write him a note that said: "Your story was darned well received, del Rey, and it's been moving up steadily in the reader's choice. But as I look through my inventory, I don't find anything more by you. I hope you'll remedy this."

It was exactly the right tone to strike with del Rey—respectful of his independence, unpresuming, and thoroughly flattering in its receptivity. It was more than Lester could resist. He set out to study just what it was that Campbell really did want, and to see if he could supply it.

He looked in the market report of the latest issue of *Writer's Digest*. There he found Campbell saying: "I want reactions rather than actions. I want human reactions. Even if your hero is a robot, he must have human reactions to make him interesting to the reader."

The message was clear to del Rey—Campbell wanted science fiction humanized. It was this element in Campbell that had responded to del Rey's story about intelligent dogs mourning the passage of man. Taking his clue from Campbell's market report, del Rey sat right down and wrote a story about a man falling in love with a selfless female robot.

Campbell bought del Rey's story, "Helen O'Loy," and published it in the December 1938 *Astounding*. It was one of the most popular stories of the year.

Shortly thereafter, Campbell wrote again to del Rey. But this time he didn't merely urge del Rey to send him another story—he suggested the idea for one: Perhaps Neanderthal man wasn't actually exterminated by Cro-Magnon, but died instead from the heartbreak and frustration of meeting culturally and technically superior human beings. Del Rey wrote his version of this in less than two hours— not sparing the human sentiment—and Campbell popped "The Day Is Done" right into the May 1939 *Astounding*.

And so it would go. During the Golden Age, del Rey would write stories for Campbell under his own name and no fewer than four pseudonyms. Some of these stories would be written completely on del Rey's own initiative, but at least as often Campbell would have to seek del Rey out, woo him away from his latest hobby, and stimulate him with story ideas—all without offending del Rey by appearing to overdirect him.

Eventually, Campbell would entrust del Rey with the major idea of disaster in an industrial nuclear plant. And the short novel that del Rey produced, "Nerves" (*Astounding*, Sept 1942), would become his best-known story.

Del Rey says of John Campbell:

> He was, as I came to know, a great and creative editor. Nobody has any idea how many of the stories in his magazine came from ideas he suggested, but a group of us once determined that the figure must be greater than half.
> ... Part of his success probably came from the fact that he gave just enough of an idea to inspire, but not so much as to stifle the writer's own ideas.

The story seeds planted by Campbell might be plots or situations as specific as those in "The Day Is Done" or "Nerves." But just as frequently, Campbell might hand a writer a universal principle that could be given fictional illustration in any number of different ways. Campbell would convey to the writer a sense of the relationship or operation he had in mind, and it was then up to the writer to elaborate his own particular example of the general case.

Fred Pohl can remember Campbell telling him: "When I think of a story idea, I give it to six different writers. It doesn't matter if all six of them write it. They'll all be different stories, anyway, and I'll publish all six of them."

But as much as Campbell might contribute to the fiction that appeared in his magazines, he asked for an even greater measure of thought and effort in return. Campbell required commitment, insight and imagination from the writers he gave story ideas to. And if a writer should prove to have no grasp of the new vision; if he was not able to perceive that Campbell was handing him a seed and expecting back a universe; if he was unable both to speak to Campbell's central concerns and also to present Campbell with wonders never seen before, then the editor would not bother to expend further energy and attention upon him.

As Campbell once said to Isaac Asimov: "If I give a story idea to a writer and get it back exactly as I told it to him, I don't waste any more story ideas on him. I want it to grow and develop inside him. I want more back than I give. I'm selfish that way."

But of all Campbell's new writers of 1938, the one he valued the most was a man who already had his own individual sense of the new vision, a self-starter who didn't have to be cajoled, stimulated, prompted or led into writing modern science fiction, but who had a natural affinity for this splendid new game. This was a tall, thin, highly erudite patrician named L. Sprague de Camp.

Lyon Sprague de Camp was born on November 27, 1907 in New York City. As a boy, he took his share of licks for being overly well-read and well-bred and for having a snooty name. However, without ever losing his aristocratic bearing, Sprague gradually managed to learn to get along in the rough-and-tumble world of the Twentieth Century by taking life as he found it, offering respect to all, cultivating a sense of humor, and becoming interested in the new science and technology.

John Carter of Mars, an early hero of his, had more than a little to do with how he met life.

De Camp majored in aeronautical engineering in college, and then did graduate work in engineering and economics. Like so many others, however, his immediate hopes for a career got sidetracked by the Depression. At the time he first met Campbell, he was the principal of the inventions and patents branch of the International Correspondence School in Scranton, Pennsylvania, a job that was much less grand than his title might suggest.

In 1937, his college roommate, John D. Clark, brought him into the informal circle of New York SF writers to which John Campbell belonged. De Camp had just sold a story to *Astounding*, but it hadn't yet been published. Campbell was then still some months away from being hired as editor of the magazine.

The two men hit it off together immediately. De Camp, the beginning science fiction writer, was impressed by Campbell, the old pro. In those scuffling days, Campbell was more reserved and less aggressively argumentative a person than he would later become, and de Camp was struck by the shrewdness and quietly voiced good sense of his observations on writing.

But Campbell saw something special in de Camp, too.

When he became editor of *Astounding*, Campbell requested and bought a story, or even several, from most of the writers who had sat in with his old circle—Edmond Hamilton, Henry Kuttner, Manly Wade Wellman, Otto Binder, Frank Belknap Long. Of these, it was the ever-adaptable Jack Williamson who would work out the best for him. Starting with *The Legion of Time* in 1938, Campbell would be able to rely on Williamson to contribute a novel and a shorter story each year to *Astounding* or *Unknown*.

However, out of all the SF writers he knew, it was the newcomer, L. Sprague de Camp, whom Campbell picked to become his first major ally in the presentation of modern science fiction.

On the face of it, that might seem strange. De Camp's first story, published in the last Tremaine-edited issue of *Astounding*, was lively and learned, but it was also clumsy. Moreover, de Camp did not know a lot about science fiction. He had never been a regular reader of the pulp magazines. His own influences in SF ran more to Edgar Rice Burroughs, Mark Twain, Lord Dunsany and E. R. Eddison than to E. E. Smith, Don A. Stuart and Stanley Weinbaum.

But three things in particular recommended de Camp to Campbell:

One was de Camp's special background and experience. He had been editor of his college newspaper at Cal Tech, and he was co-author of a new book on patents and their management. De Camp was that altogether rare individual inside science fiction or out—the man who combined a sound technical education with the ability to express himself clearly and easily. John Campbell was prepared to appreciate a scientific man who knew how to write.

De Camp's second attraction for Campbell was his temperament. To the outward eye, de Camp might be stiff, upright and thoroughly proper—a man of unimpeachable rationality. But, as Campbell soon came to recognize, lurking beneath this well-buttoned exterior there was another de Camp with urges to be a zany, a social critic and a romantic. Campbell, the professional provocateur, could respond to de Camp's heretical inclinations.

Third, and by no means least important, was "Hezekiah Plantagenet." This was the name of an oral round-robin game that de Camp had played as a boy and then came to introduce to the writers circle. In this game, one player would invent a terrific predicament for Hezekiah, the continuing hero, and then pass the story on. The challenge for the next person was to think of a way out—and then to imagine Hezekiah into a new and even tougher fix for the succeeding player to cope with.

But these science fiction writers were asked to play the game in science fiction terms. Hezekiah was to be opposed by a mad scientist, Homer Mifket. And however farfetched the problems posed and the solutions offered (and, by all means, the wilder the better) they were not allowed to run contrary to the known laws of nature.

Not only was this game of de Camp's a great deal of fun and wonderful exercise in SFish one-upmanship, but it was also highly revealing of knowledge, attitude and character. It cannot have been altogether lost on Campbell that certain writers were just too old-fashioned, too lacking contemporary scientific knowledge, or too slow to play the game well. Or, that whenever it seemed convenient to him, careless facile young Henry Kuttner might simply throw out something outrageous along the lines of, "Well, just then a hole in space happened along, and Hezekiah stepped into it"—at least until he was hooted down by his fellows.

Most of all, however, it cannot have escaped Campbell's attention that despite his impulses toward irreverence, L. Sprague de Camp was one SF writer willing and able to play strictly within the rules, paying all due respect to scientific law, and yet still able to be consistently inventive and amusing.

De Camp was a rebel within the law. And that made him just the man for Campbell.

If there was a fourth point of recommendation, it was that de Camp was available. De Camp had long been restive off in Scranton, feeling himself in exile there. At the end of 1937, he was glad to leave the place for another job as assistant editor of a fuel oil trade journal. After just a few months, however, de Camp's new job was terminated in an economy measure and he found himself out of work.

Campbell's need and de Camp's need came together. In very short order de Camp would be a free-lance writer living in New York City, producing stories and essays for John Campbell.

It didn't take Campbell long to see that de Camp had a highly developed sense of a universe of interconnection, a universe in which all things hang together. And Campbell was able to recognize this as the same in essence as the universe of his own vision—the universe of underlying operating principles.

De Camp became Campbell's right-hand man. In 1938, Campbell would publish only three short stories and one article by de Camp. But in 1939, the figures would be two two-part articles, two novels, and six stories, and Campbell would also use de Camp as a script doctor to do a complete revision of another author's not-quite-acceptable novel.

It would be hard to overstate the value de Camp held for Campbell in those early years. It was a complex and interrelated program of change that Campbell was attempting to engineer in *Astounding* through 1938 and 1939, and the writing that best exemplified the modern science fiction that Campbell was striving to bring into being was the work of L. Sprague de Camp. Until other writers finally showed up with their own versions of the new Atomic Age vision, it was de Camp who served as Campbell's corroboration and proof.

We might think of Campbell as an architect designing and erecting a mighty building—a house of many mansions—within the conceptual space over which E. E. Smith had spread his tent during the Thirties, rendering formal and permanent what had previously been improvised and temporary. And the articles and stories that L. Sprague de Camp contributed to Campbell in 1938 and 1939 were the first pillar of this edifice.

In this work, de Camp set out to answer the evolutionary conundrum that had so baffled and dismayed the Age of Technology: What was the true position of man within the universe?

To the Techno Age, it had seemed pretty evident that the universe had no liking and little tolerance for man in his present form. It appeared that if man was to survive, he must evolve. If he did not, then he would certainly be subject to supersession by more nimble Earthly creatures like octopuses or ants, or to subjugation by more ruthless and advanced beings sweeping in from the reaches of time and space. But if man were to evolve—into the alien and monstrous Big Brain, say—would that not come at the complete cost of his precious humanity?

This was the puzzle that de Camp was attempting to challenge and answer. He aimed to make a natural place for humanity within the universe by redefining "man" and "universe" and "evolution," and the connections between them, in the new terms of the Atomic Age vision.

For de Camp there was no longer a radical split between the Village and the World Beyond the Hill. No more was there a safe and tidy here-and-now that was completely known, completely controlled, and totally rational, which then stood in contrast to a wild and unfathomable out-there in which all familiar rules were suspended and anything at all might happen.

In de Camp's writing, the universe was presented as a continuum, everywhere partly known, everywhere holding surprise. This may be seen in the articles that de Camp contributed to *Astounding*. Here he was at pains to demonstrate the familiarity that might be inherent in the strange and different—and also to show the difference that could lurk within the accepted and familiar.

That something as seemingly fixed and familiar as the language we speak and write and read might become strange to us was asserted in "Language for Time Travelers" (*Astounding*, July 1938), the initial article that de Camp contributed to Campbell. Here he pointed out that our own English language that we take for granted as stable and constant, in actual fact changes and evolves continually through time.

And the complementary thought, that even the most apparently alien of beings might actually prove to be familiar and comprehensible to us, was expressed in his next article, "Design for Life" (*Astounding*, May-June 1939), in which de Camp discussed the form that intelligent life must necessarily take from an engineering point of view. He came to the conclusion that "if intelligent life did develop on another planet, it is unlikely that it would look like a chrysanthemum, or a starfish, or a fire hydrant. There are good reasons for thinking that it would probably look something like a man."

The effect of these articles—and de Camp's next essay, "There Ain't No Such!" (*Astounding*, Nov-Dec 1939), which discussed Earthly creatures as bizarre in appearance and habit as any alien being imagined by SF—was to suggest that the universe was of a common piece, that man was not out of place in the universe, and that evolution was not altogether strange and other, but was an everyday process of small increments of change in which mankind might already be participating without even being aware of it.

In the proto-ecological universe projected by de Camp, to be human was not some exclusive privilege of *Homo sapiens*—the special result of our possession of a rational soul and a personal relationship with God—but rather was a natural state of being which we might share with a wide variety of creatures. So it was that invading aliens in de Camp stories like "Divide and Rule" (*Unknown*, Apr-May 1939) or "The Warrior Race" (*Astounding*, Oct 1940) might fancy themselves to be innately superior to us, but then reveal what might be termed all-too-human frailty. Conversely, de Camp was capable of imagining what previously would have been thought of as lesser beings—a black bear experimentally raised to high intelligence in "The Command" (*Astounding*, Oct 1938), a Neanderthal man surviving into the present day in "The Gnarly Man" (*Unknown*, June 1939), and a tribe of mutated baboons in "The Blue Giraffe" (*Astounding*, Aug 1939)—and of portraying all of them as being as decent, rational and civilized as most men manage to be, and maybe even a bit more so.

De Camp was perfectly willing to concede that men of our own kind might still run afoul of the forces of evolution and pass from the scene. But if that were to happen, it would not be because evolution was some hostile outside force single-mindedly bent on bringing us down, but because we were so careless, stupid and greedy that we tripped ourselves up.

This may be seen in the short story "Living Fossil" (*Astounding*, Feb 1939). Here, the intelligent 150-pound capuchin monkeys who have succeeded a devolved and nearly extinct mankind suggest that our fall came to pass not through the operation of some iron law of growth and decay, but rather as the result of a multiplicity of human failings, not the least of which was abuse of the environment. As a monkey scientist puts it:

> "We know that Man, during the period of his civilization, was prodigally wasteful of his resources. The exhaustion of the mineral oils is an example. And the world-wide extinction of the larger mammals at the close of the last ice age was probably his doing, at least in part. We're sure that he was responsible for wiping out all the larger species of whales, and we suspect that he also killed off all but two of the twenty or more species of elephant that abounded at that time. Most of the large mammals of today have evolved in the last few million years from life forms that were small enough to sit in your hand in Man's time.
>
> "We don't know just why he became extinct, or almost extinct. Perhaps a combination of war and disease did it. Perhaps the exhaustion of his resources had a share. You know what a hardboiled materialist I am in most things; but it always has seemed to me that it was a case of outraged nature taking its revenge. That's not rational, but it's the way I feel. And I've dedicated my life to seeing that we don't make the same mistake."

But for de Camp, mankind was by no means inevitably doomed. There was an obvious way forward, and that was for us to embrace nature, and not to rebel against it.

As early as his first story for Campbell, "Hyperpilosity" (*Astounding*, Apr 1938), de Camp imagined a near-future world in which humanity has encountered a virus and suddenly sprouted fur. In Techno Age SF, human change of almost any kind had been perceived as inherently dangerous and destabilizing, the herald of coming decay. For those with this attitude, the growth of fur on human beings must be taken as a hideous sign of degeneration into animality.

Not so for de Camp, the dedicated debunker of Techno Age illusions. For him, fur on human beings was only a superficial change—something to laugh about, but nothing to get worked up over. Rather than resistance and denial, the course recommended by de Camp was adaptation to circumstances. In his story, the person who ultimately prospers in the new furry society is not the man who buys stock in hair remover, but rather the man who invests in currycombs.

In sum, the answer that de Camp presented to the evolutionary conundrum of the Techno Age in his early writing was this: The universe was not to be feared as fundamentally hostile and other. We ourselves were a natural product of that universe, so that even though we might discover much there that was strange to us, nothing that we would encounter was likely to be wholly alien. If we kept calm, used our science to learn the rules of the universe, and did what was appropriate at each turn, we could get along.

Here in de Camp's work was essentially the same message as the message of "Who Goes There?" but laid out as a complete, carefully made argument without the vestiges of horror and hysteria that had marked Campbell's story.

The science fiction short stories and the science articles that de Camp wrote during 1938 and 1939 helped to replace Techno Age emotionalism with a new tone of rationality and good humor. They made a strong case for the legitimacy, value and power of human nature. And they tended to suggest that immediate human survival and advancement would not come by way of evolution, which was a slow, gradual, long-term process that could be trusted to take care of itself, but rather through scientific progress, the cumulative mastery of universal operating principles.

Useful, even essential, as this early work was, however, it would not be de Camp's most original and significant contribution to Campbell's enterprise. This would come in the novels and short novels that he began to write both alone and collaboratively for *Unknown*, the new companion magazine of *Astounding*.

This second magazine, which started publication in March 1939, was the true measure of John Campbell's breadth and subtlety. It was the culmination of Campbell's early editorial experiments with SF form and content.

Unknown would be to *Astounding* something of what *All-Story* had once been to *Argosy*—a less dignified, less responsible and less respectable sibling. A place for SF writers to have some fun without being held to strict account for it.

In outward appearance, *Unknown* would seem not to be a magazine of science fiction at all—at least not science fiction as Hugo Gernsback might reckon it. Instead, it presented itself as a magazine of traditional fantasy, printing stories about gods, witches, genies, devils and gnomes.

But this appearance would be deceiving. To the degree that the fiction printed in *Unknown* might honestly be called a kind of fantasy, it was fantasy written as though it were a variant form of modern science fiction. The "magic" in *Unknown* would not be based upon *spirit*, as in traditional myth. Instead, it would come to be regarded as another kind of science, the result of the operation of alternative underlying operating principles—which L. Sprague de Camp and his collaborator Fletcher Pratt would call "the laws of magic."

In fact, many of the stories printed in *Unknown* would bear little or no resemblance to traditional spirit-based fantasy. Rather, they would be contemporary SF stories with some impossible twist or odd assumption.

When Campbell received a good story that did not observe the strict parameters of plausibility and subject matter that he was attempting to establish in *Astounding*, it was highly convenient for him to be able to term the story "fantasy" and print it in *Unknown*. The tale usually told about the way *Unknown* came into being is that John Campbell had a novel submitted by British writer Eric Frank Russell concerning scientifically unexplained "Fortean phenomena." Under Harry Bates or F. Orlin Tremaine, this story, *Sinister Barrier*, would have fit right into *Astounding*, but not under Campbell. So he dreamed up *Unknown* just to contain it.

L. Ron Hubbard would tell a different story. There can be no doubt that with three Arabian Nights otherworld adventure novels in *Unknown* in 1939, he was the contributor whom Campbell initially most depended upon. Late in his life, Hubbard would suggest that it was for his own personal benefit that Campbell invented *Unknown*, since he was more comfortable writing fantasy than science fiction.

At best, however, both stories are only partial truths. Campbell himself said about *Sinister Barrier*: "I can assure you that one does not start a new magazine because of the arrival of any one story alone." And he also said: "One of the things that led to the launching of *Unknown*...was the fact that more first-rate manuscripts than *Astounding* could publish were coming into the office."

Since Campbell was drawing from a common pool of manuscripts, there might at times appear to be a certain degree of arbitrariness in his decisions as to just what story would appear in which magazine. At least some of the stories that he published—de Camp's invading alien story "Divide and Rule," for instance—might as easily have appeared in one place as the other.

But in Campbell's mind, there was an essential formal distinction between his two magazines. And to aid his writers in their conceptions, he would tell them explicitly: "'I edit two magazines, *Astounding* and *Unknown*. For *Astounding* I want stories which are good and logical and possible. For *Unknown*, I want stories which are good and logical.'"

What this meant in practice was that the special business of *Astounding* was stories of the future and outer space—the mainstream of science-fictional possibility. And the province of *Unknown* was variant realities.

Within the context of the times, it was *Astounding* that was the vastly more important magazine. *Astounding* was engaged in the serious business of bringing the future of man into being. *Unknown* was just fun and games.

But beyond the immediate moment, *Unknown*—which would only last for four years and thirty-nine issues—would have a considerable importance of its own. In *Unknown*, a basis would be made for perceiving traditional fantasy and pulp magazine science fiction as being different aspects of a larger SF. And, as the first presentation of SF not just as a literature of *change*, but of *alternate possibilities*, *Unknown* would be a portent of coming things in SF just as surely as *The Steam Man of the Prairies* had been a forehint of *The Time Machine* and *The Skylark of Space*.

Of all Campbell's writers, it was L. Sprague de Camp who found the freedom of *Unknown* most necessary and most congenial. De Camp suffered from one great inhibition in producing stories for *Astounding*—the "science fiction" published in *Astounding* was supposed to be possible, and the rational side of de Camp took this injunction with the utmost seriousness. But this meant that de Camp was not able to write about either time machines or faster-than-light travel, since in his scientific heart-of-hearts he didn't believe that either of these irrational modes of travel would ever be possible.

Way back in *The Skylark of Space*, E.E. Smith might have his venturers casually dismiss Einstein and zoom away toward the stars at supralight speed, saying, "'Einstein's Theory is still a theory. This distance is an observed fact.'" But de Camp, the new Atomic Age man of reason, debunker of Techno Age credulity, was utterly incapable of this sort of imaginative recklessness.

And because he couldn't see how to leap lightly from here to there, de Camp was never fully at home writing about either the future or outer space. His strict imaginative scruples kept his science fiction stories in *Astounding* comparatively limited and Earthbound.

Ah, but for de Camp, stories thought of as "fantasy" and written for *Unknown* were crucially different from stories of "science fiction" meant for *Astounding*. Stories for *Unknown* were not *expected* to be possible—and this set de Camp's imagination free.

As one example, operating according to the standards of *Astounding*, de Camp would never have been able to imagine "The Gnarly Man," his story of a prehistoric man coping easily with the challenges of the modern world. By what *possible* means, pray tell, might a Neanderthal man survive for 50,000 years, never aging? Certainly none that de Camp the rational man of science knew. But writing in the context of *Unknown*, he was permitted to posit that his prehistoric bison hunter had been physiologically altered by a (purely conventional) stroke of lightning, and then get on with the pure fun of imagining how modern people might react to him, and he to them.

Unknown gave de Camp a license to take great leaps of the imagination—which he was then expected to develop logically and rigorously. John Campbell couldn't have devised an imaginative formula more perfectly suited to the nature and knowledge of this particular writer.

So it was, then, that in a story like *Lest Darkness Fall* (*Unknown*, Dec 1939), the de Camp who could not in all conscience write about science fiction time machines felt free to assume yet another lightning-bolt-of-convenience—"the granddaddy of all lightning flashes"—as a device to send his protagonist, archaeologist Martin Padway, back in time to a crucial moment in Western history, the final fall of Rome. Then, from that point, de Camp could play the game of *what if* and proceed to write a novel about the application of universal operating principles to the needs of an earlier moment and the transplantation of scientific progress into the past.

It was *Lest Darkness Fall* that firmly established L. Sprague de Camp as the star writer of *Unknown.* The obvious model for this story was Mark Twain's *A Connecticut Yankee in King Arthur's Court* (1889). *Lest Darkness Fall* might be thought of as an attempt to take *A Connecticut Yankee* and do it *right*—that is, in Atomic Age terms.

In both of these stories, contemporary protagonists are transferred to the past through unlikely accidents. Twain's man is sent back through time as the result of a blow on the head from a crowbar in the hands of a dissident worker, while de Camp's is sent to the past by that humungous bolt of lightning. The point of arrival in both cases is Europe in the Sixth Century A.D., the eve of the Dark Ages. And the aim of both of these modern men becomes to alter the past.

But at that point, the two books diverge subtly but significantly.

Twain's Boss, Hank Morgan, is a man of the Techno Age, a maker of tools and engines and a superintendent of labor. He's a guy who knows how to build machines and keep men in line. His natural impulse is to take the half-historical, half-legendary world he has entered and whip it into shape. Since it is what he knows how to do, he will make guns and railroads and electric lights and set out to turn Arthurian Britain into a facsimile of Nineteenth Century America whether the yokels and peasants like it or not.

But because the story of King Arthur as we know it simply doesn't *go* that way, eventually he must be slipped a sleeping draught by Merlin which has the effect of returning him to his own time. In the end we have to take all that comes between the blow on the head (which comes before the beginning of the narrative proper) and the sleeping potion at the end as some sort of dream or hallucination.

De Camp, however, was the active beneficiary of all the stories of travel in time and dimension written in the fifty years since *A Connecticut Yankee*—even though he himself might spurn Wellsian time machines of nickel and ivory and crystal as scientifically impossible. And at the very outset of *Lest Darkness Fall*, before the crucial bolt of lightning strikes, he has an Italian professor set forth a very Wells-like theory of time as a tree with many branches:

> "I was saying all these people who just disappear, they have slipped back down the...trunk of the tree of time. When they stop slipping, they are back in some former time. But as soon as they do anything, they change all subsequent history. ... The trunk continues to exist. But a new branch starts out where they came to rest."

Thus, pure device of convenience though that stroke of lightning may be, we do have a basis of argument for taking it seriously as a time travel device. And when Martin Padway finds himself transferred to a known historical period—a declining Rome in 535 A.D., ruled by an Ostrogothic king and about to suffer invasion by Justinian's brilliant general, Belisarius—it isn't a dream and he isn't going to just as suddenly find himself back in the Twentieth Century. He's in Rome for real, and he's there for good.

What is more, he isn't condemned to complete futility by what our history books say did happen then. He has some assurance that by the actions he chooses to take, he can alter the course of history. It is within his power to create a whole new reality if he is clever and able enough.

Unlike Twain's Techno Age Boss, who perceives the Sixth Century Britons as no better than children or animals, Martin Padway is an Atomic Age democrat who sincerely likes and respects the people he has fallen among. De Camp being de Camp, these various Italians, Goths, Vandals, Syrians, Jews, Greeks and such are presented as familiar, normal, decent, fallible human beings not very different in nature from ourselves.

What distinguishes Padway from them is not that he is some sort of superior human being, higher on the evolutionary ladder than they, but rather his comparatively greater degree of knowledge and objectivity. He is forearmed by knowing something of history as it would have been without him. And he is also a man of scientific training, an heir of the past few centuries of Western scientific progress.

Padway's impulse isn't to attempt to re-create the Twentieth

Century in Sixth Century Rome, erecting skyscrapers beside the Colosseum. Indeed, he doesn't for an instant believe that such a thing would be possible. But he is deeply aware of the pivotal nature of the moment in which he finds himself:

> He was living in the twilight of western classical civilization. The Age of Faith, better known as the Dark Ages, was closing down. Europe would be in darkness, from a scientific and technological aspect, for nearly a thousand years. That aspect was, to Padway's naturally prejudiced mind, the most, if not the only, important aspect of a civilization.

Almost inevitably, then, it occurs to Padway to wonder: "Could one man change the course of history to the extent of preventing this interregnum?"

It's as though Padway were some special sort of doctor brought to the bedside of this ailing culture to give it a shot of what it needs the most. That isn't an instant, inappropriate modernity, but rather transplants of appropriate inventions and techniques from the Middle Ages and the Renaissance, stuff that may serve to start up the machinery of scientific progress.

So it is that Padway introduces Arabic numerals, horse harnesses, distilling, the telescope, semaphore telegraphy, paper and printing, a postal system and schools. When he proposes this last, he says frankly, "'I'm going to have things taught that really matter: mathematics, and the sciences, and medicine. I see where I shall have to write all the textbooks myself.'"

Of necessity—there is that invasion by the armies of the Eastern Roman Emperor Justinian to consider—Padway does become involved in military and political activities like Twain's Hank Morgan, but he sees these only as means. He says: "'The end is things like the telegraph and the presses. My politicking and soldiering may not make any difference a hundred years from now, but the other things will, I hope.'"

And by the end of the story, he has grown convinced that he has been successful. Whatever befalls him, these things he has introduced are now too widespread and well rooted to disappear. History has been changed. Darkness will not fall—at least not on this one new branch of the tree of time.

What a triumph for the power of universal operating principles! To overset the primary example of cyclical history—the decline and fall of the Roman Empire—and replace the Dark Ages with a new era of scientific progress!

De Camp would take the implied argument of *Lest Darkness Fall* and give it explicit expression in the fourth of his influential articles for Campbell, "The Science of Whithering" (*Astounding*, July-Aug 1940). In this essay, de Camp examined one theory of civilization after another, including Oswald Spengler's and Arnold Toynbee's great expositions of cyclical history. But de Camp would come to the conclusion that cyclical history was not after all a grim inevitability for mid-Twentieth Century Western civilization. It might be overturned by the more effective power of modern scientific and technological development.

The transition from Techno Age SF to the new modern science fiction of the Atomic Age reached its turning point in the summer of 1939, at just about the same time that de Camp was shifting his primary attentions from *Astounding* to *Unknown*. It was then that John Campbell's patient efforts to alter *Astounding* and to change SF began to come together and take on synergetic power.

By that time, Campbell had overhauled *Astounding* inside and out. It no longer presented the same face to the world. It had a revised title, new design, and new cover artists.

The content of the magazine had gradually altered along with its outward appearance. In the pages of *Astounding*, Campbell had announced and defined a new kind of science fiction, and published examples by himself and others. And he had discovered or developed a nucleus of writers capable of producing this new SF.

Campbell had given science fiction readers and writers a new humanized universe to consider: A universe that was not hostile to mankind. A universe in which human decision and human action counted. A universe that human beings might even come to control.

And in editorials, in articles and in fiction, Campbell had set forth a new agenda of major projects for the modern science fiction writers of *Astounding* to concentrate their attention on—tests of this new universe. These central problems would be the essence of the Golden Age *Astounding*: learning to cope with the complexities of future living, developing space travel, controlling atomic power and the robot, and exploring the limits of the human mind. If men could learn to handle these operations, then surely they could master anything the universe had to offer.

Finally, Campbell had created the modern fantasy of *Unknown* as an obvious contrast to the new science fiction of *Astounding*. But also as a less obvious reinforcement and extension of the methods and values of *Astounding*.

And even so—through the first half of 1939, *Astounding* was not yet a magazine of modern science fiction, but still only striving to be one.

But then, in the summer of 1939, this condition visibly began to alter. In the space of just three months—July, August and September—

a host of new writers appeared for the first time in Campbell's magazines, lured to him by the message of the changes in *Astounding*, by the sound and smell of action, or by the simple force of Campbell's need for them.

The July 1939 issue of *Astounding* marks the sunrise of the Campbell Golden Age. This was the first issue in which the preponderance of material was in the new style:

Campbell's editorial was a follow-up to the news that the atom had been split. He foresaw both commercial atomic power plants and the explosive potential of rapid fission, noting, "For sheer violence, the fission of the uranium atom is unmatched."

There were two articles in July. One was "Tools for Brains" by Leo Vernon, a history of the development of thinking machines. The other, "Geography for Time Travelers" by Willy Ley—which owed something to de Camp's previous article, "Language for Time Travelers"—pointed out that even the shape and location of continents are subject to change.

In this issue, the cover story was "Black Destroyer," a novelet by a new writer, a Canadian named A. E. van Vogt, who had been stimulated to take up SF writing by an impulsive newsstand reading of "Who Goes There?"

Also here was "Trends," the first story in *Astounding* by young Isaac Asimov, the eager kid from the candy store whom Campbell had been tutoring for the past year.

Nor was that the end of the riches. Also in this July issue was a striking novelet of alternate futures, "Greater Than Gods," the first story for Campbell by C. L. Moore, the author of "Shambleau" and the Jirel of Joiry stories. Not only would Moore contribute a number of distinguished stories to Campbell under her own name, but after her marriage to Henry Kuttner in 1940, they would jointly become two of Campbell's most effective new wartime writers, Lewis Padgett and Lawrence O'Donnell.

And there were more new writers to come. In the August issue of *Astounding*, there appeared "Life-Line," the first SF story by former Navy officer Robert Heinlein. He would become two major writers for Campbell: himself and Anson MacDonald.

And still more. In the August *Unknown* there was "Two Sought Adventure," a first novelet by Fritz Leiber, Jr., the son of a well-known Shakespearean actor. And the September *Astounding* contained "Ether Breather," the first SF story by young merchant seaman Theodore Sturgeon.

It was this horde of new writers so suddenly arrived—together with E. E. Smith, Jack Williamson, Clifford Simak, L. Ron Hubbard, Lester del Rey, and L. Sprague de Camp—who would be the makers of John Campbell's Golden Age, the builders of his empire of the imagination.

The most central of these would be de Camp, Asimov, Heinlein and van Vogt. It would be they who would take universal operating principles and apply them to other dimensions, to the robot, to time, to space, and to the higher evolution of man.

Modern science fiction—the new, stream-lined, fact-minded, universe-manipulating science fiction designed by John W. Campbell that so visibly began to come on-line in the summer of 1939—may be seen as the culmination and fulfillment of Techno Age SF. But at the same time, it was something altogether different and new—the foundation for the following forty years of SF development.

In the pages of *Astounding* and *Unknown* during the Golden Age that lasted from the summer of 1939 through the end of 1945, the great body of scientific fiction written since 1870 would become raw material to be drawn upon, played with, summarized, consolidated and extended. It would also be completely reformulated.

The most epitomal example of this process of simultaneous fulfill-ment and transmutation is to be seen in the story "Nightfall," a novelet by Isaac Asimov published in the September 1941 issue of *Astounding*. So unique and yet so completely typical of modern science fiction is "Nightfall" that nearly thirty years after it was first published, when the members of the Science Fiction Writers of America were asked to vote for the best SF stories produced prior to the founding of the organization in 1965, they would place this story first, ahead of Stanley Weinbaum's "A Martian Odyssey."

"Nightfall" is the most pivotal story of a pivotal moment. We can learn a great deal about how Campbell's Golden Age was made and how it worked—and even catch some inklings of its eventual limitations—by taking a good look at the variety of Techno Age, Romantic, and even earlier materials that went into the inspiration and design of this central story; by looking beyond that to the nature of the apprenticeship in modern science fiction that Isaac Asimov had to undergo before John Campbell was ready to acknow-ledge him as someone capable of undertaking a project of this importance; and finally by seeing the way that old materials and the new attitudes developed by Asimov were successfully conjoined in "Nightfall" to produce a story of unique significance.

"Nightfall," in fact, was a story that was assigned to Asimov to write. As with so much else in the Golden Age *Astounding*, the idea for "Nightfall" was Campbell's. He recognized the germ of an SF story in a lyrical sentence in the opening paragraph of *Nature* (1836), the first book by Ralph Waldo Emerson, the New England Transcendentalist lecturer and essayist.

Emerson had begun his little book by proclaiming the visibility of the hand of God in Nature. In illustration of this thesis, he wrote: "If the stars should appear one night in a thousand years, how would men believe and adore, and preserve for many generations the remembrance of the city of God which had been shown!"

Asimov recalls coming to a story conference at John Campbell's office on March 17, 1941. On this occasion, Asimov's own latest idea was quickly waved aside. Campbell had something he wanted to show him—this quotation, shorn of its last four words. When he'd read it, Campbell asked:

> "What do you think would happen, Asimov, if men were to see the stars for the first time in a thousand years?"
> I thought, and drew a blank. I said, "I don't know."
> Campbell said, "I think they would go mad. I want you to write a story about that."

What a powerful idea this was for Asimov to have dropped on him from out of the blue! And all the more so since prior to this moment, Campbell had never seen fit to offer Asimov an original story idea of any kind. He had played around with Asimov's own ideas and expanded upon them, but he had never presented Asimov with a brand-new idea before.

At the same time, however, as phrased here, what a curiously old-fashioned suggestion it was! This quote from Emerson dates from the height of the Romantic Period and is an embodiment of Romantic attitudes. It proposes that if the brilliance of the stars were to be visible for only one night in a thousand years, the souls of men would still instantly recognize the handiwork of God which had been revealed to them, and adore the Creator. That is what good Romantics would do.

But the alternative reaction that Campbell was apparently touting was not new, either. It was straight out of the Age of Technology, the era when men had lost their grip on their souls, the long-cherished lifeline to God, and found themselves standing alone in the cold front yard of the new universe of space and time, dazzled and dismayed. Campbell's counter-suggestion to Asimov was that men in the situation envisioned by Emerson would not worship God at all, but would react instead like some hysteric out of H. P. Lovecraft, who on discovery of the terrifying new vistas of reality and our frightful position therein promptly goes mad. Or like Olaf Stapledon's hapless Last Men, who find the aloof and changeless presence of the constellations so horrifying, so demoralizing, and so maddening that all they can do is whimper and retreat from the stars.

In fact, however, there was much more on Campbell's mind than just these old-fashioned reactions. Emerson was only the jumping-off point for his thinking, and Techno Age cosmic fear but the first elaboration.

We may remember Campbell suggesting to Asimov that when he presented an idea to a writer, he expected to get back more than he gave. In this case, the all-but-unstated something more that Campbell wanted was the special new perspective of modern science fiction, the perspective that Campbell had so patiently been teaching Asimov month after month through the preceding two and a half years.

Something of Campbell's true underlying attitude, thinking, and expectation can be caught by taking note of the stance that he automatically assumed toward this project. He himself was in no peril of either adoring God or freaking out. He stood outside the Emersonian situation—above it and beyond it—perceiving in it the substance of a formal thought experiment, the makings of a Campbell-style SF story. And he obviously expected the same kind of calm dispassion from Asimov, the two men practicing their science fiction together as though it were a kind of science.

Campbell's confident posture of detached rational consideration may be glimpsed in Asimov's account of the balance of that crucial story conference. He says, "We talked about various things, thereafter, with Campbell seeming to circle the idea and occasionally asking me questions such as, 'Why should the stars be invisible at other times?' and listening to me as I tried to improvise answers."

It was Campbell's presumption that his new fact-manipulating modern science fiction would be able to find a way—and more than one way, many ways—to literalize, act out, and then master the uncertain Emersonian moment in which the stars are unveiled to human eyes that have not witnessed them in a thousand years. In this assumption, Campbell had the advantage—which Asimov did not share—of knowing that Robert Heinlein, the former Navy engineer who was Campbell's most reliable new writer, had already delivered a major story to him on this very same theme.

In "Universe" (*Astounding*, May 1941), Heinlein presents a pioneering spaceship that long ago was launched into the void between Earth and the nearest star. In generations past, this ship suffered mutiny and mutation. It has forgotten its purposes. What was once known to be historical and scientific fact has been turned into verse, a religious rigmarole that is committed to memory but no longer understood.

The ship has lost its way, and no one looks outside. Words like "the Earth," "a ship," and "the stars" are now taken allegorically. So it is that when the stars outside the ship are revealed to the protagonist at last, the result is neither worship nor madness, but an onrush of understanding that what had been taken as so much fudge is in fact literal truth. This is experienced as a kind of emotional/ esthetic tripout that Heinlein compares to orgasm:

> Light after jeweled light, scattered in careless bountiful splendor across the simulacrum sky, the countless suns lay before him—before him, over him, under him, behind him, in every direction from him. He hung alone in the center of the stellar universe.
>
> "Oooooh!" It was an involuntary sound, caused by his indrawn breath. He clutched the chair arms hard enough to break fingernails, but he was not aware of it. Nor was he afraid at the moment; there was room in his being for but one emotion. Life within the Ship, alternately harsh and workaday, had placed no strain on his innate capacity to experience beauty; for the first time in his life he knew the intolerable ecstasy of beauty unalloyed. It shook him and hurt him, like the first trembling intensity of sex.

Heinlein's protagonist then wants nothing so much as to show the same sight to others so that they may know the truth and beauty of the stars, too.

Campbell not only had this special story in hand, "Universe" was already set in print and would be appearing on the newsstands in only a month. But, as though in proof of his claim that he could feed half-a-dozen writers the same idea and get back six different stories, Campbell wanted Asimov to write another story containing the sudden revelation of the stars. However, this one was to be different from Heinlein's. It was to be centered around a mass reaction of madness.

Now Campbell was not requesting Asimov to write a story about the experience of madness, like Edgar Allan Poe in one of his more hallucinatory moods. Nor was he asking him to meditate on the prospect of society gone crazy from the shock of a suddenly revealed wider universe.

What Campbell was ultimately proposing to Asimov was that he resolve a fundamental problem with the aid of universal operating principles, as Don A. Stuart, Campbell's alter ego, had done in "Who Goes There?", the seminal story Campbell had so impressed Asimov with at their first meeting. But the problem Campbell was offering for solution was not merely the minor problem of mass freakout at the sight of the stars, but the larger problem of cyclical history and the failure of humanity.

Don A. Stuart's "Twilight" and "Night"—which together presented Earthbound cyclical history taken to its ultimate declination—had been published only half-a-dozen years earlier. Asimov—who was just past 21 and a graduate student in chemistry at Columbia—had read these stories of Campbell's when he was a senior in high school and a freshman in college. So when Campbell and Asimov agreed before the close of that special story conference that the tale they were planning would be entitled "Nightfall," Asimov must have recognized on some level that Campbell was deputizing him to deal with the problem that "Twilight" and "Night" had posed and then left unresolved.

Something of the attitude with which Asimov approached this assignment can be seen in the tenor of the bell-note that he struck in his mind when he sat down to write "Nightfall." He recalled the thought-variant stories once published in *Astounding* by Campbell's predecessor, F. Orlin Tremaine. Asimov says:

> The thought-variants (however noticeable their errors in science to my increasingly hypercritical self) affected me profoundly. They struck me as science fiction par excellence, and by the time I began to write science fiction myself, I yearned to write thought-variants, even though the use of the term vanished with Tremaine. My story "Nightfall" was consciously written as a thought-variant.

We should be aware—as Asimov most certainly was aware—that neither "Twilight" nor "Night" had been identified by Tremaine as thought-variants. And with good reason. Campbell's two stories had not offered any wonder-inspiring new ideas. Rather, they were late restatements of that Techno Age vision of far future Earth in decrepitude that had been presented in *The Time Machine*, "The World of the Red Sun," and many other stories. Their special virtue was the vividness with which they evoked the early Twentieth Century devolutionary nightmare.

An Asimov who had grasped the idea that "Nightfall" should in some sense be a companion piece to "Twilight" and "Night," but who was also resolved that his story should be a thought-variant, was an Asimov who had indeed gotten Campbell's message and understood the true nature of the task that had been laid out for him.

We can see, then, that even in the planning stage, it was intended that "Nightfall" should incorporate a succession of stages of Western thought, a whole range of old and new attitudes toward transcendence.

"Nightfall" would begin with a Romantic epigraph from Ralph Waldo Emerson declaring that the city of God—which we can take both as the heavenly city of traditional Christian conception and also as its successor, the rationally perfected utopian city of the Age of Reason—was not just some faded dream of *spirit*, but was actually to be glimpsed in the countenance of material nature... as men allowed to view the stars only once in a millennium would most surely be ready to testify.

In its own time, this was a thoroughly radical assertion which aimed to indicate the way out of the old spirit-based belief and into the new materialistic head-state that was then emerging. But a hundred years later, working in the context of a different era, Campbell and Asimov could elect to treat it as though it were a conservative statement, a mere reaffirmation of traditional spiritual values.

In contrast to this, the story proper would offer a situation that was a literalization of all the mental ups and downs suffered by Western scientific man since he gave up being spiritual and became materialistic. "Nightfall" would include the madness of Edgar Allan Poe and the intolerable cosmic revelations of H.P. Lovecraft. It would bow toward scientific utopia and toward the lost race story. It would invoke the red-sun-at-the-end-of-time melancholy of *The Time Machine* and "Night." Its title would be an acknowledgement of the concerns of Don A. Stuart. And the story would also be a Tremaine thought-variant.

All at the same time.

And the new Campbellian modern science fiction, with its power to imagine any special set of circumstances and conditions, and its positive eagerness to pose problems and solve them, would manage to align all of these disparate elements and turn them into the backbone of a story resolving the thorny problems of cyclical history.

At this point, Asimov, who could be as secretly unsure of himself as he could be outwardly brash, still considered himself only a tyro as a science fiction writer—a hopeful third-rater. In three years of effort, he had sold seventeen SF stories—but only four of these sales had been to John Campbell, who was his standard of measure. For Asimov, *Astounding* was the only game in town; sales other than to Campbell didn't really count.

So how was it that Campbell had sufficient confidence in Asimov to entrust him with this altogether special assignment? The answer is that John Campbell had been observing Asimov closely ever since the day he first showed up at his office, and he knew things about Asimov that Asimov himself didn't yet know.

To start, Asimov was not like his friends, other young would-be SF writers who made their way to Campbell's office, found the overbearing manner and Socratic style of the great editor too intolerable to endure, and fought with him, insulted him, or fled from him, even unto the opposite coast. Asimov alone among these bright, hungry, talented, lippy New York kids was prepared to be patient and avoid argument, to carefully attend the significance of Campbell's every word, and to find some way to follow the editor's lead even when he might be in disagreement.

Asimov says:

> I became the youngest member of the "stable" of writers he...gathered around himself. Though others still younger came his way later, I don't think that ever in his career did he have an acolyte less worldly and more naive than I was. I believe that amused him and that it pleased him to have so excellent an opportunity to do a bit of molding. At any rate, I have always thought that of all his writers I was his favorite and that he spent more time and effort on me than on anyone else. I believe it still shows.

Campbell tested him again and again. None of his other major contributors was ever asked to struggle and fight and hang in there to win acceptance from Campbell as a modern science fiction writer to the degree Asimov was. But the earnest, eager young Asimov rose to the challenge. He never gave up—never thought for a moment of giving up, even when he had written eighteen stories and Campbell had only seen fit to buy one.

Asimov labored mightily to find the key to work that John Campbell might find acceptable. Many of his early attempts were naive, irrelevant, or simply wide of the mark. But, little by little, Asimov absorbed the editor's message, and gradually but steadily his work moved in Campbell's direction.

When everything came together at last for Asimov, and he finally did succeed in transforming himself into a genuine writer of modern science fiction—and no ordinary one, at that—Campbell was there ready and waiting for him. He recognized what Asimov had managed to make of himself long before Asimov did, and knew how best to put him to use.

"Nightfall" might be thought of either as a kind of final exam, or alternatively as a first opportunity. When Campbell handed the Emerson quote to Asimov in March 1941 and asked him to write a story around it, it was the crowning moment of all those months of personal instruction. By then, Campbell had a pretty fair notion of Asimov's knowledge and abilities, and good and sufficient reason to think that Asimov might be ready to handle a challenge of this magnitude.

A look in detail at the nature of the adjustments Asimov made in his writing and thinking in order to become a Campbellian science fiction writer will show exactly why Campbell could be so confident that Asimov was ready to take on a story like "Nightfall," and also something of what was different and new and special about modern science fiction.

Let's begin with Asimov's first inadequate story, "Cosmic Cork-screw." Though it would never see publication, Asimov has described it in his collection of his earliest stories and again in the first volume of his autobiography.

In this story, a time traveler penetrates the future only to find all animal life suddenly, recently, and mysteriously vanished from the planet. He has no way to discover exactly what has happened—the nature of time and of his device prevent him from investigating. And then, when the traveler returns to our era and tells his tale, he is reckoned to be mad and placed in an insane asylum.

Pretty standard ho-hum Age of Technology stuff. A recognition of this was Asimov's first lesson in modern science fiction.

The point was made by Campbell's own new story, "Who Goes There?", which he showed to Asimov at their first meeting in June 1938. "Who Goes There?" was a prototype for SF to come. Following the example of "Who Goes There?", Campbellian modern science fiction would be concerned with posing problems of human relationship to the multiverse of space and time, and then finding the solution to these problems using the appropriate universal operating principles.

At its best, "Cosmic Corkscrew" could only be another old-time scientifiction story. It posed no solvable problem at all, but only displayed a great cosmic enigma and then retreated from it.

Asimov recognized immediately that there was a vital difference between the two stories, and he quickly gave indication that it was Campbell's game he wished to play.

In less than a month, he was back at Campbell's office with a second story, "Stowaway." This story had been heavily influenced by Asimov's reading of "Who Goes There?" It featured a deadly creature that appeared mysterious but proved to be scientifically comprehensible. "Stowaway" also owed something to "Other Eyes Watching" (*Astounding*, Feb 1937), a Campbell article on Jupiter in the series he was writing before he became editor.

But Campbell turned this second story down, too. He said that it had no particular identifiable fault, but that it was amateurish and didn't move smoothly. He advised Asimov that it would probably take him a year of effort and a dozen tries before Campbell could begin to find his work acceptable.

Although Campbell didn't say so explicitly, it was necessary for Asimov to learn that the modern science fiction story was not conceived, organized or written in quite the same way as the Age of Technology SF story.

The typical Techno Age story was a linear narrative after the fashion of *Journey to the Centre of the Earth*, *The Time Machine*, or Asimov's "Cosmic Corkscrew." It was composed of a string of *and thens*, as a character made a transition from the Village into the World Beyond the Hill, had a series of adventures there, and then returned. The meat of the story was the detailed exposition of all that was encountered and the character's reactions to it. The more adventures and the more reaction the better.

The modern science fiction story was very different. It was not framed as an endless, episodic process of probing into the unknown. Rather, it was conceived as a kind of mosaic, with every element in the story existing both for its own sake and also for its contribution to the pattern of the whole.

Like the multiverse it delineated, a modern science fiction story hung together. It could make do without a lot of the endless describing-and-reacting that earlier SF had considered indispensable. Since it was the shape of the whole that really mattered, much could now be said by implication or need not even be said at all.

As a result, modern science fiction was less emotive and more businesslike than Techno Age SF. With the coming of modern science fiction, story lengths became more compact. In giving Asimov his reasons for rejecting "Cosmic Corkscrew," Campbell had cited the fact that at 9000 words its length was awkward, too long for a short story, too short for a novelet. But in former times, that wouldn't have been an unusual length for a short story in *Astounding*.

And just that quickly, Asimov seized hold of the proper new external standards of measure. At 6000 words, his second story "Stowaway" was exactly the right length. If his story still came out as amateurish and clunky, that was because Asimov didn't yet grasp that the shorter length of the modern science fiction story was the result of packing more meaning into a smaller space.

The first real clues as to how modern science fiction was actually to be constructed came to Asimov in an exchange he had with writer Clifford Simak later in that summer of 1938. Simak, more than fifteen years older than Asimov, was the midwestern newspaperman who had published a few stories in the early Thirties and then put science fiction aside until Campbell became editor of *Astounding*.

When Simak's first new story after his return, "Rule 18," appeared in the July 1938 issue of *Astounding*, Asimov was not at all impressed by it. In his regular monthly letter to the magazine rating the stories, Asimov-the-fan ranked this relatively slight tale of time-traveling football players low.

Simak read Asimov's letter when it was printed in the September issue. And he immediately wrote a sincere and temperate letter to the youngster in Brooklyn seeking to know the details of his criticism. What was it that had been wrong with the story?

Asimov says:

> I reread the story in order to be able to answer properly and found, to my surprise, that there was nothing wrong with it at all. What he had done was to write the story in separate scenes with no explicit transition passages between. I wasn't used to that technique, so the story seemed choppy and incoherent. The second time around I saw what he was doing and realized that not only was the story not in the least incoherent, but also that it moved with a slick speed that would have been impossible if all the dull bread-and-butter transitions had been inserted.
>
> I wrote to Simak to explain and to apologize, and adopted the same device in my own stories. What's more, I attempted, as far as possible, to make use of something similar to Simak's cool and unadorned style.

By copying that unadorned style and Simak's technique of jump-cutting between significant scenes, Asimov was soon able to write stories that were sharper, sparer and more of a whole than his first few attempts. So swift a learner was young Asimov that it wouldn't take him anything like a full year to sell his first story to John Campbell, but only another six months.

What Asimov was picking up from Simak was not just a simpler, less emotional style and a technique of shifting scenes without justifying the transition. It was also the orientation toward existence that underlay them.

During the Age of Technology, as in earlier periods, the known and the unknown had been clearly separate spheres. Village Earth was a small center of consciously known things surrounded by the vast unknown of the World Beyond the Hill.

But the redesigned cosmos presented in Campbell's *Astounding* was not like this. It was a continuum, held together everywhere and at all times by constantly overlapping, interacting universal rules.

Within this multiverse of time, space and other dimensions, every single thing was accessible and potentially knowable.

In this new frame of reference, the human enterprise was no longer to be strictly identified with Village Earth. Human consciousness might have its locus anywhere in space or time, and manage to deal with things when it got there.

At the same time, however, it was apparent that any single locus or point of view within this new cosmos must have its limitations. If existence is the product of a complex net of causal factors too interwoven and far-reaching to ever be completely encompassed, then from any one vantage at any one moment some things will be clearly revealed, while others must necessarily be hidden—at least until a change in perspective occurs.

In Techno Age SF, transcendence had been found *out there* in the larger darkness. But in modern science fiction, transcendence could be located anywhere at all. Gaps, glitches and blank spots in our awareness were where mystery was now concealed.

But even in this uncertain new universe, constantly shifting in and out of focus, men could still make their way. What was essential was not that they know everything all at once, but only that they identify and master those particular principles that would produce desired results in a given set of circumstances.

It was this practical-minded engineering mentality that was central in the pages of the Golden Age *Astounding*. By contrast with the great philosophical ponderings and the fascination with vastness typical of a Wells or a Stapledon, Campbellian SF could seem small in scale and a bit nearsighted. But it would also display a compensatory immediacy, adaptability, verve and daring.

It wasn't just that a modern science fiction story might leap lightly from one meaningful moment to another, unconcerned about the spaces in between. In the new SF, *anything* might be hidden or omitted or approached from a cockeyed angle. The writers of Golden Age science fiction would delight in starting their stories at any point in space or time, with action in progress, and would expect the reader to play the game, fill in the blank spots, and put together the ongoing situation from hints and clues and bits of exposition casually dropped in passing.

In the strange reality presented in the Campbell *Astounding*— half here and half not-here—it took a very cool operator who knew the way things really work to tell what was important and what was not and make things come out his way. And a not altogether dissimilar demand for Atomic Age street-smarts was made on the readers of *Astounding*.

Isaac Asimov would gradually evolve his own personal brand of the new kind of story. More than any other of Campbell's writers, he would come to specialize in stories of formal problem-solving. The classic Asimov story would be a schematic representation of the scientific method in action. Characters so sparely presented as to be little more than disembodied voices would tackle some science-fictional conundrum. They would propound, test, and discard one theory after another until at last they lit upon the proper principle, applied it, and resolved the problem before them.

Asimov would not attain this level of sublime abstraction over-night. But John Campbell would certainly encourage his tendencies in this direction. The stories he chose to buy from Asimov's first two dozen attempts—"Trends" (*Astounding*, July 1939) and "Homo Sol" (*Astounding*, Sept 1940)—would be the two that most closely resembled the work of the later Isaac Asimov. And, in large part, this would be so because Campbell nudged and pushed until these stories became what they were.

Most of Asimov's early efforts were space operas, or invention stories, or stories of future oppression and rebellion. Campbell might take stories of these kinds from other writers, but he wouldn't accept them from Asimov. From Asimov he had to have new ideas, or nothing at all.

Campbell would spy a first hint of possibility in Asimov's ninth manuscript, "Ad Astra." The youngster happened to be earning needed money typing and taking notes for a sociology professor who was working on a book about social resistance to technological innovation. Asimov adapted the idea to science fiction, including a passing mention of social resistance to space travel in his latest story. Campbell hadn't seen that notion before, and he picked it out immediately.

It was Campbell's habit to snatch up an idea like this one, reduce it from conclusion to initial premise, and throw it back to the writer again. In this case, he called Asimov into his office for a chat and told him that his story as it was wouldn't do, but that he might have a viable piece of work if he would take this problem of resistance to space travel and make it his central concern.

So Asimov tossed away what he had and began again. He would still think it was the same story he was writing and continue to call it by the same title—"Ad Astra." Campbell, knowing better, would retitle it "Trends."

In its new incarnation, Asimov's story would show the more powerful trend of scientific progress, represented by space travel, winning out over the lesser trend of a social reaction against science in the form of a temporary religious revival. And that was a story that Campbell would happily buy. He was a strong advocate of scientific progress and it was highly important to him to see science portrayed as more fundamental, powerful and effective than society or religion, to show advances in knowledge triumphant over mere fleeting social spasms.

But after "Trends," it would be another full year and many more tries by Asimov before he came to visit Campbell with another idea that the editor responded to. In this case, it was the notion of a story in which Earth, having achieved interstellar space travel, is welcomed into the bosom of a Galactic Federation.

As in the earlier instance, Campbell perceived Asimov's original simple notion not as a sufficiency, but as a starting point. But this time it proved to be much harder for Campbell to get exactly what he wanted from Asimov. It would take several months and three versions of the story before he would be satisfied with "Homo Sol"— a tale in which the newly received Earthmen are analyzed by galactic mathematical psychologists and discovered to be both dauntingly competent and mentally distinct from every other space-traveling race.

What hung this story up for so long was personal limitation— both Asimov's and Campbell's. Asimov's limitation was that he was still groping in the dark for the key to modern science fiction. But Campbell's limitation here was, if anything, even greater.

As his authors would gradually come to learn, John Campbell had a highly conservative side as well as a radical and heretical side, and one old-fashioned notion to which he was firmly wedded was the Edwardian belief that Man must prevail and shall prevail. Ultimately, it was not scientific progress that Campbell truly cared about, but human progress and power.

This particular bias wasn't just Campbell's alone, but was shared by a number of people in his generation who were able to accept the overwhelming new universe revealed by modern science, but who had not given up their attachment to Techno Age elitism. The elitism they embraced was not the old traditional elitism of blood and birth, but rather the newer Wellsian elitism of knowledge, ability and competence. For these people, it was only this kind of specialness that might allow Man to tackle and master the vast indifference of material existence and the hostility of alien beings.

It was this generational bias, which Campbell held with an unusual purity and fervor, that he aimed to impose on Asimov's story. Writing about their conflict of aims subsequent to Campbell's death in 1971, with the advantage of thirty years of maturation and insight, Asimov would say:

"Homo Sol" has a plot of a sort that particularly appealed to Campbell. Although the human beings in the story are far behind the other intelligences of the Galaxy, it is clear that there is something special about them, that they have an unusual ability to move ahead very quickly, and that everyone else had better watch out for them.

Campbell liked stories in which human beings proved themselves superior to other intelligences, even when those others were further advanced technologically. It pleased him to have human beings shown to possess a unique spirit of daring, or a sense of humor, or a ruthless ability to kill when necessary, that always brought them victory over other intelligences, even against odds.

But in early 1940, the young Asimov didn't immediately understand what it was that Campbell really desired him to write—partly because Campbell wouldn't come right out and say what it was he wanted, and partly because Asimov simply didn't share Campbell's special attachment to the exaltation of Man.

Asimov was not the person to press notions of innate human superiority, even though he himself was brighter than almost everyone he knew. He was a Jew born in Europe, where World War II—Hitler's demonic crusade for Aryan dominance and racial purification—was already in progress.

Moreover, Asimov was a member of the post-World War I generation to whom human chauvinism and aggression seemed a more powerful and immediate threat than anything the physical universe was likely to dish out. Years before such attitudes became a commonplace in science fiction, Asimov was a committed liberal; even his very earliest stories presented earnest condemnations of racism and pleas for human tolerance.

It was because of his initial ignorance of Campbell's true intent and because their values were so divergent here, that it took Asimov so many tries before he finally adjusted "Homo Sol" into something like the shape that Campbell really wanted.

However, in the months after "Homo Sol" was finally accepted, Asimov very gradually came to the realization that he had somehow been maneuvered into writing a story he didn't altogether like. And he felt compromised. More than anything else, he wished to sell further science fiction stories to John Campbell, whom he admired and respected as he did no other man. But not if it was to be at the cost of having to espouse views that he found personally repugnant.

Asimov couldn't tackle this problem head-on. It was unthinkable to Asimov to quarrel with Campbell, possibly offend him, and thereby lose this relationship that was of such central importance to him. But neither was he willing to compromise his own personal sense of decency, equity and integrity.

So just how was he to get around this apparently inflexible rule of Campbell's that human beings must be superior, yet still write about the issues of relative power and dominance that were of central importance to him? More than any other single thing, it was Asimov's search for a solution to this problem that turned him into the unique writer of modern science fiction that he became.

The method of approach that Asimov picked was persistent experimentation. He would try one thing, and then another, and then another, until at last he found something that worked. This, in fact, was the very method that had won Asimov admittance to graduate school the previous year when it seemed that the Columbia University Department of Chemistry was determined not to let him in. And it would become the standard operating procedure of the classic Asimov character.

Asimov's first ploy would be to try another story with a galactic setting—a story related to "Homo Sol," for whatever weight that might carry—but without any human beings involved. "The Imaginary" was precisely the same length as "Homo Sol." In it, the idea of a scientific psychology operated with mathematical rigor was even more explicitly advanced. There just happened to be no human-nonhuman conflict in this one. It was only in passing that men of Earth were mentioned at all.

But this attempt to circumvent Campbell was not successful. The editor showed no interest in "The Imaginary." He may very well have been pleased and intrigued by the notion of math-based psychology; in time, it would become a central supposition of much of Asimov's work for him. Quite plainly, however, if mathematical psychology was going to be placed at the center of a story, it wasn't going to be a story without human beings.

The editor who would eventually buy "The Imaginary" and publish it in the November 1942 *Super Science Stories* was Asimov's friend and Campbell's one-time student in editing, Fred Pohl. Of the early Asimov stories that Campbell did not respond to or wasn't shown, Pohl's magazines would print no fewer than eight, and he would even commission Asimov to write a ninth. He was Asimov's first steady market—if not the market that Asimov most desired to hit.

After "The Imaginary," Asimov tried once more to evade his situation. He liked *Unknown* better if anything than *Astounding*, and *Unknown* did not involve problems of superiority and inferiority. So he wrote a fantasy story aimed at *Unknown* in which an oak tree foretells the future by rustling its leaves.

The story wasn't successful. Campbell didn't buy it, and neither did anyone else. The real significance of "The Oak" was that it would be the very last story (except for two short-shorts) that Asimov would fail to sell. Even though he had not yet mastered Campbell's special requirements, he was now able to write to a consistently professional standard.

Then twice more during the summer of 1940, Asimov tried again to write as he had been used to writing. The stories he produced were frank expressions of his own feelings—one was about overcoming groundless prejudice, and the other was about the futility of war. But neither story was particularly original as science fiction. Campbell rejected them, and it was again left to Pohl, who was another young idealist responsive to sentiments of this kind, to give them publication.

So this was the situation, with nothing that he tried working very well, that Asimov found himself in at the end of the summer of 1940, when two of his stories appeared on the newsstands at nearly the same moment. One was "Homo Sol" in the September *Astounding*. Seeing it in print made the true acuteness of his disagreement with Campbell explicitly evident to Asimov. The other story was "Strange Playfellow" in the September issue of Pohl's *Super Science Stories*. And it offered an indication of a possible way out of his dilemma.

Going over "Homo Sol" was a dismaying business for Asimov. As he read it, he discovered that even those changes and adjustments he had been chivvied into making for Campbell had not been sufficient to satisfy the editor, who had thought it necessary to insert comments of his own in several places in which he offered special tribute to the warmaking abilities of Earthmen. Asimov did not appreciate this one bit. He did not like being apparently responsible for sentiments that seemed to him both racist and militaristic.

At this point in his dealings with Campbell, Asimov was feeling frustrated and desperate and, even though he might not care to admit it, more than a little angry. In two dozen attempts he had managed to sell only two stories to the man, and he could readily wonder if he was ever going to escape the maze presented to him by Campbell's strictures, judgments and demands. Especially after what Campbell had just done to "Homo Sol."

Asimov knew he had a problem. It was clear to him that Campbell wanted him to write about universal operating principles. But it was also evident that except for a story like "Homo Sol," in which Earthmen present themselves to be measured by alien scientists and the aliens then blush, stammer and tremble at the readings they get, Campbell just wasn't going to tolerate stories in which intelligences other than human controlled these principles and mankind didn't. On this point, the editor was unyielding.

But, for his own part, Asimov would never see the day when he would be ready to write stories in which superior human beings lord it over lesser aliens. That was simply contrary to everything he believed.

He could see that something had to be done if he were to continue to try to write for Campbell. But what?

When Asimov picked up his other story, he saw that it, too, had an obvious if less acute problem—its title. He had written this little tale of the vindication of a robot nursemaid the previous year and called it "Robbie." But Pohl had seen fit to retitle it "Strange Playfellow"—and Asimov found this change exquisitely embarrassing.

It wasn't at all unusual for a pulp editor to change a title and not bother to notify the author. Campbell had casually altered "Ad Astra" to "Trends." "Stowaway" had been changed by Pohl into "The Callistan Menace" (*Astonishing*, Apr 1940). One of Asimov's titles would even be altered from "Pilgrimage" to "Black Friar of the Flame" (*Planet Stories*, Spr 1942). The crucial difference that made Campbell's change acceptable to Asimov where others were not was that it was evident to him that Campbell was attempting to express the pure, undiluted essence of things, whereas other SF editors were merely aiming for cheap and easy pulp sensationalism.

Aside from the change in title, however, Asimov wasn't displeased with what he saw. He says, "After reading 'Robbie' in cold print in the magazine, I decided I liked it more than any other story I had written yet."

"Robbie" was a story with a purpose. It had been written as a reaction to all those Romantic Era and Techno Age horror stories, from *Frankenstein* to *R. U. R.*, in which created beings turn on their human makers and destroy them.

In Asimov's story, a man buys an early model nursemaid robot to mind his little daughter, but his wife doesn't like the idea at all. She says:

" 'You listen to me, George. I won't have my daughter entrusted to a machine—and I don't care how clever it is. A child just isn't made to be guarded by a thing of metal. ... Some little jigger will come loose and the awful thing will go berserk and— and—' "

Husband George counters this old-fashioned fear of the machine out of control by saying:

" 'A robot is infinitely more to be trusted than a human nursemaid. Robbie was constructed for only one purpose—to be the companion of a little child. His entire 'mentality' has been created for the purpose. He just can't help being faithful and loving and kind. He's a machine—made so.'"

Almost always prior to this—with the notable exception of the mechanical man Tik-tok in L. Frank Baum's Oz books—an SF scientist or inventor would construct the exterior of an android or robot, but the creature's thoughts and motives and volition would still be its own. There would be no guarantee that it might not take it into its head at any moment to run amok. Here in this story, however, Asimov was ready to suggest that the values and purposes of a constructed being might be preprogrammed, built right in from the start.

Eventually, Asimov would state this aspect of his thinking about the robot this way:

> Consider a robot, then, as simply another artifact. ... As a machine, a robot will surely be designed for safety, as far as possible. If robots are so advanced that they can mimic the thought processes of human beings, then surely the nature of those thought processes will be designed by human engineers and built-in safeguards will be added. The safety may not be perfect (what is?), but it will be as complete as men can make it.

But there is still another view of the nature of the robot on display in "Robbie"/"Strange Playfellow." It is there by implication throughout the story as Asimov refers to this mute metal construct as "he." And it is stated explicitly when husband George says of his little daughter, "'The whole trouble with Gloria is that she thinks of Robbie as a person and not as a machine.'"

For Asimov, the robot was no monster, having been designed for safety. But if he was not a monster, then what was his true nature? Was he merely a reliable machine? Or was he a person, maybe a friend? Ot was he perhaps something even better and greater than that, something possibly transcendent?

Asimov would investigate these questions throughout his SF writing career. In this first robot story, however, his concern was not to pin down the exact nature of the robot, but rather to demonstrate robotic reliability.

Robbie the nursemaid is fortunate enough to be granted the opportunity to put his trustworthiness on public display. He wins a secure place in the family by saving Gloria from the threat of a conveniently onrushing tractor. We may rest assured that whatever else he might be, *first of all* Robbie is faithful and loving and kind—and prepared to keep his little charge out of trouble. He's made that way.

John Campbell hadn't seen fit to buy this story when it was submitted to him back in May 1939. It must have seemed just another of those simple first-order notions that Asimov was still offering to him then. Since this one hadn't happened to spark any next-order consequences in Campbell's mind to come back at Asimov with, he'd let the story pass.

But as Asimov read "Robbie" now, he not only found himself liking it—title change aside—but he caught a sudden glimmering of all those future robot stories he would come to write. He says, "It also occurred to me that robot stories would not involve me in any superiority/inferiority hassle with Campbell. Why not, then, write another?"

Why not, indeed?

On examining his conscience closely, Asimov saw no problem in writing more stories like "Robbie" in which human beings were at least assumed to be superior to robots that were made, directed, and controlled by universal operating principles. What is more, in a sudden access of insight, Asimov was gifted with exactly the kind of idea that Campbell in all his brilliance might have given him, but hadn't. That is, he thought of a next-order consequence of dealing with a made-to-be-reliable robot.

This time, Asimov thought, he wouldn't just write some obvious little story in which a sweet, sincere, devoted robot mutely did exactly what he was supposed to do.

What if that robot could talk?

What if he should decide to talk back?

What if a robot should argue for his own alternate view of things?

What was the maximally rebellious thing a reliable robot might think or say, and get away with? Just how contrary and insubordinate and out of hand could a robot get and still be acceptable to John Campbell?

During the Techno Age, there had been the nagging fear that because of the greater logic of their thought processes and the greater efficiency of their function, robots might actually prove superior to their makers. So, what if a safely controlled robot were to declare the obvious superiority of robotic logic and efficiency—and even present this as an article of robotic religious faith?

Asimov says:

> My notion was to have a robot refuse to believe he had been created mechanically in a factory, but to insist that men were only his servants and that robots were the peak of creation, having been created by some godlike entity. What's more, he would prove his case by reason, and "Reason" was the title of the story.

On the face of it, this was exactly the kind of idea Campbell was always asking him for. But this one had hidden teeth. It was the equivalent in story form of a technique that Asimov the precocious wiseguy kid had often used at home or in school to show up the pretensions of authority without being able to be held accountable for it. This was to wait until just the right moment, and then to slip in some apparently ingenuous remark or question that was actually intended to reveal limitation, self-contradiction, or hypocrisy, and then to wait all wrapped in a cloud of sunlit innocence to see whether his father or his teacher could cope with the implications of their dicta, and to enjoy it mightily when they proved they couldn't.

As Don A. Stuart and as the editor of *Astounding*, Campbell liked to present himself as a dedicated challenger of received opinion. Until now, Asimov had listened to Campbell, avoided conflict with Campbell, and attempted, with no great success, to please Campbell, but never had he tested his limitations. But now, after "Homo Sol," Asimov was ready to find out what stuff Campbell was really made of.

He was feeling half-conciliatory, half-rebellious. He did want to please Campbell. But he also wanted to fight him tooth and nail in defense of his own values. He was willing to do things Campbell's way. But he was also determined to retain the right to think his own thoughts and believe his own beliefs.

So he put his contrary feelings into "Reason." He would give Campbell exactly what he liked best, to the utmost of his ability. And at the same time, he would be as completely and subtly subversive as he knew how to be—and see whether Campbell could deal with that.

He would attempt to appeal to Campbell with a pair of scientifically trained space adventurers like Campbell's team of Penton and Blake. Asimov had tried a variation on Penton and Blake as early as the fourth story he'd shown to Campbell, back in the summer of 1938. Campbell had made no comment about this would-be homage then; he'd just turned the story down. But now Asimov was ready to have another go at Campbell with an improved variant—robotic field-testers Gregory Powell and Michael Donovan.

And of course "Reason" would bear an epitomal one-word, Don A. Stuart-type title. Asimov knew that Campbell had a taste for the story title that promised the quintessence of something or other. In the early years of his editorship, Campbell would print stories with titles like "Impulse," "Pressure," "Pride," "Habit," "Hindsight," "Legacy," "Jurisdiction," "Mission," and "Proof"— not to mention "Universe" and "Nightfall" and "Nerves" and a good many others. Since Campbell changed "Ad Astra" to "Trends,"

Asimov had tried this approach half-a-dozen times with no success, but he was ready to try it again.

Best of all, his story would toss Campbell a bone that Asimov thought the editor would really snap at. He would show religious belief—the religious belief of a robot—as ultimately secondary to the power of universal operating principles. That should really push Campbell's buttons.

And then, finally, the test. "Reason" would have human characters and lesser creatures of a sort. But not so much lesser that the point couldn't be argued, and continue to be argued after the story was over. Could John Campbell handle that?

On October 23, 1940, Asimov gathered his ambivalent feelings and his plans for "Reason" and set off for lower Manhattan and the Street & Smith offices to see the editor. And just as he had calculated, John Campbell did like his story idea. More than that, he was completely enthusiastic! The last thing he said to Asimov as he was setting off home to Brooklyn was a reminder that he wanted to see this story as soon as possible.

How wonderful! How unprecedented! How unnerving.

And, in fact, when Asimov sat down to work, he found himself hung up, unable to get the story under way. Four times he began it, wrote a couple of pages, and then scrapped them.

Some part of this hesitation may well have been because Asimov was trying so many different things in this story and required time to integrate them before going ahead. But it seems more likely that Asimov's need, his desire, his ambition, his calculation, and his rebellion were taken by surprise and stunned into silence by the very degree of Campbell's receptivity. It was as though he had inadvertently stumbled upon the pure mother lode of favorable response that had previously eluded him, and he was disconcerted and didn't know what to do next.

Asimov tells us quite frankly, at least, "In this case, pushing Campbell's buttons was easier than pushing the typewriter keys."

Finally, after eight days of spinning his wheels and going nowhere with this story, Asimov decided that the thing for him to do was to touch base with Campbell. So, somewhat sheepishly, he went back to see the editor and confessed that he was having a problem getting his story started.

And John Campbell rose to the occasion. He managed to give Asimov the right advice at just the right moment—the final thing he needed to learn in order to be able to write modern science fiction.

Campbell told him: "Asimov, when you have trouble with the beginning of a story, that is because you are starting in the wrong place, and almost certainly too soon. Pick out a later point in the story, and begin again."

This most certainly was not Techno Age storywriting advice. That would have been to begin at the beginning, and then to go on until the end, telling everything that happened along the way. This was fundamental modern science fiction writing advice—to start a story as late as possible and tell no more than was necessary. And it was what Asimov needed to hear just now for "Reason" to fall into place.

"Reason" does start at a strange and special advanced moment. It is some time in the not-too-distant future and we are on board one of a number of space stations that have been established to beam solar energy to Earth and the other planets. Heat, solar radiation and electron storms make a post like this a difficult one for humans to endure, so a new experimental series of robots has been developed to handle the job. As the story opens, the more thoughtful of Asimov's troubleshooters is facing the first of these robots, QT-1, and explaining the facts of life to him:

"Gregory Powell spaced his words for emphasis. 'One week ago, Donovan and I put you together.' His brows furrowed doubtfully and he pulled the end of his brown mustache."

Cutie the robot reflects on this for a moment, and then says, "'Do you realize the seriousness of such a statement, Powell?'"

If we ourselves pause to think about it, we can only wonder at this situation. Why would a sophisticated experimental robot have been shipped to a space station in a packing crate and assembled there for the very first time? Why should a great space station like this be staffed by only two men? Why does QT-1 not recall the moment of his awakening, with Powell and Donovan no doubt standing right there beaming proudly upon their handiwork? And why is it that the true state of things wasn't properly explained to Cutie then and there during that first crucial moment of awareness?

Somehow a glitch has occurred. A full week has been allowed to slip away and it is only now that Powell is getting around to telling Cutie of his origins. But for some unknown reason, Powell doesn't come across as all that certain about what he is saying. He speaks with odd overemphasis, he furrows his brow in doubt, and he yanks on his mustache. By comparison, Cutie the new-made robot is a model of composure. He may be ignorant of ordinary fact, but in no time at all this robot has turned himself into a sure-footed philosopher full of talk of intuition, assumption, reason, and the deduction of truth from *a priori* causes. Whatever has happened here?

Now, if Asimov had thought long enough and hard enough, he might have been able to come up with answers for all of these questions. Armed with Campbell's crucial piece of advice, however, he saw that he didn't need to. In the new kind of science fiction, it was all right to skip right past these irrelevancies and go straight to the heart of the matter.

In a modern science fiction story, we are wherever we chance to find ourselves. And, in this case, where we happen to be is within a special isolated artificial environment, a place where one explanation of reality may appear as plausible as another. Here a recently assembled robot with no memory and a philosophical bent can look the other member of this human team in the eye and say:

> "Look at you. ... I say this in no spirit of contempt, but look at you! The material you are made of is soft and flabby, lacking endurance and strength, depending for energy upon the inefficient oxidation of organic material—like that." He pointed a disapproving finger at what remained of Donovan's sandwich. Periodically you pass into a coma, and the least variation in temperature, air pressure, humidity or radiation intensity impairs your efficiency. You are *makeshift*.
>
> "I, on the other hand, am a finished product. I absorb electrical energy directly and utilize it with almost one hundred per cent efficiency. I am composed of strong metal, am continuously conscious, and can stand extremes of environment easily. These are facts which, with the self-evident proposition that no being can create another being superior to itself, smashes your silly hypothesis."

This special situation that we find ourselves in is a unique thought-experiment that tests the relative understanding, power and reality-structures of robot and man. We don't quibble about how we happened to arrive here. We accept it so that we may have the pleasure of seeing this game of comparisons played through to its conclusion.

But why is it such a pleasure? The fact is that we experience this story in a curious double fashion. Subjectively, we may be trapped in a pocket universe, a closed situation, with absolutely no way to prove which ordering of reality is actually so. Objectively, however, we stand outside the confines of the story and look upon it with our own knowledge of human science and society, and our previous experience of SF stories in which robots were designed and space stations constructed.

We assume we *know* which side is really right—despite Cutie's preternatural self-confidence and Powell's strange aura of doubt. And it is this special knowledge that allows us to find amusement in the sight of a Powell burying his face in his trembling hands, or a Donovan beating the air impotently with his fists in a fit of frustration.

We can afford to chuckle when Cutie comes to recognize the solar station's energy converter as "the Master," and the lesser robots of the station all acknowledge Cutie as "the Prophet." Cutie and his cohorts are no old-time cosmic threat like A. Merritt's Metal People, and we know it. We can have confidence that they aren't going to go raging off and attempt to take over the universe in the name of the Master.

What Cutie does do is bar the two men from the station's control room and engine room as deluded lesser beings whose function has been superseded. But Powell and Donovan know that an electron storm is on its way which will certainly disturb the energy beam to Earth. Unless precise control is maintained, the beam will go out of focus and hundreds of square miles of planet will be incinerated.

If they don't regain control of the situation, a major boo-boo is likely to occur for which Powell and Donovan will be held responsible. But nothing they can say or do—including assembling another robot while Cutie looks on—will serve to shake the robot's firm faith in his religion of perfect robotic rationality:

> Donovan was half in tears. "He doesn't believe us, or the books, or his eyes."
>
> "No," said Powell bitterly, "he's a *reasoning* robot, damn it. He believes only reason, and there's one trouble with that.... You can prove anything you want by coldly logical reason—if you pick the right postulates. We have ours and Cutie has his."

However, when the electron storm has come and gone, Powell and Donovan discover that the energy beam to Earth has been kept in perfect focus all the while. Even though Cutie may not be willing to acknowledge the existence of Earth, but prefers to believe that he has simply been keeping "'all dials in equilibrium in accordance with the will of the Master'"—nonetheless, the robot has performed the job he was designed to do.

Donovan continues to be upset that Cutie should be so persistent in his delusions, but Powell now knows better. He says, "'Look, Mike, he follows the instructions of the Master by means of dials, instruments and graphs. That's all *we* ever followed.'"

Powell has come to a recognition that as long as Cutie handles the job he was made for, and does it perfectly, it doesn't really matter *what* the robot believes. Since human purposes ultimately rule, the apparent threat of robotic rebellion is not actually a threat at all.

Powell is still capable of being stung by Cutie's contempt and pity. But so fundamentally reconciled to the facts of the situation has he grown that his last words to Donovan are a suggestion that later QT models be brought here to learn Cutie's belief system before they take up their posts—as though he believes that this would benefit their effectiveness of operation. And when he and Donovan are finally relieved from duty aboard the space station by two other humans, Powell is able to grin up his sleeve at the thought of these guys trying to cope with Cutie, but he doesn't think it necessary to warn them about what they will be facing.

Donovan, however, leaves the station still cursing under his breath at Cutie and turning his back to avoid having to deal with him. His sense of ordinary human reality has been sufficiently shaken that his final words to Powell are, "'I won't feel right until I actually see Earth and feel the ground under my feet—just to make sure it's really there.'"

And it does remain a fact that the question of relative truth has not really been settled. Cutie may well do things that humans think desirable in something of the same way that a human might have done them—but his personal belief system certainly hasn't been refuted. Believing his own beliefs, he has been able to run the solar station as effectively or more effectively than the humans did believing theirs. Within the robot's sphere of autonomy, it seems certain that things will continue to be done according to his frame of reference. And any humans who enter Cutie's domain are going to have to learn to recognize this and come to terms with it.

"Reason" is a story that at first appears to be about the dangers posed by a wrong-thinking robot. If that were really the problem, however, then the solution would be to straighten out the kinks in robotic thinking, perhaps by the expedient of showing QT robots some of the sights of Earth before they are taken off to serve aboard space stations. It surely wouldn't be to bring still more robots here to learn delusions firsthand from Cutie.

A better interpretation of "Reason" is that it is about the need for overdirective men to learn to relax and allow the robot to get on with the job he has been designed to do—according to his own terms.

Taken in this light, "Reason" may be seen as a message meant for John Campbell. As plainly as Asimov could bring himself to say it, this story said: *Different people live according to different structurings of reality, all founded on different premises, and all equally unprovable. But it is perfectly possible to call a goal by different names and still have it be the same goal. If you will just stand back and let me get on with it, I will do things your way. But I reserve the right to think them my way.*

Was Campbell equal to a challenge of this kind? Indeed he was. Asimov submitted "Reason" to the editor on November 18, 1940.

And just four days later, he received a check in the mail from Street & Smith. Not only did Campbell ask for no revisions, but he even went so far as to tell Asimov that he had seriously considered awarding him a bonus for this story.

Asimov's display of rebellion and original thought was everything that Campbell could have been hoping to see from the youngster through those two long years of patient personal instruction. The Asimov revealed by "Reason" was the kind of writer Campbell treasured most—the man who could do things Campbell's way, but who was also determined to think things out for himself.

It was as though the writing of "Reason" by Asimov and its acceptance by Campbell together constituted the forging of a working contract. Effectively, the writer would strive to give Campbell *exactly* what he wanted—except for any case where he happened to have his own convictions about things. And the editor would love and cherish Asimov both for his originality and for his spunk as a rebel within the law.

Two things helped to make this arrangement between Asimov and Campbell work. One was that—with the rare exception of "Nightfall"—the ideas that the two men were playing around with and building upon were Asimov's to begin with, not Campbell's. And the other was that when Asimov did take a suggestion of Campbell's and twist it into something that he found inoffensive, it was almost always done in such a skillful way that Campbell found the change inoffensive as well.

The last important thing we should note about the accommodation the two men reached is that it was tacit, no more than an unspoken working agreement. It was nothing that Asimov could ever feel completely certain about.

It wasn't that Campbell was incapable of reaching explicit understandings with his most valued authors. In the course of 1941, Robert Heinlein would, tactfully but effectively, force the acceptance of everything he might submit to Campbell by telling the editor, "I'll send you a story from time to time...until the day comes when you bounce one. At that point we're through. Now that I know you personally, having a story rejected by you would be too traumatic."

And during 1941, Campbell would decide to write to A. E. van Vogt in Canada and throw *Astounding* wide open to him. So much work was Campbell willing to contract to buy from him that van Vogt turned himself into a one-man factory all through World War II, toiling "from the time I got up until eleven o'clock at night, every day, seven days a week, for years," just to keep Campbell supplied with stories.

As time passed, Asimov would eventually come to be ranked alongside Heinlein and van Vogt as a major writer of SF—even in Campbell's eyes. What is more, so in tune would he and Campbell become that there would not be a word of fiction that Isaac Asimov would write from the beginning of 1943 to the end of the decade—with the exception of one novel written at the request of another editor—that John Campbell would not buy and print.

But Asimov would never be offered carte blanche by Campbell, and he himself would never feel entitled to deliver ultimatums or demand guarantees. Even though Asimov might eventually become capable of addressing the editor with an occasional uncomfortable "John," in his heart he would always regard his mentor as "Mr. Campbell" and treat him accordingly.

Nonetheless, there can be no doubt that despite Asimov's secret impulses to rebel and Campbell's lack of guarantees, a new working relationship had been established between the two men after "Reason." This may be seen in the fact that when Asimov came to visit Campbell at his office one month after turning in "Reason," both men had been giving thought to the implications of the story.

Campbell had been thinking about one particular passage in "Reason" that he found troubling. At the direst moment in the story, Donovan suggests that it might be possible to neutralize Cutie by squirting concentrated nitric acid in his joints. But Powell answers, "'Don't be a dope, Mike. Do you suppose he's going to let us get near him with acid in our hands—or that the other robots wouldn't take us apart if we *did* manage to get away with it?'"

John Campbell was a person who enjoyed nothing more than to confront a listener with some outrageous idea and dare him to refute it, so he could really appreciate Cutie's discomfiting arguments—just as long as he felt certain that Cutie would perform his duties and injure no one. But to Campbell, the kind of robots who might disassemble human beings as an act of retribution presented a problem that cried out for solution. And he discerned the answer lurking in Asimov's previous robot story, "Robbie": "'He just can't help being faithful and loving and kind. He's a machine—made so.'"

Asimov, for his part, came to this story conference with the idea for another robotic problem story. What if, through some accident of manufacture, a robot should prove to be telepathic, able to read human minds? He says, "Again, Campbell became interested and we talked it over at length—what complications would arise out of robotic telepathy, what a robot would be forced to lie about, how the matter could be resolved, and so on."

In the course of this discussion, Campbell found occasion to raise the issue that had been bothering him, and the grounds for its solution. Characteristically, however, the editor didn't state his true concerns in any direct and open way, but rather elected to phrase them as another Campbellian dictum. He said:

> "Look, Asimov, in working this out, you have to realize that there are three rules that robots have to follow. In the first place, they can't do any harm to human beings; in the second place, they have to obey orders without doing harm; in the third, they have to protect themselves, without doing harm or proving disobedient."

Asimov would take up these operating principles proposed by Campbell and give them formal expression in his stories as the Three Laws of Robotics, phrasing them this way:

1. A robot may not injure a human being or, through inaction, allow a human being to come to harm.

2. A robot must obey the orders given it by human beings except where such orders would conflict with the First Law.

3. A robot must protect its own existence as long as such protection does not conflict with the First or Second Laws.

The Three Laws of Robotics would become the basis for seven stories that Asimov would write for Campbell during the Forties. In 1950, these stories—together with "Robbie" and "Reason," rewritten to bring them into conformity with the Three Laws— would be collected under the title *I, Robot*. And Asimov would go on to write many more stories and novels incorporating these fundamental principles of robotic operation.

In later years, Asimov would more than once attempt to credit Campbell with responsibility for inventing the Three Laws. But Campbell would deny it, saying, "'No, Asimov, I picked them out of your stories and your discussions. You didn't state them explicitly, but they were there.'"

And that would be the truth—as far as it went. What it would overlook was the role played by Campbell's own urgent desire that human control be established over the robot.

It was not because Asimov's robots were dangerous that this control was necessary, but because they were all touched by transcendence: RB-34, in Asimov's third robot story "Liar!" is telepathic. QT-1 is a robotic prophet. Even the least-common-denominator robot, Robbie, is superhumanly faithful and loving and kind.

When Cutie claims that no being can create another being superior to itself, it seems that he must be mistaken. For apparently that is what human beings—in collaboration with the glitch factor—have done. Humanity designs the physical and mental form of the robot. The uncertainty of the universe does the rest.

We can see the glitch factor at work in "Liar!" where it is invoked at the beginning of the story to account for robot RB-34's otherwise unaccountable ability to read minds. One human says to another: "'Listen, Bogert. There wasn't a hitch in the assembly from start to finish. I guarantee that.'"

But Bogert, who is a mathematician, replies:

> "If you can answer for the entire assembly line, I recommend your promotion. By exact count, there are seventy-five thousand, two hundred and thirty-four operations necessary for the manufacture of a single positronic brain, each separate operation depending for successful completion upon any number of factors, from five to a hundred and five. If any one of them goes seriously wrong, the 'brain' is ruined."

Only not precisely ruined this time: made transcendent. This sort of accident has a way of happening to Asimov's robots. They seem to have some latent tendency toward transcendence inherited from their wild Techno Age ancestors.

It is only their bondage to the Three Laws of Robotics that makes these powerful robots tolerable to humanity. However they may choose to behave on their own time, we can have confidence that these strange servitors we have created will not injure us and that they must do whatever we tell them to do.

In fact, "Liar!" is specifically concerned with a conflict between the transcendent power of a robot and the Laws of Robotics which is resolved in favor of Campbell's and Asimov's in-built rules.

In "Liar!," RB-34 has the special ability to read human minds. But Herbie, as he is familiarly called, has the bad habit of lying to people about the thoughts he reads.

Herbie is bound by the Laws of Robotics not to do harm. But he believes that if he speaks the truth about what he knows, he will destroy people's illusions and cause them pain. To avoid this harm, he tells them whatever it is they most want to hear instead of the truth.

But this can lead to eventual greater pain, embarrassment, and chagrin. For instance, Herbie tells the spinster robot psychologist Dr. Susan Calvin that a man she has a crush on secretly loves her. But then, when she begins to reveal her own repressed emotions, she learns that the man is actually recently married and has no interest in her.

Herbie is able to identify the glitch in his manufacture that is responsible for robotic telepathic power. But a vindictive Dr. Calvin prevents him from revealing what he knows. She points out to him over and over again that if he tells the answer to human scientists, he will be showing them up, but if he doesn't, he will be depriving them of what they want to know. Whatever Herbie does, then, he must cause harm to a human, and thus break the Laws of Robotics.

Dr. Calvin's paradox is such an insoluble problem that poor Herbie is driven into a catatonic silence. There is certainly some degree of loss here—future robots will just have to do without the power of telepathy. But that must be reckoned a small cost, at least insofar as John Campbell and the modern science fiction public works project are concerned, beside Susan Calvin's potent demonstration of the power to control inherent in the Laws of Robotics.

Asimov delivered "Liar!" to Campbell on January 20, 1941. And, for a second time, Campbell would ask for no revisions and get a check to Asimov within four days.

When the story was received, "Reason" was already in production, scheduled for the April 1941 issue of *Astounding*. To give Asimov's stories of controlled robots maximum splash, Campbell rushed "Liar!" into the very next issue—where it would appear directly after "Universe," Robert Heinlein's lead novelet.

So it was, then, that when Asimov came to his story conference with John Campbell on March 17, 1941, the April issue of *Astounding* containing "Reason" was only three days from appearing on the newsstands, with "Liar!" due to follow in just one month.

If Asimov at this point could still look on himself as no more than a hopeful third-rater, this was because he had no way to appreciate the degree of importance his robot stories had for Campbell. The editor was bound to value these stories. More than any other work printed in the Golden Age *Astounding*, they visibly showed transcendent power responding to a set of explicitly stated operating principles.

But young Isaac Asimov had no basis as yet to perceive himself as a writer of bedrock modern science fiction—an exemplar of what the new Campbell *Astounding* was all about. The applause and recognition he would receive all lay in the future. In fact, Asimov tells us quite frankly:

> In time to come, van Vogt, Heinlein, and I would be universally listed among the top authors of the Golden Age, but van Vogt and Heinlein were that from the very beginning. Each blazed forth as a first-magazine star at the moment his first story appeared, and their status never flagged throughout the remainder of the Golden Age. I, on the other hand (and

this is not false modesty), came up only gradually. I was very little noticed
for a while and came to be considered a major author by such gradual
steps that despite the healthy helping of vanity with which I am blessed,
I myself was the last to notice.

"Nightfall" was the story that would first cause Asimov to be
taken as a writer of significance. When Asimov came to the crucial
story conference in March 1941 that resulted in "Nightfall," he
was right in the midst of his great leap from SF apprentice to
master of modern science fiction.

Asimov may not have been consciously aware that he was in
the middle of making this kind of shift at the moment that he
was handed the crucial quotation from Emerson's *Nature* and
asked, "What do you think would happen, Asimov, if men were
to see the stars for the first time in a thousand years?"

But Campbell most certainly did know what was happening to
Asimov, and knew what he was doing in assigning him "Nightfall."
He may even have seen this plum of a story idea as a way to provide
Asimov with an opportunity for self-recognition, the chance to wake
to his own nature and discover that unbeknownst to himself he had
become Isaac Asimov, master science fiction writer.

In the event, the youngster did make the most of his opportunity.
Asimov sat right down to work on "Nightfall," the writing went
without a hitch, and early in April, only three weeks after their
story conference, he turned in a 13,000 word novelet, the second-
longest story he had ever attempted.

Campbell was thoroughly pleased with the story, asking only
for minor revision to speed the opening. Not only did he offer
Asimov hearty and unqualified praise for "Nightfall," but this
time he kicked in a twenty-five percent bonus.

Asimov's story was placed in the lead spot of the September
1941 issue of *Astounding*, its advent heralded at length in the
"In Times to Come" column in the preceding issue. And on the
September cover, the climax of "Nightfall" was depicted in a
particularly striking picture by Hubert Rogers.

For Isaac Asimov—who had grown up treating the SF magazines
on sale in his father's candy store with the utmost reverence,
calculating the calendar of his life from one magazine on-sale date
to the next, then reading each new magazine without breathing
and putting it back on the newsstand without the slightest mar
so that he could do it again the next time—it was all a dream come
true, his fondest boyhood wish fulfilled. A lead story in *Astounding*!

And a cover by Rogers, too—that wasn't bad. Through the heart
of the Golden Age, from April 1940 until August 1942, it was

Hubert Rogers who painted every *Astounding* cover. Rogers' pictures—simple, clean-cut, modern and definite—captured and expressed the pure visual essence of Campbellian science fiction.

SF cover illustration of the Thirties had emphasized great cities and gigantic machines. People were either not visible or were tiny dots lost in immensity. Rogers' *Astounding* covers moved men into the foreground of the future, portraying them as powerful and confident citizens of the world of tomorrow, masters of the mighty machines and cities.

However, the cover for "Nightfall" was not Rogers' usual thing:

In this picture we are within a cavernous astronomical observatory dominated by a massive telescope. The aperture of the observatory dome gapes open, and in the slice of sky visible to us an overwhelming torrent of stars seems to tumble, cascade and explode in a great showering display of cosmic fireworks. A man is running toward us, his eyes bright with fear, a torch in his hand newly extinguished and trailing smoke. Behind him, other men are frozen in postures of alarm and panic. And at the horizon, a city is on fire.

Here human mastery and control have collapsed. The heavens have opened wide, and the sky is falling.

The locus of Asimov's story is the astronomical observatory of Saro University on the world of Lagash, a planet somewhere in time and space that has six suns in its sky. Four of these are named for us—Alpha, Beta, Gamma and Delta. (Presumably the two unnamed suns are Epsilon and Zeta.) Once in every two thousand forty-nine years, five suns set, while the remaining sun—Beta, a red dwarf—is eclipsed by a moon of Lagash that ordinarily cannot be seen. Then night falls on this perenially sunlit world, and the hidden stars shine forth.

This is the picture, at least, as it has been slowly and carefully pieced together by the scientists of Saro University, calling upon evidence and argument from a number of different fields of study. They may never have experienced the fall of night, they may not know what "the Stars" are, but they are ready to say that darkness and disaster are coming.

We are here at the observatory in the company of Theremon 762, a skeptical reporter who views the predicted eclipse as a failure of nerve by science, a capitulation to ancient nonsense and superstition. What the academics are proposing sounds to him and to many other people like the central myth of the Cultists, a remnant religious group.

This myth is summarized for us by Sheerin 501, a psychologist at the university:

"The Cultists said that every two thousand and fifty years Lagash entered a huge cave, so that all the suns disappeared, and there came *total darkness all over the world!* And then, they say, things called Stars appeared, which robbed men of their souls and left them unreasoning brutes, so that they destroyed the civilization they themselves had built up. Of course, they mix all this up with a lot of religio-mystic notions, but that's the central idea."

For Theremon, it is the scientists of Saro University who have become mixed up by a lot of religio-mystic notions. And he is ready to face university director Aton 77 and tell him so:

"This is not the century to preach 'the end of the world is at hand' to Lagash. You have to understand that people don't believe the 'Book of Revelations' any more, and it annoys them to have scientists turn about face and tell us the Cultists are right after all—"

But Aton cuts him off to say:

"No such thing, young man.... While a great deal of our data has been supplied to us by the Cult, our results contain none of the Cult's mysticism. Facts are facts, and the Cult's so-called 'mythology' *has* certain facts behind it. We've exposed them and ripped away their mystery. I assure you that the Cult hates us now worse than you do."

So Theremon asks to be informed of the science that lies behind the scientists' prediction of universal darkness and insanity. And in the hours before the great eclipse descends, psychologist Sheerin takes him aside for a drink and lays all the evidence out for him, bit by bit.

What a truly wonderful situation it is that we find ourselves in! Such is the power of modern science fiction to set forth any special case that it can actually locate and describe a planet like Lagash, with its six suns, its moon that is never directly seen, and its incredibly lopsided cycle of day and night.

But what turns this unique situation into a marvel is that Lagash is also a near twin of contemporary Earth. Whatever *can* be the same in both places *is* the same.

Men are men on Lagash, with teeth and with toes and with Adam's apples that bob when they swallow. Their blood is red, and they whistle and sweat and frown. They listen to the radio. They read the papers. For amusement, they ride the roller coaster. They work as photographers, astronomers, carpenters and electricians.

On Lagash, just as in 1941 America, liquor is poured from bottles and drunk in glasses, floors are covered by carpets, clothes have collars, time is reckoned in hours and minutes, and crazy people are trussed up in straitjackets and given injections of morphine to cool them out.

Even the current states of social development here and there are identical. On Lagash, a societal stage in which traditional religious belief was central has been superseded by a phase based upon rationality, science and technology—exactly as in the Twentieth Century Western culture which formed Isaac Asimov and for which he was writing this story.

There are certain differences between the two worlds. Perhaps because the people of Lagash live all their lives in a state of perpetual daylight, in the ordinary way of things they would appear to be a tad more rational than Earthmen have ever managed to be. At least they all have scientific-utopian zip-code names like Beenay 25 and Yimot 70, and apparently always have. Even a prophet in the ancient "Book of Revelations" was named Vendret 2.

But if the Lagashans are more regular-minded than we when the lights are on, they overcompensate for this by flying all to pieces when the lights go out. Sheerin tells Theremon about one particularly vivid example of the power of this phobia—a world exposition two years earlier where thrill-seekers were exposed to the Tunnel of Mystery, a fifteen-minute ride through total darkness. Most people were left breathless and trembling by this experience, but some were actually driven crazy or even outright frightened to death.

Sheerin provides Theremon with a sample of this disorienting alternate state by having him draw the curtains against the last ruddy light provided by the distant red dwarf, Beta. And sure enough, Theremon finds the darkness far more upsetting than he is willing to admit and is thoroughly relieved when the curtains are thrown open again.

The many parallels that exist between Lagash and Earth become all the more remarkable when we discover how very different Lagashan history actually is from our own. It seems that time and time again the Lagashans have worked themselves up to something like their present level of civilization, only to crash out.

This becomes one of the subjects expounded by Sheerin. He says:

"You realize, of course, that the history of civilization on Lagash displays a cyclic character—but I mean, *cyclic!*"

"I know," replied Theremon cautiously, "that this is the current archaeological theory. Has it been accepted as a fact?"

"Just about. In this last century it's been generally agreed upon. This cyclic character is—or rather, was—one of *the* great mysteries. We've located series of civilizations, nine of them definitely, and indications of others as well, all of which have reached heights comparable to our own, and all of which, without exception, were destroyed by fire at the very height of their culture."

The planet of Lagash must be the ultimate spawning ground of lost civilizations! Again and again and again these people build, they crash, they forget.

It seems that the Lagashans have been up and down, up and down forever like a yo-yo, each time putting the previous go-around out of mind completely, except for imperfect and distorted accounts like the one to be found in the "Book of Revelations." Their Stone Age now lies so deeply buried in the past that they know nothing about it at all and even imagine that men of those distant days must have been little more than intelligent apes—which, if true, would certainly make the original establishment of civilization on Lagash all the more marvelous.

If anyone ever needed to escape from the eternal round of cyclical history, it surely must be these people. And because they have finally managed to apply the tools of modern science to the problem and figure out what has been happening to them, they may actually accomplish the feat this time.

In this world, the most novel and advanced concept of science is the Law of Universal Gravitation—so abstruse a subject that popular wisdom holds that only a dozen men on the whole planet are capable of understanding it. Sheerin tells Theremon—and us—about that, too:

"After Genovi 41 discovered that Lagash rotated about the sun Alpha, rather than vice versa—and that was four hundred years ago—astronomers have been working. The complex motions of the six suns were recorded and analyzed and unwoven. Theory after theory was advanced and checked and counterchecked and modified and abandoned and revived and converted to something else. ... It was twenty years ago...that it was finally demonstrated that the Law of Universal Gravitation accounted exactly for the orbital motions of the six suns. It was a great triumph."

There is, however, one major exception to the perfection of this theory:

"In the last decade, the motions of Lagash about Alpha were computed according to gravity, and *it did not account for the orbit observed;* not even when all perturbations due to the other suns were included. Either the law was invalid, or there was another, as yet unknown, factor involved.

It was Aton 77—an astronomer as well as a university director—who solved this particular mystery by calling upon certain data held by but not understood by the Cult. This new information has led him to theorize the existence of a moon of Lagash that is too dull to be seen in the brilliant wash of light from the six suns, but whose presence would account for the deviations in Lagash's orbit. And in further leaps of insight, Aton has come to recognize that a satellite of the proper mass and distance and orbit to affect Lagash in exactly the right way would inevitably eclipse a lone Beta once in every two thousand forty-nine years. And also to realize that just such an epochal eclipse is due *now*.

If we add all these various elements of mystery together—the mystery of the periodic event described in the "Book of Revelations"; the mystery of darkness and its destabilizing effect on the Lagashan psyche; the mystery of one civilization after another inevitably destroyed at its height by fire; and the mystery of the invisible moon of Lagash—we begin to see the picture that Sheerin is drawing for Theremon.

Sheerin summarizes it like this: "'First the eclipse—which will start in three quarters of an hour—then universal Darkness, and, maybe these mysterious Stars—then madness, and end of the cycle.'"

If Aton and Sheerin and the other scientists are correct, then just one mystery remains to be unveiled: the actual nature of the Stars. And one member of the observatory staff has a speculation to offer on that score, too. He suggests that these unknown whatever-they-ares just might be other suns too distant to be detected by their gravitational effects. Perhaps as many as a dozen or even two dozen such suns. Maybe as far away from Lagash as four light years.

This great speculative leap captures the imagination of Theremon the reporter. He can't help blurting out, "'What an idea for a good Sunday supplement article. Two dozen suns in a universe eight light years across. Wow! That would shrink *our* universe into insignificance. The readers would eat it up.'"

But Theremon may never have his chance to print all the juicy stuff he has been told. The hour for good Sunday supplement articles may be past and not return again for a couple of thousand years.

Already the outline of Beta has begun to be chipped away by blackness, and at the sight, Theremon grows pale and trembles. There can be no question now about the existence of that invisible moon or about the true meaning of the mumbo-jumbo in the "Book of Revelations." Soon the mysterious Stars will become visible and then there will be no need for speculations.

Here is the climactic moment of total eclipse as Theremon experiences it:

With the slow fascination of fear, he lifted himself on one arm and turned his eyes toward the blood-curdling blackness of the window.

Through it shone the Stars!

Not Earth's feeble thirty-six hundred Stars visible to the eye—Lagash was in the center of a giant cluster. Thirty thousand mighty suns shown down in a soul-searing splendor that was more frighteningly cold in its awful indifference than the bitter wind that shivered across the cold, horribly bleak world.

This last paragraph—with its apt but almost certainly unintended pun of "shown" for "shone"—was an interpolation by John Campbell. And even though Asimov would retain the paragraph in all later reprintings of "Nightfall," he would never really be happy about it. Not only isn't it written in that cool, unadorned style that Asimov had worked so hard to cultivate, but it makes explicit mention of Earth, which Asimov had been at particular pains throughout the story not to do.

Asimov would be half-right in having negative feelings about this; no caring writer ever enjoys having his work tampered with. But he would also be half-wrong.

It is true that Earth is nowhere else mentioned directly in this story, but as we have already seen and will see further, its existence is certainly reflected everywhere. So this flaw, if it is one, may be relatively minor.

And if the paragraph isn't written in Asimov's own usual style, it also may be that a cool and unadorned modern style wasn't appropriate or adequate to express this moment of cosmic breakthrough. "Nightfall" is simultaneously an old-time scientifiction story and a story of modern science fiction. But Isaac Asimov was by now so much the modern science fiction writer that the old purple-tinged scientifictional manner didn't come easily to him, even when a touch of emoting was called for.

And that old-style scientifictional paragraph with its "soul-searing splendor," its "awful indifference," and its "cold, horribly bleak world" did have an important emotional point to put across that otherwise would not have been fully made. Ultimately, in "Nightfall," it is not just the darkness that overwhelms the people of Lagash, unbalances their reason, and causes them to trash their civilization. What gets to them and brings them down is the sudden recognition of their own cosmic insignificance.

Ordinarily the people of Lagash live in a vest-pocket universe composed of six suns, and regard that as a sufficiency, an all-in-all. By straining their imaginations to the utmost, they can envision and mentally accommodate the existence of a hidden universe that is as much as four times larger than this. Instead, however, in the space of a single instant they find themselves drowning in a great sea of stars—not the mere thirty-six hundred suns visible to us, but thirty thousand Stars blazing down on them at once.

The sudden revelation of a universe this many times more vast and complex than even imagination has allowed for could be sufficient to chill the heart and unhinge the mind of one of our own Techno Age citizens—H.P. Lovecraft, say. In the dark, it is quite enough to overtopple the poor children of Lagash.

There is a certain grand inevitability about the end of the story and the conclusion of the latest cycle of civilization on Lagash. At the sight of the Stars, all of the men present in the astronomical observatory—skeptical reporter, sober scientist and Cultist true believer alike—promptly fall to pieces without regard to what each of them may think he believes. They whimper, they scream, they cry, they giggle hysterically as they are overtaken by their ineluctable Fate:

> Someone clawed at the torch, and it fell and snuffed out. In the instant, the awful splendor of the indifferent Stars leaped nearer to them.
>
> On the horizon outside the window, in the direction of Saro City, a crimson glow began growing, strengthening in brightness, that was not the glow of a sun.
>
> The long night had come again.

And so "Nightfall" ends.

This is a scientifiction story, for sure. Just like Asimov's "Cosmic Corkscrew" or Don A. Stuart's "Night" or H.G. Wells's *The Time Machine* or a hundred other stories of the Technological Age, "Nightfall" displays a catastrophic cosmic situation before which mankind is helpless. And that is that, or so it seems: The long night has come again. Chalk up another fallen civilization and start the next cycle.

But, of course, that isn't simply that. "Nightfall" may be an epitomal presentation of cyclical history and cosmic horror, but it isn't just another scientifiction story. Even as we gaze at it, its nature alters and it stands revealed as modern science fiction.

The first things that identify "Nightfall" as modern science fiction are its distant location and its highly special circumstances.

As we have seen, a typical Techno Age scientifiction story that invoked either cyclical history or the impact of the wider universe upon the vulnerable psyche of man would be likely to find its setting at the focal point of human concern, on Village Earth. Or, at most, it might trail along after an adventurer from Earth out exploring the Solar System in search of the ruins of past civilizations.

But, for all the evocations it makes of Earth, Asimov's story is neither tied to Earth nor to a protagonist from Earth. As a modern science fiction story, "Nightfall" can take place anywhere at all. It can search through all of time, space and alternate dimensions to find exactly what it is looking for—the ultimate scientifiction-like situation, the place where cyclical history and the suddenly revealed wider universe are not only literal fact, but even turn out to be the very same thing.

However, this special effect does take a lot of arranging. Asimov has to present a situation of incredible complexity—six cooperating suns, the crucial one of which is a red dwarf so that the last light before the eclipse may appear properly terminal and melancholy; a planet that is physically and also culturally a twin of present-day Earth; a moon of exactly the right composition to be unobservable; and a race of men that is given to pyromania and amnesia under conditions of stress—with all of these peculiar elements interacting just so. Then, behind the glitches and blank spots of their natures and interweavings, the spook of cyclical history in the form of a cluster of thirty thousand suns can lurk until just the right moment to pop out and go, "Boo!"

But what an effort it all takes! Simply by the distance that must be traveled and the amount of puffing and straining that is necessary to arrange and maintain the special scientifictional situation of "Nightfall," this story contrives to make cyclical history and cosmic freakout seem a highly unlikely fate for us on Earth.

The duality of "Nightfall" also marks it as modern science fiction. Once again, as in Asimov's earlier story "Reason," we both experience the events of a story and stand outside them looking on.

We are, quite naturally, ignorant of the situation in which we find ourselves. We identify with Aton and Sheerin and Theremon in their quest for knowledge, and along with them we put together details, fragments, and scraps of information as they become available to us and do our best to make sense of them. When these citizens of Lagash break down and Saro City goes up in flames, we care about all that has been lost.

At the same time, however, we also manage to stand at a comfortable distance from the disaster. We know all kinds of things that the characters in this story do not, and our privileged knowledge separates us from the doom suffered by Lagash and allows us to look upon it with a certain objectivity.

As one example, there is the fact that what are the deepest possible mysteries to Lagash are not necessarily mysteries to us, who are fortunate enough to be permitted a wider angle of view. We are no strangers to darkness ourselves, and we have managed to survive the experience with our wits intact. We are familiar with moons and with eclipses. We have often seen the stars, and we are acquainted with the wider universe revealed by Twentieth Century science, with its suns by the billion and galaxies beyond counting. So however much we may empathize with the poor Lagashans, simply finding ourselves in the dark surrounded by a globular cluster of stars isn't going to shake our nerve and rattle our brains.

Moreover, throughout the story we are constantly flashed special signals over the heads of the Lagashans that give us assistance in understanding and assessing the situation in which we find ourselves. These aren't direct references to Earth so much as meaningful allusions to Earthly events that not only provide us with an extra measure of understanding, but also lend plausibility to the story we are being told.

We are, for instance, obviously meant to see that international exposition with its Tunnel of Mystery by the light of the recent New York World's Fair. When we are told of a series of nine civilizations that were all destroyed by fire, we are expected to recall the excavation of the nine cities of Troy, some of which were destroyed by fire. When reference is made to a theory that only twelve men are supposed to be able to understand, we are meant to hear an echo of the public marveling over Einstein's Theory of General Relativity. And if we are expected to believe the indirect detection of that invisible moon of Lagash, that is partly because we are already known to be aware of the gravitational anomalies that led to the search for the unknown planet Pluto.

The single most important piece of special information that is given to us, however, is that the scientists of Lagash are essentially correct—the great eclipse they have predicted really is going to occur. The eclipse is what we have been brought here to see, and we *know* that it is coming. John Campbell made certain of that five times over:

The title of the story was an indication of what to expect. So were the epigraph from Emerson and the powerful Hubert Rogers cover painting. And Campbell's story blurb, which ran beneath Asimov's title and right beside the quote from Emerson, said: *"How would people who saw the stars but once in two thousand years react—"*

But all of this was no more than a reminder, because in the preview of "Nightfall" that Campbell had run in the preceding month's "In Times to Come" column, he had spelled out the story situation exactly:

Next month, Isaac Asimov has a novelette, "Nightfall," inspired by a quotation from Emerson—which might, offhand, seem a curious source of inspiration for a modern science-fiction writer. Said Emerson: "If the stars

should appear one night in a thousand years, how would men believe and
adore, and preserve for many generations the remembrance of the city
of God!"

"Nightfall" discusses just that point. How *would* men believe—and what—
if the stars appeared but once in a millennium or two? Suppose there were
a planet of a multiple-sun system where there was no night, since there was
always, everywhere, at least one sun-star in the sky. Except that, once in
some twenty-five hundred years, the configuration became such that—
night fell.

Now—what would happen? Asimov has an idea, and a story—and I
think they're both darned good!

We cannot have any doubt that John Campbell wished the readers
of *Astounding* to be fully aware of the basic facts about the situation
in "Nightfall" before they began to read the story. While it might be
nice if they were able to summon an old-time scientifictional frisson
over the sad fate of Lagash, they were not in any way to be surprised
by it. They were to know better from the outset.

The duality displayed in "Nightfall" can be understood as a
demonstration of a fundamental assumption of Campbellian science
fiction—that it is possible to live, experience and suffer within the
universe, and also at the same time to stand apart from existence,
observe its workings, and influence its operation.

This leads us to one last regard in which Asimov's story is modern
science fiction. "Nightfall" isn't content to wring its hands helplessly
while an unheeding cosmos grinds the bones of all-too-mortal man,
as a story that was merely scientifictional might. It actually proposes
a solution to the eternal problem of Lagash—couched in the terms
suggested by L. Sprague de Camp in his essay on the direction of
history, "The Science of Whithering," published in *Astounding*
in 1940.

That is, this eclipse that we have been brought here to witness
may not be just one more Lagashan light show of stars and burning
cities, all so much alike that we might as readily have attended the
one that came before it, or the one that comes after. This fall of
civilization on Lagash may not be just one more fall of civilization
on Lagash. What we have been seeing may actually be the last time
around the age-old cycle.

This time, at least, having some few months to prepare for the
coming disaster, the scientists of Saro University have built a bulwark
against the power of the Darkness and the Stars. They have invented
what they describe as an "artificial-light mechanism"; we would call
them torches. They have constructed a place of refuge—"the Hideout"—for three hundred women and children and able educated

men. And they have placed all their precious scientific records there for safekeeping.

Sheerin assures Theremon: "'The next cycle will *start off* with the truth, and when the *next* eclipse comes, mankind will at last be ready for it.'"

It is possible that Sheerin is wrong. The present eclipse, when it occurs, is so much more intense an experience than the scientists have anticipated that it may be that the Hideout has not managed to survive it, either.

But then Sheerin could be right after all. And though we can't know for certain, we have to suspect that he is. There is only one regard in which this eclipse is different from other eclipses in earlier cycles. And that is the existence of that safe Hideout with its essential scientific records.

This time round, men have actually used the power of science to determine the operating principles at work in their situation, and have attempted to master them. So if the Hideout does survive, then in the morning light after the night has gone for another eon, Lagash may finally wake and begin to unchain itself from the eternal wheel of cyclical history. And that is the only viable answer there can be to the otherwise unending futility of Lagash.

Modern science fiction would like readers here on Earth to take a lesson from this, in particular those laggard folk still bogged down in the assumptions of the Age of Technology. Speaking to people like these, "Nightfall" says: *There is a way out of the nightmare of cyclical history, a way past the otherwise total certainty of your own downfall. Become a master of universal operating principles and learn to deal with whatever circumstances you find yourselves in.*

Just as Isaac Asimov intended when he first sat down to write it, "Nightfall" is a true thought-variant. It is a scientifiction story, but set in a modern science fiction location. At the same time it is a model modern science fiction story that addresses and resolves the most nagging questions of scientifiction.

Taken only as a scientifiction story, "Nightfall" is about the long night coming again. But read as modern science fiction, "Nightfall" is about the crucial transition from a state in which men have been ruled by the Stars to a new era in which free will is at last a possibility.

"Nightfall" is a bridge that links the Technological Age and the new Age of the Atom. It can be likened to Edward Bulwer-Lytton's 1871 novel *The Coming Race*, which eased the previous moment of transition from the Romantic Era to the Age of Technology through its conception of the transcendent force *vril*, which was simultaneously spiritual, rational, occult and scientific.

In something of the same way, in "Nightfall" different realms of transcendence are perceived as essentially the same. That is, the invisible moon and hidden stars of Lagash are interpreted in spiritual terms by the Cult, as the vast unknown universe by the scientists of Saro University, and as blank spots in perception by us outside observers.

But at the same time that these different frames of reference are equated, the new formulation is asserted to be superior to the old ones in aptness and power. The suggestion is made that merely by a change in perspective, a whole range of Techno Age problems—from cyclical history to cosmic horror—might finally become recognizable as a single problem which could be resolved by universal operating principles in the hands of science-minded men.

The story "Nightfall" couldn't have been written either much earlier or much later than it was. It was both the product and the representation of a moment in which perceptions were shifting.

We might think of this story as the unique result of exactly the right two collaborators—editor John W. Campbell, Jr., who had been working so long and so diligently to solve the problem of human Fate, and his star pupil, modern science fiction writer Isaac Asimov. By producing this story at precisely the one moment when it could be produced, they pointed the way out of the Techno Age, in which the destiny of man had been determined, into the new Atomic Age in which anything was possible.

A World of Change

Paradoxical though at first it might appear, the most immediate result of the arrival of John Campbell's modern science fiction at the end of the Thirties was a radical shrinking of the scope of science fiction, a withdrawal from the great vastnesses of time and space that had loomed so large to the Techno Age imagination.

In the 1939 *Astounding*, there was a retreat from the farther reaches of the future—with their grim promise of decay, devolution and the ultimate quiescence of all existence. No more were there to be stories of red suns at the end of time, and no more encounters with Big Brains domestic or foreign. Overwhelmingly powerful alien invaders of all kinds were asked to pack and shown the door.

Short stories became largely confined to the near future and to near space, and to those things that might be known, calculated and controlled. The most typical kind of story in *Astounding* in 1939 was some sort of technological space opera set amongst the worlds of our Solar System as described by John Campbell in his long-running series of articles and then depicted on *Astounding*'s new realistic astronomical covers. These might be tales about rushing urgently needed serum to Jupiter, or about the canny astrogational techniques that permit a slower ship to win a space race from Mars to Jupiter and back, or about the discovery of a young mathematical whiz in the midst of a construction gang laboring to alter an asteroid into a space station.

A measure of sweep did still remain in the novels that were published in *Astounding* in 1939. The three major serials were all super-scientific space epics in the style of the early Thirties. Clifford Simak's *Cosmic Engineers* (Feb-Apr) was a deliberate attempt to write a good old-time story about bold venturers wielding mighty science after the example of the young John W. Campbell. Jack

Williamson's *One Against the Legion* (Apr-June) was a comparatively
tame second sequel to *The Legion of Space*. And E. E. Smith's *Gray
Lensman* (Oct 1939-Jan 1940)—easily the most far-reaching story of
the year—was the first sequel to *Galactic Patrol*, the novel that had
been in serialization at the moment that Campbell assumed the
editorship of *Astounding* in 1937.

By 1940, however, even the novels that Campbell chose to print
in *Astounding* reflected the new restrictiveness. The three major
serials this year were all set on Earth in the near-to-middle future,
with neither star travel nor aliens. Robert Heinlein's short novel
"If This Goes On—" (Feb-Mar) was about the overthrow of a future
American religious dictator. L. Ron Hubbard's *Final Blackout*
(Apr-June)—written in the hour that Hitler invaded Poland, launching World War II—was about war in Europe protracted for generation
after generation. And A. E. van Vogt's *Slan* (Sept-Dec) was about the
attempts of emergent Homo superior to deal with the jealousy, fear
and rage of ordinary humanity.

One way to understand the radical indrawing of science fiction
that took place during the first two years of the Atomic Age would
be to recall the situation that existed back in 1870, just before the
publication of "The Battle of Dorking" and the opening of the
Technological Age. At that moment, the future did not yet belong
to science-beyond-science. Rather, it was still imagined to be the
land of utopian social perfection.

In a very similar way, at the onset of the Atomic Age in 1939, the
far future was the exclusive property of Techno Age SF. It was
envisioned as the country of Big Brains and red suns.

We might feel some inclination to say, then, that this was a
moment for SF to draw in its horns. Modern science fiction as of
yet had no alternative images of the most distant reaches of the
multiverse. It had no business of its own to perform at the far
ends of space and time. And consequently, it felt the need to restrict
itself to comparatively well-defined territory until it had worked
out new answers to the questions of what was to be done out there
amidst the enigmatical immensities, and how, and why.

However, there is an alternative way of regarding this early
modern science fiction of 1939 and 1940 that may catch a little
more of the truth of the matter. To see things from the proper angle,
we must recall the overwhelming degree to which the expansive super-
scientific SF of the early Thirties had emphasized mystery, while
devoting comparatively little thought to the matter of plausibility.

In that hour of political and economic desperation, with the whole
world apparently falling into collapse, a handful of exploratory
writers had flatly denied the inevitability of the decline and fall of

Western man. Instead, these bold visionaries had foreseen man bursting free of the bonds of Earth and leaping lightly to the stars. They'd imagined that men might run into alien races out there, wrestle with them for dominance, and win. So powerful would men become that they might destroy whole planets with nothing more than a seeming child's toy or the pure overwhelming power of their thought. Out of the nothingness of space, they might produce anything their hearts desired. And there would even come a day when ancient alien races saluted humanity for its maturity and breadth of vision, and men served as the guardians of the galaxy.

The young John Campbell had perhaps gone the farthest. In his SF daydreams, he had imagined man as unique and alone in his power—a creator and destroyer, well-nigh a god.

This was certainly inspiring stuff—for some people, at least—in a time that could use all the inspiration it could get. But in no way could it be called inherently likely. It was all cobbled together out of unfounded hope and barefaced assertion.

And as wonderful and mysterious as the leaps beyond current possibility might be that were tossed off with such apparent casualness in the SF of the early Thirties, they could also be more than enough to test the credibility of even so uncritical a scientific believer as Hugo Gernsback. It might seem to us that there was nothing that this man could not swallow if only the word "science" were attached to it—but the kid John Campbell proved that even Hugo Gernsback had his limits.

In the December 1932 issue of *Wonder Stories*, Gernsback wrote a special editorial entitled "Reasonableness in Science Fiction" and attached it to a new Campbell story called "Space Rays." Said Gernsback:

> In the present offering, Mr. John W. Campbell, Jr. ...has proceeded in an earnest way to burlesque some of our rash authors to whom plausibility and possible science mean nothing. He pulls, magician-like, all sorts of impossible rays from his silk hat, much as a magician extracts rabbits. There is no situation that cannot easily be overcome by some sort of preposterous scientific—(as he terms it)—gimmick. ... If he has left out any colored rays, or any magical rays that could not immediately perform miraculous wonders, we are not aware of this shortcoming in his story.

How odd of Gernsback to deliver this public rap across the knuckles! Even though his criticism may have had a certain justice to it, it would seem that the doubts and reservations he felt were not sufficient to prevent him from accepting Campbell's story and publishing it—and, presumably, even paying for it by and by.

This reprimand from Hugo Gernsback, the guardian of all that was serious about science fiction, apparently smarted considerably. "Space Rays" would be the last story that Campbell would publish in *Wonder* for four full years. He wouldn't appear there again until Gernsback had given up and sold the magazine and it had been remade into *Thrilling Wonder Stories.*

And yet, this reproof would seem to have been a turning point for John Campbell. It appears to mark the precise moment that he began to put aside his juvenile fantasies of the unstoppable power of science-wielding man and to turn his considerable critical intelligence to the task of setting forth the unresolved problems and challenging the unconsidered premises of Techno Age science fiction.

It was on the heels of Gernsback's rebuke, in December 1932, that Campbell wrote "Twilight." And by Campbell's own reckoning, it was "Twilight" that "led to the development of the Don A. Stuart stories, and thus to the modern *Astounding.*"

In fact, however, the whole variety of work that Campbell found to do during the Thirties following his initial super-scientific phase—his stories as Don A. Stuart, the Penton and Blake series, and his eighteen articles on the Solar System, beginning with one significantly entitled "Accuracy" (*Astounding*, June 1936)—can be seen as varying attempts to bring necessary plausibility to the dreams of human power and domination with which he had begun.

Campbell was not totally alone in this. We may remember, for instance, that one reason why Stanley Weinbaum's first story, "A Martian Odyssey," had such powerful impact was its relatively greater concern for plausibility. Even John Campbell himself was ready to take instruction from Weinbaum in conceiving and writing his Penton and Blake stories.

As the Thirties passed and Depression fears gradually began to wane, there was a decrease in demand for stories of escape to the far ends of space and time, or for stories of human scientific invincibility, and an increase in concern for what it might actually prove possible for human beings to be and do. More and more of the readers of science fiction—like the young Isaac Asimov—were receiving education in current science and beginning to care that the stories which inspired them should have some reasonable consonance with known fact. They wanted science fiction to be more than just made-up stuff.

By the later Thirties, so evident had the increased appetite for accurate science become that with the beginning of 1937, F. Orlin Tremaine would alter the letters column in *Astounding* from "Brass Tacks" to "Science Discussions." In a sense, it was only the confirmation of this trend when eight months later John Campbell, the chief contemporary spokesman for scientific accuracy in science fiction, was chosen to become the new editor of *Astounding*.

As we've seen, the moment he became editor, Campbell began a series of radical changes in *Astounding* that were designed to alter it into a fit vehicle for an altogether new kind of SF—a modern science fiction that was not only good, but was also logical and possible. And, as we have also seen, by then *Astounding* had a readership that was more than ready to go along with Campbell in the new direction, to support his policy of mutation and to ask for more.

To understand the radically constrained science fiction of the 1939 and 1940 *Astounding*, then, we must be aware that at the hour it was published, it was not perceived as an imaginative retreat. Rather, it was hailed as a giant step forward, a radical advance in realism, rigor and relevance.

Observers like us, shielded by the passage of time from the pure overwhelming force of John Campbell's self-confidence and the corresponding enthusiasm of his readers, might still only see that there was a moment when Campbell's vaunted new modern science fiction actually amounted to no more than a small handful of relatively trivial stories about the human race becoming hairy, or a man falling in love with a female robot, or the problems of repairing a cracked drive shaft on a Martian spaceliner. And it could be with a sense of near-embarrassment that we mentally compare these simple little stories to the ever-so-much-vaster dignity, scope and seriousness of a Techno Age work like Olaf Stapledon's *Star Maker*, published as recently as 1937.

But then we have to pause and remember that every period has its own problems, its own priorities, and its own sense of exactly where it is that plausible transcendence is to be sought and found. Just as the Age of Reason had been concerned with the rational perfection of society, while the Romantic Era was bound on a Grail-quest in hopes of healing its wounded soul, so had it been the special business of the Age of Technology to come to terms with the vastness of the wider universe.

The Atomic Age simply wouldn't be mesmerized by *vastness* in the same way. There would still be a few writers like Isaac Asimov and Arthur C. Clarke who would continue to find a measure of inspiration in the thought of vast sweeps of time and space—in something of the same way that there had still been those during the Techno Age who continued to care about the fate of the soul. But modern science fiction as a whole would not concentrate its hopes and fears on the remotest imaginable distances. It would seek its mysteries in other places.

A third way—and perhaps the best way—to look upon the apparent constriction and limitation of SF in *Astounding* in the first years of the Golden Age would be to think of science fiction under Campbell's direction as changing the focus of its vision from the far away and vague to the near and sharply defined. If that was a very small territory at the outset—the Solar System during the next hundred years or so—in short order, Campbell's careful, thoughtful, plausible, human-centered modern science fiction would begin expanding its area of authority and control, moving out into the territory of Techno Age SF and taking it over.

There would be distinct limits to how far it would ultimately go. For the most part, no farther ahead in time than about fifty thousand years, and no farther out in space than the borders of our own galaxy. But within this broad-enough area of knowability, John Campbell would stake out his science fiction empire.

The first territory that was placed under Campbellian rule, however, would not be our time or space, but rather parallel universes—that multitude of alternate realms of being asserted to exist by Dunsany and Lovecraft, among others, but perhaps most tellingly evoked by H. G. Wells in *Men Like Gods*.

Assertion of authority over these not-quite-real places would take place in the not-completely-serious pages of *Unknown* in 1940—a time when *Astounding* was still concentrating its full attention on the immediate task of straightening and tidying up around the Solar System.

The writers responsible would be L. Sprague de Camp, fresh from the triumph of *Lest Darkness Fall*, and a collaborator, Fletcher Pratt. In a pair of comic short novels, "The Roaring Trumpet" (*Unknown*, May 1940) and "The Mathematics of Magic" (*Unknown*, Aug 1940)—gathered in 1941 as a book entitled *The Incomplete Enchanter*—they imagined the power of universal operating principles as extending not just to the past and the fall of Rome, but as applying to every conceivable realm or dimension of being.

De Camp's writing partner, Murray Fletcher Pratt, was a scholar, linguist, and gourmet born in 1897 on an Indian reservation in western New York State. In his youth, he was simultaneously a public librarian and a professional boxer. In later years, he chose to wear the loudest shirts he could find, raised marmosets in his apartment, and enjoyed reading sagas aloud in the original Norse. He would write more than fifty books of many different kinds, but at the time of his death in 1956, his chief reputation was as a Navy and Civil War historian.

Along with his many other interests, Pratt had an early and continuing involvement in SF. Back in the Twenties he had contributed a handful of collaborative scientifiction stories to *Amazing*. Then, in the Thirties, he translated novels from French and German for *Wonder Stories*—contriving to collect the money he was owed by Hugo Gernsback through the simple expedient of holding onto the final installment of a novel in serialization until he received his payment in full.

De Camp and Pratt were first thrown together by de Camp's one-time college roommate, John D. Clark, the man who had introduced de Camp to magazine science fiction and also to John Campbell. At the time they joined forces, it was Pratt, ten years de Camp's elder, who was much the better-known writer—at least outside the confines of *Astounding* and *Unknown*. What's more, the initial notion of writing fantasies about modern characters in storybook settings was his, too.

As de Camp would eventually say: "With the appearance of Campbell's *Unknown*, Pratt conceived the idea of a series of novels, in collaboration with me, about a hero who projects himself into the parallel worlds described on this plane in myths and legends."

What Pratt had to offer de Camp was his broad and loving knowledge of European myth and legend, together with a more lively imagination than de Camp possessed. It would be he who picked the worlds they would have their modern characters travel to—first the realm of Norse myth, and then the world of Edmund Spenser's allegorical epic poem, *The Faerie Queene* (1589-1596).

What de Camp offered to Pratt was a keen sense of story logic, and a lightness of touch that Pratt's own fiction tended to lack. De Camp also knew how to write for John Campbell, while Pratt did not.

The two made a very odd couple: Pratt was as conspicuously short as de Camp was conspicuously tall. He was as flamboyant as de Camp was self-contained. And he was as romantic as de Camp was humorously skeptical. But the collaboration of these two proved to be a very happy blending of their separate talents. De Camp himself says, "I thought that the combination of Pratt and de Camp produced a result visibly different from the work of either of us alone."

If "The Roaring Trumpet" and "The Mathematics of Magic," their first two collaborative stories, appeared altogether marvelous and new—by a considerable margin the most wonderful stories yet to see print in *Unknown*—that would be due in some degree to the freshness of the settings selected by Pratt. Even more, however, it would be because of the originality and scope of de Camp's arguments for the existence of a multiplicity of worlds, each defined by its own individual set of operating principles, with a master set of operating principles ruling over all.

Just as in *Lest Darkness Fall*, the theory that is to be illustrated by the events of the story is set forth at the outset of "The Roaring Trumpet," this time in a conversation between senior psychologist Reed Chalmers and the members of his staff at the Garaden Institute in Ohio on the subject of "'our new science of paraphysics.'" Chalmers suggests:

> "The world we live in is composed of impressions received through the senses. But there is an infinity of possible worlds, and if the senses can be attuned to receive a different series of impressions, we should infallibly find ourselves living in a different world."

To this, a young psychologist, the rash and romantic Harold Shea, responds:

> "Do you mean that a complete shift would actually transfer a man's body into one of these other worlds?"
>
> "Very likely," agreed Chalmers, "since the body records whatever sensations the mind permits. For complete demonstration it would be necessary to try it, and I don't know that the risk would be worth it. The other world might have such different laws that it would be impossible to return."
>
> Shea asked: "You mean, if the world were that of classical mythology, for instance, the laws would be those of Greek magic instead of modern physics? ... Then this new science of paraphysics is going to include the natural laws of all these different worlds, and what we call physics is just a special case of paraphysics—"
>
> "Not so fast, young man," replied Chalmers. "For the present, I think it wise to restrict the meaning of our term 'paraphysics' to the branch of knowledge that concerns the relationship of these multiple universes to each other, assuming that they actually exist."

Here, in the crucial term "paraphysics," we can perceive a clear measure of the change from traditional thought. In former times, the nature of being and the ultimate structure of the world were the subject of *metaphysics*, a branch of philosophy concerned with non-material spiritual reality. However, in the new order reflected in modern science fiction, these fundamental questions were now to be recognized as the subject of something quite different—*paraphysics*, which might be defined as the science of higher-order universal operating principles, or what might be called universal operating principles beyond universal operating principles.

And once again, just as in *Lest Darkness Fall*, in very short order in "The Roaring Trumpet" initial speculation is borne out by actual experience. Bored and brash young Harold Shea gathers those supplies that seem appropriate to him—including a .38 revolver, a box of matches, a 1926 *Boy Scout Handbook*, and a sporty hat with a green feather—and makes an attempt to transport himself into the world of Irish legend by reciting a series of logical equations designed to attune him with the mental state of that alternate universe. However, Shea doesn't fully have the hang of what he is attempting, and instead his "syllogismobile" deposits him in the mud and snow of the realm of Norse myth, leaving him to try to cope with the likes of Odinn, Thor and Loki.

In this other universe, the science and technology of our world won't operate at all. Shea's watch doesn't tick, his matches won't light, his gun doesn't shoot, and the *Boy Scout Handbook* turns into a meaningless blur before his eyes. Lost in this other reality, Harold Shea has none of the advantages of special knowledge that permitted Martin Padway to undo the fall of Rome.

Except for one, that is. Shea has a firm grip on the principle of universal operating principles. He thinks:

> This world he was in—perhaps permanently—was governed by laws of its own. What were those laws? There was only one piece of equipment of which the transference had not robbed him; his modern mind, habituated to studying and analyzing the general rules guiding individual events. He ought to be able to reason out the rules governing this existence and to use them—something which the rustic Thjalfi would never think of doing. So far the only rules he had noticed were that the gods had unusual powers. But there must be general laws underlying even these—

In short, though magic may work in this realm and our familiar physics may not, at a stroke magic has been redefined and turned into something that looks very much like an alternate form of physics. Armed with this attitude, it isn't long at all before Shea himself is successfully constructing spells.

On the eve of Ragnarök—the ultimate confrontation between the gods of Asgard and their enemies whose outcome no one can foretell—Shea and the god Heimdall find themselves prisoners of the fire giants of Muspellheim. But Shea proves able to perform a successful job of magical plastic surgery on a troll guard who is sensitive about the size of his nose, and thereby to win his cooperation in contriving their escape.

Shea reflects:

> He couldn't get used to the idea that he, of all people, could work magic. It was contrary to the laws of physics, chemistry and biology. But then, where he was the laws of physics, chemistry and biology had been repealed. He was under the laws of magic. His spell had conformed

exactly to those laws, as explained by Dr. Chalmers. This was a world
in which those laws were basic. The trick was that he happened to know
one of those laws, while the general run of mortals—and trolls and gods,
too—didn't know them. ... If he had only provided himself with a more
elaborate knowledge of those laws instead of the useless flashlights,
matches and guns—

What a complete reordering this is of everything we ever thought
we knew! And what marvelous promises of new possibility are
made here!

The most notable previous stories of cross-dimensional travel in
Unknown had been several 1939 short novels by L. Ron Hubbard
in which contemporary guys found themselves transferred into
otherworlds out of the pages of *The Arabian Nights.* In the first
of these, "The Ultimate Adventure" (Apr 1939), the hero manages
to prevail in a strange magical country on the strength of a revolver
and a box of matches. In the second, "Slaves of Sleep" (July 1939),
the edge the hero enjoys is his cunning and his ability to take
advantage of opportunity.

But "The Roaring Trumpet" went far beyond anything in
Hubbard's stories in its explicit imposition of contemporary
authority over the worlds of the imagination. In the first place,
Pratt and de Camp did not just invoke one specific otherworld
or another. Rather, they suggested the existence of an infinity
of different worlds, and then created paraphysics, a whole new
branch of science, just to deal with them.

Moreover, in this story transference between dimensions was
not just some half-accidental result of running afoul of an ancient
talisman or a whacked-out scientist with a potent drug, as in
Hubbard's stories. Instead Pratt and de Camp offered us the
syllogismobile, a deliberate scientific means of travel that, rightly
operated, could rotate us out of the limits ordinarily set for us
and thrust us into a thousand different universes.

Most important of all, however, was the fundamental assertion
in "The Roaring Trumpet" that there must be one set of operating
principles or another at work in every last nook and cranny of the
multiverse, with ultimate operating principles to regulate the interactions of the whole. It was this new ordering of existence that
permitted conceptions like paraphysics and the syllogismobile to be
thought of at all—in much the same way that H. G. Wells's vision of
vast sweeps of post-utopian future time necessarily preceded and
made possible his conception of a time machine to explore them.

Just like an L. Ron Hubbard hero abroad in another dimension,
Harold Shea has the advantage of a flexible, questioning modern

mind. But the real edge he enjoys is his confident certainty that even though he may happen to find himself in some place where he doesn't know the local rules, nonetheless rules will exist and he will be able to work them out for himself.

His success in casting simple spells is a heady indication of potential success for the Western scientific mode of approach—but it is all the farther that Shea is able to go in this initial story. When he and Heimdall join Odinn before the gates of Hell to warn him that Ragnarök has arrived, the demonic old hag Odinn has come to consult hurls a clot of snow at Shea and bids him begone to the misbegotten place from which he came. And, forthwith, back to Ohio he travels, startling Dr. Chalmers and his colleagues with the suddenness of his arrival, the wildness of his appearance, and the size of his appetite.

It might be fair to say that unlike Martin Padway in Sixth Century Rome, Harold Shea is not yet sufficiently knowledgeable or powerful to tip the balance of the situation he has been faced with. With him departed, Ragnarök will still go on to its uncertain conclusion.

But then it is only appropriate that Shea should not be there, since he never wanted to have anything to do with Ragnarök in the first place. At the outset of his adventure, when he first learns from Heimdall that the final battle is near, his immediate impulse is to ask, "'What can I do to keep from getting caught in the gears? ... I mean, if the world's going to bust up, how can I keep out of the smash?'"

That is what Shea asks for, and that, ultimately, is what he gets.

However, in the second Harold Shea comic adventure, the significantly titled "The Mathematics of Magic," matters are carried a vital step or two further.

This story followed almost immediately on the heels of "The Roaring Trumpet": For the readers of *Unknown* in 1940, the second Shea short novel saw publication in August, just three months after the first. For Harold Shea himself, his new story begins even before he has put a period to the previous adventure with three steaks and a whole apple pie.

The check hasn't been paid before he and Dr. Chalmers are laying plans for a second trip into another world—this time with Chalmers as a participant. Shea once again proposes Cuchulinn's Ireland as their destination, but Chalmers quickly turns this down as too rough and barbaric. Then Shea suggests the world of Edmund Spenser's *Faerie Queene*—a chivalric epic telling of struggle between the knights of Queen Gloriana and various enchanters that was left half-finished at the poet's death in 1599.

Chalmers says:

"Certainly a brilliant and interesting world, and one in which I personally might have some place. But I am afraid we should find it uncomfortable if we landed in the latter half of the story, where Queen Gloriana's knights are having a harder and harder time, as though Spenser were growing discouraged, or the narrative for some reason were escaping his hands, taking on a life of its own. I'm not sure we could exercise the degree of selectivity needed to get into the story at the right point."

Chalmers' objection is that this is another deteriorating situation with an uncertain outcome, not unlike the Ragnarök of Shea's first adventure. And therefore they would be well-advised to give it the go-by.

But so great has Shea's confidence become as a result of his first foray into the unknown that he now perceives danger and impending disaster not as threats but rather as a challenge. This time he doesn't desire to avoid an hour of overwhelming crisis.

Instead, he says eagerly, "'Listen: why shouldn't we jump right into that last part of the *Faerie Queene* and help Gloriana's knights straighten things out? You said you had worked out some new angles. We ought to be better than anyone else in the place.'"

By this, of course, he doesn't mean better men. He means more adept operators of magic.

Shea's proposal is that they should take themselves and their modern magic to this world, oppose its antagonists, and alter its fate. Like Martin Padway in Rome, it is his hope to avert a fall of darkness. And Chalmers—seeing this as the chance to make a mark that has been denied him in this world—agrees.

What incredible confidence is displayed here! To imagine that one could transfer into another world entirely and immediately have a better grasp of its inner workings than its most accomplished natives! But that is the modern science fiction attitude.

And this time, as token of their increased power of command, their syllogismobile takes them just where they want to go, to exactly the right point in Spenser's *Faerie Queene*. Here is real confirmation both of their theory of multiple worlds and of the syllogismobile as a precise and reliable means of travel.

Very shortly, Dr. Chalmers is successfully attempting spells. Too successfully, in fact. When he attempts to change water into wine, instead he gets Scotch whiskey. And when he attempts to conjure up a dragon, he gets a hundred, fortunately all harmless vegetarians.

Shea asks about the problems Chalmers is having, and Chalmers answers:

"A property of the mathematics of magic. Since it's based on the calculus of classes, it is primarily qualitative, not quantitative. Hence the quantitative effects are indeterminate. You can't—at least, with my present skill I can't—locate the decimal point. Here the decimal point was too far rightward, and I got a hundred dragons instead of one. It might have been a thousand. ... Apparently the professionals learn by experience just how much force to put into their incantations. It's an art rather than a science. If I could solve the quantitative problem, I could put magic on a scientific basis."

For a time it appears that Chalmers may be allowing his new love for the study of magic to get the better of him to the point of forgetting the purpose for which they came. When speaking to the bow-and-arrow-toting woods girl, Belphebe, he can assert that magic is neither black nor white in itself, but merely another morally neutral branch of knowledge that then may be applied to ends that current governing authority happens to approve or happens to disapprove.

And indeed, when the opportunity presents itself, Chalmers seems only too happy to be elected as a qualified member by the local Enchanters' Chapter—the bad guys—and to learn whatever he can from them. When he emerges from a series of lectures on magic, including one entitled "A neue use for ye Bloud of unbaptized infants," he is even capable of looking pleased with himself and remarking, "'A trifle harrowing that session, but gratifyingly informative.'"

Shea, who has fallen in love with Belphebe, is horrified that the enchanters plan to capture her and rip her toenails out. But Chalmers is ready to wave aside these impulses to excess as nothing to get upset about, and to say, "'In a few months I shall be in a position to effect an industrial revolution in magic—'"

In this leaning toward amoral, fact-minded pragmatics, Chalmers is a true representative of modern science fiction. At his best, the new Atomic Age man would be a confident, competent manipulator of the inner workings of the universe, but at his worst he would merely be a scientific operator looking for the next button to push.

It's somewhere along this axis that Reed Chalmers' character could be said to fall. For better or for worse, he's an example of the mid-century scientific barbarian, his attention so tightly fixed on what *works* that he is all but completely oblivious to other values.

For that matter, despite his leftover impulses toward the romantic, Harold Shea is basically this type of man, too—as we can tell from his concern with "tricks" and "angles." It is precisely their narrowly focused, result-oriented cast of mind that permits Shea and Chalmers to seek out other worlds with the intention of tinkering with them and making adjustments in the first place.

Fortunately, however, at the climactic moment of "The Mathematics of Magic," when Harold Shea leads a party into the enchanters' castle to rescue Belphebe, Chalmers is able to rouse himself from his single-minded program of scientific investigation long enough to recall which side he is really on. He casts a crucial spell, sending pairs of hands swooping through the air to strangle nearly half of the enchanters. And when the battle is finally won, he can announce cheerfully, "'The really important fact about this evening's work is that I've discovered the secret of quantitative control.'"

Shea succeeds in saving Belphebe from the clutches of the last of the enchanters by using a spell that Chalmers has had the foresight to prep him with—a highly significant "spell against magicians." But the result of the use of this spell—precisely as Chalmers has warned him— is a magicostatic discharge that sends Shea zipping back to Ohio.

However, Shea doesn't really mind this second abrupt return from an otherworld adventure. His decision to use this spell was, in fact, his decision to go home. The enchanters have now been whipped— and with him he has the true ultimate object of his venturings, Belphebe, his dream-girl. That is quite enough to satisfy him.

Chalmers, however, remains behind. He has found a girlfriend of his own, he has his decimal point rightly located at last, and his eyes are all agleam with dreams of the science of magic. What at the outset of "The Roaring Trumpet" had seemed a completely unacceptable risk to him—the possibility of never being able to return to our world—by the end of "The Mathematics of Magic" has become his own deliberate choice.

Chalmers never will go back to Ohio. He prefers to remain permanently abroad in the meta-universe as an itinerant master of paraphysics.

It was no accident that these two pivotal fantasy stories by de Camp and Pratt should have been broadly humorous. There was a very real sense in which they were nothing more than affectionate travesties, games of "let's pretend" played to comic effect with favorite works of old high literature. They weren't really meant to be taken seriously—and said so by being funny.

At the same time, of course, there was also a sense in which de Camp and Pratt were undeniably serious. The Harold Shea stories said very plainly: *Such is the ubiquity and centrality of universal operating principles that if the realms described in the high literature of the past really did exist and it was possible to travel to these worlds of magic, scientifically trained modern men could move right in on them, take over their controls, and operate them with effectiveness.*

Back in the comparably humorous *A Connecticut Yankee in King Arthur's Court*, Mark Twain had imagined a man of the present seizing hold of the historico-legendary past and imposing guns and railroad trains and electricity upon it—for a time, at least. But ultimately not altering it permanently. Twain was aware that the story of King Arthur didn't go that way, and neither did Sixth Century history, and in the end thought it necessary to respect both.

De Camp, however, had just finished rearranging Sixth Century history in *Lest Darkness Fall*—without backing off from what he had done. Now in "The Roaring Trumpet" and "The Mathematics of Magic," he proved himself ready to rewrite myth and legend as well, and to leave those changes in place, too.

These changes wouldn't be anything as crude or as radical as Twain's imposition of Nineteenth Century technology on a world where it just didn't belong. De Camp and his collaborator Pratt wouldn't dream of suggesting such a thing. They allowed that alternate worlds might have their own integrity—their own special and distinct ways of working—which could very well exclude modern paraphernalia such as guns or matches or the 1926 *Boy Scout Handbook*.

They were merely ready to suggest—all in a spirit of good clean fun, mind you—that a modern man with an awareness of the scientific method might enter any of these alternate universes, discover how things work there, and then change the world permanently from within *according to its own system of rules*.

That's all.

As presented by implication in de Camp's *Lest Darkness Fall* and then more and more strongly stated in "The Roaring Trumpet" and "The Mathematics of Magic," however, this little "that's all" offered a considerable challenge to serious modern science fiction. All the more so when taken in conjunction with de Camp's two-part article "The Science of Whithering," which suggested that cyclical history must give way before the power of modern science.

Effectively, these frivolous "fantasy" stories in *Unknown* were model examples of the very sort of work that the writers of serious modern science fiction should properly be attending to in their own sphere. If de Camp was capable of imagining able and confident modern men employing universal operating principles to reverse the fall of Rome or to alter the outcome of events in the world of Spenser's *Faerie Queene*, then shouldn't the writers of *Astounding* be able to imagine men of the new kind successfully using universal operating principles to take command of the future and outer space, the mainstream of real human possibility?

Well, yes, they should. And John Campbell was expecting nothing less of them.

But there were problems to be overcome. By no means the least of these was the sheer entrenched weight of the orthodox Techno Age conception of what the future was going to be like.

This conception had been given definitive expression by Olaf Stapledon in *Last and First Men.* Here are to be found great sweeps of time, movement from planet to planet of the Solar System, and one form of future man succeeding another. But in the two billion years covered in this book, only one story is ever told— over and over, the cyclical rise and fall of civilization. Up the civilizations go, and down they come again, until the final fatal fall of Eighteenth Man on Neptune.

As we know, this view hadn't gone completely without challenge. E. E. Smith and John Campbell, L. Sprague de Camp and Isaac Asimov had all written stories that suggested the grip of cyclical history on mankind's future might not be absolute. But even so, in 1939 and 1940, it was still a herculean task to imagine the shape of a future that wasn't centered around the rise and fall of civilizations. If cyclical history wasn't to be the story of our future, then what was?

Without invading aliens to combat or red suns to wring one's hands over, what was the future for? If people of the future weren't to be utopians or decadents, what were they to do with themselves? And if the pattern of the future wasn't necessarily bound to be up and down, up and down, round and round, but essentially going nowhere, until the machinery of the universe at last came wheezing and grinding to a halt, what was its shape to be?

Seemingly, an alternative would have to be significantly different— but different in what ways? How was the differentness of a different future to be expressed?

It was all an imaginative blank spot.

In 1940, the best counterexample to the orthodox Techno Age conception of the future was the Lensman series of E. E. Smith— still recognized as the leading writer of American science fiction, just as he had been since 1928. In this series, which was the culmination of all the expansive epics of super-science of the late Twenties and Thirties, Smith envisioned not only far planets, but distant times, and a genuinely superior man to look after them and run them right. Rather than bogging down in Earth-centered cyclical history, *Galactic Patrol* and *Gray Lensman* offered an ongoing cosmic war between the forces of good and the forces of evil in which man-beyond-man was destined to play a central role.

Inspiring as the Lensman stories might be, however, they weren't exactly what John Campbell was looking for. They had too many remnant Techno Age elements, and they did not recognize the revised cosmos of universal operating principles.

The power at the center of things in these stories is the Lens, the special badge of distinction of Smith's elite Galactic Patrolmen, which is described as "a lenticular polychrome of writhing, almost fluid radiance." The Lens is a telepathy device and amplifier of psychic powers. It is individually tailored to its owner and glows only as long as he wears it. After his death, it ceases to glow and soon disintegrates.

We are told in *Galactic Patrol* that the Lens is "'not essentially scientific in nature. It is almost entirely philosophical, and was developed for us by the Arisians.'"

These alien beings, the makers and suppliers of the Lens, are an even higher form of transcendence. The Arisians appear to men in any of a variety of forms. Their actual nature may well be Big Brain. But in any event, they are so incredibly advanced that their true reality must be kept hidden even from the members of the Galactic Patrol itself. In *Gray Lensman*, an Arisian says of the Patrolmen:

> "None save a few of the most powerful of their minds has the slightest inkling of the truth. To reveal any portion of it to Civilization as a whole would blight that Civilization irreparably. Though Seekers after Truth in the best sense, they are essentially juvenile and their life-spans are ephemeral indeed. The mere realization that there is in existence such a race as ours would place upon them such an inferiority complex as would make further advancement impossible."

Much as he might genuinely admire Doc Smith—and ready as he still might be to publish his Lensman stories—John Campbell couldn't be altogether comfortable with stuff like this.

Far planets, yes. Distant times, by all means. And above all, a genuinely superior man to run them right. This is what John Campbell could accept from the Lensman stories.

But not wars between good and evil. The Atomic Age wasn't at all sure that it still believed in moral absolutes like good or evil. Most probably it did not. And John Campbell wasn't about to rely on so slender a reed as human virtue to bring mankind to the top in a universe of conflicting interests. Instead, he placed his faith in human know-how.

The Lens wouldn't do, either. Its nature was not scientific. In fact, in its tie to the individual, in its glowings, and in the extinction of its light upon the death of its owner, it was far too soul-like.

Most of all, however, what Campbell could do without was intolerably advanced alien beings tugging upon the strings of humanity and shifting us this way and that, even with the noblest of intentions. Campbell wished to present men standing tall and being subservient to no one, man taking control of the future by themselves and for themselves.

The way to do this, as Campbell saw it, was through the neutral medium of universal operating principles. They were the one sure way for men to answer all problems, to bridge all gaps, to fill in all blank spots, and to proceed from here-and-now to the farthest imaginable there-and-then—all the way to the heat death of the universe and beyond.

It would take three writers working diligently for a period of years in the pages of *Astounding* to establish the new future that John Campbell was aiming to bring into being: the Lensman future, or something like it—but without Lenses, or Arisians, or cosmic moral battle.

Former Navy officer Robert Heinlein would alter the conception of time-to-come, changing it from a place where nature and fate are determined into a place of multiplex possibility.

Canadian writer A. E. van Vogt would involve himself in a systematic inquiry into the meaning of superiority, both in aliens and in man.

Finally, the young prodigy Isaac Asimov would gather the insights of Smith, Campbell, Williamson, de Camp, Heinlein and van Vogt, and integrate them all into a story series in which human beings rule the galaxy thousands of years hence.

These crucial bodies of work—Heinlein's Future History, van Vogt's superman stories, and Asimov's Foundation stories—would mark the parameters of John Campbell's science fiction empire. Mainstream science fiction for a generation to come would be written within the conceptual limits set forth in these stories.

The most immediately influential of the three writers was the oldest among them, Robert Heinlein. He came to story writing in 1939 as a man of nearly 32, with not only a wide variety of worldly experience but also perhaps the broadest reading knowledge of earlier SF of anyone who had ever attempted to write science fiction. In 1941, a mere two years after he began, he would be chosen Guest of Honor of the Third World Science Fiction Convention, held in Denver, Colorado, following Frank R. Paul and Doc Smith in this distinction.

Robert Anson Heinlein was born in the rural county seat of Butler, Missouri on July 7, 1907, the third of what would be seven children. When Heinlein was very young, his father, a cashier and bookkeeper, moved the family north to Kansas City in search of greater opportunity.

Young Robert was a very bright, intense and private boy, much given to having his own way in things when he could get it. Though he wasn't without athletic ability, he had little taste for team sports. He was an avid reader, considered the class grind by his fellows. His real love was for science, and he told everyone that he aimed to be an astronomer when he grew up, though what he *really* wanted was to travel to the Moon.

At the same time, the young Heinlein was troubled by over-whelming doubts that he could share with no one. His family and the immediate society around him were locked in turn-of-the-century Bible Belt Fundamentalism, narrow, bigoted and reactionary. Even as a child, Robert was acutely aware that there were contradictions between what he was reading and observing, and what he was informed was the literal word of God. He would have moments in which he doubted the sanity of ordinary adult life, doubted the reality of society, doubted the existence of everything and everyone but himself.

These feelings would surface from time to time in stories written throughout Heinlein's long career. In reference to the first of them— "They" (*Unknown*, Apr 1941)—Heinlein would note:

> Idea is based on the feeling I had as a kid that everything as I saw it was a deliberate plot to deceive me, that people didn't do the things I saw them do when I wasn't watching them.... The world consists of two parts, the ego—unique and utterly alone—(how is it that I am *inside*—that is the most startling fact we deal with)—and the outside, strange, incomprehensible, and possibly hostile.

If the boy Robert had a love for science, it was because science seemed to offer the possibility of verifiable truth. It was a road that promised to lead beyond his own limitations and the restrictions of his present situation.

In Heinlein's third published story, "Requiem" (*Astounding*, Jan 1940), D.D. Harriman—the now-aged financier who made space travel possible, but who himself has never been permitted to travel to the moon—recalls the scientific dreams of his youth. Clearly speaking for Heinlein, too, he says:

> "I wasn't unusual; there were lots of boys like me—radio hams, they were, and telescope builders, and airplane amateurs. We had science clubs, and basement laboratories, and science-fiction leagues—the kind of boys who thought there was more romance in one issue of the *Electrical Experimenter* than in all the books Dumas ever wrote. We didn't want to be one of Horatio Alger's get-rich heroes, either; we wanted to build spaceships."

At the age of 13, Heinlein managed to resolve the unutterable tension he felt between the dictates of the King James Bible, literally interpreted, and his secret desire to build spaceships and travel to other worlds. It was then that he read Darwin's *Origin of Species* and *The Descent of Man*, and recognized that he was no Christian true believer at all, but rather a scientific freethinker.

Science and skepticism became the young Heinlein's chosen methods for dealing with the conflict between his immediate social surroundings and his sense of truth. He resolved that he was going to doubt everything that could be doubted, test everything that could be tested, look at anything and everything, and make up his mind for himself.

In high school, he became captain of the Negative Debate Team. He used Will Durant as a key to philosophy; Heinlein says, "He first introduced me to a wide range of philosophers; and I read 'em all; I gobbled 'em all." Heinlein sought out and avidly consumed the sassiest mockers and doubters the skeptical Twenties could offer him: before anyone, his fellow Missourian Mark Twain; the author of *The Devil's Dictionary*, Ambrose Bierce; the provocative playwright George Bernard Shaw; and the reigning iconoclast of the day, H.L. Mencken. He read forbidden literature of all kinds in search of whatever it might be that he wasn't supposed to know.

Most of all, however, Heinlein took his clues from SF. He relished every scrap of transcendent literature he could find. Until he began to write it himself, reading SF was his favorite spare-time activity.

He started at it young and persisted despite parental disapproval. A whole generation of science fiction writers, from Jack Williamson to Isaac Asimov, would discover SF in the pages of *Amazing Stories*. Alone among them, Heinlein was reading it much earlier and soaking up a somewhat different set of influences.

He was a reader of Hugo Gernsback's popular science magazines, *Electrical Experimenter*, and then *Science and Invention*. He read tattered old copies of the Frank Reade, Jr. dime novels, and he read the new Tom Swift boys' books as they were issued. He read *All-Story* and he read *Argosy*. And when *Weird Tales* came along in the early Twenties, he read that, too.

In those days before the advent of *Amazing*, a would-be reader of SF was still obliged to define and invent the literature for himself. But young Robert's reach was especially broad. He found his way to Jules Verne and H.G. Wells, but also to Lewis Carroll and L. Frank Baum. He read Jack London and Edgar Rice Burroughs, but also James Branch Cabell and H.P. Lovecraft.

And much as he might love science, in SF as Robert Heinlein was constructing it for himself the science-based story would be only one possible form among many. In years to come, he would even make the explicit suggestion that "it would be more nearly correctly descriptive to call the whole field 'speculative fiction' and to limit the name 'science fiction' to a sub-class...."

Of all the writers of speculative fiction that he read, it was H.G. Wells who influenced him the most. Wells dealt in radically changed futures and in improved alternate societies, and Robert, the boy who entertained doubts about the reasonableness and the reality of the social world around him, could like that. Moreover, Wells offered the highly attractive ideal of a dedicated scientific elite assuming control of society—from the Samurai of *A Modern Utopia* (1905) to the self-selected membership of *The Open Conspiracy* (1928)— and Robert could mentally enlist himself in their ranks.

In high school, Heinlein was a superior student, a school politician, and Major of the junior ROTC unit. But his classmates did have some inklings of his true nature. By his name in the 1924 Central High School Yearbook, they wrote, *"He thinks in terms of the fifth dimension, never stopping at the fourth."*

Robert spent his last year in high school writing letters and pulling political strings in a campaign to win himself an appointment to one of the military academies (he wasn't particular which) from Missouri Senator James Reed, a creature of the notorious Boss Pendergast machine. He was initially turned down, but after an interim year spent cooling his heels at the recently established Kansas City Junior College, his persistence was finally rewarded with an appointment to Annapolis.

At the Naval Academy, Heinlein found himself in heaven, one of a chosen elite of intelligent, dedicated and able young men, and he thrived there. The Academy took a bright bumpkin from Missouri and made a gentleman of him. He stood twentieth in the class of 1929, and he might have graduated as high as fifth if he hadn't been caught off-limits too many times.

Serving in the Navy permitted Heinlein to live for a period in an apartment in Greenwich Village, and it also gave him an opportunity to see the world. He served in a battleship, and in destroyers, and as a gunnery officer aboard the early aircraft carrier USS *Lexington.*

But by no means had he lost his outsider's eye. As early as 1930, he began to keep the first of an expanding number of files of newspaper and magazine clippings on trends in society and the eccentricities of American social behavior. And he continued to read every odd thing he could find—including, of course, the new science fiction magazines, the post-Gernsback *Amazing*, and *Wonder Stories*, and *Astounding Stories of Super-Science.*

In 1934, however, his paradise came to an end. He pressed duty too hard, and came down with tuberculosis, then still a disease that had an uncertain prognosis. And almost overnight, he found himself out of the Navy, retired on full disability pension at the age of 27.

Heinlein made a quick recovery, and decided to try graduate study at UCLA in mathematics and physics. But again he pushed himself too hard, and he suffered a severe relapse. This time he had to drop out of school and go off to Colorado to get well.

This was a very difficult and frustrating period for Robert Heinlein. He was young and tall and handsome. He was extremely bright and able, and seemingly there wasn't anything he couldn't master if he put his mind to it. He could build a radio. He could set stone. He could plot a ballistic. He could command troops. He could design and erect a house, performing all the various construction work himself, if need be. He could get along with working stiffs and roughnecks, but at a formal dinner party he knew which was the proper fork to use. He could talk philosophy, economics, psychology, or semantics. He knew a thousand different things.

But now, through a nasty caprice of fate and the failure of his body, his hard-won knowledge, his wide variety of skills and his sense of dedication were all rendered irrelevant. If he wasn't going to be able to *be* a Wellsian Samurai, what was he to do with himself? What was second best?

He tried his hand at one thing and another, including mining silver and selling real estate. But none of it was fully satisfying to him. Finally, in early 1939, he had a fling at politics. He ran in a Democratic primary in California in an effort to unseat an incumbent state representative, but he finished in second place.

The campaign left Heinlein not only completely broke, but with a mortgage payment coming due. It was then he recalled an ad he had seen in *Thrilling Wonder Stories* for an amateur story contest with a prize of $50. At that particular moment, this looked like a very attractive and useful sum of money.

The more Heinlein thought about it, the more it seemed to him that if he were seriously to attempt to write science fiction, he could do it. He had read SF practically forever. And once upon a time, for his own amusement while he was recovering from TB, he had even worked up a book-length quasi-historical account of the coming to power of an American religious dictator, the eventual overthrow of his line, and the establishment of a new rational society. Heinlein saw no reason why he couldn't produce more commercial work if he were to try.

So he sat right down to it, and in four days he turned out a story entitled "Life-Line." This was about Hugo Pinero, a man who has invented a machine that can accurately foretell the length of any person's life, and the opposition he and his machine arouse among the entrenched interests of society. It opens not with the invention of the machine, but with Pinero attempting to justify his already-invented machine to a hostile and skeptical Academy of Science. And it ends with the inventor dead—rubbed out—at the very moment he himself has predicted.

In many ways, including its determinism, this was an old-fashioned story. But in presentation, it was very new. "Life-Line" was brisk, snappy, self-confident, and immensely knowledgeable about the workings of society—more like a Paul Gallico writing in the slick magazine *Collier's* than anything ordinarily to be found in the science fiction pulp magazines of the late Thirties.

When Heinlein looked over what he had written, it struck him that it was much too good for *Thrilling Wonder Stories.* So acting boldly, he sent it off to *Collier's* instead. But *Collier's* wouldn't take it. For one thing, they already had Paul Gallico. For another, they weren't yet ready for science fiction in the spring of 1939.

Considering what to do next, Heinlein remembered that John Campbell, the new editor of *Astounding,* had declared the existence of a permanent open contest at the magazine, all comers welcome. Since *Astounding* paid a penny a word, this meant that a 7000-word story like his might earn $70 there.

So Heinlein sent his story off to *Astounding*—and Campbell not only accepted it, but paid for it immediately. Having found something that worked this well, Heinlein tried it again. He wrote a second science fiction story—"Misfit," the tale of Andrew Jackson Libby, the young mathematical genius who is discovered among a space station construction gang. And Campbell bought that one, too.

But it wouldn't continue to be quite this easy. Heinlein began his career with a simple, clean-cut, modern style, a background in science fiction, a wide range of knowledge, experience and developed opinion, and a fascination with human social behavior—just the qualities that John Campbell was looking for in 1938 and 1939. But Heinlein had not yet arrived at a sense of universal operating principles, and he would have to pick that up. And he would also have to learn which subjects and attitudes Campbell would accept and which he would not.

As an example, Heinlein was a sophisticated adult, which for the most part readers of pulp science fiction magazines in 1939 were not. Heinlein's third story, "'Let There Be Light,'" concerned the invention of cheap and efficient solar receptors by a scientific team—Archie Douglas, a physicist, and Mary Lou Martin, a "bio-chemist and ecologist"—and the threat they encounter from the powerbrokers until they find a way out by deciding to donate their discovery to the public. This was a perfectly satisfactory neo-Gernsbackian story, but it was also full of mild sexual banter. Campbell wouldn't have that—and sure enough, when it was published under the pseudonym Lyle Monroe in the May 1940 issue of Fred Pohl's *Super Science Stories*, there were readers who did protest what they perceived as smut.

However, the most significant point of contention between Campbell and Heinlein was this:

Heinlein's sense of SF had been formed back in the Teens and Twenties, and included speculative notions of every kind. The first three stories that Heinlein wrote were all relatively tame and plausible neo-Gernsbackian projections, their one real point of novelty being the degree of their concern for social context. After that, however, Heinlein was ready to try some queerer speculations.

The next story he wrote was called "Elsewhen." Here a professor of "speculative metaphysics" and his students transfer themselves by means of "hypnosis and suggestion" into a variety of alternate worlds that correspond to their respective natures. However, except for flittings-about from one world to another, nothing much really happens. By comparison with Heinlein's earlier efforts, this story was vague and flabby.

Another of his 1939 attempts—and his own immediate favorite—was a short novel called "Lost Legacy." In this one, a young doctor and a male-female team of parapsychologists join forces with mystical masters who reside on California's Mt. Shasta—including the arch-doubter Ambrose Bierce, usually thought to have vanished in Mexico in 1914 at the age of 72. Together, scientists and mystics (and the Boy Scouts, too!) wage psychic war against the vilest and most regressive elements of society, the "antagonists of human liberty, of human dignity—the racketeers, the crooked political figures, the shysters, the dealers in phony religions, the sweat-shoppers, the petty authoritarians, all of the key figures among the traffickers in human misery and human oppression, themselves somewhat adept in the arts of the mind, and acutely aware of the dangers of free knowledge—all of this unholy breed...."

Quite clearly, from the beginning Heinlein wanted to declare his long-held belief that there is a difference between real truth and what society takes to be true. He wanted to write stories in which the defects and corruptions of society are overcome and freedom is won. He wanted to give utterance to all the heresies and strange thoughts he'd kept locked inside him ever since he was a boy. And he was ready to employ any means that the broad-based SF he'd put together for himself could offer to express what he wanted to express.

But John Campbell was both more limited than this and more of a purist. He had no use for flabby occult nonsense in *Astounding*— or in *Unknown*, either. He was trying diligently to eliminate such stuff from his magazines. So he was prompt to bounce both of these stories, and several more squidgy or trivial attempts by Heinlein.

In fact, after the easy immediate success of "Life-Line" and "Misfit," Campbell rejected four consecutive Heinlein stories. Young Fred Pohl would imagine this to be a major lapse on the editor's part, snap up several of these stories for his own magazines, and count himself lucky to have them. But Campbell was quite sure that he knew what he was doing. He was in the process of creating modern science fiction, and he was determined that he would have plausible argument and universal operating principles from Heinlein, and nothing less.

In background and training and dedication, and even in their prejudices, these two men—Campbell and Heinlein—had more than a little in common. They were two highly dominant, self-willed Atomic Age engineers, so perhaps it was inevitable that they should wrestle to handle and adjust each other and to push each other's buttons. We've already seen how ready Campbell was to align and direct writers to get just what he wanted from them. But Heinlein in his own right was a well-practiced people manipulator, too. Consequently, even at their moment of greatest mutual regard, with Heinlein at one end of the continent and Campbell at the other, their relationship would never be a completely easy one.

In this early moment, however, the leverage was all with Campbell. Heinlein not only had a mortgage, but the notion of paying it off by writing science fiction stories, and Campbell held the purse strings of the best and most reliable science fiction market.

So it was Heinlein who gave way. He altered what he was writing, adapting it to the shape of John Campbell's rejections and suggestions. Where he was soft, he hardened up. Where he was fuzzy, he tightened his focus. His control of plausibility became more consistent and far more subtle and clever. And he picked right up on the idea of universal operating principles.

It had taken Isaac Asimov two and a half years of regular visits to Campbell before the penny finally dropped and he caught on to the trick of writing for the editor. By comparison, Robert Heinlein was so immediately adept, so uniquely well-prepared to write science fiction, and so generally attuned to the same wavelength as Campbell that he was able to sell the editor four (and later a fifth) of his first ten stories. By the end of 1939, only nine months after Heinlein first sat down to write, he was so well-zeroed-in on his chosen target that he could sell Campbell every story he wrote.

The pivotal sale for Heinlein was his third, which didn't come until his seventh story, four months after "Misfit." This was the short novel "If This Goes On—."

It was with this story—which was a rewriting into pulp fiction form of a portion of his old account of a religious dictatorship to come—that Heinlein made the happy discovery that it might be possible both to do the things that Campbell wanted done and also to scratch his own itches. If he wrote a story of universal operating principles at work in the future, it could also be a story of secret heresy and rebellion. And if he included enough plausible detail to satisfy John Campbell, he could also put in a substantial dollop of occultism for himself.

The result of this combination of aims was that "If This Goes On—" takes place in a curiously mixed future unlike any previously presented in SF. Things in this world are very different from now, but also oddly familiar.

The story opens with a young officer, the highly idealistic John Lyle, standing guard outside the apartments of the religious dictator of a latter-day United States. This citizen of the future (whose last name is the same as Heinlein's mother's maiden name) begins by telling us something about himself. And within the context of science fiction as it existed then, what he has to say and how he says it came across as wonderful and wild and weird.

Listen:

I was young then—a legate newly graduated from West Point, and a guardsman in the Angels of the Lord, the personal guard of the Prophet Incarnate.

At my birth my mother had consecrated me to the Church, and I was brought up to revere and venerate my spiritual elders. At eighteen my Uncle Absolom, a senior deacon, had used one of the appointments alloted to each member of the Council of Elders to send me to the military academy.

I was happy at West Point. The ideals of the service had seemed perfect and right. I hadn't minded the routine. On the contrary, I had rather enjoyed it—up at five, two hours of prayer and meditation, then classes and lectures in the manifold subjects of a military education, strategy and tactics, theology, mob psychology, basic miracles. In the afternoons we practiced with vortex guns and blasters, drilled with tanks, and hardened our bodies with exercises—the friendly monastic life of the barracks. I longed for it.

But now, in spite of prayer and fasting, I sometimes envied my brother, Lemuel, who enjoyed the easier discipline of the Rocket Patrol. He did not bother with the ritualistic spear and buckler, which I must perforce wear constantly. I patted my vortex pistol. *That* was my defense should any of the ungodly seek to approach the revered person of the Prophet.

Wow! In these few paragraphs, we can see Heinlein's major early SF influences gathered and integrated—the scientific advances beloved by Hugo Gernsback, the alternate societies of H. G. Wells, and the juicy anachronisms and narrative immediacy of Edgar Rice Burroughs. Heinlein combines all of these here to express—as science fiction—something of what it had felt like to grow up under the rule of Fundamentalist Christianity and then break free.

And what a strange mixed-up world it is that he shows us! Imagine a United States of the future so radically altered as to be ruled by a Prophet Incarnate! And yet this world is still in many ways the same as the one we know. West Point continues to be the national military academy. Cincinnati and Kansas City remain the cities they were. Even *The New York Times* continues to be published and read.

There is paradox and humor in what Heinlein writes—like the presentation of theology, mob psychology and "basic miracles" as taken-for-granted elements of a proper military education, every bit as appropriate as strategy or tactics. And there are head-bending juxtapositions, like those archaic words "spear and buckler" that appear sandwiched between the futuristic "Rocket Patrol" and "vortex pistol," but which are rendered plausible for us by the casual additional word "ritualistic."

Somehow, out of the apparently artless narrative voice, the right wrong details, and even the cockeyed relationship of one word or phrase to the next, a gestalt emerges. We find ourselves not only in a world other than our own, but identifying with a living, breathing individual who is operating within its context, and thinking and acting according to its terms.

It is very apparent that this world is highly advanced in certain ways, but backward in others. And that was also something new.

Through the Techno Age, society had been taken to be an indivisible whole in SF. Social progress and technological progress were seen as inseparable. If society progressed, it all progressed, and if it declined, it went downhill all at once and all over. It fell.

At the outset of his SF writing career, Robert Heinlein had still had it in his head that technological progress and social progress must be related. The space travel of "Misfit," his second story, had been imagined as occurring only at a considerable distance in the future, after the overthrow of the Prophet and the establishment of a better society.

By the time Heinlein wrote "If This Goes On—," however, he had begun to see things somewhat differently. To his new Atomic Age eye, society and the universe now appeared as ever-changing composites made up of many separate elements operating relatively independently and capable of being connected to each other in a variety of different ways. As one character in "Elsewhen" thinks: "There seemed to be no end to the permutations and combinations: either of matter or of mind."

This view is the key to Heinlein's presentation of the future society of "If This Goes On—." As he conceived it, if the elements of our contemporary society were to be extended into the future, some might regress, some might advance, while some might stay the same. And the new combination that resulted from these permutations might be the kind of world presented here, with spears and West Point and the Rocket Patrol, all at once.

The essence of Heinlein's new technique of the selective extension of factors is to be seen in the very title of his story. This method, which would come to be called *extrapolation*, from a term used in mathematics, would very soon become standard in science fiction.

Even from the first few paragraphs of Heinlein's short novel, it is possible for us to discern that the rule of the Prophet Incarnate over future America is maintained through manipulation of the populace, oppression, and the deliberate inculcation of false belief. And from the narrator's choice of words, we can also see that John Lyle— sympathetic though we may find him—is, or used to be, one of the deluded himself, so much the product of the society in which he has been raised that he doesn't quite realize the true nature of the forces to which he has been given over at birth.

This new use of language within SF for subtle multiple effect was no accident. Heinlein was an early student of Alfred Korzybski's General Semantics, a new linguistic discipline concerned with the true nature, meaning and use of symbols and their change through time. Within "If This Goes On—" itself, we are told that the styling of language for effective propaganda purposes has become a mathematical science.

This is explained by Lyle's friend and fellow officer, the older, more worldly wise Zebadiah Jones:

"The emotional connotation of any word is a complex variable function depending on context, age and sex and occupation of the listener, the locale, and a dozen other things. An index is a particular solution of the variable that tells you whether or not a particular word used in a particular fashion to a particular type of listener will affect that listener favorably, unfavorably, or simply leave him cold. Statistical research in this stuff provides us with the means to choose language best suited to play on the emotions."

And he adds: "'There is magic in words, if you know how to use it.'"

It is love for one of the Prophet's handmaidens that causes the scales to fall from John Lyle's eyes. At last he begins to perceive something of the true cynical, repressive and exploitative nature of the theocracy. And very soon thereafter, both he and Zeb become members of the Cabal, the revolutionary underground that is seeking to overthrow the reign of the Prophet.

The true identity of the Cabal, this small elite of the undeluded, is most interesting. Though never directly named, through allusions and signs and initiatory phrases it is made clear that these are the Freemasons, the same mystical secret society that played a key role in the American and French Revolutions of the Eighteenth Century.

Ultimately, however, it isn't mystical enlightenment that the revolutionaries count upon to win America over to their cause, but universal operating principles effectively applied. In the good cause of throwing out the theocracy and then establishing a new regime of tolerance and open-mindedness, the rebels are every bit as ready to cozen and manipulate the people at large as the Prophet and his legions whom they oppose so fervently.

The signal to begin the crucial uprising is the faking of a key annual broadcast by the Prophet, which is itself a sham. Each spring, Nehemiah Scudder, the First Prophet, is witnessed to arise out of the form of his current incarnation and confirm the rule of the incumbent. This time, however, a counterfeit broadcast is made, so that Scudder appears as usual, but only to denounce the current Prophet as Satan and bid the populace to destroy him. Through this deception, the simple belief of the people is turned against the Prophet.

What is more, when they gain control, it is the revolutionaries' intention to brainwash people into accepting a new independence of thought:

The plan concocted by Colonel Novak and Zebediah provided for readjusting the people to freedom of thought and freedom of action. They planned nothing less than mass reorientation under hypnosis. The technique was simple, as simple as works of genius usually are. They had prepared a film which was a mixture of history, theological criticism, simple course in general science, exposition of the philosophy of the scientific viewpoint and frame of mind, and so forth. Taken consciously, it was too much to soak up in one dose, but they planned to use it on subjects in a state of light hypnosis.

... More than a hundred million persons had to be examined to see if they could stand up under quick re-orientation, then re-examined after treatment to see if they had been sufficiently readjusted. Until a man passed the second examination we could not afford to enfranchise him as a free citizen of a democratic state. We had to teach them to think for themselves, reject dogma, be suspicious of authority, tolerate difference of opinion, and make their own decisions—types of mental processes almost unknown in the United States for many generations.

This is certainly Atomic Age pushbutton thinking at its least attractive. And when Heinlein came to revise and expand this story for book publication in the Korean War year of 1953, he would reject this psychological reconditioning of America as a completely unacceptable solution. When it is proposed—not by Zeb Jones or Colonel Novak—Heinlein would have an elderly man described as looking like "an angry Mark Twain" rise and declare:

"Free men aren't 'conditioned!' Free men are free because they are ornery and cussed and prefer to arrive at their own prejudices in their own way—not have them spoonfed by a self-appointed mind tinkerer! We haven't fought, our brethren haven't bled and died, just to change bosses, no matter how sweet their motives."

And almost immediately the old man drops dead, just to reinforce the point.

In 1939 and 1940, however, this mental readjustment of the population to the scientific frame of mind could still seem a work of genius, a canny application of leading-edge know-how in a noble cause.

We should clearly understand that beyond its areas of conspicuous brilliance and innovation, "If This Goes On—" was still in many ways an awkward and sketchy early effort. But very shortly, in other, increasingly confident stories, Heinlein would begin to apply some of the lessons of the breakthrough he had made.

The story that Heinlein produced immediately was "Requiem," a wish-fulfillment written in the light of his new insight that social progress and technological progress might operate independent of each other.

Heinlein's oldest and fondest dream had been to travel to the Moon. But space travel had always seemed a remote possibility, as in his story "Misfit." It was something that was going to have to wait until a better day when society had advanced enough to value and support it and permit it to happen.

But if technological accomplishment wasn't dependent on social progress, then it might be possible for men to actually reach the Moon within Heinlein's own lifetime. One determined man, working in spite of the non-comprehension of society and the resistance of those closest to him, might be enough to make it all possible. And if that man was so old and frail by the time he made space travel happen that society still wouldn't permit him to have his most cherished dream, why maybe he might step outside the rules of society—the "Space Precautionary Act"—and find a way to go to the Moon anyway.

"Requiem" would take place in a late Twentieth Century America that is still relatively familiar. It would begin with old D.D. Harriman looking over a former Moon rocket at a county fair in Bates County, Missouri—that is, in Butler, the very town that Heinlein was born in. And it would end with Harriman dying a blissful death on the Moon:

"At long last there was peace in his heart. His hurts had ceased to pain him. He *was* where he had longed to be—he had followed his need. . . . He was on the Moon!"

In Heinlein's next futuristic story, "The Roads Must Roll" (*Astounding*, June 1940), he would go a step beyond the mere fulfillment of a long-cherished dream. He would employ his new techniques of extrapolation and the recombination of factors to envision a whole new social pattern—but this time projected just thirty years into the future.

One of these factors, shrewdly extrapolated by Heinlein, was the inevitable eventual shortage of petroleum, and the effect that this might have on the existence of the private automobile.

Another factor was the notion of moving roadways. This idea had been used as striking incidental detail by H.G. Wells in two related dystopian stories, the short novel "A Story of the Days to Come" (1897) and the novel *When the Sleeper Wakes* (1899). And when the first of these stories was reprinted in *Amazing* in April 1928, Frank R. Paul had made one of these multiple-beltway systems the subject of a memorable bedsheet-sized full-page illustration. Heinlein would imagine rolling roads like these as the successor to the obsolescent automobile.

The third vital factor in the conception of this new future situation was the "Douglas-Martin Solar Reception Screens" that we saw in the process of being invented in "'Let There Be Light,'" Heinlein's risqué third story. They would serve as the power source for the rolling roads.

Putting these factors together, Heinlein envisioned a radically altered American society in the year 1970, living strung out along the length of the rolling roads. This wasn't exactly societal progress.

But it was a whole new age, with a very different orientation. It has its own slang, its own new jobs, customs and expectations, and its own new problems.

But only thirty years away!

During the Techno Age, society had been seen as innately unified, fixed and stable. It had seemed that only the impact of powerful external forces could produce social change. Hence, on the one hand, the Techno Age preoccupation with invasions and catastrophes, and on the other, its fears of social stagnation and decadence.

Heinlein's new stories suggested something very different: that social change is a constant, the natural result of the interaction of the various elements of society and the universe. Change—Heinlein was suggesting—does occur, must occur, and most certainly will occur, and maybe a whole lot sooner than you might think. It doesn't have to be imposed from outside by invading aliens, or even by a Martin Padway. Change is an inevitability.

Heinlein would say this explicitly one year later in "The Discovery of the Future," his guest-of-honor speech at the Third World Science Fiction Convention, held in Denver in July 1941. Heinlein would declare:

> There won't always be an England—nor a Germany, nor a United States, nor a Baptist Church, nor monogamy, nor the Democratic Party, nor the modesty tabu, nor the superiority of the white race, nor aeroplanes—they will go—nor automobiles—they'll be gone, we'll see them go. Any custom, technique, institution, belief, or social structure that we see around us today will change, will pass, and most of them we will *see* change and pass.

With his next story after "The Roads Must Roll," Heinlein would begin to play games with his new-found ability to envision future change and difference. "Coventry" (*Astounding*, July 1940) takes place some years after the revolution of "If This Goes On—." A new libertarian society has been established that aims to ensure the maximum possible freedom of action for every person: "Citizens were forbidden by the Covenant to damage another. Any act not leading to damage, physical or economic, to some particular person, they declared to be lawful."

Social misfits who refuse to abide by this Covenant and who will not accept psychological readjustment—like Heinlein's protagonist, who has gone so far as to punch someone in the nose—are sent to a restricted area known as Coventry that is surrounded by an impenetrable barrier. And inside Coventry, there are no less than three further societies: one of these is made up of still-faithful followers of the Prophet; one is a fascistic dictatorship; and one is a nominally democratic petty bossdom not unlike Heinlein's boyhood Kansas City.

In this story, in the most direct way possible, Heinlein showed that the future need not be monolithic at all, but might assume a variety of different guises.

There would be further demonstrations of this in Heinlein's next story, "Blowups Happen" (*Astounding*, Sept 1940). This was an exactingly researched and imagined account of dedicated engineers striving to cope with conditions of intolerable psychological stress in an atomic power plant. And just like "The Roads Must Roll," it would be indicated to be taking place about thirty years in the future.

But is this an alternative future in which solar power was never invented? Not at all. By casual cross-references in "Blowups Happen," Heinlein would tie this story to "The Roads Must Roll" and to "'Let There Be Light'" and to "Requiem," and make the point that even the near future might have a multiplicity of newness to display to us.

To keep straight this multiplex future of sun-power screens, rolling roads and space rockets that he was evolving, Heinlein even worked up a chart of the next fifty years and hung it on his wall. He would later say, "This was an idea I had gotten from Mr. Sinclair Lewis, who is alleged to maintain charts, files, notes and even very detailed maps of his fictional state of Winnemac and its leading city, Zenith."

Moreover, as a striking confirmation that factors indeed may change and new relationships result, immediately after Heinlein wrote "Blowups Happen," the balance of power between him and John Campbell began to alter radically.

By that time, early in 1940, Campbell had come to recognize what a uniquely capable and innovative writer he had found in Heinlein. He was now eager to get his hands on any new piece of work that Heinlein turned out.

However, it was at precisely this moment that Heinlein succeeded in paying off the mortgage that had caused him to take up writing in the first place, and threw a mortgage-burning party to celebrate. He no longer felt obligated to write SF. He was now master of his own options.

If Heinlein did choose to continue to write for a little longer, perhaps to the end of the year, well, that was only because he saw some convenience in it. He could certainly use a newer car, and a few other things. He had it in mind to take a trip to New York, among other reasons because he wanted to finally meet John Campbell face to face. And he did have a bunch of stories already worked out and needing to be written.

But there was this vital difference. Up until now, Heinlein had felt it necessary to please Campbell, to play along with the editor and accede to all his requests and suggestions. But no longer. Now, if he were to continue to write SF, it would be on his own terms or not at all.

The immediate test of this would be "Magic, Inc," Heinlein's first post-mortgage story. Just as he had done before with very little success, Heinlein took large chunks of personally meaningful material and put them into another strange speculative story. In this fantasy short novel, he would once more express his horrified fascination with American business and political corruption, his strong conviction that the ordinary reality of present social consensus is not the only possible reality, and his accumulated knowledge of a forbidden area of study—in this case, magic and witchcraft.

However, this time, with something between a glint and a twinkle in his eye, Heinlein would combine these factors with the very elements that Campbell had been asking for in his science fiction stories for *Astounding*: plausible argument, universal operating principles, and more fiction about the future. There would be no chance that this story would come across as vague or flabby. Every trick of plausible presentation that Heinlein had worked up for his science fiction stories, he would employ in this not-altogether-serious fantasy.

For example, in all his recent science fiction stories, Heinlein had snatched the reader into the ongoingness of a different future reality by starting with some urgent, intriguing line of dialog. "'Who makes the roads roll?'" a leader of dissatisfied technicians demands. Or "'Put down that wrench!'" a psychiatrist says to an atomic engineer.

In very much the same way, but even more provocatively, "Magic, Inc." would begin with the impertinent question: "'Whose spells are you using, buddy?'"

It is a cheap thug who asks. And coolly, the narrator, a building-materials dealer named Archie Fraser, answers back: "'Various of the local licensed practitioners of thaumaturgy.'"

This may not be very helpful to the thug, who is here to put pressure on Fraser to change the source of supply of one of the more important elements in his business, but it certainly tells us a great deal about the world we are entering.

In fact, once again we are in an altered society thirty years in the future—just like "The Roads Must Roll" and "Blowups Happen." But in this logical if not necessarily possible 1970, it is magic that is the key fact of change.

It is assumed that around 1950, magic was placed on a regular and socially accepted basis with mastery of "the arcane laws." And after a further twenty years, it has become a major facet of daily American life, regulated by law and contract and custom. As Archie Fraser's good friend, cloak-and-suiter Joe Jedson says, speaking at a small city Chamber of Commerce luncheon:

> "We all use it. I use it for textiles. Hank Manning here uses nothing else for cleaning and pressing, and probably uses it for some of his dye jobs, too. Wally Haight's Maple Shop uses it to assemble and finish fine furniture. Stan Robertson will tell you that Le Bon Marché's slick window displays are thrown together with spells, as well as two thirds of the merchandise of his store, especially in the kids' toy department."

Archie Fraser helps us to accept this magical future society. He's a hardheaded Scot, a practical weigh-and-measure man, so conventional in his cast of mind that when he explains to us that racketeers are moving in to gain an illegal monopoly in magic so that they can raise prices, it's only natural for him to compare it with the price-rigging that was once attempted locally in the Portland cement trade. At the same time, however, he is a native of this odd future, perfectly ready to take its every strangeness in stride.

Indeed, such is the spin that Heinlein puts on things that ultimately we can no longer be quite sure what is really strange and what isn't. When Archie and his more magically gifted friends figure out that it is a demon who is behind the racketeering in magic and track him down in "the Half-World," all we can do is laugh as a lesser demon rushes up to lend them a crucial hand—and then reveals himself to be an FBI agent working out of the antimonopoly division on undercover assignment. It seems only fitting.

"Magic, Inc." was a deadpan spoof, all in good fun, but it was also a bold experiment. Heinlein had become increasingly slick at slipping necessary information into his science fiction stories in such a way that it seemed only natural. In this story, however, he outdid himself. Nothing at all was given directly. All the background information that Heinlein had to impart, he wove into the fabric of his story. It was demonstrated, or it was given in the attitudes of his characters, or it was thrown away in dialog, or it was dropped in an incidental narrative comment serving some other apparent purpose.

And the result of this technique was that the reader who wanted to know where he was and what was going on here was obliged to become an active and trusting participant in "Magic, Inc." Without benefit of any obvious direct exposition, he had to gather scattered hints and references and implications and fit the overall pattern together for himself.

In years to come, showing-without-telling and asking the reader to fill in the blank spots of a pattern would become standard methods for presenting strange future societies. And Robert Heinlein would always be the supreme master of this kind of indirect presentation. But it was in "Magic, Inc." that he first brought the trick off.

When John Campbell was allowed to see this whacky, innovative story, he loved it, of course. An out-and-out fantasy that was written with the techniques of leading-edge modern science fiction was just the thing for him. He hurried "Magic, Inc." into the September 1940 *Unknown*, pausing only to change the title to "The Devil Makes the Law" to avoid any clash with Pratt's and de Camp's second Harold Shea story, "The Mathematics of Magic," published in the August issue.

On the check for this story, Heinlein traveled east. And when he got to New York, he tested Campbell again, a little harder this time. He handed the editor a short story he had written on the way, the frankly solipsistic "They," in which the familiar modern world is revealed to be no more than an elaborate stage setting designed to keep the protagonist distracted from remembering his true identity and power. Campbell bought that one, too—although he would be a good bit slower about putting it in print, sticking it at last without special notice into the April 1941 *Unknown*.

In this first meeting between the great editor and his most able new writer, there was obvious respect, geniality, and good-fellowship. Beneath the surface, however, this encounter between Heinlein and Campbell was an all-out war, a struggle between two titans for dominance and control. And it was Heinlein who emerged the winner, as he had fully intended to do when he set off for the east.

Oh, Campbell did come away with a certain number of concessions: Heinlein agreed to write more of his new line of futuristic science fiction for *Astounding*, something he hadn't done for almost six months. What is more, to provide a home for his stranger notions, Heinlein would create a Don A. Stuart-type alter ego, Anson MacDonald—a pseudonym cobbled together out of Heinlein's middle name and his wife's maiden name. And Heinlein was even willing to initiate this new name by turning an old plot of Campbell's into a quick serial novel to fill a hole in the magazine.

In actuality, however, it was Heinlein who established all of his points: He wouldn't write to command or to deadline. He would write what he wanted, when he wanted, and the way he wanted. For exactly as long as he wanted.

Immediately, yes, he would agree to write Campbell's serial for him; he could use the money just now for a new car. But in the long term, it was necessary for Campbell to understand that if the time should come when the editor rejected another of his stories, that was the end of it. Heinlein wouldn't send him anything further. And that—sweetly, charmingly phrased, of course—was The Word.

Campbell being Campbell, he would never completely give up trying to prompt and adjust and direct Heinlein, but the edge was no longer his. His need for Heinlein was greater than Heinlein's need for him—and Heinlein had let him know it.

It was in this new phase in their relationship that Campbell would tell his young fellow editor, Fred Pohl:

> The trouble with Bob Heinlein is that he doesn't need to write. When I want a story from him, the first thing I have to do is think up something he would like to have, like a swimming pool. The second thing is to sell him on the idea of having it. The third thing is to convince him he should write a story to get the money to pay for it, instead of building it himself.

The real situation, of course, was rather more complex than that. Heinlein may have done a good job of convincing Campbell that he was a gentleman of independent means and thought who really didn't have to write at all, but only did it because he happened to find it amusing and convenient to play around with SF for a time. But it wasn't strictly true.

For that matter, Heinlein may have convinced himself that he had backed into science fiction writing completely by accident, and had only continued it for sound pragmatic reasons. He was willing to tell his friends that he "was just a chap who needed money and happened to discover that pulp writing offered an easy way to grab some without stealing and without honest work." But that wasn't strictly true, either.

In fact, Heinlein did need to write.

In one year, from a standing start, Heinlein had turned out a truly prodigious amount of work—three short novels, four novelets, and seven short stories. And he had thought of at least a dozen stories more that he might write. He was just bubbling over with SF ideas.

The stories Heinlein had written contained all sorts of formal knowledge and conscious cerebration, but they were also the most intensely personal body of work any SF writer had ever produced. As we've seen, they were full of long-cherished Heinlein dreams, and private references, and a great deal of autobiography, both disguised and overt.

These were highly immediate stories. Previous science fiction stories of the future had either been brief visits or else were one-dimensional accounts. Heinlein, however, had put incredible effort into working out techniques that would allow the imagined future to feel plausible and lived-in.

Finally, these were urgent stories. Again and again, they concerned dedicated men—overseers of society—who are plagued by nightmares and unspoken doubts and are on the very verge of cracking up under the awesome weight of their responsibilities. In "Blowups Happen," for instance, he had written of his atomic engineers:

> They were selected not alone for their intelligence and technical training, but quite as much for their characters and sense of social responsibility. Sensitive men were needed—men who could fully appreciate the importance of the charge entrusted to them; no other sort would do. But the burden of responsibility was too great to be borne indefinitely by a sensitive man. It was, of necessity, a psychologically unstable condition. Insanity was an occupational disease.

And in "The Roads Must Roll," he had written of his main character, the Chief Engineer of the Diego-Reno Roadtown: "He had carried too long the superhuman burden of kingship—which no sane mind can carry light-heartedly—and was at this moment perilously close to the frame of mind which sends captains down with their ships."

But, of course, as we have also seen, in one early Heinlein story after another, society's major institutions—business, politics, religion— are indicted as short-sighted, greedy, corrupt, dishonest, dangerous, and possibly outright evil. Common folk—the sort of little people who go "'ridey-ridey home to their dinners'" via the rolling roads— are seen as easily duped, mesmerized by the moment, lost in the trivial and superficial aspects of life, oblivious to higher concerns. And when people of real knowledge do attempt to share their experience with society, ordinary citizens are apt to pay no attention, while the corrupt are likely to try to silence or kill them.

It was a complex tangle of thought and feeling that Heinlein was being driven to to try to sort out in these urgent, immediate, intense personal stories. He yearned to be an effective man of higher dedication, but he felt thwarted. He longed for a society deserving of his service, but saw instead a society of unworthiness and corruption. He wondered whether it was possible to be a Wellsian Samurai or something like it without being struck down for his pride or breaking under the strain. And he couldn't make it all come out even.

Some of the time, Heinlein might reassert the duty to society of the man of superior knowledge and ability. At other times, he might suggest the necessity for a revolution that would make society more worthy of its best men. And, in yet other moods—say, after a visit to his old boyhood surroundings in Kansas City—he might say to hell with society, and once again doubt the reality of anything and everything but himself.

Science fiction allowed Heinlein a way to express all the different facets of this dilemma, and actually to get away with it. Who cared what sort of accusations or hypothetical possibilities or personal fantasies or outright heresies were uttered in stories in some pulp science fiction magazine? Now that Heinlein had both learned to write for Campbell and presented Campbell with his terms for continuing to write, there wasn't anything he wanted to say that he couldn't say as science fiction.

What is more, science fiction stories offered Heinlein a means of working his way through his problem. As a boy reading Hugo Gernsback's magazines, Heinlein had pinned his fondest hopes and expectations on a future that would be different from his present. And in growing up, he had found exactly that—a mid-Twentieth Century America that was not the same as the early Twentieth Century America into which he had been born.

Western society had been undergoing an accelerating pace of change since the Age of Reason. But it was only now, with the transition to the new Atomic Age, that the pace had become rapid enough and insistent enough that it was possible for one man to point to the evidences of difference and say, "This is what change is. This is how it works."

Robert Heinlein was that rare individual. He *knew* that society was constantly undergoing outward and inward change. And he had the files of clippings he had been accumulating for the past ten years to prove it.

The way that Heinlein found to deal with his great problem of matching his ambition, his talent and his energy to the needs of society was to combine his dilemma with his conviction of ongoing change and future difference. The new, mutable multiplex future that Heinlein had been working out for himself in stories like "If This Goes On—," "The Roads Must Roll," and "Magic, Inc." allowed him the possibility of imagining what worthy work might be for the man of superior intelligence, training, character and responsibility, and also to imagine what kind of society might support and not oppose him in doing it.

And yet, Heinlein's right hand was not aware of what his left hand was up to. On the conscious level of his mind, Heinlein could say that he was just doing it for the money, or for a limited period of time, and believe that was the truth.

As a demonstration to Campbell and to himself that he was a strict pragmatist, Heinlein turned out the serial novel that Campbell immediately needed while he was still on his trip to the East Coast: *Sixth Column*, by Anson MacDonald (*Astounding*, Jan-Mar 1941). And it was a considerable testament to his skills that he was able to take Campbell's old-fashioned plot about Oriental invaders combatted by American super-science and write it in such a way that it could pass for modern science fiction.

But Heinlein's heart would not really be involved in this mere job of work, and *Sixth Column* would be the only story idea he would ever accept from Campbell. Whether or not he consciously realized it, Heinlein needed to write the stories he had been writing and it was imperative for him to continue.

He would find this out when the time came that he actually attempted to quit. In the summer of 1941, Campbell challenged the new order Heinlein had established by going so far as to reject a Heinlein story. And so, just as he had promised he would do, Heinlein set his science fiction aside and turned to other things.

He would recall:

> I promptly retired—put in a new irrigation system—built a garden terrace—resumed serious photography, etc. This went on for about a month when I found that I was beginning to be vaguely ill: poor appetite, loss of weight, insomnia, jittery, absent-minded—much like the early symptoms of pulmonary tuberculosis, and I thought, "Damn it, am I going to have still a *third* attack?"

But, in fact, it didn't turn out to be tuberculosis yet again. Just as soon as Heinlein had made it evident to Campbell that his threat to quit was a serious one, and Campbell had unrejected the story in question, Heinlein went back to the typewriter. And instantly his symptoms disappeared.

Heinlein was hooked—not just for now, but for a lifetime. He would write SF until the United States entered World War II and he got caught up in war work. And after the war, against his expectations, he would go back to science fiction writing—though mostly for other and better-paying markets than the Campbell *Astounding*. Heinlein would be a dominating figure in SF for the next forty years and more.

The crucial intuitive leap of integration that first established him as that was made in the late summer of 1940, just as soon as Heinlein had finished proving to Campbell and himself what a rational, competent, controlled fellow he really was by grinding out *Sixth Column* for the money to buy a car when he got home.

With the check in his pocket, Heinlein set out for California. But along the way he stopped off in Jackson, Michigan to meet the last SF writing hero of his youth, Doc Smith. And it proved to be a very happy encounter. The two men, the old master of science fiction and the new, took an immediate liking to one another.

Back home in Los Angeles, at the informal gatherings of SF writers that met at Heinlein's home on Saturday nights, which he liked to call "the Mañana Literary Society," Heinlein might point out, accurately enough, that the social and cultural dimensions of life were missing from the Lensman stories. But in the presence of Smith himself, Heinlein felt no inclination to be critical. He found himself genuinely impressed by the man's largeness of character and by the breadth and depth of his practical skill and knowledge.

So impressed was he, in fact, that on impulse he took Smith up on his offer to road-test and select a used car for him there in Michigan for the price of his *Sixth Column* check (plus, as it turned out, thirty-five cents in cash). The '39 Chevy that Smith finally chose Heinlein dubbed *Skylark Five*. And so good a car did it prove to be that he was able to keep on driving it for the next dozen years.

For his part, Doc Smith was sufficiently taken with Heinlein that he enrolled him as a member of "the Galactic Roamers," the informal brain trust that read Smith's Lensman stories in manuscript and offered him comment and special advice. This was a rare honor that had been accorded to no other SF writer of the younger generation.

So, feeling like a member of the Galactic Patrol, Heinlein headed off toward California in *Skylark Five*. And on the way to Los Angeles, a momentous thing happened. Heinlein was struck by a particularly dazzling insight, one that took all of the varied work he had been publishing in *Astounding* and made a whole of it.

In these stories from his first year of writing—along with "'Let There Be Light'" by Lyle Monroe—he had projected two separate future backgrounds.

One was the middle-distance future he'd worked out years before, with the overthrow of the rule of the Prophets and the establishment of the Covenant. This extrapolation of the most tyrannous elements of his childhood into the future, and their utter defeat by the forces of freedom and rationality, was very important to Heinlein. It was no less than his psychic autobiography.

The other future that he had been evolving for the coming half-century, with its sun-power screens, road-cities and atomic power plants, was less urgently powerful stuff—except for its climax with the death of old D.D. Harriman on the Moon. But it was much more detailed and plausible and varied.

In fact, so much had Heinlein's SF skill and insight grown during the last year that this near-range future was starting to make his other future of "If This Goes On—," "Coventry" and "Misfit" seem fuzzy, static and remote. It now seemed a much less likely development from the present. It was old-fashioned, utopian and romantic.

Could it be possible to apply the new tricks and techniques of presentation he had been working out in such a way as to give this more distant future greater believability and substance? In "Magic, Inc." he had managed to make spirit magic and tea-leaf reading and all sorts of other arrant nonsense seem the very stuff of tomorrow. Why couldn't the Prophets and the Covenant be made as plausible as that?

For that matter, what was to prevent the farther future from being made to seem every bit as immediate, detailed and self-consistent as the short-range future outlined on his wall chart?

All in a flash, then, Heinlein saw that his wall chart could be extended well beyond fifty years; and also that the future waiting there just might be—why not?—the world of "If This Goes On—." He could actually combine the old future of his historical outline and the new future of his wall chart. His two futures might be one future!

The wall chart would then have more extension, while the future of the Prophets would take on greater definition; one set of stories would give support and credence to the other. Not only that, but this new combined future would necessarily be not merely a place of change, but of change after change after change. Now wouldn't *that* be something!

Oh, some things would get lost in the process. He would have to kill off the rolling roads. There certainly could be no place for road-cities in the world of the Prophets. Space travel would have to be imagined as starting with Harriman, then stopping for a time, and then starting up again under the Covenant. And the rule of the Prophets couldn't possibly appear as total, overwhelming and demonic as once it had. Instead of being *the* future, it would only be an episode, just one phase in a kaleidoscopic, ever-changing future of multiplicity.

But these losses would be as nothing next to what would be gained: a future that wasn't all of one piece. This future would have room for rolling roads *and* for Prophets armed with spears and vortex guns *and* for the libertarian society of the Covenant. And more besides. Almost anything you cared to put in could find its place in the framework.

In order to make his two sets of stories fit together, Heinlein radically reworked and expanded his wall chart when he got home. In this new form, it covered two hundred years, marked off in decades from 1940 to 2140. Eight written stories were included, from "Life-Line" in more-or-less the immediate present to "Misfit" in 2105 or thereabouts.

In itself, this chart was a brilliant, multifaceted work of modern science fiction, both plausible and mysterious:

The main body of the chart was divided into a number of different areas presenting biographical, technical, social, economic and historical information. There were lines measuring off the life-spans of his various characters and the periods of use of different inventions. There were notations of particular achievements and innovations. There was one vertical column devoted to sociological notes, and another reserved for general remarks.

Looking at the chart, it was possible to see that Douglas and Martin, the inventors of the sun-power screens, were imagined as dying together around 1985. The rolling roads existed for about fifty years, from 1955 until just after the beginning of the Twenty-First Century. And, as Heinlein worked it out, the life of Nehemiah Scudder, the First Prophet, necessarily had to be short. He was born around 1985 and was dead shortly after 2015.

A large number of facts and events that existed as yet only in Heinlein's imagination, but not in his stories, were noted on the chart: "The 'FALSE DAWN,' 1960-70...the Voorhis financial proposals...Revolution in Little America...The Travel Unit and the Fighting Unit...Parastatic engineering...the end of human adolescence and the beginning of first mature culture." And a great deal more.

Even after Heinlein had finished integrating his further future into his wall chart, however, a considerable problem still existed. The fit between the two sets of stories really wasn't all that snug.

"Requiem" was the last in time of Heinlein's five near-future stories. But if old D.D. Harriman had been a reader of the *Electrical Experimenter* as a boy, there was no way this story could take place much later than 1990.

"If This Goes On—" was the earliest in time of Heinlein's three middle-distance stories. And there we had been told that the era of the Prophets had lasted "for many generations." The absolute earliest moment that Heinlein dared to place "If This Goes On—" was around 2070.

This left a considerable hole—an eighty-year blank spot from 1990 to 2070—right in the center of a two-hundred-year history. But this gap seemed like no particular problem to Heinlein. Such was his confidence at this moment that it seemed to him there was nothing he couldn't put in his chart. He could throw off the most outrageous sort of idea, employ almost any kind of plot, leap anywhere in space and time, and still make it all part of his great schema.

And he set out to demonstrate as much to himself in the next three stories he wrote:

The first of these was "'And He Built a Crooked House'" (*Astounding*, Feb 1941), a mathematical jape about a contemporary Los Angeles house built in the shape of an unfolded tesseract, or four-dimensional super-cube. When an earthquake jolts the house into its "normal" configuration, it becomes a place of irrationality, offering doorways into alternate worlds and strange, frightening glimpses of the back of one's own head.

Although this story had no ties to any other Heinlein story, he entered it on his chart anyway, right after "Life-Line." When the charted stories were published in book form after the war, Heinlein would have second thoughts about including "'And He Built a Crooked House'"—but right now such was his mood that he saw no reason not to put it in.

The next story that Heinlein wrote after his return to Los Angeles was his proof that the gap in the chart could be filled in. This was a novelet called "Logic of Empire" (*Astounding*, Mar 1941), set around the year 2010.

Taken as an independent story, "Logic of Empire" was a bit of a mess. It combined two standard Thirties story formulas—the tale of the man of privilege who gets a taste of what real life is like, and the space opera story about slavery on some other planet—and turned them into something like a lecture in economics:

Heinlein's protagonist, lawyer Humphrey Wingate, begins by doubting that slavery actually exists on Venus, and then learns better at first hand when he signs himself up for a term of service while on a drunken lark. But when he has escaped from servitude in the swamps of Venus and returns to Earth to try to tell about what he has experienced, nobody really wants to hear it.

It is explained to him by a friend that slavery in the colonies is an old, old story, the inevitable result of expanding free-market economics. And that ordinary Earth people just seem to find matters like this too difficult and abstract to be bothered with.

The story ends with Wingate asking, "'What can we *do* about it?'"

And his friend replies: "'Nothing. Things are bound to get a whole lot worse before they can get any better. Let's have a drink.'"

Futile, scattered and inconclusive though "Logic of Empire" may have been as a story, it was quite a bit more effective as an element in Heinlein's evolving future. Not only did it cut twenty years out of the gap in the middle of his chart, but for the first time, it bound Heinlein's two sets of stories together. "Logic of Empire" was connected to "Requiem" by references to Luna City and the Space Precautionary Act. And it was linked to "If This Goes On—" through several mentions of "a rabble-rousing political preacher" by the name of Nehemiah Scudder.

But it was the third story that Heinlein wrote after his visit to the East Coast that was his ultimate statement of just how far he thought the principle of his chart could be extended, and of how strange and special a story might be and still fit into the whole. This was "Universe" (*Astounding*, May 1941), Heinlein's tale of the lost spaceship that has forgotten the existence of the stars.

"Universe"—this utterly unique situation—would take place long after the two-hundred-year time frame of Heinlein's chart. And yet Heinlein would make provision for it within his schema. Notations on his chart would indicate that the ship in question was launched about 2120 by the society of the Covenant.

So what was there that wouldn't fit into the chart?

Well, Heinlein had been thinking about a near-future story in which the United States has developed atomic weapons but can't trust anyone else with them, and so, contrary to its inclination, must take over the world. As he had first conceived it, this was to have been one more story on his chart, set around 1950.

But real-world atomic research was not holding still. Even in late 1940, a year before active entry of the United States into World War II, and two years before the first sustained fission reaction at the University of Chicago, it had begun to seem likely to Heinlein— and to Campbell, too—that atomic weapons would be developed before the end of this current war.

Heinlein chose to say as much as Anson MacDonald in an extended fiction/essay written completely outside the bounds of his wall chart. He imagined World War II brought to an end in 1944 by a bombing raid that scatters radioactive dust over Berlin, followed almost immediately by a short, intense struggle for domination between the United States and Russia.

He called this grim novelet "Foreign Policy." Campbell would retitle it "Solution Unsatisfactory" and publish it, along with "Universe," in the May 1941 *Astounding*.

Heinlein's next story, "'—We Also Walk Dogs'" (*Astounding*, July 1941), would also appear as the work of Anson MacDonald. It may be taken as Heinlein's demonstration to himself that even though almost anything might be fitted into his charted future, he wasn't necessarily bound to that future.

This story concerns a special company, General Services, that will perform any lawful undertaking for an appropriate fee. They have accepted the task of providing comfortable quarters on Earth for a conference of "'representatives of each intelligent race in this planetary system'"—including Martians, Jovians, Titans and Callistans.

Just now, this story would not be part of Heinlein's charted future— presumably because of all the various local intelligent alien races, who make no appearance in any of his other pre-war stories. But after the war, Heinlein would apparently once again say, "Why not?" and "'—We Also Walk Dogs'" would assume a place in the official canon, marked in around the year 2000.

It was only at this point, early in 1941, with all this burst of experimentation behind Heinlein, that the first formal notice of his interconnected future was made by John Campbell. After announcing "Logic of Empire" in the "In Times to Come" column of the February *Astounding*, the editor went on to say:

> I'd like to mention something that may or may not have been noticed by the regular readers of *Astounding*: all of Heinlein's science-fiction is laid against a common background of a proposed future history of the world and of the United States. Heinlein's worked the thing out in detail that grows with each story; he has an outline and graphed history of the future with characters, dates of major discoveries, et cetera, plotted in. I'm trying to get him to let me have a photostat of that history chart; if I lay hands on it, I'm going to publish it.

In this announcement by Campbell, there was, of course, a not altogether untypical element of well-calculated insincerity, or salesmanship. He knew full well that not all of Heinlein's science fiction was laid against a common background, including the installment of *Sixth Column* by Anson MacDonald in this very issue. And prior to the actual publication of "Logic of Empire," which would be the first link between Heinlein's two major sets of stories, no reader of *Astounding* could reasonably have been expected to see them all as one.

Having been given this tip, or heavy nudge, however, readers could now hardly overlook the cross-connections that did exist in "Logic of Empire." And that was what the editor was really after. He wanted Heinlein's future history to be taken note of.

Back in the June 1940 *Astounding*—an issue featuring on its cover a Rogers' painting of the inner workings of Heinlein's rolling roads—Campbell had suggested in passing in his editorial, "Mapping out a civilization of the future is an essential background to a convincing story of the future." And now he had his example: a model presentation of just how a multiplex, ever-changing Atomic Age future was to be imagined.

But Campbell was not content merely to have his readers and writers perceive the existence of Heinlein's history of the future. He wanted them to study the blueprints and see how it fit together. So he didn't rest until the Future History chart appeared spread across two pages of the May *Astounding*.

The May 1941 issue of *Astounding* was the most significant since July 1939, and can be seen as one of the two or three most stellar issues of Campbell's Golden Age. It contained "Universe" and "Solution Unsatisfactory," and Asimov's second robot story, "Liar!" as well as the concluding installment of L. Sprague de Camp's only pre-war *Astounding* serial, "The Stolen Dormouse." But the center-piece of the issue was Heinlein's Future History chart.

This was recognized in Campbell's editorial, which was entitled "History to Come." Here, Campbell formally redefined science fiction in terms of Heinlein's accomplishment. He declared, "Funda-mentally, science-fiction novels are 'period pieces,' historical novels laid against a background of a history that hasn't happened yet."

Science fiction hadn't been seen in these terms previously. But the publication of Heinlein's Future History chart would force a general alteration of perception of what science fiction was about and how it was made.

Through the years, other writers of SF had turned out story series aplenty. But these had always been the adventures of a particular character or group of characters, invariably operating within the bounds of some well-defined formula. No one had ever thought of reversing figure and ground and writing a story series that had no consistent central character, but rather was concerned with the twists and turns and reversals of social and psychological change to come.

However, not only was this what Heinlein had done, but his chart was incontrovertible proof that he had done it. The chart took a handful of parts and made a visible whole of them. It was the most detailed, multifaceted and interconnected picture of the future that anyone had ever produced, so persuasive in appearance that it might almost be a couple of pages ripped out of some history book of tomorrow.

And now that it could be seen clearly as a whole, how wonderfully persuasive and real Heinlein's Future History was, with its picture of a coming world of change and difference! The future envisioned by Olaf Stapledon in *Last and First Men* might be vaster and grander, yet somehow the immediate two hundred years outlined in the Future History managed to encompass a wider range of human social activity, more mental variety, greater liveliness, and more sheer differentness than all of Stapledon's two billion years put together. Next to Heinlein's Atomic Age future of change upon change, Stapledon's old-fashioned Techno Age view of the future seemed static and single-noted.

By aiming to break free of determinism and find a future of free will for himself, Heinlein had found the means for all modern science fiction to break out of the extreme constriction in time and space that had been so typical of the *Astounding* of 1939 and 1940. Taken in sum, Heinlein's stories—not just the Future History, but also "Magic, Inc." and his futuristic Anson MacDonald stories—proclaimed that the future was waiting to be invented, and that practically anything might be plausibly imagined as happening there.

Heinlein blazed the way for all Atomic Age futures to come, not in detail, but in approach and method. Because of Heinlein's pre-war experiments, SF writers of the Atomic Age would be able to see the future both as historically connected to the present and as a wide-open playground of the imagination. On the strength of Heinlein's example, they would feel licensed not only to make up their own alternate future histories, but also to set forth any free-floating future possibility they could imagine.

Prior to the announcement and publication of the Future History chart, Heinlein had been a well-respected new writer, acknowledged as a steady, reliable storyteller. But he had been the special favorite of only a very few readers.

However, this changed with the revelation that all of Heinlein's separate stories in *Astounding* were in fact so many fragments in a far larger and more complex pattern. He was now seen to stand by himself as the most ambitious and inventive writer of modern science fiction. It was this new, more sizable Robert Heinlein who was asked to be Guest of Honor at the Third World Science Fiction Convention in Denver in July 1941.

In that same month, *Methuselah's Children*, the longest Future History story yet, began three-part serialization in *Astounding*. This story was the culmination of all the work Heinlein had done to knit together a connected but ever-changing future. It was also the fulfillment of a promise.

One of the more intriguing mysteries of Heinlein's chart as it saw publication was five "Stories-to-be-told," listed in parentheses. These not only filled out some of the thinner portions of the chart, but intimated Heinlein's power to see more and to tell more of his future:

("Word Edgewise") was penciled in around 1960, between "'Let There Be Light'" and "The Roads Must Roll."

Shortly after "Requiem"—c. 1995—there was ("Fire Down Below!")

Shaving another ten years off the great gap in the center of the chart, there was ("The Sound of His Wings") around 2015, and ("Eclipse") around 2020.

Finally, as the very last entry on the chart, around 2125, twenty years after "Misfit," there was ("While the Evil Days Come Not").

It was this last story that saw publication as *Methuselah's Children.* This was not only Heinlein's proof that it was possible for him to redeem his promises, but it showed that he could further extend his vision of future change and difference.

In its very conception, this novel was a striking demonstration of Heinlein's new philosophy of factors in combination and permutation. To make *Methuselah's Children*, Heinlein took two originally separate story ideas from his file and ran them together, and then turned the result into a further phase in his Future History.

One of the ideas that went into the pot was for a story called "Shadow of Death," about a group of people selectively bred for long life, and their persecution by ordinary short-lived men. It was to have been set entirely on Earth.

The other idea—less seriously titled "Peril in the Spaceways... or...Who Shot the Baby???"—was for a space epic in the grand tradition. It may be thought of as the kind of answer the young planet-busting John Campbell might have made to the ultimate unsolvable problem of Stapledon's *Last and First Men.*

In this projected story, our Sun is failing. A group of human adventurers sets off for the stars in search of a solution. After encounters with two alien races—"the Rapport People" and "the Dog People"—men find their answer in towing the Earth through interstellar space and placing it in orbit around a friendlier star.

As Heinlein fit these ideas together to make *Methuselah's Children*, it was the long-lived people of the first projected story who would serve as his space explorers. And, rather than the threat of yet another cosmic catastrophe, it would be Earthly persecution that would be their reason for traveling to the stars and meeting the Dog People and the Rapport People.

In *Methuselah's Children*, the Howard Families are a select group of Americans bred for longevity beginning in 1875. Some two hundred and fifty years later, in the days of the Covenant, there are 100,000 of them. Among their number are people who can stand up and say, "'I was here when the First Prophet took over the country. I was here when Harriman launched the first Moon rocket.'"

Oldest of them all is Lazarus Long, Heinlein's central character. Lazarus may be 213 years old and still counting, but at heart he is another ageless perpetual adolescent, not unlike Edgar Rice Burroughs' John Carter.

It is Lazarus more than any other single thing that ties the Future History together and makes a whole of it. He was born before the Future History chart begins and remains alive after it ends. Long, long ago, Hugo Pinero of "Life-Line" took his reading, and then returned his money. Andrew Jackson Libby, the boy genius of

"Misfit"—who proves to be another Howard Family member—becomes Lazarus's best buddy. Lazarus embraces the entire Future History from beginning to end; he can vouch for it all.

Because they are different from the ordinary run of mankind, the Howard Families have done their best to remain publicly invisible. Fifty years after the overthrow of the Prophets, however, they finally feel secure enough to reveal the fact of their existence to society-at-large.

This turns out to be a mistake. Greedy and powerful men, jealous for longer life, suspend the Covenant and begin to arrest and torture the members of the Howard Families to extract their supposed secret of immortality.

Lazarus isn't really surprised. He says, "'If there is any one thing I have learned in the past couple of centuries, it's this: These things *pass*. Wars and depressions and Prophets and Covenants—they pass. The trick is to stay alive through them.'"

Back during the difficult years when the Prophets ruled, Lazarus chose to sit things out on Venus. Now he proposes that the Families pack up and leave Earth until this current wave of hysteria passes.

With the connivance of one responsible short-lived politician, Administrator Slayton Ford, Lazarus steals the giant spaceship *New Frontiers*—a twin to that in "Universe." Andy Libby whips up a superior space drive, and the Families, plus Ford, flee to the stars.

Here, however, things do not go well for them.

The Families have left Earth because the very fact of their existence is intolerable to ordinary men. As one member puts it:

> "It is clear to me now that our mere presence, the simple fact of our rich heritage of life, is damaging to the spirit of our poor neighbor. Our longer years and richer opportunities make his best efforts seem futile to him—any effort save a hopeless struggle against an appointed death. Our mere presence saps his strength, ruins his judgment, fills him with panic fear of death."

But amongst the stars, the long-lifers find beings who are even more dismaying to them than the Howard Families are to normal humanity.

The first stop of the Families is the planet of the Dog People—or, as they call themselves, the Jockaira. These tall thin humanoids are scientifically and mathematically advanced. Not only is their planet a near-twin of Earth, but they are very hospitable folk. They empty a city and turn it over to the Earthmen for their use.

After a time, however, a price is demanded. The Jockaira talk constantly of their gods. Now they say that the Earth people must pick a temple and a god to worship.

The Earthmen decide to play along with this charade. Administrator Ford is the first to be initiated. He and Lazarus go to the temple of Kreel; Ford enters, while Lazarus waits for him outside.

However, when Ford comes out of the temple again, he is a broken man. He can't even communicate what has happened to him. But Lazarus believes he knows what has occurred. He says:

> "Here's my opinion: we've had these Jockaira doped out all wrong from scratch. We made the mistake of thinking that because they looked like us, in a general way, and were about as civilized as we are, that they were *people*. But they aren't people at all. They are...*domestic animals*. ... There are people on this planet, right enough. Real people. They lived in the temples and the Jockaira called them gods. They *are* gods!"

By this, Lazarus makes clear, he doesn't mean they are supernatural beings. He means these are beings so evolutionarily advanced that next to the Jockaira—or to humanity—they might as well be gods.

And, very quickly, these higher beings demonstrate their power. Through the Jockaira, they inform the humans that they must leave this planet and go to another thirty-two light years away. The gods then enforce this dictate by teleporting the humans through the air, stuffing them into their ship, and then directing the ship through space to the destination they have selected.

This second planet is gentle and sweet and tranquil. It is populated by the Little People, small furry androgynous beings who are not individuals in themselves, but exist in telepathic rapport groups. These creatures are far superior to us in physical science, although they avoid employing physics and machines any more than they absolutely must. They are even more superior to us in biology. So adept are the Little People that they can create plants that taste like steak and mushrooms or mashed potatoes and gravy.

In a state of considerable disquiet, Lazarus mentally reviews the situation of the Howard Families:

> The hegira of the Families had been a mistake. It would have been a more human, a more mature and manly thing, to have stayed and fought for their rights, even if they had died insisting on them. Instead they had fled across half a universe (Lazarus was reckless about his magnitudes) looking for a place to light. They had found one, a good one—but already occupied by beings so superior as to make them intolerable for men...yet so supremely indifferent in their superiority to men that they had not

even bothered to wipe them out, but had whisked them away to this—this overmanicured country club.

And that in itself was the unbearable humiliation. The *New Frontiers* was the culmination of five hundred years of human scientific research, the best that men could do—but it had been flicked across the deeps of space as casually as a man might restore a baby bird to its nest.

The Little People did not seem to want to kick them out, but the Little People, in their own way, were as demoralizing to men as were the gods of the Jockaira. One at a time they might be morons but taken as groups each rapport group was a genius that threw the best minds that men could offer into the shade. Even Andy. Human beings could not hope to compete with that type of organization any more than a backroom shop could compete with an automated cybernated factory. Yet to form any such group identities, even if they could, which he doubted, would be, Lazarus felt very sure, to give up whatever it was that made them *men*.

And almost immediately, the question of what makes a man is put to the test. One of the oldest humans, fearing death, chooses to swap her individuality for a permanent continuing existence as an element in a Little People rapport group. And a human child is born that has been modified and improved by the Little People:

> It lacked even the button nose of a baby, nor were there evident external ears. There were organs in the usual locations of each but flush with the skull and protected with bony ridges. Its hands had too many fingers and there was an extra large one near each wrist which ended in a cluster of pink worms. There was something odd about the torso of the infant which Lazarus could not define. But two other gross facts were evident: the legs ended not in human feet but in horny, toeless pediments—hoofs. And the creature was hermaphroditic—not in deformity but in healthy development, an androgyne.

At this point, only a very few of the long-lifers wish to continue exploring among the stars. A larger handful is content to remain with the Little People. But the vast majority, Lazarus chief amongst them, wants to go home.

So homeward they go. When they arrive, they find that seventy-four years have passed on Earth. They aren't received as outlaws and fugitives as they had feared, but rather as heroic stellar explorers. Nobody is mad or jealous anymore. Thanks to positive thinking and radioactive vitamins everyone is a long-lifer now, and everything is just swell.

The story concludes with Lazarus whistling *"California here I come! Right back where I started from!"* and hoping that his favorite Dallas chili house from way back when is still in business.

What an unsatisfactory ending this is! Here we have Robert Heinlein—the man who assured us that any custom, technique, institution, belief, or social structure *must* change—concluding a novel about a stellar voyage longer than the entire reign of the Prophets with the earnest hope that nothing has changed on Earth and that things will still be the same as when the Families left.

More than that. The early chapters of *Methuselah's Children* were Heinlein's most futuristic work yet, filled with casually fantastic detailing like this: "When Lazarus went to bed he stepped out of his kilt and chucked it toward a wardrobe...which snagged it, shook it out, and hung it up neatly. 'Nice catch,' he commented...."

But it isn't even this world that Lazarus seems to expect to find upon his return. What he actually has in his head, at least, are the songs and cuisine of his boyhood, way, way back in the Twentieth Century. Seemingly Lazarus has encountered more than he can handle among the stars and it has shocked him out of 275 years or so of growth.

A fundamental Techno Age problem is presented for solution in *Methuselah's Children*—the problem of evolutionary superiority. It is set forth no fewer than five times: by the Howard Families; by the gods of the Jockaira; by the Little People; by a human choosing to join a Little People rapport group; and by the human baby that the Little People redesign and improve.

The first of these cases, the longevity of the Howard Families, proves in time not to be a true example of evolutionary difference after all. Mere longer life doesn't make the long-lifers any wiser or more competent or more successful as human beings. As Lazarus is frank to say in criticism of one Family member: "'Bud, you strike me as a clear proof that the Foundation should 'a' bred for brains instead of age.'"

In fact, it is precisely because this difference is only a superficial one that ordinary humanity can catch up to the Howard Families so quickly and that the long-lifers can be welcomed back to Earth at the end of the story.

But the other examples are far more serious challenges. They represent the prospect of fundamental change in human form and human mentation, of encounter with beings who can out-compete us on our own terms, and, most trying of all, of discovery of the existence of beings of another and higher order than our own.

The Howard Families and Lazarus Long simply are unequipped to cope with any one of these possibilities. Instead, they are left feeling bullied and baffled, horrified and demoralized. Like kids who have dared to cross the street to the next block and discovered more than they can deal with there, they must turn tail and scoot for home to climb into the safety and comfort of a nice hot bowl of chili.

But as hard as Lazarus and the others might try to pretend that nothing at all really happened on the voyage of the *New Frontiers*, we, who were along for the ride, certainly know better. We can remember Administrator Slayton Ford—a man of such "superior ability and unmatched experience" that he was able to take over executive direction of the Howard Families even though not a long-lifer himself—as he ran weeping and distraught from the temple of Kreel, gazed on Lazarus with "horror-stricken eyes" and then clutched him desperately for security.

With his ideal of an elite of human competence, Robert Heinlein was easily able to imagine coming to terms with a future of social and psychological change. But evolutionary change was another matter. Could even the most competent of men cope with creatures like Kreel? Maybe not. Probably not. As one character says ruefully to Lazarus: "'Those creatures the Jockaira worshiped—it does not seem possible that any amount of living could raise us up to that level.'"

We should note that Heinlein would not always feel this way. In 1958, a moment when faith in the efficacy of universal operating principles had reached its maximum, Heinlein would publish the revised and expanded book version of *Methuselah's Children*. There he would drop out this line that we have just quoted, and he would add a concluding conversation between Lazarus and Andy Libby in which Lazarus expresses renewed zest for interstellar exploration and a determination to grow up enough someday to take on the gods of the Jockaira.

Libby says: "'They weren't gods, Lazarus. You shouldn't call them that.'"

And Lazarus answers:

> "Of course they weren't—I think. My guess is that they are creatures who have had enough time to do a little hard thinking. Someday, about a thousand years from now, I intend to march straight into the temple of Kreel, look him in the eye, and say, 'Howdy, bub—what do *you* know that *I* don't know?'"

With these changes, Heinlein would reduce the gap between Kreel and Lazarus from an evolutionary difference that can't possibly be surmounted to a mere difference in state of knowledge. In the same way that the ordinary people left behind on Earth managed to scuffle and scramble and catch up to the Howard Families, so may Lazarus aspire to catch up to Kreel in another thousand years or so.

In 1941, however, Heinlein had reached his sticking point. His Future History had carried him just as far as it could and then run him into a brick wall, or what looked like a brick wall. After one last Future History story—a relatively weak and unconvincing sequel to "Universe" entitled "Common Sense" (*Astounding*, Oct 1941)—Heinlein was ready to put his whole connected future on the shelf.

And, in fact, at this moment the Future History was about as complete as it was ever going to be. After World War II, Heinlein might shuffle stories around, add some new stories to the near end of the chart, and rewrite and tidy the Future History for book publication. But he would never get around to writing any of the other "Stories-to-be-told" that were promised on the chart as it first saw publication in May 1941. And neither would he ever do anything to close the sixty-year gap remaining between "Logic of Empire" and "If This Goes On—." Eventually, Heinlein would simply declare, "I probably never will write the story of Nehemiah Scudder; I dislike him too thoroughly."

Now, rather than filling in the Future History, Heinlein beat his head some more against the problem that *Methuselah's Children* had raised but not resolved.

In the intricate time travel novelet "By His Bootstraps" (*Astounding*, Oct 1941) by Anson MacDonald, a contemporary graduate student named Bob Wilson is hauled thirty thousand years into the future by a man of lined face and gray beard who calls himself Diktor. Diktor informs Wilson that the Palace they are in and the Time Gate through which he has come are the work of "the High Ones," superior beings who came, ruled humanity for twenty thousand years, and then departed, leaving mankind a pretty, placid, doggish species, like some cross between the Jockaira of *Methuselah's Children* and the Eloi of Wells's *The Time Machine*.

Diktor horses Wilson around, tricking him into making loop upon loop through time to meet himself and argue with himself and even punch himself in the mouth. And the poor befuddled Wilson finds himself helpless to do anything more than compulsively repeat lines he has already heard himself say twice over.

This callous treatment only leaves him suspicious, resentful and rebellious. Eventually, Wilson dodges ten years into Diktor's past—where Diktor proves not to be—and sets himself up in Diktor's place as boss of the docile local folk.

In time, however, being top dog here grows to be a bore, and Wilson conceives a desire to know more of the High Ones. He uses the Time Gate to search for them, and at last he sees one.

We aren't told what it looks like, only what Wilson does: He screams. He runs away. He gets a fit of the shakes. He reacts like Slayton Ford in the temple of Kreel.

We are told: "He felt he had learned all about the High Ones a man could learn and still endure."

Wilson's sleep is ruined—he has night sweats and bad dreams. His face becomes lined and his hair and beard turn gray.

It is years before he can bring himself to fool around with the Time Gate again. And when he does, it is only to find himself inadvertently snatching young Bob Wilson, the graduate student, into this future moment.

At last, then, the heretofore unrecognized truth dawns on Wilson: "He was Diktor. He was *the* Diktor. He was *the only* Diktor!"

By no means does he fully comprehend what has happened even yet: "He knew that he had about as much chance of understanding such problems as a collie has of understanding how dog food gets into cans."

At this point, all he can think to do is to go on with the fore-ordained game, secure in the bittersweet certainty that what *has* happened *must* happen. And so, with the supreme false assurance of a used car salesman who has a live one on the hook, he smiles on his younger self and says, "'There is a great future in store for you and me, my boy—a great future!'"

And Heinlein-as-narrator echoes wryly: "A great future!"

Like so much of Heinlein's fiction in this year since his declaration of artistic freedom, "By His Bootstraps" was a confidently brilliant work of science fiction. Nobody had ever written a time travel story of this order of complexity before, and readers were dazzled by its intricacy.

But as ordinary readers were less likely to notice, "By His Bootstraps"—like most of Heinlein's stories of the past year—was filled with undertones of bitterness, resignation and defeat, accentuated by Wilson/Diktor's disastrous encounter with the High One. This story was one more "solution unsatisfactory."

The one reader who could not help but notice Heinlein's inability to cope with superior beings was John Campbell. In August 1941, Heinlein sent him yet another such story, a novelet called "Goldfish Bowl" in which this Earth is suggested to be the home of atmospheric intelligences who are as far beyond humanity as men are beyond fish.

In this story, two American scientists attempt to investigate a strange phenomenon—two gigantic waterspouts that have appeared in the Pacific Ocean near Hawaii and remained in place for months. Instead, however, they find themselves taken prisoner and kept in the mysterious somewhere at the top of the spouts. From the manner in which they are held, it is possible for them to deduce that their keepers are highly advanced beings.

In *Methuselah's Children*, Slayton Ford encountered Kreel in his temple, even though he could remember nothing of it afterward. And in "By His Bootstraps," Bob Wilson was able to see the High One through the Time Gate, though again it would be a blank to him later. But the scientists in "Goldfish Bowl" aren't permitted even this much. They never meet their captors, they never see them, and they are never able to communicate with them. They are just *kept*.

One of the men, "an oceanographer specializing in ecology" named Bill Eisenberg, says in despair:

> "We've had some dignity as a race. We've striven and accomplished things. Even when we failed, we had the tragic satisfaction of knowing that we were, nevertheless, superior and more able than the other animals. We've had faith in the race—we would accomplish great things yet. But if we are just one of the lower animals ourselves, what does our great work amount to? Me, I couldn't go on pretending to be a 'scientist' if I thought I was just a fish, mucking around in the bottom of a pool. My work wouldn't *signify* anything."

And, after his older companion has died and his body has been removed, Eisenberg thinks to himself:

> They were outclassed. The human race had reached its highest point— the point at which it began to be aware that it was not the highest race, and the knowledge was death to it, one way or the other—the mere knowledge alone, even as the knowledge was now destroying him, Bill Eisenberg, himself.

Despite the fact that by his own reasoning this knowledge can do humanity no good, what it occurs to him to do is to painfully inscribe a cryptic message in scar tissue on his body: "BEWARE—CREATION TOOK EIGHT DAYS." And then he waits to die and to have his body thrown out like a pet goldfish flushed down the toilet.

This was the Heinlein story that John Campbell would attempt to turn down, as though he hoped a timely rejection might serve as a shock to bring Heinlein to his senses and help him escape from the grip of this compulsive funk. "Goldfish Bowl" would see publication— after Heinlein went on his strike and Campbell backed down and took the story—in the March 1942 *Astounding* as another work by Anson MacDonald.

But Heinlein may have had his batteries recharged by his short vacation. When he did return to storytelling, it was with his longest and most ambitious piece of fiction yet, Anson MacDonald's *Beyond This Horizon* (*Astounding*, Apr-May 1942), a novel that he would complete all in a rush on the eve of the Japanese attack on Pearl Harbor and the beginning of official U.S. participation in World War II.

Beyond This Horizon would be many things at once, as though with his time for writing SF visibly running out, Heinlein aimed to say everything he had to say in the pages of one story:

This novel would be a late scientific utopia, a vision of a society-to-come attempting to make itself better by the deliberate selection and cultivation of its citizens' soundest and most desirable genetic qualities. In this, it would be a deliberate retort to Aldous Huxley's dystopian satire *Brave New World* (1932), which itself had first been conceived as an attempt to answer H. G. Wells's *Men Like Gods* (1923).

Beyond This Horizon would also be a modern science fiction story, Heinlein's most masterful presentation of a future America that is radically altered and yet still recognizable. The strange kind of skew that Heinlein had put on the opening pages of "If This Goes On—" and the first few chapters of *Methuselah's Children*, he would manage to sustain for the entire length of this novel.

In the world of *Beyond This Horizon*, men wear their names back-to-front, pass through doors that dilate, compare shades of nail polish, surprise their ortho-wives by visiting them two days in a row, and sleep on beds filled with water (something Heinlein had conceived and designed, but not built, during the time he was bedfast with TB). They have colonies and research stations throughout the Solar System, including Pluto, but they have not yet made the big jump to the stars.

This future is not like the society of the Covenant. There a man might be sent off to Coventry for the deviant act of punching someone in the nose and refusing therapy. In the urbane survival-of-the-fittest society of *Beyond This Horizon*, however, first class citizens carry sidearms and fight duels to the death when their manners are called into question—and should they survive, they go back again to their dinners and think no more about it.

The world Heinlein presents in this story is the product of an entirely different course of future development from the one he had evolved for his official Future History. If "Magic, Inc." was the story in which Heinlein had first shown that he could construct an imaginary future society around any state of knowledge or belief, *Beyond This Horizon* was Heinlein's proof that he could just as readily invent future histories to order, now that he knew the method.

Heinlein had made it clear in his guest-of-honor speech in Denver in July—a mere two months after the publication of his Future History chart—that he wasn't attached to the particulars of his prototype. He had said, "I do not expect my so-called *History of the Future* to come to pass, not in anything like those terms. I think some of the trends in it may show up; but I do not think that my factual predictions as such are going to come to pass, even in their broad outlines."

What was actually central to him was the process of "time-binding," a Korzybskian term that meant the making of mental projections into time-to-come as an exercise of preparation for future change.

So it was, then, that in *Beyond This Horizon*, the future historical thread given is all different. Rather than the rolling roads, we are referred to the "Atomic War of 1970." And instead of being reminded of the overthrow of the Prophets, we are bidden to recall "the Empire of the Great Khans."

In this variant line of development, it would seem that after the overwhelming horror of the Atomic War people were so shocked at what they had done that they deliberately did their best to breed aggressiveness out of the species. Some resisted this, however, and set themselves apart. Eventually there was a war between the new pacific strain of humanity and unaltered man—the First Genetic War. We are told:

"The outcome was...a necessity and the details are unimportant. The 'wolves' ate the 'sheep'."

The Second Genetic War, some three hundred years later, was fought against the Great Khans over the issue of human general adaptability vs. special adaptation. Like Wells's non-human Selenites in *The First Men in the Moon* or Aldous Huxley's society in *Brave New World*, the Great Khans were willing to bend the basic form of man to produce specialized creatures for specialized tasks:

They tailored human beings—if you could call them that—as casually as we construct buildings. At their height, just before the Second Genetic War, they bred over three thousand types including the hyper-brains (thirteen sorts), the almost brainless matrons, the clever and repulsively beautiful pseudo-feminine freemartins, and the neuter "mules".

In fighting mule soldiers directly, generalized men did not fare well. But in the end, they won the war:

The Empire had one vulnerable point, its co-ordinators, the Khan, his satraps and administrators. Biologically the Empire was a single organism and could be killed at the top, like a hive with a single queen bee. At the end, a few score assassinations accomplished a collapse which could not be achieved in battle.

No need to dwell on the terror that followed the collapse. Let it suffice that no representative of *homo proteus* is believed to be alive today. He joined the great dinosaurs and the sabre-toothed cats.

He lacked adaptability.

With this history, it is no wonder that the society of *Beyond This Horizon* should be genetically oriented and survival-minded. However, in its genetic selection it avoids the mistakes of the past. It rejects tampering with either human nature or the human form. Instead, it strives to eliminate heritable defects and to conserve and generalize positive qualities:

> Infants born with the assistance of the neo-Ortega-Martin gene selection techniques are normal babies, stemming from normal gene plasm, born of normal women, in the usual fashion. They differ in one respect only from their racial predecessors: they are the *best* babies their parents can produce!

And we are allowed to see that they are getting somewhere. In the course of *Beyond This Horizon*, in a satiric modern science fiction reversal of an old-time scientifiction situation, an anomaly— "the Adirondack stasis field"—is finally opened and proves to contain a time traveler, a wide-eyed, bushy-tailed, young go-getter from 1926 named J. Darlington Smith. Smith, looking for something to do, introduces football to this latter-day world, but though he was twice an All-American himself, he can't play now. Nor does he dare to wear a gun. His reflexes simply aren't fast enough to allow him to compete with genetically improved future man.

The central story line of *Beyond This Horizon* would be Heinlein's best attempt to phrase and resolve his great dilemma about the relationship between the man of competence and his society. Heinlein's protagonist, Hamilton Felix, is a man of superior ability who fritters his time away as a designer of what he terms "'silly games for idle people.'" Though the District Moderator for Genetics, Mordan Claude, informs Hamilton that he is a biological crown prince, a genetic star line, the best of the best, he feels like a failure. He lacks a photographic memory, and this has disqualified him from being what he dreamed of becoming as a boy—"an encyclopedic synthesist."

The occupation of synthesist was something that Heinlein had called for in his speech in Denver. His suggestion was that these men of encyclopedic understanding would "make it their business to find out what it is the specialists have learned and then relay it to the rest of us in a consolidated form so that we can have, if not the details of the picture, at least the broad outlines of the enormous, incredibly enormous, mass of data that the human race has gathered."

And he had offered his boyhood hero, H. G. Wells, as his example of a pioneer synthesist. He called him "so far as I know the only writer who has ever lived who has tried to draw for the rest of us a full picture of the whole world, past and future, everything about us, so we can stand off and get a look at ourselves."

This was the kind of man that Hamilton Felix had aimed to be:

> All the really great men were synthesists. Who stood a chance of being elected to the Board of Policy but a synthesist? What specialist was there who did not, in the long run, take his orders from a synthesist? They were the leaders, the men who knew everything, the philosopher-kings of whom the ancients had dreamed.

But when it became apparent to Hamilton that he wouldn't be able to become a synthesist because of his lack of an eidetic memory, everything else available came to look no better than second-best to him. Life seems pointless. His society wants him to have children and fulfill four generations of genetic planning, but he isn't disposed to cooperate. He says to Mordan:

> "You can probably eliminated my misgivings [in my children] and produce a line that will go on happily breeding for the next ten million years. That still doesn't make it make sense. Survival! What for? Until you can give me some convincing explanation why the human race should go on at all, my answer is "no."

However, when a revolution by people who fancy themselves superior and aim to emulate the Great Khans comes along, and they ask Hamilton to join them, he isn't flattered or attracted. The society of *Beyond This Horizon* was the soundest and most uncorrupt, the purest and most ideal that Heinlein could imagine at this moment, and Hamilton Felix, for all his disaffection, finds it worth defending. He serves as a spy and does his best to see the revolt put down.

And when it is, Hamilton's society does him return service. The synthesists of the Board of Policy deem it worthwhile to launch a project to scientifically investigate the fundamental questions of human meaning and purpose, and Hamilton is offered a place in this "Great Research" for the unorthodox quality of his imagination.

At last he has something to do that he finds worth doing. So reconciled does Hamilton become that he even marries the girl picked out as his genetic match and fathers the children the Planners wish him to have.

Along with everything else that *Beyond This Horizon* had to offer—its utopianism, its satire, its future-building, its alternative history-making, and its philosophical ventures—this novel would go at least partway toward solving the intractable evolutionary problem that Heinlein had been banging his head against throughout 1941.

This novel suggested that even human evolution might sometime be domesticated, brought under the conscious direction and control of mankind. So far, so good—especially if you should happen to be a genetic crown prince like Hamilton Felix and not a despised, discriminated-against "control natural," or unimproved man.

However, in *Beyond This Horizon* the larger and more difficult part of the evolutionary question—how humanity might learn to cope with the fact of the existence of superior beings—was scamped. It was acknowledged as a potential problem, but then put out of mind.

That is, in this story there are no other intelligent races in the Solar System. (Mention is made of a news report of the discovery of intelligent life on Ganymede which proved to be erroneous.) And though the Great Research is perfectly willing to concede the possibility of non-human intelligence somewhere else, lacking the starships to go and check, human beings are not soon going to be put on the spot and embarrassed again as they were on the voyage of the *New Frontiers* in Heinlein's other future.

Hamilton Felix does consider the question:

> If there were such [non-human intelligences], then it was possible, with an extremely high degree of mathematical probability, that some of them, at least, were more advanced than men. In which case they might give Man a "leg up" in his philosophical education. They might have discovered "Why" as well as "How".
>
> It had been pointed out that it might be extremely dangerous, psychologically, for human beings to encounter such superior creatures. There had been the tragic case of the Australian Aborigines in not too remote historical times—demoralized and finally exterminated by their own sense of inferiority in the presence of the colonizing Anglish.
>
> The investigators serenely accepted the danger; they were not so constituted as to be able to do otherwise.
>
> Hamilton was not sure it *was* a danger. To some it might be, but he himself could not conceive of a man such as Mordan, for example, losing his morale under any circumstances. In any case it was a long distance project. First they must reach the stars, which required inventing and building a starship. That would take a bit of doing.

In short, the genetically refined society of *Beyond This Horizon* is spared from suffering a rude evolutionary awakening by its own comparative technological ineptitude. Though privately we may wonder whether Mordan Claude really would fare any better in the temple of Kreel than Slayton Ford did, this question is not about to be tested.

Heinlein, however, had clearly not rid himself of his own fear and doubt. This is indicated by his very last pre-war story, "The Unpleasant Profession of Jonathan Hoag," written in April 1942 while he waited to take up war work as an engineer in the Philadelphia Navy Yard. He sent this fantasy short novel to Campbell with the new pseudonym John Riverside, and it would be published in the October 1942 issue of *Unknown*—by then called *Unknown Worlds*.

In this unsettling story, the contemporary world is once again revealed to be a sham. We are offered two Twenties-style explanations to account for its true nature:

There are "the Sons of the Bird"—horrid, powerful Lovecraftian creatures who lurk in the space behind mirrors and yearn to torment and demean us with the knowledge of our own true inferiority. Are they right in their claim to be the proper rulers of our world?

Or is prissy, creepy Jonathan Hoag right when he offers the alternative Cabellian explanation that this world, including the Sons of the Bird, is actually only an interesting botch by a promising young artist on a higher plane of existence? It is Hoag's claim that he is an "art critic" from that superior dimension, here in the form of a man to experience this world from within and determine how much of it, if any, is worth saving.

In either case, however, ordinary human beings and their efforts cannot amount to very much. The best the frightened protagonists of this story, a private detective and his wife, are allowed is to hang on tight to each other and wait to find out what may happen to them.

And on this note, after three intense years at the typewriter, Robert Heinlein ceased storytelling and went off to war. The conundrum of evolutionary superiority was left for somebody else to resolve.

This would be the Canadian writer A. E. van Vogt. But to understand the basis of van Vogt's accomplishment and why it was possible for him to achieve what Heinlein could not, we must first take a look at an aspect of the Golden Age and of universal operating principles that we haven't examined previously.

15

Consciousness
and Reality

The starting place of our story was the great mythic and religious crisis that was initiated in the Western world during the Seventeenth Century—the ultimate impact of which is only being felt now, some three hundred years later. This crisis resulted from the decision by the leading lights of Western thought to draw a basic distinction between matter and spirit, and to cast the fate of the West with matter.

By the Twentieth Century, with the loss of spirit and the misplacement of God, many of the people of the West would come to feel rootless, disoriented, without purpose, and disconnected from reality. Without the moral compass of spirit to guide them, they would be in a quandary to know how to proceed in this new universe of malleable materiality.

If we should say that the citizen of the Age of Technology at his most pitiable was a poor lost lamb, a solitary soul trying his best to be brave even as he was ground into extinction by the vast uncaring material universe, then Atomic Age man at his most bewildered was an amnesiac orphan child awakened to consciousness in a kaleidoscopic world of matter, not quite certain who he was, or where he was, or how he came to be here, yet somehow saddled with an imperative obligation to make choices and to take actions.

But our story hasn't been about the poor fish who were left to gasp and flop on the rough shoals of materiality when the tide of transcendent spirit receded leaving them high and dry. Instead, the story we've had to tell has been of the way in which a succession of dreamers, drug-takers, mystics and science-minded speculators— each generation recognizing and building on the one before it, incorporating its insights and attempting to go it one better—were able to gradually evolve new expressions of transcendence in terms of materialism during the 175 years between the beginning of the Romantic Era and the end of the Age of Technology.

This new matter-based literature of transcendence did not come into being without rejection from both of the great contending parties of the West. To the defenders of spirit, science fiction was impious materialism carried to an extreme of presumption and pride. To simple kick-a-rock materialists, science fiction was contrary to self-evident reality. It was idle fancy. But whichever your belief might be, SF appeared excessive.

It was necessary, then, for SF to make its way where it could, as it could, most usually operating near the fringes of social acceptability. Ultimately, during the Great Depression, even as it was failing in Europe, science fiction would find a small safe niche for itself as the last-established of the specialized American pulp magazine story genres.

But yet, for the relatively small but devoted audience that was able to find it, to read it, and to accept it, SF was the truest, most effective guide that society had to offer to the direction in which the West was headed. It was genuine myth. In the science fiction of one period would be outlined the daily reality of the next. To read SF would be a means of preparation for new jobs, new styles of life and thought and relationship, for change after change after change.

Inventors and explorers, submariners and pioneers of rocketry, theoretical and applied scientists, engineers and technocrats—all of these would grow up finding their ideas of possibility and their sense of direction in SF, and when they went forth to bring the modern world of science and technology into being, it was with images from the stories of Jules Verne, H. G. Wells, Edgar Rice Burroughs and E. E. Smith dancing in their heads.

However, by the end of the Age of Technology, science fiction as a myth of scientific materialism was approaching a dead end—not least because of the very degree of its success.

Material science was losing its former mystery. All the old super-scientific wonders so long imagined in science fiction stories—rockets, computers, television, atomic power—were beginning to come true. As they did, they were ceasing to be transcendent. They were changing from a *might-be* into an *is*.

Even the dark corners of knowledge where the Techno Age had hoped to find wondrous unknowns were being exhausted. As one example, between 1939 and 1945, the last three empty slots in Mendeleev's periodic table of 92 elements were filled in. This meant no more beakers of X the unknown metal, capable of sending a Richard Seaton hurtling off to the stars.

To be on the verge of a new world made in the image of science fiction was intensely exciting for the heirs of Hugo Gernsback. And John Campbell and the writers he influenced were motivated to get things right—to bring their imaginary science into line with the new reality. This meant that the science-beyond-science in *Astounding* became more plausible than it had ever been before. But it also became less mysterious.

Where was new mystery to be found?

In the 1920s and 1930s, at the very moment that Techno Age science fiction was mastering space and time with the aid of transcendence based in matter, advanced Western thought had taken a very strange new turn. Atomic physicists, seeking to locate and identify the ultimate fine grit out of which existence is made, fell through matter entirely and out the other side.

Underlying the visible material world, they found a hitherto unknown subatomic level of existence. This substrate was more fundamental than our familiar realm of being—it was the stuff out of which the things we see and hear and smell and taste and touch are made. But this stuff, whatever it was, wasn't matter in the usual sense. It was something very different, paradoxical and elusive.

In our world—as science was accustomed to dealing with it—matter has surface and substance. It can be observed directly. It can be weighed and measured and manipulated. Most important of all, in interactions of matter it is possible to attribute effects to antecedent causes. All of the efforts and successes of material science had been based upon this premise.

In the microcosmic world, however, none of these things would prove to hold true. As Werner Heisenberg, the brilliant young physicist who won the Nobel Prize in 1932 for his contributions to the foundation of quantum mechanics, would eventually come to put it: "All the words or concepts we use to describe ordinary physical objects, such as position, velocity, color, size and so on, become indefinite and problematic if we try to use them of elementary particles."

Here are some of the strangenesses and difficulties that arise in dealing with the microcosm:

In contrast to the mass and extension that characterize our sphere, the world within the atom would be overwhelmingly empty. The apparent solidity of the things we see around us would be revealed as an illusion.

In the world of conventional scientific experience, elements are what they are. In the microcosm, however, matter could be energy in another form, light would be simultaneously a wave and a particle, and elements might be transmuted from one kind to another.

This underlying level of being could not be observed directly, but only by means of its impact upon scientific instruments. But human-made recording devices would be severely limited in what they could report about the microcosm.

In the subatomic realm, cause-and-effect would not hold true. Here events would occur in terms of probabilities.

What is more, for scientists to make any attempt to spy upon the workings of the microcosm would inevitably be to influence what was observed. Whatever they selected to look for would absolutely determine the nature of the results they got.

This new subatomic level of being might not be the old spirit realm. But, clearly, neither was it any simple cause-and-effect, weigh-and-measure world of tangible lumps where the kicking of rocks could serve as a sufficient test of reality. It was a whole new facet of existence.

It was undeniable that the quantum world did exist. It would be confirmed, in all its strangeness, by experiment after experiment. Its actuality would underlie one aspect of the coming Atomic Age after another, from the atom bomb to the computer chip.

But what *was* it that was lurking down there beyond the range of our ability to see and touch?

Max Born would think that it was probability waves.

Werner Heisenberg would suggest that it was mathematical forms, which he would identify with Platonic Ideas.

A.S. Eddington would simply say, "Something unknown is doing we don't know what."

The kind of understanding human beings were to have of our interactions with this realm of uncertainty and indeterminacy was even more problematic. What were we to make of the fact that poking it with one kind of stick gave one kind of result, and that poking it with another kind of stick would just as consistently yield the contrary?

The first construction of this to be offered would be the so-called "Copenhagen interpretation" of Danish physicist Niels Bohr in 1927. Bohr would suggest that quantum phenomena come into being only as they are observed. That human intention partly determines what the structure of the physical world shall be. That the human mind is a creator of reality.

Albert Einstein couldn't accept this, and at physics conferences in the late Twenties, he did his best to overturn Bohr. At last, however, he ran out of arguments and had to step back out of the way of the further development of physics.

Other physicists, however, would be more ready than Einstein to accept quantum mechanics—and to take in stride the fact that to do so was to admit the previous insufficiency and the future incompleteness of modern Western science.

There was a considerable irony here. Science had routed spirit in large measure by its claim to be able to answer all questions through weighing and measuring. But at the very moment of spirit's failure, here was advanced science ready to admit that perhaps it had been a bit over-optimistic in the claims it had formerly made. It would appear that there were undeniable fundamental entities that Western science was inherently unable to weigh and measure.

The old-time language of spirit had largely been left behind during the long passage through materialism, so when the time came for the Twentieth Century physicist-turned-philosopher to step forward and attempt to explain this new-found mystery to the general public, he was unlikely to resort to the bygone vocabulary of traditional religious belief. Instead, he was apt to speak in the contemporary terms of mind and consciousness.

Here is how Eddington would say it:

> To put the conclusion crudely—the stuff of the world is mind-stuff. As is often the way with crude statements, I shall have to explain that by "mind" I do not here exactly mean mind and by "stuff" I do not at all mean stuff. Still, this is about as near as we can get to the idea in a simple phrase. The mind-stuff of the world is, of course, something more general than our individual conscious minds, but we may think of its nature as not altogether foreign to the feelings in our consciousness. The realistic matter and fields of force of former physical theory are altogether irrelevant—except in so far as the mind-stuff has spun these imaginings.

And he would say further:

"The mind-stuff is the aggregation of relations and relata which form the building material for the physical world."

We might compare this to A. Merritt writing in *The Metal Monster* in 1920, half-a-dozen years before the devising of quantum mechanics:

> Is there a sea of this conscious force which laps the shores of the farthest-flung stars; that finds expression in everything—man and rock, metal and flower, jewel and cloud? Limited in its expression only by the limitation of that which it animates, and in essence the same in all.

The answer that scientists like Bohr and Jeans and Eddington would come to give to Merritt's question would be: "Yes, indeed. Allowing for poetic expression, this is very much the way we suppose things to be."

But there should be no surprise that they and Merritt should perceive things in such highly similar terms. In the early Twentieth Century, a considerable number of Western artists and scientists were beginning to look to *consciousness* as an emerging name for mystery.

This new awareness of mind as an unknown—perhaps the fundamental unknown—was an almost inevitable result of the failure of spirit.

Mind had figured centrally in the origin of the modern Western adventure back in the Seventeenth Century. It was a series of three vivid dreams on the night of November 10, 1619 that prompted the young René Descartes to begin the radical philosophical inquiry that resulted in the foundation of the modern scientific method. And, even before he made his basic division between matter and spirit, Descartes' initial conclusion in his seminal work, *A Discourse on Method* (1637)—the first principle of his philosophy—was "I think, hence I am."

In elaboration upon this, Descartes would go on to say:

> I...concluded that I was a substance whose whole essence or nature consists only in thinking, and which, that it may exist, has need of no place, nor is dependent on any material thing; so that "I," that is to say, the mind by which I am what I am, is wholly distinct from the body, and is even more easily known than the latter, and is such, that although the latter were not, it would still continue to be all that it is.

This is where modern Western science would begin: with one man's dream of himself as being in essence a disembodied thought—a placeless, immaterial atom of consciousness observing itself and the material world around it, including its own accidental outward trappings of flesh and blood—and that man's ability to convince others that they were creatures of this same kind.

Until the 1920s and the advent of quantum physics, the dream of complete objectivity would be a continuing unexamined assumption of modern science. Western scientists would believe that they could stand outside materiality and observe it without affecting it, or, for that matter, being affected by it.

But the immaterial pea of consciousness at the center of things, watching and thinking, would be largely forgotten or ignored. Indeed, as the Western concentration upon the study of matter came to prove more and more fruitful, there was a tendency on the part of the heirs and successors of Descartes to identify completely with matter and to lump mind with spirit as an ephemerality that was outside the scope of legitimate scientific investigation. Mind was something that couldn't be seen, heard, touched, smelled or tasted. At best, it could only be inferred. Perhaps it was some kind of effervescent froth bubbling up spontaneously out of matter. Or maybe it was all an illusion. In any event, to a good simple materialist, mind was a very doubtful area of inquiry.

Psychology—a word that was used to mean knowledge of the soul before it was adapted to changing times and employed to mean the study of the mind—was the last of the major scientific disciplines to be established, arising in the Nineteenth Century out of natural philosophy and medicine. And, perhaps because it was so lacking in material substance and so vulnerable to suspicions of being spiritualism in covert guise, psychology struggled all the harder to establish itself as serious exact science.

Thus it was that in the early Twentieth Century psychometricians would come forward with tests that were claimed to measure human mental capacity with precision. And by the early Twenties, the victory of matter over spirit would even lead to the establishment of one American school of psychology, the behaviorists, that would attempt to model itself upon the prototypical hard science—Nineteenth Century cause-and-effect physics.

The behaviorists would recognize no necessity at all for the hypothesis of mind. They would completely repudiate both consciousness and purpose. Instead, they would presume to account for all human behavior in terms of external stimulus-and-response.

The founder of behaviorism, Dr. John B. Watson, would say: "Psychology, as the behaviorist views it, is a purely objective, experimental branch of natural science which needs introspection as little as do the sciences of chemistry and physics."

At this very moment, contemporary physicists like Eddington might be rising to declare that the Nineteenth Century verities on which the science of behavior had so recently been founded—materialism, mechanism, determinism and objectivity—actually amounted to no more than irrelevant imaginings spun by the underlying mindstuff. But to behavioral engineers like Watson, or his Atomic Age disciple and successor, Harvard University's B. F. Skinner, remarks such as this could only appear dismayingly mentalistic, a craven retreat from the clarity and certitude of objective science into some very thinly disguised last-minute attempt to hang on to spirit.

However, there would be other Techno Age scientific investigators of mind who would be led in the opposite direction from behaviorism by the failure of spirit and the triumph of matter, toward a widening instead of a narrowing of their subject. These would mainly be physiologists and psychiatrists—medical doctors—rather than academic psychologists. These medical men had practical experience of the sometimes untidy facts of actual human thinking and behavior, as well as intimate experimental knowledge of the functioning of the human brain, sense organs, and nervous system, not merely thumbs grown calloused from clicking stopwatches over the heads of laboratory rats being taught to run through mazes.

The more doubtful spirit came to appear, the less possible these doctors found it to continue lumping the phenomena of mind in with spirit as a convenient way to dismiss them without having to give them serious consideration. To men like this, it was evident that even if spirit were to be thrown out completely as a legitimate explanation of anything and everything, all the strange thoughts, beliefs, practices and happenings associated with the mind would continue to remain as something requiring careful scientific investigation and explanation.

A. Merritt's friend and instructor, Dr. Silas Weir Mitchell, is an example of one such physician. So early in the game was his work done that he wouldn't be known as either a physiologist or a psychiatrist, but rather as a specialist in nervous disorders. To Dr. Mitchell, it would be apparent that the human mind was a mystery, and he would attack the problem both through the direct examination of the human brain and nervous system and through the investigation of bizarre and anomalous mental phenomena.

Techno Age physiologists would directly address the question of how the brain gathers data from the sensory organs, and at every step in the process they would find limitation and the possibility of error:

First, years of experimentation demonstrated that the discriminating powers of the human senses are distinctly limited, both in comparson with the sensory powers of other creatures and in comparison with the ranges of data detected by scientific instruments.

It was also shown that sensory data encountered by human beings had first to be turned into nerve impulses that then travel at finite speed to the brain—and only there become processed into the sights and sounds and smells we believe ourselves to be experiencing directly.

Physiologists and their psychologist allies would further demonstrate that of the limited data that are received by the senses and passed along to the brain, only a comparatively small portion actually make their way through the mental veils of awareness into conscious attention.

And, finally, they would prove again and again that human beings could be tricked by illusion, ambiguity, unexpectedness, and their own preconceptions into seeing and hearing what wasn't there and into misinterpreting what actually did occur. It would become a favored ploy of instructors in Twentieth Century introductory psychology courses to stage some sudden unanticipated dramatic happening as a means of showing students what partial and subjective witnesses they actually are.

Taken in sum, these various physical and perceptual investigations amounted to a heavy assault on the unexamined bases of modern Western science. Certainly, they cast considerable doubt on René Descartes' initial conclusion that the essence of a human being like himself was some remote objective intelligence that could operate alone and apart from the body and examine the nature of matter with a rational and dispassionate eye.

We might recall that Descartes' initial sense of himself as a disembodied mind had had its origin in a dream—certainly not the most rational and dispassionate of mental states. And, indeed, at the beginning of the Twentieth Century, the Viennese psychiatrist Sigmund Freud would take studies of the mind into a whole new dimension through a close examination of the unconscious significance of dreams.

Freud's study of dreams would convincingly demonstrate their non-rational nature. Beyond this, he would show the existence of a number of mental processes whose existence and import were not known to the ordinary conscious awareness.

However, Freud's own explanatory model of what he discovered would still be limited and mechanistic in its origin. He would think in terms of compartments, pipes and valves, as though the mind were a kind of steam boiler, and he would see the new dimension of mind as an overload chamber into which materials that the conscious mind was unable to handle, primarily sexual, could be shunted to relieve excessive pressure.

Freud's one-sidedly sexual orientation and the narrowness and rigidity of his mechanistic and deterministic thinking would eventually cause all of his earliest allies and disciples to leave him and go off on their own paths.

In 1912, Freud's most favored early disciple, the Swiss psychiatrist Carl Jung, would break with him after five years of connection. To all appearance, the disagreement would be over the significance of dreams and how they were to be interpreted. But this would only be the outward sign of a more fundamental unspoken quarrel between them about the nature and scope of the new mental dimension.

Dreams for Freud were symptoms of repressed thought. But for Jung, dreams were messages from the unconscious, not always immediately comprehensible because they were couched in the language of symbol, but nonetheless purposeful in their structure and intention.

The real difference between the two pioneer psychiatrists, however, was that Freud perceived the new unknown aspect of mind as a *sub*conscious, a closed auxiliary basement chamber. For him, dreams were clues to the sexual sludge that must be cleaned out of the system if the conscious were to function properly.

Jung, however, visualized the new reaches of mind as an *un*conscious, a great undiscovered country much vaster in its dimensions than the meagre territory encompassed by the individual conscious mind. Some of what might be discovered there assuredly did consist of thoughts repressed by the individual, but by far the greater part of the unconscious was common to the collectivity of man. For Jung, dreams were messages from out of this darkness, demanding interpretation.

Dreams would not be his only clues. Jung would look everywhere for points of entry into the labyrinth of the unconscious. He might be thought of as a medically trained investigator sifting through all the purported evidences of transcendent mystery that had been collected by the Romantics during the previous century, but then left to gather dust in the attics of the Western world. Among these were alternate states of consciousness, anomalous happenings like poltergeist phenomena, the expressions and beliefs of past cultures and foreign cultures, literary and artistic symbology, myth and religion.

To Sigmund Freud, Jung could only seem a prodigal son who had elected to turn his back on Freud's authority and the certainty of material science in order to go scrambling and panting after that old whore *spirit*. In truth, however, it was in the realm of the unconscious mind and not in the spirit world that Jung was searching for contemporary transcendence. It wasn't that he was using mind as a veil for old-fashioned religiosity so much as that he was attempting to preserve for his time whatever was still viable in former vocabularies of transcendence and to translate this into the new terms of mind.

To Jung, accepting the plunge into the unconscious was the necessary road to self-transcendence—the overcoming of limitations and the attainment of higher states. For the patient, the hope was for the integration of the conscious and the unconscious mind. For the artist, the aim was acts of genuine creativity. And for Western culture in general, the goal was the successful surmounting of the current state of excessive rationality.

On each of these levels, Jung would have his natural allies. These would include all of those who had sufficiently come to terms with the new existential Twentieth Century reality that they were prepared to trust their own individual experience above received authority of whatever stripe—and who had come to recognize mystery in the workings of their own minds. Included, too, would be all of those artists and writers of the day, from James Joyce and Pablo Picasso to A. Merritt, who were starting to look to consciousness for their orientation and inspiration. And finally, included would be the new quantum physicists with their challenge to the completeness and sufficiency of Western science and their tendency to suggest that the apparent material world is spun out of mind-stuff.

In the end, Jung would be able to progress about as far in his line of inquiry as the quantum physicists would get in theirs. That is, both of these new areas of study—the psychology of the unconscious and quantum mechanics—demonstrated the existence of heretofore unrecognized aspects of being lurking as near to us as the napes of our own necks. Both of these unknowns would persistently elude precise rational scrutiny. Both called into question the basic assumptions of modern Western thought. And, ultimately, the two might even be identical, even though one was nominally the understructure of matter and the other was nominally the night side of mind.

Taken together, quantum mechanics and Twentieth Century psychology—the psychology of the unconscious, in particular—may be understood as the first steps in the emergence of a new phase in Western social and psychic evolution that could be termed post-materialistic.

SF, dealing as it always does in best knowledge and in the areas of mystery beyond best knowledge, could not be oblivious to these new developments. But recognizing what they meant and then applying the implications to science fiction stories was no simple and obvious task. Not only would it take years to assimilate the new physics and the new psychology, but in the process SF literature would be altered into something different from the fiction of transcendent science that it had formerly been.

The first major agent of this change—in part knowingly, but in even larger part despite himself—would be John W. Campbell, the editor of *Astounding*. For exactly as long as he was able to hold together states of mind that were ultimately incompatible through a pure faith that he would be able to make them come out even in the long run, Campbell was the perfect person to oversee the transformation of materialism into emergent post-materialism. The contradictions in his own thought and character were exactly suited to the needs of this moment.

The inner conflict that was the driving force of John Campbell's nature was that he loved science, but hated finality and constraint.

John Campbell was born the son of a scientific man in the midst of an era of unprecedented scientific and technological achievement. For someone living in this hour and raised in this family, science was the only possible path to follow. And at some very early moment in his life, John did make a fundamental identification with the precision of science, the curiosity of science and the practical power of science to get things done.

At the same time, however, the young Campbell deeply resented his father's authoritarian style, his claims of scientific objectivity, and his automatic presumption in any conflict that he must be the possessor of the true facts. John gradually discovered that the way to successfully oppose and confound his father was to be more scientific than he was—to be more objective, to know more of the actual facts of the matter, and to argue them better.

The young Campbell extended this attitude to school. He began to challenge the pronouncements of his instructors, refusing to accept that they could be any kind of final word. After all, most of his teachers knew a good bit less than his father did, and his father was very often wrong.

By the time he got to college, he was so established in this pattern that when one professor stated that the amalgamation of iron was an impossibility, John brought an experimental apparatus into chemistry class and showed that he was mistaken. And when another declared that ball lightning could not exist because there was no theoretical basis for such a phenomenon, Campbell was ready to stand and say that he himself had witnessed ball lightning and knew for a fact that it did exist, whether it could be explained theoretically or not.

Eventually, the young Campbell grew to perceive himself as a person committed to a nobler and purer standard of science than that observed by the ordinary scientific man. He was more open to strange facts. He was more ready to ask difficult questions. His frame of reference was larger.

As a corollary of this line of thought, it would begin to seem more and more clear to him that he could no longer continue to accept the authority and sufficiency of present-day science. In the scientific romances and scientifiction stories that he'd read, Campbell had caught convincing glimpses of the wonders of man's progress to come. And Campbell was also aware that from Newton to Einstein, those scientists who were genuinely of the first rank had always been frank to admit their true degree of ignorance and limitation.

To Campbell, it appeared an absolute certainty that whatever modern science might have managed to accomplish thus far, and whatever it might think it knew at the present moment, there was yet much more to be learned—and much, much more to be accomplished. Present formulations were bound to be superseded. New discoveries would be made. What was not possible now would become possible in time.

That was the kind of science that John Campbell wanted to associate himself with. If he was going to be a scientist, it seemed to him that the only kind of scientist worth being was a meta-scientist—one who was able to separate himself from the orthodoxy and ignorance of the current moment and look beyond them to perceive what might *really* be possible.

Henceforth, the only authority that Campbell would agree to acknowledge was the authority of the universe—the final arbiter. But nobody else and nothing less than that.

This would mean that at the first moment and again at the last, John Campbell would be ready to rise and join more conventional scientists in their ritual pledge of allegiance to the power and truth and inviolability of the laws of the universe as indicated by modern science. But at every other instant, as a measure of his true respect for them, he would be attempting to test these rules to discover for himself how aptly they had been phrased and how well they were actually understood.

The true scientific challenge, as Campbell perceived it, had to be the discovery of the overlooked principle, the odd implication, the unconventional application, the hidden clause, the loophole or the exception that would permit the accomplishment of all those things that lesser men were content to assume could never be done.

This ideal of science would be written large in Campbell's earliest SF, produced while he was still in college and published under his own name. These stories were simple exuberant dramatizations of the wondrous power of science-to-come. His characters would twist the tail of the universe, produce a new principle of super-science, and then hie themselves off to have some fun with it, traveling to the stars or another dimension, blowing up planets and suns, and showing off in front of alien races.

It was only natural that a young John Campbell with an eye for the unorthodox but undeniable should glance in the direction of quantum physics and Twentieth Century psychology. These new areas of mystery were exactly the sort of exceptions to the completeness of contemporary science that he was seeking.

Quantum mechanics was a center of heated scientific debate when Campbell first went off to study at M.I.T. in 1928. He had to become fascinated by advanced science that was inherently paradoxical, that didn't make any sense at all in the familiar terms of received physics, and yet that was able to stand up to one challenge after another from the likes of Albert Einstein. If he hadn't gotten caught up in writing science fiction—and if he hadn't flunked German—he liked to think that he would have become an atomic physicist playing with the nature of possibility.

Then at Duke, Campbell's second university, he wandered somewhat farther afield in his search for science reaching beyond the bounds of science. He offered himself as an experimental subject—of no special distinction, as it turned out—in the pioneer efforts of Dr. Joseph Rhine to study telepathy and other forms of extrasensory perception scientifically.

It would, of course, be no accident that of all the different investigations of mind that Campbell might have chosen to involve himself with, the one that he did pick—Rhine's parapsychology— was designed along the lines of an experiment in physical science. As avid as he was for strangeness, it was Campbell's long-term expectation that the powers of the mind, and quantum uncertainty, too, would eventually be brought within the rule and understanding of material science.

But yet, despite all the interest Campbell was taking in the new Twentieth Century wild science, neither consciousness nor probability was more than peripheral matter in his earliest stories of men having fun with science-beyond-science. However, during his second and more thoughtful writing career as Don A. Stuart, this would gradually come to change.

The alternate writing persona of Don A. Stuart was invented by Campbell to deal with a problem that was completely beyond the scope of simple, super-scientific "John W. Campbell, Jr." This problem was the Techno Age dilemma—which was the same as the essential contradictions at the core of his own nature:

It was science that had brought the Western world, and John Campbell, too, to their present state of thought and development. And both the society (with a certain amount of doubt) and Campbell, Jr.-the-science-fiction-writer (with no apparent doubts at all) were counting on further science to be the means that would carry mankind beyond the limitations of the present moment.

But it seemed that this very same science in which so much faith was placed was also prepared to declare that do whatever he would, in time man must inevitably be brought low. The laws of nature—whether they be called fate, determinism, cyclical history or entropy—guaranteed that humanity must fail and the universe must perish.

Here was a thoroughly nasty fact that had to be faced:

Underneath the apparent invitation of its smile, the science that supported man today and promised him marvelous new accomplishments tomorrow wore the chilly grin of a messenger of death.

How was that to be dealt with? If John Campbell couldn't find an answer, it seemed that all the whooping and hollering he'd been doing on behalf of the power, fun and noise of science-to-come was only so much whistling past the graveyard.

To his credit, once he had recognized this basic conundrum, Campbell didn't shy away from it. Clearly and unflinchingly, in "The Last Evolution" under his own name, and in "Twilight" and "Night" as Don A. Stuart, Campbell dramatized the scientific case for the passing of mankind, the passing of man's mechanical off-spring, and the passing of the universe.

Having done this, Campbell then set out to take the true measure of this ultimately final finality. There was nothing he wasn't ready to examine, no question he dared not pursue, no authority he wasn't prepared to challenge.

In the stories that he wrote during the Thirties in the person of Don A. Stuart, Campbell put man and universe to the test. He tested humanity's ability to cope with advanced aliens. He tested mankind's relationship with the machine. He tested the scientific process. He tested natural law. And at each turn, he looked for the crucial misunderstanding or ignorance or alternate possibility that would permit men to survive and to prevail.

Campbell's ongoing interest in consciousness and probability began to become more specific during this second science fiction writing career as Don A. Stuart. If in former times he'd only thought of these new areas of study as exceptions to the completeness of contemporary science, now he began to value their common ability to contradict the absolute power of determinism.

Eventually, Campbell managed to evolve an argument, a provisional answer to the problem of human fate that he had set himself to solve. Effectively, the argument ran like this:

What appears determined to us now may only be the reflection of our current state of limited understanding. The brilliant but still rudimentary achievements of modern science give us cause to believe in the existence of the Laws of the Universe, but as of yet we don't know what those Laws actually are. Indeterminacy suggests the possibility of free will. Wild talents suggest the existence of possible higher states of consciousness. The best course for humanity is to keep striving to learn and apply the real Laws of the Universe, and to deal with problems as they arise. In due course, Man will find out what is actually possible, and anything that is possible he will contrive to do.

We can see this argument unfolding in the last few stories that Campbell wrote under the Stuart name. In "Forgetfulness," he said that humanity was not yet finished growing up, and that man's future would ultimately lie not with his artifacts, but in the full development of his mental powers. And in "Who Goes There?," Campbell suggested that if natural law was truly universal, applying everywhere and to everything, then men might be able to turn that universality into a tool which no alien creature, however awful or powerful it might be, could possibly deny.

The final Don A. Stuart story was "The Elder Gods," a short novel written in a rush by Campbell to fill a hole in the October 1939 issue of *Unknown*. Here Campbell linked consciousness and indeterminacy and pitted the two against the forces of mechanism and fate.

"The Elder Gods" takes place in a remote future moment, long after our civilization has destroyed itself. Its setting is a country where men "'know more of minds and the works of the power of mind than any people of the Earth.'"

But this island society has grown isolated and static. It has fallen under the sway of a set of man-created "gods," mechanistic in nature, who deal in inflexible logic and the "'absolutes of nature's laws.'"

However, set in opposition to these entities is another, older group of gods, who are described as crystalized thought-forms and identified with chance. These elder gods draft a shipwrecked adventurer into service as their chosen instrument, and this bold fellow proves able to overturn the usurper gods and re-establish free will amongst the people of this land.

Don A. Stuart went off into permanent retirement after this story with a public explanation that the press of work made him too busy to continue writing science fiction. But the special line of inquiry that Campbell had been pursuing under the Stuart name would go on. In fact, John Campbell would tell his writers that it was really Don A. Stuart who was now editing *Astounding*.

The most pressing item that Stuart/Campbell had on his agenda as editor of *Astounding* was to counter the perceived power of cyclical history and the certainty of eventual human decline and failure. In place of Techno Age fatalism, he aimed to open up the future and outer space and offer man his fair chance to master them.

Any tool that promised to advance this work, Campbell would employ. But the tools he most favored were the ones he had been working out in his Don A. Stuart stories: indeterminacy/free will, consciousness/wild talents, and universal operating principles.

Campbell would feature stories of unusual states of consciousness and stories of shifting realities in *Astounding* from the beginning of his editorship. In fact, the very first story that he would deem new and different enough to dub a "Mutant" in 1938, that initial year of constant deliberate change in the magazine, was Jack Williamson's serial novel *The Legion of Time*—originally announced in "In Times to Come" under the title *The Legion of Probability*. And the first two contributions to *Astounding* by L. Ron Hubbard, "The Dangerous Dimension" and *The Tramp*, would be wild talent stories concerning teleportation and the mental power to kill and to heal.

At this early moment, it wouldn't yet be clear which of Campbell's chosen weapons was truly paramount. But, if anything, the implicit weight of presumption was on the side of universal operating principles.

That is, if there were no problems the universe could present to man that he couldn't grab by the tail and turn to his own advantage, then it seemed likely that one way or another mental phenomena and quantum reality, too, would eventually be tamed and placed under the rule of law. And if in the meantime mind and reality were to run a little bit wild, that was quite all right as long as the cast-iron future which condemned men to decline and extinction was controverted.

Once more, we ought to stress that the phrase "universal operating principles" was never used in the pages of the Campbell *Astounding*. We coined it ourselves in the course of writing this book, taking our cue from Buckminster Fuller, as a way of expressing the characteristic attitude and approach to natural law favored by Campbell, by Fuller, and by other systems-minded innovative thinkers of their generation.

However, as we've seen in some detail, what we are electing to call universal operating principles were implicit in the way that John Campbell wrote and talked and related to his writers. They were the key assumption underlying the changes that Campbell made in the structure and direction of *Astounding* after he became editor. Most especially, they were depicted in all of those new laws and systems that he and his chief writers were so busily imagining into existence.

At the same time, it is necessary for us to recognize that even in this exhilarating golden moment of creativity, this most central concept was still tacit, unspoken, inexpressible. It was picked up. It was caught. It was snatched out of the air. But it was never defined and it was never explained.

However, if we range ahead in time a little to November 1953, we can locate a moment in which the parameters—and the contradictions—of Campbell's universal operating principles would be expressed about as clearly as they ever would be. Here in the handclap between two different Campbellian statements we can recognize the basis upon which the Golden Age *Astounding* was constructed.

The first statement comes from a letter that John Campbell wrote to Dr. Joseph Rhine on November 23, 1953, seeking recognition from the parapsychologist for all the wild talent stories he was publishing in *Astounding*. In the course of this letter, Campbell said, "Almost any first-rate, young, experimental research director will most freely and happily assure you that physics doesn't know its ABC's yet—and certainly hasn't reached D!"

He went on:

> Your group, you know, is not the only group that finds the laws of physics seem to be breaking down at the edges. The nuclear physicists find that. So do the men at White Sands, where rocket research is probing out into something called "space," and coming back with answers that don't match anything the hypotheses of physics, sometimes known as "laws" of physics, call for....
>
> Physicists aren't one whit disturbed; physicists never did think the "laws" were anything more than temporarily useful methods of organizing data for reference and filing. It's the non-physicists who consider physical law to be final.

Clearly enough spoken. But even while Campbell was writing these words to Rhine, the latest issue of *Astounding* was just appearing on the newsstands. Campbell's editorial in this December 1953 issue was entitled "The Scientist," and what he had to say here was very different from what he was saying to Rhine.

In "The Scientist," Campbell wrote:

> Many of the fine scientists I know and have known appear to me to act on a system of beliefs somewhat like this:
>
> They believe in the existence of a Supreme Authority in the Universe, an Authority they call "Natural Law." They hold that that Authority is above and beyond the opinions and beliefs, the will or willfulness, of any human being. That that Authority can, moreover, be directly consulted by any man, at any time—and that every man is, at every time and in every place, directly and specifically obedient to that Authority, to Natural Law, whether he recognizes that fact or not.
>
> They believe that the highest task of Man is to seek to understand more fully the nature of the Laws of the Universe.
>
> That the highest good of Man is achieved by understanding and working with those Laws, and not by seeking to defy them.
>
> That the system of laws is absolutely inescapable, but that any *individual* law can be offset by proper use of the others of the total system of laws....
>
> That Man thus has free choice with respect to any situation—but he cannot rationally speak of having free choice as to whether he will or will not obey the total system of the Laws of the Universe.

So which was it really? Were physical laws nothing more than temporarily useful methods of organizing data for reference and filing, or were they the Supreme Authority in the universe, above and beyond the opinions and beliefs of any human being?

The truth is that Campbell would have it both ways, depending on which interpretation was more convenient. When law appeared ready to give him what he wanted, he would suggest that law was something that human beings could consult at any time, understand and work with, and thereby achieve their ends. But when law seemed to forbid and deny his hopes, then Campbell would claim that what was being taken for law was only inadequate contemporary understanding, and look beyond it for the sounder comprehension or the effective combination of other laws that would allow Man to have his way.

Universal operating principles were Campbell's attempt to bridge the gap between "law" and Law—between human half-knowledge and Ultimate Authority. They were an assertion that there was an intimate connection between the two, and that the more closely that humanity could make its "law" conform to True Law, the more power and authority would pass into the hands of Man.

At the same time, universal operating principles were a flexible, pragmatic, engineering approach to the question of "law" and Law. To Campbell, it didn't actually matter which one he had hold of, as long as the job got done.

As he put it in his letter to Rhine:

"The engineer is a hard-working man, and in his frame of reference, theory is an interesting side-light—anything that he can use effectively, on the other hand, is a good and respected tool. 'To hell with *why* it works! Let's make it work.'"

But always at the heart of Campbell's version of natural law there would remain an area of fundamental ambiguity that in its way was not unlike the uncertainty lurking at the heart of the atom.

To conservative interpreters among his authors, universal operating principles could continue to look like old-fashioned, rigid, deterministic, now-and-for-all-time Laws. Seen this way, they were a last attempt to maintain the original tenets of modern Western science, a final expression of Cartesian and Newtonian cause-and-effect thinking.

To more radical writers, however, universal operating principles would just be "law," convenient approximations, reflections of the particular biases of human perception and presumption. In this mode, it is possible for us to recognize universal operating principles as an early attempt to express emergent post-materialistic concepts—specifically, that both the patterns of human thought and the habits of the universe may be subject to change.

In practice, the writers of the Golden Age would flip-flop between one interpretation and the other, just like Campbell. A good example is to be seen in the fantasy novels contributed to *Unknown* by Fletcher Pratt and L. Sprague de Camp.

In "The Roaring Trumpet" and "The Mathematics of Magic," it appears to be "law"—an imperfectly understood and operated system of symbolic equations—that is used to transfer Harold Shea and Dr. Chalmers to other worlds. But within a given alternate world, it would seem to be Law that holds sway. At least, once the proper decimal place has been found, the "laws of magic" operate with something like the predictability and exactitude of our own laws of chemistry and physics.

However, what if an alternate world did not observe fixed Law? Such would be the case in de Camp's and Pratt's last published pre-war fantasy novel, *The Land of Unreason* (*Unknown Worlds*, Oct 1941).

In this story, an American diplomat, Fred Barber, is carried off as a changeling to Fairyland—that realm of magic presented in Shakespeare's *Midsummer Night's Dream*.

And early on, Oberon, the King of Fairyland, tells Barber:

"'Look you—you come from a land where natural law is immutable as the course of the planets. But in our misfortunate realm there's nought fixed; the very rules of life change at times, altogether, without warning and in no certain period.'"

The truth of this statement would be explicitly demonstrated late in the story. Barber has this crucial exchange with the apple dryad Malacea, which is initiated by a protest from Barber that things in this world aren't logical. Malacea asks:

"What does that mean? A magic word?"

"No, it means according to the laws of consistent reasoning. Things equal to the same thing are equal to each other, nothing can be both true and false, and two and two make four."

"A mortal word; and like most such, not true."

"Oh, but it is." Barber disengaged himself and picked up four pebbles, two in each hand. "Look," he said, "two!" and then opened the other hand to show the others. "Two!" He clapped the two hands together and opened them again. "Four!"

"No," said Malacea.

Barber looked and gaped. His opened hands held five pebbles.

It might have been an accident, or she might have dropped one in. He tossed away the extra stone, shut both hands resolutely, and clapped them together again.

"Now will you admit there are four?" he demanded belligerently.

"No," said Malacea. She was right. There were eight pebbles....

So disconcerting is this to Barber that he not only drops Malacea, with whom he has become intimate, but henceforth will never take another apple dryad as a lover. There is logic for you!

However, the fact that really must be taken account of is that Pratt's and de Camp's Land of Unreason was not essentially different from the cosmos that Campbell was constructing in *Astounding* and *Unknown* with the aid of universal operating principles. The closer we look, the clearer it becomes that indeterminacy and mentalism were to be found everywhere within the Campbellian multiverse.

We can find our example in the Harold Shea stories. In the course of this series, de Camp and Pratt offer two conflicting rationales for the existence of a multiplicity of alternate worlds:

In "The Mathematics of Magic," Shea asks Dr. Chalmers how it is that even though the laws of magic do not operate in our own universe, they do make an appearance in our fantasy stories. Chalmers answers:

> "The question is somewhat obvious. You remember my remarking that dements suffered hallucinations because their personalities were split between this universe and another? The same applies to the composers of fairy tales, though to a lesser degree. Naturally, it would apply to any writer of fantasy, such as Dunsany or Hubbard. When he describes some strange world, he is offering a somewhat garbled version of a real one, having its own set of dimensions quite independent of ours."

However, at the outset of the third story in the series, "Castle of Iron" (*Unknown*, Apr 1941), Harold Shea and his friends go astray in their travels and find themselves watching belly dancers at an Oriental banquet in the world described by the Romantic writer Samuel Taylor Coleridge in his poem "Xanadu." And Harold Shea takes this as a crisis.

He says: "'That puts us in a jam. You remember the poem was unfinished. It might refer to an incomplete universe, one that is fixed in a certain set of actions, like a phonograph needle in a groove. If that's the case, this performance might go on forever.'"

So which of these is true? Do these alternate realms of being have independent existence that is glimpsed by writers of fantasy and participated in by madmen? Or are these other worlds constructs of the mind of some poet that exist with only the degree of completeness with which they were first imagined?

The answer is indeterminate. Pratt and de Camp have it both ways, and give us no reason to prefer one explanation to the other. But either way, whether alternate worlds are merely glimpsed from afar, or whether they are constructs of a poet's imagination, consciousness underlies the human experience of these other worlds.

Not only would the multiverse be mental in nature, but it would also be true that in every single instance of universal operating principles that we have discussed to this point, some crucial mental aspect can be discerned.

We might recall, for instance, the very first official mutation in *Astounding*—those bold new scientifically accurate astronomical covers featuring spacesuited human beings at large in the most distant reaches of the Solar System.

Where did consciousness intrude in these scenes? In publishing the first of them—a picture of the Sun as seen from the surface of Mercury—on the cover of the February 1938 issue of *Astounding*, Campbell made an editorial point of declaring that what was being depicted was not reality, but *things as they would appear to human perception.* He presented sketches showing how much larger the Moon rising above the horizon seems to a human observer than it actually is. And he promised, "As in this first, *mutant* cover, so in all of the series to come, our astronomical color-plate covers will be as accurate an impression as astronomical science and knowledge of human reaction can make them."

A closely parallel instance is to be seen in Isaac Asimov's pivotal novelet "Nightfall." Here again what would be presented would appear to be a natural, factual situation—a problem to be settled by science—that instead would prove to be a question of human thought and perception.

Simply put, if the disasters on the planet Lagash that regularly attend eclipses and the revelation of the stars are ever going to come to an end, what is necessary isn't a change in physical circumstances, but rather an alteration in the state of knowledge and mental responses of the people of this planet.

What's more, exactly this was implicit in the initial conversation between Campbell and Asimov that led to the writing of "Nightfall." We may remember Asimov telling us that Campbell asked:

> "What do you think would happen, Asimov, if men were to see the stars for the first time in a thousand years?"
>
> I thought, and drew a blank. I said, "I don't know."
>
> Campbell said, "I think they would go mad. I want you to write a story about that."

It wasn't just a physical situation that Campbell wanted represented, either in his astronomical covers or in "Nightfall." He wanted mental reaction as well.

We might recall Campbell saying specifically in the market report in *Writer's Digest* at the outset of his editorship: "I want reactions rather than actions. I want human reactions. Even if your hero is a robot, he must have human reactions to make him interesting to the reader."

With some assistance from the editor, Asimov would follow Campbell's lead here, too. In the series of robot stories that began with "Reason," robot behavior has seemingly been brought under the control of universal operating principles. "Robopsychology" and the Three Laws of Robotics assure human beings that robots are safe and reliable.

However, at the same time, these robots keep thinking their own private thoughts and keep acting as though they have free will. Persistently. So persistently that Chip Delany, a young black reader of science fiction in Harlem during the Fifties who would himself grow up to be a leading writer of SF, would find it only natural to interpret Asimov's robots as wily slaves evading the unreasonable dictates of their masters.

And it is certainly true that in "Reason," just as in "Nightfall," it is human mental attitudes that must ultimately be adjusted—not the universe or the robot.

However, it would be precisely the acceptance of this crucial fact—that changes in human thinking are not merely possible, or even desirable, but with the passage of time must be inevitable—that would open wide the imagined future in *Astounding*. This was the key insight of Robert Heinlein, master builder of future societies.

Mental bent, far more than gadgets or inventions, would characterize and define Heinlein's various futures. For all the difference it would make, it could as easily be the people of *Methuselah's Children* who sleep on water beds and the folk of *Beyond This Horizon* who have wardrobes with the ability to snag a tossed garment out of the air and hang it up neatly, rather than the other way around. What really sets his societies apart is their radically different values, ideas and assumptions. They don't think the same way.

Taken in sum, Heinlein's pre-war futuristic stories, such as "If This Goes On—," "The Roads Must Roll," "Coventry," "Magic, Inc." and "Universe," would present a broad array of distinctly different frames of mind. This was an even more significant accomplishment than Heinlein's formal framework of the Future History. By viewing futurity as a smorgasbord of potential mental states to choose from, Heinlein transformed time-to-come from The Future— a procession of inevitabilities destined to culminate in the guttering out of the Sun—into a realm of multiplicity and indeterminism.

However, there would be a certain number of stories published in Campbell's magazines during the Golden Age which presented the new post-materialistic expressions of transcendence without even bothering to nod respectfully in the direction of universal operating principles. For as long as it continued to be published—until the fall of 1943—*Unknown*, the magazine of alternate possibilities offered in a spirit of good clean fun, was a more receptive home for these stories of shifting realities and the stranger side of consciousness than *Astounding*, the serious and responsible magazine of human control over the future and outer space.

Of all Campbell's writers, it was L. Ron Hubbard who was perhaps the most persistently drawn to the subject of reality and consciousness. Arguably, the best work that Hubbard would produce for Campbell was two mind-based short novels published in *Unknown* in 1940—"Fear" (July) and "Typewriter in the Sky" (Nov-Dec).

In "Fear," an over-rational, spirit-denying college professor named James Lowry, misunderstanding the circumstances in which he has discovered his wife and his best friend together (they are planning a surprise party for him), has murdered them both with an ax. Lowry then spends the next several days flipping in and out of what appear to be fantasy episodes, but are eventually revealed to be psychotic states, before he is finally able to acknowledge to himself and to us what he has done.

The even more provocative "Typewriter in the Sky" offers Mike de Wolf, a contemporary piano player, who suddenly finds himself living out the role of a character—specifically, the antagonist, Spanish Admiral Miguel de Lobo—in a buccaneer novel, *Blood and Loot*, which is in the process of being banged out by his best friend, a cynical, slapdash writer named Horace Hackett.

As de Wolf thinks, when he discovers the truth of his situation:

> That would mean that he was Horace Hackett's villain in truth and in the flesh. And it would mean that he was in a never-never land where anything might and probably would happen. Where time would be distorted and places scrambled and distances jumbled and people single-track of character—

Hackett sits around in his customary dirty bathrobe and pounds the typewriter keys. And again and again de Wolf within the inner narrative is compelled to do and say what he would rather not.

No real solution is ever worked out for this uncomfortable situation—only an eventual storm-tossed transference of de Wolf back to his familiar world, which leaves him wondering if that "reality," too, could be the product of a God who on his own plane is no more than another cheap word merchant like Horace

Hackett. The short novel ends with this intimation by de Wolf of what, under the circumstances, just might be L. Ron Hubbard himself, hovering behind the scenes of his story:

"Up there—

"God?

"In a dirty bathrobe?"

"Typewriter in the Sky" can be understood as an old-fashioned alien exploration story, but with a new basis of transfer from one world to another—the thoughts of an outside intelligence. Except for the radical discontinuities that result from the struggle for control between Hackett and de Wolf, the realm of being that is reached—which previously would have been the World Beyond the Hill—wouldn't be notably marvelous. No more so than the world presented in any conventional pulp pirate story. But the ordinary Village "reality" to which Mike de Wolf returns—like the world of James Lowry in "Fear"—has been altered into a place of utter uncertainty.

One story originating in *Unknown* would stand apart from the rest for its presentation of the new transcendence of probability and the new transcendence of mental power, and for its successful equation of the two, without any invocation of universal operating principles. This was Jack Williamson's novel *Darker Than You Think*, first published in the same December 1940 issue as the second installment of "Typewriter in the Sky," and then expanded for book publication in 1948.

Like other late pioneer children we have met, Jack Williamson, one-time dweller in the Stone Age and traveler by covered wagon, had grown up with awe and love for the amazing new science of the Twentieth Century. As a youth, he picked up whatever scientific information he could from magazine articles and encyclopedias. Though he had no money to speak of and very few resources available to him, young Williamson still did his best to follow the path of science. He constructed batteries and motors which never quite managed to work. He attempted to build an adding machine out of pine sticks. And he even put together a steam engine of sorts with a lye can for a boiler, which promptly blew up.

At last, after his graduation from an unaccredited rural New Mexico high school, Williamson got his opportunity to go off to college and study real science. What a keen disappointment it was, then, for him to find himself being instructed in Nineteenth Century physics by a professor who knew nothing whatever about the new science of radioactivity and subatomic particles that Williamson found so fascinating. By the time he finished two years at West Texas State College, it had become evident to Williamson that he would much rather be an SF writer than an actual practicing scientist, and he dropped out of school to seek wider experience.

But the consequence of traveling this road was that Williamson had much less in the way of formal instruction in orthodox science and engineering than did the likes of Campbell, de Camp, Heinlein or Asimov, and so, perhaps, had less of a predisposition to have faith in universal operating principles. He wasn't as committed to Newtonian science as they.

Even so, when John Campbell became editor of *Astounding*, Williamson was able to find ways to produce science fiction that he would buy, while others who had written successfully for Hugo Gernsback or even F. Orlin Tremaine couldn't get anywhere with Campbell.

Williamson had two things in particular going for him. One was that great degree of personal adaptability which had made him the only writer able to sell SF stories to every market and every editor from *Argosy* to *Weird Tales*. The other was his active continuing interest in the new post-materialistic forms of transcendence.

We've already seen Williamson offering an early fictional representation of the assertion that this is a world of probability rather than certainty in his novel *The Legion of Time*, with its different contending futures struggling to come into existence. But he was also very quick to pick up on the new Twentieth Century psychology of the unconscious.

Even though he might appear amiable and undemanding to others, Williamson himself was far from being content with his own soft-voiced, stoop-shouldered diffidence and his backwardness in social relationships. In 1936-37, a time when such things were far from commonplace, especially for farm boys from New Mexico, he undertook a year of psychoanalysis with Dr. Charles Tidd at the Menninger Clinic in Topeka, Kansas. Dr. Tidd later moved to Southern California, and in 1940-41, Williamson followed him to Los Angeles and underwent a second year of analysis and therapy.

Darker Than You Think, which Williamson wrote shortly after his arrival in Los Angeles, would become his personal favorite among all his stories. It was a by-product of the self-work he was doing, an expression of both the reluctance and the exuberance involved in his "growing willingness to accept bits of myself that I had always feared or hated."

The protagonist of *Darker Than You Think* is Will Barbee, an orphan raised in institutions who has grown up to be a hard-drinking and none-too-happy young newspaper reporter. Barbee has never managed to get over his unaccountable rejection by his one-time college mentor and surrogate father, a professor of anthropology named Dr. Lamarck Mondrick.

At the opening of the story, Barbee is at the airport to attend a press conference called by Dr. Mondrick and his assistants—in former times Barbee's closest friends—who have just flown back from an archaeological expedition to Inner Mongolia. Dr. Mondrick, not looking at all well, speaks to the newsmen of a hidden enemy of mankind and the coming of "'a Black Messiah—the Child of the Night—whose appearance among true men will be the signal for a savage and hideous and incredible rebellion.'" But then, before he can say anything more substantial, he drops dead from an apparent heart attack.

Will Barbee is left deeply troubled. It seems that Mondrick was allergic to cats, and prior to the news conference Barbee had seen a black kitten in the hands of April Bell, a young and beautiful red-haired reporter whom he finds both alluring and unsettling. He can't help wondering if she deliberately triggered a fatal asthmatic seizure in Mondrick.

He is even more bothered when he discovers the abandoned body of the little black kitten. It is dead twice over—strangled with the red ribbon that had been tied in a bow around its neck, and stabbed to the heart with the pin of April Bell's jade brooch.

When Barbee confronts April with this seeming bit of witchery, she confesses to him that indeed she is a witch. And Dr. Mondrick was her dedicated enemy.

Long ago there existed many of her kind, who were eventually tracked down and exterminated by normal mankind—but not before they had interbred with humanity. Now, in a materialistic era in which black magic and shape-shifting are no longer given credence by most people, the witches are selecting for their own genes and backbreeding themselves into existence once more. Not only was Mondrick aware of this, but he had come back from Mongolia having discovered what he sought, the ancient secret of how to detect and combat witches. It was utterly necessary that he be killed.

Barbee is more than a bit of a modern skeptic himself, and furthermore is bedazzled by April, and he finds it hard to accept this story at face value. In the original short novel, he attempts to explain it to himself in terms of Freud's study of the unconscious mind and Rhine's investigations of extrasensory perception.

In the book version, however, there is more. To make sense of what he has been told, Barbee attempts to translate it into terms of quantum reality. He thinks:

Probability—he recalled a classroom digression of Mondrick's on that word, back in Anthropology 413. Probability, the bright-eyed old scholar said, was the key concept of modern physics. The laws of nature, he insisted, were not absolute, but merely established statistical averages. The paper weight on his desk...was supported, Mondrick said, only by the chance collisions of vibrating atoms. At any instant, there was a slight but definite probability that it might fall through the seemingly solid desk.

We may recognize this, in itself, as a very near repetition of what Williamson had already suggested in *The Legion of Time*, serialized in *Astounding* in 1938. However, in the book version of *Darker Than You Think*, Barbee takes this line of thought and couples it with the mentalistic speculations of his original short novel:

The direct mental control of probability would surely open terrifying avenues of power—and the Rhine experiments had seemingly established that control. Had April Bell, he wondered uneasily, just been born with a unique and dangerous mental power to govern the operation of probability?

In this rationalization of witchcraft, then, we have a direct linkage of quantum mechanics and Joseph Rhine's experiments in ESP. The suggestion is that the same mind power that can predict symbol cards and tip dice will be able to directly affect atomic reality, seen as the source of multiple possibility.

Barbee immediately discounts his speculations. But as soon as he goes to bed, he finds himself caught up in a queer vivid dream in which he changes into the form of a wolf and joins April, also in the shape of a wolf, and runs the night with her.

In the course of this experience, April explains the ability to change shape, and her account matches Barbee's own probabilistic and mentalistic line of speculation. She says:

"I don't know physics enough to explain all the technical ramifications, but my friend made the main point seem simple enough. The link between mind and matter, he says, is probability....

"Living things are more than matter alone.... The mind is an independent something—an energy-complex, he called it—created by the vibrating atoms and electrons of the body, and yet controlling their vibrations through the linkage of atomic probability—my friend used more technical language, but that's the idea of it.

"The web of living energy is fed by the body; it's part of the body—usually. My friend is a pretty conservative scientist, and he wouldn't

say whether he thinks it's really a soul, able to survive long after the body
is dead. He says you can't prove anything about that. . . .

"But that vital pattern in us, is stronger than in true men—his experiments
did prove that. More fluid and less dependent on the material body. In the
free state, he says, we simply separate that living web from the body and use
the probability link to attach it to other atoms, wherever we please. . . ."

In these speculations and explanations, three post-materialistic
ideas are proposed that later SF would find useful and return to
again and again. One is that mind and matter are not separate, but
linked. Another is that mind is an energy-complex or pattern. And
the third is that natural laws are not absolute, but rather constitute
a range of possible outcomes whose average has been mistaken for
hard-and-fast "law."

In *Darker Than You Think*, the strange dreams continue. Barbee
assumes one new shape after another and, with April to goad him
on, commits crime after crime against his former friends. As a sabre-
toothed tiger, he kills one buddy by slashing his throat and forcing
his car off the road. As a giant snake, he crushes another and throws
his body out of a ninth-floor window.

And when Barbee is awake again, he discovers that indeed his
friends are dead from causes as superficially plausible as Dr. Mondrick's heart attack. One was driving a car with bad brakes much
too fast down a notoriously dangerous hill. The car crashed and
the windshield broke and cut his throat. The other was a sleepwalker
who accidentally tumbled out a high window to his death.

The conscious rational Barbee is in a state of turmoil. He drinks
too much and ties himself into knots of jealousy over April. He
would like to be a support to his friends and to oppose evil. He
also wants to doubt all that is happening, even to the point of
undertaking psychoanalysis. And in the meantime, the shape-shifting
nighttime Barbee keeps running wild with April.

It is only gradually that Barbee comes to recognize and admit his
own true nature: He is not the person he always took himself to be.
He, too, is a witch. More than that, he is the awaited one, the Child
of the Night, his powers all the greater for being slow to waken.
It is his task to seize probability and lead the witch-people to final
victory over a disbelieving mankind.

At last, however, Barbee does assent to his destiny. After another
auto accident on that dangerous hill, he takes leave of his familiar
material body for good and begins to exist as a mental pattern
capable of weaving any form he wishes out of convenient atoms.
The story ends with him once more assuming the shape of a wolf
and following April's exciting scent off into the shadows.

A fascinating mixture of psychology, morality and emotion is presented in this novel. The unconscious is perceived as a source of free will—but also of possibly evil behavior. The ambivalence and highly charged feelings associated with separation from the nuclear family and initiation into sex are powerfully set forth. Ultimately, however, the central issue of *Darker Than You Think* becomes the willingness to accept a protean personal nature—represented by Will Barbee's ability to cloak himself in any form he desires.

We may understand this more flexible individuality as the consequence toward which all of the rejection of received religion, of traditional cultural roles, and of historical determinism that we have been witnessing in the course of our story had been tending, made visible and explicit at last. That is, the long-term result of the modern Western adventure into materialism and out the other side was the development of a new kind of man, not predefined by society and its expectations, but flexible enough to respond appropriately to whatever circumstances he might encounter.

Jack Williamson himself was an early example of this new type of man. This is the explanation for his slow maturation and his highly individual life path. It accounts for his singular ability to write successfully for every SF market when no one else could do this. And it also explains his somewhat uncomfortable fit within a society that taken as a whole had not yet gone as far as he had in shaking off the constraints of tradition.

But no matter how badly adjusted to conventional mid-Twentieth Century American life Williamson may sometimes have felt, the psychic twinges he suffered were growing pains rather than signs of illness. The fact of the matter was that Williamson was an existential child whose experience of life stretched from covered wagons on the American frontier to the streets of modern-day New York and Los Angeles, and from a Stone Age existence to the exploration of the stars—and there simply was no familiar social pigeonhole offered by Western society that was capacious enough to contain him. Except, of course, to eke out a living as a science fiction writer.

Darker Than You Think was the expression of Williamson's own recognition and acceptance of his unfixed nature. And even so— as with every new imaginative step into the unknown taken by SF during the course of its development—there was in this story a central element of uncertainty, disquiet and fear.

Indeed, whenever the new forms of transcendence were not presumed to be under the control of universal operating principles, they could arouse feelings of wariness, apprehension and self-protectiveness in the science fiction writers of the Golden Age.

This is perhaps most precisely illustrated by "Waldo" (*Astounding*, Aug 1942), Robert Heinlein's final bow as Campbell's resident iconoclast, Anson MacDonald. This short novel was Heinlein's next-to-last pre-war story, written between *Beyond This Horizon* and "The Unpleasant Profession of Jonathan Hoag" during the months after Pearl Harbor when Heinlein was making arrangements for the wartime job he would hold as a civilian engineer at the Philadelphia Navy Yard.

Here, as in "Magic, Inc."—with which "Waldo" would eventually be paired in a hardcover volume—Heinlein once again deliberately mixed futuristic science fiction and outright fantasy, but this time with the weight of appearance more toward the science-fictional side. And even so, "Waldo" was overtly metaphysical enough to be upsetting to certain of the more determinedly materialistic readers of *Astounding* who would write letters wondering about the legitimacy of such a story in their science-based magazine.

In the next-century world presented in "Waldo," people fly air cars and live in underground dwellings. Their power is supplied not through wires but by broadcast radiation. Now, however, the power receptors—"the deKalbs"—are beginning to fail and the air cars are starting to drop out of the sky.

This is highly upsetting. North American Power-Air, the great energy conglomerate which supplies more than half of the energy of the continent, is understandably anxious to resolve this problem quickly, whatever its nature may be. Their fear is that power to the cities may soon begin to fail, too—and, in fact, it does.

The most troubled of the NAPA executives is Dr. Rambeau, head of research. In this day, Heisenberg's Uncertainty Principle has been overturned and overturned again, and physics is once more considered an exact science. But Rambeau can't find anything wrong with those malfunctioning deKalbs. And yet they still refuse to work properly.

This is contrary to everything that Rambeau knows and believes. His religious faith in modern science is being severely shaken, and he doesn't know what to do.

In the face of this disintegrating situation, North American Power-Air's Chairman of the Board and its Chief Engineer, who are more practical and less theoretical men than Rambeau, have no hesitation in soliciting the special problem-solving talents of Waldo Farthing-waite-Jones. This self-taught genius is a grossly fat invalid, rich, nasty, greedy and selfish, who lives with his two pets, a mastiff and a canary, in a space station parked twenty-five thousand miles above the Earth.

Waldo deals impersonally with his fellow human beings. He communicates with them either by means of a TV-phone or through a full-size dummy replica of himself that sits in an outer room of the space station. The things that are around him, and things below on Earth, Waldo manipulates with the aid of power-multiplying remote-control mechanical hands of his own devising, known as "waldoes" after him.

The basis for this character had been with Heinlein for a long time. He would explain:

Back in 1918 I read an article in *Popular Mechanics* about a poor fellow afflicted with *myasthenia gravis*, pathological muscular weakness so great that even handling a knife and fork is too much effort. In this condition the brain and the control system are okay, the muscles almost incapable. This man—I don't even know his name; the article is lost in the dim corridors of time—this genius did not let *myasthenia gravis* defeat him. He devised complicated lever arrangements to enable him to use what little strength he had and he became an inventor and industrial engineer, specializing in how to get maximum result for least effort. He turned his affliction into an asset.

Beyond this obvious model, however, in Waldo's cool, unsympathetic intelligence, his rotundity, and his helplessness in Earth's gravity, we can catch a strong afterwhiff of Big Brain. Waldo and his situation also express something of the original Cartesian aspiration to be a remote disembodied mind riding high above all material things and studying them from afar.

At the outset, Waldo will have nothing to do with North American Power-Air. He bears the company a grudge over a patent dispute. But eventually, having been made aware of his dependence on a functioning civilization down below, Waldo agrees to tackle NAPA's unsolvable problem.

Waldo is a man of universal operating principles. It's his belief that he can make the cosmos do what he wants it to do. If no answer to a problem presently exists, he believes that he can always invent one. Moreover, he sees his confidence that he can wring answers out of a reluctant universe as something that distinguishes him from Rambeau, who is a more old-fashioned man of natural law:

"To Rambeau the universe was an inexorably ordered cosmos, ruled by unvarying law. To Waldo the universe was the enemy, which he strove to force to submit to his will. They might have been speaking of the same thing, but their approaches were different."

In the event, however, Waldo proves no more able than Rambeau to get the dead deKalbs to work again.

But there is one man who can. This is Gramps Schneider, an ancient Pennsylvania hex doctor. As a personal favor for a local boy,

he has fixed the malfunctioning deKalbs of the assistant to NAPA's
Chief Engineer. The catch is that the deKalbs now work in a way
they never did before. The rigid antennae that draw broadcast
radiation from the air now behave like so many wriggling worms.

Dr. Rambeau is the first to examine the altered machine. He even
manages to learn how to duplicate the anomalous effect, but only
at the cost of his sanity. He calls Waldo up on the viewphone to tell
him what he is able to do:

> "I've learned how to do it," he said tensely.
> "How to do what?"
> "Make the deKalbs work. The dear, dear deKalbs." He suddenly thrust
> his hands at Waldo, while clutching frantically with his fingers. "They go
> like this: *Wiggle, wiggle, wiggle!* ...
> "Listen carefully: Nothing is certain. ... Hens will crow and cocks will
> lay. You are here and I am there. Or maybe not. Nothing is certain.
> Nothing, *nothing*, NOTHING is certain! Around and around the little
> ball goes, and where it stops nobody knows. Only I've learned how to
> do it."
> "How to do what?"
> "How to make the little ball stop where I want it to."

It is clear that Rambeau has flipped his wig completely. And very
shortly, NAPA officials have him strapped to a confining stretcher
and carried off to the hospital. Somewhere en route, however,
Rambeau manages to escape from his restraint, leaving the straps
of his stretcher still buckled in place, and disappears into thin air.

Waldo is left with the squirming, writhing deKalb receptors.
But they are every bit as baffling to him as the deKalbs that ought
to work but don't:

> Waldo was forced to conclude that he was faced with new phenomena,
> phenomena for which he did not know the rules. If there were rules....
> For he was honest with himself. If he saw what he thought he saw, then
> rules were being broken by the new phenomena, rules which he had
> considered valid, rules to which he had never previously encountered
> exceptions.

At last, all he can think to do is go visit Gramps Schneider, who
not only declines to own modern machinery but won't even communicate with Waldo by viewphone. The consequence is that it is
necessary for Waldo to venture down into the overwhelming gravitational field of Earth for the first time in seventeen years.

However, when he arrives, he finds Gramps Schneider as sweet and helpful as he can be. The old hex doctor feeds Waldo coffee and cake and tells him everything he desires to know, and more. Not only does he show him how to fix the ailing deKalbs, but also how to repair his own woefully inadequate muscles.

Schneider tells him:

> "One of the ancients said that everything either *is*, or *is not*. That is less than true, for a thing can both *be* and *not be*. With practice one can see it both ways. Sometimes a thing which *is* for this world is a thing which *is not* for the Other World. Which is important, since we live in the Other World. ... The mind—not the brain, but the mind—is in the Other World, and reaches this world through the body. That is one true way of looking at it, though there are others."

Schneider goes on to suggest to Waldo that it is because of the doubt and fatigue of their pilots that the air cars have been failing. It is belief in modern science that has kept them up in the sky, and when that lapses, down they fall. To fix the deKalbs—and to heal Waldo's ineffective muscles—it is necessary to draw on the power of the Other World.

This is not only a lot for Waldo to absorb, but it is contrary to everything he ever thought he knew, and it takes him a while to come to terms with what he has been told. But he is a pre-eminently practical man, and by the time he can produce the Schneider effect in the deKalb receptors himself, Waldo has altered much of his previous thinking.

For one thing, he has begun to give magic credence as a mode of thought with its own measure of validity—which in some cases has been confirmed by modern science, but in other cases may have been too hastily dismissed by science and its reductionist either-or logic.

Waldo goes on from this to convince himself that the Other World of which Schneider speaks really does exist, and that this is the source of power that the altered deKalbs are drawing upon. He tries to picture the alternate realm in his mind, knowing as he does so that the image is probably inadequate, but still finding it convenient: "'I think of it as about the size and shape of an ostrich egg, but nevertheless a whole universe, existing side by side with our own, from here to the farthest star.'"

From conceding that there might be something to magic after all, and further postulating that there really might be an alternate realm of being with the power to affect this world, Waldo somewhat reluctantly abandons the safety and security of natural law to experiment with a mentalistic point of view:

Waldo was not emotionally wedded to Absolute Order as Rambeau had been; he was in no danger of becoming mentally unbalanced through a failure of his basic conceptions; nevertheless, consarn it, it was convenient for things to work the way one expected them to. On order and natural law was based predictability; without predictability it was impossible to live. Clocks should run evenly; water should boil when heat is applied to it; food should nourish, not poison; deKalb receptors should *work*, work the way they were designed to; Chaos was insupportable—it could not be lived with.

Suppose Chaos *were* king and the order we thought we detected in the world about us a mere phantasm of the imagination; where would that lead us? In that case, Waldo decided, it was entirely possible that a ten-pound weight *did* fall ten times as fast as a one-pound weight until the day the audacious Galileo decided in his mind that it was not so. Perhaps the whole meticulous science of ballistics derived from the convictions of a few firm-minded individuals who had sold the notion to the world. Perhaps the very stars were held firm in their courses by the unvarying faith of the astronomers. Orderly Cosmos, created out of Chaos—by Mind!

The world was flat before geographers decided to think of it otherwise. The world was flat, and the Sun, tub size, rose in the east and set in the west. The stars were little lights, studding a pellucid dome which barely cleared the tallest mountain. Storms were the wrath of gods and had nothing to do with the calculus of air masses. A mind-created animism dominated the world then.

More recently it had been different. A prevalent convention of materialistic and invariable causation had ruled the world; on it was based the whole involved technology of a machine-served civilization. The machines *worked*, worked the way they were designed to work, because everybody believed in them.

Until a few pilots, somewhat debilitated by overmuch exposure to radiation, had lost their confidence and infected their machines with uncertainty—and thereby let magic loose in the world.

This is a most remarkable sequence of speculation. There is nothing that matches it elsewhere in the Golden Age *Astounding* or *Unknown*.

In the first place, it is a direct philosophical statement of the great insight that is expressed again and again by Heinlein's early futuristic stories: Over the course of time, thought patterns accepted at any one moment as normal, self-evident and completely sufficient can change and do change.

"Waldo" may further be seen as a prescient attempt to recognize and come to terms with the very same succession of mental orientations in Western society that has been of concern to us throughout this account of the story of science fiction—the transition from spiritual belief to materialism, and the further shift from materialism to emergent post-materialism.

Finally, in Waldo's own modes of thinking we can glimpse the spectrum of thought typical of Campbell's Golden Age, from his initial pragmatic belief in his ability to force answers out of an uncooperative universe, to his brief moment here on the heady heights of mentalism and probabilism.

But, as story titles like "Fear" and *Darker Than You Think* should indicate to us, at this early hour the new transcendence could still seem so intense, untamed and perverse as to be well-nigh intolerable. Consciousness and uncertainty were almost as frightening to the new Atomic Age as wild science had been to the Romantics or as the enigmatical immensities of time and space had appeared to the Age of Technology.

So it is for only a very brief moment that Waldo can tolerate this much transcendent possibility. As we have just overheard him thinking, he isn't at all sure that it is possible to live without predictability. And the new uncertain, indeterminate reality in which "'a thing can both *be, not be*, and *be anything*'" looks like Chaos to him.

In Jack Williamson's *Darker Than You Think*, Will Barbee is able to accept a new personal state where he can *be, not be*, or *be anything*—even though he might have to be goaded and enticed into it by April Bell. But Waldo isn't able to cope with this degree of freedom. He has to hastily back away and re-establish control.

Waldo's clampdown comes immediately. He thinks:

> The world varied according to the way one looked at it. In that case, thought Waldo, he knew how he wanted to look at it. He cast his vote for order and predictability!
>
> He would *set* the style. He would impress his *own* concept of the Other World on the cosmos! ... He would think of it as orderly and basically similar to this space.

In sum, offered infinite possibility, the possibility that Waldo opts for is to have things continue much as they have been. He never really was Big Brain at all. In fact, he isn't even as adventurous as mad Dr. Rambeau. When you come down to it, he's just another guy with a hunger to be liked.

So it is that for his own need, Waldo will draw on enough of the power of the Other World to heal his bodily weakness and turn himself into a dancer, brain surgeon and popular personality. And, for society's sake, he will keep the window to the Other World open a crack, just enough to make it the new source of technological power replacing the old debilitating radiation.

Society is maintained, and Waldo receives the adulation he has been craving. And that is enough to satisfy Waldo. But any more of the freedom allowed by the Other World would be Chaos, and that would be insupportable. He won't allow it.

But Waldo is only fooling himself. He hasn't really imposed his point of view on the cosmos at all. Only on his society, and only for a time.

Before the end of the story, Gramps Schneider does what he can to remind Waldo of this. The old hex doctor is no more enamored of clocks that run evenly and the technological civilization they regulate than he ever was, and he sends Waldo a note politely refusing his offer to take part in the Other World power project. Gramps goes on to say:

"'As for the news of your new strength I am happy, but not surprised. The power of the Other World is his who would claim it.'"

That is, the power of the Other World belongs to anyone with the breadth of vision to venture beyond the limits of current social belief, and the courage to *be*, *not be*, or *be anything*—even if it is, like Waldo, only for the briefest moment.

The new post-materialistic transcendent power of consciousness and reality was there to be claimed by any of the SF writers of Campbell's Golden Age. But there was only one among them who was consistently able to avail himself of it and to exercise it without fear or retreat. This was A. E. van Vogt.

16

A New Moral Order

In the most central stories of the early Campbellian Golden Age, two fundamental tenets were affirmed and reaffirmed. One of these was that change and difference are always possible. The other was that men armed with a knowledge of universal operating principles can always find a way to cope with any difficulty that change and difference may present.

These tenets were asserted in one important story after another by L. Sprague de Camp, Campbell's first ally, and Isaac Asimov, his most able student. And yet, brilliant as these stories were, nonetheless there was something about them that was distinctly limited—something of the special case, something untested.

The various novels that de Camp published in *Unknown* were only humorous fantasies, games of *what if*. They didn't make any claim to be serious. If *Lest Darkness Fall* invoked the historical past, before the end of the story this was indicated to no longer be our own past, but rather some brand-new branch sprouting from the tree of time. And, at best, the Harold Shea stories, with their extension of scientific control to storybook worlds, might be taken as a kind of theoretical exercise in the application of universal operating principles, but no more than that.

Asimov's stories were more serious-minded science fiction, published in *Astounding*. But "Nightfall" was the most special of special cases, a laboratory experiment in cyclical history set off in some remote place in space and time with no direct connection to men of Earth and their history. And even though his series of robot stories was the most explicit presentation of universal operating principles to be found anywhere in Campbell's magazines, it was also true that the sphere of control that they established was only over a handful of man-created machines during the next fifty years or so.

Of all Campbell's writers, it was Robert Heinlein who applied the new beliefs where they were of greatest relevance—to the course of humanity's own future development, from the present moment to the human attainment of the stars. But even as he was doing this, Heinlein ran into a problem that he couldn't get past.

The difficulty didn't lie with the initial Golden Age tenet, the principle of change and difference. To Heinlein, it seemed clear that change not only might happen, but that it does happen, and that it will continue to happen. In his various futuristic stories written between 1939 and 1942, he imagined time-to-come as a kaleidoscopic whirl of permutation and combination, of change upon change upon change.

Heinlein's sticking point came with the second tenet—the presumption that men with a knowledge of the way the universe really works could contrive to cope with any difficulty they might encounter. Heinlein had been a relatively late convert to the doctrine of universal operating principles, and even though at his most confident he might envision a dedicated elite of competent men, the overseers of society, who could solve any problem that might present itself and manage to ease ordinary folk past the rough spots, when he put his beliefs to the test, he wasn't able to maintain confidence. The truth was that shepherding mankind from the present to the stars looked like no easy task to him.

He had little trust in the willingness and ability of normal less-than-competent humanity to do the right thing. He could wonder whether the capable, responsible few could manage to raise stupid, greedy, unheeding humanity up to the stars without snapping under the strain. But what really haunted Heinlein was the possibility that when mankind did reach the stars, it would find beings more able and advanced already established there.

In a universe responsive to competence, these aliens might effortlessly outstrip the most brilliant human genius, even Andy Libby of *Methuselah's Children*. They could be more adept manipulators of universal operating principles—like the rapport groups of the Little People who by the power of thought alone can convince plants to bear fruit that tastes like mashed potatoes and gravy. Or, like the gods of the Jockaira, they just might be so highly evolved that try as men could it would never be possible for them to catch up.

It is this spectre that causes Heinlein's long-lived people in *Methuselah's Children* to turn back from the stars and retreat to Earth. Heinlein's Best of Breed are motivated and sustained by the confident knowledge of their own superiority. Without this assurance, they despair of life, wilt, go mad, and die.

Until World War II finally intervened, and he went off to serve his country at the Philadelphia Navy Yard, Heinlein went round and round with this problem in one story after another. But he never came close to resolving it.

Heinlein's limitation was his lingering attachment to Techno Age notions of survival of the fittest and evolutionary superiority. These caused him to look upon transcendent aliens if not as hostile, certainly as dismaying. To someone who craved to have the edge, to know all the answers, and to be in charge as badly as he, the imagined indifference of higher beings could seem shattering—as he indicated in *Methuselah's Children,* "By His Bootstraps" and "Goldfish Bowl."

There was another writer for *Astounding,* however who would tackle the thorny questions of fitness, evolution and the future development of man and deal with them more creatively than Heinlein had been able to do. This was A. E. van Vogt, the most radical and visionary of all Campbell's authors.

Alfred Elton van Vogt was born on his grandparents' farm in Manitoba, Canada on April 26, 1912. At this time, van Vogt's father and three of his uncles were partners in a general store in the village of Neville, Saskatchewan and his father was studying by correspondence to earn a law degree.

Like Isaac Asimov, who developed a case of double pneumonia at the end of his second year from which it was feared he wouldn't recover, van Vogt had an early brush with death. When he was two, he fell from a second-floor window onto a wooden sidewalk, knocked himself unconscious, and remained in a coma for three days.

Van Vogt was like Asimov in another regard—the original language of this writer-to-be was not English. Until his mother put her foot down on the matter when Alfred was four, it was a dialect of Dutch that was spoken in the van Vogt household.

Young Alfred had something of a divided nature. He was an insatiable reader who for many years devoured two books a day and knew early that he wanted to be a writer when he grew up. But there were also moments when he was "an extrovert of extraordinary energy"—as he put it in a 1981 memoir entitled "My Life Was My Best Science Fiction Story."

Van Vogt was a horseback rider as a youth. In summers during his teens, he worked as a separator man on a threshing outfit and drove a truck for a combine. He was a good rifle shot, and even came close to going off on a trapping expedition to northern Canada.

In later years, van Vogt would look back upon his younger self and try to determine just when it was that the more outgoing part of himself had gotten suppressed. Did it stem from that traumatic fight with another boy that occurred when he was eight? Was it the teacher who had caused him to doubt himself for reading fairytales at twelve? Or was the crucial event when he was 17½ and killed a snake, and then suffered a revulsion against doing harm to any wild creature?

Though van Vogt might make guess after guess, he would never be able to pinpoint the exact moment when it happened. And, in fact, even well into his twenties, when he was an advertising space salesman and writer of interviews for a string of trade papers, van Vogt could still call on some lingering residue of brashness in his character to gain the attention of businessmen and store owners—as long as no one challenged him.

The truth of the matter seems to be that van Vogt's withdrawal into himself took place over a considerable period of time. The beginning of it may lie in the fact that young Alfred was a highly idealistic small town boy with a number of wide-eyed notions about right and truth and justice in his head. When the world failed to conform to his expectations, he found that a substantial shock.

Beyond this, it was also true that Alfred was a boy who had something a little strange and left-footed about him. He didn't think or talk exactly like everyone else, and reaction to this may have had its effect on his developing personality.

As the Twenties boomed, van Vogt's lawyer father moved his family once and then again, first to the larger town of Morden, Manitoba, and then to the city of Winnipeg, where he became the western Canadian agent of the Holland-American Shipping Lines.

These moves were very difficult for van Vogt. He would recall: "Childhood was a terrible period for me. I was like a ship without anchor being swept along through darkness in a storm. Again and again I sought shelter, only to be forced out of it by something new."

Morden was twice as large as Neville. It was a conservative community with a predominantly English population, and here van Vogt was made aware that Canada was British but that he was not.

Winnipeg was even more trying. It was a city of 250,000—two hundred times the size of Morden—and Alfred felt lost there. He quickly fell behind in school "in the five subjects that you just can't catch up on easily: algebra, geometry, Latin grammar, Latin literature, and one other that I can't recall." In consequence, he was asked to repeat the tenth grade.

The broader horizons offered by science fiction—still not yet called this—were one answer he found to his difficulties. He came across SF first in Morden at the age of eleven in a British boys' magazine called *Chum*, the yearly collected volume of which he contrived to borrow for a dime from another boy who soon became his best friend.

Then, in Winnipeg, in his dark days of failure in school, he discovered the November 1926 issue of *Amazing Stories* on a newsstand and recognized it as what he was seeking. During the next three years—until Hugo Gernsback lost control of the magazine and it came under the more conservative editorial direction of ancient T. O'Conor Sloane—van Vogt would read *Amazing* assiduously, seeking signs of another and higher order of being than that which was to be found in Winnipeg, Manitoba in the late 1920s. As van Vogt would eventually come to express it:

> Reading science fiction lifted me out of the do-be-and-have world and gave me glimpses backward and forward into the time and space distances of the universe. I may live only three seconds (so to speak), but I have had the pleasure and excitement of contemplating the beginning and end of existence. Short of being immortal physically, I have vicariously experienced just about everything that man can conceive will happen by reading science fiction.

If *Amazing* had defects and limitations, this wasn't apparent to young Alfred. What he saw in the pioneer magazine of science fiction was the wonders of man's progress-to-come, and his imagination was fired by one grand new concept after another: "ESP; trans-light speeds; exploration of space; the infinitely small turning out to be another universe; new super-energy sources; instant education; the long journey; shape changing; vision at a distance; time travel; gravity minimization; taking over another body; etc."

A considerable impression would be made on van Vogt by E.E. Smith's *The Skylark of Space*, of course. But the writer in *Amazing* who had the most to say to him was A. Merritt.

When Gernsback left the magazine, the youngster couldn't help but notice the change. *Amazing* lost the magic it had held for him and became dull. Consequently, in 1930, in one of the utterly abrupt transitions that were to become typical of his conduct of life, van Vogt put science fiction aside.

Lack of spare cash was one reason for his ceasing to buy science fiction magazines. The stock market crash of 1929 took place at the beginning of van Vogt's last year in high school. Before that school year was over, van Vogt's father had lost his shipping-lines job and it was apparent there wouldn't be sufficient money available for Alfred to go to college. Although in later life, van Vogt would sit in on college courses in many subjects from economics to acting, this was to be the end of his formal education.

For the next six months, he hid out in his bedroom and wondered what to do with himself. Mostly he continued to read. He read hot pulp fiction—historical romances, mysteries and Westerns. He read serious turn-of-the-century British fiction and Nineteenth Century French novels. He read history and psychology. And he also read books of science.

The science that interested van Vogt the most was not familiar Newtonian science. It seems possible that the unrecallable essential subject he flunked in tenth grade, along with Latin and math, just might have been chemistry or physics. Unlike a John Campbell or a Robert Heinlein, van Vogt hadn't spent his youth building radios or carrying out a search for a better way to blow up the basement. There was never much likelihood that he would grow up to become an aeronautical engineer like de Camp or a biochemist like Asimov.

The science that van Vogt did care about was the new wider science of atoms and galaxies. But even here, what interested him was not the details, but rather concepts and overviews—the philosophy and meaning of science. And so it was only natural that he would find his way to the writings of Arthur Eddington, James Jeans and J. B. S. Haldane.

However, the book that had the greatest influence on the formation of his thinking may have been Alfred North Whitehead's *Science and the Modern World* (1925). At one time or another, this pioneering work of post-materialistic philosophy passed through the hands of most of the youngsters who would grow up to become the science fiction writers of Campbell's Golden Age. But it was van Vogt alone amongst them who would be able to take insights derived from this difficult little book and make them the basis for his SF writing.

Until the year preceding the publication of *Science and the Modern World*, Alfred North Whitehead's career had been spent as a mathematician, first for twenty-five years at Trinity College, Cambridge, and then, from 1911, at the University of London. We might recall Whitehead in his role as Bertrand Russell's collaborator on the *Principia Mathematica* (1910-13), a heroic three-volume attempt to reduce all mathematics to logic. Some thirty years after it was published, Pratt and de Camp would draw upon the opening pages of this work for the symbolic equations which Harold Shea employs to transfer himself from one reality to another.

We might also remember that in his brilliant 1931 metamathematical paper, "On Formally Undecidable Propositions," the German Kurt Gödel had demonstrated that it was impossible for either the *Principia Mathematica* or any like system to be self-consistent and complete. Certain statements must necessarily be admitted as true that the system itself was incapable of either proving or disproving.

Even before the publication of Gödel's paper, however, Alfred

North Whitehead himself had already come to perceive the inadequacy of his and Russell's monumental effort. In fact, Whitehead had been led by his understanding of mathematics, of the new quantum physics, and of physiology and psychology to doubt the sufficiency of the entire modern scientific philosophy.

He would object: "We are content with superficial orderings from diverse arbitrary starting points." And, with disarming gentleness, he would further inquire: "Is it not possible that the standardized concepts of science are only valid within narrow limitations, perhaps too narrow for science itself?"

So it was that in 1924, at the advanced age of 63, Whitehead traveled across the Atlantic to join the faculty of Harvard University as a professor of philosophy. And the first fruit of this new career was *Science and the Modern World*, based in the main on eight Lowell Lectures that he delivered in 1925.

Two complementary lines of argument were to be found intertwined in this remarkable book. In one, Whitehead reviewed the entire history of Western objection and exception to scientific materialism: The philosophical arguments that had been raised against it at the outset of the modern Western scientific adventure, during the Age of Reason. The experiential objections—often phrased in poetic terms—of the Romantic Era. And finally, the problems that had been recently raised for scientific materialism by the strange new science of the later Age of Technology.

And meanwhile, in his other, concurrent line of argument, Whitehead sketched out a basis for an alternative post-materialistic philosophy—"a system of thought basing nature upon the concept of organism and not upon the concept of matter."

As Whitehead would draw the distinction:

> The materialistic starting point is from independently existing substances, matter and mind. The matter suffers modifications of its external relations of locomotion, and the mind suffers modifications of its contemplated objects. There are, in this materialistic theory, two sorts of independent substances, each qualified by their appropriate passions.
>
> The organic starting point is from the analysis of process as the realisation of events disposed in an interlocked community. The event is the unit of things real.

Following the arguments that Whitehead was setting forth in *Science and the Modern World* was not at all easy. His presentation was intricate, wide-ranging, dense and elusive, as though Whitehead himself wasn't always completely sure just what it was he was attempting to say.

In the course of his discussion, Whitehead would draw a contrast between thinkers who are clear, yet limited, and thinkers who are muddled, but fruitful. Beyond question, he himself was a thinker of the second sort. In consequence, following out the nuances and implications of Alfred North Whitehead's arguments and attempting to determine exactly what they meant would remain something of a challenge even for professional students of philosophy.

It was little wonder, then, that van Vogt's contemporaries—the other boys who would grow up to write the science fiction of the Golden Age—should largely find *Science and the Modern World* unintelligible. Or that in the places where these earnest young scientists of the basement could comprehend Whitehead—as in his repudiation of scientific materialism—they would not be prepared to accept and follow him.

However, it would be quite otherwise with van Vogt, in large part precisely because he was not a professional student of philosophy, and neither did he have any special allegiance to the given assumptions of Western science. He was just an out-of-step kid from farther Canada who above all things desired to broaden his mental horizons and was ready to take his ideas wherever he could find them.

For van Vogt, reading *Science and the Modern World* provided him with exactly what he was seeking. From out of the general murk of Whitehead's argumentation, certain key remarks leaped forth to speak directly to him.

As one example, there was this:

My theory involves the entire abandonment of the notion that simple location is the primary way in which things are involved in space-time. In a certain sense, everything is everywhere at all times. For every location involves an aspect of itself in every other location. Thus every spatio-temporal standpoint mirrors the world.

What a mind-boggling suggestion this was—that everything is everywhere at all times, so that each and every standpoint to some extent mirrors all that exists! Now that was food for thought.

So was this:

"If organisms are to survive, they must work together. Any physical object which by its influence deteriorates its environment, commits suicide."

And this:

"Successful organisms modify their environment. Those organisms are successful which modify their environments so as to assist each other."

It mattered little to van Vogt that he might not be picking up every last detail of Whitehead's reasoning. What did matter was that he grasped the whole: In place of a universe of constantly competing particles effectively going nowhere, Whitehead was offering the alternative vision of an organic and interconnected universe evolving through creativeness and cooperation.

Thinking such as this—neither spiritual nor materialistic, but holistic, organic, environmental and evolutionary—was a genuine rarity in the Twenties. But the young Alfred van Vogt found it highly appealing and took to it eagerly.

The extraordinary ideas that he stumbled upon in *Science and the Modern World* would linger in the back of his mind. Eventually, after they had incubated long enough and become his own, they would emerge again as the philosophical basis for the science fiction van Vogt would write for John Campbell's *Astounding*. And the fundamental difference distinguishing his stories from the Golden Age SF produced by all the writers who still remained card-carrying scientific materialists would be van Vogt's Whitehead-inspired post-materialistic sense of a universe of interconnected organisms evolving together.

As the months that followed high school wore on, it became clear that there was a limit to the length of time that young Alfred could go on burying himself in his books and insisting to everyone that he was a writer even though he had never written anything. Early in 1931, van Vogt took a Civil Service examination, was offered a temporary government job, and accepted it. He traveled east to Ottawa, the capital city of Canada, where he would spend ten highly formative months as a clerk tabulating the Canadian census.

Van Vogt's imagination was captured by the holistic quality of the census, with its populations of information to be examined first from this angle and then from that. One result of this fascination would be that in years to come, when a Doc Smith was still describing the thinking machine of tomorrow as no more than a gigantic card sorter, and a Robert Heinlein had gotten no further than to conceive of a ponderous and unreliable "ballistic calculator" used for the single specialized purpose of working out spaceship rocket burn requirements, A.E. van Vogt would be envisioning the computer of the future as an information machine capable of containing a quadrillion facts all cross-referenced by names, dates and key words, and available to an inquirer at the touch of a button.

Another thing that would stick in van Vogt's imagination from his sojourn in Ottawa—and eventually find expression in his SF stories—would be a powerful secret that he was let in on by his boardinghouse roommate, a young man who had recently been brought over to Canada from Scotland. He informed Alfred that his flag-waving neighbors back in Morden, Manitoba had had it all wrong: the English didn't rule the British Empire at all; they only thought they did. The actual covert masters of empire were the Scotch, taking their revenge for the defeat of Bonnie Prince Charlie at Culloden. And just as soon as the roommate had earned his college degree, he expected to assume the place that was being held for him behind the scenes in the Canadian government.

Since van Vogt enjoyed no comparable secret support from well-placed Dutch-Canadian cabalists, he had no alternative but to catch a freight train back to Winnipeg when the work of compiling the 1931 census was over. But during his time in Ottawa, he'd made a serious start toward learning how to become the writer he was already claiming to be. From the Palmer Institute of Authorship, he took a correspondence course in "English and Self-Expression." The long-term consequence of this course would be to set him thinking about the possible subliminal effects of particular sounds and unorthodox word selections.

Then, back home in Winnipeg, he took out of the library Thomas Uzzell's *Narrative Technique*, and two highly useful books by John Gallishaw, *The Only Two Ways to Write a Story* and *Twenty Problems of the Short-Story Writer*—precisely the manuals of instruction that a young Jack Williamson, newly dropped out of college to become a full-time writer, was choosing to study at about this same time. From Gallishaw, van Vogt learned the necessity of writing sentences that conveyed either emotion, imagery or suspense, and how to break a story down into a series of short scenes, each with its own distinct purpose. From Uzzell, he took the idea that a story should make a unified impact upon the reader.

At last, after all this study, the 20-year-old van Vogt felt ready to try writing a story of his own. But what kind of story should it be?

He didn't read confession magazines himself, but van Vogt had noticed that *True Story*, the top such magazine, had a prize contest in every issue. So he decided to be audacious and take a shot at that. He went off to the library, and with Uzzell and Gallishaw backing him at either elbow, he managed to write the first scene of a story.

What he was attempting seemed chancy to van Vogt. All the time he was working, he kept waking in the night and going round and round about what was to come next. But after turning out one scene each day for nine days, he managed to finish a story which he called "I Live in the Streets." This was about a girl who had run into hard times in the Depression and been thrown out of her rooming house. It didn't win any prizes, but *True Story* did buy and publish it.

During the next three years, from 1932 to 1935, van Vogt had regular success selling simple, emotional, anonymous little stories to the confession magazines, and even won a thousand dollar prize with one. But then—as though his inner being had come to the sudden conclusion that if practice was what he had been after in writing these stories, he had had practice enough—in the middle of another true confession he felt disgusted with himself, threw down his pen, and wrote no more of them.

But if it was not sufficient to write whatever was easiest to sell, then what was his writing for? Van Vogt wasn't altogether sure. In the middle Thirties, he would write trade newspaper interviews, short radio plays, and an occasional short story for a newspaper supplement or a pulp magazine. He learned from this work, but none of it was completely satisfying. At the same time, he had been told that he had the ability to write for the slick magazines, but he felt a strong aversion to attempting this which he couldn't altogether explain.

Because he was a reader, a writer, and a thinker, van Vogt regarded himself as an intellectual. But if he was an intellectual, it was not of the usual sort. He wasn't silver-tongued or swift-witted. He had very little ability to remember a precise fact or an exact niggle, and no talent at all for linear thought and logical analysis. He was not a conventional man of reason.

Rather, van Vogt's usual method was to fix on some question or subject in a highly single-minded way—to surround it and dwell upon it and absorb it. He might get nowhere with a problem for the longest time, but then at last the penny would drop and some insight would pop into his mind.

When van Vogt had enough insights accumulated on a topic, they would assemble themselves into what he would come to think of as a system—a methodology or mode of approach that had its own consistency, if only in the manner in which it was applied by him. In later days, van Vogt would even take pride in describing himself as "Mr. System."

The insight that he might write science fiction, and that he *should* write science fiction, dawned on him in the summer of 1938. It came with typical suddenness and indirection. After eight years in which he had not read any science fiction, one day when he was in McKnight's Drug Store in Winnipeg, van Vogt casually picked up the latest issue of *Astounding*, a magazine he had never paid any attention to before. He flipped on through to the middle pages, and began to read a story.

But not just any story: Amazingly... coincidentally... significantly... perhaps even inevitably... the story that he singled out in this apparently completely random fashion was "Who Goes There?" by Don A. Stuart—the prototypical example of modern science fiction.

Van Vogt was immediately hooked by the mood and the flavor of what he was reading. And so he bought the magazine and hurried on home to finish the story he'd started—to savor it, to linger over it, and to think about it.

What struck van Vogt most forcibly about "Who Goes There?" wasn't exactly the same thing that would catch the attention of those readers who were still staunch scientific materialists. All that they would see was the morally neutral message that even a shape-shifting otherworldly monster might be subject to the universal power of human scientific knowledge. We might recall, for instance, that Isaac Asimov, responding to this very same story, would write his first attempt at modern science fiction—"Stowaway," or "The Callistan Menace"—about another threatening alien creature that human beings come to understand scientifically.

But what van Vogt took from his reading of "Who Goes There?" was something quite a bit different from this. What intrigued him about this story was its intimation of a cooperative ethic— a new ordering of value appropriate to the post-materialistic universe he had been turning over and over in his mind since he first read Whitehead.

That is, van Vogt noticed that those human beings in the Antarctic party of "Who Goes There?" who retained their sanity were able to work together to overcome a creature who on an individual basis was far more powerful than any of them. And conversely, he saw that the horrific alien, even though it might be both telepathic and originally one being, was not able to join its various parts together to take concerted action. Indeed, its selfishness and egoism were so complete as to affect even samples of its blood, so that at the threat of a hot wire these would scream and strive to escape, and thereby betray their non-human nature.

And this all had a rightness for van Vogt. It seemed to him that in an organic, interconnected universe, cooperation would be a fundamental value, a reflection of the purposes of the whole. And selfishness would be a fatal ethical defect no matter how outwardly powerful the entity might appear to be.

"Who Goes There?" altered van Vogt's life. Just as surely as if someone had seized him by the shoulders and physically realigned him, reading this story turned van Vogt around and pointed him in a new direction.

In the science fiction stories that he would come to write during the next half-dozen years, van Vogt would work out the answers to a cluster of questions that were first aroused by his reading of "Who Goes There?"

In an organic universe, wherein does true superiority lie?

Does might in and of itself make right?

What connection exists between evolution and altruism?

And—his most persistent line of inquiry—how would a genuinely superior creature behave? What would it do? How would it act? And how would it be perceived by lesser beings?

For us to say all this, however, is not only to anticipate the direction in which A.E. van Vogt would travel, but to state with some clarity what was not necessarily at all clear to him in the summer of 1938 when he put aside the August *Astounding* to reach for a sheet of letter paper and an envelope. It is perfectly possible, perhaps even probable, that he had no explicit memory of *Science and the Modern World,* or thoughts of post-materialism, or formed convictions about the moral nature of transcendent being in his mind at all. In the immediate moment, all that he may have known for certain was that he had an urgent idea for an SF story.

In complete unawareness that Don A. Stuart, the nominal author of "Who Goes There?," and the editor of the magazine he'd been reading were one and the same, van Vogt drafted a letter of inquiry. As an indication of his serious intent, he summarized his past experience as a writer. Then, in a paragraph, he outlined his idea. Would *Astounding* be interested in taking a look at a story like this?

He mailed the letter off to New York, and then waited for some sort of answer to come. One moment he was rarin' to go—ready to take over the whole universe and transform it with his imagination. He knew how to tell a story, after all. And from his teenage reading of *Amazing,* he knew his way around science fiction. So why shouldn't he write SF and do it well? In the next instant, however, he would start to feel all unsure of himself, like a shy kid new to the neighborhood who has to have an invitation before he can bring himself to come outside and play.

But if encouragement was what he had to have in order to begin writing SF, John Campbell did not let him down. Van Vogt would say later:

> I feel pretty sure that if he hadn't answered, that would have been the end of my science fiction career. I didn't know it at the time, but he answered all such letters.
>
> When he replied, he said, "In writing this story, be sure to concentrate on the mood and atmosphere. Don't just make it an action story."

This was precisely the right thing to say to van Vogt. It had been that splendidly atmospheric opening sentence—"The place stank."—which had first hooked him into reading "Who Goes There?" And the creation of story mood was the very thing van Vogt felt he knew how to do best.

So, feeling under some real obligation to follow through now that he had received this go-ahead from Campbell, he set to work on his story. He called upon the familiar methods he'd derived from the Palmer Institute, John Gallishaw and Thomas Uzzell: particular words and sounds used strangely for effect; sentences of constant suspense, imagery and emotion; one purposeful scene after another; all aiming toward a final unified impact.

The eventual title of the story would be "Vault of the Beast." It began:

> The creature crept. It whimpered from fear and pain. Shapeless, form-less thing yet changing shape and form with each jerky movement, it crept along the corridor of the space freighter, fighting the terrible urge of its elements to take the shape of its surroundings. A gray blob of disinte-grating stuff, it crept and cascaded, it rolled, flowed and dissolved, every movement an agony of struggle against the abnormal need to become a stable shape. Any shape!

This creature bears an immediately apparent resemblance to the menace of "Who Goes There?" It, too, is a telepathic shapeshifter capable of assuming the form of any human it encounters. But it also has its differences from Campbell's monster. It isn't able to proliferate and take over other beings, and it isn't autonomous.

In fact, this half-hysterical, half-terrified, yet casually murderous thing—which van Vogt called both a "robot" and an "android" and described both as organic and as a machine—is a construct that has been made by "great and evil minds" from another and slower dimension than ours. It has been dispatched to Earth to find a mathematician capable of freeing one of their kind who millions of years ago fell into our space and while helpless was imprisoned in a vault by the Martians of that day, who sensed its underlying ill intent.

If this mighty prisoner should become free, it can show its fellows the way to transfer from one dimension to another. And that is what they yearn for. As they admit, at the moment they think their designs have finally been achieved: "Our purpose is to control all spaces, all worlds—particularly those which are inhabited. We intend to be absolute rulers of the entire Universe."

The malevolent aliens use their shape-changing robot creature to manipulate, delude and sweet-talk an Earthman into divining how the vault might be opened. But when this has been accomplished, they give their true nature away. They propose to use the android as the key to the lock, and take evident pleasure in the pain it suffers as they wrench it out of the human form it has assumed and twist it into the requisite shape.

Brender, the Earthman, cannot avoid the recognition that he has been tricked. At exactly the same moment, however, he also comes to the sudden realization that the act of opening the ancient sand-buried Martian prison is going to cause the destruction of its occupant and ruin the aliens' schemes for conquest.

The poor screaming robot can still read Brender's mind. It knows what he knows. Even yet it might warn its makers and possibly save its own life—but it elects not to. It permits itself to be sacrificed. The vault is opened, and the evil alien within perishes—and with it its knowledge of how to travel from one dimension to another.

As the now-dying robot struggles in vain to return to human form, it explains to Brender:

"'I didn't tell them...I caught your thought...and kept it... from them.... Because they were hurting me. They were going to destroy me. Because...I liked...being human. I was...somebody!'"

The aliens, it seems, have been undone by their own remoteness, deviousness and casual cruelty. And while Brender looks on in pity, the android dissolves into a puddle of gray, which then crumbles away into dust.

When he had finished this story, van Vogt mailed it off to *Astounding*. And just as van Vogt had managed to recognize "Who Goes There?" when he needed to, so John Campbell was able to reciprocate and to perceive from the outset that in this new Canadian storyteller he had discovered someone most unusual.

The very first thing that he noticed in reading "Vault of the Beast" was just how immediate and raw-nerved and intense it was. It didn't sit still for one minute, but moved ahead with the inexorable pace of a fevered dream. Writing as relentless as this had never been seen in the SF pulp magazines.

The story was also boldly, even extravagantly science-fictional. We may recall that only five years earlier, the venerable H.G. Wells had suggested that to include more than a single wonder in any SF story was to step over the line into irresponsible silliness. He had declared, somewhat testily, "Nothing remains interesting where anything can happen."

But here was a rank beginner who seemed to have no compunctions at all against throwing a profusion of marvels into one brief novelet: a protean monster/robot/android; space travel; telepathy; malevolent

higher aliens; a multiplicity of dimensions operating at different time rates; inter-dimensional transference; a long-vanished
Martian civilization; antigravity; the "'ultimate prime number'";
no less than two different kinds of "'ultimate metal'"; and an
irresistible universal force. What's more, van Vogt came very close
to making this superabundance of wonders add up to a real and
meaningful story.

But the most original and impressive aspect of "Vault of the
Beast" was that a considerable portion of the story was told from the
point of view of a whimpering, blobby, shape-altering *thing*. Not
only this, but van Vogt even asked the reader to empathize with the
creature and to regret its passing. This was completely unheard of.
Nobody had ever dared before to write from inside the psyche of
so different and monstrous a being.

As powerful, imaginative and unusual as van Vogt's story recog-
nizably was, however, Campbell couldn't help feeling that it wasn't
yet as sound and effective as it might be.

To begin with, it wasn't altogether plausible. If the headlong pace
of the narrative should be interrupted for even an instant and exact
questions be asked, there was much in this story that would not hold
up under examination.

This would, in fact, always be van Vogt's weakest point. Like his
mentor, Alfred North Whitehead, he would be muddled and fruitful,
rather than limited but clear.

In later times, van Vogt would say of the writers of the Golden
Age: "In a sense we were all One Great Big Author." And there
would be considerable aptness to this observation. However, to the
extent that the body of Campbellian modern science fiction did
amount to a whole—the synergetic product of many separate and
partial individual contributions—it would be writers other than
A.E. van Vogt who would supply it with its detailed plausible
arguments. Without the comparatively restrained and careful work
of de Camp, Heinlein, Asimov and the others, van Vogt's flights of
dreamlike imagination might very easily have seemed completely
unfounded—just as without his work, many of their stories might
have seemed lacking in mystery.

There was a further difficulty with "Vault of the Beast" beyond
its imperfect plausibility. Despite the sound advice of Thomas
Uzzell, it wasn't unified in its effect.

The central questions raised by the story appeared to be how the
android creature was to contrive to win the freedom of the long-
imprisoned alien, and what this evil being and its kind might do if
it were allowed to escape from the Martian vault. At the climax of
the story, however, all this possibility and danger prove to be nothing

more than illusion. At any time that the vault should be opened, it appears, the alien inside must inevitably perish.

So the main story problem was not a problem at all—and never had been. At this point, the emotional weight of "Vault of the Beast" shifted over to the death of the shape-changing robot, and the flattering taste this wretched creature has acquired for the assumption of human form.

This alteration of emphasis did not work perfectly. At the very least, it appeared to Campbell that if the reader was to be hooked into identifying with this monster and looking upon it with pity, then more emphasis would have to be placed upon the emotions of the creature early in the story.

So Campbell returned the manuscript to van Vogt. He praised it highly, but suggested that it still needed some fine-tuning. The Earthman, Jim Brender, could use additional motivation. And the monster should be made more pitiable from the outset. Would van Vogt have a try at that?

Instead, however, his new would-be contributor overleaped Campbell's expectations entirely. By the time he heard from the editor, van Vogt was already at work on a second SF story that incorporated all he had learned in writing the first one. And it was going so well that he didn't want to set it aside.

It would be a good while before van Vogt got back to "Vault of the Beast" to rewrite it. In this form, arguably stronger, yet still not wholly satisfactory because of the central non-problem of the imprisoned alien—it would appear in the August 1940 issue of *Astounding* as his fifth published SF story. And this one extended delay for revision would be as close as he would ever come to having a story rejected by John Campbell until after the end of World War II.

It was the novelet "Black Destroyer," his second science fiction story, which convinced Campbell that this "Alfred Vogt"—as he would address him at the outset—wasn't just another highly promising beginner who required tutoring and guidance. On the basis of this singular story, it became evident to the editor that this 26-year-old from Winnipeg—just two years younger than Campbell himself—had already arrived as a wild imaginative talent unmatched in science fiction.

Van Vogt demonstrated in "Black Destroyer" that the apparent virtues of his first effort had been neither an illusion nor a fluke. His new story had the very same strengths: Once again, he started his story with a dynamic and gripping first line—"On and on Coeurl prowled!"—and then hurtled along from there. Once again, he asked the reader to identify with the drives and purposes of a powerful alien creature. And once again, he offhandedly mixed together a multiplicity of SF concepts, any one of which another writer might have thought more than sufficient to serve as the basis for a story.

But this time his plot was more integrated. Better than that— unlike "Vault of the Beast" and its model, "Who Goes There?", which still retained overtones of the conventional Techno Age alien invasion story—"Black Destroyer" had a situation that was completely new and different.

And still better yet was that this novelet was a brilliant anticipation of science fiction as John Campbell thought it ought to be and wished it to become.

The direction in which the great editor desired to move science fiction was toward human dominion over the future and outer space. And in "Black Destroyer" van Vogt imagined an exploration vessel from a future human civilization which spans the galaxy landing on a planet of a red sun that is separated from its nearest neighbor by nine hundred light years.

What a premise this was! An interstellar survey team from an Earth-derived human civilization that is as broad as the galaxy! Some fifteen years later, in the mid-Fifties, a story background of this kind would be commonplace in *Astounding*. But in 1939, nothing quite like it had ever been imagined before.

It was John Campbell's conviction that if it was going to be possible someday for men to travel to the planets and the stars and establish control over the wider universe, the necessary job for science fiction had to be to identify every possible problem or hindrance to this, and then imagine how each one might be dealt with. The real flaw in "Vault of the Beast" from the editor's point of view was that it didn't actually pose any problem of responsibility and control for men to resolve.

But "Black Destroyer" did.

In this story, the human scientists exploring the isolated world they have discovered set their spherical ship down near the remains of a long-destroyed city. And here they encounter the bizarre and powerful Coeurl, a catlike creature with fangs and massive forepaws, tentacles that grow from his shoulders, and tendrilled ears, whom they will eventually identify as a degenerate survivor of this ruined civilization.

As the Techno Age would reckon matters, Coeurl is a clearly superior being, more than a match for any one man. Not only is he immensely long-lived, but he is quick, strong and deadly. He is able to breathe chlorine or oxygen indifferently. Through his ear tendrils, he can hear sounds, pick up the vibrations given off by the precious life-substance *id*, and also detect, broadcast and control electro-magnetic phenomena. And with his prehensile tentacles, he can instantly operate sophisticated machinery he has never encountered before, including the great globular human spaceship itself.

Coeurl is a living example of cosmic hostility. He is a ruthless and practiced killer. He and his kind have leveled their civilization, fought amongst themselves, and devoured all other living things in this world in a desperate death struggle to obtain "the all-necessary id"— eventually identified by a human scientist as the element phosphorus.

Before the humans manage to recognize Coeurl's true nature and power, this utterly rapacious being has ripped one man to pieces to obtain his id, and then murdered another twelve men as they sleep. When he is found out at last—his carnage discovered—Coeurl escapes to the spaceship engine room, barricades himself there, and then launches himself and the human party into interstellar space.

However, if Coeurl is a representative of unrelenting Techno Age cosmic hostility, it is as perceived through revisionist Atomic Age eyes. And the Atomic Age would not only doubt that there can be such a thing as total difference or absolute superiority, but would boldly assert that men may scientifically investigate anything and everything that exists in search of the most convenient handle to grab it by.

We might think back to the members of the Antarctic party in Campbell's "Who Goes There?" Though confronted by a shape-shifting alien monster, they are able to calmly say, "'This isn't wildly beyond what we already know. It's just a modification we haven't seen before. It's as natural, as logical, as any other manifestation of life. It obeys exactly the same laws.'"

In highly similar fashion, even though the human scientists of "Black Destroyer" may find themselves up to their knees in corpses and gore as their spaceship screams toward the stars under the guidance of an id-crazed cat-creature endowed with powers like none they have ever encountered before, Commander Morton, the leader of the expedition, is able to overcome any impulses he might be feeling toward fear and panic and deal coolly with the situation. He declares: "'We're going to find out right now if we're dealing with unlimited science, or a creature limited like the rest of us. I'll bet on the second possibility.'"

And that's a pretty good bet. Capable and dangerous Coeurl may be, but he is by no means either all-powerful or invulnerable. He has a number of weaknesses and limitations—crippling defects of ability, knowledge, mentation and perspective.

Foremost among these is Coeurl's animalism. Ever since H.G. Wells's invading Martians, alien beings had displayed a taste for human blood and proved their own superiority by looking upon men as cattle. For van Vogt, however, Coeurl's insatiable appetite for id identifies him, and not his human victims, as the animal.

Coeurl is driven by lusts and hungers and lacks self-control. It doesn't take a lot to unbalance his psyche.

He can be thrown by his greed for phosphorus: "The sense of id was so overwhelming that his brain drifted to the ultimate verge of chaos."

Unexpectedness—even so little as the closing of a door and the movement of an elevator—can unsettle him: "He whirled with a savage snarl, his reason whirling into chaos. With one leap, he pounced at the door. The metal bent under his plunge, and the desperate pain maddened him. Now, he was all trapped animal."

And mayhem can make him manic and cause him to forget his purposes: "It was the seventh taste of murder that brought a sudden return of lust, a pure, unbounded desire to kill, return of a millennium-old habit of destroying everything containing the precious id."

Over and over, Coeurl gives himself away by these descents into animality. They cause him to act prematurely, to betray his intentions, and to reveal his awesome but combatable powers.

Moreover, when Coeurl isn't acting like a heedless beast, he is a blind egotist. All that he can see in the human scientific expedition is new inferiors to serve as a fresh supply of essential id. And beyond that, an opportunity for himself and the others of his kind who still survive to leap to the stars and seize even more id:

> For just a moment he felt contempt, a glow of superiority, as he thought of the stupid creatures who dared to match their wit against a coeurl. And in that moment, he suddenly thought of other coeurls. A queer, exultant sense of race pounded through his being; the driving hate of centuries of ruthless competition yielded reluctantly before pride of kinship with the future rulers of all space.

At every turn Coeurl believes himself to be more powerful and able and in control than he actually is, and he automatically dismisses the human opposition he faces without ever pausing to think very deeply about its true nature.

But, in fact, there is a profound difference between the humans and him. Their galactic civilization has solved the problem of cyclical history, while Coeurl and his kind have not, so they know a great deal about him while he knows nothing about them.

The men can look at his historical context and his behavior and gauge Coeurl accurately as a degenerate and a criminal. As the archaeologist Korita observes: "In fact, his whole record is one of the low cunning of the primitive, egotistical mind which has little or no conception of the vast, organization with which it is confronted.'"

It is wholly typical of Coeurl that he should take over the engine room of the spherical spaceship under the apparent assumption that being where the power is located will be sufficient to make him master of the situation—and also typical that he should be mistaken. In fact, it is the humans who occupy the ship's control room who actually direct the ship and its machines.

What's more, they possess science that Coeurl does not, and dares not face. He may be able to blank out remote pictures of himself, to take a shot in the head from a vibration gun without suffering harm, to disrupt electric locks, and to harden the door to the engine room by increasing "'the electronic tensions of the door to their ultimate.'" But he cannot redirect, ward off, or absorb atomic power. Consequently, once the humans do manage to break into the engine room, they have an effective weapon with which to attack him.

Coeurl must escape from this threat. So able is he, within his limits, that he can throw together an individual spaceship right then and there in the machine shop of the great ship. And in this little ship, he attempts to flee back to his own planet to gather his kind.

But alone in space is just where the humans would like to see Coeurl. They have vast experience there, while he has none. As Korita says: "'We have, then, a primitive, and that primitive is now far out in space, completely outside of his natural habitat.'"

And, indeed, Coeurl does find space disconcerting. Given his tendency to lose his head, it isn't surprising that he should be thrown into confusion when all his usual expectations begin to be overturned.

First, the human ship suddenly disappears from view. Then it seems that he is going backward, away from his planet, rather than toward it, as he should. And finally, the human ship—which by Coeurl's reckoning should be far behind—suddenly proves to be waiting in front of him.

It is all too much for Coeurl, and he becomes overwhelmed by panic. Fearing the flames of men wielding atomic disintegrators, he wills his own death:

> They found him lying dead in a little pool of phosphorus.
> "Poor pussy," said Morton. "I wonder what he thought when he saw us appear ahead of him, after his own sun disappeared. Knowing nothing of anti-accelerators, he couldn't know that we could stop short in space, whereas it would take him more than three hours to decelerate; and in the meantime he'd be drawing farther and farther away from where he

wanted to go. He couldn't know that by stopping, we flashed past him
at millions of miles a second. Of course, he didn't have a chance once
he left our ship. The whole world must have seemed topsy-turvy."

And, in fact, with this brilliant novelet, van Vogt would turn all
Techno Age perception upside-down. In previous science fiction, it
had always been invading aliens who had the universe on their side
and men who had to overcome a limited Earth-bound perspective.
But in "Black Destroyer," these values were reversed. Despite their
power as individuals, it is Coeurl and his kind who are the limited
offspring of a small and isolated planet, and it is human beings who
have the knowledge and resources of the galaxy behind them.

What a promise! When he saw this, John Campbell's heart had
to leap.

The editor wrote to van Vogt, saying, "You've done a perfectly
beautiful job on this yarn about the Black Destroyer." And he
would place this new writer's first published SF story on the cover
of the July 1939 *Astounding*, the issue which marked the beginning
of the Golden Age.

In his letter accepting "Black Destroyer," Campbell described
Unknown, a fantasy magazine he was starting, at some length,
and asked van Vogt to consider it a wide-open market. Campbell
thought that writing fantasy would come naturally to van Vogt,
with his gift for evoking mood and horror. The editor declared,
"If this 'Black Destroyer' had not been interplanetary, had not
involved atomic power, mechanism, etc., it would have been grand
for the new magazine."

And van Vogt did his best to oblige Campbell by giving him
what he was asking for. More or less immediately, he wrote a
story about a Polynesian shark-god—"The Sea Thing" (*Unknown*,
Jan 1940)—that was his attempt to do something like "Black
Destroyer" in fantasy dress. And in 1942-43, he would contribute
three more stories to the magazine, including a novel, *The Book
of Ptah* (*Unknown Worlds*, Oct 1943), in the very last issue.

But even though van Vogt might not be a man for facts and
exactitude, and had a certain talent for evoking moods, writing
rational fantasy just wasn't his thing. Ultimately, stories like
that hinged on providing material explanations for bits and pieces
of remnant spiritualism, and playing that game wasn't what van Vogt
had returned to SF to do. Consequently, he wrote stories he thought
of as fantasy only with the utmost difficulty, and his work for
Unknown was no match for his science fiction in either originality
or effectiveness.

Van Vogt only caught fire when he was writing what he believed in, and his true beliefs were post-materialistic. His great aim in writing SF was to look deep into the time and space distances of an organic, interconnected, evolving universe and imagine man transcending himself.

Between the sale of "Black Destroyer" and its publication, van Vogt married Edna Hull, a woman seven years older than he. She was a former executive secretary, a freelance writer of newspaper features and short-short stories for church magazines whom he had met at the Winnipeg Writers Club. After their marriage, Mrs. van Vogt would transcribe her husband's handwritten drafts on the typewriter and in the process become sufficiently intrigued by SF that she would eventually write a dozen stories of her own for *Astounding* and *Unknown* under the name E. Mayne Hull.

The first story van Vogt completed after his marriage was a direct sequel to "Black Destroyer" entitled "Discord in Scarlet" (*Astounding*, Dec 1939). Here the same human survey ship, this time traveling from our own galaxy to another, comes upon Xtl, a red six-limbed alien being even older, more powerful and more frightening than Coeurl, floating there in the void where a cosmic explosion had hurled him eons ago.

Once he has been permitted inside the barriers that protect the human ship, Xtl proves to be able to rearrange his atomic structure so as to pass through floors and walls at will. Then he begins playing an elaborate game of hide-and-go-seek in which he suddenly appears out of nowhere, seizes and paralyzes a man, preferably a nice fat one, and carries him away to deposit one of his eggs in.

The humans are awestruck by the creature's ability to survive in space and to walk through walls. And one of them declares, "'A race which has solved the final secrets of biology must be millions, even billions of years in advance of man.'"

Psychologically, however, Xtl is much less advanced. Despite the opportunity he has been granted for heavy meditation all alone there in the timeless quiet of the extra-galactic darkness, his thinking remains cycle-bound. And Korita the archaeologist is able to recognize that Xtl displays the blinkered vision typical of a peasant.

As a peasant, his first aim is to safeguard his posterity. It is his overriding concern to find hosts for the eggs he carries within his breast that gives men the time they need to organize themselves and to devise plans against him.

Furthermore, having a peasant's personal attachment to his own little territory, Xtl is unable to conceive until too late that the men might actually halt their ship in the middle of intergalactic space and then abandon it in order to trap him alone inside while they temporarily turn their ship into "a devastating, irresistible torrent of energy" to rid themselves of him.

After Xtl has fled into the intergalactic dark, one crew member suggests that they had a natural advantage over the creature: "'After all, he did belong to another universe and there is a special rhythm to our present state of existence to which man is probably attuned.'"

But another replies:

> "You assume far too readily that man is a paragon of justice, forgetting apparently that he lives on meat, enslaves his neighbors, murders his opponents, and obtains the most unholy sadistical joy from the agony of others. It is not impossible that we shall, in the course of our travels, meet other intelligent creatures far more worthy than man to rule the universe."

In these first three science fiction stories by van Vogt—"Vault of the Beast," "Black Destroyer," and "Discord in Scarlet"—there were two common elements. The more readily apparent of these was monsters possessing more-than-human powers. Indeed, so obvious was this that it would begin to seem to some—van Vogt himself among them—that it was possible he was only a one-plot author.

A more complete and sympathetic assessment, however, would understand that van Vogt was yet another intuitional SF writer following his nose wherever it chose to lead him—and, moreover, one who had rather less conscious awareness of where he was bound and what he was really up to than was usual even amongst this gang of creative sleepwalkers.

Van Vogt would begin writing a story when he had nothing more to work with than some faint glimmering—an image, or a mood— and then grope his way toward the end one scene at a time, working by feel and by inspiration. He would say frankly: "I have no endings for my stories when I start them—just a thought and something that excites me. I get some picture that is very interesting and I write it. But I don't know where's it's going to go next."

He would throw in every single idea that he had during the time he was writing a story, holding back nothing. And when he got stuck, van Vogt found that the necessary new turn he needed would arrive in a dream that night or in a flash sometime the following morning:

> Generally, either in a dream or about ten o'clock the next morning— bang!—an idea comes and it will be something in a sense non-sequitur, yet a growth from the story. I've gotten my most original stories that way; these ideas made the story different every ten pages. In other words, I wouldn't have been able to reason them out, I feel.

As we have had more than one occasion to notice, earlier writers of SF, in imagining their stories, had again and again taken their cue from some dream or sudden insight. But A. E. van Vogt was the first writer of science fiction to attempt to turn this into a system and rely upon non-rational processes to light his way through one story after another.

However, the truth of the matter may be that he simply couldn't help but do this. Writing out of mental imagery, lack of conscious foreknowledge of what was to come next, and dreamstuff was the only effective way that van Vogt knew to produce science fiction at all. He says, "I have tried to plot stories consciously, from beginning to end, and I never sell them. I know better, now, than to even attempt to write them that way."

The less obvious, less superficial, common element in van Vogt's earliest stories—the message from his unconscious that he was forced to repeat until at last he understood it—was *morality*, or, as the more psychologically minded Atomic Age would prefer to call it, *sanity*. In each of his first three science fiction stories, super-powered monsters are undone by their drives and hungers, by their egotism, ruthlessness and cruelty, and by their inability to surrender cherished attachments, while men constituted much like ourselves are able to prevail over them through decency, self-sacrifice, cooperation and breadth of vision.

After three of these science fiction monster stories—plus that paler imitation for *Unknown*—and just when he was beginning to think that this might be all he could write, van Vogt finally came to a conscious recognition of what his unconscious mind had been getting at all along. It was telling him that true superiority was not a matter of age or biology or personal power. Rather, it lay in being able to distinguish between mere self-interest and the good of the whole.

Having finally gotten this message, van Vogt would state it as explicitly as he could in his next science fiction story, the aptly titled "Repetition" (*Astounding*, Apr 1940).

In this story, an envoy has been sent from Earth to persuade the stubbornly defiant colonists of the Jovian moon Europa to allow their world to be ceded politically to Mars in order to bring Mars into union with Earth and Venus and forestall a Solar System-wide war. The envoy admits that short-term suffering for this colony is a real possibility, but argues that it should lead to a greater long-range good:

"Remember this, it's not only Europa's recoverable metals that will be used up in a thousand years, but also the metal resources of the entire Solar System. That's why we must have an equitable distribution now, because we can't afford to spend the last hundred of those thousand years fighting over metal with Mars. You see, in that thousand years we must reach the stars. We must develop speeds immeasurably greater than light—and in that last, urgent hundred years we must have their co-operation, not their enmity. Therefore they must not be dependent on us for anything; and we must not be under the continual mind-destroying temptation of being able to save ourselves for a few years longer if we sacrifice them."

The envoy's concluding exhortation, which convinces a young Europan to switch from being his enemy to being his earnest protector, is this:

"I have talked of repetition being a rule of life. But somewhere along the pathway of the Universe there must be a first time for everything, a first peaceful solution along sound sociological lines of the antagonisms of great sovereign powers.

"Some day man will reach the stars, and all the old, old problems will repeat themselves. When that day comes, we must have established sanity in the very souls of men, so firmly rooted that there will be an endless repetition of peaceful solutions."

The story had little of the intensity, heat and drive that had made van Vogt's three previous science fiction stories different from all other SF. Next to them, "Repetition" was merely conventional—similar in appearance and scope to other short fiction in *Astounding* in 1940. More than that, it was a talky story, in essence no more than a dramatized lecture.

Even so, it did have one highly important statement to make. If men were ever to become the beings that van Vogt had described in "Black Destroyer"—if they were ever to reach the stars at all, let alone inherit the galaxy—they would first have to learn simple sanity: breadth of vision, surrender of self-interest, and peaceful cooperation. And if they couldn't achieve this, they would be just so much chopped liver for creatures far simpler and less powerful than Coeurl.

That this indeed was the point implicit for van Vogt in "Black Destroyer" and "Discord in Scarlet" would be confirmed in 1950 when he put these stories together with two others and added new material to make what he would call a "'fix-up' novel"—*The Voyage of the Space Beagle*. The overall point made by this book would be the necessity for integrated vision. Sanity.

In the novel, van Vogt would introduce a new central character, Elliot Grosvenor, a Nexialist, or applied holist. He might be understood as the van Vogtian equivalent of Heinlein's ideal man—the "encyclopedic synthesist" or master of all knowledge. The difference between them was that in Heinlein's version the weight of emphasis was on photographic memory and perfect command of fact, while in van Vogt's case the emphasis was on holistic vision.

At the outset of the story, Grosvenor is something of an odd man out aboard the exploration vessel. He is all but invisible:

> He was becoming accustomed to being in the background. As the only Nexialist aboard the *Space Beagle*, he had been ignored for months by specialists who did not clearly understand what a Nexialist was, and who cared very little anyway. Grosvenor had plans to rectify that. So far, the opportunity to do so had not occurred.

Grosvenor intends to apply Nexialism to the splintered viewpoints of the various scientific specialists aboard the ship and to resolve the small-minded political infighting that divides the men of the *Space Beagle*. His opportunity to demonstrate the value of holistic thinking arrives in the encounters with Coeurl and Xtl—here given as Ixtl—and other bizarre life forms. With his broader view of things, Grosvenor becomes the person most responsible for the survival of the expedition.

By the end of the book, the need for Nexialist thought has become sufficiently well-established that Grosvenor is giving classes in holism to the men of the *Space Beagle* which even his former chief antagonist has begun to attend. Grosvenor says:

> "The problems which Nexialism confronts are whole problems. Man has divided life and matter into separate compartments of knowledge and being. And, even though he sometimes uses words which indicate his awareness of that wholeness of nature, he continues to behave as if the one, changing universe has many separately functioning parts. The techniques we will discuss tonight...will show how this disparity between reality and man's behavior can be overcome."

In late 1939, however, van Vogt's thinking had not yet explicitly progressed as far as this. Rather, we can say that with "Repetition," he had answered one question for himself, but then raised another. He had satisfied himself that men who were well-integrated into the universe could face any selfish Village-minded creature to be found in this galaxy or beyond it, and prevail. But he had also begun to wonder what men must become if they were to be successful in making their own transition from the Village Solar System to the wider universe.

It seemed to him that men would have to transcend themselves and become better attuned to the universe as a whole. So to John

Campbell, van Vogt suggested the possibility of a novel about Homo superior emerging out of man as we presently know him. This story, *Slan*, would be told from the point of view of the new higher order man.

Campbell's immediate reaction to this proposal was that what van Vogt wanted to do simply couldn't be done. It wasn't possible.

Some twenty-five years later, in a letter to Doc Smith, Campbell would recall what he told van Vogt: "I pointed out to him that you can't tell a superman story from the superman's viewpoint—unless you're a superman. He pulled a beautiful trick in that yarn, and proved me 100% wrong."

What Campbell threw at van Vogt was nothing less than orthodox wisdom, received truth. During the Age of Technology, it had been presumed that superior meant *superior*—clearly better in every significant regard. If a being were to be acknowledged as a superman, by definition that must mean that his thoughts and motives and values were completely beyond the ability of lesser men to understand.

The very unfathomability of the superman would be a central evidence of his superiority. Consequently, a superman story in the Techno Age, like Olaf Stapledon's *Odd John*, would invariably be told by some uncomprehending but tolerated human who is allowed close enough to the New Man to look upon his radiant splendor in something of the same way that a dumb but adoring cocker spaniel might gaze upon its lord and master.

The "beautiful trick" that van Vogt would pull off in *Slan* was to tell his story from the point of view of an isolated, ignorant and immature superman—a young and vulnerable boy on the run, seeking to learn more about himself and his kind.

And this was something that John Campbell could accept. Not only would he be willing to concede that a superman who wasn't very old and didn't know all that much might be within the power of ordinary human beings to comprehend, but he would be thoroughly delighted with van Vogt for demonstrating the insufficiency of an accepted truth. There was nothing Campbell liked better than that.

So much did Campbell like it, in fact, that he would adopt the narrative argument of *Slan* as his own and attempt to pass the lesson he'd learned on to others. Here is how Campbell would phrase that lesson in a letter to Clifford Simak:

> The super-*man* can't be fully portrayed. But since ontogeny recapitulates phylogeny, a super-human must, during boyhood and adolescence, pass through the human level; there will be a stage of his development when he is less than adult-human, another stage when he is equal to adult-human— and the final stage when he has passed beyond our comprehension. The

situation can be handled, then, by established faith, trust, understanding and sympathy with the *individual as a character* by portraying him in his not-greater-than adult human stages—and allow the established trust-and-belief to carry over to the later and super-human stage.

This Campbell-eye view of *Slan* would be accurate and perceptive—but only as far as it went.

For instance, it would be quite true that van Vogt would portray his superman, Jommy Cross, at different moments in his early life—in boyhood, in adolescence, and as a young man. But to van Vogt, these different points would not represent a series of discrete stages, climaxed by a leap to some single final stage of supermanhood in which Jommy passes beyond our power to understand. Rather, they would delineate a steeply rising curve of growth that might well continue on to even higher levels.

For van Vogt, being a superman was a relative condition, not an absolute one. Because he was more able and together than an ordinary human being, Jommy Cross would be *a* superman. But he wouldn't be *the* superman—the one and only kind of superman there could be—in the old Techno Age sense.

Again, Campbell would be perfectly correct in noting that trust and belief in Jommy's motives and behavior were established when it was easiest, while he was a helpless, hunted, innocent kid. There can be no doubt that van Vogt, the writer who had evoked empathy with blobby creeping androids and id-thirsty tentacled cat-monsters, spared no effort to hook the reader into making an emotional identification with his nine-year-old telepathic boy with golden tendrils in his hair, separated from his mother on a city street and forced to flee for his life.

What's more, he would make the boy an unflagging idealist as well, and completely convince the reader of Jommy's constant desire to find out the truth and to do right.

Where Campbell would be mistaken, however, would be in thinking that Jommy Cross's innocence and idealism were only a narrative ploy, a device to gain reader identification and sympathy. In fact, Jommy Cross's purity would have its own reason for being. It would be the very essence of what van Vogt was attempting to express in this novel.

The central plot-problem of *Slan* would be young Jommy's struggle against all the old Techno Age stereotypes which insisted that the superman must be a remote, unfeeling, hyper-intellectual—Big Brain's younger brother. Jommy would be told that this was the true nature of his own kind, the tendrilled slans. Again and again he would be offered reason to perceive them as utterly cold and ruthless and cruel.

In the meantime, however, through his own maturation and gradual self-discovery, Jommy would demonstrate what it really might be like to be a superior human being. We'd see for ourselves that a superman didn't necessarily have to be brainy, heartless and amoral, because Jommy himself would not be at all like that.

Jommy Cross would be the first example of a new and radically different sort of Earth-born superman—good and noble and altruistic.

It was van Vogt's holistic sense of an organic, evolving, interconnected universe that permitted him to reconceive the superman in these terms. More than permitted him—compelled him.

If the universe was indeed a whole and not merely a jumble of unrelated parts, then it was obvious to van Vogt that true superiority must consist in being relatively more in tune with the purposes of the whole. To be superior was to be more integrated and less partial. To better approximate the wholeness of the whole.

However, it would be one thing for van Vogt to come to an apprehension of this *gestalt*—to have a sudden gut awareness that there was a novel demanding to be written about a superman whose superiority ultimately lies in his relatively greater integration with the purposes of the universe—and another to actually write the story. Like most of van Vogt's work, *Slan* was completed only with considerable effort.

Because van Vogt was so often vague and implausible and had so little concern for exact factuality, there would be those among the readership of *Astounding* who would take him for a hasty and careless writer. That wouldn't exactly be the case, however.

The truth of the matter was that A. E. van Vogt toiled endlessly over the stories he wrote. He wasn't facile—anything but. It was often difficult for him to find any words, let alone the right words set down in the right way to express the images and relationships that came to him in dreams or sudden flashes.

Like a Romantic of the previous century, he struggled to express the all-but-inexpressible: his sense of where transcendence was to be found. And with his eye fixed on the whole of things, he was always capable of tripping over the English language and taking a header.

It wasn't that van Vogt had no ear at all for the language. One of his real pleasures in writing lay in coining names like Coeurl and Xtl and Jommy Cross. And he loved what he liked to call "the great pulp music," and aimed to emulate it, most successfully in his ringing final lines.

But the truth must be admitted—his prose wasn't as consistently clear as Asimov's, as consciously clever as Heinlein's, or as exquisitely cadenced as Theodore Sturgeon's. Van Vogt was capable of bashing words together in the most dismaying manner without seeming to take any notice of the damage he was inflicting. One example of this is the phrase "'fix-up' novel"—but there have been and will be others that we may quote without lingering over.

At the same time, however, it is also true that a considerable portion of what looked to be clumsiness on van Vogt's part was in fact deliberate and hard-won technique: A word used more for its sound value than for its meaning in order to set up some subliminal resonance. Or a provocative vagueness deliberately introduced in order to prevent his readers from understanding too clearly and exactly what was happening and thereby losing their sense of mystery. As van Vogt would eventually say:

> Each paragraph—sometimes each sentence—of my brand of science fiction has a gap in it, an unreality condition. In order to make it real, the reader must add the missing parts. He cannot do this out of his past associations. There *are* no past associations. So he must fill in the gap from the creative part of his brain.

On several different occasions, van Vogt would offer this passage as an example of what he meant by this kind of writing: "The human-like being reached into what looked like a fold of skin, and drew out a tiny silver-bright object. It pointed this shining thing at Hagin."

But so difficult and trying did van Vogt find it to write in this way—in dream-born, emotion-charged, headlong sentences, each with its own special element of oddness or not-thereness—that there were times when he would more than half-envy those SF writers like L. Ron Hubbard who could just sit down at the typewriter and bang out finished story copy as fast as they could type.

He would think of writers like that as intuitional—and himself as not. Indeed, van Vogt's own self-description would be: "The writer with the slowest natural intuition—meaning the least naturally talented, in terms of normal creativity availability—of any successful writer that I, personally, have ever met."

It was van Vogt's firm belief that it was only his systems for contacting his unconscious processes and for writing stories that allowed him to produce science fiction at all. He would say: "People do not seem to realize that form does not bind. It frees. If your form seems to constrain you, learn others. . . ."

We should also take note, however, that at another moment he would say: "I mean, I'm always trying to write by methods, see. I'm mad about methods and I sometimes feel that's the only thing that makes my stories worth it, but it's really not true. There is a place for method in writing, but I've overdone that many times and had to back away from it and start all over."

So here we have A.E. van Vogt, for whom words always came with a certain difficulty, systematically at work on his first novel, the revisionist superman story *Slan*. It would take considerable self-alignment and constant self-monitoring to produce this story. But, with the aid of his methods for contacting his creativity and engaging the intuition of his reader, and the further systems he used to guide him in the construction of his stories science-fictional sentence by science-fictional sentence and scene by scene, van Vogt would inch his way along, only occasionally having to back away and start over.

Making *Slan* go slower, however, was the fact that van Vogt was a part-time SF writer who had to steal his moments to work as best he could. Most of his attention was required elsewhere.

Until two months after the publication of "Black Destroyer," van Vogt still continued to write trade paper interviews for the likes of *Hardware and Metal, Sanitary Engineer* and *Canadian Grocer*. But then, in September 1939, Hitler's armies invaded Poland and World War II began, and Canada was carried into the war along with the rest of the British Empire.

Poor eyesight rendered van Vogt unfit for active military service. But the Civil Service, rummaging through its files, recalled him as someone who had worked on the census eight years before. A telegram was sent to van Vogt offering him a job as a Clerk II in the Department of National Defence.

In his heart, van Vogt didn't really want to take this job. Working as a low-level paper-pusher once again felt like taking a big step backward. But he thought that everyone should try to be of some use in the war effort, so he accepted the offer.

He traveled to Ottawa by bus, leaving Edna in Winnipeg to pack, sell their furniture, and follow. It was November by then, and the newspapers told them there were only fourteen apartments to be had in the entire city. They felt highly fortunate to locate a nice place to live, even though the monthly rent was $75 and van Vogt's take-home pay was just $81.

The gap between his pay and their actual living expenses could be made up for a time out of the money for the furniture they had sold back home. But it was evident that if they wished to eat, to meet the time payments on their new furniture, and to have such amenities as a phone, a working stove, or lights, it was going to be necessary for van Vogt to push ahead and finish that novel of his and bring home some writing income.

But the new job didn't leave him very much time for it. Van Vogt had his Sundays free, and half a day on Saturday, but for the most part he did his writing in the evenings, when he wasn't too tired. He'd come home from the job, eat dinner, take a short nap, and then press on with *Slan* until eleven at night.

At the times when it was going well, he could complete a scene in longhand during a single writing session. And sometimes, especially toward the end when the narrative had gained a momentum of its own, it might be two scenes. Then, the next day while he was off at work, Edna would transcribe what he had written.

It took six months for van Vogt to write his story, all the time existing in such a state of tension that he was constantly waking and worrying over his novel in the middle of the night. Somehow, however, between Campbell's pronouncements, his own vision of things, his conscious methods for writing, his dreams, his urgent need for money, and the ever-dwindling amount of time he had in which to write, he finally managed to complete *Slan* in the late spring of 1940.

Van Vogt rushed his novel off to John Campbell, who not only received it with considerable pleasure but backed his enthusiasm with a swift check which included a highly welcome quarter-of-a-cent per word bonus.

Van Vogt says: "Checks from Campbell were always prompt. He evidently knew writers starved, because you could send him a story and, apparently, he'd read it almost immediately, and put the check through."

Slan would be serialized in *Astounding* from September to December 1940, and would be far and away the best-liked story published in the magazine that year—more popular than either Robert Heinlein's story of the overthrow of the Prophets, "If This Goes On—" or L. Ron Hubbard's endless war story, *Final Blackout.*

But what a completely unusual story *Slan* actually was! The more closely it was examined, the stranger and more elusive it had to seem. Like all of van Vogt's early stories, except for his most recent, "Repetition," it had that bizarre, intense, dreamlike quality—but this time at the extended length of a novel.

At the outset of *Slan*, nine-year-old Jommy Cross and his mother are on a city street, surrounded by an unseen but mentally sensed circle of hostile humans. People blame the slans for their use of the mutation machines of ancient scientist Samuel Lann, which have caused ordinary humanity to give birth not only to slan babies, but also to grotesque failures and botches. They aim to exterminate the tendrilled telepaths.

As the humans close relentlessly in on them, Jommy's mother sends her son running in a desperate but successful try for life that has him clinging with super-strength to the rear bumper of a speeding "sixty electro Studebaker." But before she is cut down, she gives Jommy a final mental admonition to kill the man behind the anti-slan campaign, the dictator of Earth, Kier Gray. She thinks:

"Don't forget what I've told you. You live for one thing only: To make it possible for slans to live normal lives. I think you'll have to kill our great enemy, Kier Gray, even if it means going to the grand palace after him."

When he is 15, Jommy follows a hypnotic command from his long-dead scientist father. He enters the catacombs underneath the city to recover his father's great discovery, the secret of controlled atomic power, from the place where it has been hidden. However, he is caught in the act, and in order to escape he must use an atomic weapon to kill three guards. This is something that causes him continuing remorse, and which he becomes determined not to repeat.

In his own right as a teenage super-scientist, Jommy develops "ten-point steel," a metal that approaches the theoretical ultimate in hardness. And he invents "hypnotism crystals," which enable him to control the thinking of ordinary human beings.

Jommy also roams the world looking for other slans with golden tendrils in their hair—but he is never able to find any. Where can they be?

However, again and again he stumbles across a widespread network of "tendrilless slans," who are also products of Samuel Lann's mutation machines but lack telepathic ability. They have mastered anti-gravity and built spaceships, and established settlements on Mars that are completely unknown to ordinary Earthbound humanity.

But these half-slans look on Jommy as an enemy, too. It seems that when the tendrilled slans were in ascendancy, they persecuted the slans without tendrils, and the tendrilless slans have neither forgiven nor forgotten. They call Jommy "'a damned snake'" and strive even more diligently than the simple humans to kill him.

Jommy steals a spaceship from them, and has the opportunity to kill a tendrilless slan, Joanna Hillory. But he forbears in spite of the enmity she shows him. Instead, he assures her of his good will:

"Madam, in all modesty I can say that, of all the slans in the world today, there is none more important than the son of Peter Cross. Wherever I go, my words and my will shall rule. The day that I find the true slans, the war against your people shall end forever."

And he sets Joanna Hillory free.

Then, at last, when he is 19, Jommy finds another slan like himself, a girl, Kathleen Layton, seeking refuge in a long-abandoned slan hideout, an underground machine city. Kathleen has been kept for observation by Kier Gray ever since she was a child, but now, with her life in imminent danger from the slan-hating secret police chief, John Petty, she has fled the palace.

The meeting of Jommy and Kathleen is a wonderful moment of mutual recognition:

"And she was a slan!

"And he was a slan!

"Simultaneous discovery!"

But almost in the moment in which they find each other and fall in love, John Petty invades the cave hideout and surprises Kathleen there alone. He shows her no mercy at all, but straightaway puts a bullet into her brain.

Jommy arrives on the scene with Kathleen's dying telepathic goodby to him still ringing in his mind. He might pay John Petty back in kind by blasting him into nothingness with his atomic weapon, but he stays his hand. He leaves the crucial button unpressed, and withdraws under heavy fire in his car made of ten-point steel.

Then, when Jommy is 26—still not fully mature by slan standards— the tendrilless slans launch an all-out attack upon his secret laboratory and his spaceship, hidden under a mountain twenty miles away. But Jommy signals his spaceship, and it tunnels its way to him, and he escapes.

He travels to Mars to spy upon the tendrilless slans. Posing as one of them, he confirms his speculation that they soon intend to make a general attack upon the Earth.

But no sooner is he certain of this than he is suspected of being himself. He is taken to the office of Joanna Hillory, now the tendrilless slan military commissioner who has the job of tracking him down. She has written no less than four books on the subject of Jommy Cross.

While he waits, he is allowed the opportunity to consult what we today would think of as a computer:

Inside the fine, long, low building, a few men and women moved in and out among row on row of great, thick, shiny, metallic plates. This, Cross knew, was the Bureau of Statistics; and these plates were the electric filing cabinets that yielded their information at the touch of a button, the spelling out of a name, a number, a key word.

Jommy asks these electric filing cabinets to tell him about Samuel Lann—and in no time he is reading Samuel Lann's diary for 1971, and then further random entries from 1973 and 1990, and from them is discovering that there never was a mutation machine at all. From the very outset, the tendrilled slans were and always have been a purely natural mutation.

Then, when he is called into the office of Joanna Hillory, he finds that his idealism as a 15-year-old was so convincing to her that she has spent the years since maneuvering herself into a position to help him in just such a moment as this. She aids him to escape and to return to Earth with the knowledge of a secret entrance to the slan-built palace of Kier Gray.

Van Vogt has said, "From a fairly early time, towards the end of my stories...I would launch my subconscious into free associations, and, within the frame of what I was writing—roughly—would just let it rattle on." This kind of creative process would seem to underlie what happens next in *Slan*.

In a very strange scene, Jommy hurls himself down a hole in the palace garden, and when he reaches the bottom he is two miles beneath the surface. There he encounters signs which presume him to be a slan and tell him where he is and what his circumstances are. Then walls close together around him, and in a kind of prison-elevator he is raised high up into the palace to the most private inner sanctum of Kier Gray.

And once again, as in the Greek plays that van Vogt had read, a scene of recognition takes place. Jommy looks on the ruthless and powerful, but noble, face of Kier Gray and knows him for what he really is:

"Kier Gray, leader of men, was—
"'*A true slan!*' exclaimed Cross."

At first, Gray's manner is cold and hard. He even threatens to amputate Jommy's tendrils. But then Jommy demonstrates his own power by effortlessly freeing himself from his bonds, and the recognition becomes mutual. Kier Gray knows that this must be the son of Peter Cross, the master of atomic energy, and immediately his manner completely alters:

> "Man, man, *you've done it!* In spite of our being unable to give you the slightest help! Atomic energy—at last."
>
> His voice rang out then, clear and triumphant: "John Thomas Cross, I welcome you and your father's great discovery. Come in here and sit down. .... We can talk here in this very private den of mine."

And Gray then proceeds to tell Jommy all.

Slans, he says, really rule the world from behind the scenes—something like those Scotsmen running the British Empire: "'What is more natural than that we should insinuate our way to control of the human government? Are we not the most intelligent beings on the face of the Earth?'"

Slans are "'the mutation-after-man.'" Despite the fact that ordinary humanity hates and fears them, the slans are watching out for poor feckless old-style man, who is now growing sterile and beginning to pass from the scene. And if the slans in the past gave the tendrilless slans something of a hard time, well, that was all for their own good, to keep them tough.

The fact of the matter is that all unknown to themselves the tendrilless slans *are* the true slans. Their special characteristics— tendrils, double hearts, more efficient nervous systems, and so on— have been temporarily genetically suppressed to keep them safe from the wrath of humanity. But one by one the slan characteristics have been re-emerging. And in another forty or fifty years, the tendrils and telepathic power will start coming back, too.

The problem for the slans-behind-the-scenes is to make the transition from man to slan a smooth one. They would like to keep the humans from launching one last desperate anti-slan witch-hunt. And they would also like to keep the tendrilless slans from exterminating ordinary man before he passes naturally from the scene.

Now, however, it appears that both problems can be solved. With the aid of Jommy's atomics, the tendrilless slan attack from Mars can be turned away. Those slans who are in the know will "'make a big noise with a small force'" that should send the invaders back to Mars until the tendrils of their children grow in. Then, with the hypnotism crystals that Jommy has developed, it will be possible to soothe the hysteria, jealousy and fear of man-as-he-has-been, and make his passing painless and happy.

With this solution worked out, *Slan* concludes with a dramatic entrance, and a final recognition scene. A young woman comes into Gray's private study—and it is Kathleen. Kathleen resurrected! Kier Gray then introduces her to Jommy....

"It was at that moment that Kier Gray's voice cut across the silence with the rich tone of one who had secretly relished this instant for years:

"'Jommy Cross, I want you to meet Kathleen Layton—my daughter!'"

And so the story ends, leaving us all aglow. But also with a thousand rational questions that we might ask if we were of a mind to:

If Kathleen Layton really is Kier Gray's daughter, why should he have endangered both her and himself by keeping her near him as she grows up? And if Gray is such a sentimentalist that he must have her close by, why is it that when Kathleen first meets Jommy, she doesn't yet have the slightest suspicion that Kier Gray might really be a slan, let alone her own father?

It only takes Jommy a matter of moments to find out from the tendrilless slans' electric filing cabinets that there never was a mutation machine. Why is it that the tendrilless slans don't know this fundamental fact? And if the tendrilless slans suspect him of being their most feared adversary, Jommy Cross, why do they so casually allow him free access to their data banks without anyone even bothering to take a peek over his shoulder just to see what he might be up to?

And, in its own way, perhaps the greatest oddity of all: What in the world is a Studebaker car with a protruding rear bumper in the style of the 1930s doing on the streets six hundred and thirty, or eight hundred, or fifteen hundred years in the future? (The figures for how much time has passed between now and then keep shifting, like so much else in this story.)

Of the thousand questions that might be asked about the novel, van Vogt himself would attempt to address perhaps fifty or a hundred in the revised second hardcover edition of *Slan*—but with mixed results. Some matters for doubt, like that anomalous Studebaker, could be tidied up easily enough with the help of an eraser. But the effect of some of the other changes that van Vogt made would just be to swap one question for another.

The truth is that the essence of *Slan* did not lie in logic and reason, and no amount of tidying could ever be enough to make this story add up neatly and consistently. It might even be argued that the unintended result of those 1951 revisions aiming to make *Slan* more reasonable was actually to diminish some of the irrational power of the original serial novel.

In either version, however, the fundamental non-rationality of this story can't be emphasized strongly enough. In fact, if there is any obvious defect in our brief account of *Slan*, it is that by the very act of compressing and summarizing the story line, we have necessarily made the novel appear a good deal more transparent and coherent than the unsuspecting reader is likely to find it.

In *Slan*, things operate according to the dictates of dream logic. Characters gifted with unaccountable knowledge, and equally unaccountable ignorance, suddenly loom into view, only to disappear again just as abruptly. Anything that seems fixed—like a date, or an attitude, or an identity—may alter without warning and become something other than it was before. In this story, coincidences, unlikelihoods and radical transitions abound—but as within a dream, this just seems the way that things naturally ought to happen.

Far more even than we've managed to indicate, van Vogt's future world is filled with secret passageways, underground hideouts, caves, catacombs and tunnels. Here it seems perfectly normal for a spaceship to be parked within a building or underneath a flowing river, or for someone to leap down a rabbit hole two miles deep, and then rise again. The world of tomorrow and the labyrinths of the mind become one and the same place in *Slan*.

The Golden Age *Astounding* had plenty of writers who were prepared to be rational, plausible and responsible in what they imagined. But it had only one A.E. van Vogt, a writer convinced that he could be most true to the real underlying actualities of existence if he gave control of what he wrote to his non-rational mind and allowed it to go wherever it wished to go and say whatever it pleased to say.

In placing his unconscious in charge of his storytelling this way, van Vogt took the risk that it might blurt out something outrageous or paranoid or sexual or stupid. And, indeed, his stories were capable of being any or all of these things. However, there was one great redeeming virtue to his method, and this was that again and again van Vogt was able to evoke vistas of transcendent possibility and human becoming in his stories such as no other SF writer of his era could begin to equal.

To be sure, among the readers of the Campbell *Astounding* there would be some who were too rational-minded to swallow van Vogt. They couldn't bring themselves to cast aside all logic and common sense to read him in the uncritical fashion in which he had to be read in order to be effective. Not only would the cheering that greeted *Slan* be baffling and annoying to these logicians, but the exasperation they felt would only increase as time passed and van Vogt just continued to persist in his perversely left-handed approach to science fiction writing.

When *Slan* was serialized in the fall of 1940, however, most of the readers of *Astounding* found themselves swept up by the hurtling power of van Vogt's narrative. And so exhilarating would they find the breathless motion of the story and the constant changes they were given to experience that they wouldn't be able to bring themselves to stop and worry about whether or not it all happened to be making strict logical sense.

After the roller coaster ride was over and the concluding emotional glow of Jommy and Kathleen rediscovering each other had faded, these wide-eyed readers might not be able to say where they had been, or how it was that van Vogt had worked his special magic. But they would be certain that *Slan* had somehow managed to reach right into their minds and stir their imagination in ways they couldn't begin to utter or explain.

We might recall that John Campbell had told van Vogt at the outset that it would take a superman to write a story from the viewpoint of a superman. And, of course, A.E. van Vogt himself was no superman—at least, not in the old absolute Techno Age sense of the word. But then, it wasn't actually necessary that he should be a perfected being. It was enough that he had a grasp of emerging post-materialistic thinking at a time when others did not.

In something of the same way in which Jommy Cross was a relatively superior human being, able to do what the ordinary person could not do, so may we see van Vogt as a relatively superior SF writer, able to imagine what the ordinary science fiction writer of 1940 could not imagine.

Throughout the modern scientific era, as we have taken some pains to notice, existence had been divided into two parts—an area of securely known things and another area of unknownness. But van Vogt no longer observed this distinction between *here* and *out there*, between the Village and the World Beyond the Hill. To his way of thinking, knowledge and mystery were inextricably intertwined in all times and places.

As van Vogt saw it, so great was the imperfection of our perception and thought that even the here-and-now was all but a total mystery to us. At the same time, however, the farthest star and the most remote moment were part of the same ultimate Unity as we, and consequently in some sense might be knowable by us.

This new construction of things allowed van Vogt to operate freely and easily in mental and physical territory that was too far out for his more conventional colleagues. And it also allowed him to imagine utter strangeness close at hand where ordinary perception would never expect to find it.

To an audience that was still struggling to come to terms with materialism and the apparently accidental and meaningless nature of existence, van Vogt's new perspective seemed mysterious and elusive. It permitted him to come at his readers from impossible directions and to show them marvels completely beyond their ability to anticipate.

Even John Campbell was captivated, charmed and awed by the sheer inexplicability of A. E. van Vogt. Shaking his head in wonder, Campbell would say, "That son of a gun is about one-half mystic, and like many another mystic, hits on ideas that are sound, without having any rational method of arriving at them or defending them."

However, nearly fifty years after the original serialization of *Slan*, with the advantages lent to us by hindsight, by the changes that have taken place in thinking patterns during the intervening time, and by van Vogt's own self-explanations, we don't need to be quite as baffled or as hypnotized by the story as readers were in 1940. We can see that what was present in *Slan* to be taken away by a reader—whether consciously or not—was precisely those elements that van Vogt had labored so long and so hard to put into his story in the first place: Names of significance. A sense of the mutability of things. Sudden emotional and intellectual recognitions. Patterns and relationships. Awareness of the whole.

In *Slan*, far more explicitly than in van Vogt's subsequent stories, the names chosen for key characters were emblematic of their roles. The slan-hating secret police chief was Petty. The ambiguously regarded dictator of Earth was Gray. And the name of the young protagonist—J.C./Cross—was a sign to the reader that this particular superman, at least, was no cold, ruthless amoralist, but someone striving to be decent and noble and good.

As we've seen, a sense that things move and change was central to *Slan*. Perhaps as much as Robert Heinlein, another SF writer who had been brought in childhood from a small town to the big city, van Vogt was convinced that things must change and do change. But van Vogt's mode of expression of this crucial insight was completely different from Heinlein's, and, in its way, was far more subtle.

Heinlein, the engineer, student of math, and compulsive keeper of clipping files, envisioned change in terms of permutations and combinations of existing and potential factors. Through his keen powers of analysis, his encyclopedic knowledge, and his ability to combine and permute elements in an almost algebraic way, Heinlein was able to imagine modes of thinking and states of social possibility that were not the same as our own: future societies variously organized around a charismatic religious dictator, or moving roadways, or even the laws of magic.

But A. E. van Vogt, the systematic intuitionist, had little or none of Heinlein's special gift for observing change, considering it intellectually, and then portraying it in objectified terms. Instead, he sensed change as a kind of kinetic force, and that would be the way in which he would represent it.

By making his stories up as he went along, by constructing them as a series of individual scenes, each of which had its own purpose, and by allowing dream flashes to constantly alter the direction of his narrative, van Vogt wove change into the very fabric of what he wrote. A story like *Slan* didn't discuss the dynamics of change. It didn't depict the effects of change. It just kept changing and changing.

The result of this variance in expression was that from Heinlein's 1940 stories like "If This Goes On—" and "The Roads Must Roll," a reader could anticipate the intellectual convictions that Heinlein would express directly in his 1941 guest-of-honor speech, "The Discovery of the Future." Heinlein's stories said quite clearly that the society of tomorrow would necessarily be different from the society of today, and that consequently the man of knowledge and competence would be well-advised to make himself ready for change to come.

But the reader of van Vogt wouldn't be invited to think about change so much as to experience it. And he would put *Slan* down not just intellectually convinced that change was a potential of the future, but with a gut feeling that change was an immanent aspect of existence, something that might occur within the context of any given instant.

Likewise embedded in the structure of van Vogt's novel would be his conviction—based upon his own experience—that understanding comes as the result of sudden accesses of insight. Not only would there be recognition scene upon recognition scene in *Slan*, but also instance after instance where Jommy suddenly arrives at some answer or conclusion on the basis of what would seem to be insufficient evidence or no evidence at all, but then proves to be correct.

There would be no discussion of this in the novel, and no lingering upon it when it occurs. Rather, Jommy just *knows* something, the story moves on, and yes, indeed, what Jommy thinks he knows is actually the way things turn out to be.

We can, of course, recognize this as exactly the same ability that van Vogt himself had for hitting upon sound ideas without having any rational method of arriving at them or defending them. To Campbell, this talent in van Vogt would appear half-mystical—but that would not be the way the writer would see it. For him, as for many others in his generation, "mystic" was something of a dirty word, an epithet indicating spiritualistic woolly-mindedness. And, most definitely, van Vogt was not a spiritualist of any kind.

A more acceptable explanation would be that van Vogt was an organic holist, a pattern-perceiver, and so was his character, Jommy Cross. And it was their respective abilities to read patterns as wholes that would allow each of them to arrive at sound conclusions that could not be logically demonstrated or defended.

Here is van Vogt on his own thinking processes:

> For years I may mentally stare at something that has aroused my interest, and, in a manner of speaking shake my head the entire time. This means that, for me, the pieces do not seem to be falling into a coherent shape. Years later, I'm still looking, still patient, waiting for *the* insight that will bring it into focus. Suddenly—and I do mean suddenly—the pattern flashes into view.

Similarly, within *Slan*, the achievement of holistic perception would be Jommy's most important mental attainment during the seven years from age 19 to age 26. In this new state, he is able to be aware of his surroundings as a whole. Nothing significant escapes him. As van Vogt-the-narrator describes Jommy's new condition of mind: "Details penetrated, a hard, bright pattern formed where a few years before there would have been, even for himself, a blur."

One example of such a pattern falling into place in *Slan* might be Jommy's sudden realization that Kier Gray, leader of the humans of Earth and the archenemy of all tendrilled slans, is in actuality himself a true slan. Here, to be sure, is an unusual relationship: what at first seem to be separate contending parties, which ultimately prove to have common leadership.

What is more, variations upon this situation would appear in one early van Vogt novel after another. What ever should we make of that?

Van Vogt's first serious critic—a young fan named Damon Knight, who in time would himself become an SF writer and editor of note—would single out this recurrent relationship as a major flaw in van Vogt's work. He would characterize the situation as "the leader of the Left is also the leader of the Right" and condemn it as a plot device of "utter and imbecilic pointlessness."

And, admittedly, so it might very well seem to a sober, rational, rule-abiding person of democratic convictions, certain that in any contention between parties the apparent issues must in fact be the real issues and one side more correct than the other.

As we cannot help being aware, however, Twentieth Century history has not been altogether devoid of examples of political parties which were infiltrated and subverted by their rivals, or of revolutionary leaders who turned out to be secret police agents as well. To a person of this cast of mind—authoritarian and conspiratorial, contemptuous of rules and hungry for the exercise of power—the situation presented by van Vogt might not appear quite so stupid or pointless as it did to young Damon Knight writing his criticism in 1945.

And certainly there are some grounds for thinking that Kier Gray might be just this kind of man. He is a dictator over ordinary human beings. His arrival to power came via devious means, and to retain his grip he shows himself perfectly ready to plot, conspire, misrepresent, threaten and even kill. And there is no doubt that he does anticipate a coming day when ordinary men are gone from the face of the Earth and true slans are all that exist.

Given a person this ruthless and cunning, it seems possible that he might not care particularly about nominal distinctions like Left and Right, or trouble himself overly about the illusory issues pursued by people who know less than he does. To someone like Kier Gray, it might very well be the separate contending parties that seem stupid and pointless, and not his ultimate power over both.

Now, admittedly, a Kier Gray who was this kind of man would be a megalomaniac, fully as crazy, suspicious and dangerous as the Adolf Hitler with whom van Vogt's country was currently at war. Nonetheless, there would be sufficient basis for this kind of reading of van Vogt's stories that the writer himself would develop his own measure of concern with the question. He would wonder about the compulsion he felt to write again and again about the emergent superman, and say, "I had become aware of all the things I'd done that were somewhat on the paranoid, the schizophrenic side."

To make completely certain that he had a clear grasp of the difference between a genuinely superior man and the kind of unbalanced, self-justifying, and violent human male who becomes a Hitler or Stalin, van Vogt would undertake a systematic study of this aberrated type of person and eventually write a realistic contemporary novel, *The Violent Man* (1962), on the subject.

However, it isn't necessary for us to take Kier Gray as a player of pointless games. And neither do we have to interpret him as a power-seeker with a twisted psyche. A third and better reading of him and his dual leadership of man and slan is possible. And this is that Kier Gray is a genuine caretaker with a concern for things as a whole.

There is no doubt that Kier Gray can be coolly pragmatic and even sometimes outright ruthless. In the interest of making the transition from man to slan as untraumatic as possible, Gray shows himself ready to pamper and soothe failing mankind, to intimidate and bamboozle tendrilless slans, and to treat true slans coldly and roughly. He is even capable of raising his own daughter Kathleen as a kind of zoo exhibit in order to test contemporary reaction to the presence of a revealed tendrilled slan.

Nonetheless, Kier Gray—as van Vogt suggests in describing him—is a noble man. Despite the unique degree of power he wields, we never see him being greedy, lustful, vicious, vengeful or self-aggrandizing. When Jommy suddenly appears in his private study bearing the gifts of controlled atomic energy, ten-point steel, and hypnotism crystals, Gray doesn't pause for an instant to consider how these might be used for his own personal advantage. Instead, he immediately begins to plan how they may be applied to the problems of the ongoing transition.

If Kier Gray really does aim to be a dispassionate universal caretaker with a concern for the welfare of all, then it might not be altogether pointless or crazy for him to be the leader of more than one party. Especially if the various sides aren't actually as separate and opposed as they believe themselves to be.

We might consider that what at first seem to be ordinary human beings prove instead to be communities of tendrilless slans living unnoticed amidst the general population. And further that what are initially identified as tendrilless slans eventually turn out to be all-unknowing true slans. And finally, that what are at first suggested to be the unnatural and inhuman product of a monster-making machine—the tendrilled slans—are ultimately revealed to be not only a completely natural mutation, but the next stage in the evolutionary development of man.

The truth is that behind the appearance of difference and the assumption of difference, man, tendrilless slan, and true slan are one.

This is the pattern that suddenly flashes into view in the climactic scene of *Slan* at the moment in which it is revealed that Kier Gray, the great human antagonist of the slans, is in actuality the most powerful and visionary of true slans, and that the slans are the mutation-after-man. Even more than Jommy Cross's intelligible character and good intentions, it is the unifying nature of Kier Gray that demonstrates the continuity of man and slan to the reader.

Slan isn't really a story of politics or power relations at all. It's a story about a difficult species-wide transition of man to a new and higher state of body and mind.

The audience that received *Slan* had lately been reading stories about the passage from Neanderthal man to Cro-Magnon, like Lester del Rey's "The Day Is Done." And they had found themselves able not only to look back upon poor vanished Neanderthal and pity him for his grossness and imperfection, but also to feel a genuine human kinship with him.

Van Vogt asked his readers to make a corresponding leap of imagination and empathy, but this time in the opposite direction, and to perceive the beauty and desirability of becoming man-beyond-man. He offered the opportunity and challenge of identifying with the tendrilled slans, and of seeing them not as intolerably Other but rather as the manifestation of the transcendent potential waiting within us.

If the underlying message of van Vogt's novel was that the possibility of transcendence exists even within our present moment and condition, this communicated itself to John Campbell. One year after *Slan* began serialization—in the same September 1941 issue of *Astounding* containing Isaac Asimov's "Nightfall"—Campbell would publish an article entitled "We're Not All Human." Here he would suggest that superior human beings already exist among us without fully appreciating their own specialness. And he would name *Slan* as the initial stimulus for this line of speculation.

There would be readers of *Astounding* who not only got this message from *Slan*, but who were prepared to take it personally.

Some fans, for instance, would give their boardinghouses or communal living places joking names like "Slan Shack" or "Tendril Towers."

Another, much more earnest about his identification with the idea of imminent human self-transcendence, would declare in the first issue of his amateur magazine, *Cosmic Digest*:

> Man is still evolving toward a higher form of life. A new figure is climbing upon the stage. Homo Cosmen, the cosmic men, will appear. We believe that we are mutations of that species. We are convinced that there are a considerable number of people like ourselves on this planet, if only we could locate and get in touch with them. Someday we will find most of them, and then we will do great things together.

This youngster would announce a new organization called "the Cosmic Circle" and attempt to rally his fellow SF readers to its banner with the slogan "Fans are slans!" And even though his efforts would be greeted with more amused tolerance than visible success, nonetheless it is clear that van Vogt had done his work in making slanhood seem a desirable condition to aspire to.

A. E. van Vogt became the first superstar of Campbell's Golden Age on the strength of two special stories—"Black Destroyer" and *Slan*. But then, with the serialization of *Slan* complete and van Vogt at a peak of popularity as an SF writer, he all but disappeared from the pages of *Astounding*.

During the fourteen months that followed *Slan*, through all of 1941 and into 1942, while Robert Heinlein/Anson MacDonald was dominating the magazine with a great burst of stories—*Sixth Column*, "Logic of Empire," "Universe," "Solution Unsatisfactory," *Methuselah's Children*, "By His Bootstraps," and a good many others—van Vogt would only manage to contribute two short stories to *Astounding*. And after the second of these, "The Seesaw" in July 1941, he would be completely absent for the next eight months.

The reason for this difference was that Heinlein was waiting for the war to catch up with the United States, and while he waited he filled his time, earned some money and scratched an old itch by writing science fiction stories. Van Vogt, however, was already caught up in World War II and scarcely had time in which to take a deep breath.

There had been months of inaction following the original declaration of war in September 1939. But just about the time that van Vogt was finishing *Slan* in the late spring of 1940, Hitler launched a lightning flank attack that swept across the Netherlands,

Belgium and France and pushed the remnant Allied armies into
the sea at Dunkirk. Then, in the summer and fall of 1940, the
Germans sent wave after wave of aircraft across the English Channel
to bomb Britain, their last surviving opposition in Western Europe.

The worse that things went for the mother country, the more
hours the Canadian Department of National Defence required
of van Vogt. He was fortunate to find enough time in the space
of the next year even to write two short stories.

Brief and rare as "The Seesaw" was, however, it would manage
to be one of the most remarkable of all Golden Age science fiction
stories. The line of thought that culminated in "The Seesaw" was
set in motion when van Vogt read John Campbell's editorial note
in the February 1941 *Astounding* officially announcing that all of
Heinlein's stories of the future fit together in one common historical
framework. Seeing that note got van Vogt to thinking about the
unity of his own fiction.

He says:

> Being a system thinker and a system writer, I realized at once that
> in the area of overall purpose I had no system, except, yes, hey, wait
> a minute; yes, I had already started one but not called it anything. ...
> The underlying premise was: In every rock, in every grain of sand, in
> every cell, there is a "memory" of ancient origins, and of the history
> of that cell going back to the beginning of things. If we could but read
> the signals that these bits of matter are showing us, we would have the
> answers we seek.

Once his own continuing concern with identity and organic wholeness had become apparent to van Vogt, he set out to express this in
the structure of his next story. "The Seesaw," more explicitly than
any other van Vogt story, would be a representation in narrative form
of his Whiteheadean sense of the holistic interconnection of all things.
No writer who was working from a rational, linear, materialistic
Village-centered point of view could possibly have conceived it.

"The Seesaw" begins with a newspaper story dated as recently as
the middle of last week—that is, the week before the on-sale date of
this very issue of *Astounding*. The clipping tells of the materialization
of a strange building in the space on a city street normally occupied
by a lunch counter and a tailor shop, and the eventual disappearance
of this anomalous store. The entire episode is presumed to have been
the work of some unknown master illusionist.

It seems that across the front of the strange building, but directly
readable from every angle, there was a large sign that said: "FINE
WEAPONS. THE RIGHT TO BUY WEAPONS IS THE RIGHT TO

BE FREE." And in the window of the store, along with a display of curiously shaped guns, another sign read: "THE FINEST ENERGY WEAPONS IN THE KNOWN UNIVERSE."

The newspaper clipping says that the door of the shop would not open when a police inspector made an attempt to gain admittance. But that it did open for a reporter, C.J. McAllister, who thereupon entered the building.

The story proper then proceeds to relate what happened to McAllister after he went into the gun shop—and saw the handle of the door swinging shut behind him writhe to avoid the grasp of the policeman trying to follow him inside.

Within the store, the reporter discovers that here it isn't June 1941 at all. Instead, the girl and her father who run this weapon shop inform him that it is "'eighty-four of the four thousand seven hundredth year of the Imperial House of Isher.'"

This weapon shop and other similar shops, connected in a network by matter transmitters, serve as an independent force that counterbalances the power of this long-enduring empire. And the temporal displacement of McAllister is a sign to the gunmakers that something is seriously awry. Very quickly they determine that he has been jerked into this present moment as an accidental by-product of an invisible attack that has been launched against all of the weapon shops by the forces of the empress.

McAllister is informed that in his passage through time he has accumulated a charge of "'trillions and trillions of time-energy units.'" If he should step outside the confines of the weapon shop or even be touched by another person, he would cause a monumental explosion. However, if he can be returned through time to 1941, this would have a significant effect on the great machine behind the Isher attack.

As one representative of the weapon shops explains to him:

> "You are to be a 'weight' at the long end of a kind of energy 'crowbar,' which lifts the greater 'weight' at the short end. You will go back five thousand years in time; the machine in the great building to which your body is tuned, and which has caused all this trouble, will move ahead in time about two weeks."

This maneuver will give the gunmaking guild the opportunity it must have to counter the threat of the Isher Empire and maintain its independent existence.

However, when McAllister is sent back through time, something completely unforeseen happens. He arrives where he started from in 1941—but he doesn't stay there long. Instead, he begins careening

back and forth through time in a great series of pendulum swings
that takes him ever further into the future and into the past.

If the great Isher machine is on the other end of this wild seesaw
ride, then it seems certain that the attack by the empress on the
weapon shops has been successfully disrupted. But even if someone
were aware of what is happening to poor McAllister, there is nothing
to be done for him.

The story concludes with a burst of van Vogtian music as a calm
and contemplative McAllister comes to a recognition of what the
eventual conclusion of his bizarre adventure must be:

> Quite suddenly it came to him that he knew where the seesaw would
> stop. It would end in the very remote past, with the release of the
> stupendous temporal energy he had been accumulating with each of
> those monstrous swings.
>
> He would not witness, but he would cause, the formation of the planets.

What an altogether unusual story! Taken in terms of characteri-
zation or social observation or simple plausibility, there was nothing
at all to it. The central character, McAllister, has no specific personal
nature whatever; he is more a function than an individual. The world
of five thousand years hence is not a complete, complex, ongoing
society. All that we ever see of it is the eternal naked polarity—
weapon shops vs. Isher Empire—and not a single thing more. And
the explanations and interpretations that are offered in the course
of this story are at best simple images or metaphorical indications
like "crowbars" and "seesaws," but nothing more consistently
reasoned or fully imagined than this.

However, if we agree to leave aside the questions of plausible
argument and fullness of detail and take this little story instead
as a kind of pattern or general statement, there is a great deal more
to be found in it. In fact, we can get the most from "The Seesaw"
if we elect to look on it as an active meditation on the nature of
the cosmos and our place within it.

Casting about for precedents and antecedents, we might say
that it has a kinship with that "prehistoric daydream" in Verne's
Journey to the Centre of the Earth in which Axel the narrator
travels back in his imagination through past evolutionary ages to
the fiery creation of things. And it also has a relationship to all
those tales of time travelers brooding over red and chilly suns and
the fate of man, from Wells's *The Time Machine* to Don A. Stuart's
"Twilight" and "Night."

But there was a crucial difference between "The Seesaw" and
these older cosmological meditations. In the Age of Technology, a

narrative overview of existence would be sure to present a story of
birth in primal gas and fire, which in good time would necessarily
be followed by entropic death in darkness, cold and rubble.

However, that wasn't the story that van Vogt had to tell. Instead,
he wrote of a Yin-and-Yang universe of reciprocal maintenance. In
the cosmos as presented in "The Seesaw," there is no such thing as
strict linear cause-and-effect. Rather, the whole universe is seen as
existing through the mutual collaboration and support of its subordinate aspects, and the aspects as existing through the overallness
of the whole.

At least four obvious examples of fundamental interdependency
can be seen in van Vogt's short story:

First, there is the title and central metaphor—the seesaw. A
teeter-totter in action is an instance familiar to everyone of a
dynamic equilibrium that requires the active participation of two
different parties.

Second, there is the interpenetration of 1941 A.D. and the year
4700 of the Isher Empire. Here we have a cross-connection of
elements from very different eras, so that McAllister becomes a
pivotal factor in the doings of time-to-come, and the slogan that
the right to buy weapons is the right to be free—a message that
most assuredly had a point for a democratic yet still nominally
neutral United States in early 1941—becomes impressed upon the
here-and-now.

Third, there is the symbiotic nature of the weapon shops and the
Isher Empire. Though one party can be seen as standing for the force
of determinism, authority and control, and the other for the power
of free will, free thought and free action, the two appear to be
absolutely necessary to each other.

And fourth, there is the chicken-and-egg question of which comes
first, the universe that will produce McAllister, or the McAllister who
will not witness but will cause the formation of the planets?

With all the intertwining, mutual dependence and reversal of
temporal sequence here, how are we to say what is really a cause
and what is an effect?

It is because of the Isher Empire's attack on the weapon shops
five thousand years from now that McAllister is snatched out of
the year 1941 A.D. And it is for the purpose of defending themselves against the forces of the empress that the weapon shops send
McAllister back through time again. And it is because of this joint
effort by the Isher Empire and the weapon shops, and because of
McAllister's movements back and forth through time that a primal
explosion will result which in due course will produce the conditions
for McAllister, and subsequently the weapon shops and the Isher

Empire, to come into existence. Somehow, through their own mutual yearning to be, 1941 A.D. and 4700 I.E. work together to call themselves into being.

But even this can't be the whole story. It fails to take into account the counterweight on the other end of the seesaw. In order for McAllister to do his stuff, it seems essential for the great Isher machine to serve as a balancing force. And even though van Vogt may say nothing about the fate of the machine, imagination suggests to us that at the moment that McAllister is going *bang* at one end of existence, the great machine must necessarily be going *ka-boom* at the other.

By this reading, the various collaborations between the future and the present, the weapon shops and the Isher Empire, and McAllister and the Isher machine all add up to one crucial action-event that begins creation and also brings it to an end.

And were our perspective even broader, we might be able to see this as nothing exceptional. Perhaps as a result of collaborations just like these, the universe is created and destroyed at every instant.

Just this would be the case in van Vogt's very next story, "Recruiting Station" (*Astounding*, Mar 1942). Here it is said, "Every unfolding instant the Earth and its life, the universe and all its galaxies are re-created by the titanic energy that is time.... The rate of reproduction is approximately ten billion a second."

In any case, it is clear that van Vogt had accomplished something quite significant in "The Seesaw." In place of the old Village-centered orientation held for so long by the Western world, with its arrogant assumptions of self-importance alternating with tremulous fears of cosmic insignificance, van Vogt offered a universe in which man and the present moment were completely essential—but were not sufficient.

Shortly after van Vogt finished this potent little story, the conditions under which he was attempting to live and to write finally became too much for him. His wife Edna had needed operations in both 1939 and 1940. His monthly expenses continued to exceed his monthly income. The money the sale of *Slan* had brought in was all but gone. And the Canadian Department of National Defence wanted still more hours of work from him.

He says: "By April, 1941, they had me working my full day plus four evenings a week plus all day Saturday and every other Sunday, all without a raise in salary. And so, since I could no longer support the job by part-time writing (no part-time being available), I resigned."

However, as much as van Vogt may have been pushed toward this decision by his lack of income, we shouldn't underestimate the part that was played by the inner need he felt to write more science

fiction. Ultimately, that may have been his most compelling reason
for resigning.

As he would say about this inner drive:

> I write on the basis of uneasiness. I should be working is my feeling,
> and so, when that reaches a certain level, I'm working. If it doesn't,
> I'm not. This has nothing to do with whether or not I am completely
> solvent right now. I feel as if I should be working all the time, and if
> I've been wasting time in some way too much, then this feeling intensifies.
> It's like a feedback system. It reaches a certain point and I'm at work,
> and that's all.

When this inner urgency was on him, van Vogt *had* to write
stories, even if he didn't consciously know why:

> I was being swept along in an entirely compulsive situation—funda-
> mentally a compulsive situation. I didn't know why I was doing it. I
> didn't know why I was interested in it. I *was* interested; I enjoyed it.
> I got fun out of it. I read my stories, when they were published, with
> interest: "Did I write that?"

As long as he was still permitted to have a few minutes every
now and then in which to write, van Vogt could continue to go
on working at the Canadian Department of National Defence.
But when he saw his last precious moments of writing time about
to be snatched away from him, he *had* to resign.

And once again, he was served by his uncanny sense of timing.
If van Vogt had resolved to try to stick it out for even a few more
months, he would have been frozen in place for the duration of
the war. His request to resign would have been denied, no matter
how impossible his personal living circumstances.

As it was, van Vogt was set free: Free from the demands of a
grinding and unfulfilling job. Free from the burden of somehow
managing to pay each month for his over-expensive apartment.
Free from the close confines of the city of Ottawa. Free to pause
for a long moment and catch his breath. Most of all, however, free
once again to satisfy the compulsion he felt to write science fiction.

Just as soon as it was possible, the van Vogts sublet their apartment and moved up the Gatineau River into Quebec, where they
rented a summer cottage five miles beyond the end of the nearest
paved road. Van Vogt let Campbell know that he had quit his job
and would now have more writing time available, and set to work
on a short novel.

Then, in September 1941, while van Vogt was still up on the

Gatineau, he got a letter from Campbell saying that Robert Heinlein had it in mind to retire. And even though the editor had not totally given up hope of seeing further stories from Heinlein, it was evident that he would be needing a high quality writer to take his place as a reliable regular supplier of material. If van Vogt was willing to have a try at it, Campbell declared himself ready to accept what amounted to 20,000 to 25,000 words of material a month from him for the two magazines, *Astounding* and *Unknown*.

What a splendid opportunity this was! Van Vogt had never previously had the chance to be a full-time science fiction writer. And after all the days he had spent trying to survive on $81 a month take-home pay, the prospect of an income of two or three hundred dollars every month was truly welcome.

But also, what a challenge it was! Over the space of three full years, van Vogt had only managed to contribute one novel and seven pieces of short fiction to Campbell—a total of about 140,000 words. But now he was being asked to deliver quite a bit more than this every year—an average of a short story and a novelet, or a short novel, or an installment of a serial, each and every month.

Van Vogt was still a painfully slow writer, but nonetheless he decided to accept Campbell's offer. What others seemed to be able to do with speed and ease, he would attempt to accomplish by method and by diligent persistence.

As he would come to say: "In order to produce what I was producing, I worked from the time I got up until eleven o'clock at night, every day, seven days a week, for years."

No wonder van Vogt could speak of having been in the grip of a compulsion!

The first eight stories that van Vogt turned out after quitting his job would see publication in *Astounding* between March 1942 and January 1943. Not only would several of these rank among his all-time best, but in this initial burst of work as a full-time science fiction writer, he would confirm, consolidate and extend the special lines of thought he had begun to set forth and explore in his earlier fiction.

Taken as a whole, these stories would declare that we live in a responsive universe with different levels of being and consciousness. They would assert again and again the necessity for cooperation among sentient creatures. And they would suggest that the natural business of truly superior beings must be to serve as the guardians and protectors of lesser entities.

The moral responsiveness of the universe can be seen most clearly stated in "Secret Unattainable" (*Astounding*, July 1942), a novelet that may in part have been van Vogt's self-justification for having given up on his war effort. The story is in the form of a file of documents brought to the United States after World War II which charts the beginning and end of a secret German scientific project.

It seems that in 1937 a scientist named Kenrube proposed the construction of a machine capable of bridging hyper-space and extracting limitless quantities of raw materials from distant planets to serve the purposes of the Fuehrer and the German Reich.

Professor Kenrube is another holist. He is reported as believing in "the singleness of organism that is a galactic system" and that "all the matter in the universe conjoins according to a rigid mathematical pattern."

Kenrube's conclusions seem doubtful to more orthodox scientists. And he is by no means trusted by the regime, his brother having been executed in 1934 for opposing the National Socialists. But his machine is of such potential usefulness to Hitler's plans for world conquest that Kenrube's project is given official approval and funding.

The Nazis take every precaution they can think of to guard against any treachery that Kenrube may have in mind. And they are pleased and excited when the model machine that he builds works exactly as anticipated—except for an eventual unfortunate accident in the professor's absence that destroys the test model and kills an assistant who has been set to spy on Kenrube.

Indeed, so promising are the results of the project that the Nazis are encouraged to act upon their lust for power and launch World War II. And just as soon as a full-scale machine is completed and successfully tested in the spring of 1941, Professor Kenrube is placed under arrest and thrown into prison under constant guard.

However, at the formal demonstration of the hyper-space machine for the benefit of the assembled Nazi hierarchy, there is a great disaster. The machine is completely destroyed, many notables are killed, and the Fuehrer himself only narrowly escapes death.

More than this—it seems that Kenrube himself mysteriously escaped from confinement on this very same day, managed somehow to appear hours earlier at the scene of the disaster even as it was unfolding, and then disappeared for good. From statements he made to his guards just before he vanished, and from a further declaration made at the site of the demonstration, it becomes apparent that the entire project has been an elaborate plot of revenge by Kenrube for the death of his beloved brother.

Kenrube has successfully turned the greed and power-hunger of the Nazis against them. He has lured them into launching a war that they must inevitably come to lose by promising them a secret weapon that they are inherently incapable of putting to use.

As he says to his guards just before his disappearance from his cell:

"'My invention does not fit into our civilization. It's *the next*, the coming age of man. Just as modern science could not develop in ancient Egypt because the whole mental, emotional and physical attitude was wrong, so my machine cannot be used until the thought structure of man changes.'"

And to those assembled for the demonstration of the hyper-space machine, he says:

"Here is your machine. It is all yours to use for any purpose—provided you first change your mode of thinking to conform to the reality of the relationship between matter and life.

"I have no doubt you can build a thousand duplicates, but beware— every machine will be a Frankenstein monster. Some of them will distort time, as seems to have happened in the time of my arrival here. Others will feed you raw material that will vanish even as you reach forth to seize it. Still others will pour obscene things into our green earth; and others will blaze with terrible energies, but you will never know what is coming, you will never satisfy a single desire. ...

"It is not that the machine has will. It reacts to laws, which you must learn, and in the learning it will reshape your minds, your outlook on life. It will change the world. Long before that, of course, the Nazis will be destroyed. They have taken irrevocable steps that will insure their destruction."

Here in "Secret Unattainable" is an assertion of the moral responsiveness of the universe in the most immediate and relevant terms that van Vogt could imagine. The Nazis, his story declared, must inevitably lose World War II because of the deficiencies inherent in their fundamentally short-sighted, hostile, greedy, barbaric and paranoid mode of thought.

When Professor Kenrube tells Hitler and his henchmen that their thinking fails to conform to the "'reality of the relationship between matter and life,'" we might well be reminded that in *Science and the Modern World* Alfred North Whitehead had suggested that any being which by its influence deteriorates its environment commits suicide. And that those organisms are successful which modify their environment so as to assist each other.

We should remember, too, that in his 1940 story "Repetition," van Vogt had specifically declared that if our species was ever to leave the Solar System and reach the stars, both individual men and human governments would have to learn to actively work together. Now, no less than three times over in his stories of 1942, van Vogt would assert the positive value of mutual assistance between mankind and alien beings. The first of these stories would even bear the explicit title "Co-operate—or Else!"

In this short novelet published in the April 1942 *Astounding*, humans have managed to attain the stars. There they have encountered a wide variety of sentient creatures. And through their conviction of the essential desirability of cooperation, men have managed to unite no fewer than 4874 non-human races in one common alliance.

"Co-operate—or Else!," which concerns human relations with two lately encountered alien races, might be taken as a specific demonstration of how this was accomplished.

One race, the ezwals, are huge, three-eyed telepathic creatures native to Carson's Planet, which men have recently colonized. The ezwals, who live a life in nature, have no use for the artifice and constraints of human civilization. They are doing their best to drive men from their world by violent attacks—without giving away the fact that they are actually an intelligent species.

The other race, the wormlike Rull, are advanced and able enough to have spread among the stars. However, unlike humanity, they are so implacably vicious, intolerant and bellicose that they will not allow any other thinking beings to survive within their sphere of control. Just as soon as they become aware of man's existence, they launch an interstellar war against him.

One human, Trevor Jamieson, has discovered that the ezwals are sentient, which nobody else suspects. He is in the process of taking one to Earth to demonstrate his case when a Rull attack on his spaceship causes him and the ezwal to crash-land on a primitive planet. In order for the two of them to survive both the blind, unthinking hostility of the jungle world and the threat of the Rull, Jamieson must and does convince the ezwal that cooperation is a necessity.

In a minor related short story, "The Second Solution" (*Astounding*, Oct 1942), a young ezwal gets loose in the wilds of northern Canada and is hunted as a dangerous animal. If it isn't to be executed, it must demonstrate the ability to overcome its immaturity, discipline its prejudices, and develop trust in a human being, an assistant of Trevor Jamieson who has also figured out the truth about ezwals.

At the same time, the man who has striven the hardest to kill the ezwal—doubting its intelligence and fearing the savage physical power that has led to the death of thirty million humans on Carson's Planet—must likewise learn to revise his own thinking and behavior. And, indeed, it is he who will ultimately prove to be the narrator of this story.

"Co-operate—or Else!" and "The Second Solution," together with a radically revised "Repetition," would eventually be included in a van Vogt "'fix-up' novel" on the subject of cooperation—*The War Against the Rull*, published in 1959.

Also forming part of the material of this book would be another novelet, "The Rull" (*Astounding*, May 1948). In this story, van Vogt would bring on stage one of the Rull—who in the two 1942 stories are no more than an incentive for man and ezwal to make common cause—and show that if they were only banged on the head hard enough to get their attention, they, too, might alter their behavior and be brought within the circle of cooperation.

The third van Vogt story in 1942 on the theme of mutual assistance between unlike beings would be "Not Only Dead Men," published in the November issue of *Astounding*. In this short story, however, instead of mankind being the style-setter, teaching other races the value of cooperation, it would be humans who would be moral pupils learning from more advanced beings.

In "Not Only Dead Men," a spaceship directed by reptilian aliens from a galaxy-wide civilization is attacked by a Blal, a fierce and mindless space-dwelling monster, while in the course of passsing through our solar system. The creature is wounded, but the spaceship is severely damaged, and both fall to Earth on the Alaskan coast. There the scaly aliens manipulate an American whaling vessel into having no choice but to aid them in destroying the space creature.

It is a firm galactic rule that low-level beings such as we are not to be allowed to know of the existence of interstellar civilization. And we have been led to believe that when the usefulness of the whalers is past, they will be casually destroyed to keep the disturbing knowledge of galactic civilization from humanity in general.

Instead, however, the aliens consider it a moral necessity to pay their debts, while still protecting Earth from an order of knowledge it isn't yet prepared to handle. In consequence, as the story ends, the decision has been made to lift the crew of the whaling ship from our planet and transport them through space to the green and wonderful world from which Earth was originally colonized at some moment long past.

In this reward for services rendered, and also in the rules that protect vulnerable and immature beings from premature awareness of the existence of galactic civilization, it is possible for us to catch a glimpse of van Vogt's most profound and original new theme— the obligation of superior beings to look out for the welfare of those less advanced.

The first half-indication of this emergent insight came in Kier Gray's dual leadership of the tendrilled slans and ordinary mankind in *Slan.* And there would be a further hint of it in the first story van Vogt wrote after he resigned from his clerical job in the Department of National Defence, the highly provocative but overly complex short novel "Recruiting Station" (*Astounding*, Mar 1942).

502 THE WORLD BEYOND THE HILL

In this story, the Glorious, an arrogant Earth-centered future race of man, is shanghaiing contemporary men and turning them into automatons to fight in a war between Earth and the planets that mankind has settled. But the very existence of the universe has become imperiled by their careless manipulations of time. A race of the farther future, who will be the heirs and successors of the Planetarians—that is, if they manage to win the war—has become aware of the danger, but so tenuous has their past become that they are unable to travel back through time to correct the situation.

However, with their assistance, Norma Matheson, a young woman of the present day whom we have understood to be completely under the control of the ruthless Dr. Lell of the Glorious, develops superpowers far beyond his, and with her serving as a focal point, space and time can be manipulated to minimize damage to existence. At the conclusion of "Recruiting Station," Norma has been returned to the moment in 1941 when we first met her, where she will work to cancel all of Dr. Lell's efforts in our era.

The story ends with another of van Vogt's striking last lines: "Poor, unsuspecting superman!"

"Recruiting Station" would be notable for its presentation of a future containing not just change upon change, but level upon level of possible human becoming. And beyond any doubt, superior humans do lend a hand to comparatively backward Twentieth Century people in a moment in which they are being victimized. The single point about which we might have question, however, is whether these highly developed human beings are acting out of a sense of altruism or out of a desire for self-preservation.

But there would be no doubt of this kind in three other van Vogt novelets—"The Weapon Shop," "The Search," and "Asylum"—that would easily be his best work of the year. In each case, the altruism of those more gifted or insightful or intelligent would not only be established beyond any doubt, but in fact would be a central point of the story.

"The Weapon Shop" (*Astounding*, Dec 1942) would be set against the same future background first glimpsed in "The Seesaw," with one (possibly careless) difference: the time, which in the earlier story was given as five thousand years in our future, is here said to be seven thousand years from now.

In this story, the central character, Fara Clark, is a very ordinary person, a motor repairman and totally loyal supporter of the empress—"the glorious, the divine, the serenely gracious and lovely Innelda Isher, one thousand one hundred eightieth of her line." When a weapon shop appears in his village, he is the local citizen who is most adamantly opposed to it.

However, very shortly thereafter, an interplanetary bank and a giant corporation conspire to swindle him out of his life savings and force him out of business. And there is no one who will give Clark any help. Even his own family turns against him.

With his life in ruins, and driven to the depths of despair, Clark enters the weapon shop with the intention of purchasing a gun and killing himself. Instead, he finds himself transferred *somewhere* to a place called "'Information Center.'" Here, inside an immense building that is also a machine, the weapon shops keep constantly amended census data for all the settled planets of the Solar System—and individual files on every living person.

Fara Clark is directed to a particular room, and there, in a most mysterious and summary fashion, his case is reviewed. He is informed that both the bank and the corporation that took advantage of him are among the many enterprises secretly owned by the empress. And somehow fines are instantly levied and collected against the offending businesses, with Clark getting back all he has lost and a good deal more.

He is also told a little about the history and nature of the weapon shops. It seems that some four thousand years past, "'the brilliant genius Walter S. DeLany invented the vibration process that made the weapon shops possible, and laid down the first principles of weapon shop political philosophy....'"

This philosophy is moral and idealistic:

> "It is important to understand that *we do not interfere in the main stream of human existence.* We right wrongs; we act as a barrier between the people and their more ruthless exploiters. ... As always we shall remain an incorruptible core—and I mean that literally; we have a psychological machine that never lies about a man's character—I repeat, an incorruptible core of human idealism, devoted to relieving the ills that arise inevitably under any form of government."

The practical instrument of this philosophy of protection and justice for the common man is the man himself—armed with the guns that the weapon shops sell. A weapon shop gun is attuned to its owner, and whenever it is needed it will leap instantly to his hand. Not only does the gun present a complete defensive shield against energy weapons of the kind carried by the soldiers of the empress, but there is no material object that its beam cannot penetrate or destroy. However, a weapon shop gun absolutely may not be used—and perhaps cannot be used—for either aggression or murder.

Here is a weapon whose nature is not so much scientific as moral. A gun of justice! With a sidearm like this, it would seem that any oppressed man could look tyranny in the eye and never need to blink.

And, indeed, back home in his village with a weapon shop gun on his hip and a new outlook on life, Fara Clark is able to stand up for his rights, re-establish his family, and regain his repair shop—and in the process discover that others besides himself are in actuality supporters of the weapon makers.

When van Vogt finished "The Weapon Shop" and sent it to John Campbell, the story proved to have a very strange effect on the editor. As he was reading this novelet, he recognized that he was enjoying it thoroughly. But when he attempted to analyze the story intellectually, he just couldn't see why it should be so effective.

Campbell's head assured him that nothing of any real consequence happened in "The Weapon Shop." A simple motor repairman loses his business, is given justice, and then gets his shop back again. Was that the stuff out of which a proper science fiction story should be made? The editor just couldn't think so.

And yet, at the same time, Campbell was aware that whatever his head might be telling him, in his heart he liked this novelet so much that he intended to pay van Vogt a bonus for it and use it for a cover story.

It was a highly intriguing puzzle—all the more so since it seemed to Campbell that it was the business of any proper editor to know exactly why a given story did or didn't work. He was even willing to share his perplexity with the author himself. Along with the check for the story, he sent van Vogt a letter in which he said quite frankly:

"Weapon Shop" was, like much of your material, good without any detectable reason for being interesting. Technically it doesn't have plot, it starts nowhere in particular, wanders about, and comes out in another completely indeterminate place. But, like a park path, it's a nice little walk. I liked it, as you may have gathered from the 25% extra.

To understand the problem that Campbell had in coming to terms with his affection for the Canadian's unorthodox but curiously effective science fiction, it is necessary to look at van Vogt's stories with the eyes of an early Forties pulp editor, a man expected to put a magazine on the newsstand each month that would grab a browser's attention and make him eager to buy and read.

The first rule in science fiction as Campbell knew it—and in pulp fiction in general—was that things must happen. There must be visible action.

In the stories that the young Campbell had made his initial

reputation with, for instance, there had been clashes between cosmic antagonists contending for dominance, climaxed as like as not by a titanic space battle with rays of various colors shooting off and whole planets exploding like rotten tomatoes. Now there was visible action for you!

And even in the more thoughtful modern science fiction that the editor was pioneering in *Astounding*, there would typically be some well-defined public problem—a strike on the rolling roads, or a robot who can read human minds, or a disaster in an atomic plant—which would then be resolved through a timely application of the proper universal operating principle.

But van Vogt's fiction wasn't like that. Despite all the powerful forces, the overwhelming personalities, and the levels and levels of possible becoming that were represented in his stories, in most of them very little overtly happened.

Van Vogt's stories were dreamlike—made up as he went along, deliberately written in such a way as to elude the reader's conscious grasp, altering with each new intuitional flash, changing direction completely every ten pages. And, like dreams, they didn't seem to observe ordinary daylight standards of cause and effect. Instead, the reader would find himself in the midst of some ongoingness, and then, after an abrupt transition, find himself dealing with some other given state—and then another, and then another. In a van Vogt story, things didn't seem to *happen* so much as they just *were*.

In van Vogt's work there was also very little in the way of public problem-solving, and almost no direct physical conflict. A typical van Vogt story would be far more likely to climax with a conversation than with a fight.

Even when we look for outright physical contention where we might most expect to see it, in van Vogt's earliest human vs. monster stories, we simply don't find it. Rather, those powerful, hostile creatures would ultimately fall victim to their own flawed natures, or panic and commit suicide, or turn tail and flee whimpering into the intergalactic darkness.

The true plane of action in van Vogt's fiction would not be physical, but mental and moral. The classic van Vogt story would start with the presentation of some limited attitude or level of understanding, and after all the changes were done, conclude with another that was more sane and inclusive—which might well be the complete opposite of the original point of view.

At the outset of *Slan*, for instance, Kier Gray is taken to be the principal persecutor of the tendrilled slans, the archenemy whom Jommy must someday seek out and kill. But at the climax of the story—which is not the scene of violent contention we have been led to expect, but rather a moment of recognition—Jommy sees Kier Gray in a new light, as a caretaker of mankind in all forms with whom he must henceforth ally himself.

In similar fashion, the powerful yet still less than self-sufficient ezwal in "Co-operate—or Else!" learns from the harsh reality of the jungle planet that it is necessary for him to alter his attitudes, surrender his prejudices, and learn to cooperate with whoever is there to be cooperated with. He must give up being a special partisan of his own kind and become a citizen of a galactic federation of unlike beings.

And in "The Weapon Shop," Fara Clark must cease to be a slavish idolizer of the empress—and a helpless victim of her exploitations—and become a self-responsible member of an alternate society of free and just men. At the conclusion of the story, Clark marvels that his sleepy native village can look so unchanged to his outward eye—the ordering of the universe within his mind is now so utterly different.

It was just this kind of rearrangement that van Vogt aimed to bring about in the minds of his readers. If at the outset they presumed, in conventional mid-Twentieth Century fashion, that the nature of the universe must be inherently amoral, accidental, competitive and fragmented, van Vogt would cast doubt on these assumptions with his sudden unveilings of the new organic reality, and perhaps even succeed in transforming them completely with the impact of his brilliant revelatory flashes.

Again and again, the bold ringing lines that concluded so many of van Vogt's stories would zap home a startling new apprehension of the way things are. In a single lightning phrase like "Poor, unsuspecting superman!" or "He would not witness, but he would cause, the formation of the planets," the order of the universe would be wholly remade.

When John Campbell suggested that "The Weapon Shop" was a nice little park path walk, good without any detectable reason for being interesting, there was no rational answer that van Vogt could conceivably make to this left-handed compliment. He couldn't explain to the editor what he was actually up to; it was all that he could do to *do* it. The only effective response available to him was to write a story, "The Search," that was more of the same, send it to Campbell, and see what happened.

And, no doubt, John Campbell did find "The Search" another strangely fashioned piece of work. Like "The Weapon Shop," this new novelet was an access-of-knowledge story. But, if anything, it had even less action to offer—not even the implicit potential for purely defensive violence inherent in a weapon shop gun seated in a holster on the hip of a Fara Clark. In "The Search," everything was accomplished with a glance, a word, at most a touch.

In true van Vogtian style, the story began with a state of ignorance and limitation. It shifted abruptly from one queer set of circumstances to another. It climaxed with a conversation. And it concluded with a striking final line in which the conventional ordering of the universe was stood on its head. Along the way, it displayed haunting dream imagery and introduced a powerful new science fiction concept.

"The Search" was one of van Vogt's more effective stories, and John Campbell was the first to recognize it. Whatever the puzzlement and disquiet he might feel where van Vogt's fiction was concerned, he would buy this novelet with his usual promptness and publish it the month following "The Weapon Shop," in the January 1943 issue of *Astounding.*

As "The Search" begins, Ralph Drake, the protagonist, is lying in a hospital bed with a case of amnesia. This acute state of personal ignorance was a device that van Vogt would come to employ on a number of occasions in his fiction.

It seems that Drake was found in a ditch with papers identifying him as a salesman for a writing supply company. But the most recent events he can remember happened two weeks previously. He had just been rejected by his draft board for an odd but harmless reason—the location of his internal organs is reversed from the normal. And as his next move, he had decided to apply for this job as a traveling salesman.

There in the hospital, he is told that the territory he had been assigned to cover includes the area of farms and small towns around Piffer's Road—the little community where he was born and spent his boyhood. Drake determines that he will go back to the beginning of his route and retrace his steps in hopes of discovering the events he cannot remember.

Along the way, he falls in with another traveling salesman, who informs him that the two of them had been sitting together on his previous trip when a girl, Selanie Johns, boarded their train at a local stop with her basket of souvenirs. The girl's father is a buyer of old metal who makes a number of strange and wonderful gadgets—among them fountain pens that offer a choice of different colored inks and never need refilling, and cups that provide a variety of refreshing liquids to drink. Young Selanie sells these, one to a customer, for only a dollar.

When the salesman had showed him the pen that he had bought from her, Drake had been astounded by it. His company simply couldn't match its quality or value, let alone its marvelous nature.

But while Drake was examining the pen, a fine-looking old man seated across the aisle asked to see it, and when it was passed to him somehow it snapped in two.

Selanie was told of this accident as she passed through the train with her basket. Looking at the old man, she had gotten back such a powerful stare that she'd fled the train at the very next stop—Piffer's Road. Drake had followed after. And that was the last the salesman had seen of either of them until now.

Drake pursues the trail of his lost memory to Piffer's Road. He hopes to find the Johnses there, but the trailer they live in has been moved somewhere else. And when he makes inquiries at the house of a woman neighbor, he hears another strange story:

Two weeks earlier, the neighbor's son had seen Drake come from the train and enter the Johnses' trailer. And he'd spied on him as Drake found even more super-gadgets there—glasses that serve as anything from a microscope to a telescope, and cameras that deliver developed pictures instantly.

But when Selanie and her father had come to the trailer in a state of agitation, the boy had anticipated trouble and run away. When he looked back, the trailer was gone—not driven away, but suddenly vanished—with Drake still aboard.

Furthermore, it seems that very shortly after this, a fine-looking old gentleman had come around asking people about the gadgets they had bought from Mr. Johns. And two days later, every one of these items was missing, with a dollar left behind as payment.

Drake goes back to his hotel wondering what to make of all this, and there he sees a splendid-looking old man who has just broken another man's pen and is offering him a dollar in compensation. Drake confronts him on the sidewalk outside the hotel. But the old man suddenly seizes Drake's wrist with a grip impossible to resist and hustles him into a car, and there he loses consciousness.

When Drake opens his eyes again, he is lying on his back under a high domed ceiling in some immense building. A great marble corridor stretches farther than his eye can see in either direction.

He follows the main corridor, ignoring all the many doors and side corridors and branch corridors he passes, until it seems to him that the building must be fully ten miles long. At last he comes to a great final door that opens onto clouds of fog. He descends a course of one hundred steps, and there he discovers that the building hangs unsupported in the mist.

Back inside the building, he enters an office. It contains journals, ledgers and reports concerning the affairs of "Possessor Kingston Craig." This man is apparently capable of traveling nine hundred years into the future—or twenty-five thousand—in order to right wrongs, avert murders, or convince ruthless rulers to behave themselves, even though to do so means the creation of new "probability worlds." On one occasion, Craig spent months quietly working to establish "the time of demarcation between the ninety-eighth and ninety-ninth centuries." And whenever he has completed a job, this Possessor returns to "the Palace of Immortality."

It would seem that we are privileged to have a peek into the intimate file cabinets of an organization that has undertaken a truly vast responsibility—the care and direction of mankind through future time. We may recall that the weapon shops only dedicated themselves to the righting of individual wrongs; they didn't presume to interfere with the main stream of human existence. But these Possessors from the Palace of Immortality apparently have no such reservations. They have both the ability and the moral confidence necessary to range ahead through time, altering, shaping and guiding the future development of man.

When Drake is through examining the papers of Kingston Craig, he discovers a magnificently furnished apartment at the head of a flight of stairs off a side corridor. He eats there and then goes to sleep.

He wakes to find a handsome woman beside him in the bed and she speaks to him as though they know each other well. And when he goes outside the apartment, he finds that the previously deserted building is now busy with people.

A man approaches Drake, calling him by name. And shortly they are joined by the handsome woman, who is introduced as Drake's wife—the former Selanie Johns.

It is explained that this place is the Palace of Immortality. It was built in the only known reverse time eddy, so that whoever lives here grows younger instead of older.

There are three thousand Possessors—people gifted with the innate ability to travel through time. All were born during a five hundred year period beginning in the Twentieth Century in the area around an infinitesimal rural American community called Piffer's Road. These Possessors share a common physical characteristic—the location of their internal organs is reversed from that of an ordinary person.

Selanie's father, it seems, is a Possessor who does not believe that the work the Possessors are doing is right. Through the influence of the gadgets he sells and the removal of metal from the area around Piffer's Road, he means to alter the conditions that originally caused the Possessors to be born.

If Mr. Johns succeeds, he will bring into being a probability world in which the Palace of Immortality stands silent and empty—just as

Drake saw it yesterday. The only way in which he can be thwarted is for an untrained Possessor—specifically, Ralph Drake—to approach him and seize him by the shoulder with a special glove. Will Drake agree to do this?

As an influence on Drake's decision, Selanie then recounts her memory of what was said and done while Drake was hiding in the trailer that disappeared from Piffer's Road:

Her father was mightily upset by the appearance of the pen-breaking old man on the train. As their trailer moved off through time to evade this Possessor, Mr. Johns exclaimed: "When I think of the almighty sacrilege of that outfit, acting like God, daring to use their powers to change the natural course of existence instead of, as I suggested, making it a means of historical research—'"

And that was the moment in which Drake stepped forth from hiding, seized Mr. Johns by the shoulder with a gloved hand, and destroyed forever his power to pass through time.

Mr. Johns was completely downcast by this abrupt termination of all his efforts, but Selanie remembers her younger self being relieved and glad. At last she was free to admit her true feelings about the Possessors to her father and to herself.

She declared to him: "'*They're* in the right; *you're* wrong. They're trying to do something about the terrible mistakes of Man and Nature. They've made a marvelous science of their great gifts, and they use it like beneficent gods.'"

When he has heard her account, Drake's mind is made up—whether it be by the mutually consistent stories he has been told about himself by one witness or another, or by the fascinating prospect of marriage to this magnificent woman, or by the attraction and challenge of becoming a trained Possessor capable of roaming at will through time-to-come, using power like a beneficent god and never growing old. He smiles at Selanie and he says that he doesn't think he will muff what he has to do.

As the novelet comes to an end, Drake is walking down the great steps into the mist, toward Earth and the fulfillment of his destiny. The concluding lines of the story are:

"His memory search was over. He was about to live the events he thought he'd forgotten."

What a reversal of perspective! What a powerful and alluring dream of human possibility! What an Olympian park path walk!

"The Search" was the first science fiction story to imagine that a continuing organization of human beings might stand apart from the flow of history and then dip back in wherever it seemed appropriate to positively affect the direction of human affairs. Van Vogt's Possessors, ranging forth from their Palace of Immortality to play beneficent god with history and then returning to file reports on the subject, would stimulate the imaginations of many SF writers. During the Forties and Fifties, there would be stories aplenty about Eternals and Time Patrols and Paratime Police and Change Wars, all of which would reflect the influence of this novelet.

More immediately and specifically, however, "The Search" offered a heady promise of new possibility to the egalitarian children of the Atomic Age. This story said that anyone at all might prove to be super. The most apparently ordinary of contemporary guys—even, say, a farm boy from Nowheresville, USA, a draft reject turned traveling salesman—might discover a truer nature as a meta-man, a supra-man, a person capable of ignoring the normal constraints of society and time and matter, and of assuming a responsibility for the guidance and direction of humanity's future.

What's more, this was a story that had a basis in truth. "The Search" was nothing less than A.E. van Vogt's own life story cast in the form of science fiction:

Van Vogt was an essentially ordinary guy who was born and raised in rural Manitoba and Saskatchewan in places even more unheard-of than Piffer's Road. He had lived in boardinghouses, and hopped freight trains, and been turned down by his draft board for physical reasons. And he'd worked at totally commonplace jobs like driving a truck, clerking for the government, writing true confession stories, and selling advertising space in the pages of *Stationers Magazine* and *Canadian Paint and Varnish.*

But van Vogt had managed to step out of this background of ordinariness and obscurity and assume a new calling as a science fiction visionary. He had discovered that he had the ability to disengage his imagination from the ongoingness of the present moment and allow it to wander freely through the time and space distances of the universe in search of wondrous glimpses of what humanity could aspire to become. And it was his belief that the visions he put down on paper would have their influence on the future direction that mankind would elect to take.

As van Vogt would say in regard to his intentions: "Science fiction, as I personally try to write it, glorifies man and his future."

In this aim, we can see the answer to the riddle of how it was that John Campbell could manage to love van Vogt and even pay bonuses for his work despite everything his professional judgment had to tell him about the formal inadequacy of van Vogt's stories. If Campbell had no other reason for putting aside all he thought he knew about the way that stories should be constructed in order to buy every single bit of fiction that A.E. van Vogt could produce, this purpose of van Vogt's would certainly have been reason enough.

It was, after all, Campbell's passionate wish for modern Western man to overcome his paralyzing fears of the vast material universe, and of older, more powerful beings, and of the inevitable decline and fall guaranteed by cyclical history, and reach out to grasp the stars. Toward the accomplishment of this end, he had armed the writers of *Astounding* with the power of universal operating principles, and filled them with faith in the ability of man to learn whatever he needed to know, and then he'd sent them forth to clear away every obstacle standing between humanity and its higher destiny.

There is no doubt that Campbell's authors had labored diligently and often brilliantly at this task. Yet none of them, not even the omni-competent Robert Heinlein, had been brave enough to take the crucial imaginative leap and portray human beings who actually possessed the necessary confidence and moral authority to successfully establish control over the wider universe.

None of them, that is, but not quite plausible, not quite rational, not quite technically sound A. E. van Vogt, with his dream-visions of a glorious human future.

As early as his first published SF story, van Vogt had suggested that one day the human race might be capable of ruling the entire galaxy. And, as we have seen, when considered as a whole, the overall body of fiction that he had published in *Astounding* from "Black Destroyer" to "The Search" may be understood as a multi-faceted meditation on the subject of how man would have to alter and what he would have to become if human beings were ever to assume responsibility for themselves, for their fellows, for other beings, for time and for space, and for the entirety of existence.

There was no way that John Campbell could possibly turn away from that. It was too close to his own heart's dream. And yet, there would be fundamental aspects of van Vogt's thinking that would continue to baffle and elude the editor.

Campbell was a materialist, pragmatist and holist—a person with an engineer's appreciation for things which work. What was important to him was establishing human control over the universe, and anything that served to bring this about was good enough for him. We could fairly say of him that he still saw the nature of the universe in Twenties' terms, as a great machine—but modified by his advanced Thirties' recognition of the synergetic power of whole systems. It was Campbell's belief that if human beings could only get hold of the handbook of rules by which the great cosmic machine-system was run, they could take command of its operation and direct existence as they wished.

If van Vogt was also a holist, it was of a more subtle kind. He was not just a materialist and a pragmatist. To him the universe wasn't merely an assemblage of dead parts, a motiveless hunk of machinery that men could take over and operate in any way they pleased. Rather he saw existence as an integrated, living Whole that must be dealt with carefully and respectfully—according to its own terms, and not ours.

It was a new moral order that van Vogt was offering in his stories, crucially different from the traditional moral order whose threatened collapse had been such a central issue in the great Technological Age contention between the embattled defenders of soul and spirit and the barbaric partisans of visible materiality. The difference was that the inherited cosmic and social order had been based upon degrees of descent from God and spirit, but van Vogt's new morality was based upon the relative ability of beings to incorporate and exemplify the essential qualities of higher Wholeness.

John Campbell was about as innocent of morality as a Twentieth Century scientific barbarian could be. But he was able to travel a certain distance in company with van Vogt by electing to treat his new moral order as though it were a variant form of Campbell's own doctrine of universal operating principles. That is, if the way in which the universe actually *does* function is what you mean by the word "right," then right behavior and effective use of universal operating principles would be one and the same thing. Campbell could go along with that.

Of course, this highly selective interpretation of van Vogt would be something like the old woman of fable who had never encountered a hawk, and when she did was unable to rest content until she had clipped its wings and beak and turned it into a proper bird. Similarly, Campbell's reasoning would deprive van Vogt of nothing that was of any real importance—merely his sense of the essential connection between matter and life, and his imperative conviction of the cosmic necessity of moral behavior.

The truth was that if John Campbell was sometimes willing to do the right thing, it wasn't because he recognized it as the moral thing to do, but because it seemed the thing most likely to get the job done on a particular occasion. Other times, other expedients. But for van Vogt, doing the right thing was not just a means or an option. It was the only thing. It was mankind's road upward.

The result of this underlying disparity in perception and aim was that Campbell could willingly accept van Vogt's stories with their potent images of human beings ruling the stars, defeating monsters, traveling between galaxies, creating the planets, besting supermen, standing off the power of empire, and policing time-to-come. But the means by which van Vogt was able to arrive at these wonderful possibilities would always escape him.

With our advantages of perspective, however, we can see that, taken as a whole, the first eight stories that van Vogt produced after he left the Canadian Department of National Defence to become a full-time SF writer were an outline of a program for human conduct and human advancement within a moral, purposeful, interconnected and organic universe. These stories said that in such a cosmos the way for mankind to move forward was through responsibility, cooperation and altruistic behavior. They said that one level of becoming after another was possible, each of which was defined by its own relative degree of integration. And they said that a natural imperative attendant upon human progress from one level to the next must be for those had managed to advance to reach back and lend assistance to those lagging behind and aid them in overcoming oppression and limitation, in widening their horizons, and in learning how to participate in higher patterns and systems of being.

Of these eight stories, the one that indicated the farthest range of potential human integration and action, and the one that van Vogt himself considered his best piece of early fiction, was an extended novelet entitled "Asylum." This story was published following "Recruiting Station" and "Co-operate—or Else!" in the May 1942 issue of *Astounding*.

In "Asylum," the human form is given as the standard for all intelligent life throughout the galaxy. But within the framework of this basic form, it seems that many different levels of organization are possible. We see six in this story, identified in terms of IQ scores.

At the bottom of the scale comes ordinary Earth humanity, represented by a young reporter named William Leigh. He is a normal guy with a slightly-above-average IQ of 112.

In his future world, psychology machines invented by Professor Garret Ungarn, a noble but reclusive scientist who lives with his daughter in a "meteorite" home near Jupiter, had been thought to have eliminated all war and crime. But Leigh is now covering a story about several bizarre and brutal murders—"the first murders on the North American continent in twenty-seven years"—which left the victims drained of blood and of static electricity, and with burnt and bruised lips.

These killings are in fact the work of two space vampires called Dreeghs, a male named Jeel and a female named Merla. This unsettling couple has super-swift reflexes, overwhelming psychological presence, and IQs of 400. But if they are to sustain themselves, they must have constant supplies of blood and "life force" drained from other human beings.

As Merla eventually explains to William Leigh, a million years ago, the Dreeghs were a party of interstellar holidayers who were caught in the grip of a deadly sun:

> "Its rays, immensely dangerous to human life, infected us all. It was discovered that only continuous blood transfusions, and the life force of other human beings, could save us. For a while we received donations; then the government decided to have us destroyed as hopeless incurables.
>
> "We were all young, terribly young and in love with life; some hundreds of us had been expecting the sentence, and we still had friends in the beginning. We escaped, and we've been fighting ever since to stay alive."

Jeel and Merla have come stumbling upon Earth while suffering an agony of need for blood and life force. Beyond the borders of our solar system, their spaceship encountered an "*ultra*" information beacon which signaled to them that Earth is a Galactic colony just seven thousand years old: "'It is now in the third degree of development, having attained a limited form of space travel little more than a hundred years ago.'" The beacon tells them that at such an early stage in its development, this culture isn't yet ready to cope with knowledge of the existence of the older, wider, ongoing Galactic world. Galactic ships are warned to stay clear.

Merla and Jeel are elated to hear this. To them, an ignorant, isolated third degree planet like this represents a rich and easy source of blood and life energy for themselves and for the other members of the Dreegh tribe.

The one obstacle between them and what they crave is the resident Galactic Observer in this solar system. But Jeel and Merla do not anticipate any problem in identifying and then eliminating this man. The job of being Galactic Observer in a primitive backwater like this is the kind of menial work assigned to Kluggs, a human type with an average IQ of just 240 or so—and no match at all for the likes of a Dreegh.

The only thing the Dreeghs actually do fear is the possible intervention of a vastly superior sort of human being, a "Great Galactic" with an IQ of 1200. Thus far, however, in the course of a million years, these exalted beings have never taken personal action against them.

Jeel and Merla make an appearance in William Leigh's hotel bedroom—their spaceship somehow held coincident in space-time with what would otherwise be his bathroom—and turn the reporter into their helpless tool. Using his knowledge and resources, they identify Professor Garret Ungarn as the local Galactic Observer. Then they hypnotize Leigh into fancying himself in love with the professor's daughter Patricia, and send him off to Jupiter to gain entry to the Ungarn meteorite and lower the defensive screens that protect it.

Leigh accomplishes exactly what they desire of him—but in the process something most peculiar happens. While he is aboard the meteorite base, there is a sequence of events that plays itself through again and again:

In the first version, Leigh is being taken to an interview with a highly suspicious Patricia Ungarn when he knocks out his escort and escapes. He runs to an elevator. This carries him to a room of utter blackness. Here he encounters a *something* that flashes and sparkles and then seems to penetrate his head.

Abruptly, Leigh finds himself back at the moment of his escape. He is bidden to enter Patricia Ungarn's apartment, which he finds marvelous and magnificent.

In a state of some confusion, he tells her of the elevator and the blackness room, but she denies that either one exists. She even demonstrates to him that what he is certain is the elevator door is in fact the door to another corridor.

When Leigh declares his love for her, Patricia becomes convinced that he must have been hypnotized. She determines to put Leigh aboard a small spacecraft and send him off to take his chances with the Dreeghs outside.

Abruptly, however, Leigh once more finds himself returned to the moment of his initial escape. As he is bidden to enter Patricia Ungarn's apartment, it seems to him that Jeel must be dissatisfied with the way that things have gone and is somehow forcing them to repeat until they come out the way he wants them to.

Leigh now begins to sense the presence of another mind within his head—and then suddenly he sees things with a strange new clarity. Patricia's apartment, which had seemed so fine to him before, now seems marked by flaws and disharmonies. And when he studies Patricia herself, she appears very different to him than in the moment of his declaration of love:

> On all Earth, no woman had ever been so piercingly examined. The structure of her body and her face, to Leigh so finely, proudly shaped, so gloriously patrician—found low grade now.
>
> An excellent example of low-grade development in isolation.
>
> That was the thought, not contemptuous, not derogatory, simply an impression by an appallingly direct mind that saw—overtones, realities behind realities, a thousand facts where one showed.

This time, Leigh is able to effortlessly dominate the situation. He overpowers Patricia and her father, and then he cuts the power supporting the screens that protect this Galactic outpost.

Leigh has done exactly what he was bidden to do by the Dreeghs. And when he is back in their hands once more, an exultant Jeel binds him and turns him over to a rapacious Merla. The female Dreegh has been lusting after Leigh with a passion and greed that seem as much sexual as hunger for his life force.

Merla begs Leigh to cooperate with her kiss of death. However, when their lips meet, it is not *from* him but *to* him that energy flows. There is a searing flash of blue and Merla collapses.

As Jeel revives her with some of his own supply of life force, a terrified Merla confesses that she has been cheating. She has secretly killed dozens of men on Earth for their energy, and now Leigh has it all!

We might remember that at the climax of *Slan*, Jommy's bonds dropped away, thereby identifying him to Kier Gray as the son of Peter Cross. Now Leigh's bonds fall away from him. The being who was William Leigh stands revealed as a Great Galactic!

It seems that the Dreegh discovery of Earth was anticipated. This Great Galactic has deliberately suppressed nine-tenths of his energy and mental power in order to take on the persona of an ordinary Earthman. Now his normal level of energy has been restored, and he is prepared to collect the two hundred and twenty-seven Dreegh ships gathered here to fall upon Earth.

This supremely confident and able being dismisses the now-docile Jeel and Merla, telling them, "'Return to your normal existence. I have still to co-ordinate my two personalities completely, and that does not require your presence.'"

To this point in "Asylum," we have seen five different levels of intelligence portrayed: William Leigh, Earth reporter, IQ 112; Professor Ungarn and his daughter Patricia, Kluggs, with IQs around 240; the Dreeghs, Merla and Jeel, with IQs of 400; the beginning-to-awaken Leigh who is able to perceive the flaws and disharmonies evident in Patricia and her apartment; and the re-energized Galactic being who is able to dismiss the likes of Jeel and Merla with no more than a word.

But another level now remains to be attained—the fully reintegrated Great Galactic with an IQ of 1200.

Whatever any such fabulous number as that might actually mean!

A. E. van Vogt, more than most, had reason to be aware that real intelligence was a far deeper and more complex matter than just the conscious, rational ability to juggle facts and figures. And so we shouldn't make the literal-minded error of interpreting the various IQ numbers given in "Asylum" as some exact index of relative skill at checking off the proper boxes in a cosmic pencil-and-paper test. Instead, we would do better to take these numbers as a rough indication of the variety of effective levels possible in the integration of all the different aspects of which "intelligence" is comprised.

If this wasn't specifically emphasized in "Asylum," it would be in a long-delayed but closely connected sequel, a short novel entitled "The Proxy Intelligence" (*If*, Oct 1968). Here, Professor Ungarn would comment that standard Earth IQ tests omit a number of relevant intelligence factors, including mechanical ability and perception of spatial relations. And Patricia Ungarn would look a Dreegh in the eye and say scathingly: "'If altruism is an I.Q. factor, you Dreeghs probably come in below idiot.'"

What an awesome challenge it was for van Vogt to attempt to imagine the likes of a fully integrated Great Galactic! As a gauge of how difficult it could be in 1941 to conceive of an encounter with a radically transcendent being, we might remember Slayton Ford returning a broken man from his interview with the gods of the Jockaira in Heinlein's *Methuselah's Children*, or the brief, unrecallable glimpse of a High One in Heinlein's "By His Bootstraps" which demoralizes Bob Wilson/Diktor, turns his hair gray overnight, and leaves him feeling like a bewildered collie who can't fathom how it is that dog food manages to get into cans.

But it wasn't just a less traumatic meeting with radical superiority that van Vogt was proposing to imagine. What van Vogt aimed to show was nothing less than a normal Earthman—or something like one—being transmuted and melded and assumed into the highest state of awareness and responsibility that the writer was capable of conceiving.

Van Vogt says:

> The problem was to describe how a being with an I.Q. of 1200 would operate—what he would see, feel and think. I couldn't have him on the stage too long, because he'd become unreal. I slept on it for several nights and I finally got it. I think it was completely satisfactory; nonetheless, even the writing was kind of an anguished hurt.

He also says, "That was the hardest scene I ever wrote."

Here are the concluding paragraphs of "Asylum" with the frightened and resistant subsystem that still imagines itself to be merely William Leigh, Earth reporter, IQ 112 and proud of it, facing its moment of integration into the Great Galactic:

> Amazingly, then, he was staring into a mirror. Where it had come from, he had no memory. It was there in front of him, where, an instant before, had been a black porthole—and there was an image in the mirror, shapeless at first to his blurred vision.
>
> Deliberately—he felt the enormous deliberateness—the vision was cleared for him. He *saw*—and then he didn't.

His brain wouldn't look. It twisted in a mad desperation, like a body buried alive, and briefly, horrendously conscious of its fate. Insanely, it fought away from the blazing thing in the mirror. So awful was the effort, so titanic the fear, that it began to gibber mentally, its consciousness to whirl dizzily, like a wheel spinning faster, faster—

The wheel shattered into ten thousand aching fragments. Darkness came, blacker than Galactic night. And there was—

Oneness!

There is a holistic ending for you!

What a great distance we've traveled from those earlier days when a venturer from Earth who encountered what might be a higher being could only think to stomp it or shoot it. And, in fact, no other modern science fiction story would ever manage to take a greater leap than this into the arms of transcendent mystery!

But this novelet would signify more than just a successful act of identification with transcendent being. For those of us who have been following out the full life cycle of science fiction—the mythic representation of modern Western scientific materialism—the holistic pattern that stands revealed in the body of work which A. E. van Vogt contributed to *Astounding* from July 1939 to the beginning of 1943, and that is epitomized in this final scene in "Asylum," must be taken as an intimation that our story is now nearly complete.

The Golden Age of modern science fiction that John Campbell fostered coincided almost exactly with the duration of World War II. This wonderful period of constant ongoing creativity and change began with the publication of A.E. van Vogt's "Black Destroyer" and Isaac Asimov's "Trends" in the July 1939 issue of *Astounding*, just two months before Germany triggered the Second World War by marching into Poland. And it would come to an end more than six years later in the final months of 1945, after the Atomic Bomb had been dropped and Japan had surrendered, with the serialization in *Astounding* of novels by van Vogt and Asimov that had been written while the war was still in progress.

The Golden Age had two phases. Roughly speaking, we can say that the line dividing them was the Japanese attack on Pearl Harbor in December 1941, the event which brought the United States into active participation in the war.

It was during the first phase of the Golden Age—the nearly two-and-a-half years that America spent hovering on the sidelines of this new and even greater Great War, waiting for the moment when it would prove necessary to take an active hand and tip the balance in this fight, too—that John Campbell directed a final assault upon the intractable Techno Age problem of fate. Under his banner of modern science fiction, and armed with his potent new weapons of consciousness, indeterminacy and universal operating principles, the writers he published in *Astounding* and *Unknown* ventured forth in imagination from what had formerly been Village Earth, aiming to establish control over everything they encountered and to place mankind in charge of the multiverse.

And all of this basic work by the likes of de Camp, Heinlein, van Vogt and Asimov was written—and almost all of it was published—prior to December 7, 1941.

In fact, it was at the beginning of August 1941 that Isaac Asimov brought John Campbell the basis for the last great conceptual conquest of the early Golden Age. This was the defeat of cyclical history in the vast arena of the galaxy and the establishment of human authority over the stars and the farther future.

Asimov had just earned his M.A. in chemistry at the tender age of 21. That summer, he was taking one intensive course at Columbia University in the subject of phase rule, working toward qualification for the Ph.D. program. He was following the latest turn in the war—the sudden invasion by Germany of its sometime ally, the Soviet Union—with the closest attention. He was, of course, still serving his usual hours behind the cash register in his family's little neighborhood store in Brooklyn. And, in his spare time, he managed to write three SF stories.

The boundaries of Asimov's tightly circumscribed personal world were beginning to expand that summer. In June, his parents persuaded him to leave home for a week's vacation by himself at an inexpensive resort in the Catskills—a new experience for Isaac. For the first time, he had enough cash in his pocket to begin experimentally taking a variety of girls out on movie dates. In another year's time, he would be a married man living in another city and employed in war work as a chemist.

At this moment, August the first, 1941—Asimov was also right in the middle of his sudden emergence as a science fiction writer of the first rank. "Reason" and "Liar," his third and fourth stories for Campbell, had been published in the spring without making any overwhelming impression upon the readers of *Astounding*. However, other SF writers had taken note of them—Asimov's law-abiding robots had been a subject of conversation at gatherings of the informal Mañana Literary Society at Robert Heinlein's house in Los Angeles.

In just a few more weeks, the September issue of *Astounding* would see publication, with the youngster's first lead story, "Nightfall," illustrated on the cover with one of Hubert Rogers' most effective paintings. From that point, Asimov's presence as a science fiction writer would be impossible to ignore.

When his class in phase rule at Columbia was over on Friday, the first of August, Isaac caught the subway to go pay one of his regular visits to John Campbell at his office in the Street & Smith printing plant in lower Manhattan. He always liked to have an idea for a story ready for discussion when he went to visit Campbell, but this time he hadn't been able to think of one so far.

Asimov recalls:

On the way down I racked my brain for a story idea. Failing, I tried a device I sometimes used. I opened a book at random and then tried free association beginning with what I first saw.

The book I had with me was a collection of the Gilbert and Sullivan plays. I opened it to *Iolanthe*—to the picture of the Fairy Queen throwing herself at the feet of Private Willis, the sentry. Thinking of sentries, I thought of soldiers, of military empires, of the Roman Empire—of the Galactic Empire—aha! ... Why shouldn't I write of the fall of the Galactic Empire and the return of feudalism, written from the viewpoint of someone in the secure days of the Second Galactic Empire?

How wonderfully expansive a chain of free association this was— to begin with a randomly chosen picture of a Fairy Queen from a Nineteenth Century light opera, and only a moment later to be lost in a vision of the fall of one Galactic Empire and the rise of another!

And yet it wasn't entirely an accident that Asimov should have been tripped off into this particular line of speculation by some stimulus or other. From our later vantage, at least, the establishment of structure and control over the stars has the appearance of an idea just waiting to occur to someone, with Isaac Asimov as a highly likely candidate.

De Camp and Pratt had already carried scientific authority from one parallel universe to another. Robert Heinlein had structured time-to-come. The next big job on the agenda of modern science fiction surely had to be the application of universal operating principles to the wider stellar universe.

The person to establish this was not going to be de Camp. His strict scientific scruples didn't permit him to imagine travel faster than the speed of light—which meant that he could not envision human beings traveling to any but the very nearest stars.

Heinlein wasn't likely to accomplish it, either. In his novel, *Methuselah's Children*, which was in serialization at this very moment, his characters were finding life among the stars so overwhelming and disconcerting that they would eventually have to scoot back to Earth to soothe their frazzled nerves with hot bowls of Dallas chili.

But Isaac Asimov wasn't hampered by doubts and fears like these. The light of the stars shone in his eyes.

As a reader of the science fiction magazines of the late Twenties and the Thirties, Isaac had been a particular fan of epics of super-science and tales of alien exploration set amongst the stars. The stellar pioneers—E. E. Smith, Edmond Hamilton, Jack Williamson and the young John Campbell—were all among his favorite writers.

In fact, thinking back on it, Asimov would identify the absolute high point of his pleasure in reading the SF pulp magazines as the first installment of *Galactic Patrol*—the initial story in Doc Smith's immense Lensman series—in the September 1937 *Astounding*. He would say of it, "Never, I think, did I enjoy any piece of writing more, any piece of any kind."

To a degree unmatched by Campbell's other new authors, Asimov yearned to write modern science fiction set in the wider stellar universe. So far, however, the editor had only allowed him to do so in highly limited ways.

Asimov's first attempt at a story with a galactic setting—a novelet entitled "Pilgrimage"—had been submitted to Campbell as early as March 1939, following the sale of "Trends." And when Campbell turned it down, Asimov had insisted on rewriting and bringing it back again, and then again, and even a fourth time before the editor firmly and finally decided against it. In the end, this would be the most worked-over story Asimov would ever write, revised seven times and rejected ten times before it finally saw publication in the Spring 1942 issue of *Planet Stories* under the editor-chosen title "Black Friar of the Flame."

And we may remember that Asimov's second sale to Campbell, "Homo Sol," had been a story about a Galactic Federation of humanoid beings who welcome the first men from Earth to reach the stars. But the editor was only willing to accept this story after he had had Asimov place particular emphasis on galactic recognition of our kind as a special race of "'mad geniuses.'"

Then, when Asimov had proceeded to write a sequel of sorts to "Homo Sol," a story called "The Imaginary" involving these same sentient galactic beings, but not Earth humans, Campbell had been prompt to turn that one down.

Most recently, with "Nightfall," Asimov had written a story to order for Campbell that was set on a distant planet with six suns, located in the midst of a giant cluster of thirty thousand stars—but populated by beings who were physically, socially and psychologically just like us.

For Asimov to move from stories like these to thoughts of human stellar empire was not such a large step, especially since the concept of Galactic Empire was already a part of his science-fictional vocabulary. The idea had been introduced two-and-a-half years earlier in a Jack Williamson short novel, "After World's End," published in the February 1939 *Marvel Science Stories*. This was an SF pulp that put out nine irregular issues between 1938 and 1941.

John Campbell had been given first look at this story, of course, but he'd turned it down. Although it had points of originality, taken as a whole it was too much in the old style for the new *Astounding* that Campbell was making.

Not the least of this was its structure. In form, "After World's End" was one more Techno Age tale about someone who travels into the World Beyond the Hill, has adventures there, and then returns home.

The story's narrator, Barry Horn, is a contemporary adventurer and pioneer rocketeer. During Horn's attempt to be the first person to reach another world, his spaceship, the *Astronaut*, goes astray and misses its target, the planet Venus. He falls into a cold sleep in space and does not revive again for another twelve hundred thousand years.

The future he wakens to is one in which a powerful renegade robot named Malgarth has been striving to enslave, tyrannize and destroy mankind for a million years. It would seem that the creator of this colossal being was a descendant and namesake of the explorer, another man named Bari Horn, who was murdered by Malgarth as his initial act of rebellion against human authority.

It is the duty and destiny of the reawakened legendary figure, the original Barry Horn, to penetrate the hundred-foot-tall body of Malgarth within "'his guarded temple on Black Mystoon,'" and kill him by tearing out a crucial fluid-tube at the center of his black brain. And the instant this is accomplished, Horn is hurled back across time to the moment of his original departure from Earth in October 1938. Here he writes down his tale, and then he dies.

There was no way that Campbell was going to buy an old-fashioned story like this one, all romantic postures and poetic diction. In 1938, the editor was doing his best to eliminate from the pages of *Astounding* stuff like robots in revolt against their makers, affinities (ultimately soul-based) that o'erleap a million years, and journeys into other worlds that are followed by returns that last just long enough to produce a manuscript account of the adventure.

Yet it is also true that despite being unacceptable to John Campbell, within its own late-Techno-Age frame of reference, "After World's End" did have at least one major new concept to offer to science fiction: Instead of being confined to the environs of Earth, or to our own Solar System, as stories of this type had previously been, the conflict between Malgarth and mankind was given as taking place against the backdrop of a human-occupied galaxy— a Galactic Empire.

Barry Horn is made aware of this during his long slumber through space and time. He finds himself able to eavesdrop mentally on the course of future human development (a capacity explained with a reference in passing to "Rhine's famous experiments in 'parapsychology.'")

In this telepathic dream-state, Horn perceives the rise of human interstellar empire. He tells us:

Men multiplied and grew mighty. Commerce followed exploration, and commerce brought interstellar law. For a hundred thousand years—that seemed, in that uncanny sleep no more than an hour—I watched the many-sided struggle between a score of interplanetary federations and the armada of space pirates that once menaced them all. ...

Spreading from star to star, the rival federations drove the pirates at last to the fringes of the galaxy, and then turned back upon one another in ruthless galactic war. For ten thousand years ten million planets were drenched with blood. Democracies and communes crumbled before dictatorship. And one dictator, at last, was triumphant. The victorious League of Ledros became the Galactic Empire.

A universal peace and a new prosperity came to the world of stars. Enlightened Emperors restored democratic institutions. Ledros, the capital planet, became the heart of interstellar civilization.

With this account, Jack Williamson was suggesting something wonderful and previously unheard-of—the possibility of a human political empire that was capable of reaching out and encompassing all the stars of our galaxy. Up until now, science fiction stories had always treated the farther future and the stars as realms of fierce evolutionary struggle, testing grounds of cosmic fitness to survive. But here, in a bold imaginative move, Williamson was elbowing all evolutionary rivals aside to lay claim to the galactic future as a playground for human historical development.

When he read "After World's End," Williamson's young fan, Isaac Asimov, had to find this new line of speculation thrilling. Asimov was a history buff as well as a science fiction reader, and it was a revelation to him to see the stars and human history united this way under the name of Galactic Empire.

At the same time, however, to the Isaac Asimov who had lately become John Campbell's pupil in the new discipline of modern science fiction, there were certain aspects of this story that were downright exasperating. And they would continue to bother him until he presented answers to them in his own SF stories.

One example of this was Williamson's perpetuation of the "hundred-times-told" convention of the arrogant and ungrateful robot who turns upon his creator and destroys him. It was Malgarth and his like that Asimov would be reacting against in "Reason" when he presented Cutie, a robot who might be argumentative and contrary, but who was ultimately to be counted upon to do the job he was made to do.

Another troublesome point for Asimov was that despite all that "After World's End" did to indicate the possibility of future human historical development, it wasn't historically minded enough. With its galactic wars that go on for ten thousand years at a stretch, family names that survive the passage of two hundred thousand years, and robots whose contempt and hostility for mankind never vary for an instant, even over the course of a million years, it was just too simple and static a picture of history-to-come to suit Asimov.

More than that—in the instant that Malgarth and his robot minions appear on the scene, the two hundred thousand years of future human galactic development indicated in this story would abruptly come to an end. After this, there would be a million years in which men and robots do nothing but endlessly arm-wrestle, until at last the first Barry Horn is roused to deal with Malgarth.

For Asimov, with his newly awakened taste for galactic history, this lapse into one more struggle for evolutionary dominance would seem an unnecessary step backward.

In fairness to Williamson, however, we should note that the historical element in "After World's End" was of less concern to him than the question of whether it would be possible for humanity to maintain its sense of confidence and purpose in a universe in which robots do all the meaningful labor. Eventually, Williamson would take this question up again, together with many of the key materials, circumstances and relationships of "After World's End," and would restate them more effectively in the new terms of modern science fiction in the novelet "With Folded Hands" (*Astounding*, July 1947), and its sequel, the serial novel ...*And Searching Mind* (*Astounding*, Mar-May 1948)—which is better known by the title of its rewritten book version, *The Humanoids* (1949).

In late 1938, however, what was centrally important to Williamson's reader, Isaac Asimov, was his new-found conviction that the human future in space, from the first landing on the moon to the attainment of interstellar empire, would necessarily have to have a historical dimension that SF so far had not seriously begun to consider. And within just a few weeks of reading "After World's End," Asimov wrote a story that presented the first trip to the moon, not in terms of personal adventure, but in terms of its social and historical impact.

With his imaginative eye looking beyond toward the farther goal, Asimov named this story "Ad Astra"—Latin for "to the stars." But John Campbell, wishing to place emphasis upon the originality of Asimov's socio-historical stance, retitled it "Trends."

After this first sale to *Astounding*, Asimov's next story aimed at Campbell was called "The Decline and Fall." We know very little about it. It was never published, the manuscript was eventually lost, and even Asimov can remember nothing more of it than its title. But that title is an allusion to Edward Gibbon's immense pioneer historical study, *The Decline and Fall of the Roman Empire* (1776-1788), which Asimov had read and then read again. Even if it was employed only facetiously or trivially, this title is an indication that Asimov continued to have history on his mind, and specifically the passing of empires.

Then, with his next effort, "Pilgrimage," Asimov attempted to write a story that was simultaneously galactic and historical. In this novelet, human colonies among the stars that have allowed themselves to forget their Earthly origins rediscover their sense of historical awareness and purpose and return to liberate Earth from its long-time occupation by the Lhasinu, reptilian aliens who are the one other intelligent race in our galaxy.

What is more, in framing the particular circumstances of "Pilgrimage," Asimov drew upon one historic parallel after another. The occupation of Earth was imagined as being like the Roman rule of Judea at the beginning of the Christian era. The campaign to liberate Earth was modeled after the Christian Crusades of the Middle Ages. And the climactic space battle was based upon the Greek defeat of Persia at the naval battle of Salamis in 480 B.C.

Despite being worked over again and again, however, "Pilgrimage" would never be a completely successful story in any of its incarnations, including the one ultimately published in *Planet Stories*. The reason for this was that even though it was far and away the most substantial and ambitious piece of work that Asimov had yet attempted, nonetheless it was only 16,000 words long—about the same length as Heinlein's "The Roads Must Roll" or van Vogt's "The Weapon Shop." In his inexperience, Asimov was attempting to make a pint pot hold the ingredients of an epic.

However, as breathless and sketchy as this novelet was, it would still be an intimation of the style and direction of much of Asimov's future work. In fact, it could fairly be said that it would take him the better part of fifteen years and fully half-a-dozen books to work his way through all the issues, materials, attitudes and situations that he had originally tried to cram into "Pilgrimage."

After this story—or, more properly, during the period in which he was writing and rewriting "Pilgrimage"—Asimov eased back somewhat on his galactico-historical aspirations while he experimented with other sorts of science fiction and learned to write consistently in terms that John Campbell would accept. But he never let go of the insight into human stellar history that had come to him as a result of reading "After World's End."

In sum, then, on August 1, 1941, when young Isaac Asimov got on the subway without a conscious idea for a story in his head, and, seeking inspiration, opened his Gilbert and Sullivan at random to an illustration from *Iolanthe*, he was about as well-prepared as a modern science fiction writer could possibly be to receive a sudden vision of the fall of Galactic Empire and the return of feudalism, written from the viewpoint of someone in the secure days of the Second Empire.

As soon as this idea burst upon him, Asimov knew that it was a dandy. He held on tight to it for the remainder of his subway ride, thinking about Gibbon's *Decline and Fall of the Roman Empire*, working out the direction his story might take, and trying to anticipate what John Campbell's reaction was going to be.

However, as filled with Galactic Empire as Asimov's thoughts were, the fact of the matter is that he hadn't yet grasped the full potential of the idea that had just come to him. It is true that he couldn't stop himself from grinning compulsively—he knew that what he had was *that* good—but he didn't have the least suspicion of how big this idea would eventually prove to be.

It took John Campbell to see more. Not everything, but more. And just as soon as he realized what it was that Asimov had brought to him, Campbell set out to broaden the youngster's awareness.

Here, from Asimov's autobiography, is the way he remembers things going between them:

> I was bubbling over by the time I got to Campbell's, and my enthusiasm was catching. It was perhaps *too* catching, for Campbell blazed up as I had never seen him do.
> "That's too large a theme for a short story," he said.
> "I was thinking of a novelette," I said, quickly, adjusting my thoughts.
> "Or a novelette. It will have to be an open-ended series of stories."
> "What?" I said, weakly.
> "Short stories, novelettes, serials, all fitting into a particular future history, involving the fall of the First Galactic Empire, the period of feudalism that follows, and the rise of the Second Galactic Empire."
> "What?" I said, even more weakly.
> "Yes, I want you to write an outline of the future history. Go home and write the outline."

Since elsewhere Asimov says that they talked for two hours, this has to be a highly compressed version of their conversation. But even in this spare account, certain things are clear.

One is that John Campbell immediately recognized that Asimov was thinking once again in terms of pint pots. He only aimed to write a short story, or, just possibly, a novelet, and that wasn't space enough to do this subject justice.

In order to shift Asimov's thinking in the right direction, the editor told him that what he wanted to see was an open-ended series of stories of various lengths, including serial novels, about the full sequence of events from the fall of the First Galactic Empire to the rise of the Second.

Hearing that took Asimov completely by surprise. Up until this time, he had sold just half-a-dozen stories to *Astounding*, only one of which was longer than a short story, and he had never written a novel. The suddenness of Campbell's enthusiasm and the wide-openness of his receptivity were sufficient to leave the youngster speechless.

This is what Asimov tells us—but there is even more that he leaves out: the specifics of the story he originally proposed; the reasons why Campbell was so sure that a series of stories would be more appropriate than just one; and the details of Campbell's criticism and advice. However, with the aid of scattered clues from other places, together with our knowledge of Asimov and Campbell and of the story that Asimov actually did come to write, it is possible to fill in a little more of what passed between them during their two hours of talk.

It would seem that when Asimov came rushing into Campbell's office, all eager to share his latest story idea, he was primarily thinking about the period of interstellar feudalism following the fall of empire.

As Asimov had it, a planet of men of learning—encyclopedists—located on the fringes of the galaxy would be working to offset the effects of the great collapse. During the Galactic Dark Ages, these scholars would be caretakers of humanity's best knowledge in much the same way that Irish monks on the periphery of Europe had served as custodians of classical culture after the fall of Rome.

And (we can imagine Asimov saying) as a demonstration of the ultimate success of their enterprise, a quote could be included from the *Encyclopedia Galactica*—published in the secure days of a new and better Second Empire that their efforts have helped to bring into being.

The more closely we look at these story circumstances, the clearer it will become that this is the final situation of "Nightfall"—in which all hope of ever bringing cyclical history to an end on the planet Lagash depends upon the survival of the scientific knowledge that is stored for safekeeping in the Hideout—only written large and carried a step further. We can also see a reflection of Asimov's respect and love for the *Encyclopaedia Britannica*, which he longed to own a copy of, and had ambitions of reading from one end to the other.

While Asimov sketched his idea, John Campbell, as usual, leaned back in his swivel chair and puffed on a cigarette in a black holder. But even while the editor listened, his mind was busy weighing and assessing each word and testing alternative possibilities.

He could see immediately that Asimov had reason to be excited. It was a highly promising situation that he was setting forth—if only it could be grabbed by the right handle.

At the same time, however, Campbell couldn't help but be aware of the limits of the youngster's proposal. He was never satisfied by first order answers, and this story that Asimov was suggesting was too simple and static and easy.

Specifically, the editor was sure that it could never be sufficient to just preserve and codify the imperfect state of understanding of some civilization in collapse. As he would say in the blurb that he attached to Asimov's story, "Foundation," when it was published in the May 1942 *Astounding*: "It's a characteristic of a decadent civilization that their 'scientists' consider all knowledge already known—that they spend their time making cyclopedic gatherings of that knowledge."

In Campbell's book, knowledge—real knowledge—was the ability to deal successfully with a problem never encountered before, including the fall of Galactic Empire. And if what you thought you knew didn't work, then it ought to be discarded in favor of better answers. But he saw no point in attempting to turn ineffective "knowledge" into an icon.

As he listened to Asimov, the editor felt there had to be a better way to deal with the problem of the fall of Galactic Empire than making encyclopedias, and he looked for a hint of wider possibility that he could snatch up and toss back to Asimov. And then he was given exactly what he was looking for. He heard Asimov declare that out of the rubble of the First Galactic Empire a later Second Empire would arise.

That was enough to make Campbell straighten up in his chair. He saw at once that if the attainment of the Second Empire was made the center of concern, then this promising idea of Asimov's would become a spectacularly good idea!

The fall of the old Galactic Empire was just the starting point. The challenge for the modern science fiction writer was to imagine men who knew what they were doing as they strove to countermand the power of cyclical history and bring a new and better Galactic Empire into being!

And so, in the very instant that Asimov finished laying out his story idea to Campbell, the editor was ready to answer him. And each and every thing he had to say was aimed to alter Asimov's thinking in the direction of this new and wider conception.

It was a lot for Asimov to take in at once—a radical shift in both scope and emphasis—and he gave signs of needing some time to absorb it all. So after a while Campbell decided that the discussion had gone on long enough. He suggested to Asimov that he work up an outline of this future history and sent him off to Brooklyn.

And when he got home, Asimov dutifully spent the next ten days attempting to produce the outline Campbell had asked for. But he just couldn't get it to work. He says that it "got longer and longer and stupider and stupider until I finally tore it up."

Three months earlier, when Robert Heinlein's Future History chart had been published in *Astounding*, Asimov had been as impressed by it as everybody else. Perhaps more impressed, since he was both an appreciator of history and Heinlein's earliest fan. But banging his head against this outline was enough to convince him that if Campbell wanted him to be another Heinlein and base all his stories on detailed charts and 70,000 word background manuscripts, it wasn't going to happen.

It was Asimov's conviction that he was incapable of planning a story out on paper, all in advance, and then following that plan exactly—let alone doing this for an entire series of stories. It was just the opposite of how he actually worked.

Asimov didn't build up a whole out of an accumulation of details. He started with a sense of something—a glimmering—and eventually found the specific form and words that would express it.

First would come the inkling. Then, after he had moved factors and insights and potentialities around and around in his mind, a story pattern would fall into place. This might happen almost instantaneously, or it might take considerable thought, but the process couldn't be talked about, let alone pinned down on paper in any meaningful way.

At last, when Asimov had enough of a design in his head to begin writing, he would sit down at the typewriter and throw himself into a state of intense concentration. His inner eye would remain fixed on the shape and direction of the whole, while his typing fingers took on a life of their own. Words would then pour onto the page almost as though they were being dictated to him—until at last he looked up and found himself with another completed story.

In this process of creation, Asimov was sure there was no place for written outlines. His conclusion was that if the editor's head had been turned by Heinlein's example, so that he desired Asimov to do exactly what Heinlein had done, then Campbell had to be mistaken.

We might go even further than this, however, and say that if Asimov was correct in thinking that this was what Campbell wanted of him, then the editor was doubly wrong, since we know that this wasn't what Heinlein had done, either. When Robert Heinlein wrote science fiction, including his Future History, he made things up as he went along—just like Asimov.

But another possibility does exist, and this is that John Campbell never seriously intended for Asimov to produce an exact outline of what he would write. The editor, after all, was asking Asimov for "an open-ended series," and a story series that constantly surprises itself by going off in unexpected new directions has to be an unlikely candidate for complete outline in advance.

What Campbell may actually have wanted was for a little time to pass for an overwhelmed Asimov to catch his breath and regain his balance. And setting him to work on an outline, however useless it might prove, at least ensured that he must do some thinking about a series of stories and the way to seek Second Empire.

In either case, after ten days there came a moment when Asimov was ready to shrug off the command to produce an outline, and just go ahead and write. In this mood of readiness and determination, he was prepared to forget about what might happen in later stories, and simply try to deal with a single story in his usual way.

He tells us: "I started the story I had originally intended to write (with modifications that resulted from my discussions with Campbell) and the heck with possible future stories. I'd worry about them when the time came—and *if* the time came."

In "Foundation," the story that Asimov wrote, it is fifty thousand years after the discovery of atomic power. Humanity has expanded into a galaxy devoid of other intelligent beings, and there it has settled on millions of different planets. An Empire centered on the planet Trantor has ruled the galaxy for thousands of years, but now the Empire is in decline and soon it must fall.

The demise of the Empire has been predicted by Hari Seldon, the greatest psychologist of the age, who is able to mathematically anticipate the thought patterns of whole populations, and thereby to affect them. Seldon says:

> "And after the Fall will come inevitable barbarism, a period which, our psychohistory tells us, should, under ordinary circumstances, last from thirty to fifty thousand years. We cannot stop the Fall. We do not wish to; for Empire culture has lost whatever virility and worth it once had. But we can shorten the period of Barbarism that must follow—down to a single thousand of years."

As the story opens, Seldon is addressing the final meeting of fifty of the best philosophers, psychologists, historians and physical scientists in the Galactic Empire. After twenty years of effort, the work of this team of wise men is now complete.

Seldon declares:

> "We have done; and our work is over. The Galactic Empire is falling, but its culture shall not die, and provision has been made for a new and greater culture to develop therefrom. The two Scientific Refuges we planned have been established: one at each end of the Galaxy, at Terminus and at Star's End. They are in operation and already moving along the inevitable lines we have drawn for them. ...
>
> "We began in secret; we have worked throughout in secret; and now end in secret—to wait for our reward a thousand years hence with the establishment of the Second Galactic Empire."

Thus it was that in the opening paragraphs of "Foundation" the ultimate goal was explicitly set forth—the re-establishment within a thousand years of a new, improved Galactic Empire.

But we can also see much else of importance either stated or implied by Hari Seldon: a human-ruled Galaxy that may be falling of its own weight, but is not threatened by alien equals or superiors; a new science of "psychohistory"; and the existence of two different Scientific Refuges, one at each end of the Galaxy.

When he imagined a human empire occupying a galaxy that was lacking in all alien competitors, Asimov was following the precedent set by Jack Williamson in "After World's End." Looking back in more recent time, Asimov has frankly acknowledged that "the multi-intelligence Galaxy is, to my way of thinking, more probable than the all-human one." But when it came to the making of his science fiction stories, it was never the calculation of probabilities that guided Asimov.

Modern science fiction, as Asimov had been learning to write it from Campbell, consisted of thought experiments—the imagining of possible problems and their solutions. And just as it was legitimate in a scientific experiment to arrange all sorts of improbable conditions in order to tease an event into being and then observe what occurred, so did Asimov regard it as perfectly legitimate in science fiction thought experiments like "Reason" or "Nightfall" to present unlikely yet possible circumstances for the sake of working through what might result from them.

Even though it was cut from a larger bolt of cloth, "Foundation" was not different from "Reason" or "Nightfall." It was a thought experiment, too. And in this particular case, Asimov had at least three good reasons for not including able, contentious aliens in the galaxy of his imagination.

One of these reasons—it seems quite likely—was shared with Jack Williamson in "After World's End." And this is that if you wish to write a story about a human Galactic Empire, it is altogether simpler and easier to allow men to set up shop in a universe that is wide-open and ready for the taking than to require them to contend with other beings for the privilege of establishing and maintaining their Empire.

A second reason was that Asimov didn't crave any unnecessary struggles with John Campbell. He says, "It was my fixed intention not to allow Campbell to foist upon me his notions of the superiority and inferiority of races, and the surest way of doing this was to have an all-human Galaxy."

Asimov's third reason for omitting aliens was that they had no role to play in the story he was aiming to tell. It was human social, political and historical forces that Asimov desired to set upon the galactic stage and observe in action. Alien beings would only be a distraction.

Ultimately, however, all three of Asimov's reasons for choosing an all-human galaxy were one and the same: He didn't wish to write about mankind contending for evolutionary dominance in the old familiar Techno Age manner. He wanted instead to pose problems and then work his way through to solutions in the emerging style of the Atomic Age.

So, in choosing the conditions of his particular thought experiment, Asimov simply elected to leave out all aliens. In fact, so ruthless was he in setting his parameters that he even excluded the robots he had brought under human control in his other series of connected thought experiments.

Campbell would have no complaints to make about Asimov's radical simplification. The editor might still be enough of an unregenerate Techno-Ager to never want to concede that any alien being could be permanently or absolutely superior to man, but he suffered no compulsive need to hunt up strange beings and pick fights with them. His real interest, too, was in human problem-solving. If Asimov's streamlined galaxy allowed men to get on with their proper business of solving problems without distraction or dismay, that could only be a recommendation in Campbell's eyes.

Other writers would find Asimov's expedient a convenience, too. In years to come, so many of the stories printed in *Astounding* would follow Williamson and Asimov into the humans-only galaxy that it could even be taken by some to be the mainline human future.

Asimov's new science of psychohistory would also be congenial to Campbell. With the prompting and encouragement of the editor, Asimov had been trying out the idea of a mathematically exact science of psychology in one form and then another. In "Homo Sol," it was galactic masters of mathematical psychology who take the measure of mankind and then declare us awesome. In the series of stories about robots-under-control that Asimov was evolving, it was mathematically founded robot psychology, epitomized in the Three Laws of Robotics, that guaranteed the grip of man over his mechanical offspring. And now, here in "Foundation," it was a statistically based psychology of human populations that was to furnish the basis for shortening the hiatus between Galactic Empires to a mere thousand years.

At different moments in "Foundation" and its sequels, "psycho-history" would be spelled in different ways—sometimes with a capital, sometimes without, sometimes with a hyphen and sometimes not. But in all its variants, this would be a most powerful and penetrating science. Asimov would summarize its nature this way:

> Psycho-history dealt not with man, but with man-masses. It was the science of mobs; mobs in their billions. It could forecast reactions to stimuli with something of the accuracy that a lesser science could bring to the forecast of a rebound of a billiard ball. The reaction of one man could be forecast by no known mathematics; the reaction of a billion is something else again.

From this we can see that in form psychohistory would bear a resemblance to kinetics. That is, it would not be able to measure and predict the psyche of an individual human being any more than kinetics was able to account for the behavior of a single molecule in a volume of gas. But when it came to the behavior of the whole—the psychological reactions of the entire human population of the galaxy—psychohistory would be remarkably exact. Its accuracy would approach the ability of classical mechanics to predict the ricochet of a billiard ball.

Most provocative of all, however, would be the suggestion that after these comparisons to physics had been made, such was the true power and significance of psychohistory that next to it, physics must be reckoned a lesser science!

The last point of importance introduced by master psychohistorian Hari Seldon—the existence of two Scientific Refuges from the fall of Galactic Empire, and not merely the one that Asimov had originally envisioned—was the result of a suggestion from John Campbell. According to Asimov:

"I'm sure that it was Campbell who first said, 'Let's have *two* Foundations, one at each end of the Galaxy.'

"Naturally, I said, 'Why?' and he said, 'You may need the second one later on.'"

What a highly useful provision to have tucked away for the hour when it might be needed! And, indeed, Asimov would eventually discover that he did have good use to make of this second Foundation.

Now, however, after its establishment in the initial scene of Asimov's story, the second Scientific Refuge at Stars's End would be set aside. The remainder of "Foundation"—after Hari Seldon has finished making his valedictory speech to his team of sages—would take place fifty years later at Encyclopedia Foundation Number One on the planet Terminus.

Once again here, as in "Reason" and "Nightfall," Asimov would be dealing in terms of states of relative knowledge and ignorance. That is, there are fundamental things that Hari Seldon and his associates know—and which have been revealed to the reader—that the scholars of this Foundation do not know.

They haven't been informed that the Galactic Empire is falling, for instance. Nor are they aware of the plans that Hari Seldon has for them to serve as the seed from which a new Empire will grow. There has even been a deliberate exclusion of psychologists and psychohistorians from the Foundation to prevent them from knowing too much too soon and interfering with the course that has been charted for them.

At this moment, the political balance of power at the edge of the Galaxy is starting to shift rapidly. The territories of the Periphery are breaking away from the Empire. The Royal Governor of Anacreon—the area lying between Terminus and the heart of the Empire—has just declared himself a King.

The men who are in charge of Terminus, the Board of Trustees of the Encyclopedia Committee, do not perceive this as a problem. They have their attention firmly fixed on their assigned task, the compilation of "'the definitive Encyclopedia of all human knowledge,'" the first volume of which is just five years from publication.

As far as the Trustees are concerned, this Foundation of theirs has nothing to do with such political maneuverings. It is a harmless scientific project. It was established by authority of the Emperor. It has his personal protection. And that is the end of the matter.

However, there is one man who has a better understanding of practical realities and is able to grasp more of the truth. This is Salvor Hardin, the first Mayor of Terminus City. It was Hardin's original intention to be "'a psychological engineer,'" but the Foundation was lacking in the necessary teachers and facilities. So, as the nearest alternative, he has made himself into a politician.

Hardin is able to look at the Galaxy and recognize abundant signs of failure and decay where the Trustees perceive nothing but life as usual.

The Mayor is a practical man, and it bothers him that Empire science—the Foundation project most definitely included—should be content with comparing, categorizing and recapitulating past authority. Men of science no longer bother to gather evidence and conduct experiments. They don't aim to extend the known and improve upon it.

Hardin can already see one-time knowledge beginning to slip away. The new states of the Periphery have lost their former command of atomic power—and the same thing has even begun to happen inside the Empire.

It is significant to Salvor Hardin, the man of political awareness, that after ruling the Galaxy for thousands of years, the Empire has begun to fray at the edges. The edge of the Galaxy happens to be precisely where Terminus is located. It seems that very shortly the Encyclopedia-makers are going to find themselves all alone in the midst of a gang of petty kingdoms with sharp teeth and grand ambitions.

Already Anacreon has begun to insist that Terminus place itself under its protection, and pay for this service with military bases and estates for its nobles. Terminus is a poor planet with no natural resources, not even the common metals, and no military power. How is it to resist these demands?

And still the Foundation Trustees remain blind to what Hardin sees as plainly evident. They find all the reassurance they require in a visit paid to Terminus by Lord Dorwin, diplomatic representative of the Emperor. When Dorwin insists that Anacreon is not in fact independent of the Empire and its authority, they are ready to believe him. They send a note off to Anacreon refusing its demands and invoking the might of Empire.

But Salvor Hardin doesn't believe that there is any coercive power left in that particular stick. What the Mayor perceives is an Anacreon that has just been dared to prove its strength, and a Terminus that is about to have its freedom taken away from it.

Soon enough, an answer is received from Anacreon, and Hardin's précis of it is finally enough to get the attention of the Trustees: "'You give us what we want in a week, or we beat the hell out of you and take it anyway.'"

Now that they finally grasp their true situation, the Trustees have two reactions. There are those who see no alternative but to surrender before the greater strength of Anacreon. But there are others who want to hang on until a time vault opens on the occasion of the fiftieth anniversary of the establishment of the Foundation. They hope for a message from their far-seeing founder, Hari Seldon, anticipating this bind and showing them some way out.

By this time, Salvor Hardin has had quite enough of all this heedlessness and helplessness. He is one man who isn't afraid to think for himself and to take action when it is necessary to do so. He sets a plot in motion that will throw out the Foundation Trustees—who are not elected and do not represent the interests of most of the million people who live on Terminus—and replace them with a strong mayor system of government. The coup is scheduled to take place while Hardin and the Trustees are in the time vault.

At the proper hour, the lights in the vault go dim. A figure in a wheelchair appears. It is Hari Seldon, and the grand old man does indeed have an assessment of their situation to share. However, it isn't at all what the Trustees have been hoping to hear. What they are offered is a reorientation very much like the one Campbell had presented to Asimov when he first brought in the idea for this story.

Hari Seldon tells them:

> "The Encyclopedia Foundation, to begin with, is a fraud, and always has been! ... Neither I nor my colleagues care at all whether a single volume of the Encyclopedia is ever published. It has served its purpose, since by it we attracted the hundred thousand humans necessary for our scheme, and by it we managed to keep them preoccupied while events shaped themselves, until it was too late for any of them to draw back.
>
> "In the fifty years that you have worked on this fraudulent project— there is no use in softening phrases—your retreat has been cut off, and you have no choice but to proceed on the infinitely more important project that was, and is, our real plan."

Then, for the first time, Hari Seldon explains the true situation to them—that future historians will come to place the Fall of the Galactic Empire at some point during the past fifty years. He talks of the psychohistorians' hope to shorten the period of Barbarism to a thousand years, and of the role that Terminus and its companion Foundation are to play as founders of a Second Galactic Empire.

Seldon says:

> "To that end we have placed you on such a planet and at such a time that in fifty years you were maneuvered to the point where you no longer have freedom of action. From now on, and into the centuries, the path you must take is inevitable. You will be faced with a series of crises, as you are now faced with the first, and in each case your freedom of action will become similarly circumscribed so that you will be forced along one, and only one path. ...
>
> "This, by the way, is a rather straightforward crisis, much simpler than many of those that are ahead. To reduce it to its fundamentals, it is this:

You are a planet suddenly cut off from the still-civilized centers of the Galaxy, and threatened by your stronger neighbors. You are a small world of scientists surrounded by vast and rapidly expanding reaches of barbarism. You are an island of atomic power in a growing ocean of more primitive energy; but are helpless despite that, because of your lack of metals.

"You see, then, that you are faced by hard necessity, and that action is forced on you. The nature of that action—that is, the solution to your dilemma—is, of course, obvious!"

But Hari Seldon doesn't reveal this solution. He simply repeats that no matter how convoluted the way may seem, the path has been marked out, and at the end of it lies the Second Galactic Empire. Then his image disappears and the lights come up.

The only person in the time vault who doesn't have to begin radically revising his thinking, the one person with any idea of what must be done next, is Salvor Hardin. He doesn't need someone else to tell him how to cope with this crisis. The first spaceships from Anacreon may be landing on Terminus tomorrow, but the Mayor is confident that he will have them off the planet again within six months.

The story ends with him affirming to himself: "The solution to this first crisis was obvious. Obvious as hell!"

However, he doesn't reveal the solution, either. And neither does Asimov-the-narrator. The story simply ends with old Hari Seldon and Salvor Hardin, fifty years apart in time, both knowing the answer—and us not. What a strange, unresolved conclusion!

But that's the way that Asimov had it. And John Campbell bought the story. Its acceptance was the sealing of a bargain between them.

We may remember that Asimov began "Foundation" after resolving that he was going to write one self-sufficient story and only worry about sequels at some later time. But while he was at work on "Foundation," he changed his mind.

From the moment that Asimov had first started writing science fiction and submitting it to John Campbell, he had yearned to establish an ongoing story series in *Astounding*. When "Reason" and "Liar" clicked with the editor, he had thought himself on top of the world. But it was only as he was working on "Foundation" that it finally sank in that to every appearance, Campbell had now committed himself to two different Asimov story series!

Once this thought had crossed his mind, he couldn't rest easy until he had confirmed the reality of this dream come true. And leaving the conclusion of "Foundation" dangling was a way of testing whether he did indeed have an open door at *Astounding* for a new series of stories.

As Asimov would come to say (with a certain note of wry bemuse-
ment at the machinations of his younger self): "The idea was that
Campbell would have to let me write the sequel now, and would,
moreover, have to take it. How clever of me!"

When his scheme worked, and Asimov got Campbell's acceptance
and a check for "Foundation" on September 17, he couldn't help
feeling pleased with himself. Just recently, he had received a con-
gratulatory note from Robert Heinlein upon the publication of
"Nightfall." And the very next night following receipt of the check
for "Foundation," he would see the colored streamers of the Northern
Lights hanging in the sky over Brooklyn for the first time in his life.
At the moment, it seemed to Asimov that he had the universe by
the tail.

There was only one thing that he was failing to take into account.
This was the two-way nature of the tacit deal he'd just made. The
acceptance of "Foundation" as it stood didn't merely mean that he
had John Campbell in a position where he had to take a sequel and
couldn't back out. It also meant that Asimov had committed himself
to sitting down and writing this companion story, and that the
editor was expecting to see it delivered pretty damn quick.

With its incomplete ending, "Foundation" could only be published
after the sequel was on hand, so that the two stories could be scheduled for consecutive issues. Together they would make a rough short
novel, with a cliff-hanger at the end of the first installment.

It was a sign of real trust on Campbell's part, and also a measure
of how much he wanted to see this particular series, that he could be
willing to buy "Foundation"—a story that as it stood was unpub-
lishable—and be confident that Asimov was not going to let him
down. By this time, however, the editor had begun to count Asimov
as one of his major new authors, even if he wasn't yet telling him so.

But Campbell wouldn't be shy about telling others. In a letter to
Jack Williamson a few weeks after the acceptance of "Foundation,"
he was ready to say:

> At present, the strongest science-fiction writers are Heinlein and
> van Vogt—two brand-new men. Asimov is really pushing upward, too.
> Reason, I think, is that neither of the first two ever really liked the early
> scf styles—they were free to roll their own. ... Asimov, a little later,
> has actually formed his stuff on theirs.

What a mixture of truth and non-truth this was!

It wasn't true, for instance, that neither Heinlein nor van Vogt had
ever really liked the early science fiction styles. A. E. van Vogt loved
A. Merritt's vivid and sensuous use of language, and had a desire to

make great pulp music of his own. And such was Robert Heinlein's passion for H.G. Wells that in 1935, when he ought to have been in bed recovering from tuberculosis, he'd made a pilgrimage to hear Wells speak in California, and taken along his treasured copy of *The Sleeper Awakes* for Wells to autograph.

Neither was it strictly true that Asimov had specifically modeled his work on that of Heinlein and van Vogt. He had certainly learned much from Heinlein, and absorbed something from van Vogt, as well—as these two writers in turn would find stimulation in Asimov's science fiction. But where fundamental influence was concerned, it would be a lot closer to the mark to suggest that it was the most imaginative (and also the most humanistic) writers of the Thirties—not the least important among them John W. Campbell and Jack Williamson—whom Asimov was really aiming to integrate, answer and extend in his stories.

At this moment, however, Campbell was less interested in speaking with absolute accuracy than in having a desired effect. And in the letters he was sending to Jack Williamson just now, the editor was attempting to convince this senior SF writer—who was still only 33 years old, one year younger than Heinlein—to rid himself of his remaining Techno Age storytelling habits and make himself over as a modern science fiction writer in the emerging style.

Williamson took this instruction with good grace, even gratitude. He was aware that science fiction was changing rapidly under Campbell's direction, and that he wasn't yet fully in tune with the new, more rigorous SF.

He replied to Campbell that while living in Los Angeles this past year, he had been paying close attention to Heinlein's ideas about the writing of science fiction at gatherings of the Mañana Literary Society. And he was trying to apply them now in a novel that he was writing about the Fall of a Galactic Empire: "Bob has been commenting on the inadequate social and cultural backgrounds of Doc's interstellar stories, and I hope to do something better."

What a wonderful coincidence we have here! It would seem that the very same idea of a failing Galactic Empire had struck two different writers at almost the same exact moment!

During the summer, Williamson had been writing a novelet, "Breakdown," which Campbell would make the cover story of the January 1942 *Astounding*. Here, an empire that encompasses our Solar System has reached its climax and is now collapsing. But, as its culminating achievement, it has produced a spaceship which will preserve something of human civilization and plant the seed of man among the stars.

The inventor of this "interstellar cruiser" expects to find every normal star accompanied by its own family of planets, even though planet-formation seems contrary to the processes presently at work in the universe. He accounts for his expectation with an argument expressing a favorite Williamson proposition—that natural law may not be the same in all times and places. He says:

> "The old cosmologists went wrong because they didn't know their own universe. They thought their constants of mass and energy were really constant. Now we know that the only real constant is the unitron itself— a basic underlying unit common to both the subatomic particles of mass and the quanta of energy. I've been working with the unitron equations that treat mass and energy as changing functions of time. They show that our universe was a very different place, five or six billion years ago—a sort of place the old astronomers never imagined. Processes worked then that would be impossible now."

When he finished this novel in August, Williamson was pleased with what he had done. It occurred to him then that he might write another story that was doubly related to it. This novel, the working title of which would be *Star of Empire*, would follow "Breakdown" in time, depicting the long-term results of its intended seeding of the stars. It would also be a further exploration of the theme of "Breakdown," in that it would tell of the simultaneous coming to completion and collapse of a human empire that spans the galaxy.

Here, in two stories, Williamson's *Star of Empire* and Asimov's "Foundation," we can see an index of change in SF. Back in the Romantic Era, the urge to write a story of science-beyond-science might overcome a rare writer once or twice in a lifetime. But now, in the early Atomic Age, there were so many dedicated writers of science fiction at work on the same set of problems that it was possible for two of them to conceive stories with the same new idea at the very same time.

And this wasn't the only occasion during the Golden Age when such a coincidence of inspiration and effort would take place. It was almost as though the One Great Big Writer imagined by van Vogt as producing the science fiction printed in *Astounding* were tuned in to One Common Wavelength, so that if one writer didn't express a particular story idea, another surely would.

In the case of this novel of galactic downfall, *Star of Empire*, Campbell didn't undercut Williamson's effort by informing him that Asimov, too, was at work on the subject, and had already delivered a short novelet, with more soon to follow. Rather, he made a suggestion to Williamson much like the one he had made to Asimov—that he should broaden his canvas and turn his novel into "'the chronological background for a dozen or two dozen shorts and novelettes.'"

As it happened, at the time that Campbell and Williamson were exchanging their notes concerning *Star of Empire* and what Williamson must do to make himself into a modern science fiction writer, Asimov had not yet begun to work on the sequel to "Foundation" that he had bound himself to write. Through the remainder of September and most of October, he took it easy and busied himself with other things.

He registered for the new term at Columbia and settled into a course in food analysis that he needed in order to pass his Ph.D. Qualifying Exams. He was feeling so chipper this fall that his professor received a number of complaints about Asimov's incessant singing and joking in the lab. Asimov offset these by telling his teacher that although he might make his living by writing, it was chemistry that was the delight of his heart and he just couldn't help showing it.

Then, when he did return to the typewriter early in October, it still wasn't to work on the story that Campbell was waiting to see. Instead, as though he needed to prove to himself that he really did have two different series established with the editor, Asimov devoted the first three weeks of the month to turning out a new robot story entitled "Runaround."

In itself, this story would be relatively trivial. An expensive robot named Speedy is being field-tested on Mercury when it gets stuck going round and round a pool of molten selenium in an endless approach/avoidance pattern, and nothing that our old friends Greg Powell and Mike Donovan can do will snap it out of its funk.

At last, however, Powell puts himself in danger of too much exposure to the Sun, and then calls upon the robot to save him. So powerful is the grip of the First Law—"'A robot may not injure a human being, or, through inaction, allow a human being to come to harm.'"—that Speedy is compelled to respond, thereby breaking him free of his futile round and restoring him to rationality.

"Liar!," Asimov's previous robot story, had served to show that one of his mechanical men would short out and do nothing at all rather than cause even psychic distress to a human being. Now, in "Runaround," he demonstrated that his law-abiding robots would ignore previous orders, put aside the impulse to protect themselves, and even overcome mental imbalance in order to save a human being from peril. What firmer assurance of robotic reliability and subservience to man could be asked for?

As the first story in which the Three Laws of Robotics were explicitly stated, "Runaround" was immediately acceptable to John

Campbell. The editor may have hesitated for a full week before he bought "Foundation" with its inconclusive ending, but he put through a check for "Runaround" on the very same day he received the story.

It was only then, at the beginning of the last week in October 1941, that Asimov finally took up the problem of writing the sequel to "Foundation" that he had been putting off for a month and a half. The new story was called "Bridle and Saddle," and at the outset it went very smoothly. After just three days of writing, Asimov had accumulated seventeen pages of manuscript.

In this story, thirty years have passed since the events of "Foundation," but Salvor Hardin is still Mayor of Terminus City and director of the affairs of the planet. Early in the novelet—in that portion which had just come so easily to Asimov—Hardin at last offers an answer to the question of how the threat posed to Terminus by Anacreon was countered and the first crisis resolved. Hardin says:

> "What I did...was to visit the three other kingdoms, one by one; point out to each that to allow the secret of atomic power to fall into the hands of Anacreon was the quickest way of cutting their own throats; and suggest gently that they do the obvious thing. That was all. One month after the Anacreonian force had landed on Terminus, their king received a joint ultimatum from his three neighbors. In seven days, the last Anacreonian was off Terminus."

Ever since then, the Foundation/Terminus has been performing a delicate balancing act. It preserves its existence by making itself indispensable to the rulers of the Four Kingdoms—Anacreon, Smyrno, Konom and Daribow—but not so useful as to allow any one of them to gain advantage over the others.

Because advanced science is regarded with awe by the ordinary populace of the Four Kingdoms, the Foundation offers its technical, economic, medical and educational assistance under the guise of a new religion of the Galactic Spirit. In each of the Four Kingdoms, the most promising young men are picked out to travel to Terminus and be educated in the priesthood.

The best of the best are brought within the Foundation as genuine scientific researchers. The second-raters are trained in technology, but not in science, and then sent back to their home worlds to run the new atomic power plants, give support to the current rulers, and minister to the people.

However, there are political firebrands on Terminus—the Actionist Party—who despise this religion as flummery and perceive the provision of any kind of assistance to the Four Kingdoms as craven truckling that in the long run must be dangerous to the security of the planet. They would prefer to build up the military strength of Terminus and impose their will on the Four Kingdoms before the time comes when the barbarians have learned too much and launch their own inevitable attack.

Salvor Hardin's response to their contempt for his presumed weakness and their transparent greed for power is to repeat his favorite slogan: "'Violence is the last refuge of the incompetent.'"

This was about as far as Asimov had managed to move "Bridle and Saddle" along when he went to pay one of his regular visits to John Campbell. This time the editor greeted him by finally declaring, "'I want that Foundation story.'" And that was sufficient to throw Asimov completely off balance.

For the next five days, nothing he tried would convince the novelet to move ahead another inch. Asimov was completely stymied.

By a synchronicity of the kind we've encountered so often, the other Fall of Galactic Empire story, *Star of Empire*, was running into trouble during October, too. In fact, so badly stuck did his novel get that Jack Williamson would at last find it necessary to set it aside and go on to other things. A dozen years later, with the aid of a co-writer, James E. Gunn, he would be able to start the story moving again, and it would finally see publication as a book in 1955 under the title *Star Bridge*.

Asimov would get over his own block more easily, but by much the same method—bringing an outside judgment to bear on the problem. On Sunday, the second of November, he went to Lower Manhattan to visit his friend and age-mate, Fred Pohl, who at different times had been his editor, his agent, and his collaborator.

They had first gotten to know each other in 1938 as two of the founding members of the Futurians, a small pack of hungry, bright and radical young New York City SF fans. As it turned out, Asimov was too busy trying to be an "A" student, a candy store clerk, and a science fiction professional all at once to have the time to be an active fan. But his peripheral participation in this group did lead to an abiding friendship with Pohl.

The two were drawn together by their commonalities of age, intelligence and ambition—but also by their extreme differences in background, temperament, education and experience. Pohl was a cool young fellow, a self-taught high school dropout who was already making his own way in the world by bluff and wit and luck. By 1940, he was a married man at a time when Asimov, the wiseacre immigrant kid become precocious chemistry grad student, was still living at home with his parents.

But Pohl had respect for the self-discipline and diligence that permitted Asimov to work and to succeed within the tight parameters of his life situation, and he envied Asimov's ability to sell stories to *Astounding*. And Asimov, for his part, admired Pohl's ability to deal with his own more chancy path in life with self-reliance and nerve, and counted Pohl's science fiction judgment second only to John Campbell's among the people he knew.

The two would exchange visits. When Pohl walked over to Brooklyn, he would hang around the candy store and be treated to free milk shakes by Asimov's mother. But it was a different situation when Asimov went to see Pohl. Although Asimov was never made aware of it, Pohl's then-wife was unfond of him and didn't like having him around the apartment. Pohl's solution was to take him for strolls around nearby Chinatown—which Asimov in his own way found a treat.

On this occasion, they wound up walking out onto the Brooklyn Bridge. There they talked over this story of Asimov's that had gotten stuck but absolutely had to be finished at the earliest possible moment. In later years, neither man would be able to recall the details of what they said to each other, but a grateful Asimov would swear that it was the suggestions Pohl made to him here that settled his case of nerves and freed up his imagination again.

Asimov came off the Brooklyn Bridge knowing just where his tale needed to go next. "Bridle and Saddle" would prove to be the longest story he had yet written—half again longer than "Foundation"—but it would only take him another two weeks to see it finished.

In "Bridle and Saddle," the balance of power that has allowed Terminus to survive for the past thirty years is in the process of being overturned. Anacreon—which has never surrendered its ambitions to rule the Periphery and as much more of the universe as it can manage to bring within its grip—has stumbled upon a centuries-old Imperial Navy battle cruiser, an immense and powerful ship constructed back in the days when "'they could *build*,'" drifting abandoned in space. And now Wienis, the Prince Regent of Anacreon, has presented a formal request that the Foundation use its knowledge to put the cruiser back in fighting condition, and then give the ship over to the Anacreonian Navy.

It is plain that if the cruiser actually is repaired, it is the intention of Anacreon to turn the ship's atom blasts against Terminus and against the three rival kingdoms. But if the Foundation should refuse to repair the cruiser, that, too, would be sufficient excuse for a suspicious and power-hungry Prince Regent to pick the fight he wants.

Terminus is in a double bind. Whether it chooses to cooperate with Anacreon's wishes or not, it seems that a war is going to come that the Foundation cannot win. And if Anacreon isn't able to get the war started all on its own, the Actionist Party on Terminus seems committed to doing the job for it.

Beyond this, Salvor Hardin, the one person who desires to avoid war, appears to be caught in the grip of a double bind all his own. However he elects to act, whatever he chooses to do, it would seem that either the Actionists or Wienis will succeed in finding reason and means to have him thrown out of office, and then oversee the ruination of the work of thirty years and more.

When Salvor Hardin was young, he was not unwilling to take direct action—as he is frequently reminded. Now, however, in his maturity, he is content to wait and wait and wait. By agreeing to the repair of Anacreon's battle cruiser, he is able to buy himself six months of time. Through this period, he works to stall and confuse the Actionists, all the while assuring them that the government is of the opinion that it knows what it is doing.

It isn't that Hardin has mislaid his ability to sense danger. But he remembers clearly that when Hari Seldon made his appearance in the time vault, he had said that at each crisis Terminus would be facing on the road to Second Empire, its freedom of action would become circumscribed to the point where only one course of action was possible. It is that moment of complete inevitability for which Hardin is waiting.

When his associates urge him to act now while peril is identifiable but not yet imminent, Hardin answers, "'Force the issue now? Before the crisis comes? It's the one thing I mustn't do. There's Hari Seldon and the Plan, you know.'"

In this declaration, we can recognize a highly significant change in emphasis from "Foundation." There, all that Hari Seldon had actually said to the people of this Scientific Refuge was: "'You have no choice but to proceed on the infinitely more important project that was, and is, our real plan.'"

But here in "Bridle and Saddle," this seemingly casual one-time use of the word "plan" has become an article of faith. It is now "the Plan." And Salvor Hardin, the one remaining witness to the miraculous visitation of Hari Seldon in the time vault, is totally committed to acting in accordance with the necessary operation of the Plan.

With the passage of time, events do fall together: The repair of the ship is completed. Young King Lepold of Anacreon is due to come of age. The Actionists are readying themselves to attempt a coup. And the eightieth anniversary of the establishment of the Foundation is almost at hand.

This is the moment Hardin has been anticipating. He leaves word that a second appearance of Hari Seldon in the time vault is to be expected three weeks hence, and then departs to attend the coronation of Lepold on Anacreon.

There, in the last hour before a haloed Lepold is scheduled to rise in the air on a levitating throne to receive the adulation of his people, Hardin is drawn aside by the Prince Regent. Wienis informs the Mayor that the spacefleet of Anacreon under the command of his son, Admiral Lefkin, and led by its mighty new flagship, the battle cruiser *Wienis*, has just departed to deliver a decisive strike against Terminus. Hardin is to consider himself a prisoner of war.

Hardin's answer is to reveal that he has prepared a counterstroke of his own which is due to take effect at midnight, the moment of Lepold's accession. From that hour, Anacreon is placed under religious interdict. Hardin invites Wienis to witness what this means.

And sure enough, at midnight the true command of the new religion of the Galactic Spirit is made manifest:

The priest-technicians who tend the atomic power plants pull the plug on the power supply. The lights in the palace fail.

Signs of religious favor are withdrawn from the new monarch. The halo surrounding Lepold is suddenly taken away and his flying throne thumps to the floor.

There is only one building in the whole city not in darkness—the Argolid Temple of the Galactic Spirit. And very shortly, a priest-led mob of outraged worshipers is surrounding the palace, crying out against the attack on the Foundation and demanding the release of Salvor Hardin.

The Prince Regent, himself an utter cynic and non-believer, is taken aback by the unanticipated demonstration of strength. But still he is able to exult over the fact that the attacking spacefleet is now beyond recall.

He declares: "'Let the mob howl and let the power die, but we'll hold out. And when the news comes back that the Foundation has been taken, your precious mob will find out upon what vacuum their religion has been built, and they'll desert your priests and turn against them.'"

Wienis is in error, however. The pre-arranged interdiction applies to the spacefleet as well as to Anacreon. And at the appointed hour, the head priest aboard the flagship, Theo Aporat, addresses the fighting men of the fleet and denounces the sacrilege of this attack upon the blessed Foundation. Aporat intones:

> "In the name of the Galactic Spirit and of his prophet, Hari Seldon, and of his interpreters, the holy men of the Foundation, I curse this ship. Let the televisors of this ship, which are its eyes, become blind. Let its

grapples, which are its arms, be paralyzed. Let the atom blasts, which are its fists, lose their function. Let the motors, which are its heart, cease to beat. Let the communications, which are its voice, become dumb. Let its lights, which are its soul, shrivel into nothing. In the name of the Galactic Spirit, I so curse this ship."

And instantly, this curse has results:

> With his last word, at the stroke of midnight, a hand, light-years distant in the Argolid Temple, opened an ultrawave relay, which at the instantaneous speed of the ultrawave, opened another on the flagship *Wienis.*
> And the ship died!
> For it is the chief characteristic of the religion of science, that it works, and that such curses as that of Aporat's are really deadly.

When Admiral Lefkin is dragged before the ultrawave relay and is forced to announce that the Anacreonian spacefleet now stands with the Foundation, it is more than his beleaguered father can handle. Wienis orders his soldiers to shoot Hardin, who is now encompassed in a modest aura of his own, and when they refuse to obey, he snatches an atomic gun from a guard and turns it on the Mayor himself. But Hardin's aura is the outward sign of a force field, and the beam from the gun can do him no harm.

In one final act of desperation, the Prince Regent points the atom blast at his own head and pulls the trigger, leaving Hardin to tut-tut over his corpse: "'A man of "direct action" to the end. The last refuge.'"

It appears that Hardin was right—there was never any need to resort to violence. The government of Terminus did know what it was doing, and its long-range strategy and quiet competence have been all that is necessary to deal with this second crisis.

Salvor Hardin's rightness is confirmed yet again when ancient Hari Seldon in his wheelchair shows up in the time vault at the predicted hour. What is more, even the founder himself is now speaking of "the Plan."

The image of Hari Seldon says: "'My figures show a ninety-eight point four percent probability there is to be no significant deviation from the Plan in the first eighty years.'"

Wow! What a thoroughly impressive confirmation this is, not merely of Mayor Hardin and his choice of methods, but also of the anticipatory powers of psychohistory!

Seldon is declaring that way back at the time his message was set down, he had known with a certitude of 98.4% that whoever would be in charge of Terminus would elect to employ a religio-techno-logical strategy in attempting to deal with the threat posed by its wild neighbors, and that the effectiveness of this solution would be demonstrated exactly eighty years after the establishment of the Foundation.

We can discern even more striking evidence of the exact predictive power of Seldon's science in a central difference between his two messages from out of the past. We may remember that when Hari Seldon appeared in the time vault at the end of "Foundation," he had been completely confident that the first crisis would already be in progress, but that the answer for it would not yet have been arrived at. Accordingly, he had held his tongue, alluding to an obvious solution, but not divulging it. On this second occasion, however, Seldon is just as certain that when he appears in the time vault, the crisis will already be over, and there will be no impediment to talking about the means by which it was resolved.

Thus it is that Seldon is prepared to say quite openly:

> "According to our calculations, you have now reached domination of
> the barbarian kingdoms immediately surrounding the Foundation. Just as
> in the first crisis you held them off by the use of the Balance of Power, so
> in the second, you gained mastery by use of the Spiritual Power as against
> the Temporal."

What a most remarkable suggestion this is to come upon in a science fiction story—that given the right crucial difficulty, Spiritual Power might prove to be the most appropriate solution, superior in effectiveness to mere worldly might!

As we are aware, throughout the course of the modern Western adventure, there had been a continuing struggle between the representatives of the worldview of established religion and partisans of the worldview of emerging science and technology to settle the question of which of the two more nearly expressed the best knowledge and highest hopes of Western civilization. This struggle can be seen in key events like the silencing of Galileo by the Inquisition in 1633, the public debate over evolution between Thomas Huxley and Bishop Samuel Wilberforce in 1860, and the Scopes trial in Tennessee in 1925. And for just as long as the issue remained unsettled, neither party—the religious nor the scientific—had any desire to be confused with the other.

But here in Asimov's "Bridle and Saddle," we have a very different situation—one in which religion and science have somehow become intertwined and identified with each other as Spiritual Power, which is pitted against the lesser power of a would-be conqueror. Whatever are we to make of this turning?

The first thing to be said is that Asimov derived the idea of Spiritual Power mastering Temporal Power from his reading of Edward Gibbon. In *Decline and Fall*, he found two different examples of this principle: first the ability of the Catholic Church to establish and maintain dominance over the fragments of the former Western Roman Empire during the Middle Ages; and second, the startling military success of early Islam against every army it encountered from Persia to Spain.

But then we need to pause and ask if this is the same sort of power that we see at work in "Bridle and Saddle." Does the religion of the Galactic Spirit function in the same way as actual historical religions like Christianity and Islam? Or is it only an artificial construct cobbled together to manipulate the sentiments of ignorant and gullible barbarians?

If we find it necessary to ask questions like these, it is partly because on previous occasions during the early Golden Age when science and religion had gotten mixed together in story, the result had tended to be something more nearly akin to mind control than to Spiritual Power. The most striking examples of this are to be seen in Robert Heinlein's first two serial novels.

We may recall that in "If This Goes On—," the religion of the Prophets uses the fruits of science—mob psychology, mathematically calculated propaganda, and television special effects—to shape and direct the beliefs of the American people. And the spell of the Prophets is only broken when rebel forces demonstrate their superior skill at this kind of scientific manipulation of thought and perception.

Then, again, in the first Anson MacDonald story, *Sixth Column*, American super-science is pitted against the military might of an Oriental invader. Because the defenders are few in number, they find it expedient to combine genuine scientific power with "flubdub and hokum" in a new religion of the Lord Mota (*atom* spelled backward), and to use this as a front to hide behind while they misdirect, unsettle and terrify the PanAsians with apparent miracles.

Without a doubt, Asimov's religion of the Galactic Spirit in "Bridle and Saddle" does share a willingness with the religions in Heinlein's stories to play games of scientific miracle-fakery, impressing the simple citizens of the Four Kingdoms with flubdub and hokum like halos and levitating thrones. And within the story itself, more than one character is willing to stand up and accuse the religion of being a barefaced fraud.

The leader of the Actionist Party, for instance, is distressed that genuine science should be presented to the barbarian kingdoms dressed up in phony religious trappings. He criticizes Hardin to his face, saying, "'You were forced to surround these scientific gifts with the most outrageous mummery. You've made half religion, half balderdash out of it. You've erected a hierarchy of priests and complicated, meaningless ritual.'"

The religion also seems a sham to the Prince Regent. Speaking to Lepold about the religious pronouncements of the high priest of Anacreon, Wienis declares: "'He believes in that mummery a good deal less than I do, and I don't believe in it at all. How many times have you been told that all this talk is nonsense?'"

There is even a moment in "Bridle and Saddle" that we have already witnessed when the hokum gets turned in our direction, and we as readers are actually asked to join the ignorant Anacreonians in applauding scientific game-playing just as though it were true religious power. At the moment that the flagship *Wienis* is floating silent and dark in space after the curse of the head priest, the narrator—completely contrary to his usual habit, which is to let events speak for themselves—intrudes to claim: "For it is the chief characteristic of the religion of science, that it works, and that such curses as that of Aporat's are really deadly."

This boast has to fall flat with us, and not just because it trips over its own grammar. The power in the ship doesn't really fail because of the special deadliness of Theo Aporat's curses. The ship goes dark because there is someone standing by in the Argolid Temple ready to throw open an ultrawave relay at the prearranged hour of midnight. And the ability of this stooge to wink the lights off and on from a distance doesn't exactly make the case for a claim that the religion of science (is this the same as the religion of the Galactic Spirit?) is the religion set apart from all others by the fact that it works.

Science speaking as science and not as would-be religion would say that when the Foundation is invited to renovate a powerful spaceship, it is capable of installing a secret control system for its own benefit, and that this technology, operating within its usual parameters, will then work as effectively and reliably as technology is expected to work. What's more, science as science would expect the ultrawave relay system to work for Wienis, too, if he happened to discover its existence, even though he is no believer in the religion of science.

And yet, after all this has been said—after we have admitted the fakery, doubt and pretension which attend the religion of the Galactic Spirit—a crucial fact remains:

What actually determines the outcome of "Bridle and Saddle" isn't halos and flying thrones and other hokum, nor is it the genuine science that underlies them. Rather, what really counts is the allegiance to the new religion that is displayed by the people of

Anacreon—the outraged mob which surrounds the palace to protest the attack on the Foundation; the gang of soldiers that seizes Admiral Lefkin instead of obeying his orders; the palace guards who refuse to fire their guns at Salvor Hardin when the Prince Regent commands them to.

These are sincere believers. For them, this religion is clearly more immediate and compelling than the ambitions of Anacreon's royal family. When they have to choose between one and the other, again and again they decide in favor of the religion of science, the Foundation, and the Galactic Spirit.

A number of different states and conditions of belief may be seen among the people of Anacreon:

Many, perhaps most, are superficialists, ignorant of the realities of science, but capable of being awed by scientific smoke and mirrors.

Others less credulous may take halos and flying thrones only as symbols of power, but revere the Foundation as the mysterious source of all that is most positive in society—atomic energy, medicine, education and trade.

More sophisticated yet are the bright young fellows who are picked out to travel to Terminus for training, and then return as priests to their native planet to operate the marvels of technology, even though they do not clearly and completely understand the science that underlies what they are given to say and do.

Finally, the most advanced people of Anacreon are those youngsters who demonstrate that they have sufficient intelligence, perception and personal balance to be brought within the Foundation and introduced to the pure, unmediated study of science.

It seems apparent from this hierarchy of understanding that if the priests of the religion of the Galactic Spirit found it necessary to begin their work with the people of the Four Kingdoms by offering them social and scientific gifts wrapped up as mummery and balderdash, it wasn't just because they were seeking to mislead and take advantage of the ignorant. It was because they were obliged to deal with the state of thought that they actually encountered in Daribow, Konom, Smyrno and Anacreon.

As Salvor Hardin puts it: "'I started that way at first because the barbarians looked upon our science as a sort of magical sorcery, and it was easiest to get them to accept it on that basis.'"

But though the religion of the Galactic Spirit may have had to deal in flubdub and hokum at the outset, flubdub and hokum aren't where it ends. Instead, it takes people from an initial state of ignorance and superstition and leads them along mentally from one stage to the next until they have accumulated the experience, the knowledge and the insight that are a necessity if they are to be able to encounter science on its own terms.

We might recall Salvor Hardin's favorite slogan: "'Violence is the last refuge of the incompetent.'"

In their initial condition, the people of the Four Kingdoms automatically resort to violence for lack of any more appropriate and practical methods of getting what they crave. However, Hardin's religion of the Galactic Spirit teaches how they may develop the basis, one step at a time, for another, more effective approach to life—namely scientific competence—and thereby eliminate their need for violence.

This program of educational development marks a significant difference between the religion of "Bridle and Saddle" and the fictional religions presented by Heinlein in "If This Goes On—" and *Sixth Column*. The religion of the Prophets and the religion of Mota both aim to keep people in the dark for the advantage that it brings. But the religion of the Galactic Spirit actively works to take those who are in darkness and give them understanding.

Unlike Heinlein's religions, then, Asimov's religion isn't a total lie. It is more than just a con game or a power trip.

But yet it does have an element of human manipulation that cannot be denied. Just as the title "Bridle and Saddle" suggests, Salvor Hardin and the Foundation are engaged in a subtle, long-term program to domesticate the wild men who surround Terminus.

With every resource at their command—from the simulation of miracles to the construction and maintenance of atomic power plants—the priests of the Galactic Spirit labor to increase the psychic and social dependence of Anacreon, Smyrno, Konom and Daribow upon advanced technology.

The more involved the barbarians get, and the more committed they become to the new religion, the more necessary and desirable it is for them to pass from awe of science to mastery of science.

But the price exacted for this development is that the people of the Four Kingdoms must sacrifice the heedlessness, belligerence and self-aggrandizement exemplified by Prince Regent Wienis. They have to learn to discipline their passions and widen their horizons.

As the barbarians grow more peaceful, and more competent, and more indebted to the Foundation, they become bound ever more tightly into a single religious, scientific and economic community consisting of all of the Four Kingdoms plus Terminus. In no small measure, what we see taking place in "Bridle and Saddle" may be understood as the refusal of this greater community of the Galactic Spirit to allow Wienis to divide it against itself.

And—as ancient Hari Seldon is ready to confirm upon his second manifestation in the time vault—this grand strategy of scientific education, social therapy and communal interdependence, all passing under the name of religion, is indeed the answer to the internal and external political threats with which the story began.

If the Four Kingdoms and Terminus perceive themselves as component parts of a single body that includes them all, there can be no need for an Anacreon to attempt to conquer its neighbors and to wrest away the scientific secrets of the Foundation, nor for an Actionist Party to strive at all cost to hang onto precious scientific advantage. Just as soon as they can arrive there, everyone within this community is going to be equally scientific—and equally well-prepared to deal with it.

So Salvor Hardin has successfully guided the Foundation through a second crisis. But a central question still remains unanswered: Why does the shade of Hari Seldon choose to describe the necessary course of action that has been taken as "Spiritual Power" rather than as what it appears to us to be—an effective job of psychological engineering?

We are, after all, in the time vault at the Foundation on Terminus, not off somewhere in the Four Kingdoms. And here at home, Salvor Hardin isn't identified as a religious figure, but rather as a politician looking out for the welfare of his planet. Moreover, whatever doctrine he may have his priests teaching the barbarians, he himself is no believer in the religion of science in any of its variants.

So why should the grand old man, Hari Seldon, sitting there so knowingly in his wheelchair eighty years in the past, have considered it appropriate to characterize what Hardin and his helpers would be doing—and indeed have been doing—as a case of Spiritual Power overcoming Temporal Power?

The answer could be this: In the religion being promulgated by Salvor Hardin, there are two separate levels of understanding, one of which is a preparation for the other. Hardin isn't a believer in the religion of science; he is past the need for that. But he is the most fervent of believers in the religion of the Galactic Spirit—otherwise known as the Plan.

We are never told directly about Salvor Hardin's conversion to this higher order transcendence. But clearly it occurred during Hari Seldon's first appearance in the time vault, in the exhilarating moment when the founder made the announcement that the true destiny of Terminus was not just to be a maker of the ultimate encyclopedia, but to be one of the seeds from which a new and better Second Galactic Empire would grow.

Hearing this great psychohistorical Plan set forth was an experience for Salvor Hardin something like the vision on the road to Damascus that turned Saul the Pharisee into Saint Paul, the tireless organizer of the early Christian church. The very next day, at least, or the day after that, Hardin founded his new religion and set out to unify the wild barbarians. And above and beyond the religion of science—that necessary preliminary—it was in the name of the Galactic Spirit and his prophet, Hari Seldon, that Salvor Hardin would present himself as acting.

The Mayor is completely sincere in this. What he preaches is what he believes. The question is, how much of what he believes and preaches does he himself truly understand?

The new higher order transcendence that he would like to serve is many different things at once:

It is religious.

It is scientific.

It has a mathematical component.

It deals in states of actual and potential human consciousness.

It is also occult—with secret masters and forgotten knowledge, and an inner core of truth hidden within an inner core of truth, concealed in a universe falling into ruin.

Above all, it is holistic, an overarching vision of the entire Galaxy restored to an awareness of its own intrinsic unity, and unified once again in fact.

Salvor Hardin, however, can only dimly appreciate the higher reality that underlies all these apparently different aspects. The truth is that he knows nothing at all about the actualities of psychohistory. As much as this science has always fascinated and attracted him, he has no education or training in it, and no real understanding of how it operates. All his contact with it comes at second hand, chiefly in the wonderful promises set forth by Hari Seldon.

Beyond this, his own personal conceptual framework is so limited and parochial that it actively serves to prevent him from comprehending the true higher wholeness. Hardin may appear to be a model of competence and wisdom when he is measured against an ignorant barbarian like Prince Regent Wienis. But when he is placed next to someone like Hari Seldon, who possesses the interstellar experience, the breadth of vision, and the higher knowledge that he lacks, Hardin stands revealed for what he really is—a hick from the Galactic outback.

The narrator tells us frankly that the Mayor is "one whose habits of thought had been built around a single planet, and a sparsely settled one at that." As long as Hardin's state remains so primitive that he can experience the Kingdom of Anacreon as staggeringly vast, even though it consists of only twenty-five stellar systems, he can't possibly be prepared to deal with the true magnitude of the Galaxy, with its hundred billion stars.

In fact, just as with the religion of science, we can discern the existence of a hierarchy of understanding here, with each stage relating to the new transcendence by a different name.

Hari Seldon and his team of wise men are masters of the meta-science of *psychohistory*. So far and wide are they able to see, and so great is their power, that they can expect the work they do to affect the entire human population of the Galaxy over the span of a thousand years and more.

However, when the founding father communicates with Salvor Hardin and the other leaders of the Scientific Refuge on Terminus, he can't talk in terms of the ways and means of psychohistory, about which they know nothing. It is necessary for him to simplify radically. More than that, to accommodate their peculiarities of thought and their limitations of understanding, it is even possible that Seldon may have to resort to what is, for him, flubdub and balderdash.

In any case, what is a certainty is that Seldon's initial message to the Foundation is a variation upon a most ancient and powerful mythic theme: The story of the child of destiny, offspring of gods and kings, who is raised in exile ignorant of his true identity. It is his fate to return to the center of things, dethrone the usurpers of power, and reign in righteous glory.

This is the story of many a hero of Iron Age legend, of the renowned Persian king, Cyrus the Great, and of the long-anticipated Jewish Messiah, as well as of every ambitious orphan from the provinces who ever tried to make good in the city. In Seldon's version, of course, it is the Foundation that is this fortunate child, unaware of its true origins and its own real nature, but destined after many trials to return in triumph from the Periphery and redeem the unity of the Galaxy.

This mythic promise that they were born for a purpose—the making of a New Galactic Empire—from the man they revere as their founder and guardian, is known by the people of the Foundation as *the Plan*.

But when Salvor Hardin and his fellows travel to the Four Kingdoms to spread the message of Galactic holism and reunification, they can't possibly talk to the barbarians about Hari Seldon, the master psychohistorian, and the wonderful secret Plan that he has for the Foundation. That would only rouse their fear and suspicion.

Once again it is necessary to address the people of Daribow, Konom, Smyrno and Anacreon at their own level of understanding. Consequently, Hardin and his priests elect to speak to them in religious terms, of *the Galactic Spirit* and his prophet, Hari Seldon.

But whether the name is given as *psychohistory*, or as *the Plan*, or as *the Galactic Spirit*, it is always the same transcendence that is being referred to. The only thing that changes is the perspective from which it is seen.

In exactly the same way, whether Hari Seldon is regarded as the prophet of a religion of Galactic unity, or as the founding father of a planet of destiny, or as a super-scientist-supreme who is capable of practicing the principles of his craft on a Galactic scale, depends entirely on the state of comprehension of the viewer.

For his part, Salvor Hardin, when looked at from the higher vantage of the psychohistorian, resembles one of those half-educated priest-technicians from the Four Kingdoms who can be counted upon to watch dials or to throw open switches on command, but who doesn't actually grasp the whys and wherefores of the advanced science he aspires to serve.

The Mayor operates on the basis of his highly limited understanding, on what remains of the initial burst of enthusiasm that struck him upon his first encounter with Hari Seldon, and on continuing faith. As best he can, he tries to imitate the founder's example, and hopes that what he elects to do will prove to be in accordance with the Plan:

He may not be able to make calculations based upon the essential continuity of human consciousness throughout the Galaxy the way Hari Seldon did—but he can set out to organize the immediate neighborhood.

He may not at first be able to talk to the barbarians about the awesome and wonderful Plan for New Galactic Empire that leads him—but he can teach them the self-control, scientific competence and sense of community that they must have before the subject of the Plan can be raised.

Most of all, Hardin may not be able to duplicate for others the heady rush of insight and conviction that swept over him when he first saw Hari Seldon in the time vault and heard him speak, and caught—beyond the founder's words and calculations and super-science—a brief unfathomable glimpse of underlying transcendent wholeness. But he can express the essence of his intuitive recognition in terms of a new religion of the Galactic Spirit, and carry the word to the Four Kingdoms.

And thirty years later, these actions by Salvor Hardin would prove to be exactly the right steps to have taken!

From the point of view of Hari Seldon, of course, that would be something of a foregone conclusion. After all, he *knew* with a certainty of 98.4% that if he showed up on the fiftieth anniversary of the Foundation and stimulated the imaginations of those assembled in the time vault with the Cyrus the Great/New Galactic Empire origin-and-destiny story, that their reaction would be to start a new religion and carry it to the surrounding barbarians. Seldon is only getting the results he anticipated.

But that kind of assurance has never been available to Salvor Hardin. After his crucial initial decision to found a new religion and use it to tame the wild barbarians, it has been thirty long years of patience and effort and hope. And until everything finally fell into place so neatly and completely, he could never be certain that his religion of the Galactic Spirit would stand up to the test and prove a sufficient answer to the likes of Wienis. From Hardin's point of view, it has all been a blind leap of faith.

No wonder that on his second appearance in the time vault, Hari Seldon should think it appropriate to treat the Foundation's success-ful resolution of this crisis as a triumph of Spiritual Power!

But then, having endorsed Salvor Hardin's methods and results, Hari Seldon goes on to play a new game of thought modification with those gathered in the time vault. Before he disappears again, he warns that there are crises ahead that Spiritual Power cannot resolve, and he names three sources of potential conflict:

One is other centers of local stellar allegiance, which he terms the force of Regionalism or Nationalism.

Another is the dying giant, the failing but still mighty First Galactic Empire.

As for the third...Hari Seldon says: "'And never forget there was *another* Foundation established eighty years ago; a Foundation at the other end of the Galaxy, at Star's End. They will always be there for consideration.'"

Now whatever is that supposed to mean? Previously, it had always been taken for granted that the two Scientific Refuges were sister organizations devoted to a common purpose. But now, at a word from Hari Seldon, the other Foundation has become transformed into an unknown that must constantly be worried about.

With this concluding set of provocative remarks by Hari Seldon, Isaac Asimov had certainly provided himself with plenty of room for further stories in this series, if and when the time came that he was ready to write them!

Asimov finished "Bridle and Saddle" on Sunday, the 16th of November. And the next day, exactly two months after he had received the check for "Foundation," he took the long-awaited sequel to Campbell's office.

So eager was the editor to lay hands on this novelet that he did something he'd never done before in the more than three years that Asimov had been bringing him stories: He sat right down with the manuscript and read it then and there, while Asimov waited to learn what his reaction would be.

In accepting a story that had been deliberately left unfinished, and then trusting that Asimov would come through promptly with an acceptable sequel, John Campbell had put himself out on the end of a very thin limb. Right now, he had a most urgent need to prove to himself that the high opinion of the youngster he'd been expressing lately was really warranted.

Did "Bridle and Saddle" get the job done? Did it complete "Foundation" satisfactorily and then carry the tale of the rise of New Galactic Empire on another step?

Could Campbell buy this story and put it right into the schedule as it stood, or was he in for even more delay while he waited for Asimov to rewrite?

What if this novelet turned out to be a complete disaster? What was the editor to do then?

As he settled to reading the manuscript, Campbell wasn't looking for nits to pick. His only concern was for the effectiveness of the whole as a whole: Did the story work, or didn't it?

However, we ought to be aware that if he had been actively interested in identifying points in "Bridle and Saddle" that deserved to be questioned, he could most certainly have found some. That is, this story, like both of Asimov's previous important thought experiments, "Reason" and "Nightfall," was built on a whole series of relatively unlikely premises.

As one instance of this, we are told in "Bridle and Saddle" that atomic power had been forgotten by Anacreon until it was reintroduced by the priests of the Galactic Spirit. And it is further revealed in the course of the story that Anacreon lacks the power of instantaneous interstellar communication.

But if Anacreon didn't have atomic power or some even more sophisticated mode of propulsion, how was it able to send a fleet of spaceships between the stars to occupy Terminus? And if it doesn't have the ultrawave relay, or some other system just like it, how does it coordinate its military forces and maintain its control over twenty-five different stellar systems?

We are also informed that right after the conclusion of the events of "Foundation," a coalition of the other Kingdoms confronted Anacreon and compelled it to withdraw its men and ships from Terminus. Does it really seem likely that on the heels of such a forced retreat, Anacreon's barbarian rulers—arrogant, small-minded and suspicious at the best of times—would be in any mood to receive "priests" from Terminus bearing some religion newly invented by Salvor Hardin, the architect of their great humiliation? Would they then give this doubtful lot permission to meddle as they pleased in every important aspect of society, or would they hedge them about as tightly as possible with regulations, ordinances and customs, stupidity, inaction and refusal, while carefully scrutinizing their every move? Can we believe that they would be so anxious to have the false prestige lent by halos and flying thrones that they would allow these red-robed intruders to make off with the allegiance of the people in the space of only thirty years?

There are questions that might be asked, too, about the immediate cause of the Foundation's second crisis, the battle cruiser *Wienis*. How likely is it that at the conclusion of some great space battle of yesteryear, an Imperial Navy warship two miles long, in readily repairable condition, would have gone unaccounted for, allowed to gently drift out of the realm of human ken and be forgotten among the stars? What are we to suppose happened to its crew?

And further, how probable is it that after being invisible, or misplaced, or nonexistent for three hundred years, this derelict should come floating back into history at precisely the right moment to foment a long-predicted psychohistorical crisis? If this is a random stroke of fortune, it is an altogether marvelous one. Or was it somehow prearranged to happen by Hari Seldon and his gang of psychohistorical guardian angels?

We might also wonder what Prince Regent Wienis could possibly have been thinking about to insist that the people of the Foundation repair this mighty battle cruiser for him so that he may turn right around and attack them with it—and then neglect to oversee and double-check every last detail of the work performed by the Foundation's technician-priests. It seems strangely trustful of him.

Finally, there is the peculiar periodicity of the crises faced by the Foundation. The fact that one of these coincides with the fiftieth anniversary of the Scientific Refuge, and the other takes place on the eightieth, makes them appear to have been specially timed to occur by someone with an eye to the calendar and a sense of what dates might seem significant to the yokels of Terminus, and not the result of cosmic and historical forces operating according to their own dynamic. Does Hari Seldon really enjoy that kind of fine control over the course of events?

Of these different points that we've raised for possible question in "Bridle and Saddle," none is wholly impossible or beyond explanation. What we really do need to note, however, is that added all together, they amount to a case that is fully as special in its own way as, say, the unique set of circumstances presented in "Nightfall."

This wasn't important to John Campbell. The relative probability or improbability of the various premises of Asimov's thought experiments didn't concern him.

What he did care about was the results. As an editor who had a magazine to put out every month, he needed to know whether the story was sound enough to publish. And, as a man with an agenda in his head, he wanted to know if it advanced his program of imagining the establishment of human control over the stars, including the overturning of the force of cyclical history on the galactic scale.

In these matters, Campbell wasn't disappointed. "Bridle and Saddle" did everything the editor expected of it and more:

It did work as a story, moving along so smoothly and hanging together with such apparent plausibility that—as it was told—it seemed a highly realistic view of the possible human future, particularly when compared with previous galactic stories such as Doc Smith's Lensman series and Jack Williamson's "After World's End."

And it did advance Campbell's cause. It rounded off the dangling conclusion of "Foundation," with its initial problem of ensuring the independent existence of the Scientific Refuge on Terminus in the face of barbarian threat, and then presented a further stage of development in which the local stellar neighborhood gets drawn together to form the nucleus of the greater galactic community to come. That was exactly the sort of thing that Campbell wanted to see.

But this wasn't all that Asimov's novelet had to offer the editor. In "Bridle and Saddle," a crucial Campbellian tenet was restated, refined and extended. Again and again, first in one way and then in another, the story asserted that the fate of mankind isn't ultimately determined by material objects, but rather by human attitudes, knowledge and states of mind.

We may recall Campbell stating in his March 1938 editorial, six months after assuming control of *Astounding*: "We presuppose, in these stories, two things: that there is yet to be learned infinitely more than is now known, and that Man can learn it."

Only a few months later, young Isaac Asimov, who would be John Campbell's most attentive and diligent pupil, began to sit at the master's knee and absorb his new beliefs—that humanity can learn and change; that one stage after another of human advance is possible; and that the arrow of future human development points away from matter and toward mind.

Now, in "Bridle and Saddle," Asimov was handing these ideas back to his teacher, but with an important difference. That difference was Asimov's sense of the stars as a locus of future human history.

Campbell's late scientifiction story, "Forgetfulness," had been visionary in nature, but not historical. It leaped ahead ten million years to show us a glimpse of potential future man—not Wells's grotesque Big Brain flopping about futilely in a pool filled with nutrient broth, but mental man, outwardly simple and ordinary, even backward, but inwardly mature and masterful. This novelet didn't have much to say about the details of how we were to get from here to there; it just asserted that it was possible for us to do.

As an early modern science fiction story, however, Asimov's "Bridle and Saddle" was specifically concerned with the method, process and context that were absent from Campbell's "Forgetfulness." Asimov's story took a much smaller leap into the future—only fifty thousand years—to show us men far more like ourselves than like Campbell's advanced men of mind as they strive to rise from their current fallen condition to create a New Galactic Empire free of the weaknesses that caused the First Empire to fail. In the dynamics of their struggle, much is revealed.

We can see, for instance, that in the contention between Mayor Salvor Hardin and Prince Regent Wienis which occupies so much of the foreground of "Bridle and Saddle," Hardin is the representative of the evolutionary power of mind, while Wienis stands for the more rigid and static power of matter.

In the Prince Regent's frame of reference, the only things that count are brute force and will. He thinks that a two-mile-long spaceship with mighty atom blasts is all the license he needs to seize control of the universe and make everybody else bow down before him and his progeny.

It is intriguing to note that even so dedicated a non-believer as Wienis has been touched by the new transcendence-of-many-names which guides both Hari Seldon and Salvor Hardin. The end they desire and the end he desires are one and the same. This becomes clear when the Prince Regent, seeking to influence young King Lepold, suggests to his ward: "'Together we will recreate an empire—not just the kingdom of Anacreon—but one comprising every one of the billions of suns of the Galaxy.'"

However, Wienis resolutely rejects the religious and scientific and psychohistorical pathway that would eventually ready him—or, more likely, some descendant of his—to become a participant in New Galactic Empire. It seems to be his assumption that having a lust for the goal and a willingness to kick aside anything that stands in his way is all the self-preparation he requires to become Emperor of the Galaxy.

But other people are more conscious than he of the personal shortcomings that render him unfit for the job. For instance, Hardin's personal observer, the high priest of the Galactic Spirit on Anacreon, says of Wienis: "'He's the most egregious fool on the planet. Fancies himself as a shrewd devil, too, which makes his folly the more transparent.'"

That's not just one man's opinion, either. From the beginning, Isaac Asimov tips a wink to the reader over the heads of his characters that there is something definitely lacking about the Prince Regent and his methods. It's not by accident that this would-be ruler of the universe and his mighty flagship should be blessed with a name insinuating laughable impotence. Who could be expected to take with total seriousness a threat from anybody or anything named "Wienis"?

Not altogether surprisingly, then, under test it proves to be simplicity itself for the Mayor to outthink, outplan and outmaneuver this belligerent but ineffectual deadhead. In the spirit of Hardin's favorite slogan, we may say that his competence easily wins out over Wienis's mere violence. Mind over matter.

But that is the way things were set up to be when the Foundation was established with a vast store of human knowledge on a beleaguered peripheral planet completely lacking in natural resources. Clearly, Hari Seldon wanted the people of the Foundation to think their way to the goal, and not to win by overwhelming material force.

By setting forth this order of value and explicitly demonstrating its power in "Bridle and Saddle," Isaac Asimov was making the auctorial promise that henceforth on the long road to New Galactic Empire, knowledge, skill and insight might always be counted upon to prevail over brute force and ignorance. Human states of mind would determine the outcome of the Plan, not armies and spaceships and atom blasts.

But Asimov didn't stop there. He went on in this story to assess the relative effectiveness of one frame of mind and another. Taken as a whole, "Bridle and Saddle" portrayed a kind of ladder of consciousness—a series of modes of thought which must be worked through in the proper order if men are ever to defy the power of cyclical history and avert thirty to fifty thousand years of galactic darkness and barbarism.

The most elementary of these is religion. This mental framework is limited and emotional, but one that is effective in organizing the otherwise chaotic thought of local communities such as Anacreon.

Next, there is the scientific approach. Because it is willing to look at the facts and to revise itself, it is a less excitable and more pragmatic ordering of thought than religion. Yet it is still capable of becoming mesmerized by the special conditions that happen to hold true in some particular time and place, such as Village Earth in the early Twentieth Century, or Lagash in the long seasons between eclipses, or Terminus in the uncertain days after the withdrawal of the Old Empire.

Finally, beyond this scientific nearsightedness, there lies a more comprehensive and effective state of mind which might be called holistic perception.

This mode isn't anything so advanced as the ability of the men of "Forgetfulness" to annihilate the ordinary bounds of space and time with the power of mind. Rather, it is the more modest ability to perceive complete patterns, with their necessary interconnections, and thereby to be aware of the true nature and demands of a given situation.

Asimov was thinking in this way when he found it impossible to outline his stories logically and linearly in advance of writing them, but instead had to follow an inner sense of their design and put them down whole.

And his character, Salvor Hardin, would also be thinking this way in the approach he takes to the Foundation's second crisis. Long before there is any visible necessity to take action, Hardin does what seems utterly irrational—he founds a new religion. Then, thirty years later, when those around him are getting themselves all worked up over the renewed threat from Anacreon, Hardin never loses his composure. He has already done what had to be done at the time when it was most appropriate to do it, and now he just needs to wait for the pattern to complete itself.

The best model that Asimov had of a person who was able to think in holistic terms was, of course, John W. Campbell. Though the youngster might be a little distance ahead of his mentor in the specialized knowledge of advanced chemistry, from the moment they first met Asimov was in no doubt that Campbell was someone who saw farther and perceived more than he did.

Again and again, Asimov had the experience of bringing the editor some idea for a new science fiction story, only to have him alter it into something a great deal larger and more meaningful, such as the Three Laws of Robotics, or a program for the attainment of New Galactic Empire. Campbell might declare, modestly enough, that he was just expressing what was already implied in the original story idea, but over and over Asimov was left marveling at his breadth of vision.

In "Foundation" and in "Bridle and Saddle," Asimov would deliberately imagine a fictional counterpart to John Campbell in the great psychohistorian Hari Seldon. These two masters of holistic thought would be alike in setting the goal of a unified Galaxy and then standing back out of the way of its accomplishment—except for the occasional interjection of a provocative remark at just the proper moment for it to have maximum effect.

"Bridle and Saddle" declared that it was by climbing the ladder of consciousness from religion to science to holistic thought—and, presumably, on beyond—that mankind would thwart the power of Fate and succeed in shaping its own destiny. That was the way to deal with the Fall of Galactic Empire.

It was also the answer to the perennial problem of Lagash in "Nightfall." The ultimate solution to recurrent mass freakout can come only when the people of Lagash develop sufficient holistic appreciation of their cosmic situation that sudden variations in the number of visible stars no longer faze them.

And it was the answer, too, to the Techno Age dilemma faced by Western man. Indeed, in the sequence of thought-modes offered by Asimov here in "Bridle and Saddle" we can recognize a précis of the story we have been telling in this book.

Just as soon as John Campbell finished reading the last page of Asimov's manuscript, he picked up the phone and put in a call to Street & Smith's accounting department to ask them to strike a check for Asimov. But perhaps because Asimov's delay in delivering the story had left him with a scheduling problem that he still had to resolve, this time he didn't see fit to throw in a bonus.

Campbell found his way out of his scheduling tangle by moving "Runaround," the robot story, into the next issue that he made up for the printer—the March 1942 *Astounding*. He then held back "Foundation" until May—an issue that was perhaps the most impressive in the entire Golden Age, containing not only Asimov's novelet, but van Vogt's "Asylum" and the final part of Heinlein/ MacDonald's *Beyond This Horizon*.

"Bridle and Saddle," of course, would follow in June. Despite the lack of bonus payment, it proved to be Asimov's second lead story in *Astounding*, illustrated on the cover.

After that, however, more than two years would pass before Campbell would be able to publish another Foundation story. Three weeks to the day after Asimov brought him "Bridle and Saddle," the United States was at war. And that meant radical changes for *Astounding* and for science fiction.

Man Transcending

In the second portion of the Golden Age, the years from 1942 through 1945 during which the United States was an active participant in World War II, *Astounding* would become a very different place than it had been in the intial universe-conquering phase of John Campbell's editorship. In part, this would be a result of Campbell's own thought and action—his sense of what was possible and necessary at this moment, and the corresponding changes in course that he elected to make in the magazine. But also, in part, it would be the result of wartime conditions that were utterly and completely beyond his control.

It isn't always easy to say exactly where the line should be drawn between what the editor consciously intended to do, and what would be done by him unknowingly, or even contrary to his belief, his judgment and his preference. As best he was able under trying circumstances, Campbell would attempt to go on serving as the master of provocation and farseeing coordinator of the new science fiction that he had been since assuming direction of *Astounding* at the end of 1937. But the war years would have their own necessities to impose that the editor could do nothing whatever about.

For one thing, the World War II years would be the period in which the United States did its best impression of the machine-state first dreamed of in Edward Bellamy's *Looking Backward.* That might be no impression at all when compared to totalitarian regimes like Nazi Germany and Communist Russia which attempted to treat their people like cogs in a machine. Even so, during the war American society would be mobilized as a whole—organized and prioritized, rationed and regulated, ordered and compelled as it had never been before. The entire country would be turned into a war industry.

The most fit, able and well-educated young men would be snatched away from the careers they had been attempting to put together out of the shambles left by the Depression, and set to the work of fighting and winning the war. And among those called away to the armed services, defense plants and research laboratories would be the brightest and best of the modern science fiction writers that John Campbell had been laboring so hard to gather and train. This could not help but have a great impact upon *Astounding*.

Between missing manpower and the new national priority of defeating Germany and Japan and their allies, limitations would be imposed on many aspects of ordinary life. Not the most important of these, but also not the least, would be that there were fewer lumberjacks on the job, and fewer railroad cars available to transport logs, and paper and printed pulp magazines. That would have its effect on *Astounding*, too, and upon science fiction in general.

But the American people would be ready to accept shortages, disruptions and extraordinary impositions of authority. There was great anger in the country over Japan's all-too-successful surprise attack on the U.S. Pacific Fleet based in Hawaii, and a deep accumulated dislike of the fanaticism, arrogance, brutality and treachery that had been displayed by Germany ever since the rise to power of Adolf Hitler and the Nazi Party.

From the time the United States entered World War II, a public consensus rare in American history would exist that this war was just and had to be fought. This wasn't merely one more conflict imposed upon the people by rich men in high places out to line their pockets and prove their power. Ordinary Americans had a pretty good notion that if the likes of Hitler and Mussolini and the military party that had recently seized control in Japan were allowed to win this war and rule the world, the cost would be their own freedom, and they were ready to fight to see freedom preserved.

In American eyes, the Axis powers would be looked upon as the embodiment of old-time attitudes that were now revealed as excessive and unacceptable. This was to be a war fought against all those who would set themselves up as superior to everyone else because of their race or nation or class, against those incapable of accepting difference in thought or diversity of kind, and against those who would seek to impose their will on the world through the rule of force and violence.

Offered in opposition to this elitism, intolerance and determination to prevail at any cost would be the recently emerged American ideal of democratic pluralism, the conviction that each man has his own individual value and ought to be allow the opportunity to demonstrate it. If the people of the United States were ready to overlook their differences and work toward a common goal, it wasn't because they were forced to, or because some monolithic central authority permitted them to think no other thought, but because they aimed to show the totalitarian states what free men working together in voluntary cooperation could manage to do if they were of a mind to.

America's new ideal can be seen in its simplest and purest form in World War II combat movies—particularly those made in the decade of reassessment that followed the war. The standard World War I story had been about the futility and waste of sending a generation of young men out of the trenches and over the top to be cut down by gas and machine gun fire in No Man's Land, or about dashing but doomed young pilots attempting to face fate and the end of Western civilization with a smile. But the archetypical movie of the Second World War would feature a squad of infantrymen— a Texan, an Italian, a Jew, a spoiled rich kid, an immigrant Slavic coal miner, a farm boy, and a wiseguy from Brooklyn—learning to get along together and win the war.

The actual conduct of the United States during World War II wouldn't always be equal to its best new ideal, of course. For instance, the American people may have believed that they were fighting for the principles of free thought and free speech, but during the war the actual willingness of the U.S. government to trust in the power of free thought and speech would be something less than total, and the American people would be subjected to internal censorship and propaganda.

The government was capable of a measure of Techno Age excess, particularly at the beginning of the war. The most flagrant example of this was the doubting of the loyalty of Japanese-Americans living on the West Coast. Anger against Japan over Pearl Harbor and lingering fears of the Yellow Peril—an unstoppable horde of invading Asians—would be discharged upon these American citizens. They would be arbitrarily deprived of their liberty and property and herded off into desert concentration camps.

If indeed that all-American infantry squad ever did exist during the war, it most certainly would not have included Nisei, or Negroes, let alone women. During World War II, each of these would be kept in segregated military units, separate and apart from the central melting pot of male American soldiery.

More than this, women would be allowed to serve only in highly limited roles, such as clerk, typist and nurse. And blacks in uniform would be treated, if anything, with even greater prejudice, confined to assignments such as cook, stevedore, manual laborer and truck driver, but not permitted to fight.

Even after all this has been said, however, it nonetheless remains true that Americans would be convinced they were waging this war for the ideal of democratic pluralism. While the war was on, certain sacrifices and compromises in personal freedom might be demanded.

And yes, the United States might display some highly visible imperfections in its current ability to live up to its own highest ideals. But the unprecedented degree of social assent and cooperative effort that would be achieved in the U.S. during the Second World War would only be obtained through a mutual understanding between government and people that when this war was over, a more just and equitable society would emerge.

And even while the war was being fought, the United States would start becoming more genuinely pluralistic. Women and Negroes would begin to be offered opportunities and responsibilities that previously had been denied them. A woman might put on pants and go to work on an aircraft assembly line. A black man might become a streetcar conductor in Philadelphia.

It would also be during the war years that teenagers, who through the Techno Age had been considered either older children or young adults, would first begin to define themselves as a separate age group with its own distinctive clothing and music. This was the period of teenage girls in bobby socks and saddle shoes swooning over Frank Sinatra.

The ongoing broadening of society would even affect the American armed forces. Before the war was over, Negroes would be allowed a limited combat role, and Nisei from the West Coast and Hawaii would distinguish themselves fighting as a unit in Europe.

Such would be the success of these experiments in the toleration and trust of difference that shortly after the war, President Truman would issue an executive order ending all racial segregation in the military. And that would be the first major step in the tearing down of legal barriers based upon race, religion and sex which would be a central American preoccupation throughout the Atomic Age.

The pluralization of society that began taking place during the war years would have its parallel in the pages of *Astounding*. Aliens, robots and mutants would shed their former aura of fundamental otherness and be seen in new light, not as evolutionary competitors, but as variations upon the larger theme of being human.

Before the U.S. entered the Second World War, L. Sprague de Camp had stood out for his insistence that a Vandal could be the equal of a Goth, and that a talking bear, a mutant baboon, or a surviving Neanderthal might be every bit as much *a man* as the ordinary Joe in the street. But by the last two years of the war, humanistic pluralism would become the insight of the hour in science fiction.

John Campbell would be swept along by the tide of change. However, there would be aspects of the new expanded humanism that he would never wholly accept or completely understand. In this instance, he would clearly be led by his writers rather than leading them, as he had always been able to do before.

But democratic pluralism wouldn't be the only aspect of the contemporary state of mind to have its effect on Campbell's modern science fiction. An even greater impact would be made upon *Astounding* by the wartime mood of radical disequilibrium.

These years were heady, upsetting and uncertain, a wild emotional roller-coaster ride of stomach-churning lows and giddy highs:

There was a great overturning of familiar customs and habits in American society. All sorts of folk would use the war as their excuse for ignoring established behavior and start acting in ways that to an older generation had to seem casual, heedless, disrespectful and individualistic.

Nothing was to be counted upon, time was fleeting, anything at all might happen tomorrow, and no one could say for certain what the outcome of the war would prove to be—who would survive and by what measures, which things would prosper and which would fade away, or what the world was going to look like when all the jumbled and scattered pieces of existence were finally fit back together again. Beneath America's public face of confidence, solidarity and good cheer, World War II would be a time of subjectivity, introspection and strange flights of mind.

It was the war years that would see the appearance of abstract expressionist painting, a form of art whose purpose was not to represent the external world, but rather the artist's own mental and emotional state. It would be a common thing for movies and plays of the time to feature questionings of personal sanity, psychiatric probings into the unconscious mind, dream sequences, and drunken hallucinations that just might prove to have their own reality. And there would also be a resurgence of interest in spirit-based horror and fantasy.

For its part, science fiction in *Astounding* would become a good deal queerer after America entered the war than it had been in the first phase of the Golden Age, with much more interest in mystery than in plausibility. But rather than SF writers seeking out one unknown realm of existence after another, as they had done when the constraints of the imagination had become loosened during the First World War, this time it was the universe of consciousness that they would explore.

What an alteration in perspective had taken place in the years between the two World Wars!

Taking their intial clues from the otherworld adventures of the Teens, science fiction writers of the Twenties and Thirties had traveled joyfully into the furthest reaches of time and space. They had explored what it might mean to be citizens of the wider universe and had offered the exhilarating possibility that humanity's true business might be the assumption of responsibility for the entirety of existence.

John Campbell's first aim on taking over the editorship of *Astounding* in 1937 had been to place a grounding of plausibility beneath this wonderful glimmering vision of a new and better human destiny. He offered his writers a powerful new set of arguments and assumptions and then demanded that they use them to resolve the great Techno Age conundrum—the haunting certainty that man was ultimately doomed to failure and extinction.

So it was that in the modern science fiction stories that Campbell published, men left Village Earth to tame our own solar system and then reach out to grasp the stars. Again and again the power of cyclical history to spell an end to man was gainsaid by characters able to show that they could respond effectively and creatively to any challenge they encountered. And the most constructive of Campbell's contributors—L. Sprague de Camp, Robert Heinlein and Isaac Asimov—went even further to imagine new systems, laws and sciences that harnessed major aspects of the multiverse to the power of human knowledge and will.

But what was not recognized and assimilated in this exuberant initial phase of problem-solving and empire-building was that in the course of resolving the Techno Age dilemma, the modern science fiction of John Campbell had placed itself outside—or beyond—the Western scientific frame of reference made by men like Galileo, Descartes, Newton and Darwin.

The universe as presented by Campbell was no longer the same universe that the followers of these great scientists had striven to deal with. It wasn't exclusively material in nature. It wasn't a simple machine like a clock. It wasn't a cold, remote, lifeless wasteland. Nor was it a place of unceasing hostility, competition and struggle for survival. Rather, the cosmos he was asking his writers to deal with was a super-system, a responsive whole, a natural blabbermouth that was always ready to give the right answer to any properly phrased question put to it by one of its children.

In this new ordering of existence, humanity was no longer a cosmic orphan, a fluke of nature to be eliminated by the blind grindings-on of matter, or by other creatures determined to knock mankind off his precarious perch on the evolutionary ladder, or by the inevitable senescence and failure of the race. Instead, man belonged in the universe and had a part to play there—perhaps a crucial one. And if he kept learning and maturing and accepting every challenge that came his way, there was no limit to what he could become.

A universe of consciousness giving birth to an ever-more-aware humanity... Mankind contriving to raise itself higher by asking

questions, solving problems, and growing in understanding...
Consciousness arising out of consciousness by means of consciousness... That was the picture of existence underlying all of the
triumphs of the Campbell *Astounding.*

But the writers of modern science fiction didn't immediately
realize that this was so. The giants of the early Golden Age still
thought of themselves as writing about transcendent science, just
as their predecessors had done. Except that instead of dreaming
of new drugs, new machines and new forces, it was new orders of
scientific command that they were aiming to envision. That's all.

They didn't recognize that the new laws and systems and sciences
they were imagining were vitally different in one central respect
from the science-beyond-science they had grown up with. Old-time
transcendent science had always been conceived in material terms.
Even the Lens in Doc Smith's Lensman stories—a telepathic device
and mental amplifier with certain lingering soul-like characteristics—
was still presented in the form of a physical object strapped to
the wrist of a wearer.

But the likes of paraphysics and the Future History and the
Laws of Robotics had no physical correlatives of any kind, not
even a button to push. They were new mental constructs—new
states of knowledge and control.

These thought systems were something more and something other
than material super-science. And it was precisely their extra-scientific,
extra-rational and extra-physical transcendent nature which made
them so effective in dealing with the intractable problems that the
Atomic Age had inherited from three hundred years of Western fixa-
tion upon the rational scientific consideration of material existence.

All of the factors in this initial pattern—a universe understood
in more-than-materialistic terms; a humanity reoriented within
the cosmos; and transcendence in the new form of a knowledge
system, yet still treated as though it were one more manifestation
of super-science and applied to the old Western problems—would
be on display in *Astounding* as late as Isaac Asimov's first two
Foundation stories, written on the eve of U.S. involvement in the
Second World War and published in the spring of 1942:

In "Foundation" and "Bridle and Saddle," as we have seen, the
universe is presented as a stairway of consciousness for mankind to
ascend, with "science" the name of just one step. But this radical
reconception of the nature of existence is buried in background
and in story structure. It is never explicitly stated.

In these stories, there has also been a dramatic shift in the psychic
orientation of man. His ties to Village Earth have been cut with such
completeness that he can no longer remember on which planet it

was that he originated. So much a child of the universe as a whole has he become that galaxy-wide empire is now the normal, accustomed human frame of reference.

The highest manifestation of transcendence to be seen in the Foundation stories is psychohistory, a mode of understanding that is presented as a new form of science, but which might as readily be taken as religious, or occult, or mathematical, or psychological, or historical, or holistic. But the problems to which this multifaceted new form of transcendent knowledge are applied are the old Techno Age problems of survival in the face of stronger material power and of overcoming the threat posed to humanity by cyclical history.

The one writer in the pre-war *Astounding* who understood most clearly that he was no longer dealing with old-time science-beyond-science, but rather with a holistic universe, the powers of non-rational thought, and the higher potential of mankind was A. E. van Vogt. And, as we know, in the burst of stories that he published in 1942, after he had quit his job at the Canadian Department of National Defence and become a full-time writer for John Campbell, van Vogt would insist that the universe had to be related to as a responsive whole with level upon level of potential being and becoming.

In the altered context of a World War II America that not only was psychically unsettled, but also was becoming aware of different states of mind and learning how to speak of them in the new terms of Twentieth Century psychology, other writers would begin to join van Vogt in acknowledging the holistic universe of consciousness. With more than a little trepidation, particularly at the outset, they would start to investigate the nature and meaning of this new interactive reality.

John Campbell would have a considerable part to play in this process of probing and testing the holistic universe. Over and over again, he would point to van Vogt as a model for others to follow. And he would nudge and urge and challenge his authors as only he knew how to do to convince them to deal with the van Vogtian mysteries of indeterminacy, non-rational thinking, wild talents, and higher levels of human becoming.

But we should also know that there would come a time at the end of the war when the great editor would wake with a start and a splutter to find that somehow he had contrived to get himself in way over his head. Between one thing and another—the momentum of his investigations into the new van Vogtian reality, his need during the war to accept almost any story, however strange, that was of publishable quality, and the peculiar headiness of the night air—he had allowed himself to be lured into far deeper and darker psychic waters than he was prepared to cope with. And this postwar Campbell would hastily beat a retreat to safer ground.

However, for as long as the war lasted and as long as it still seemed to Campbell that he was leading his writers in a scientific inquiry into non-logical phenomena, he would print a much queerer line of story in *Astounding* than he would have been ready to find acceptable in the first phase of the Golden Age, or would be able to tolerate once the war was over.

As a whole, then, we can say that some of the radical changes that took place in *Astounding* during World War II were due to wartime circumstances, some to the altering mood of the time, some to Campbell leading writers onward, some to Campbell being led, some to the pursuit of science and reason, and some to the siren call of the new transcendence. However, the very first change that occurred in *Astounding* after the United States entered the war was not only the sign of the beginning of a new phase, but was wholly and solely John Campbell's doing.

When the January 1942 issue of *Astounding* appeared on the newsstand less than two weeks after the attack on Pearl Harbor, the magazine was no longer the same 7 by 10 inch pulp size it had always been throughout the dozen years of its existence. Instead, it was now 40% larger, expanded in its dimensions to the 8½ by 11½ inch bedsheet size of the old Gernsback *Science Wonder Stories*.

For Campbell, altering the size of *Astounding* (and *Unknown*) was intended to accomplish a number of different purposes at once. It was a bold try for more prominent display on the magazine racks, for better sales, and for increased advertising revenue. More than anything else, however, it was a bid for greater respect and dignity.

The truth of the matter is that Campbell felt compromised and held back by the juvenile pulp company that his magazines were forced to keep. He wanted nothing so much as to shake free from it.

He knew how original and special *Astounding* and *Unknown* were, and how superior to their competition. He was well aware that they were read and appreciated by able, intelligent people—scientists, engineers, college professors and professional men. And he longed for them to be taken just as seriously by society in general.

The first step in this process, as he saw it, was to put some distance between his magazines and the others on the sales racks. But this was not at all easy to do.

The new *Astounding* and *Unknown Worlds*, as the magazine was now renamed, might indicate by their size that they would like to be thought of as different from all the other SF pulps. In actual fact, however, they still had to appeal to the popular audience that bought and read story magazines. They were still printed on cheap, rough, pulp paper. And they still had the style and appearance of large, skinny, pulp magazines.

Since there was no other reasonable place for them to be put, they continued to be grouped on the newsstand with the other SF pulps. And instead of receiving better display, now Campbell's oversized magazines were all too likely to be tucked away behind the others so as not to block their covers from being seen.

The upshot was that there was no sudden leap in sales for *Astounding* or *Unknown*. They garnered no classy new audience. And there was no change at all in the nature or amount of advertising they attracted—only the same old ads as always for razor blades, trusses, correspondence courses, and other Street & Smith publications.

A fair assessment of this attempt to take on greater respectability might be that in fact no large, untapped market of bright, influential readers such as Campbell hoped for actually existed, and that he was already reaching the entire American audience which was capable of appreciating the modern science fiction and fantasy he published. A mass audience for SF was still a generation away.

At the same time, the change in size was something of an esthetic disaster. The pulp *Astounding*s of the early Golden Age, with their simple, clean-cut, definite modern design, and their bright, confident, human-centered Hubert Rogers covers, had been bold, dynamic and graceful physical objects. But in the redesign of the magazine, that artless pulp perfection was lost.

The taller, thinner issues, held together by only a single staple, were awkward, floppy and fragile. The new covers, with a central picture framed by broad borders, no longer had the old boundary-bursting immediacy. Individual pages were now less attractive and harder to read. Illustrations of a formerly sufficient size now seemed small and shoved off into the corner of the page.

Sixteen issues of *Astounding* and ten issues of *Unknown Worlds* would be published in the large size before this experiment was brought to an end by the wartime paper shortage. But *Astounding* would never manage to recapture the confidence, balance and perfect proportion that had seemed to come so effortlessly and naturally in the days before the war. . . .

Even before the disaster at Pearl Harbor, the U.S. had begun the process of rearming itself, designing and building new ships, planes and tanks, and increasing the size of its armed forces. In the fall of 1940, unmarried young men began to be drafted into the military for a year's service.

Once the United States had joined the war, conscription was expanded to take in men from the ages of 18 to 45, with registration of all men up to age 65. The term of service was to be the duration of the war, however short or long that proved to be, plus an additional six months.

Campbell lost his first writer to the war effort as early as the summer of 1941, when L. Ron Hubbard joined the Naval Reserve as an officer and was called to active duty. But that was just the beginning. During the spring and summer of 1942, all of the major players in *Astounding* and *Unknown*—with the exception of A. E. van Vogt—ceased to write and turned to war work.

E. E. Smith's third Lensman story, *Second-Stage Lensman* (*Astounding*, Nov 1941-Feb 1942), was in the middle of its serialization even as the United States joined the war and *Astounding* increased in size. Doc Smith was 51 years old and had a family, and he had already served as an officer during the First World War. But after Pearl Harbor, he applied to the War Department for a job that would make use of his technical expertise.

He was thanked but turned down. So Smith followed up a want ad and took a job as a Junior Chemical Engineer in an ordnance works in Kingsbury, Indiana, making mines and bombs. He would work his way up to Chief Chemist, and then to Head of the Inspection Division.

Robert Heinlein, who only a few months earlier had feared that he might be suffering a third flare-up of his tuberculosis, wanted nothing so much as to get back into uniform and join the fight. But Navy doctors had their look at him and refused to restore him to active duty.

Heinlein's oldest Navy friend was currently the director of the Materials Laboratory of the Naval Aircraft Factory at the Philadelphia Navy Yard, so Heinlein arranged to have himself taken on there as a civilian research and development engineer. And with him, he brought Isaac Asimov as a civilian chemist, and L. Sprague de Camp, a new-made Naval Reserve officer, as an engineer. These three leading writers of modern science fiction would spend the war years working on the same floor of the same building.

Hubert Rogers, whose bold, bright cover paintings had formed the outward image of the exuberant pre-war Golden Age, went north and joined the Canadian Army. His final cover, in August 1942, was an illustration of Heinlein's last story for *Astounding*, Anson MacDonald's "Waldo." His successor during the next four years was William Timmins, an artist who was no match for Rogers in technique, artistry, or vision. Under Timmins' hand, the face of *Astounding* would grow dark and murky, as though even warmth and color had been rationed for the duration.

As soon as U.S. involvement in the war began, John Campbell understood that he would very shortly be losing the technically trained men who were his leading contributors. And he tried to prepare his readers for the inevitable with an editorial in the April 1942 issue of *Astounding* entitled "Too Good At Guessing."

The pose he took was that in the ordinary way of things *Astounding* stories were only one short step beyond actual fact, but that henceforth it would be the patriotic duty of the magazine not to compromise actual secret research by publishing stories of near-future invention. He said, "We will, in the future, try to be wilder guessers, place our stories further in the future, or base them on themes that can't lead to those too-good guesses."

This was utter bushwah, of course.

The truth of the matter was that Campbell would continue to be just as receptive to SF based upon actual science and technology as he had ever been—when he was able to get it. He would try a variety of expedients in hopes of increasing the supply. And it wouldn't bother him that he might be intruding into areas of real secret research. In fact, he wouldn't mind at all if he did.

When the editor got even the slightest hint that a new writer had scientific or technical training, he would encourage him to make use of it in his fiction. In January 1942, just about the time that Campbell was writing this editorial, he received an unsolicited story submission from Detroit. Its author was George O. Smith, a 31-year-old electronics engineer who until recently had been laboring long hours trying to work the glitches out of an automatic tuner for car radios which refused to hold a station without drifting. In the switchover to wartime engineering, he temporarily had a little spare time on his hands, and he was using it to fulfill a long-standing urge to write science fiction.

His first submission wasn't acceptable, but it did indicate to Campbell that Smith had writing talent, and also that he was someone who almost certainly had been technically educated. Just the kind of guy the editor needed most.

So Campbell wrote back to say that while he couldn't use what Smith had written, he did like its style. And what's more, he had a pretty good notion that Smith was someone with a technical background. Would it be possible for him to try writing another story which used his special knowledge and experience as a foundation?

Smith's response to this Campbellian letter of invitation and indication was to write "QRM—Interplanetary," a story about wisecracking engineers aboard an interplanetary radio relay station in the orbit of Venus who have to cope with their supervisor's incompetence. Campbell received it with delight and ran it in the October 1942 *Astounding*.

It was in June and August 1942 that Campbell published the first stories by Harry Stubbs, an astronomy student at Harvard who wrote in his free time under the name Hal Clement. More than any other SF author before or after him, Clement would be concerned to write imaginative science fiction that employed and respected the facts of known science. His particular pleasure would be in conceiving of alternate forms of alien life.

In addition to these new writers, Campbell dug up an old one— Will F. Jenkins, the prolific storyteller who for years had produced science fiction with his left hand under the name Murray Leinster, but who had written no SF at all during the period that John Campbell had been editing *Astounding*. Jenkins, as a hobby, was a self-taught inventor who would eventually develop the front projection system that would revolutionize motion picture special effects and make possible SF movies like *2001: A Space Odyssey* (1968) and *Star Wars* (1977), but he had seldom attempted to apply his scientific knowledge to his SF writing in any serious way. For him, the story had always been the primary thing.

The editor invited him to try his hand at the new, more exact, modern science fiction. And Jenkins/Leinster responded with "The Wabbler" (*Astounding*, Oct 1942), a fictional account of a semi-sentient air-dropped robot torpedo feeling its way into an enemy harbor to destroy a ship.

In a similar way, Campbell did what he could to adjust the approach to SF of another old-time writer, Jack Williamson. We may remember that when Williamson's Galactic Empire novel, *Star of Empire*, was drying up in the fall of 1941, the editor had suggested to him that he might look to Heinlein, van Vogt and Asimov as models of the new science fiction.

More than this, Campbell told Williamson that he really ought to try adopting a pseudonym and write the new style of story from behind this screen. He said, "Fundamentally, I think a 'Don A. Stuart' stunt would help you a hell of a lot..."

Williamson decided to go along with Campbell's suggestion. He says of himself:

Looking for a new name and something entirely new to write, I come up with "Will Stewart" and the idea for a series about the planetary engineers who would "terraform" new planets to fit them for colonization— the word, I think, is my own coinage. He likes the idea and suggests the interesting problems they might meet on contraterrene worlds. "Contraterrene" was the term for antimatter, then. Campbell's abbreviation was CT, and I spelled it out, "seetee."

The editor had previously tried without success to interest Robert

Heinlein in writing about contraterrene matter. Now he prompted Williamson with so much material on the subject that the writer would say, "The seetee stories, bylined Will Stewart, were almost collaborations with John Campbell."

Over the next eight months, Williamson wrote three seetee stories— a novelet, a short novel, and a two-part serial. If these ultimately proved to be something less than his best work, it may have been because the stories pulled in two different directions, with Williamson's original idea of terraformed worlds tugging one way and Campbell's intense desire to see fiction about men establishing their mastery over antimatter yanking another.

Campbell would feed specialized scientific information to other established SF writers who had only a limited amount of formal education in science, occasionally with very happy results. Early in 1942, after Lester del Rey had been rejected by his draft board for extreme tachycardia and it looked as though he might be available as a writer for a while, Campbell sent him the idea for a story about a catastrophic accident in an atomic plant.

Del Rey's line as a writer had always been emotion-laden short stories, and it seems likely that Campbell was only expecting to get back a relatively brief glimpse of atomic disaster as it was experienced by the plant's doctor. But del Rey had been secretly itching for some time to write a story of suspense, and he perceived the makings of a good one in this idea. He spent more time in research, preparation and plotting than he ever had before, and the result was his longest, most serious science fiction story to date, the short novel "Nerves" (*Astounding*, Sept 1942).

In May, however, del Rey followed his girl friend to a new government job in St. Louis. And soon he himself was working for McDonnell Aircraft hammering tail assemblies into shape for DC-3 planes.

It went like that whenever Campbell thought he had a writer lined up whom he could count on. Jack Williamson was 34 years old and seeing a psychiatrist, and Campbell had high hopes for regular contributions from him. But at the end of July, Williamson finished "Opposites—React!," his third and longest seetee story, and then joined the Army, which made him into a weatherman, and eventually promoted him to sergeant.

It became harder and harder for Campbell to arrange a continuing supply of science-minded SF for *Astounding.* Will F. Jenkins was occupied working for the Office of War Information in Washington. Harry Stubbs graduated from Harvard in 1943 and became an Air Force bomber pilot. George O. Smith was living in Cincinnati and working as a project engineer on the development of "the so-called 'radar' proximity fuse."

Campbell had to be content with the occasional story that he could get from these busy men writing in odd moments. But the editor never stopped prompting and adjusting, stroking and challenging in hopes of getting a good sound technically based story for his magazine.

After the publication of "QRM—Interplanetary" in the fall of 1942, for example, Campbell sent a letter off to George O. Smith in Cincinnati. After discussing his own basement experiments in electronics for a few pages, the editor let it drop that he was ready for Smith to send him another story as good as the one he had just published. He was waiting to see it.

Smith was flattered by this attention and moved by Campbell's expectations of him. So when he was able to, he sat down and turned out another Venus Equilateral story. He says, "Hoping... not to be hauled off before a firing squad, I took some liberties with what little was known about radar, and wrote 'Calling the Empress.'"

Altogether, then, we can see that not only did John Campbell continue to publish SF based in science after the beginning of the war, and do whatever he could to generate more of it, but he knowingly and deliberately published stories about atomic power plants, air-dropped torpedoes and radar. He got into trouble over this playing with fire only once, when he published Cleve Cartmill's story "Deadline" in the March 1944 issue of *Astounding*.

Cartmill was a California newspaperman who had fallen in with Heinlein's Mañana Literary Society in the days before the war, and then begun to write for Campbell, first for *Unknown* and then for *Astounding*. In this case, the editor had primed Cartmill with detailed information about the construction, shielding and detonation of an atomic bomb made of U-235, and Cartmill had embedded this data in an otherwise lame and unimaginative story set during a World War on some other planet. This story was filled with names like "Sixa" and "Seilla" and "Ynamre," as well as other names that looked just as strange but were not as easily deciphered.

All this seemed suspicious enough to bring out agents of Military Intelligence, who feared that the security of the Manhattan Project had been compromised. So they looked up John Campbell and discussed the matter with him. They talked to Cleve Cartmill in California. They talked things over with the illustrator of the story, Paul Orban. An investigator even dropped by the Office of War Information to have a chat with Will F. Jenkins, who had a security clearance and presumably could be trusted.

Jenkins was able to tell the agent that "Deadline" was a perfectly ordinary science fiction story of a kind that *Astounding* was accustomed to publishing and that it was based on material that was public knowledge:

"I told him what I could about where Cartmill could have gotten the idea. There was a book published by the Bureau of Mines, a US Government publication, that stated definitely that when atomic energy was achieved it would be achieved through uranium."

John Campbell was not only ready and willing to point out to his own interrogators the unclassified pre-war publications that were his sources, but even had the audacity to argue that *Astounding* should be allowed to continue to publish stories of atomic power. If the Germans were watching (and it would turn out that some of them, at least, had been; Werner von Braun, the mastermind of the German rocket program, for one, would arrange to keep getting his own personal copy of *Astounding* all through the war), then it might very well seem suspicious if the magazine were to suddenly cease printing stories on this long-established topic.

Indeed, it is quite possible that Campbell went on to argue that since he had declared so publicly that actual secret research wouldn't be compromised in *Astounding*, for the magazine to continue to publish atomic stories would be to actively mislead the enemy into thinking that we weren't working on the Bomb. Whatever he actually said, the arguments the editor made were accepted by his questioners and their superiors, and *Astounding* was left to go its own way.

"Deadline" wasn't all that much of a story, and it wasn't innovative SF. But for years to come, this episode would be recounted with pride, and not a little glee, as evidence of the reality and seriousness of science fictional prediction.

Another squeeze suffered by Campbell after the beginning of the war--a direct result of the loss of his full-time authors, and the time pressures on those writers who remained—was in serial novels. There would be several long stretches during the war when no serial story was running in *Astounding*.

Typically, Campbell would attempt to pass off these periods of shortage as the result of well-considered editorial policy. He would suggest that *Astounding* was not publishing serial novels out of concern for servicemen in the field, who might find it difficult to catch up with every installment of a multi-part story. In actual practice, however, it seemed that whenever the editor was able to get his hands on a halfway decent serial story, he wouldn't hesitate to publish it, even though it might have to be spread out over four issues.

The one top writer who was left to Campbell with the departure of the other giants of the early Golden Age was A. E. van Vogt. He would be the editor's great surety in the difficult days of 1942 and early 1943, when one after another of Campbell's writers was putting the cover on his typewriter and stowing it away in the closet.

Van Vogt's presence lent continuity to the magazine which other-wise would have been lost, and his industry assured that Campbell had a good head start each month toward filling the pages of his next issue. Beginning with his return to writing with "Recruiting Station" in March 1942, van Vogt would have contributions in eleven of the fourteen remaining issues of the bedsheet *Astounding*.

In these stories, as we have seen, van Vogt insisted upon the connectivity and responsiveness of the universe, and the necessity for sentient beings to cooperate with each other. By the time he wrote "The Weapon Shop" and "The Search," he had moved beyond this to imagine men and women with the character and capacity to serve as a permanent opposition force guaranteeing individual justice and freedom within a tyrannical society, or even the ability to function as an organization of immortal observers who have the power to stand outside the stream of time and direct the ongoing flow of human history like beneficent gods.

The culmination of this sequence of visions of potential human responsibility came with the serialization of van Vogt's second novel, *The Weapon Makers*, from February to April 1943, the last three issues of the bedsheet *Astounding*. Here van Vogt attempted to give a definitive answer to the question he had raised two years earlier in "Repetition": What quality in man would render him fit to attain the stars and to rule the galaxy?

The structure of *The Weapon Makers* was quite unusual, and perhaps not altogether successful, with frequent inversions of time sequence and with separate narrative lines that never quite managed to meet. It was perfectly possible that a reader might find this story frustrating, fragmented and incoherent—even for A. E. van Vogt.

However, if we look at *The Weapon Makers* from just the proper angle with just the proper squint, it is possible for us to see it as having less of the nature of a conventional novel of any kind we are familiar with, and more of the form and approach of an out-of-time Greek play in science fiction clothing. Here, even before the story begins, a central happening of cosmic importance has taken place. In the story proper, human beings of varying role and stature must react to that event, and, as they contend, they reveal something of the essential quality of being human. Finally, at the conclusion of the story, a cathartic assessment of the situation is rendered by a non-human higher observer.

The offstage universe-altering event that underlies *The Weapon Makers* is the invention of the "infinity drive" and the human attainment of interstellar travel.

A brilliant scientist and his assistants have made the first flight between the stars, only to be marooned by a greedy subordinate on a desert planet hurtling in a figure-eight orbit around the twin suns of Alpha Centauri. That underling has now returned to an Earth society marked on every level by immorality and amorality, where he has entered into secret negotiations with the Empress Innelda Isher to sell her the interstellar drive, which she intends to suppress.

The Empress is the living embodiment of the conservative aspect of human nature, even though she is "'restless and adventure-minded'" and surrounds herself with a personal retinue of young hotbloods. It is her fear that public knowledge of the interstellar drive will send human beings hurtling off in all directions and mean the end of the 5000-year history of the Isher Empire.

The continuing counterforce to the Empire is, of course, the Weapon Shops—"an independent, outlawed, indestructible, altruistic opposition to tyranny." Here, too, paradox is involved, since even though this organization represents the rebellious, individualistic, questing element of human nature, the men of the Weapon Shops Council seem a personally restrained and cautious lot who must act in concert if they are to act at all. However, when the most farseeing of the Weapon Makers, Edward Gonish—a "No-man" or trained intuitionist who only has to know ten percent of the facts of any situation in order to grasp the entirety—understands in a flash that there is such a thing as the interstellar drive and that the Empress aims to keep it a secret, there is no question but that the Weapon Shops will do whatever they can to see it made public.

The Weapon Makers has two different protagonists. One is an ordinary man, an asteroid miner named Dan Neelan. His twin brother, Gil, with whom he has an extraordinary degree of rapport, was one of the assistants of the scientist who invented the infinity drive. Neelan, having lost his lifelong sense of contact with his brother and believing that this must mean he is dead, has returned to Earth to discover what happened to him.

This is certainly one selfless and single-minded man. After he has discovered that his brother has been marooned among the stars, and then is able to gain control of the interstellar drive, Neelan falls into the hands of the Empress. But neither desire for the riches she has to offer, nor fear of the torture she threatens him with and then subjects him to, can cause him to divulge the secret he is holding. His only concern is to follow his brother to the stars and help him in any way he can.

The other protagonist, Robert Hedrock, is a personage of greater size and broader aims. He is described to us as someone of "striking appearance, mental brilliance and strong personality." Even though he is an acknowledged agent of the Weapon Shops, a member of their Council, he has presented himself at Innelda Isher's palace, the one man bold enough to seek her hand in marriage, and has been made a Captain in her Guard.

In fact, as we will come to be told, "he is Earth's only immortal man, with private long-range purposes of his own, transcending any temporary commitment he might make." Robert Hedrock is only his latest name. This man has had many different identities.

Long ago, he was the first Isher Emperor.

He was also Walter S. de Lany, the founder of the Weapon Shops.

At various moments since, when balance and reinvigoration have been called for, he has served as the husband of an Isher Empress. On other occasions, he has been a leader of the Weapon Shops. At still other times, he has pursued the mystery of his own immortality and sought to make it a universal condition of man.

What these different persons and forces—the Empress, Dan Neelan, Robert Hedrock, and the Weapon Shops—have in common is the quality of altruism:

It is a given that the Weapon Makers are altruistic, as even Innelda Isher is ready to admit at those moments when she isn't doing her best to annihilate them. In one unusually candid moment, she describes them as "'a stabilizing influence'" in the current societal atmosphere of pervasive selfishness and corruption. And she even goes on to say, "'I am counting particularly upon a new method of mind training recently released by the Weapon Shops, which strengthens moral functions as well as performing everything that other methods are noted for.'"

The mysterious Robert Hedrock is an idealist and an altruist beyond even the ability of the Weapon Makers to comprehend. They are made so nervous by his unfathomable nature and motives that they are prepared to execute him just to have life once again be something they think they understand.

Even Edward Gonish, the No-man, cannot get his head around the whole of Hedrock. However, enough of Hedrock's pattern is visible to him that Gonish feels able to say, "'Everything the man has ever said or done shows an immense and passionate interest in the welfare of the race.'"

Next to Hedrock, Dan Neelan is an ephemeral being. But within his more limited frame of reference, he, too, is an altruist, caring far more for his brother's welfare than his own. And as soon as he has escaped from the control of the Empress, Neelan heads straight for the stars in search of his lost twin.

While he is in the depths of space, he is encountered by an immense ship full of spider-like higher aliens. These are cool, remote, thoughty beings whose lives have been conducted in accordance with the old Techno Age rule of the survival of the fittest. As they eventually describe themselves to Neelan: "'All of us here present are immortal, the winners in the struggle for supremacy and existence on our planet. Each and every one of us is supreme in some one field by virtue of having destroyed all competition.'"

The immediate judgment the spiders make of Neelan is that he is not very bright—"'Intelligence type nine hundred minus....'" But gradually these emotionless Big Brains become intrigued by his devotion to his brother, and by the rapport that exists between the two. Such a bond is unique in their experience and deserving of special study.

Even the Empress Innelda Isher—who can be selfish, willful and cruel—is capable of behaving altruistically. We know that she fears what the interstellar drive will do to the secure eternal Isherness of things. We are also aware that she is afraid of death, and that she has been told by her doctors that if she should ever have a child, it will be at the cost of her life.

But yet, as soon as she gains even an inkling of Robert Hedrock's special role in human affairs, she is ready to offer knowledge of the infinity drive to the Weapon Shops in exchange for his life. What is more, despite the fact that she is unable to tolerate the fact of his immortality or the personal relationships he has had with past Isher empresses, she will marry Hedrock in order to have his child and continue the Isher line—even though she knows that to do so means her death.

The spiderish alien observers—whose assessment of themselves is that they have taken the wrong path and are ultimately not to be reckoned one of Nature's successes—are puzzled and awed by Innelda Isher's readiness to sacrifice herself, just as they were previously impressed by the unselfish behavior of Dan Neelan.

The last line of *The Weapon Makers* is their final judgment of mankind:

"'This much we have learned; here is the race that shall rule the sevagram.'"

What an epitomally thunderous van Vogtian exit line! And what a marvelously exotic and resonant word to introduce without any explanation at the very end of a story!

As it is used here, "sevagram" seems clearly intended to stir images in the reader's mind of the broadest conceivable vistas. It would appear to mean at least this galaxy, maybe other galaxies, perhaps even the entire multiverse.

At the same time, however, while this word might be obscure to van Vogt's American readers, it was in contemporary use. Sevagram was the name of the ashram recently established by Mahatma Gandhi in India. In Hindi, this word meant "village of service."

The wider universe perceived as a mere village... The ruler whose true obligation is recognized as service to others... Above all, the identification of altruistic behavior as the essence of mankind's higher potential, uniting the aspect of humanity which remembers and maintains, man's restless questing spirit, his ephemeral individual nature, and his mysterious immortality... Wonderful ideas indeed to find expressed in a sometimes clumsy and disorganized pulp science fiction serial in the middle of World War II!

But A.E. van Vogt, though he might labor valiantly all of the day and into the night to produce stories for John Campbell, couldn't fill the pages of *Astounding* all by himself. Campbell had to have other regular writers to keep the magazine going. The place where he looked for them was *Unknown*.

Back in 1939 and 1940, the weight of editorial pressure had all been in the other direction, with Campbell doing his best to convince science fiction writers like van Vogt, Heinlein and Williamson to produce stories for his new fantasy magazine. Now, however, with *Unknown Worlds* on a bimonthly schedule and only half the market it had formerly been, and with *Astounding* losing all of its most dependable contributors, it made sense to Campbell to drop a line to one after another of his fantasy authors and suggest that *Astounding* would welcome submissions if they cared to have a try at writing science fiction.

Cleve Cartmill, the author of "Deadline," was one of these. Another was William Anthony Parker White, a writer of mysteries under the name H.H. Holmes (including the 1942 novel *Rocket to the Morgue*, set in Heinlein's Mañana Literary Society of happy memory), who in recent times had become an occasional writer for *Unknown* under the pseudonym Anthony Boucher. Yet another was Fritz Leiber, Jr., who had just finished an experimental stint as a teacher at Occidental College and delivered a fantasy novel to Campbell about witchcraft in academe based on his experience. The editor was pressing him to have a try at a science fiction novel next.

But the one writer whom Campbell singled out from *Unknown* to write for *Astounding* on a full-time basis was Henry Kuttner. On past record, this was a most unlikely choice.

Henry Kuttner was born in Los Angeles on April 7, 1914. His father, a bookseller, died when he was only five. Kuttner's mother then took him and his older brothers to San Francisco, where, for a time at least, she ran a boardinghouse.

Beyond this, what happened to him as a child isn't clear, except that it was traumatic. Kuttner wasn't a person who was much given to talking about himself. After his death in 1958, however, John Campbell would speak in a letter to Isaac Asimov about the "rotten start" Kuttner had had in life and "the terrible psychic wounds he'd been given," without elaborating on the subject.

The effect of his injuries is somewhat easier to see. Kuttner grew up a reader and a loner, with an acute sense of having been excluded from the world of literature and intellect that was his birthright. He started drinking at an early age, and often drank too much, and when he did he would flip-flop between feelings of bitterness and rage and feelings of total personal worthlessness.

Kuttner the man was a shy, bright-eyed mouse with a wry, deadpan sense of humor, a tendency to quote someone he'd been reading rather than offering an opinion of his own, and an infinite ability to say no by saying nothing at all. If you wanted to pick up on his wit, you had to lean in his direction and overhear him.

His wife, C.L. Moore, tells us that expressed over and over again in his work was a fundamental theme: "Hank's basic statement was something like, 'Authority is dangerous and I will never submit to it.'"

(Her own essential fictional statement, she says, was "'The most treacherous thing in life is love'"—though a possibly more accurate rephrasing might be: "The most threatening thing in life is overwhelming sexual passion.")

Kuttner's first published story, "The Graveyard Rats" (*Weird Tales*, Mar 1936), was written in imitation of H.P. Lovecraft. Lovecraft, who was then very near the end of his life, was an assiduous correspondent with the other writers of *Weird Tales*, and it was he who first put Kuttner and Moore in touch with each other.

The young Kuttner was a facile wordsmith, turning out a great deal of copy that had the look and sound of storytelling, but all of it was totally lacking in both original imagination and conviction. He imitated Lovecraft. He imitated Robert E. Howard. He turned out yard goods to order, including mildly sexual or sadistic material for marginal science fiction and horror magazines—which did his reputation as a writer no good. His best-known science fiction stories, a series of imitations of Stanley Weinbaum's Ham and Pat Hammond stories, which began with "Hollywood on the Moon" (*Thrilling Wonder*, Apr 1938), were an assignment that was handed to him to write.

During the late Thirties, Kuttner kept traveling back and forth between Los Angeles and New York. When he was in Los Angeles he worked as a reader in a literary agency. Then he'd head off to New York to make contacts and arrange assignments, and even to try to live as a full-time writer. But he would soon get to hate it there and retreat to Los Angeles.

On his way back and forth, he would stop to see Catherine Moore in Indianapolis. She was older than he by three years, and a much more highly regarded writer. Their relationship was largely carried forward by letter, but when Kuttner was living in California, Moore came out to visit him there. The two were married at last at City Hall in New York City on June 7, 1940, four years after they first began corresponding.

Kuttner had met John Campbell during his early visits to New York, and had sat in on his writing circle. After Campbell became editor of *Astounding*, he asked Kuttner for a contribution, but the story he received from him was a Techno Age cliché, and the editor didn't ask for another.

The problem was that Kuttner had no education whatsoever in science, and wasn't very interested in it. Nor did he have sufficient faith in the regularity and manageability of the material world to write stories of universal operating principles. In the initial phase of the Golden Age, he had nothing to offer *Astounding*.

He did somewhat better in the context of *Unknown*. Over a three-year period, he sold Campbell half-a-dozen fantasy stories. But he was by no means a mainstay of the magazine. He was a filler of pages and very little more.

C. L. Moore was far more sincere and original, but she had never been able to produce much work. From 1934 to the beginning of 1942, she had a total of five novelets in *Astounding*, plus a sixth novelet in *Unknown*.

This, then, was the couple that Campbell decided to approach in the spring of 1942 to supply him with as much material as they could write: Moore, the author of highly regarded, but widely spaced stories; and Kuttner, the complete hack, who punished himself by turning out derivative junk that was an insult to his own intelligence, but who lacked the confidence and self-esteem necessary to attempt work of greater ambition.

No account exists of the conditions and suggestions that Campbell made in offering them this deal, but it is possible to make some likely guesses, partly based on what we know of his indications to other writers and partly based on the work that Kuttner and Moore actually produced for *Astounding*.

The first condition that Campbell laid down was that they should write together. Individually, they each had weaknesses. Moore was a slow writer and much stronger on emotion than on plot. Kuttner was a technician, a student of story mechanics, but his own stories were thin and derivative. Campbell knew him to be a sophisticated and well-read man, but he didn't write like one. The two should combine their strengths and produce more work of better quality.

Second, it was an entirely new writer that Campbell wanted to see— not Kuttner, not Moore, but a flashy new talent he could present as a find, an *Astounding* exclusive. The editor would still use work under their own names, but what he really wanted was a whole new personality—a Don A. Stuart, as it were—who would say new things in a new way.

Third, what he primarily needed from them was short fiction—short stories and novelets. He needed to be able to count on a contribution from them for every issue.

Fourth, they should avoid space opera. In fact, they should forget entirely about the old-fashioned sort of science fiction. Instead, they should invent a future, throw in some strange new possibility, and then play the game through to its logical conclusion. Heinlein, van Vogt and Asimov were models of this new kind of science fiction.

There is something else that Campbell may have said. It is possible that he reminded Kuttner of the game "Hezekiah Plantagenet" that they used to play in the old writers' circle, and how Kuttner had gotten howled down when he would say something like, "'Just then a hole in space happened along, and Hezekiah stepped through it....'"

Campbell may have said: "Well, Kuttner, you're allowed to write stories like that now. Take a look at Heinlein's '"And He Built a Crooked House"' and 'By His Bootstraps' and van Vogt's 'The Seesaw.' And then think about that when this new fellow gets ready to sit down at the typewriter."

The name of the new writer that Kuttner and Moore chose to become was a token of their determination to write together. They combined the maiden names of Kuttner's mother and Moore's grandmother and came up with Lewis Padgett.

Their initial collaborative method had Kuttner writing first drafts and Moore doing final copy, smoothing out the rough places and adding touches of emotion, color and imagination. However, as they grew more adept at working together, their talents blended, even on stories that were published under the individual byline of one or the other. As Moore says, "We collaborated on almost everything we wrote, but in varying degrees."

George O. Smith would be a weekend house guest while the couple was at work on a story that is generally credited to Moore alone. He remembers one of them sitting with him for morning coffee while the typewriter rattled away upstairs, and then husband and wife swapping places. Smith says, "They worked at it in shifts, in relays, continuously, until about two o'clock that Saturday afternoon, when the one downstairs did not go upstairs when the one upstairs came down. This time the typing stopped." Story completed.

Moore's own view of their working habits was:

After we'd established through long discussion the basic ideas, the background and the characters, whichever of us felt like it sat down and started. When that one ran down, the other, being fresh to the story, could usually see what ought to come next, and took over. The action developed as we went along. We kept changing off like this until we finished. A story goes very fast that way.

Lewis Padgett would become the primary voice of their fiction in *Astounding*. From the spring of 1942 through the end of 1945, Moore would have a two-part serial and a novelet in the magazine, and Kuttner would contribute two short stories and two short-shorts. Three stories would be published under the name Lawrence O'Donnell. But no less than twenty stories would be presented as the work of Lewis Padgett.

Who was this new writer?

Well, to every appearance, he was a man of education, refinement and wit. His stories were full of allusions to Lewis Carroll, James Branch Cabell, Rudyard Kipling, Thomas Wolfe, Gilbert and Sullivan, the Venerable Bede, Omar Khayyam, Longfellow, Shakespeare and Shelley. It seemed that he might be a college professor, or perhaps a *New Yorker* writer on a holiday.

It was clear that this urbane fellow had studied van Vogt's audacious intrusions of strangeness into the familiar world, Heinlein's future societies, and Asimov's robots. But the stories he wrote weren't exactly like theirs, or any other pulp SF. His storytelling seemed more akin to that of John Collier, Dashiell Hammett and Thorne Smith.

Some of Padgett's early tales were ironies or horror stories, while others were whacky little comedies, exercises in alternative logic. His settings were the Village—America in the near future, or the present day. His favorite subjects were uncooperative robots, corrupt business practices, crooked lawyers, intuitive inventors, bright young couples, intolerably gifted children, time travel, drinking, and glitches in reality.

The initial stories by Kuttner and Moore written in the guise of Lewis Padgett were published during the last half of 1942 and 1943. They can be seen as an attempt to achieve the effects of A. Merritt and H.P. Lovecraft—the sense of imminent incomprehensible strangeness trying to break through into conventional reality—within the new terms of modern science fiction.

Clearly, these stories had many derivative aspects. They were also marked by great fear and reservation. Nonetheless, they had two areas of fresh insight.

More than any previous SF, the stories of Lewis Padgett brought the World Beyond the Hill into the heart of the Village and then denied that there was any essential difference between these two places. Transcendent mystery was capable of appearing anywhere at all, and it might involve the most ordinary of contemporary people.

Padgett's second great insight was into the nature of transcendence and how human beings might most effectively relate to it. If the World Beyond the Hill was the Village, and the Village was also the World Beyond the Hill, how then was transcendence to be recognized? Padgett's answer was that anything transcendent to us, wherever it is encountered, must have an appearance of bizarre strangeness, of irrationality, and that the way for humanity to bring itself into alignment with this higher aspect of existence must lie in the cultivation of non-rational thought processes.

The first Lewis Padgett story—which sported an allusion to Oscar Wilde's "The Ballad of Reading Gaol" in the third paragraph—was "Deadlock," published directly after Heinlein/MacDonald's "Waldo" in the August 1942 issue of *Astounding*.

In a near future dominated by ruthless corporate struggle, the supposedly "'indestructible'" robots that are the monopoly of one such company are going crazy. At last, one robot, Thor, cobbles together a strange new machine which looks like "the sort of toy an erratic child might construct with a mechano set." This is a two-foot-long cylinder, with a lens for an eye, which buzzes and floats unsupported in mid-air.

The first thing the machine does is to blast its maker to pieces. It then goes zipping around the factory grounds performing a variety of weird stunts. It eats its way through steel doors, stops watches, gives heart twinges to company owners, turns people invisible, and nullifies the force of gravity.

The most amusing and imaginative passage in the story is the description of the machine's pranks during one fifteen-minute period:

> The gadget, as though demoniacally inspired, tried to visit each separate branch of the gigantic plant. It changed a valuable shipment of gold ingots into dull, comparatively worthless lead. It neatly stripped the clothes from an important customer in the upper tower. It caused all the clocks to begin working again—backward. It revisited the wretched Twill, giving him another heart attack, and causing him to shine with a vague, purplish glow which did not wear off for more than a month thereafter.

For what purpose was the machine constructed? A second Thor robot thinks he knows, and proposes to test his solution. He steps in front of the machine—and it blasts him to pieces, too.

The human understanding of this situation is that it is all a consequence of inquisitive robots at the mercy of an irresistible impulse
to discover whether they are actually indestructible or not. Either
the problem drives them crazy, or they resort to this odd transcendent solution.

However, there is an underlying half-implication in the story
structure that this whole queer episode may actually be the result
of these robots being ordered to perform tasks by their human
makers that the robots find morally repugnant. Since they are
incapable of saying no directly to their masters, this is their way
out of an intolerable situation. The strange machine that Thor has
made says their no for them.

The second Lewis Padgett story, "The Twonky" (*Astounding*,
Sept 1942), would begin comically enough with another instance
of radical strangeness intruding into the familiar world. As it
progressed, however, it would alter into a tale of horror.

The story opens with a bewildered little man with a big head
wandering vaguely out onto the floor of a contemporary radio
factory, fingering a bump on his forehead. The plant foreman calls
him "Joe," in the same spirit that he might call anyone "Joe," and
shoos him back to work.

The only thing Joe can remember is that "his job was to make
Twonkies." And so he proceeds to construct a Twonky that to
outward appearance looks just like one of Mideastern Radio's latest
radio-phonograph consoles. Only after he is done and has taken a
nap under a workbench do the mists begin to clear from his mind:

> "Great Snell!" he gasped. "So that was it! I ran into a temporal snag."
> With a startled glance around, he fled to the storeroom from which he
> had first emerged. The overalls he took off and returned to their hook.
> After that, Joe went over to a corner, felt around in the air, nodded with
> satisfaction and seated himself on nothing, three feet above the floor.
> Then he vanished.

So far, so funny. And the story continues to be amusing as we
observe young professor Kerry Westerfield watching his wife Martha
pack for a trip, and contemplating his brand-new radio-phonograph—
and then being shocked when it uses a tendril to light his cigarette
for him. Soon after that, it is out in the kitchen washing dishes.
All without needing to be plugged in.

But then the story begins turning nasty. First the Twonky starts
deciding what music it will or won't play. When Kerry comes home
after having downed fourteen brandies, it won't allow him to be
drunk, but counteracts the effects of alcohol with a beam of yellow

light. There are certain books it won't permit him to read, including a detective novel, *Alice in Wonderland*, and a book on literary history that he needs to consult in order to teach a class. And when he persists in trying to read the forbidden, it uses another ray on him which leaves him unable to read and comprehend certain ideas.

Martha Westerfield returns home from her trip to find her husband blank-faced and dazed. When she understands what has been happening and attempts to attack the radio-phonograph with a hatchet, it makes note of her hostile intent and zaps her with a beam of light, and she vanishes. Kerry rouses himself sufficiently to pick up the hatchet, and it zaps him, too.

The Twonky says: "'Subject basically unsuitable. ... Elimination has been necessary.' *Click!* 'Preparation for next subject completed.'"

As the story concludes, a young couple is being shown through the Westerfields' empty house by a rental agent. And, in the living room, the Twonky is switching itself on, *click*, ready to do its job once more. We are left anticipating that this new couple will be treated just as roughly and unforgivingly as Kerry and Martha Westerfield have been.

Padgett was effective in presenting mysterious intrusions into ordinary reality in "Deadlock" and "The Twonky," but as yet his characters didn't have a clue how to cope with this wildness. In the next Lewis Padgett story to deal with a glitch in reality, however, this would begin to change.

"Time Locker" (*Astounding*, Jan 1943) would resemble "The Twonky" in beginning with humor and ending with horror. It would also be a morality play like "Deadlock," but a far more explicit one. However, its most innovative aspect would be its presentation of a character whose response to irrational transcendence was to be irrational, too.

The comic opening of "Time Locker" is a description of this man, a drunken near-future inventor named Galloway, and his bizarre laboratory:

> There was a little of everything in the lab, much of it incongruous. Rheostats had little skirts on them, like ballet dancers, and vacuously grinning faces of clay. A generator was conspicuously labeled, "Monstro," and a much smaller one rejoiced in the name of "Bubbles." Inside a glass retort was a china rabbit, and Galloway alone knew how it had got there. Just inside the door was a hideous iron dog, originally intended for Victorian lawns or perhaps for Hell, and its hollowed ears served as sockets for test tubes.

The crowning feature of Galloway's laboratory is his liquor organ:

He could recline on a comfortably padded couch and, by manipulating buttons, siphon drinks of marvelous quantity, quality, and variety down his scarified throat. Since he had made the liquor organ during a protracted period of drunkenness, he never remembered the basic principles of its construction.

This is standard operating procedure for Galloway. He'll get drunk and then invent some marvelous gadget, but when he is sober again he can't necessarily remember how he did the trick or even what the gadget is for. As he says, "'I think my subconscious mind must have a high I.Q.'"

Galloway's most recent invention is a standing metal locker that has been treated in such a fashion that the objects placed inside it shrink and change in appearance. A smock placed within turns into a tiny, pale-green spherical blob. A bench larger than the locker, fed into it a little at a time, becomes a four-inch-long "spiky sort of scalene pyramid, deep purple in hue."

The best explanation that Galloway can come up with to account for this phenomenon is, "'I suppose the inside of the locker isn't in this space-time continuum at all.'"

The locker is purchased from the inventor by an unscrupulous lawyer, Horace Vanning, who makes his living by advising and aiding criminals. Then, when a suitcase of stolen bonds is brought to Vanning, he places the valise inside the other-dimensional locker, where it takes on "the shape of an elongated egg, the color of a copper cent piece."

But even as Vanning watches, he sees that something is moving within the locker: "A grotesque little creature less than four inches tall was visible. It was a shocking object, all cubes and angles, a bright-green in tint, and it was obviously alive."

The creature is attempting to pick up the copper-colored egg and carry it away. So Vanning reaches into the locker and crushes it with his hand. Later, however, when Vanning looks into the locker once more, both the creature and the suitcase containing the bonds are gone.

Vanning is suspected by the police of complicity in the theft of the bonds. And the man who stole them is anxious and doubtful. He wants Vanning to hand the suitcase back, and is ready to hurt him if he doesn't.

Attempting to avoid these people one week after the disappearance of the bonds, Vanning ducks inside his office—and there is the missing valise. With policemen treading close on his heels, Vanning has to get the stolen bonds out of sight as quickly as he possibly can. But when he picks up the suitcase, a gigantic hand reaches out of mid-air and squashes him to death.

The one person who has any idea at all of what has actually happened is Galloway the inventor. He now knows why it was that a bench briefly materialized in his laboratory. The strange locker doesn't give access to some other dimension of being after all. Rather, it opens into our own time and space one week hence.

Talking to his dynamo, Monstro, Galloway says, "'I guess Vanning must have been the only guy who ever reached into the middle of next week and—killed himself! I think I'll get tight.'"

In all of these early Lewis Padgett stories—"Deadlock," "The Twonky" and "Time Locker"—the weirdness that breaks loose in the Village, the intrusions from elsewhere that coerce and manipulate us, and the holes that we manage to pry open in the fabric of reality are all seen as dangerous, incomprehensible and other. They threaten not only greedy and dishonest people like Vanning, but also normal, ordinary, contemporary folk like Kerry and Martha Westerfield. The one exception to this is the drunken inventor Galloway, who seems to have made his peace with strangeness.

There would be gestures in the direction of this same kind of fear and horror in the next Lewis Padgett story, "Mimsy Were the Borogoves," published in the same February 1943 issue of *Astounding* as the first installment of A. E. van Vogt's *The Weapon Makers*. Starting with the title taken from Lewis Carroll's "Jabberwocky," with its intimations of lurking jaws that bite and claws that catch, "Mimsy Were the Borogoves" would be full of hints and forebodings which indicated that at least one of its authors intended it to be read as another horror story like "The Twonky."

But that isn't the way the story would be taken by the readers of *Astounding*. They would pick up on counterhints—possibly the work of the other author—and instead of being horrified by the outcome of "Mimsy Were the Borogoves," they would be enthralled. Even divided against itself, this would be one of the most popular stories ever to be published in the magazine.

To see exactly what happened, let's look first at the aspect of the story which was expected to strike the reader as horrifying:

In "Mimsy Were the Borogoves," a contemporary little boy, Scott Paradine, is playing hooky from grammar school one day when a box full of marvelous toys and gadgets pops out of nothingness nearby. Scott takes the toys home and shares them with his baby sister Emma, who proves to understand them better than he does.

One of the marvels from the box is a crystal cube. When Scott peers into it, he sees tiny mechanical people building a house. He wishes there could be a fire so that he could see it put out. And that is exactly what happens:

"Flames licked up from the half-completed structure. The automatons, with a great deal of odd apparatus, extinguished the blaze."

Yet when Scott's philosophy professor father looks into the cube, he can see nothing coherent there, only "a maze of meaningless colored designs."

Another gadget, a tangle of wires and beads, is said to resemble "a tesseract," or four-dimensional supercube, when it is unfolded. To Scott's father, this device simply looks *wrong*. The angles at which the wires join appear shocking and illogical to him. And the beads, which slide along the wires, have a disconcerting ability to pass right through the points of juncture.

The gadget exasperates grown-ups, but the children persist in playing with it, even though the beads sting their fingers when they choose the wrong one or slide one in the wrong direction. And very shortly, Scott is crowing in triumph: "'I did it, Dad! ... I made it disappear. ... That blue bead. It's gone now.'"

The disquiet the Paradine parents feel intensifies when they discover that Scott has lied in telling them that the toys were given to him by a family friend, and even more when they find that toys such as these are not available in any store. They consult a child psychologist who feeds their fears by talking in terms of madness and of conditioning to a fundamentally other mode of thought. The psychologist says:

> "Let's suppose there are two kinds of geometry; we'll limit it, for the sake of the example. Our kind, Euclidean, and another, we'll call it x. X hasn't much relationship to Euclid. It's based on different theorems. Two and two needn't equal four in it; they could equal y^2, or they might not even *equal*. A baby's mind is not yet conditioned, except by certain questionable factors of heredity and environment."

The psychologist suggests that the toys may be training the children's minds to think in terms of x logic. So the toys are taken away from the children, and all seems well again, except that baby Emma makes earnest scrawls on paper which Scott is apparently able to interpret, but which no one else can make anything of. And Scott has moments when he may say disconcerting things like, "'This is only—part of the big place. It's like the river where the salmon go. Why don't people go on down to the ocean when they grow up?'"

As the end of the story approaches, Emma has made annotations all over the first verse of the poem "Jabberwocky," and Scott, in response, has built an apparatus of some kind out of vaseline-covered

pebbles, candle ends and other junk. Their father, standing outside
the door to Scott's room, witnesses their transference to elsewhere:

> The children were vanishing.
> They went in fragments, like thick smoke in a wind, or like movement
> in a distorting mirror. Hand in hand they went, in a direction Paradine
> could not understand, and as he blinked there on the threshold, they
> were gone.

From the point of view of a parent left behind, this could certainly
be horrifying. And Padgett plays it that way in the concluding
paragraphs of his story, using words like "ghastly," "crazy," "sense-
less," "defeated," "insane," "lunacy," "crumpled," "horror," and
"dead."

And yet, despite these strong intimations of a negative outcome,
the readers of *Astounding* would simply refuse to be frightened.
Instead of taking "Mimsy Were the Borogoves" as a mere horror
story, they elected to read it as a vision of glorious science fictional
possibility. And there would be material within the story that would
provide a basis for this alternate positive reading.

To begin with, the readers found those marvelous toys and gadgets
just too delightful and too intriguing to be fearsome. Rather than
interpreting what was happening to the children as negative psychological conditioning, they chose to take it as education of a special
and wonderful sort. And when Scott and Emma moved off hand
in hand into a new dimension of being beyond the ken of their
parents, with no fear at all of what they might find, the imagination
of the audience was ready to travel with them, rather than remaining
behind with the limited perceptions and apprehensions of Mr. and
Mrs. Paradine.

By way of contrast, if "The Twonky" was an effective horror
story, it was because we are given no clear idea of what kind of
world it is that Joe comes from. We don't know the true purposes
of the Twonky he builds. And we don't know what ultimately
happens to Martha and Kerry Westerfield when the Twonky turns
its beam of light on them and they disappear.

It is our strong suspicion, however, that Joe comes from a narrow
and rigid society, that the Twonky is some kind of mind control
device, and that the Westerfields are dead as dead can be. We fear
what we don't know, and we imagine the worst.

But in "Mimsy Were the Borogoves," we have too much positive
information available to us to be frightened. In the same way that
we were allowed to know more about the planet Lagash than the
natives do as we were reading Asimov's "Nightfall," and therefore

felt no temptation to join them in hysteria and freakout, so here
do we know a number of vital things that Mr. and Mrs. Paradine
do not.

We know, for instance, where the wonderful toys came from.
"Mimsy Were the Borogoves" does not begin when the box of toys
plops down on the muddy creek bank near Scott Paradine, but
rather with an account of where the box and the toys originated
and what their purposes are.

The story starts:

> There's no use trying to describe either Unthahorsten or his surroundings,
> because, for one thing, a good many million years had passed and, for
> another, Unthahorsten wasn't on Earth, technically speaking. He was
> doing the equivalent of standing in the equivalent of a laboratory. He
> was preparing to test his time machine.

For all of our inability to grasp the complete actuality of Unthahorsten, we are allowed to know that he is enthusiastic, impulsive,
and more than a bit of a kid at heart. As objects to send back to the
past in his time machine, he uses "some of the discarded toys of his
son Snowen, which the boy had brought with him after he had
passed over from Earth, after mastering the necessary technique."
Unthahorsten sends two batches of toys to the past, but neither
comes back, and so he drops the project.

Not a lot to be frightened of there—in inventors, children, toys,
and another dimension of human existence.

It is also revealed to the reader that the second set of toys fell
into the hands of a Nineteenth Century English girl named Alice.
From them, she learned a queer little verse which she sang for her
courtesy uncle Charles—whom we may take to be Charles Dodgson,
the man behind the pseudonym Lewis Carroll.

We are told:

"The song meant a great deal. It was the way. Presently she would
do what it said, and then...

"But she was already too old. She never found the way."

As presented, this would seem to be more of an occasion for
sadness than for relief at the narrow escape she has had.

With these two scenes, which the Paradine parents aren't privy to,
the reader is given a basis for an alternative, non-horrific interpretation
of "Mimsy Were the Borogoves." With our knowledge of Unthahorsten's son Snowen and poor English Alice, we can't help but have
confidence in Scott Paradine, with his certainty that the true path
of human maturation lies in travel to a greater realm of being which
is imperceptible to ordinary contemporary adults, and in his little

sister Emma, with her recognition that the first verse of "Jabber-wocky" is the map they need in order to go there.

It was only natural for the readers of *Astounding* to take the story this way. They were predisposed to do so.

Ever since "Who Goes There?", the modern science fiction to which they were committed had declared over and over again that the unknown, however horrifying it might appear, could be dealt with by human beings if only they kept their heads and put them-selves in tune with the way the universe really works. And these SF readers had all encountered "Jabberwocky" as children and shared the tantalizing feeling that somehow it made sense of a sort they could almost but not quite grasp.

Most of all, however, if they were prepared to identify with Scott and Emma Paradine, it was because they perceived themselves as trapped in a mid-Twentieth Century that was brutal, limited and unworthy when compared to the visions of wider and higher human possibility that they were finding in science fiction. Many would have liked nothing better than to chuck World War II America and travel with the children to "the big place," wherever and whatever that might prove to be.

"Mimsy Were the Borogoves" would seem to mark some sort of transition in the perception of transcendent non-rational conscious-ness. As recently as the summer of 1942, in stories like van Vogt's "Secret Unattainable" and Heinlein's "Waldo," the new transcendence had been seen as something that contemporary humans were not yet ready for, or as something to be constrained and circumscribed as completely as possible with bonds of rationality. Non-rational transcendence was dangerous and unpredictable. As Padgett had it, it might play pranks on you, stripping you of your pants or clutching your heartstrings and causing you to glow purple, like the robot-constructed machine in "Deadlock." Or it could zap you into nothingness, like the false radio-phonograph in "The Twonky."

Now, however, in early 1943, this was starting to change. To Padgett and van Vogt, it had begun to seem that the new irrational transcendence—even though it might appear strange and mysterious— did not necessarily have to be feared, evaded and struggled against.

Human beings might get along a lot better with the new transcend-ence if they would only learn non-logical modes of mentation more in tune with the actual nature of reality. Padgett's drunken inventor, Galloway, in "Time Locker," does very well with weirdness by being whacky himself. The Paradine children in "Mimsy Were the Borogoves" seem able to rise to a higher state of humanness through their special training in x thinking. And, with all his education in intuitive thought, the No-man, Edward Gonish, in van Vogt's

The Weapon Makers, has apparently learned how to take bizarre occurrences and random happenings and perceive them as aspects of meaningful higher patterns.

The one science-fictional character who would most effectively exemplify this revised attitude toward the irrational would be Padgett's inventor, Galloway. Renamed Gallegher, and given ample room to be himself, he would be featured in three novelets published in *Astounding* during 1943—"The World Is Mine" in June, "The Proud Robot" in October, and "Gallegher Plus" in November.

Galloway had only been a comic sideshow in "Time Locker," which was basically a horror story. But Gallegher would be the focal character in the three later novelets of 1943, all of which were out-and-out comedies.

Gallegher isn't exactly a super-scientist in the old-fashioned Techno Age sense. He is no discoverer of new laws of science. He is more of a transcendent tinkerer, a casual genius who plays at science by ear and produces wonders through new arrangements of known things: "Sometimes he'd start with a twist of wire, a few batteries, and a button hook, and before he finished, he might contrive a new type of refrigeration unit."

All of Gallegher's marvels of invention are achieved through the processes of his subconscious mind: "It did the most extraordinary things. It worked on inflexible principles of logic, but that logic was completely alien to Gallegher's conscious mind. The results, though, were often surprisingly good, and always surprising."

On the level of conscious understanding, it would seem that Gallegher has had only a limited education. He may toss off literary and philosophical references, but he seems to have no formal grasp of science. At one point, for instance, a robot of his own invention—who is sometimes known as Joe and sometimes as Narcissus—says to him:

"A positron is—"

"Don't tell me," Gallegher pleaded. "I'll only have semantic difficulties. I know what a positron is, all right, only I don't identify it with that name. All I know is the intensional meaning. Which can't be expressed in words, anyhow."

"The extensional meaning can, though," Narcissus pointed out.

"Not with me. As Humpty Dumpty said, the question is, which is to be master. And with me it's the word. The damn things scare me. I simply don't *get* their extensional meanings."

"That's silly," said the robot. "Positron has a perfectly clear denotation."

"To you. All it means to me is a gang of little boys with fishtails and green whiskers. That's why I never can figure out what my subconscious has been up to."

In the terms of a later era, it would appear that Gallegher is weak in the logical, rational faculties associated with the left hemisphere of the brain, and is much stronger in the non-verbal, non-linear processes attributed to the right hemisphere. We might view him as an artist whose materials are the objects and interactions usually assumed to be the exclusive property of rational scientific study.

Gallegher's standard method of procedure is to give control over to his right brain by disrupting the 1-2-3-4 thinking of the left brain with copious amounts of alcohol. The trouble is that come the following morning, his conscious self isn't likely to have much memory, knowledge or understanding of what his subconscious self has been doing.

In fact, the pattern in all three comic novelets is that Gallegher has taken on some problem while in a state of drunkenness and solved it before the story begins. The conscious, rational Gallegher is then challenged to remember just what that problem was and to recognize the solution in whatever bit of unlikeliness the other Gallegher has most recently constructed.

Two things are particularly worth noting about Gallegher and his operations. One is his lack of fear of the unknown. And the other is the multifaceted nature of the things he invents.

Gallegher isn't afraid of his subconscious—though he does find it a bit awesome. Basically, he looks on it as his stronger, more knowledgeable, more able side. When the crunch is on, it is his subconscious that Gallegher relies upon to bring him through.

This is made clear in "The Proud Robot." In this story, Gallegher is caught in the middle of an entertainment industry struggle. A beautiful blonde television star, also in the middle, asks Gallegher's advice. If she knows what is good for her, which side of the fence should she contrive to land on? Should she stick with Brock, her employer, or should she go along with the apparent power of his thuggish competitors, who are stealing Brock's pay TV programs and running them in illegal theaters?

> "Truth will triumph," Gallegher said piously. "It always does. However, I figure truth is a variable, so we're right back where we started. All right, sweetheart. I'll answer your question. Stay on my side if you want to be safe."
>
> "Which side are you on?"
>
> "God knows," Gallegher said. "Consciously, I'm on Brock's side. But my subconscious may have different ideas. We'll see."

It would appear that Gallegher has made a leap of faith. His

conscious mind may not always recognize truth, but he believes that
his subconscious will. He trusts it more.

Which side is Gallegher on? He's on the side of his subconscious.
In a world of variable truth, his subconscious will know the right
thing to do and bring him through safely.

The result of this trust of the unknown is that the universe is
transformed. Through the offices of his subconscious, Gallegher
is faced with what during the Techno Age would have been fearsome
monsters. But in the altered atmosphere of his state of calm acceptance of whatever strangeness he encounters, these one-time bogies
reveal themselves as comically humanlike in their foibles and limitations.

In "The World Is Mine," the threat which is no longer a threat is
invaders from outer space. Three of them arrive through a Gallegher-
made time machine from Mars five hundred years in the future,
asserting their intention to take over the world.

Except that these Lybllas, as they call themselves, look rather like
white bunny rabbits with round ears and golden eyes and are about
as dangerous. It turns out that they have been reading Techno Age
scientifiction and taking it to heart. They want to destroy cities and
hold pretty girls to ransom, and all the other fun stuff invading aliens
get to do.

Gallegher deals with them by clumsily faking a news broadcast in
in which it is declared that a bloodless revolution has taken place
all around the world:

> "The Lybllas are unanimously acclaimed as our sole rulers—"
>
> "*Whee!*" cried a small voice.
>
> "—and the new form of government is already being set up. There will
> be a different fiscal system, and coins bearing the heads of the Lybllas are
> being minted. It is expected that the three rulers will shortly return to
> Mars to explain the situation to their friends there."

Gallegher then shakes their paws, gives them one more cookie
apiece, and sends them back to future Mars to tell everyone about
their adventures.

In "The Proud Robot"—the best-remembered of the Gallegher
stories—the threat that isn't a threat is the robot Joe. He is another
of those robots in the same family as Jack Williamson's Malgarth
and Isaac Asimov's QT-1 who have an exalted opinion of themselves,
but think far less well of mere human beings.

Joe won't do anything that he is told to do. He insults every
person who crosses his path. Like the Glass Cat in L. Frank Baum's
Oz books, he admires his own inner workings and invites everybody

else to as well. He wants nothing more than to spend long hours before the mirror watching the wheels within his transparent hull go around and around.

There can be no doubt that this robot does have highly unusual powers and abilities. Joe can watch Gallegher throwing an apple core on the floor and snicker to himself for ten minutes over the probability that Gallegher will slip on it when he goes for the mail—which indeed he does. Joe has X-ray vision. He can hypnotize people. And, at one point, when he wants to locate Gallegher, he does so by "vastening" him:

> "What's vastened?" Gallegher wanted to know.
> "It's a sense I've got. You've nothing remotely like it, so I can't describe it to you. It's rather like a combination of sagrazi and prescience."
> "Sagrazi?"
> "Oh, you don't have sagrazi, either, do you. Well, don't waste my time. I want to go back to the mirror."

Superior being though Joe may be in certain respects, however, he is never treated for a single moment as a danger to humanity. In large part, this is because Joe has no active purposes of his own beyond self-admiration. He's just too comically vain to be a threat to anyone.

The worst that Joe does is to hypnotize some visitors he finds particularly irritating and wants to get rid of. He makes them think that it is Gallegher they are dealing with and forges Gallegher's signature to a long-term contract at pitiful wages.

This is certainly trying from Gallegher's point of view. All the more so since this is the act that places him in the middle of that ugly entertainment industry struggle. Even so, however, Gallegher doesn't get more than exasperated with the robot, in much the same way that a parent might be put out with a child who has been acting irresponsibly.

Gallegher's solution to the Joe problem is to get drunk—but not too drunk—and then talk Joe into hypnotizing himself, the better to appreciate his beauty from a new perspective. Then, when Joe is in the grip of his subconscious, Gallegher asks the robot why he created him, and the robot is forced to answer:

"'You were drinking beer,' Joe said faintly. 'You had trouble with the can opener. You said you were going to build a bigger and better can opener. That's me.'"

Now that Gallagher knows what Joe is good for, he orders the robot to open a can of beer for him, and Joe does it deftly. My what a good can opener he is! And with his basic function established, it seems that henceforth the robot will be compelled to obey all of his maker's commands.

But that isn't all that Joe does. He also emits a subsonic noise which Brock is to broadcast underneath all his pay TV programs. When amplified within one of his competitor's illegal theaters, this noise will be sufficient to put the audience into a panic and send it rushing out the door.

And yet, even this isn't all that Joe is good for. It seems that the subconscious Gallegher has a yen for a singing partner. And the story ends with a drunken Gallegher singing "Frankie and Johnnie" in a duet with his can opener.

This isn't untypical of Gallegher's solutions. In "Gallegher Plus" (the plus is his subconscious), he is being assailed by three different people who have hired him to solve their problems while he was drunk past the point of remembering. And the answer to all three of the problems turns out to be one machine. It is a dirt excavator, a hole maker. And the dirt that it eats, it converts into super-strong, super-fine wire which can be used variously as a manual spaceship control or as the basis for a three-dimensional TV screen.

It sings, too. The story ends with Gallegher—drunk, of course— harmonizing with this new machine on "St. James Infirmary."

This year—1943—in which Kuttner and Moore were for a brief period the leading writers in *Astounding*, was the trippiest and most uncertain of the war. It might be compared to that deep dark moment in the midst of World War I when writers began to cut loose from old notions of a fixed reality and set forth to explore other realms of being.

By the middle of 1943, the initial thrusts of the Axis powers into Russia, North Africa and the Western Pacific had all become stalled, but the Allies had yet to take the offensive in the war and begin to force Germany, Italy and Japan out of the territories they had seized. During this temporary moment of stasis, with the imme- diate pressure to survive relieved but no end to the war yet in sight, there was space to catch a breath, but also an opportunity for strange thoughts to enter the mind.

The old familiar living patterns of the Western countries had been thoroughly disrupted by the demands of the war, and "normality"— whatever that might be—seemed a distant dream. It was at this hour that art forms of all kinds started to perceive the mind as a new unknown and began to probe its uncertainties.

People were ready to reach out and try new and weird states of mind. And non-rational states of mind were also ready to force themselves upon people's attention.

As an example of this latter, we might consider the discovery in

April 1943 of the mind-altering properties of LSD, the first man-made hallucinogenic drug.

In the years before the war, a young Swiss biochemist named Albert Hofmann had been doing research in the alkaloids of the poisonous fungus ergot. It was his hope to find a circulatory and respiratory stimulant which could be marketed by his employers, the pharmaceutical firm Sandoz, Ltd.—and, indeed, he would eventually prove successful in this.

In 1938, Hofmann had synthesized d-lysergic acid diethylamide tartrate, the twenty-fifth in a series of lysergic acid derivatives. But when animal experiments indicated that this wasn't the drug he was seeking, he had set it aside.

Now, however, in the spring of 1943, he decided to prepare another batch of LSD-25. There was no pressing reason for him to do so. In fact, reflecting on the subject at a later time, Hofmann would say, "This was quite unusual; experimental substances, as a rule, were definitely stricken from the research program if once found to be lacking in pharmacological interest."

What is more, in handling the substance, Hofmann suffered an uncharacteristic laboratory accident. While crystallizing LSD-25, he apparently got a trace of the substance on his fingers and it was absorbed through a cut in the skin. Very shortly, the chemist had to leave work and go home to cope with the effects of the world's first acid trip.

To Hofmann, perhaps the most marvelous part of the whole affair was the minuteness of the dose that he took compared with the power this new drug had to affect his mind.

It would almost seem that LSD had nagged, schemed, shouted and pushed to force an awareness of its effects upon a heedless human intermediary—and that 1943 was somehow the appropriate moment for such a thing to happen.

Another example of a light suddenly dawning during 1943 where the powers of the non-rational mind are concerned may be drawn from the experience of A. E. van Vogt. Here was a writer who was strongly oriented toward the holistic function of the right brain—but who worked with excruciating slowness and who felt himself to be out of touch with his powers of intuition. Van Vogt wanted nothing more than to discover a system that would allow him regular contact with what he (like Padgett) thought of as the subconscious mind.

From the very beginning of his writing career, van Vogt had had repeated anxious moments when he would wake during the night not knowing where his current story was going next. He would lie awake and mull over the problems of the story until he fell back to sleep. But then, in the morning, a solution to the problem he had been so anxious about would suddenly come to him. He says, "All my best plot twists came in this way."

However, it was only in July 1943, a dozen years after he first began writing stories, that the penny finally dropped and van Vogt at last became consciously aware that this same sequence of events had happened to him again and again. He immediately determined to induce it deliberately rather than accidentally, to force himself to lie awake thinking about his latest story and see whether an appropriate creative flash came to him the next day:

> That night I got out our alarm clock, and moved into the spare bedroom. I set the alarm to ring in one and one-half hours. When it awakened me, I reset the alarm for another one and one-half hours, thought about the problems in the story I was working on—and fell asleep. I did that altogether four times during the night. And in the morning, there was the unusual solution, the strange plot twist. Exactly as when I had awakened from anxiety. So I had my system for getting to my subconscious mind. During the next seven years I awakened myself about three hundred nights a year four times a night.

Just as with Albert Hofmann and LSD, the basis for this breakthrough in consciousness had been there for years and years, right under van Vogt's nose, before he finally took notice of it. But it was in 1943, that strange, unsettled time of mind, that the eyes of both men finally became opened to what they hadn't been able to see before.

Astounding would go through a series of physical changes during this same volatile year. The stimulus for its radical reconstruction would be government-imposed restrictions in the amount of paper available to magazine publishers.

In the year before the United States entered the war, there had been a great over-expansion in the number of science fiction magazines being published, followed by a severe die-back that left about a dozen titles at the end of 1941. Now, however, with the imposition of paper rationing, there would be a further die-off of SF pulp magazines. Only half-a-dozen titles would still survive by 1944, and to maximize sales, all would be quarterlies.

All of them, that is, but *Astounding*. It was a very different strategy that John Campbell would elect to follow.

The first decision that he made, in May 1943, was to change *Astounding* and *Unknown Worlds* from bedsheet size to pulp size—a slightly compressed pulp size, 7 by 9½ inches, with too much type jammed onto each page, so that the magazine had an overcrowded look. Six issues of *Astounding* and three issues of *Unknown Worlds* would be published in this format.

Then, after the October 1943 issue of *Unknown Worlds*, the editor would make the decision to kill off his magazine of modern fantasy. It would be one of the SF magazines that was unable to survive the wartime paper crunch.

At the same time—after the October 1943 issue of *Astounding*—Campbell would change the dimensions of his science fiction magazine again, to so-called digest size, that is, the size of *Reader's Digest*, 5½ by 8 inches. The result would be one dark, squat, ugly little magazine.

But it would still be a monthly. By appropriating the former paper budget of *Unknown* and by making this second reduction in the dimensions of *Astounding*, Campbell was able to hold his magazine to a monthly schedule at a time when other SF magazine publishers were deciding to keep more than one title alive but to publish each of these less frequently than before. What is more, because of its new smaller size, it was now *Astounding* which got placed at the front of the magazine rack, and the pulp magazines which were stuck away behind.

At last, Campbell's magazine was effectively set apart from all the others!

In this new smaller size, the editor was even able to add an expanded science article section that was printed on paper of Sunday supplement quality, paper that would reproduce photographs. This increased concern for the presentation of actual leading-edge science may have been an attempt on Campbell's part to compensate for the smaller proportion of science-based stories now appearing in *Astounding*.

More and more, the leading edge stories in *Astounding* were based in transcendent consciousness rather than in transcendent science. A turning point may be seen in the October 1943 issue of *Astounding*, its last as a pulp-sized magazine. In this issue, whether by chance or by design, every one of the stories would be consciousness-based.

In the digest-sized *Astounding*, a number of writers would pick up themes that Lewis Padgett had presented in "Mimsy Were the Borogoves" and the Gallegher stories and enlarge upon them: the acceptance of the primacy of non-rational thought; toleration of aliens and robots and other creatures who would previously have been taken to be evolutionary competitors of mankind; and recognition of education in new forms of thought as the key to higher human development.

But Lewis Padgett would have no part to play in these explorations.

At about the same time that *Astounding* was switching over to digest size, Henry Kuttner was drafted into the Army, despite a heart murmur, and made into a medical corpsman.

This was the man, we will remember, whose most fundamental belief was that all authority is dangerous, and that, bend though he might, he must never give in to it. It would take the Army a little more than a year to come to the conclusion that Kuttner was someone with a total inability to accept military discipline, and to give him a medical discharge on psychoneurotic grounds.

In the meantime, Lewis Padgett would be silent as a writer, and when he was able to return to work for Campbell at the beginning of 1945, it was to find that others had pressed on beyond his limits in dealing with the new reality. Kuttner and Moore would write well for Campbell, but never again as innovatively as in 1942 and 1943.

As an example of just how queer and non-scientific SF could be in *Astounding* in the last years of the war, we might look at the short story printed immediately before Lewis Padgett's "The Proud Robot" in the October 1943 issue—Fredric Brown's "Paradox Lost."

Fredric Brown was born in Cincinnati on October 29, 1906. He was a student at two different colleges without being able to finish. He sold his first mystery story in 1936, but until he began publishing mystery novels after the war and was at last able to write full-time, he would earn his primary living as a proofreader for the *Milwaukee Journal* while turning out pulp magazine stories on the side.

Like Kuttner, Fredric Brown was another small, soft-spoken, hard-drinking man with a love for Lewis Carroll and doubts about the sufficiency of our ordinary notions of reality. Among his mystery novels would be one entitled *Night of the Jabberwock* (1950) that would lead off with the very same verse which figures so centrally in "Mimsy Were the Borogoves."

Brown found the plotting and writing of mystery stories extremely hard work, and turned to SF writing as a form of relief. He knew nothing and cared nothing about science. His SF stories would be primarily philosophical in nature, but with the philosophy made sweet and simple by means of cockeyed humor and a spare, highly readable pulp writing style.

His first SF story was "Not Yet the End" (*Captain Future*, Win 1941), but more than half of the stories that he published before the end of the war would appear in *Unknown* or *Astounding*. Altogether, about a quarter of his work, including five novels, would be science fiction.

In the introduction to his first collection of SF stories, Brown would say:

Science-fiction stories are the least painful of all stories for me to write, and when I have put THE END on the final page of one, I feel greater satisfaction than with any other kind of story. ... The important reason is that science-fiction, by giving greater scope to the imagination and by imposing fewer rules and limitations, comes closer than any other type of fiction to being honest writing.

Whatever rules and limitations science fiction did have would certainly be tested by "Paradox Lost," the second story by Brown to be published in *Astounding*. As its title would suggest, it was an exercise in playfulness, full of humor, puns, paradox and uncertainty.

In this story, a paleontology student named Shorty McCabe is seated in the back row of a logic class in 1943, wondering what he is doing there. He has more interest in watching the erratic flight of a blue bottle fly than in listening to the professor.

As he is watching, the fly passes through a hole in reality and disappears. McCabe puts his hand into this space. When he brings it back, he can still feel with the hand, but he can no longer see it.

After determining the size and shape of the hole with a series of tossed paper clips, McCabe decides to follow his hand into the other space. He stands up in the aisle and finds himself elsewhere.

It is dark here, but a sneeze reveals that someone else is present. For this person, it apparently isn't dark. Not only can he see McCabe, but he is also aware of what is going on back in the classroom—but in 1948. He is having a hoot listening to a professor tell a class that the dinosaurs died out because they got too large to keep themselves fed and starved to death. As far as the observer is concerned, that isn't at all the way it happened.

The speaker identifies himself as a crazy man locked in a padded cell in a local mental institution and McCabe as a normal person. He says, "'I'm an inventor, what they call a nut inventor. I think I invent time machines, for one thing. This is one of them.'"

He says that McCabe has stumbled into his time machine through a warp. He invites McCabe to reach out into the classroom where he was formerly sitting, and when McCabe does he feels something which jerks out of his grasp:

"'Yow!' said the voice beside him. 'That was funny!'"

And the voice explains that a knockout of a red-haired girl was sitting in the same seat that McCabe had occupied five years before, and that she had jumped and let out a yip when he pulled her hair. But it was okay because the professor looked like he had his eye out for her and was using this incident as an excuse to have her stay after class.

The voice then declares that he is bored and invites McCabe to go hunting:

"'We always hunt with slingshots. It's more sporting.'

"'Hunt what?'

"'Dinosaurs. They're the most fun.'"

And indeed, when they step out of the darkness, it is to find themselves in the bright sunshine of an archaic landscape. The voice turns out to be a man even smaller than Shorty. He is armed with a slingshot.

The "time machine" is nowhere to be seen, and Shorty asks where it is:

> "Huh? Oh, right here." The little man reached out a hand to his left and it disappeared up to the elbow.
>
> "Oh," said Shorty. "I wondered what it looked like."
>
> "Looked like?" said the little man. "How could it look like anything? I told you that there isn't any such thing as a time machine. There couldn't be; it would be a complete paradox. Time is a fixed dimension. And when I proved that to myself, that's what drove me crazy."

He has done better at inventing time machines as a crazy person, since he is no longer bound by the laws of logic. As far as he is concerned, he is at once in his padded cell and here in the Jurassic with a McCabe who has wandered into his conceptual time machine by accident.

Shorty asks:

> "Is this world we're sitting in, the Jurassic, part of your...uh...concept, or is it real? It looks real, and it looks authentic."
>
> "This is real, but it never really existed. That's obvious. If matter is a concept of mind, and the saurians hadn't any minds, then how could they have had a world to live in, except that we thought it up for them afterward?"

Feeling in a giddy mood after hearing this assertion, McCabe suggests that if it is sporting to hunt dinosaurs with slingshots, why not use flyswatters? The little man lights up at this, and for a moment—until Shorty insists he is only kidding—he is even ready to consider the possibility that McCabe might be eligible to be another non-logical person.

In a little while, a dinosaur comes along. It proves to be a lizardlike creature a foot and a half high. The little man plinks it between the eyes with a stone from his slingshot and it falls dead.

As a student of paleontology, McCabe recognizes the creature:

"'A struthiomimus!' he said. 'Golly. But what if a big one comes along? A brontosaurus, say, or a tyrannosaurus rex?'

"'They're all gone. We killed them off. There's only the little ones left, but it's better than hunting rabbits, isn't it?'"

The two then return in the invisible time machine to 1948, where that professor is still carrying on with his lame ideas about what happened to the dinosaurs. McCabe asks the little man how the big dinosaurs *were* disposed of, and gets the answer that it took bigger slingshots. Shorty then receives a push that leaves him sprawling in the aisle back in his philosophy class in 1943.

Where has he been? It takes him a day to convince himself that this was just a particularly vivid dream. And five years later, he has completely forgotten that he ever had such a dream. McCabe is now an associate professor of paleontology lecturing to a class on the extinction of the dinosaurs—it seems they starved to death— and wondering how to approach the pretty red-haired graduate student in the last row for a date.

Just then a blue bottle fly starts droning around the room. And the girl in the last row lets out a sudden yip.

"He looked at her—severely, because the eyes of the class were upon him. But this was just the chance he'd been waiting and hoping for. He said, 'Miss Willis, will you please remain after class?'"

And so the pattern completes itself. This story is typical of Fredric Brown—light and breezy and harmless on the surface, but, if thought about seriously, utterly subversive of our conventional notions of reality, logic and sanity.

About all we can say for certain in regard to "Paradox Lost," this story in which we may be adrift in the hopeful dreams of a student having a snooze in philosophy class, or be off on a trip to the Jurassic in an invisible time machine to hunt dinosaurs with a slingshot, or be sharing the delusions of a mad inventor locked up in the local loony bin—or all three at once!—is that the crazy little man seems far more at home amidst this multiplicity and flux than does Shorty McCabe. He has a much wider range of possible thought and action.

Do crazy people know something that normal rational citizens of the Twentieth Century do not? That wouldn't be an altogether inapt question to raise at a time when the purportedly normal and rational people of the world were engaged in a furious global struggle for power and control.

This line of speculation would be taken a step further in a story by Fritz Leiber entitled "Sanity" (*Astounding*, Apr 1944). Leiber, who considered himself a pacifist, was another of those writers for *Unknown* who had been more influenced by H.P. Lovecraft than by E. E. Smith, and was now crossing over to write reality-challenging modern science fiction for *Astounding*.

"Sanity" would follow the example of Robert Heinlein and show a strange yet still recognizable future society which is based upon its own unique history, assumptions and order of value. In this case, the crucial formative event-cluster from which all else has followed was a moment that saw the founding of a world state, the abolishment of war, and a universal amnesty for deviant thought of all kinds.

In the society that has resulted, everyone is at least a little bit insane if judged by the standards of the Twentieth Century. But one man named Carrsbury, who has read the literature of the past and considers himself "'a throwback to a time when human mentality was far sounder,'" is able to muster the objectivity necessary to see the true facts of the situation. His assessment is that just as with an unstable person who is able to hold himself together as long as he is striving for a goal but who falls apart with success, the achievement of a world state has allowed mankind so much slack that it has cracked up in all of the ways described in the old medical texts he has studied.

It is apparent to Carrsbury that the people who presently staff the World Management Service display disturbing signs of catatonia, manic depression and other disorders. The one we see at closest range is his nearest working associate, Phy, the general secretary of the world, a man Carrsbury looks upon with a mixture of liking and pity. There is no doubt that Phy seems a crippled personality, vacuous, childish and weak.

Carrsbury's solution to this problem is to assume control of the world and see to it that humanity starts behaving in a rational manner once again. Through connivance, he has made himself World manager and instituted reforms designed to calm society down and restore some of the old-time sense of human direction and discipline. He has re-instituted the eight-hour working day. He has legislated against wasteful and irrational acts like the contemporary fad for incomplete staircases and roads to nowhere. He has passed decrees prohibiting the reading of over-stimulating literature. And he has forbidden people to indulge in unusual or indecent impulses, with a long list of specific examples.

But even his present degree of control seems insufficient to him. If things are ever to work properly again, Carrsbury will have to sweep out all the aberrants in positions of power and replace them with sounder people. Toward this end, he has been engaged in a personal Ten Year Plan—"'the training, in comparative isolation, first in small numbers, then in larger, as those instructed could in turn become instructors, of a group of prospective leaders carefully selected on the basis of their relative freedom from neurotic tendencies.'"

Today is the day of Carrsbury's coup, and he is on his way to the conference chamber on the one hundredth floor—the top floor—of the World Managerial Center to meet with his new staff. On the elevator with him is Phy, the former general secretary.

Phy is aware of the coup, but somehow he won't concede that Carrsbury has assumed control. In fact, he suggests that things in general have actually been somewhat different than Carrsbury has imagined them to be.

Carrsbury has been sitting in his office for ten full years, receiving information and turning out edicts. But the information hasn't all been strictly accurate, and the edicts haven't all been obeyed:

> "For instance, your prohibition, regarding reading tapes, of all exciting literature...oh, we tried a little of the soothing stuff you suggested at first. Everyone got a great kick out of it. They laughed and laughed. But afterwards, well, as I said, it kind of got changed—in this case to a prohibition of all *unexciting* literature."

And as for that ban against yielding to unusual or indecent impulses—"'it went into effect all right, but with a little rider attached: "unless you really want to." That seemed absolutely necessary, you know.'"

As corroboration of what he is saying, Phy asks Carrsbury how many floors there are in this building. Carrsbury has no problem answering an elementary question like that:

"'One hundred,' he replied promptly.

"'Then,' asked Phy, 'just where are we?'"

And, indeed, the numbers on the elevator board are blinking higher and higher. The one hundred and twenties... The one hundred and forties...

"'As if you were rising through consciousness into an unsuspected realm of mentality lying above,'" Phy says to Carrsbury.

And when they have stopped on the one hundred and fiftieth floor and emerged to find themselves standing on apparent nothingness far above the visible building—one more example of this society's taste for non-rational construction projects—Phy adds:

> "For ten years now you've been spending most of your life in that building below. Every day you've used this elevator. But not once have you dreamed of those fifty extra stories. Don't you think that something of the same sort may be true of your observations of other aspects of contemporary social life?"

Sanity, it seems, is a relative and not an absolute measure. It is the ability to conform to the norms of a particular society. And by the standards of this society, Carrsbury is actually less sane and less able than most people—however normal he might have looked in the context of the Twentieth Century.

So why was he ever allowed to be World manager at all? Phy answers that for Carrsbury:

"You interested us, don't you see? In fact, you were practically unique. As you know, it's our cardinal principle to let every individual express himself as he wants to. In your case, that involved letting you become World manager. Taken all in all it worked out very well. Everyone had a good time, a number of constructive regulations were promulgated, we learned a lot—oh, we didn't get everything we hoped for, but one never does. Unfortunately, in the end, we were forced to discontinue the experiment."

Now it is time for Carrsbury to depart. An aircraft lands on the invisible 150th story to carry him away. Where he is going, he will have comfortable quarters, adequate facilities for exercise, and a complete library of Twentieth Century literature to while away his time.

"Sanity" would be an effective answer to the question of whether our familiar Twentieth Century habits of mind are final and sufficient— and also to the larger question of whether non-rational modes of thought should be considered sane. After this story, states of mind other than logic and reason would have to be given the benefit of the doubt and allowed a fair chance to demonstrate their value.

At about the time that "Sanity" was being published in the spring of 1944, the girlfriend whom Lester del Rey had been trailing after was transferred in her job from St. Louis to New York City, and del Rey was replaced in his aircraft-building job by a machine that anyone could run. So del Rey moved to New York, too, and returned to serious science fiction writing.

In the first story that he sold to Campbell after getting to the city—"Kindness" (*Astounding*, Oct 1944)—he would take up the same device that Fritz Leiber had used of comparing a throwback to our own mental state with a new human mental order. But the gap between the two that was imagined by del Rey wouldn't be due to a mere change in society and its standards of belief and behavior, but rather to a fundamental change in the nature of the species.

We might remember that del Rey's third story, "The Day Is Done," had been about the last Neanderthal man dying from feelings of overwhelming inferiority in the face of new-style Cro-Magnon man.

Now, in "Kindness," del Rey had an analogous story to tell about the last surviving *Homo sapiens* in the new world of *Homo intelligens*.

In the case of every species distinction known to the science of taxonomy, it has always been some difference in outward form which has been reckoned to separate one species from another. But not so here. In del Rey's story, what divides the new species of man from the old is an internal difference:

> Outwardly, Jack Thorpe's body might have been the twin of Danny's own well-muscled one, and the smiling face above it bore no distinguishing characteristics. The mutation that changed man to superman had been within, a quicker, more complex relation of brain cell to brain cell that had no outward sign.

Danny—del Rey's ordinary human character—is a sweet kid, but he simply isn't able to keep up with new-style people like Thorpe. Even their children are able to outstrip him:

> Homo intelligens had a new way of thinking, above reason, where all the long, painful steps of logic could be jumped instantly. They could arrive at a correct picture of the whole from little scattered bits of information. Just as man had once invented logic to replace the trial-and-error thinking that most animals have, so homo intelligens had learned to use intuition. They could look at the first page of an old-time book and immediately know the whole of it, since the little tricks of the author would connect in their intuitive minds and at once build up the missing links. They didn't even have to try—they just looked, and knew. It was like Newton looking at an apple falling and immediately seeing why the planets circled the sun, and realizing the laws of gravitation; but these men did it all the time, not just at those rare intervals as it had worked for homo sapiens once.

Thorpe and the other supermen do what they can to ease poor Danny's situation, eventually setting him up to steal an old-time human spaceship and make his way to a paradisiac planetoid they have prepared for him. To them, it seems a small enough favor to do for the last member of a predecessor race to whom they feel they owe a considerable debt.

The story ends with one of the supermen musing: "'I wonder... what kindness Neanderthaler found when the last one came to die. Or whether the race that will follow us when the darkness falls on us will have something better than such kindness.'"

Along with the expanded circle of consciousness presented in these leading edge stories of the later Golden Age, there was a corresponding increase in tolerance of beings with other standards of behavior and modes of thought than our own—as though to understand more was to be more accepting of difference. We can see this new trend at work in "Kindness" and in "Sanity," as well as in Padgett's "The World Is Mine" and "The Proud Robot."

The old concept of a single evolutionary ladder which all creatures must climb offered humans no option but to compete with other beings for the privilege of survival within a basically hostile universe. It was all or nothing. Either we would prevail or we would perish. There was no middle ground.

But the new holistic view of existence left room for everyone to be himself without necessarily posing a threat to anyone else. There could be different paths and different kinds of being without inevitable war to the death.

A formal test of the new live-and-let-live attitude would come in Murray Leinster's novelet "First Contact" (*Astounding*, May 1945). In this story, a spaceship from Earth on a scientific expedition to explore the Crab Nebula encounters the first ship of another spacefaring race that humanity has ever met.

The two sides establish communication. The captains are hesitant to fight, but both fear that a fight is inevitable. It is clear that if either ship should be trailed back to its home planet, its people would find themselves at an intolerable disadvantage.

Within the story, the state of affairs is phrased like this:

> The first contact of humanity with an alien race was a situation which had been foreseen in many fashinns, but never one quite so hopeless of solution as this. A solitary Earth-ship and a solitary alien, meeting in a nebula which must be remote from the home planet of each. They might wish peace, but the line of conduct which best prepared a treacherous attack was just the seeming of friendliness. Failure to be suspicious might doom the human race—and a peaceful exchange of the fruits of civilization would be the greatest benefit imaginable. Any mistake would be irreparable, but a failure to be on guard would be fatal.

This is a classic war game problem set forth in the form of a science fiction story. But the real question is actually one of attitude and perception. Are human and alien inevitably bound to see each other in old-fashioned Techno Age terms as hostile competitors, or are they capable of finding some way of tolerating each other's existence in the emerging style of the Atomic Age?

"First Contact" is a story about the shift from one attitude to the other. The solution to the problem of these two isolated ships which don't want to fight but are afraid not to is finally found when each side determines to threaten the other into accepting the same peaceful settlement or be blown to pieces!

Both ships are to be fixed so that they can do no trailing of each other. Their weapons are to be dismantled and their maps and records removed. Then the humans and the aliens will swap ships and take them back home to their respective home planets.

This will provide maximum information to both sides at a minimum of risk to either. Then, if the two parties decide they wish to meet again, they can do so here in the neutrality of the Crab Nebula at an agreed-upon time.

Not surprisingly, the more that is known of the aliens, the less alien they seem. At the conclusion of the story, it seems likely to at least one member of the human crew that despite their great physical differences, the two races are going to be able to get along together psychologically, and he reports as much to his captain:

> "There was the one I called Buck, sir, because he hasn't any name that goes into sound waves," said Tommy. "We got along very well. I'd really call him my friend, sir. And we were together for a couple of hours just before the two ships separated and we'd nothing in particular to do. So I became convinced that humans and aliens are bound to be good friends if they have only half a chance. You see, sir, we spent those two hours telling dirty jokes."

Dismaying though we may find it to see these two males of different species discovering their commonality through a mutual humorous bashing of the sex left at home, we have to recognize that it may be easier to accept difference when it is at a distance, and rather more difficult to accept it at close range. First things first...and we must be content that these two ships full of aggressive and competitive males are able to agree that the universe is large enough to contain them both without their having to fight to the death. It would have been otherwise in earlier times when every explorer from Earth packed a .45 automatic on his hip and was ready to use it on anything that looked at him the wrong way.

A. E. van Vogt would bring the question of tolerance of difference a good deal closer in a series of three stories in *Astounding*—"Concealment" (Sept 1943), "The Storm" (Oct 1943), and "The Mixed Men" (Jan 1945).

In the first of these stories, a battleship from Earth under command of a woman, Lady Gloria Laurr, is on an expedition to survey the stars of our satellite galaxy, the Lesser Magellanic Cloud, when it comes upon an interstellar weather station manned by a solitary human being. But when this man is interrogated, his resistance proves to be five times greater than his IQ would indicate him to be capable of. Rather than answering the questions he is asked, he launches a desperate physical attack on Grand Captain Laurr and has to be killed.

Only after he is dead is his true nature identified. He is one of the Dellians, who are described both as supermen and as perfect robots invented by an Earthman named Joseph M. Dell some fifteen thousand years ago. (The word "robot" is used here by van Vogt not in its more familiar sense of a mechanical construct, but in its original meaning of an artificial organic being, as in Capek's 1921 play *R. U. R.*) Ultimately, the Dellians were hunted down and wiped out by ordinary humans.

But not all of them were killed, apparently. In the second story, we learn that when this massacre took place, a number of Dellian and non-Dellian robots fled from the main galaxy to the Lesser Magellanic Cloud and established their own civilization there, which now encompasses fifty suns.

The Dellians are the stronger and more resilient of the two types of robots, while the non-Dellians are the more creative. These two get along harmoniously, but there is also a third kind of robot, the Mixed Men, lately crossbred from the other two by a method involving "'cold and pressure.'" The Mixed Men have two brains—one inherited from each of the two parent stocks—and consider themselves superior to the other types. After a failed attempt to seize power, they have had to go into hiding.

The great problem here for all parties, and particularly for the Earth humans to whom "robot" is a dirty word, is the overcoming of xenophobia and the acceptance of all types of man on a basis of equality. As the chief psychologist aboard the human battleship—another woman—puts it to Grand Captain Laurr:

> "Excellency, we come from a long list of ancestors who, in their time, have felt superior to others because of some slight variation in the pigmentation of the skin. It is even recorded that the color of the eyes has influenced the egoistic in historical decisions. We have sailed into very deep waters, and it will be the crowning achievement of our life if we sail out in satisfactory fashion."

A basis for reassurance comes in the third story, when research demonstrates that the so-called "non-Dellian robots" are actually human beings who long ago aided the Dellians to escape from the main galaxy and who have lived with them ever since without prejudice. Indeed, they have been willing to take on the one-time odious label of "robot" themselves.

The great conciliator who discovers this fact and mediates a settlement acceptable to all sides—one Captain Peter Maltby—is himself the living exemplar of the necessary solution to this situation. He is the hereditary leader of the Mixed Men. He was captured as a child by the forces of the Fifty Suns and has grown up to be a sworn military officer who has proven himself in test after test. He is also a man of such character and ability that he is able to win the heart and hand of Grand Captain Gloria Laurr of Imperial Earth. By caring about the welfare of all parties, Maltby cannot be untrue to the real interests of any one of them.

However, the greatest challenge to the sufficiency of human parochialism presented in the digest-sized *Astounding* would be neither the problem of learning how to be friends with alien competitors nor the difficulty of acknowledging "robots" and robot-human crossbreeds as our brothers. On several occasions during 1944, readers of the magazine would be asked to imagine the transformation of human beings into new forms, and to perceive these metamorphoses not as monstrous and awful, but as something to be accepted and even desired.

The person to whom this prospect presented the biggest psychological hurdle may have been John W. Campbell. The editor had a large psychic investment in the idea of mankind taking charge of the universe without losing its essential nature—which he identified with the outward human form.

Several years earlier, in a story entitled "Sunken Universe" published in the May 1942 *Super Science Stories* under the pseudonym Arthur Merlyn, biology student James Blish had imagined miniaturized human beings who have been adapted to life among the microorganisms of a freshwater pond on a planet of the star Tau Ceti. This was the first of a number of stories that Blish would eventually write on the subject of "pantropy," his name for the reshaping of men to fit the conditions found on particular planets.

But none of Blish's pantropic stories would be published in *Astounding*. John Campbell would vastly prefer Jack Williamson's alternate notion of "terraforming," or the reshaping of planets to fit mankind.

However, whether because of an urgent need to fill a hole in the magazine or out of wartime recklessness, the editor would publish a pantropic short story by Clifford D. Simak entitled "Desertion" in the November 1944 *Astounding*. Simak had produced science fiction for a dozen years, but it was only with the new expanded humanism of the wartime *Astounding* that he would begin to come into his own as an SF writer.

In "Desertion," human beings have managed to establish themselves on the planet Jupiter, but only within the protection of special quartz-coated domes.

They are restricted in their direct contact with the surface of the planet by the difficult conditions here—the tremendous atmospheric pressure, the overwhelming gravity, and the wild corrosive ammonia rainstorms.

The only way that men can explore the surface of Jupiter is to change themselves into the dominant life-form of the planet, which they have dubbed "Lopers." But none of the seven men who have been put through the conversion machine and sent out into the living hell of Jupiter have managed to make their way back to the dome, and it begins to look as though the planet's extremes have defeated man.

In one last desperate attempt to fulfill his mission, the dome commander, Kent Fowler, has himself and his old dog Towser converted into Loper form and put outside the dome. They are only to go a short distance into the maelstrom and then return.

But man and dog, who can now communicate directly in "thought symbols that had shades of meaning words could never have," find everything changed in this new form. Two-hundred-mile-an-hour winds now seem gentle breezes. There are wonderful odors and waterfalls of ammonia that sound like music.

We are told:

> He, Fowler, had expected terror inspired by alien things out here on the surface, had expected to cower before the threat of unknown things, had steeled himself against disgust of a situation that was not of Earth.
>
> But instead he had found something greater than Man had ever known. A swifter, surer body. A sense of exhilaration, a deeper sense of life. A sharper mind. A world of beauty that even the dreamers of Earth had not yet imagined.

Strange, complex thoughts swirl through the minds of man and dog in their new Loper form:

> "It's our brains," said Fowler. "We're using them, all of them, down to the last hidden corner. Using them to figure out things we should have known all the time. Maybe the brains of Earth things naturally are slow and foggy. Maybe we are the morons of the universe. Maybe we are fixed so we have to do things the hard way."

And, a few moments later, he adds (speaking as though both he and Towser were of the same kind):

"We're still mostly Earth. . . . We're just beginning to learn a few of the things we are to know—a few of the things that were kept from us as human beings, perhaps because we were human beings. Because our human bodies were poor bodies. Poorly equipped for thinking, poorly equipped in certain senses that one has to have to know. Perhaps even lacking in certain senses that are necessary to true knowledge."

As the person in charge of this outpost, Fowler recognizes that they ought to return to the dome—but it is more than he can quite bear to resume his former condition, which now seems muddled, ignorant and squalid to him. His pal Towser helps him put the matter into perspective:

"I can't go back," said Towser.
"Nor I," said Fowler.
"They would turn me back into a dog," said Towser.
"And me," said Fowler, "back into a man."

The other, and perhaps even more provocative, story of human mental and physical metamorphosis was "Environment" by Chester S. Geier, published in the May 1944 issue of *Astounding.* It seems very unlikely that John Campbell would have considered printing such a story as this at any other moment.

In "Environment," a spaceship from Earth lands in a great deserted city on a planet of a distant sun. The two men aboard the ship, Jon Gaynor and Wade Harlan, are seeking to discover what happened to a party of religious traditionalists who came to this place one hundred and twenty years ago under the leadership of an ancestor of Gaynor's.

From bas-reliefs around a fountain, they conclude that the builders of the city were a humanoid race. But the only life forms they encounter are strange aerial creatures:

They were great, faceted crystals whose interiors flamed with glorious color—exquisite shades that pulsed and changed with the throb of life. Like a carillon of crystal bells, their chimings and tinklings rang out— so infinitely sweet and clear and plaintive that it was both a pain and a pleasure to hear.

The two men explore apartments within the deserted city. And in each room they enter, the walls are covered with murals whose meaning escapes them. Also in each room is a niche containing a jewel, and when one of them concentrates his attention on one of these jewels, things that might be furniture or machines half-materialize: "Watching, Gaynor saw the ghostly outlines for the first time—misty suggestions of angles and curves, hints of forms whose purpose he could not guess."

They fly over the city on antigravity units and discover first one spaceship and then another—including the *Ark* of old Mark Gaynor and his band of Purists. Each of the ships they come across was apparently built by a different humanoid race. And every one of them is deserted, with no clue as to what happened to those aboard.

Eventually, Harlan and Gaynor conclude that the city bears a certain resemblance to a book. There is an order to the rooms and the wall pictures, and if they are to have any hope of understanding what is going on here, it is necessary for them to begin at the beginning. And so they locate the right end of town and begin to study the meaning of the city.

At the outset, the surroundings adapt themselves to the humans. In these first apartments they find furniture that is recognizable to them and familiar music, food and drink.

The wall paintings offer instruction in what they are to do at each step. And as they move on from room to room and from building to building, they encounter one machine after another which they are challenged to master:

"The machines grew larger, more intricate, ever more difficult of solution. Each was a new test upon the growing knowledge of Gaynor and Harlan. And each test was harder than the last, for the wall paintings no longer pointed out the way, but merely hinted now."

After the machines have gotten huge, they begin to get smaller and more subtle, until at last there are no more of them. The two men have reached the rooms with the form-producing jewels which baffled them so when they first came to the city. But now they are at a higher level of understanding and know what must be done here. Gazing at the wall paintings, Gaynor says:

"The Third Stage. The tasks will be very difficult, Wade—but interesting. We'll be putting our knowledge into practice—actually creating. This means we'll have to deal directly with the powers of the various soldani and varoo. As these are extradimensional, control will be solely by chol-thening at the sixth level, through means of the taadron. We'll have to be careful, though—any slightest relaxation of the sorran will have a garreling effect—"

On and on they proceed through the city—rising through the Third Stage and into the Fourth. They become telepathic, and then pass beyond that. They no longer require food, but materialize nourishment out of subatomic energies. They learn to fly without the aid of any device. And their bodies begin to seem "impedimenta of their childhood" to them.

At last, they vogelar to the very last tower of the city and narleen its paintings. With this ultimate knowledge, they pass into crystalline form themselves. Flashing different colors and chiming musically, they join the others of their kind high in the sky.

And the city, that unique educational device, then returns to waiting for the next set of inquisitive humanoids to come along and receive instruction.

In the new consciousness-based universe, it would seem, how you think and what you are capable of learning would be much more important than where you happen to come from or what you might look like. Starting from very different initial conditions, we might all become Lopers together, or crystalline beings tinkling in the air, or some further state even more exalted.

Of all the writers of the wartime *Astounding*, it was A. E. van Vogt who was most insistent that in a universe of holistic consciousness the human way forward lay in higher education.

Back in 1940, in his first novel, *Slan*, van Vogt had imagined that it would be necessary to have an evolutionary mutation and a whole new breed of man to replace man-as-he-presently-is before humanity could begin to think holistically. But implicit in *Slan* were hints of Techno Age elitism, racism and genocide that van Vogt couldn't be completely comfortable with. Ultimately, those were the very issues that World War II was being fought to settle.

During the involuntary hiatus in his SF writing which followed *Slan*, van Vogt was given a space of time in which to think carefully about the question of human mental and moral advancement. And while he didn't manage to resolve all problems at once, he did begin to view mutation as a less-than-fully-satisfactory answer to the question and to look for alternatives.

This may be seen in "Recruiting Station," his first published story after his return. Here, van Vogt had pitted a genetic superman against an ordinary Twentieth Century woman, and made the superman and his kind a danger to all existence and the woman humanity's savior.

In this story, van Vogt envisioned one kind of superior man after another, as though to say that no one fixed form of man could ever be final and sufficient. But the superman we are shown at closest range is immortal, telepathic Dr. Lell of the Glorious, an arrogant, exploitative race who are prepared to sacrifice the entire universe if they are not allowed to have things their own way.

Set in opposition to him is Norma Matheson, whose first name may be taken as an indication of her normal human nature. Through mental contact with post-humans of the remote future and specific training by them, she has her latent powers of mind awakened to the point where she is easily able to fool, manipulate and forestall that poor, unsuspecting superman, Dr. Lell.

The same relative order of value, in which education is seen as superior to mutation, would be presented in van Vogt's second novel, *The Weapon Makers*, at the beginning of 1943, in the two friends, Edward Gonish and Robert Hedrock. Gonish, the No-man, is not a mutant, but he has been enabled by special Weapon Shop training to become a master of holistic perception. Hedrock, the immortal man, is a unique sport of nature, but for all his advantages of longevity and his concern for the welfare of the entirety of mankind, he also has distinct limitations of mind.

Hedrock thinks about this just prior to his arrival at a crucial meeting with the Weapon Shop Council:

> Despite all his years of experience, these Weapon Shop supermen with their specialized training had inexorably forged ahead of him in a dozen fields.
>
> He could not even plan for his own protection because the techniques of education that had molded their brains from childhood were useless applied to his mind, which had been cluttered with confused, unplanned integrations ages before the techniques now so dangerous to him were invented.

If our minds weren't already cluttered with prejudices, with errors of perception and understanding, with outmoded and inadequate information, and with confused, unplanned integrations, could any of us and every one of us learn to be a superman like the members of the Weapon Shop Council?

If a natural man-beyond-man like Hedrock were deprived of all special education, would he ever be able to put his superior qualities to use?

Is it possible that appropriate mental training could produce a whole society of superior men who were more sane, more adaptable, and more able than that random accident, the untutored genetic superman?

Van Vogt would give questions like these considerable thought. And writing in a later day, he would have these speculations to offer about the relationship between human potential, society and education:

> —God made man in his own image (meaning perfect).
> (Man loused it up.)
> —A complex computer, even when it's a neural one—the human brain—has the capacity to reason perfectly.

Early training and conditioning loused it up.

—Under hypnosis, it has been established that the human memory has stored *everything* seen, heard, felt, touched and tasted, since at least early childhood.

Also loused up.

Of course, in this middle period of history, lousing up doesn't take long in any single individual's life, because of the haphazard way the person is brought up, which all too quickly turns him into the average type we see around.

We are entitled to speculate that every human being is at some bottom of his being endowed with total memory, total creativity, total intelligence; in short, down in there somewhere is a perfect brain.

We have beautiful glimpses of what is potential. One person has an open line to writing poetry. Another can draw with marvelous accuracy. A third has musical ability. Others masterfully design carpets, build cabinets, conceive vast architectural marvels; and so on, through all the arts, and sciences, and crafts, that the world, and the individual, has produced.

But the time for the brain to be handled correctly by schools and parents, and to operate freely, is not yet.

In his third serial novel, *The World of Null-A* (*Astounding*, Aug-Oct 1945), van Vogt would try to envision that better time. He would present a future society whose first priority is to educate men and women to be more able and clear-thinking than they are today. And, by way of contrast, he would also imagine an immortal superman with a second brain, like the Mixed Men, who for lack of self-knowledge and training is hopelessly bewildered and ineffective.

The mental training presented in *The World of Null-A* would differ from that offered in van Vogt's previous stories in having a plausible contemporary referent—Alfred Korzybski's psycholinguistic system, General Semantics.

Count Alfred Korzybski was another of the pioneer holists of the Thirties. Born in Poland in 1879, he was trained as an engineer, and later taught physics, mathematics and foreign languages in Warsaw. During World War I, Korzybski was a member of a Russian military mission to America. When the Russian Revolution occurred in 1917 and Russia withdrew from the war, he took up permanent residence in the United States.

The aim behind Korzybski's original work was to engineer a closer fit between human thought and behavior and the actual facts of the surrounding environment. He wanted to make human thinking both more exact and more flexible.

Korzybski's central statement was a 1933 book entitled *Science and Sanity: An Introduction to Non-Aristotelian Systems and*

General Semantics. In his analysis, our modern problems in thinking could all be traced back to the logic of Aristotle, with its either-or, black-white, this-and-therefore-not-that approach to the world. The effect of the radical science of the Twentieth Century was to reveal the inadequacy of such over-simple methods. The times demanded new, more effective, multivalued, non-Aristotelian (or null-A) systems of thought.

General Semantics was an example of such a system. In linguistics, semantics is the study of the relationship between symbols and the things they refer to. General Semantics was an extension of this—a study of the relationship between the limited ways in which human beings ordinarily think and the real world in which they must act.

Again and again, Korzybski pointed out that the map is not the territory. One moment in time is not the same as another. And if events are to be understood, it is necessary for them to be interpreted within a total context.

Korzybski's work had first been used as background in science fiction in 1940 when Robert Heinlein had made it the plausible basis for the persuasive psychology at the heart of his short novel, "If This Goes On—." But it took three years after that before van Vogt was able to catch up with a copy of *Science and Sanity* and read Korzybski for himself.

As it happened, during World War II, Canada saw fit to protect the tender sensibilities of its citizens by banning all American science fiction magazines. A partial exception was made for van Vogt, who needed to read *Astounding* for professional reasons, and he continued to receive his copies forwarded to him through the Canadian censor's office.

In the course of 1943, a science fiction reader named O.C. Wilson got in touch with van Vogt. He worked for the Canadian Broadcasting System, and his job had taken him to the censor's office, where he had happened to notice a science fiction magazine addressed to van Vogt. Was it possible that he might borrow back copies of *Astounding* and *Unknown*? Van Vogt let him have the magazines, and in return Wilson lent van Vogt his copy of *Science and Sanity*.

Korzybski's work was exactly what van Vogt the systematician was most eager to see—a system for the development of clearer human thought. Heinlein, in his story, had used Korzybski's studies as the basis by which those in society who do think with clarity could manipulate and direct that part of the populace still a slave to limited thinking. But what van Vogt perceived in General Semantics was the means by which all mankind might set itself free.

In van Vogt's novel, *The World of Null-A*, it is the year 2560, and everyone on Earth has the opportunity to absorb education in the super-General Semantics of his imagination. The result is an egalitarian society: "There simply weren't any special people in the null-A universe. ... People were people, normally born equal, requiring the simple, straightforward null-A training to integrate their intelligence. There were no kings, no archdukes, no supermen, traveling incognito."

Every year, during a special month, people who wish to advance themselves come to the capital city from all over the world to be tested by a great Games Machine. Those who do well are honored and placed in positions of social authority. And the few who do well enough—those who can demonstrate that they are completely functional human beings—graduate to another society on Venus where people live in peace and harmony without any need for the coercions of government and law.

In the course of the story, human beings from an ongoing galactic civilization who are powerfully armed, but mentally are still "*uninte-grated* men," invade this superior civilization. But the null-A men of Venus meet this threat with such clarity of mind, tenacity of purpose and uncompromising resistance that a galactic observer is soon saying to the leader of the invasion, "'Haven't you realized that null-A cannot be destroyed?'"

In this society in which supermen traveling incognito have no place, van Vogt's natural superman, Gilbert Gosseyn, would be far less effective.

At the outset of the story, Gosseyn has just arrived in the capital city from his small hometown in California to be tested by the Games Machine. But it is very quickly revealed to him that everything he thinks he knows about himself and his background is false or inadequate. The identity he has accepted as sufficient is not his true self.

Reflecting on the situation of this character, van Vogt would come to remark: "Analogically, this is true of all of us. Only, we are so far gone into falseness, so acceptant of our limited role, that we never question it at all."

In his search for who he really is, and for what he can really do, Gosseyn (whose name can be pronounced "go-sane"—van Vogt's own personal preference once his literary agent had pointed this out to him) would consult a psychiatrist, Dr. Kair. The doctor examines his "extra-brain" and reports in awe:

> "The evidence shows, Gosseyn, that what you have resembles not so much a brain as the great control systems in the solar plexus and the spine. Only it is the most compact set-up of controls that I have ever seen. The number of cells involved is equal to about a third of the total now in your brain. You've got enough control apparatus in your head to direct atomic

and electronic operations in the microcosm, and there just aren't enough objects in the macrocosm to ever engage the full potential control power of the automatic switches and relays now in your brain."

But when Gosseyn asks for aid in actualizing this potential, Dr. Kair can be of no help. He likens Gosseyn's case to that of a boy named George who was raised by a pack of wild dogs from the age of two to eleven. After his capture, George proved beyond socialization, never learning to walk and talk and take part in normal human society:

"He died at twenty-three, still an animal; a wizened up creature-boy looking hardly human in the bed of his padded cell. A post-mortem revealed that his cortex had not fully developed, but that it existed in sufficient size to have justified belief that it might be made to function."

This—or something like it—is Gosseyn's situation. For all his incredible potential, in actual practice he is pitifully underdeveloped.

The best that Gosseyn can do is attempt to remember himself—to discover who he really is. And, indeed, at the conclusion of the story, he does learn that he is nothing less than the latest clone of the immortal superman who long ago was originally responsible for setting up null-A society.

(In the 1948 book version of the story, it is explained that because of an accident suffered by the eldest current Gosseyn, it has proved impossible for him to transfer to his younger clone the cumulative memory that is the true immortality of the line. And this is the reason why this latent superman has been condemned to wander about so aimlessly from Earth to Venus—as he himself puts it, "'like a bewildered child.'")

This elder Gosseyn is killed, but as he dies he indicates to his younger clone-successor that the best thing he/they have been able to accomplish was to take the obscure system of null-A and make it into the basis for a society:

"'I nourished null-A, which was then like a tiny flowering plant in a wilderness of weeds.'"

(In the second revision of the book in 1970, the dying elder superman adds this indication that his/their immortality in itself is meaningless in comparison to the sanity of null-A man: "'I was looking for a place to settle, and for something to be that was more than mere continuity; and it seemed to me that Non-Aristotelian Man was it....'")

If van Vogt was correct in his stories of the later Golden Age, the human way forward lay not merely in being dominant, or in having greater firepower, or conquering more and more territory, and neither did it depend on mankind changing in form and developing special powers like telepathy or immortality. What was actually required was for men and women of our own kind to learn how to actualize their present untapped potential and become beings who were completely sane and fully effective.

We should recognize that the various stories of 1943 to 1945 which we've been looking at were not in the majority in *Astounding*. They were only one element in a mix which included old-fashioned stories of scientific invention, time-travel paradoxes, stories in which technical problems were posed and solved, and even a line of patriotic SF in which various dire fates were imagined for the Axis powers, in particular the Nazis and their leaders.

At the same time, however, there can be no doubt that these stories were far and away the most original and visionary work published by Campbell during the war—the model for SF written throughout the rest of the Atomic Age. Here, transcendence, like a snake that has been struggling to shed its old skin, cast off the appearance of science-beyond-science which had served it through the modern scientific era, and presented itself in the shining new raiment of consciousness-beyond-consciousness.

The shift in the perceived locus of transcendence that took place in these wartime stories was every bit as significant as the earlier shift from transcendent spirit to transcendent science with which our story began. We may understand it as the sign of the start of a whole new era in the social and psychic development of the Western world, which, as it unfolds, will necessarily be as different from the modern scientific era as that was from the preceding era of spirit-based religion.

It is possible to catch this shift in the very act of taking place in the SF stories that were written during World War II by John Campbell's most diligent pupil, Isaac Asimov—even though Asimov was someone who was scientifically educated and scientifically employed, and consciously dedicated to the proposition that science fiction was fiction about imaginary science and its possible effects upon human beings.

For a time, Asimov wasn't writing science fiction of any kind. He stopped in the spring of 1942 when he left his parents' candy store and suspended work on his Ph.D. at Columbia in order to go off to Philadelphia to serve as a chemist in the Navy Yard. He was fully occupied in learning to live on his own, adjusting to his new job, and preparing to be married in July to a girl he had begun dating in February.

Asimov had always looked upon his science fiction writing as a convenient and enjoyable means of earning money to support his studies in college and graduate school. But he didn't need to do that anymore. Now that the Navy was paying him to be a chemist, he was bringing in more money more regularly than ever before in his life.

It went further than this, however. Now that he wasn't spending those long hours behind the counter of the candy store in Brooklyn, he no longer had the inclination to go on reading the science fiction pulp magazines that had been so important to him for so many years. He did continue to buy *Astounding* each month, but he got farther and farther behind in reading that, too. It was almost as though science fiction were part of some other life which he had now left behind.

During this vacation from SF, Asimov was content to do his job and settle into his marriage. He didn't stop reading—he read a lot, especially in history. And if he felt the need for intellectual stimulation, he had Robert Heinlein to talk to, and L. Sprague de Camp, and de Camp's friend John D. Clark, a science fiction fan and chemist who was doing wartime work in explosives and who lived within convenient walking distance of Asimov's apartment.

To be sure, Asimov's relationship with Heinlein wasn't an altogether easy one. Almost from the moment they first met, there was a strong personality clash between them, which only increased with the passage of time.

Heinlein was a man with an overwhelming need to dominate and control other people, and he was only fully comfortable in social situations in which he was the one setting the terms and conditions. Because of the difference in their ages, and because of the great respect in which Asimov held Heinlein's science fiction writing, Heinlein had the psychological jump on Asimov from the beginning of their acquaintance, and he was bent on keeping things that way.

But Asimov, as we have seen, had just as strong a drive not to let anybody—not his father, not his teachers, not even John Campbell— tell him what to do and think. Over the years, he had developed a thousand tricks for undermining and evading authority while still maintaining apparent deference and respect.

Asimov had impressed his wife-to-be early in their courtship when she had asked him the old conundrum about what happens when an irresistible force meets an immovable object, and he had explained that it was impossible for the two to co-exist in the same universe. That was precisely the problem in the relationship between Heinlein and Asimov. One was irresistible, the other was immovable, and it wasn't possible for the two to comfortably co-exist in the same little Navy Yard universe.

The biggest battle between the two men was fought over the nominal issue of lunch. Asimov, never one for exercise, disliked

the half-mile trek to the Navy Yard cafeteria, and found the food
that was served there next to inedible. It was his preference to bring
a bag lunch to work, eat in the quiet, air-conditioned comfort of the
lab, and read in peace. Asimov cherished that hour, having spent a
lifetime bolting down food and then hustling back to the candy store
so that someone else could have a meal.

But Heinlein wouldn't leave well enough alone. He wanted Asimov's
presence to fill out his lunch table in the Navy Yard cafeteria, and he
wouldn't take no for an answer. He bullied Asimov into joining his
party by portraying eating at the cafeteria as a matter of patriotic
duty. And when Asimov made disparaging remarks about the food
he was being forced to choke down, Heinlein instituted fines of a
nickel for each complaint, with the money to go toward the purchase
of a war bond.

Asimov finally got him to agree that if he could find some way of
complaining about the food which wasn't on the face of it a complaint, Heinlein would drop this game. But then, when Asimov would
saw away at a slab of haddock and innocently ask, "'Is there such a
thing as tough fish?'", Heinlein would reply, "'That will be five
cents, Isaac. The implication is clear.'"

Asimov says, "Since Bob was judge, jury and executioner, that was
that."

In the long run, however, Asimov was able to make his point. It
happened like this:

"Someone new joined the table who did not know the game that
was going on. He took one mouthful of some ham that had been
pickled in formaldehyde and said, 'Boy, this food is awful.'"

That was the opportunity Asimov had been waiting for, and he
didn't let it get past him. He immediately rose to his feet, raised
his hand for attention, and declared with feeling: "'Gentlemen,
I disagree with every word my friend here has said, but I will defend
with my life his right to say it.'"

Not only was that the end of this particular game, but it demonstrated to Heinlein that Asimov was simply not a person he could
handle any old way he pleased. In consequence, when Heinlein
shortly thereafter started to put together regular social evenings
for SF writers along the lines of his old Mañana Literary Society,
with the nominal purpose of brainstorming an answer to Japanese
kamikaze attacks on U.S. warships, he saw fit to invite everyone
he knew who was then living between New York City and Washington, D.C., from John Campbell to Will F. Jenkins. But he didn't
ask Isaac Asimov to come.

If Asimov never noticed, it was partly because he had a rare ability
to be oblivious to anything that didn't concern him, and partly

because he had turned his attention back to science fiction writing. Something like fourteen months after he finished "Bridle and Saddle," it dawned on him that in fact money wasn't his primary motive in writing. If he wrote SF, it was because he felt a compulsive urge to write SF—and the urge was on him again.

So, while others, like Heinlein, forgot about science fiction writing for the duration, donning as many as three different hats in an earnest attempt to see the war brought to a conclusion as quickly and decisively as possible, Isaac Asimov was content to do his job at the Navy Yard during the day, and then go home at night to work on his latest SF story.

The first piece he wrote, a novelet entitled "Author! Author!" was a fantasy aimed at *Unknown*, a market he had never been able to crack. It took Asimov the better part of three months to finish, writing in his none-too-copious spare time, but when he was done, Campbell not only bought it, but threw in a bonus. Unfortunately, the story was still in inventory when *Unknown Worlds* was killed off in the fall of 1943, and it wouldn't see publication until more than twenty years later when it was included in an anthology of stories drawn from *Unknown*.

If Asimov had known that such a thing was going to happen, he might have been discouraged from writing further stories. As it was, however, he was so elated by his sale to his favorite magazine that he sat right down and started another story, and never looked back.

It took him a while to regain his stride. The first two science fiction stories he wrote were relatively trivial exercises that depended on snappy punchlines for their impact.

But Asimov's fourth new story, a long novelet entitled "The Big and the Little" (*Astounding*, Aug 1944), was more serious and substantial. It was another Foundation story, set seventy-five years after "Bridle and Saddle."

The central character of "The Big and the Little" is an interstellar trader named Hober Mallow, who was born in Smyrno—which we will remember as one of the old Four Kingdoms—but who was bright enough to have received a lay education at the Foundation. Such is Mallow's strength of character and his ability to recognize what the moment requires that before the end of the story he would even be elected Mayor of Terminus and successfully deal with yet another of the crises foreseen by the great psychohistorian Hari Seldon.

The big and the little of the title are the Galactic Empire and the Foundation. Though the two aren't in direct contact, they are locked in contention over the direction that is to be taken by a stellar state which lies between them, the hereditary dictatorship of Korell, ruled by a man named Commdor Asper Argo.

But "the big and the little" also refers to the respective technologies of the Empire and the Foundation. The Empire depends on machines of tremendous size, built to last for generations and run by a caste of technicians who are no longer capable of performing repairs when the machines break down. By contrast, the gadgets and machines produced by the Foundation and sold by traders like Hober Mallow are small things like refrigeration units and dust-precipitators and items of personal adornment. As Mallow puts it:

> "The Empire has always been a realm of colossal resources. They've calculated everything in planets, in stellar systems, in whole sectors of the Galaxy. Their generators are gigantic because they thought in gigantic fashion.
>
> "But we,—*we*, our little Foundation, our single world almost without metallic resources,—have had to work with brute economy. Our generators have had to be the size of our thumb, because it was all the metal we could afford. We had to develop new techniques and new methods,—techniques and methods the Empire can't follow because they have degenerated past the stage where they can make any really vital scientific advance."

One of the particular strengths of this story was that it presented in dramatic form, a full year before the publication of van Vogt's *The World of Null-A*, some of the key ideas associated with Alfred Korzybski.

Among these was the Korzybskian dictum that the map is not the territory. In the course of "The Big and the Little," Hober Mallow, following a star map 150 years old, makes a foray into territory closer to the galactic center to check on current conditions within the Empire. He lands on what he takes to be the capital planet of an Imperial Sector, only to discover that his map is no longer accurate. When he asks a scholarly informant if this is Siwenna, the man replies:

"'Siwenna, yes. But Siwenna is no longer capital of the Normannic Sector. Your old map has misled you. . . . The stars may not change even in centuries, but political boundaries are all too fluid.'"

Things do change through time—even the location of the stars. And one moment in time is not the same as another.

This Korzybskian insight—which Asimov may, in part, have picked up from his reading of Heinlein's Future History stories—is further illustrated by a crucial conversation between Hober Mallow and a political rival who is wedded to the notion that the Foundation, having successfully dealt with the Four Kingdoms through its religion of the Galactic Spirit, ought to continue to promote it forever.

The rival politician says: "'You see, of course, that your attempt at trade for its own sake...can only end with the overthrow and complete negation of the policy that has worked successfully for a century.'"

To this, Mallow replies:

"And time enough, too...for a policy outdated, dangerous and impossible. However well your religion has succeeded in the Four Kingdoms, scarcely another world in the Periphery has accepted it. ... There isn't a ruler in the Periphery now that wouldn't sooner cut his own throat than let a priest of the Foundation enter the territory."

Mallow perceives that in new times marked by different conditions, the way forward isn't to insist upon old solutions to old problems. Indeed, to do this must inevitably prove counterproductive.

Commdor Asper Argo of Korell may be politically oriented toward the Galactic Empire, and be ready to accept its gifts of atomic-powered warships. He may even declare war against Terminus, so that the Foundation must duck and run and stall for time. Over the long haul, however, what will prove decisive in the conflict is the economic ties that have been established by interstellar traders like Hober Mallow. Mallow explains:

"The whole war is a battle between those two systems; between the Empire and the Foundation; between the big and the little. To seize control of a world, they bribe with immense ships that can make war, but lack all economic significance. We, on the other hand, bribe with little things, useless in war, but vital to prosperity and profits.

"A king, or a Commdor, will take the ships and even make war. Arbitrary rulers throughout history have bartered their subjects' welfare for what they consider honor, and glory, and conquest. But it's still the little things in life that count—and Asper Argo won't stand up against the economic depression that will sweep all Korell in two or three years."

In the relative balance of forces presented in "The Big and the Little," it is possible for us to see a reflection of ideas then current about big, slow, stupid dinosaurs lumbering around while under their noses swift, bright little mammals were breaking their eggs, eating their young, and condemning them to extinction.

We might also think of Chester Geier's story "Environment," in which the men from Earth who make their way through the rooms of the deserted school-city are at first introduced to machines that grow ever larger and more complicated but then, at a certain point, begin to become smaller and more subtle.

The trend toward machines that accomplish more and more with less and less would be one of the major differences between the Atomic Age and the Techno Age. And, to the extent that Asimov's story was a harbinger of transistors and printed circuits to come, it would be fresh and new and insightful.

In other respects, however, "The Big and the Little" would not be representative of the ongoing changes that were taking place in *Astounding* during the last years of World War II. In fact, it was to an extent retrogressive inasmuch as this novelet, far more than the two Foundation stories which had preceded it, was concerned with matters of physical science.

One reason for this old-fashionedness was that the period during which Lewis Padgett and others were establishing the new type of SF frankly based in transcendent consciousness was exactly the same period in which Asimov lapsed in his reading of *Astounding*. He hadn't caught on to the change as yet.

But there was another limitation to the stories that Asimov produced when he took up writing SF again. Perhaps because of doubts engendered by the uncertainty of the war, perhaps because of the Techno Age thinking that Asimov was exposing himself to in the history books he was reading so assiduously, there was a strong undercurrent of fatalism in the stories he wrote at first. We can see this expressed in the titles of his new stories: "Death Sentence" (*Astounding*, Nov 1943), "Blind Alley" (*Astounding*, Mar 1945), and "Dead Hand" (*Astounding*, Apr 1945).

This last story, another long Foundation novelet set forty years after "The Big and the Little," was explicitly deterministic. It was heavily influenced by Arnold Toynbee's *A Study of History* (1934-54), of which six volumes out of an eventual ten had then been published. Asimov began to borrow them one at a time from L. Sprague de Camp in the spring of 1944, just prior to writing "Dead Hand."

The historical model upon which this story was based was the life and deeds of the Sixth Century general Belisarius. This able man recovered the lost territory of North Africa from the Vandals for the Eastern Roman Empire, and fought in Italy against the Ostrogoths who were then ruling Rome. Belisarius might have accomplished even more than he did had it not been for the envy of his ruler, the Emperor Justinian, who gave him insufficient troops and support, recalled him more than once to Constantinople at inopportune moments, and eventually confiscated his property and had him thrown into prison.

In "Dead Hand," for the first time, the Empire and the Foundation face each other in direct conflict. Asimov's parallel to Belisarius, a young general named Bel Riose, denies the inevitable power of Hari

Seldon's psychohistory and launches a war against the Foundation. He has considerable success, too, retaking for the Empire a number of planets that the Foundation had brought under its political and economic sway.

The Foundation not only fights desperately, but tries one trick after another to stave off the general and drive a wedge between him and his Emperor, Cleon II. But nothing that it tries accomplishes more than a temporary postponement of what appears to be inevitable defeat. Then, however, just when all seems lost, Bel Riose is recalled by Cleon for his own reasons, is placed under arrest, tried and executed.

The son of the Siwennian scholar whom Hober Mallow met in "The Big and the Little" explains to men of the Foundation why they were right to think that the key lay in disunion between the Emperor and his general, but wrong in thinking that it was they who could bring this about:

> "You tried bribery and lies. You appealed to ambition and to fear. But you got nothing for all your pains. In fact, appearances were worse after each attempt.
>
> "And through all this wild threshing up of tiny ripples, the Seldon tidal wave continued onward, quietly—but quite irresistibly. ... There was a dead hand pushing all of us; the mighty general and the great Emperor; my world and your world—the dead hand of Hari Seldon. He knew that a man like Riose would have to fail, since it was his success that brought failure; and the greater the success, the surer the failure."

And he adds:

> "What keeps the Emperor strong? What kept Cleon strong? It's obvious. He is strong, because he permits no strong subjects. A courtier who becomes too rich, or a general who becomes too popular is dangerous. All the recent history of the Empire proves that to any Emperor intelligent enough to be strong.
>
> "Riose won victories, so the Emperor grew suspicious. ... So he was recalled, and accused, condemned, murdered. The Foundation wins again.
>
> "Why, look, there is not a conceivable combination of events that does not result in the Foundation winning. It was inevitable; whatever Riose did, whatever we did."

The extreme degree of the historical parallelism and the overwhelming determinism in "Dead Hand" would trouble Asimov himself after he had had some time to consider the matter. And he would trace this to the influence of Toynbee. Asimov would say:

As I continued to read Toynbee, my admiration waned. More and more, it was obvious to me that he was essentially a classical and Christian scholar and that the order he found in history was an imposed one produced by his seeing reflections of classical history wherever he looked. The final stories of the Foundation series were once more relatively free of his influence, therefore.

One person who was explicitly troubled by the determinism of "Dead Hand" was John W. Campbell, even though he not only bought and published the story but paid Asimov a bonus for it. Cyclical history—originally based upon the model of the fall of the Roman Empire—was precisely what all his efforts with modern science fiction had been designed to confute, and it could hardly serve his purpose of making man master of the universe if Hari Seldon and his psychohistorical predictions ultimately proved to be as great a dead weight upon the being and becoming of humanity as cyclical history ever was. And that was clearly the direction in which Asimov's Foundation series was tending.

Consequently, when Asimov paid a rare wartime visit to the editor's office in New York on January 8, 1945, two months before the publication of "Dead Hand," and the two men discussed the next Foundation story, Campbell informed Asimov that he wanted to see Seldon's Plan overturned.

Asimov still had a deep attachment to Seldon and his Plan, and he hadn't yet completely cast off the spell of Toynbee. He tells us: "I was horrified. No, I said, no, no, no, no. But Campbell said: Yes, yes, yes, yes, and I knew I wasn't going to sell him a no, no."

Asimov wasn't just being pushed in a direction he didn't want to go, however. By this time, he had already begun to work his way out of the mood of extreme determinism that had gripped him, and to respond to the new current of non-rational transcendence. This may be seen in the positronic robot story which was the specific stimulus for his trip to New York to see Campbell.

The title of this story is a clue to the role that it had in Asimov's progression of thought. He called it "Escape." However, since a story with that title had already appeared in the April 1943 *Astounding*—one of the issues that Asimov hadn't read—when Campbell published it in August 1945, he altered the title to "Paradoxical Escape."

In this story, U.S. Robot & Mechanical Men is locked in a race with a rival robotic company to develop an interstellar drive, but the data that the other company has fed to its "Super-Thinker" have caused the computer to break down. Now the other company wants to hire U.S. Robot to process the same data with its own thinking machine, "The Brain."

The people at U.S. Robot suspect that the intention of their rivals is to cause The Brain to break down in the same way just to keep matters even between the two. At the recommendation of robot psychologist Dr. Susan Calvin, however, U.S. Robot agrees to accept the deal. She says:

"Consolidated's machines, their Super-Thinker among them, are built without personality. They go in for functionalism, you know—they have to, without U.S. Robot's basic patents for the emotional brain paths. Their Thinker is merely a calculating machine on a grand scale, and a dilemma ruins it instantly.

"However, The Brain, our own machine, has a personality—a child's personality. It is a supremely deductive brain, but it resembles an *idiot savante*. It doesn't really understand what it does—it just does it. And because it is really a child, it is more resilient. Life isn't so serious, you might say."

To attack the space-drive problem, the data are broken down into smaller units to try to isolate the area of difficulty. And since it seems that it is a threat to human life that has caused the breakdown of Consolidated's Super-Thinker, The Brain is instructed to not become excited over that possibility, but just to spit out the problematic sheet when it comes to it.

Contrary to expectation, however, The Brain manages to calculate all factors through to a conclusion. And under its direction, a test interstellar ship is built by robots.

Our old friends, the robotic field-testers Powell and Donovan, are given the assignment of trying out the ship to see if it works. When they do, however, the ship runs away with them.

Susan Calvin suspects that something may have gone wrong with The Brain. It is certainly acting oddly. When she questions it, however, it insists that the men will be all right. But then it adds—"slyly," we are told—that the experience will be an interesting one for Powell and Donovan.

And indeed it is. The ship proves to be set up in such a way that they cannot communicate with Earth. The only food aboard is beans and milk. And when they pass into the space-warp which permits them to travel between the stars, the two men fall into a state that may not be death, but is weirdly hallucinatory and filled with images of death.

After their return, Susan Calvin is finally able to figure out what has happened. She says:

"Strictly speaking...this was my fault—all of it. When we first presented this problem to The Brain, as I hope some of you remember, I went to great lengths to impress upon it the importance of rejecting any item of information capable of creating a dilemma. In doing so I said something like 'Don't get excited about the death of humans. We don't mind at all. Just give the sheet back and forget it.' ...

"When that item entered its calculations which yielded the equation controlling the length of minimum interval for the interstellar jump—it meant death for humans. That's where Consolidated's machine broke down completely. But I had depressed the importance of death to The Brain—not entirely, for the First Law can never be broken—but just sufficiently so that The Brain could take a second look at the equation. Sufficiently to give it time to realize that after the interval was passed through, the men would return to life—just as the matter and energy of the ship itself would return to being. This so-called 'death,' in other words, was a strictly temporary phenomenon. You see? ...

"So he accepted the item, but not without a certain jar. Even with death temporary and its importance depressed, it was enough to unbalance him very gently. ...

"He developed a sense of humor—it's an escape, you see, a method of partial escape from reality. He became a practical joker."

In "Escape," both The Brain and the field-testing team of Powell and Donovan are pressed by circumstances into thinking in ways to which they are not accustomed.

Consolidated's Super-Thinker, which is merely an overgrown calculator, runs into the gap in continuity represented by passage through a space-warp, takes it for human death, and shorts out. But The Brain's larger sympathy for men and their goals enables him to suspend judgment and get past the point where he might otherwise have flipped a switch. In the process of dealing with this non-linear problem, he develops a whole new ability—most unmachinelike by any previous standard—to think non-logically. This is represented by his newly acquired sense of humor.

He's a child. He's a joker. He's a *person*. From this point, the robots in Asimov's stories would become increasingly humanlike until it was all but impossible to tell meat-people and metal-people apart.

Even more significant is the hallucinatory passage between the stars which Donovan and Powell experience as a kind of death and resurrection. One message of "Escape" would seem to be that if men are going to travel to the stars, it will be necessary for them to pass beyond their local Village nature—"to die"—and then to begin to think in new terms.

But the most striking instance of the change in Asimov's orientation would come in his final Foundation story of the war years—"The Mule" (*Astounding*, Nov-Dec 1945). This is the story which resulted from the editorial conference in which John Campbell had insisted that Seldon's Plan must be overturned.

If Asimov felt pressured by Campbell to write this story, the way he found to get his own back was to make it his longest yet—as long as "The Big and the Little" and "Dead Hand" put together. "The Mule" would not only be his first published serial, it would be the culmination of the ever-widening-and-altering viewpoints which were the true strength of the Foundation series.

In this story, it is another hundred years after "Dead Hand." It seems that Trantor, the capital planet of the old Galactic Empire, was long ago sacked and ruined by barbarian invaders. The Empire itself, that once-great enterprise encompassing the entire Galaxy, has been reduced to twenty agricultural worlds.

Now it is the Foundation which has become the most advanced and concentrated area of industry remaining within the entire Galaxy. But it, too, has been greatly altered by the passage of time. The Mayoralty of Terminus has become a hereditary office which is now held by a man described as "an excellent bookkeeper born wrong." And there is great strain between the greedy fat-cat manufacturers of the Foundation and the Traders who sell their goods to other worlds.

As one character—a female descendant of Hober Mallow named Bayta—declares:

"'Every vice of the Empire has been repeated in the Foundation. Inertia! Our ruling class knows one law; no change. Despotism! They know one rule; force. Maldistribution! They know one desire; to hold what is theirs.'"

Now, however, a new power has appeared on the Galactic scene— a mysterious general who calls himself the Mule. In time, we learn that he is a mutant, a superman in the new van Vogtian style who has the singular ability to control and direct the emotions of other human beings, even against their will. In the space of only a few years, he has risen from a bandit leader to become the conqueror of many worlds and a threat to the safety and independence of the Foundation itself.

In this latter day, there is one man of the Foundation, Ebling Mis, who has managed to make himself into a psychologist. Though by no means the equal of a high master of Psychohistory like the great Seldon, Mis does have enough of the old knowledge at his command to be able to predict when the climax of the next Seldon Crisis will occur, and to arrange for an audience to be present to hear Hari Seldon speak.

But what Hari Seldon's shade has to say this time comes as a considerable shock to the people who have gathered—not least because of the serene confidence with which he says it.

As though no one like the Mule had figured in his calculations, he says:

"Let us take up the problem of the moment, then. For the first time, the Foundation has been faced, or perhaps, is in the last stages of facing, civil war. Till now, the attacks from without have been adequately beaten off, and inevitably so, according to the strict laws of psycho-history. The attack at present is that of a too-undisciplined outer group of the Foundation against the too-authoritarian central government. The procedure was necessary, the result obvious."

As he speaks, it becomes clear that what Hari Seldon was able to foresee was the conflict existing between the Independent Traders and the central government of Terminus. And the conclusion that he saw as necessarily occurring was defeat for the Traders—but one which would be followed by a coalition government and an increase in democracy.

But Seldon has completely failed to anticipate the appearance of an emotion-controlling mutant conqueror like the Mule. And this significant blind spot in Seldon's omniscience fills his audience with panic and dread.

However, just as in "Nightfall," this might not necessarily be so for us as readers. Rather, it could be that after suffering the immense weight of Seldon's dead hand in Asimov's last Foundation story, what we actually feel is relief and even glee in seeing that eternal know-it-all, Hari Seldon, speaking from his wheelchair-throne of prophecy and being caught out in a whoppingly inadequate assessment.

All due respect to Seldon as a mighty mighty man, the one and only Psychohistorian, as marvelous and special in his own way as Isher/de Lany/Hedrock or the ur-Gilbert Gosseyn...but surely John Campbell was right in his editorial command: For the sake of freshness of story and the continued viability of Asimov's series, as much as for the larger cause of free action and human possibility, Seldon's Plan did have to be overturned. Yes, yes, yes, yes.

And give Asimov full credit. Having decided to go along with Campbell's suggestion, he did a thoroughgoing job of it: In his story, hardly has the image of Hari Seldon faded from view when the sound of sirens is heard. Just that quickly, Terminus has come under attack by the forces of the Mule!

Now that it is bereft of the protection hitherto afforded it by Hari Seldon's infallible foreknowledge, it seems that the Foundation—that seed of New Galactic Empire—is fair game for the mutant general. And very soon it falls.

Before it does, however, four people manage to escape from Terminus in a spaceship. These are the psychologist, Ebling Mis; Hober Mallow's descendant, Bayta; her husband Toran; and a strange, ungainly character named Magnifico Giganticus, or Bobo, once a clown for the Mule, but now a runaway.

Mis maintains that it should yet be possible to defeat the Mule by attacking his weaknesses. He says:

> "A mutant means a 'superman' to the ignoramuses of humanity. Nothing of the sort.
>
> "It's been estimated that several million mutants are born in the Galaxy every day. Of the several millions, all but one or two percent can be detected only by means of microscopes and chemistry. Of the one or two percent macromutants, that is, those with mutations detectable to the naked eye or naked mind, all but one or two percent are freaks, fit for the amusement centers, the laboratories, and death. Of the few macromutants whose differences are to the good, almost all are harmless curiosities, unusual in some single respect, normal—and often subnormal—in most others. . . .
>
> "Supposing the Mule to be a mutant then, we can assume that he has some attribute, undoubtedly mental, which can be used to conquer worlds. In other respects, he undoubtedly has his shortcomings, which we must locate. He would not be so secretive, so shy of others' eyes, if these shortcomings were not apparent and fatal."

After this shrewd analysis of the Mule and his limits, the party decides that their best hope of overturning him has to lie in finding the Second Foundation, wherever it may be, and enlisting its resources in the struggle against the mutant general. Consequently, they travel to Trantor, the old capital planet of the Empire, hoping to locate records there that will offer them clues toward discovering the nature and location of the Second Foundation.

Ebling Mis is the one person capable of solving this puzzle, but in the course of their journey he turns into a declining, dying man. Nonetheless, when they arrive, the old psychologist insists on setting himself up in the twisted ruins of Trantor, with only poor Magnifico as a companion and helper, and begins to sift through the records for information about the Second Foundation.

The first thing he becomes certain of is that while establishment of the First Foundation on Terminus was an openly known fact, all that was ever given out about the Second Foundation and its nature and purposes is that such an organization did come into existence. Mis takes this difference as meaningful. He says:

"'Its significance—and all about it—are better hidden, better obscured. Don't you see? It's the more important of the two. It's the critical one; *the one that counts!* And I've got the minutes of the Seldon Conference. The Mule hasn't won yet—'"

Now what is this that we are being told? It is the *Second Foundation* which is the one that really counts?

Does this mean that up until now we have only been being led astray in believing it is the First Foundation that is of central importance in the re-establishment of Galactic Empire. Apparently, it does.

When the failing psychologist has managed to learn more, knitting together the all-too-sparse facts and his own knowledge and insights, he explains further:

> "Foundation Number One was a world of physical scientists. It represented a concentration of the dying science of the Galaxy under the conditions necessary to make it live again. No psychologists were included. It was a peculiar distortion, and must have had a purpose. The usual explanation was that Seldon's psycho-history worked best where the individual working units—human beings—had no knowledge of what was coming, and could therefore react naturally to all situations.
>
> "Foundation Number Two was a world of mental scientists. It was the mirror image of our world. Psychology, not physics, was king."

It would seem that a revised order of power in the universe is being presented here:

At the bottom is the mere material force of the old Galactic Empire.

Above that comes the more subtle physical science commanded by the First Foundation.

That, however, can be trumped by the Mule's ability to mentally control the emotions of other people.

But he is a sport, a freak with one talent. The one thing that can possibly defeat the Mule is the advanced mental science wielded by the Second Foundation. Whoever they are. Wherever they are. Whatever they may be doing.

But where are these marvelous masters of mental power to be found?

On his deathbed, Ebling Mis calls Bayta, Toran and Magnifico to him. He tells them that he knows where the Second Foundation is. Having destroyed all his notes, he is now ready to confide the secret to them.

He whispers: "'I am convinced the Second Foundation can win, if it is not caught prematurely by the Mule. It has kept itself secret; the secrecy must be upheld; it has a purpose. You must go there; your information is vital...may make all the difference.'"

But then, just as the psychologist is opening his mouth to tell them the location of the Second Foundation, Bayta draws a blaster and shoots him dead.

She explains to Toran that the grotesque clown Magnifico is in actuality the mutant conqueror, the Mule. Ebling Mis was about to tell the secret to exactly the one person who must not be allowed to hear it.

Magnifico then admits that indeed he is the Mule. While traveling the galaxy with them, he has readied one world after another for conquest with his concerts on a "'Visi-Sonor'"—the hallucinatory sound-and-image instrument that he plays. He has held Ebling Mis under his direct control, driving him to the utter limits of his strength and health in order to gain this information so vital to his designs.

The great mistake of the mutant lay in his all-too-human frailty. Because Bayta has liked him for himself, he has left her mind uncontrolled, and that has been his undoing. But though he may have lost this time, he declares that he will yet again try to locate the Second Foundation.

But to this, Bayta replies:

"We have defeated you *entirely!* All your victories outside the Foundation count for nothing, since the Galaxy is a barbarian vacuum now. The Foundation itself is only a minor victory, since it wasn't meant to stop *your* variety of crisis. It's the Second Foundation you must beat— *the Second Foundation*—and it's the Second Foundation that will defeat you. Your only chance was to locate it and strike it before it was prepared. You won't do that now. Every minute from now on, they will be readier for you. At this moment, at this *moment*, the machinery may have started. You'll know—when it strikes you, and your short term of power will be over, and you'll be just another strutting conqueror flashing quickly and meanly across the bloody face of history."

In a final triumphant shot, Bayta assures the Mule that he will prove to be the last as well as the first of his line. And, because this is nothing less than the literal truth, the comment strikes home. As he departs, the mutant general permits himself to reveal to Bayta and Toran that one reason for the selection of his name is that he is sterile. There will be no offspring of his own kind to follow him.

The Mule may be a mutant superman, but it seems that the character and action of one very ordinary human being have been sufficient to counter all of his efforts. For all the momentary power he may wield, in the long run history will account him little more than a hiccup.

If we check to see what actual changes have been made by the conquests of the Mule, we would have to say that his brief, brilliant appearance on the galactic stage has served one purpose and one purpose only. Through his activities, he has explicitly demonstrated the limitations of the science-beyond-science of the First Foundation, and caused it to be replaced in our admirations by the transcendent mental powers commanded by the Second Foundation. He has overturned the old king, physics, and brought forth the new king, psychology.

The First Foundation is now a closed chapter—either an only partially successful experiment of some kind, or a galactic sideshow, or (just possibly) a tool in the unwitting employ of more knowing hands. From now on, the presumption in this series would be that wherever it is that the masters of mental power of the Second Foundation are located must be the place where the *real* galactic action is happening.

Here in "The Mule," the answer to the perennial problem of Lagash implicit in "Nightfall"—alteration in thought—would at last be made both explicit and universal. Henceforth, the solution to any and all challenges to the glorious future of man would have to be found in higher states of consciousness, and not in higher science.

Isaac Asimov's "The Mule" was the climactic contribution to the great imaginative work project that John Campbell had been directing since becoming editor of *Astounding.* Here was the final guarantee—or as near to that as Campbell would ever have—that determinism, even the marvelous determinism of Hari Seldon, had no ultimate grip on humanity. The future was ours to make.

The two halves of the Golden Age, with their apparently very different natures, were reconciled in "The Mule." The Foundation series had been the culmination and synthesis of all the new thought systems and laws presented in the pre-war *Astounding* and *Unknown.* But now Psychohistory—and, by extension, all the other great codifications—were subsumed within the new mysteries of the war years: non-rational consciousness and human self-transcendence.

Taken as a step-by-step whole, the Foundation series said more loudly and completely what Asimov had just said in "Escape": *If mankind wishes to overcome the limits of Village Earth and attain the stars, it will be necessary for us to change the way we think.*

As the series began, our attention was directed to the rational materialists of the original Foundation project, bent on carrying out their dream of the ultimate static codification of human knowledge, the *Encyclopedia Galactica.* Now, in "The Mule," after many changes of perspective, we are asked to see transcendence in the mind-bending abilities of a mutant and the unknown powers of the super-psychologists of the Second Foundation.

Taken altogether, this progression of viewpoints offers us an altered understanding of human consciousness. Following Asimov through his series of stories, we have to acknowledge that thought is not a static or unitary process. Human mentation is actually multi-faceted and dynamic.

If the material science of the First Foundation is not sufficient to deal with the problems of Asimov's galactic future, then by implication, the scientific understanding of our modern Western world cannot be a universally valid and adequate approach to existence, either. At best, it is just one possible state of mind among many, and by no means the most advanced.

Once this is accepted, our perspective on the whole modern Western adventure must change. No more can it be the utmost that mankind may dream and do. Now it becomes reduced to a necessary phase that we had to pass through in order to stop looking over our shoulders at transcendence in the guise of spirit and start looking ahead to transcendence perceived as higher states of thinking and being.

A phase that began around 1685 and was over after the end of 1945.

But how much the myth of transcendent science managed to accomplish while it lasted! It took us from shivering under the bedclothes at the first disconcerting intimations of non-spiritual transcendent power and it showed us the infinite possibilities of the future and the wider universe. And it told us that these might be ours if only we could learn to think in new ways.

That is the ultimate promise of the stories of the Golden Age. They tell us that if we are only able to change the way we think, and to keep changing it when that is appropriate, we may have a future of difference upon difference, we may build a world of meaning for ourselves as broad as the galaxy, and we may become a higher order of man.

Since the time in which they were written, these stories have accumulated a vast audience. A generation has grown up trying to absorb the mythic lessons of the basic works of modern science fiction.

The world-that-is continues to be dominated by the values and accomplishments of the old rational scientific order. But, in terms of our new best knowledge, these seem increasingly hollow and inadequate.

And, in the meantime, throughout Western society, there are people who by their conduct and goals are attempting to bring into being a new world of ecological wholeness and higher consciousness. If we judge their efforts by the story that has been told in this book, we have to believe that they will have their opportunity to see their dreams made real...and also to discover their limitations.

Afterword

"The Mule" marks the end of science fiction, and the end of our story of the myth of science fiction.

But, of course, it was nothing like the end of SF, the re-oriented mythic stream. That has continued to this day, constantly changing and developing.

The imaginative ground assumed in this latter-day SF—which has continued to be known as science fiction out of habit, even though it is no longer about transcendent science—has been the territory staked out in the Golden Age *Astounding* and *Unknown*: the de Campian multiverse, the Heinleinian future, the Asimovian galaxy, and the van Vogtian sense of the potential of humanity.

But in this new SF of the Atomic Age, the Village and the World Beyond the Hill would no longer be separate. They would be intermingled, so that utter strangeness might appear suddenly in our midst, and we also might find elements of familiarity at the most remote removes of existence.

And the subject matter of this new myth would be transcendent consciousness.

As usual, however, that wasn't clear to anyone in 1945.

All that was clear was that the world was changing with great rapidity.

Isaac Asimov finished "The Mule" shortly after the surrender of Germany in the middle of May 1945. A little more than two months later, while van Vogt's *The World of Null-A* was in serialization, the first atomic bomb was dropped on Japan. And that was the end of World War II.

George O. Smith reached John Campbell first with the news that an Atom Bomb had been used to destroy the city of Hiroshima. And the editor's immediate reply was: "'Oh, my God! It's started.'"

The new world made by science fiction—the world of nuclear

648

bombs and atomic power, jet planes and rocket ships, television and computers—was upon us. Of all the items on Campbell's science-fictional agenda, control of the atom, with its nerves, deadlines, blowups and unsatisfactory solutions, was the one that his writers had dealt with least well. Now it was an actuality, and he wasn't ready yet. He wasn't *finished*.

With the dropping of the Bomb, the transcendent had been made real, and in the process the factors that had made the great mythic moment of the Golden Age possible had been decisively and permanently altered. As rapidly as Campbell's writers had come together in 1939, they now scattered in every direction, seeking to pick up the thread of long-interrupted lives and trying to work out for themselves where and how they fit into the new post-war world.

Each of them did what seemed appropriate:

Jack Williamson, that slow-maturing adaptable man, returned from army service in the South Pacific. He would marry a divorced woman he had known since primary school, and eventually go back to college after more than twenty years away, work his way through to a Ph.D. in English, and begin a new career as a university professor. All the while, he would continue to write SF stories.

After the war, L. Sprague de Camp remained in Philadelphia. More than any other writer, he missed *Unknown*. The best he was able to do for *Astounding* was a relatively weak story series in which a future Brazil has established a highly tentative form of interstellar space travel and placed outposts on planets of nearby suns. His main energies were reserved for a mammoth book he was writing debunking spirit-based belief systems.

Robert Heinlein returned to California. Not only did he not go back to writing for Campbell, he also neither completed the great central gap in the Future History nor faced up to the problem of coping with the superiority of higher aliens. Instead, he wrote essays warning of nuclear peril, which he was unable to get published. He wrote simple science fiction stories for the *Saturday Evening Post* which both paid him well and allowed him to carry the SF point of view to a wider public. And for youngsters, he wrote a series of juvenile science fiction novels which summarized and encapsulated the triumphs of Techno Age science fiction for a new audience.

A.E. van Vogt moved from Canada to Los Angeles—a new city in a new country—at the end of 1944. Here he wrote *The World of Null-A*. But after that was done, he fell into an inability to write that lasted for almost a year. It may have been that he took a wrong mental turning. The stories he wrote when he broke through his block lacked the fire and power of his wartime work. And they looked for the future of man in the genetic superman rather than in the superman-by-education.

Henry Kuttner and C.L. Moore went back home to California, too. A. Merritt had died in 1943, and they now began to write Merritt-influenced otherworld fantasies for *Startling Stories*, the companion magazine of *Thrilling Wonder*. And, for *Astounding*, as Lewis Padgett, they wrote short novels of human madness and nuclear holocaust.

With the conflict over, Isaac Asimov was no longer an essential war worker. He was drafted into the Army. When he got out again, he returned to Columbia University, where he finished his Ph.D. in chemistry. The stories he wrote for *Astounding* in his leisure time were accounts of ever-more-humanlike robots, until at last one secretly serves in the job of World Co-ordinator, and of a series of searches for the psychic masters of the Second Foundation.

As for John Campbell, he took to his basement, his lifelong refuge in times of trouble. His most recent hobby was experiments in hi-fi sound reproduction, which at this early stage of the game chiefly consisted of the attainment of maximum possible volume. Campbell turned the music way up loud and wondered just what was to be done about the atomic demon which science fiction had dreamed into being.

How was humanity to be saved from this out-of-control monster it had made?

If mankind destroyed itself tomorrow in a ball of incandescent flame, how were we ever to get to the stars and fulfill our higher destiny?

It seemed to Campbell that some answer had to be found to the great gap between the awesome new power at our command and the limitations of present human thought and behavior. And so he wondered about ways of engineering the human psyche so as to avert the disaster that he saw as imminent.

When the choice had to be made, it was universal operating principles that Campbell chose instead of the attainment of higher states of consciousness. And that was the point at which John Campbell found his imaginative limit.

In the meantime, the transcendent spirit underlying SF moved on. . . .

But that is another story to tell.

THIS BOOK WOULD NOT HAVE BEEN POSSIBLE WITHOUT

All the men and women who have written and read and loved SF: This story is yours, with thanks.

Our parents—Alexis and Lucie Panshin, and Ralph and Delle Seidman: Thank you for your patience, your support and your love.

The pioneers of science fiction study, bibliography and criticism. In particular, Sam Moskowitz, Donald H. Tuck, Donald B. Day, and those associated with Advent:Publishers of Chicago: Thank you all. Without your work as a foundation, this book would have been inconceivable.

The teachers from whom we learned context, method and perspective for our own approach to the study of science fiction; especially John W. Campbell, Joseph Campbell, Idries Shah and J.R.R. Tolkien: Our thanks can never be sufficient to the debt we owe them.

The many, many people, beginning with Dean McLaughlin and culminating with Paul Crawford, who through the years recounted some anecdote, shared a letter or an unpublished manuscript, handed us a speech, sent us a crucial fan magazine article, or shared research: Thank you, everyone. As you can see, it has all contributed to the story.

The libraries we have consulted—The M.I.T. Science Fiction Society, Cornell University, and Syracuse University, with special gratitude to the Bucks County Free Library of Bucks County, Pennsylvania for all the books that it has located for us in libraries from Texas to Connecticut, and to the Rare Book Collection at Temple University, and its curator, Thomas Whitehead, for the access we have been afforded to research materials: Thank you.

The writers, editors, agents and scholars who read part or all of this book in manuscript and offered us encouragement, supplied information, caught mistakes and cast useful doubt: Thanks are due in particular to Isaac Asimov, Arthur C. Clarke, L. Sprague de Camp, David Hartwell, Don Maass, Hank Stine, Leon Stover and Jack Williamson.

Our friends—in particular Frank Lunney, and Ted Wachtel and the Community Service Foundation—who at various times offered us work, money, food, typing paper, photocopying, moral support and other necessities: Thank you, and thank you again.

Thanks are due to each other, since neither of us could have written this book alone. We are grateful that we were granted the opportunity: Thanks be.

References and Notes

CHAPTER 1

THE MYSTERY OF SCIENCE FICTION

2 "We really: Hugo Gernsback, "Editorially Speaking," *Amazing Stories*, September 1926, p. 483.   **2** These evocative words are related: Definitions and derivations used in this analysis from *Webster's New World Dictionary of the American Language, College Edition* (Cleveland and New York: World, 1960).

CHAPTER 2

A MYTHIC FALL

7 "By 'scientifiction': Hugo Gernsback, "A New Sort of Magazine," *Amazing Stories*, April 1926, p. 3.   **9** "they had: Madame d'Aulnoy, "Princess Rosette," in Andrew Lang, ed., *The Red Fairy Book* (New York: Dover, 1966), p. 89.
12 "I waked: Horace Walpole, quoted by W.S. Lewis, "Introduction," in Horace Walpole, *The Castle of Otranto* (London: Oxford, 1964), p. ix.   **12** "I gave: Ibid, p. x.   **13** "an enormous: Horace Walpole, *The Castle of Otranto*, p. 17.   **13** "A clap: Ibid, p. 108.   **13** "which wants: Horace Walpole, quoted by Lewis, op. cit., p. x.   **13** "The following: Horace Walpole, op. cit., p. 3.   **14** "an artful: Ibid.   **14** "The solution: Ibid, p. 4.   **15** "It was: Ibid, p. 7.   **15** *The Castle of Otranto* is given credit: entry under Walpole, *The Encyclopaedia Britannica*, Eleventh Edition (New York: Encyclopaedia Britannica, 1911, Vol. 28, p. 289.   **16** "within the: Clara Reeve, quoted in Lord Ernle, *The Light Reading of Our Ancestors* (London:Hutchinson, 1927), p. 290.

CHAPTER 3

THE NEW PROMETHEUS

22 "Some volumes: Mary Wollstonecraft Shelley, "Introduction (to the 1831 edition)," in *Frankenstein, or the Modern Prometheus* (New York: Collier, n.d., but published 1961), p. 8.   **22** "I busied: Ibid, p. 9.   **23** "poor Polidori": Ibid.   **23** "Many and: Ibid, p. 10.   **23** "When I: Ibid.   **24** "Swift as: Ibid, p. 11.   **25** "It was: Mary Wollstonecraft Shelley, *Frankenstein*, p. 48.   **25** "I see: Ibid, p. 45.   **26** "I had: Ibid, p. 40.   **26** "'The ancient: Ibid, pp. 40-41.   **27** In a preface—written as Mary later recalled, by Percy, Mary

Wollstonecraft Shelley, "Introduction (to the 1831 edition)," in *Frankenstein*, p. 11.   **27** "The event: Percy Bysshe Shelley (?), "Preface," in Mary Wollstonecraft Shelley, *Frankenstein*, p. 5.   **30** "the most: Mary Wollstonecraft Shelley, *Frankenstein*, p. 189.   **32** "It was: Fitz-James O'Brien, "The Diamond Lens," in H. Bruce Franklin, ed., *Future Perfect: American Science Fiction of the Nineteenth Century*, Rev. Ed. (New York: Oxford, 1978), p. 346.   **32** "They say: Ibid, p. 351.   **33** "density is: Edgar Allan Poe, "The Unparalleled Adventure of One Hans Pfaall," in *The Complete Edgar Allan Poe Tales* (New York: Avenel Books, 1981), p. 26.   **33** "In 'Hans: Ibid, p. 55.   **34** "'a strange: Jules Verne, *From the Earth to the Moon* in Walter James Miller, ed., *The Annotated Jules Verne: From the Earth to the Moon* (New York: Crowell, 1978), p. 13.   **34** "'Hurray for: Ibid.   **34** "the incomprehensible: Edgar Allan Poe, op. cit., p. 50.   **34** "those dark: Ibid.   **34** "manufactured entirely: Ibid, p. 22.   **34** "tasteless, but: Ibid, p. 26.   **34** "instantaneously fatal: Ibid.   **35** "Many unusual: Edgar Allan Poe, *The Narrative of Arthur Gordon Pym of Nantucket*, in *The Complete Edgar Allan Poe Tales*, p. 700. **35** "And now: Ibid, p. 702.   **35** "sudden and: Ibid, p. 703.

CHAPTER 4

INTO THE UNKNOWN

38 "From now: Jules Verne, quoted in Russell Freedman, *Jules Verne: Portrait of a Prophet* (New York?: Holiday House, 1965), p. 25.   **39** "The only: Ibid, p. 52.   **40** "Science-Fiction": William Wilson, quoted from *A Little Earnest Book Upon a Great Old Subject* (1851), in Brian M. Stableford, "William Wilson's Prospectus for Science Fiction: 1851," in *Foundation*, No. 10, June 1976, p. 6.   **40** "the revealed: Ibid, pp. 9-10.   **40** "prophetic vision": Hugo Gernsback, "A New Sort of Magazine," *Amazing Stories*, April 1926, p. 3. **40** "the amazing: Hugo Gernsback, "Editorially Speaking" *Amazing Stories*, September 1926, p. 483.   **40** "lingering on: Jules Verne, quoted in Freedman, op. cit., p. 61.   **40** "a pale: Ibid, p. 57.   **40** "'I have: Ibid.   **40** "'We shall: Ibid, p. 60.   **42** "Formerly, to: Ibid, p. 100.   **42** "discoveries are: Ibid, p. 104.   **43** "I am: quoted in Peter Costello, *Jules Verne: Inventor of Science Fiction* (New York: Scribners, 1978), p. 72.   **44** "The most: Jules Verne, "The Bizarre Genius of Edgar Poe," in Peter Haining, ed., *The Jules Verne Companion* (New York: Baronet, 1979), p. 28.   **45** "I try: Mary Wollstonecraft Shelley, *Frankenstein* (New York: Collier, n.d.), p. 13.   **46** "whose dusky: Edgar Allan Poe, "The Unparalleled Adventure of One Hans Pfaall," in *The Complete Edgar Allan Poe Tales* (New York: Avenel Books, 1981), p. 44. **46** "In recent: Jules Verne, quoted in Costello, op. cit., p. 82.   **47** "Descend into: Jules Verne, *Journey to the Centre of the Earth* (New York: Penguin, 1965), p. 32.   **48** "It was: Ibid, pp. 163-164.   **49** "I gazed: Ibid, p. 165. **49** "prehistoric daydream": Ibid, p. 179.   **49** "The whole: Ibid.   **49** "brief hallucination": Ibid.   **50** "That's wonderful!": Ibid, p. 170.   **50** "No, it's: Ibid.   **50** "So that: Ibid, p. 218.   **50** "who for: Ibid.   **50** "Now that: Ibid, p. 219.   **53** "Instead of: Jules Verne, *Around the Moon* in *The Omnibus Jules Verne* (Philadelphia and New York: Lippincott, n.d.), p. 768.   **55** "Take the: Hugo Gernsback, "A New Sort of Magazine," *Amazing Stories*, April 1926, p. 3.   **55** "The Italians: Jules Verne, quoted in "Jules Verne Re-Visited" by Robert H. Sherard, in Haining, op. cit., p. 60.   **56** "Take for: Jules Verne, quoted in Costello, op. cit., pp. 186-187.   **56** "Before going: Jules Verne,

20,000 Leagues Under the Sea (New York: Bantam, 1962), p. 82.   **57** "There was: Ibid, p. 86.   **57** "'Captain,' I: Ibid, p. 84.   **58** "It seemed: Ibid, p. 365. **58** "Navel of: Ibid, p. 369.   **58** "Thus ended: Ibid, p. 370.

CHAPTER 5
THE HIGHER POWERS OF SCIENCE

69 "looking like: Edward S. Ellis, *The Huge Hunter, or The Steam Man of the Prairies*, in E.F. Bleiler, ed., *Eight Dime Novels* (New York: Dover, 1974), p. 108. **69** "'the ould: Ibid.   **69** "No wonder: Ibid.   **69** "...their previous: Ibid, p. 115.   **70** "It required: Ibid, p. 109.   **70** "a mere: Jules Verne, quoted in Peter Costello, *Jules Verne: Inventor of Science Fiction* (New York: Scribners, 1978), p. 187.   **70** It has been estimated that 75% were the work of one man: our information about Luis Philip Senarens is derived from Sam Moskowitz, "Ghost of Prophecies Past, or, Frank Reade, Jr., and 'Forgotten Chapters in American History,'" in Moskowitz, *Explorers of the Infinite* (Cleveland and New York: World, 1963).   **71** "The Case of Summerfield": our information about this story and its author is derived from Sam Moskowitz, *Science Fiction in Old San Francisco, Vol. I: History of the Movement* (West Kingston, R.I.: Grant, 1980), pp. 43-45.   **72** "held at: entry under Charles Cornwallis Chesney, *The Encyclopaedia Britannica*, Eleventh Edition (New York: Encyclopaedia Britannica, 1911), Vol. 6, p. 93.   **73** "Science fiction: Hugo Gernsback, "The Prophets of Doom" (unpublished address dated October 25, 1963), p. 1.   **74** "But what: Sir Thomas More, *The "Utopia" and the History of Edward V* (London: Walter Scott, n.d.), pp. 81-82. Scyllas, Celenos, and Loestrygonians are all references to monsters found in *The Odyssey* and *The Aeniad*.   **75** *Memoirs of the Year 2440*: our information about this story and contemporary reactions to it is derived from I.F. Clarke, *The Pattern of Expectation* (London: Cape, 1979), pp. 26-28.   **77** "What Happened After the Battle of Dorking": our information about this story is derived from an unpublished book-length manuscript by Brian M. Stableford on the literature of the scientific imagination.   **78** "to exhibit: entry under Edward George Earle Lytton, Bulwer-Lytton, 1st Baron Lytton, *The Encyclopaedia Britannica*, Eleventh Edition (New York: Encyclopaedia Britannica, 1911), Vol. 17, p. 186. **79** "So important: The Right Hon. Lord Lytton, *The Coming Race* (Quakertown, Pa.: Beverly Hall, 1973), p. 40.   **79** "I should: Ibid, pp. 31-32.   **80** "In another: Ibid, p. 84.   **80** "on the Darwinian: Bulwer-Lytton, quoted in I.F. Clarke, op. cit., p. 143.   **80** "And now: Lytton, op. cit., pp. 10-11. **83** "God's Will," etc.: Emerson M. Clymer, "Foreword," in Lytton, op. cit. p. v.   **84** like the Sacred Locomotive: the work referred to is William R. Bradshaw, *The Goddess of Atvatabar* (1892).

CHAPTER 6
A UNIVERSE GROWN ALIEN

86 "No one: H.G. Wells, *The War of the Worlds*, in H.G. Wells, *Seven Famous Novels* (New York: Knopf, 1934), p. 265.   **91** "beyond all: H.G. Wells, *Experiment in Autobiography* (New York: Macmillan, 1934), p. 161.   **93** "an artificial: Edward Page Mitchell, "The Ablest Man in the World," in Edward Page Mitchell, *The Crystal Man: Landmark Science Fiction*, ed. by Sam Moskowitz (Garden City, N.Y.: Doubleday, 1973), pp. 37-38.   **93** "Social progress:

Thomas Huxley, "Evolution and Ethics," abridged, in Eugen Weber, ed., *The Western Tradition: From the Enlightenment to the Atomic Age* (Boston: Heath, 1959), p. 646.   **93** "Let us: Ibid, p. 647.   **94** "luminiferous ether": The concept of the ether was the product of Newton's contemporary, Christiaan Huygens (1629-95).   **96** "The movement: Edward Bellamy, *Looking Backward* (New York: Magnum/Lancer, 1968), p. 60.   **97** "'...To speak: Ibid, p. 68.   **97** "a Cockney: William Morris, quoted in I. F. Clarke, *The Pattern of Expectation* (London: Cape, 1979), p. 166.   **98** "Somehow, every: Mark Twain, *A Connecticut Yankee in King Arthur's Court* (New York: Bantam, 1981), p. 240.   **99** "I started: H. Rider Haggard, *She*, in *Works of H. Rider Haggard* (New York: Black, 1928), p. 256.   **100** "Science is: H.G. Wells, "The Rediscovery of the Unique," quoted in Norman and Jeanne MacKenzie, *H. G. Wells* (New York: Simon and Schuster, 1973), p. 56.   **102** "The Education: H.G. Wells, *Experiment in Autobiography*, p. 426.   **102** "New books: Ibid, p. 427.   **102** "I was: Ibid, p. 428.   **103** "There grows: H.G. Wells, "The Man of the Year Million," in Peter Haining, ed., *The H. G. Wells Scrapbook* (New York: Potter, 1978), p. 30.   **104** "We think: H.G. Wells, "The Extinction of Man," quoted in James Gunn, *Alternate Worlds: The Illustrated History of Science Fiction* (Englewood Cliffs, N.J.: Prentice-Hall, 1975), p. 92.   **105** "I touched: Lewis Hind, *Authors and I*, quoted in MacKenzie, op. cit, p. 105.   **105** "The Time: H.G. Wells, *The Time Machine*, in Wells, *Seven Famous Novels*, p. 3.   **105** "'There are: Ibid, p. 4.   **106** "a glittering: Ibid, p. 6.   **106** "Parts were: Ibid, p. 9.   **106** "I do: Jules Verne, quoted in "Jules Verne Re-Visited" by Robert H. Sherard, in Peter Haining, ed., *The Jules Verne Companion* (New York: Baronet, 1979), pp. 59-60.   **107** "There is: Jules Verne, quoted in Peter Costello, *Jules Verne: Inventor of Science Fiction* (New York: Scribners, 1978), p. 186.   **107** "I have: Ibid, pp. 186-187.   **108** "great and: H.G. Wells, *The Time Machine*, p. 15.   **108** "a profoundly: Ibid, p. 19.   **108** "What might: Ibid, p. 16.   **108** "The air: Ibid, p. 23.   **108** "Face this: Ibid, p. 29.   **109** "Gradually, the: Ibid, p. 34.   **109** "So, in: Ibid, p. 36.   **109** "frail creatures: Ibid, p. 45.   **109** "the white: Ibid.   **110** "Did he: Ibid, p. 66.   **113** "a beautiful: Edward Page Mitchell, "The Balloon Tree," in Mitchell, *The Crystal Man*, p. 21.   **113** "Migratory Tree": Ibid, p. 18.   **114** "that men: J.-H. Rosny aine, "The Shapes" ("Les Xipehuz"), in Damon Knight, ed., *One Hundred Years of Science Fiction* (New York: Simon and Schuster, 1968), p. 103.   **114** "Those who: H.G. Wells, *The War of the Worlds*, in Wells, *Seven Famous Novels*, p. 276.   **115** "octopuses": Ibid, p. 288.   **115** "huge, round: Ibid, p. 348.   **115** "hands": Ibid.   **115** "eliminated them: Ibid, p. 351.   **115** "slain by: Ibid, p. 380.   **116** "Dim and: Ibid, p. 387.

CHAPTER 7
THE RELATIVITY OF MAN

119 "opaque to: H.G. Wells, *The First Men in the Moon*, in H.G. Wells, *Seven Famous Novels* (New York: Knopf, 1934), p. 399.   **119** "It's this: Ibid, p. 447.   **119** "insurmountable": Ibid, p. 448.   **121** "In brief: H.G. Wells, *Experiment in Autobiography* (New York: Macmillan, 1934), pp. 182-183.   **122** "Would it: Bertrand Russell, "A Free Man's Worship," in Bertrand Russell, *Mysticism and Logic* (Garden City, N.Y.: Doubleday Anchor, 1957), p. 44.   **123** "the cruel: Ibid.   **123** "And God: Ibid, p. 45.   **123** "Such, in:

Ibid, pp. 45-46. **124** "Brief and: Bertrand Russell, op. cit., p. 54. **125** "It must: H.G. Wells, *The Island of Dr. Moreau,* in Wells, *Seven Famous Novels,* p. 156. **125** "the little: Lord Dunsany, quoted by Lin Carter, ed., in his Introduction to his selected anthology of Dunsany stories, *At the Edge of the World* (New York: Ballantine, 1970), p. viii. **125** "the Third: Lord Dunsany, as in his collection, *Tales of the Third Hemisphere* (Boston: Luce, 1919). **126** "'Once I: Lord Dunsany, "The Hashish Man," in Dunsany, *At the Edge of the World,* p. 121. **128** "Let me live out my years: Jack London, *Martin Eden* (New York: Review of Reviews, 1912), opposite copyright page. This is an unacknowledged quotation from the poem "Let Me Live Out My Years" by John G. Neihardt. **129** "soft and: Jack London, "The Scarlet Plague," in Groff Conklin, ed., *Omnibus of Science Fiction* (New York: Crown, 1952), p. 515. **129** "The gunpowder: Ibid, p. 523. **130** who was heavily influenced by London: our information about the influence of London on Burroughs is derived from Irwin Porges, *Edgar Rice Burroughs: The Man Who Created Tarzan* (New York: Ballantine, 1976), pp. 316, 437-438. Within a month of London's death, Burroughs proposed to write a biography of London. **132** the pseudonym Normal Bean: Edgar Rice Burroughs, discussed in Porges, pp. 29, 32. **132** "Uncle Jack": Edgar Rice Burroughs, *A Princess of Mars* (New York: Ballantine, 1973), p. v. **133** "I am: Ibid, p. 11. **133** "a typical: Ibid, p. v. **133** "I could: Ibid, p. 77. **134** "As I: Ibid, p. 20. **134** "I was: Ibid. **135** "During the: Ibid, p. 62. **136** "She was: Ibid, p. 46. **137** "As he: Ibid, p. 29. **138** "'You are: Ibid, p. 90. **139** "...In all: Ibid, p. 14.

CHAPTER 8

THE DEATH OF THE SOUL

142 "a great: entry under Wells, *The Encyclopaedia Britannica,* Eleventh Edition (New York: Encyclopaedia Britannica, 1911), Vol. 28, p. 514. **143** "'Hello,' said: Perley Poore Sheehan, *The Abyss of Wonders* (Reading, Pa.: Polaris Press, 1953), p. 188. **144** the most significant and influential was A. Merritt: our account of Merritt's life is primarily based on materials contained in Sam Moskowitz, ed., *A. Merritt: Reflections in the Moon Pool* (Philadelphia: Oswald Train, 1985). **145** "our world: A. Merritt, *The Moon Pool* (New York: Collier, 1966), p. 204. **146** "In this: A. Merritt, *The Metal Monster* (New York: Avon, 1966), p. 9. **147** "gained a: A. Merritt, "A. Merritt—His Life and Times," by A. Merritt and Jack Chapman Miske, in Moskowitz, ed., *A. Merritt: Reflections in the Moon Pool,* p. 344. **148** "garden of: Ibid, p. 345. **148** "which was: A. Merritt, letter to Wallace Palmer, dated January 14, 1929, in Moskowitz, ed., op. cit. **149** "'I think: A. Merritt, *The Moon Pool,* p. 188. **149** "'The Englishman: Ibid. **151** "Consciousness itself: A. Merritt, *The Metal Monster,* p. 116. **152** "For in: Ibid, p. 238. **155** "'Fact! sanity!: James Branch Cabell, *Jurgen: A Comedy of Justice* (New York: McBride, 1922), p. 138. **158** "Serpentine proceeded: H.G. Wells, *Men Like Gods,* in *28 Science Fiction Stories of H.G. Wells* (New York: Dover, 1952), pp. 39-40. **158** "And yet: Ibid, p. 263. **161** "center for: Eugene Zamiatin, *We* (New York: Dutton, n.d.), p. 86. **161** "I am: Ibid, p. 217. **161** "'sole purpose: Karel Capek, *R. U. R.,* in Bennett A. Cerf and Van H. Cartmell, eds., *Sixteen Famous European Plays* (New York: Modern Library, 1943), p. 741. **161** "'a gasoline: Ibid, p. 742. **161** "'Oh! Perhaps: Ibid. **161** "'No. The: Ibid. **164** "From a wild: Edgar Allan Poe, "Dreamland," in *Great Tales and Poems of Edgar Allan*

Poe (New York: Washington Square/Pocket Books, 1940), p. 405.   **166** "What do: H.P. Lovecraft, "From Beyond," in H.P. Lovecraft, *The Doom That Came to Sarnoth* (New York: Ballantine, 1971), p. 87.   **166** "The most: H.P. Lovecraft, "The Call of Cthulhu," in H.P. Lovecraft, *The Colour Out of Space and others* (New York: Lancer, 1964), p. 45.

CHAPTER 9
EVOLUTION OR EXTINCTION

168 "new sort: Hugo Gernsback, "A New Sort of Magazine," *Amazing Stories*, April 1926, p. 3.   **169** "extremely easy: Charles Agnew MacLean, editor of *Popular Magazine*, quoted in Irwin Porges, *Edgar Rice Burroughs: The Man Who Created Tarzan* (New York: Ballantine, 1976), p. 637.   **169** "too bizarre: Ibid.   **170** "If we: Hugo Gernsback, "Fiction Versus Facts," *Amazing Stories*, July 1926, p. 291.   **172** "Not only: Hugo Gernsback, "A New Sort of Magazine," p. 3.   **172** "The plain: Hugo Gernsback, "Editorially Speaking," *Amazing Stories*, September 1926, p. 483.   **173** "We knew: Ibid.   **174** "The man: Hugo Gernsback, "Science Wonder Stories," *Science Wonder Stories*, June 1929, p. 5.   **175** "Extravagant Fiction: slogan printed on the editorial page of each issue of *Amazing Stories* beginning with April 1926, p. 3.   **175** coined the word television: This is stated by Sam Moskowitz in his essay, "Hugo Gernsback: 'Father of Science Fiction,'" in Moskowitz, *Explorers of the Infinite* (Cleveland and New York: World, 1963), p. 232. The article by Gernsback, published in *Modern Electrics*, was entitled "Television and the Telphot."   **176** "F.R.S.": *Amazing Stories*, April 1926, p. 3. That Gernsback was a Fellow of the Royal Society was denied in a letter to Alexei Panshin from A.J. Clark, Deputy Librarian of the Royal Society, dated 8 October 1985.   **176** invent the word *scientifiction*: Stated by Hugo Gernsback in his editorial, "$300.00 Prize Contest," *Amazing Stories*, April 1928, p. 5.   **177** "excellent science: introduction to Edgar Rice Burroughs, *The Master Mind of Mars*, in *Amazing Stories Annual*, 1927, p. 7.   **178** "Hugo the: H.P. Lovecraft, quoted in L. Sprague de Camp, *Lovecraft: A Biography* (Garden City, New York: Doubleday, 1975), p. 282.   **178** In February 1929, his printer: this account of the bankruptcy of Hugo Gernsback's Experimenter Publishing Co. is largely based on Tom Perry, "An Amazing Story: Experimenter in Bankruptcy," in *Amazing Science Fiction*, May 1978, p. 101.   **179** "science fiction": this phrase was used in *Science Wonder Stories* from the first issue in June 1929. See Sam Moskowitz, "How Science Fiction Got Its Name," in Moskowitz, op. cit., p. 322.   **179** "Prophetic Fiction: slogan printed on the editorial page of each issue of *Science Wonder Stories* beginning with June 1929, p. 5.   **179** "The Future: slogan printed on the editorial page of each issue of *Air Wonder Stories* beginning with July 1929, p. 5.   **180** *"Amazing Stories!*: Harry Bates, "Editorial Number One," in Alva Rogers, *A Requiem for Astounding* (Chicago: Advent, 1964), p. x.   **181** "thought variant": F. Orlin Tremaine, quoted in Alva Rogers, op. cit., p. 18.   **182** In January, *Startling Stories* was created: Henceforth, for the sake of simplicity, magazine issues will be dated by their cover or off-sale date rather than their actual date of publication, generally one to three months earlier.   **183** "Either you: Hugo Gernsback, "The Prophets of Doom" (unpublished address dated October 25, 1963), p. 2.   **185** "To-day there: Sir James Jeans, *The Mysterious Universe* (New York: Macmillan, 1930), p. 158.   **185** "Quantum mechanics: Albert Einstein, letter to

Max Born dated December 12, 1926, quoted in Ronald W. Clark, *Einstein: The Life and Times* (New York and Cleveland: World, 1971), p. 340.   **185** "Now my: J.B.S. Haldane, *Possible Worlds* (New York and London: Harper, 1928), p. 298.   **188** "one morning: J.R.R. Tolkien, *The Hobbit* (Boston and New York: Houghton Mifflin, 1938), p. 13.

CHAPTER 10
MASTERY OF TIME AND SPACE

193 "Wells has: Hugo Gernsback, introduction to H.G. Wells, *The War of the Worlds*, in *Amazing Stories*, August 1927, p. 423.   **199** "A being: Olaf Stapledon, *Last and First Men*, in Stapledon, *Last and First Men & Star Maker* (New York: Dover, 1968), p. 13.   **199** "Our aim: Ibid, p. 9.   **200** "ethereal vibrations: Ibid, p. 236.   **200** "Drenched for: Ibid, p. 243.   **200** "general spiritual: Ibid.   **201** "Recently an: Ibid, pp. 217-218.   **201** "But one: Ibid, p. 246.   **204** The principal author of *The Skylark of Space*: our account of the life of E.E. Smith is primarily based on the chapter on Smith in Sam Moskowitz, *Seekers of Tomorrow* (Cleveland and New York: World, 1966).   **207** *The Skylark of Space* begins: *The Skylark of Space* has appeared in a number of variant forms. Where possible, reference is made to the most familiar edition, the Pyramid paperback, which is somewhat abridged. Where necessary, however, reference is made to the original magazine serial.   **207** "Petrified with: E.E. Smith, *The Skylark of Space* (New York: Pyramid, 1958), p. 5.   **207** "the wide: Ibid, p. 7.   **207** "the firm: Ibid.   **207** "'That bath: E.E. Smith and Lee Hawkins Garby, *The Skylark of Space*, in *Amazing Stories*, August 1928, p. 392.   **208** "'She flies!': Ibid, p. 414.   **208** "'A fellow: Ibid, p. 392.   **208** "'You are: E.E. Smith, *Skylark Three* (New York: Pyramid, 1968), p. 197.   **209** "the object: E.E. Smith, *The Skylark of Space* (New York: Pyramid, 1958), p. 37.   **210** "At one: Ibid, p. 85.   **210** "The scene: Ibid, pp. 87-88.   **211** "Suddenly the: Ibid, p. 88.   **211** "nothings": Ibid, p. 90.   **211** "'Keep on: Ibid, p. 92.   **212** "'A strange: Smith and Garby, *The Skylark of Space*, *Amazing Stories*, September 1928, p. 548.   **212** "Well clear: E.E. Smith, *Skylark Three*, p. 26.   **212** "'I'm scared: Ibid, p. 200.   **213** "'Know you: Ibid, pp. 51-52.   **214** "'Doctor Seaton: Ibid, p. 107.   **215** "a genus: Philip Francis Nowlan, *Armageddon 2419 A.D.* (New York: Ace, 1972), p. 191.   **215** "a vacuum: Ibid.   **216** "the most: Ibid, p. 189.   **216** "My formative: Edmond Hamilton, quoted in the introduction to Hamilton, "The Pro," in *The Magazine of Fantasy and Science Fiction*, October 1964, p. 21.   **217** "the gigantic: Edmond Hamilton, "Crashing Suns," in Hamilton, *Crashing Suns* (New York: Ace, 1965), p. 8.   **217** "'For the: Ibid, p. 11.   **217** "'If we: Ibid, p. 13.   **217** "etheric vibrations": Ibid, p. 12.   **218** "even more: Ibid, p. 15.   **218** "They were: Ibid, pp. 24-25.   **218** "'It was: Ibid, p. 54.

CHAPTER 11
THE LAWS OF CHANCE

222 "*The Skylark*: John W. Campbell, in Dick Eney, ed., *The Proceedings; Discon* (Chicago: Advent, 1965), p. 124.   **223** "What use: John W. Campbell, *Invaders from the Infinite* (New York: Ace, 1961), pp. 152-153.   **224** "Tellus":

E.E. Smith, *Galactic Patrol* (New York: Pyramid, 1964), p. 42, et passim. Tellus was the Roman goddess of the earth. The adjective "Tellurian" is used as early as page 9 of the novel.   **224** "lenticular jewel": Ibid, p. 11.   **225** "'The Lens: Ibid, p. 15.   **226** "the Savage": Aldous Huxley, *Brave New World* (New York: Bantam, 1968), p. 104, et passim.   **226** "The supernormals: Olaf Stapledon, *Odd John* (New York: Berkley, 1965), p. 190.   **226** "The word: Ibid, p. 7.   **226** "Despite the: E.E. Smith, *Gray Lensman* (New York: Pyramid, 1965), p. 45.   **227** "I sometimes: Clifford D. Simak, quoted in Sam Moskowitz, *Seekers of Tomorrow* (Cleveland and New York: World, 1966), pp. 268-269.   **229** "He-Who-Came-Out-of-the-Cosmos": Clifford D. Simak, "The World of the Red Sun," in Isaac Asimov, ed., *Before the Golden Age* (Garden City, N.Y.: Doubleday, 1974), p. 206.   **230** "150,000,000 galaxies: Donald Wandrei, "Colossus," in Isaac Asimov, ed., op. cit., p. 461.   **230** *"He had*: Ibid, p. 482.   **230** "'I do: Ibid, pp. 487-488.   **230** "Her lips: Ibid, p. 497.   **231** "Hawk Carse: Anthony Gilmore, "Hawk Carse," in *Astounding Stories*, November 1931, p. 166.   **232** "Sometimes I: H.P. Lovecraft, "The Whisperer in Darkness," in Lovecraft, *The Colour Out of Space and others* (New York: Lancer, 1964), p. 150.   **232** "an older: C.L. Moore, "Shambleau," in Moore, *The Best of C.L. Moore* (New York: Ballantine, 1975), p. 29.   **233** "He knew: E.E. Smith, *Galactic Patrol* (New York: Pyramid, 1966), p. 223.   **234** "Life there: Jack Williamson, *The Early Williamson* (Garden City, N.Y.: Doubleday, 1975), p. x.   **234** "Here is: Jack Williamson, "Scientifiction, Searchlight of Science," in *The Early Williamson*, p. xvi.   **235** "the Mother": Jack Williamson, "The Moon Era," in Asimov, ed., op. cit., p. 312, et passim.   **235** "'The new: Jack Williamson, "Born of the Sun," in Asimov, ed., op. cit., p. 535.   **235** "more like: Jack Williamson, *The Legion of Space* (New York: Pyramid, 1969), p. 68.   **235** "What a: Ibid, p. 173.   **236** "Two little: Ibid, p. 185.   **236** Wells published a highly revealing preface: This same preface saw publication one year earlier in the British edition of this novel collection, published under the title *The Scientific Romances of H.G. Wells* (London: Gollancz, 1933). The British edition also included *Men Like Gods*, omitted from *Seven Famous Novels*.   **236** "Anyone can: H.G. Wells, "Preface," in Wells, *Seven Famous Novels* (New York: Knopf, 1934), p. viii.   **238** "Dick Jarvis: Stanley G. Weinbaum, "A Martian Odyssey," in Weinbaum, *The Best of Stanley G. Weinbaum* (New York: Ballantine, 1974), p. 1.   **239** "'Weighed about: Ibid, pp. 3-4.   **240** "'Our minds: Ibid, p. 9.   **240** "'That queer: Ibid, p. 15.   **240** "'We are: Ibid, p. 24.   **240** "'might be: Ibid, p. 26.   **242** "conflicting possible: Jack Williamson, *The Legion of Time* (New York: Pyramid, 1967), p. 23.   **242** "'The world: Ibid, p. 19.   **243** "'Probability, in: Ibid, p. 24.   **243** "It must: C.L. Moore, "Jirel Meets Magic," in Moore, *Jirel of Joiry* (New York: Paperback Library, 1969), p. 28.   **244** "'We talk: Murray Leinster, "Sidewise in Time," in Asimov, ed., op. cit., p. 553.   **244** "'Certainty is: Jack Williamson, *The Legion of Time*, p. 37.   **245** "'I start: Stanley Weinbaum, "The Lotus Eaters," in Weinbaum, op. cit., p. 259.   **245** "'Oscar, I: Ibid.   **245** "'An animal: Ibid, p. 261.   **246** John W. Campbell was born: our account of the early life of John W. Campbell, Jr. is primarily based on the chapter on Campbell in Sam Moskowitz, *Seekers of Tomorrow* (Cleveland and New York: World, 1966).   **247** "'Man can: John W. Campbell, *Invaders from the Infinite*, p. 191.   **248** "They had: John W. Campbell, *The Black Star Passes* (New York: Ace, 1972), p. 250.   **248** "'The swiftest: John W. Campbell, *Invaders from the Infinite*, p. 139.   **248** "'Here's an: John W. Campbell, *The Mightiest Machine* (New York: Ace, 1972), p. 50.   **249** "the Outsiders": John W. Campbell,

"The Last Evolution," in Campbell, *The Best of John W. Campbell* (New York: Ballantine, 1976), p. 4, et passim.   **249** "'The end: Ibid, p. 14.   **249** "pure force: Ibid, p. 20.   **250** "They stand: John W. Campbell, "Twilight," in Campbell, op. cit., p. 26.   **250** "And now: Ibid, p. 39.   **251** "The city: John W. Campbell, Jr., "Night," in Campbell, *Who Goes There?* (Chicago: Shasta, 1951). This composite quotation draws together examples from a continuing theme. The individual sentences are to be found on pages 216, 214, 214, 215, 230, and 220.   **251** "the one: Ibid, p. 229.   **251** "In many: John W. Campbell, Jr., "Introduction," in Campbell, *Cloak of Aesir* (Chicago: Shasta, 1952), pp. 10-11.   **253** slavetraders trekking through the jungles of Saturn: "The Drums" by Clifton B. Kruse, *Astounding Stories*, March 1936. **254** "'Seun is: John W. Campbell, "Forgetfulness," in Campbell, *The Best of John W. Campbell*, p. 190.

CHAPTER 12
UNIVERSAL PRINCIPLES OF OPERATION

257 "When I: John W. Campbell, in Dick Eney, ed., *The Proceedings; Discon* (Chicago: Advent, 1965), p. 123.   **257** "He was: Frederik Pohl, *The Way the Future Was: A Memoir* (New York: Del Rey, 1978), p. 88.   **257** "Every word: Ibid, pp. 87-88.   **258** "Fred, you: Ibid, p. 91.   **258** "When I: Catherine Crook de Camp, "Preamble," in L. Sprague de Camp and Catherine Crook de Camp, *Footprints on Sand* (Chicago: Advent, 1981), p. viii.   **259** "Does evolution: John W. Campbell, "Editor's Page: Mutation," *Astounding Stories*, January 1938, p. 151.   **260** "*Mutant* issues": Ibid.   **260** "In each: Ibid. **260** "genuine, fundamentally: Ibid.   **266** "To many: Isaac Asimov, "Introduction," in Asimov, ed., *Before the Golden Age* (Garden City, N.Y.: Doubleday, 1974), p. xv.   **267** "His sense: Harry Harrison and Brian W. Aldiss, "Introduction," in Harrison and Aldiss, eds., *The Astounding-Analog Reader, Vol. One* (Garden City, N.Y.: Doubleday, 1972), pp. ix-x.   **269** "I have: John W. Campbell, "Editor's Page: Invitation," *Astounding Science-Fiction*, October 1939, p. 5.   **269** "Nature is: John W. Campbell. The earliest use of this Campbellian maxim of which we are aware was Campbell, "Editor's Page: "'—but are we?'", *Astounding Science-Fiction*, January 1946, p. 6.   **269** "I made: R. Buckminster Fuller, quoted in his obituary, "Buckminster Fuller, Futurist Inventor, Dies at 87," *The New York Times*, July 3, 1984, p. 17. **270** "The new: John W. Campbell, "Editor's Page: Editorial Mutants," *Astounding Science-Fiction*, December 1938, p. 6.   **271** "The old: John W. Campbell, "Editor's Page: Science-Fiction," *Astounding Science-Fiction*, March 1938, p. 37.   **271** "We presuppose: Ibid.   **272** "Three mad: John W. Campbell, "Who Goes There?", in Campbell, *The Best of John W. Campbell* (New York: Ballantine, 1976), pp. 301-302.   **273** "The place: Ibid, p. 290. **274** "Copper stared: Ibid, pp. 308-309.   **274** "literature of: Howard Phillips Lovecraft, *Supernatural Horror in Literature* (New York: Dover, 1973), p. 15. **274** "A certain: Ibid.   **274** "'This isn't: John W. Campbell, "Who Goes There?", in Campbell, op. cit., p. 314.   **276** "I once: Isaac Asimov, "Introduction: The Father of Science Fiction," in Harry Harrison, ed., *Astounding: John W. Campbell Memorial Anthology* (New York: Random House, 1973), p. xiv.   **277** "The trouble: Edmond Hamilton, letter to Alexei Panshin, September 1, 1970.   **278** Simak told his wife: According to Sam Moskowitz in his chapter on Simak in *Seekers of Tomorrow* (New York and Cleveland:

World, 1966), p. 273.   **279** This was L. Ron Hubbard: Of the biographies
of Hubbard which have appeared since his death, the best account of his early
life is to be found in *Bare-Faced Messiah: The True Story of L. Ron Hubbard*
by Russell Miller (New York: Henry Holt, 1987), and the best account of his
later years in *L. Ron Hubbard: Messiah or Madman?* by Bent Corydon and
L. Ron Hubbard, Jr. (Secaucus, N.J.: Lyle Stuart, 1987).   **279** on March 13,
1911: In Miller, *Bare-Faced Messiah*, an alternate date of March 11, 1911 is
suggested, p. 12.   **279** "Now you: L. Ron Hubbard, lecture circa 1952,
quoted in Corydon and Hubbard, *L. Ron Hubbard*, p. 229. Ellipses in Corydon
and Hubbard.   **280** For the claim that Hubbard: The story is told by Hubbard
in the introduction to his novel *Battlefield Earth* (New York: St. Martin's,
1982), pp. vi-vii, and also in Charles Platt, *Dream Makers, Vol. II* (New York:
Berkley, 1983), pp. 181-182.   **280** "I'm damn: John W. Campbell, letter to
L. Ron Hubbard, dated January 23, 1939, in Perry A. Chapdelaine, Sr., Tony
Chapdelaine and George Hay, eds., *The John W. Campbell Letters, Vol. 1*
(Franklin, Tenn.: AC Projects, 1985), p. 44.   **282** In June 1938, Isaac Asimov:
This account of the relationship between Asimov and Campbell is based upon a
number of statements by Asimov, but chiefly upon Isaac Asimov, *In Memory
Yet Green: The Autobiography of Isaac Asimov 1920-1954* (Garden City, N.Y.:
Doubleday, 1979), pp. 194-197, etc.   **283** "delight mingled: Isaac Asimov, ed.
Before the Golden Age, p. 296.   **283** "Many years: Isaac Asimov, *In Memory
Yet Green*, p. 202.   **285** "Dogs. They: John W. Campbell, "Twilight," in John
W. Campbell, Jr., *Who Goes There?* (Chicago: Shasta, 1951), pp. 197-198.
285 "Your story: John W. Campbell, quoted from memory in Lester del Rey,
The Early Del Rey, Vol. 1 (New York: Ballantine, 1976), p. 21.   **285** "I want:
John W. Campbell, quoted in ibid, p. 22.   **286** "He was: Lester del Rey,
ibid, p. 33.   **286** "When I: Frederik Pohl, op. cit., p. 87.   **287** "If I: Isaac
Asimov, *In Memory Yet Green*, p. 202.   **287** patrician named L. Sprague
de Camp: Our account of the relationship of Campbell and de Camp is chiefly
based on an unpublished manuscript by L. Sprague de Camp entitled "Campbell
and I."   **289** "Well, just: Henry Kuttner, quoted by de Camp in ibid, p. 4.
291 "if intelligent: L. Sprague de Camp, "Design for Life," in *Astounding
Science-Fiction*, June 1939, p. 103.   **292** "'We know: L. Sprague de Camp,
"Living Fossil," in Groff Conklin, ed., *A Treasury of Science Fiction* (New
York, Crown, 1948), p. 109.   **293** "the laws: Fletcher Pratt and L. Sprague
de Camp, *The Incomplete Enchanter* (Philadelphia: Prime Press, 1950), p. 8.
294 The tale usually told: Alva Rogers, *A Requiem for Astounding* (Chicago:
Advent, 1964), p. 64, gives the typical version.   **294** "Fortean phenomena":
This phrase is not used in *Sinister Barrier*, but Charles Fort is cited in a concocted
newspaper clipping that precedes the story. Eric Frank Russell, *Sinister Barrier*
(New York: Paperback Library, 1964), p. 5.   **294** L. Ron Hubbard would tell
another story: L. Ron Hubbard, "Introduction," in Hubbard, *Battlefield Earth*,
p. viii.   **294** "I can: John W. Campbell, "Editor's Page: *Unknown,*" *Astounding
Science-Fiction*, February 1939, p. 72.   **294** "One of: Ibid.   **294** "I edit:
John W. Campbell, quoted by Theodore Sturgeon in Earl Kemp, ed., *The Pro-
ceedings; Chicon III* (Chicago: Advent, 1963), p. 122.   **295** "'Einstein's
Theory: E. E. Smith, *The Skylark of Space* (New York: Pyramid, 1958), p. 55.
296 "the granddaddy: L. Sprague de Camp, *Lest Darkness Fall* (Philadelphia:
Prime Press, 1949), p. 4.   **297** "'I was: Ibid, pp. 1-2.   **298** "He was:
Ibid, p. 48.   **298** "Could one: Ibid.   **298** "'I'm going: Ibid, p. 172.
298 "'The end: Ibid.   **300** "For sheer: John W. Campbell, "Editor's Page:
Addenda," *Astounding Science-Fiction*, July 1939, p. 7.

303 "If the: Ralph Waldo Emerson, "Nature," in Brooks Atkinson, ed., *The Selected Writings of Ralph Waldo Emerson* (New York: Modern Library, 1964), p. 5. Emerson here seems to be drawing upon Abu-Hamid ibn-Muhammad Al-Ghazzali (1058-1111), the theologian turned Sufi, who wrote in his *Confessions*: "To prove the possibility of inspiration is to prove that it belongs to a category of branches of knowledge which cannot be attained by reason. It is the same with medical science and astronomy. He who studies them is obliged to recognise that they are derived solely from the revelation and special grace of God. Some astronomical phenomena only occur once in a thousand years; how then can we know them by experience?" Al-Ghazzali, in Claud Field, ed., *The Confessions of Al Ghazzali* (Lahore, Pakistan: Sh. Muhammad Ashraf, n.d.), p. 61. This may well be a reference to the supernova of 1054—four years before Al-Ghazzali's birth—which gave rise to the Crab Nebula.   **303** "'What do: conversation between Campbell and Asimov, in Isaac Asimov, *In Memory Yet Green* (Garden City, N.Y.: Doubleday, 1979), p. 295.   **304** "We talked: Ibid.   **305** "Light after: Robert Heinlein, "Universe," in Groff Conklin, ed., *The Best of Science Fiction* (New York: Crown, 1946), p. 604.   **306** "The thought-variants: Isaac Asimov, ed., *Before the Golden Age* (Garden City, N.Y.: Doubleday, 1974), p. 498.   **308** "I became: Isaac Asimov, in Isaac Asimov and Martin H. Greenberg, eds., *Isaac Asimov Presents the Great Science Fiction Stories: Volume 1, 1939* (New York: DAW Books, 1979), p. 229.   **309** Let's begin with that first inadequate story: "Cosmic Corkscrew" is summarized in Isaac Asimov, *The Early Asimov: Book One* (Greenwich, Conn.: Fawcett Crest, 1974), p. 10, and again in Asimov, *In Memory Yet Green*, pp. 170-171.   **311** "I reread: Isaac Asimov, in *The Early Asimov, Book One*, p. 90, and Asimov, *In Memory Yet Green*, p. 213.   **315** "'Homo Sol': Isaac Asimov, in *The Early Asimov, Book One*, p. 218.   **318** "After reading: Isaac Asimov, *In Memory Yet Green*, p. 280.   **318** "'You listen: Isaac Asimov, "Strange Playfellow," in Isaac Asimov and Martin H. Greenberg, eds., *Isaac Asimov Presents the Great Science Fiction Stories: Volume 2, 1940* (New York: DAW Books, 1979), pp. 210-211.   **318** "'A robot: Ibid, p. 210.   **319** with the notable exception of the mechanical man Tik-tok: "Yet Tik-tok was popular with the people of Oz because he was so trustworthy, reliable and true; he was sure to do exactly what he was wound up to do, at all times and in all circumstances." L. Frank Baum, *The Road to Oz* (Chicago: Reilly and Lee, 1909), p. 171.   **319** "Consider a: Isaac Asimov, *The Rest of the Robots* (Garden City, N.Y.: Doubleday, 1964), p. xiii.   **319** "'The whole: Isaac Asimov, "Strange Playfellow," in Asimov and Greenberg, eds., *Isaac Asimov Presents: Vol. 2, 1940*, p. 215.   **320** "It also: Isaac Asimov, *In Memory Yet Green*, p. 280.   **320** "My notion: Ibid, p. 281.   **322** "In this: Ibid.   **322** "'Asimov, when: Ibid.   **323** "Gregory Powell: Isaac Asimov, "Reason," in Damon Knight, ed., *A Century of Science Fiction* (New York: Dell, 1962), p. 27.   **323** "'Do you: Ibid.   **324** "'Look at: Ibid, p. 31.   **325** "the Master": Ibid, p. 32.   **325** "the Prophet": Ibid, p. 34.   **325** "Donovan was: Ibid, p. 40.   **325** "'all dials: Ibid, p. 42.   **325** "'Look, Mike: Ibid.   **326** "'I won't: Ibid, p. 43.   **327** "'I'll send: Robert A. Heinlein, *Expanded Universe* (New York: Grosset & Dunlap, 1980), pp. 93-94.   **327** "from the: A.E. van Vogt, *Reflections of A.E. van Vogt* (Lakemont, Georgia: Fictioneer Books, 1975), p. 65.   **328** "Mr. Campbell": Isaac Asimov, *In Memory Yet Green*,

p. 196, footnote 1.   328 "'Don't be: Isaac Asimov, "Reason," in Damon Knight, ed., *A Century of Science Fiction*, p. 37.   328 "Again, Campbell: Isaac Asimov, *In Memory Yet Green*, p. 286.   329 "'Look, Asimov: Ibid. 329 "'No, Asimov: Ibid, pp. 286-287.   330 "'Listen, Bogert: Isaac Asimov, "Liar!" in Asimov, *I, Robot* (Garden City, N.Y.: Doubleday, n.d.), p. 99. 330 "'If you: Ibid.   331 "In time: Isaac Asimov, *The Early Asimov, Book One*, p. 88.   333 "the Stars": Isaac Asimov, "Nightfall," in Raymond J. Healy and J. Francis McComas, eds., *Famous Science-Fiction Stories: Adventures in Time and Space* (New York: Modern Library, 1957), pp. 378-411, passim. 334 "'The Cultists: Ibid, p. 385.   334 "'This is: Ibid, p. 380.   334 "'No such: Ibid, pp. 380-381.   335 "'You realize: Ibid, p. 384.   336 "'After Genovi: Ibid, p. 386.   336 "'In the: Ibid.   337 "'First the: Ibid, p. 387. 337 "'What an: Ibid, p. 404.   338 "With the: Ibid, p. 410.   339 "Someone clawed: Ibid, p. 411.   341 *"How would*: Blurb for Asimov's "Nightfall," *Astounding Science-Fiction*, September 1941, p. 9. This page is reprinted in a picture section in Isaac Asimov, *In Memory Yet Green*, after page 372. Also reproduced in black-and-white is the September 1941 *Astounding* cover illustrating "Nightfall."   341 "Next month: John W. Campbell, "In Times to Come," in *Astounding Science-Fiction*, August 1941, p. 36.   342 "artificial-light mechanism": Isaac Asimov, "Nightfall," in Raymond J. Healy and J. Francis McComas, eds., *Famous Science-Fiction Stories*, p. 405.   342 "the Hideout": Ibid, p. 382.   343 "'The next: Ibid, p. 387.

CHAPTER 14

A WORLD OF CHANGE

347 "In the: Hugo Gernsback, "Reasonableness in Science Fiction," in David Kyle, *A Pictorial History of Science Fiction* (London: Hamlyn, 1976), p. 80. 348 "led to: John W. Campbell, Jr., "Introduction," in Campbell, *Who Goes There?* (Chicago: Shasta, 1951), p. 2.   351 "With the: L. Sprague de Camp, "Pratt and His Parallel Worlds," in *Fantastic Stories*, December 1972, p. 87. 351 "I thought: Ibid, p. 93.   352 "'our new: L. Sprague de Camp and Fletcher Pratt, *The Incomplete Enchanter* (Philadelphia: Prime Press, 1950), p. 4. 352 "'The world: Ibid, p. 5.   352 "'Do you: Ibid, pp. 5-6.   353 "syllogis-mobile": Ibid, p. 10.   353 "This world: Ibid, p. 62.   353 "He couldn't: Ibid, p. 128.   355 "'What can: Ibid, p. 38.   356 "'Certainly a: Ibid, p. 158. 356 "'Listen: why: Ibid, p. 159.   357 "'A property: Ibid, p. 249.   357 "A neue: Ibid, p. 282.   357 "'A trifle: Ibid, p. 291.   357 "'In a: Ibid, p. 292. 358 "'The really: Ibid, p. 320.   358 "spell against: Ibid.   361 "a lenticular: E.E. Smith, *Galactic Patrol* (New York: Pyramid, 1966), p. 12.   361 "'not essentially: Ibid, p. 16.   361 "'None save: E.E. Smith, *Gray Lensman* (New York: Pyramid, 1965), p. 109.   363 "Idea is: Robert A. Heinlein, note in File No. 17, "They," in the Robert Heinlein Special Collection, University of California at Santa Cruz, Santa Cruz, California.   363 "'I wasn't: Robert A. Heinlein, "Requiem," in Heinlein, *The Past Through Tomorrow* (New York: Putnam, 1967), p. 205.   364 "He first: Robert A. Heinlein, in J. Neil Schulman, *"New Libertarian Notes* Interviews Robert A. Heinlein," Part V, *New Libertarian Notes* No. 33, August 1974, p. 8.   365 "it would: Robert A. Heinlein, "Ray Guns and Rocket Ships," in Heinlein, *Expanded Universe* (New York: Grosset & Dunlap, 1980), p. 373.   365 *"He thinks*: yearbook motto quoted in H. Bruce Franklin, *Robert A. Heinlein: America as Science Fiction*

(New York: Oxford, 1980), p. 9.   **367** "bio-chemist and: Robert A. Heinlein, "'Let There Be Light'" in Heinlein, *The Man Who Sold the Moon* (Chicago: Shasta, 1950), p. 41.   **368** "speculative metaphysics": Robert A. Heinlein, "Elsewhen," in Heinlein, *Assignment in Eternity* (Reading, Pa.: Fantasy Press, 1953), p. 92.   **368** "hypnosis and: Ibid, p. 95.   **368** "antagonists of: Robert A. Heinlein, "Lost Legacy," in Heinlein, op. cit., p. 211.   **370** "I was: Robert Heinlein, "If This Goes On—," in *Astounding*, February 1940, p. 10. **372** "There seemed: Robert A. Heinlein, "Elsewhen," in Heinlein, *Assignment in Eternity*, p. 117.   **372** "'The emotional: Robert Heinlein, "If This Goes On—," in *Astounding*, March 1940, p. 130.   **373** "There is: Ibid.   **373** "The plan: Ibid, p. 141.   **374** "an angry: Robert A. Heinlein, "If This Goes On—," in Heinlein, *The Past Through Tomorrow*, p. 460.   **374** "'Free men: Ibid, p. 461.   **375** "Space Precautionary: Robert A. Heinlein, "Requiem," in ibid, p. 206.   **375** "At long: Ibid, p. 210.   **375** "Douglas-Martin Solar: Robert A. Heinlein, "The Roads Must Roll," in Heinlein, *The Past Through Tomorrow*, p. 36.   **376** "There won't: Robert A. Heinlein, "Heinlein on Science Fiction," in *Vertex*, April 1973, pp. 47-48.   **376** "Citizens were: Robert A. Heinlein, "Coventry," in Heinlein, *The Past Through Tomorrow*, p. 501.   **377** "This was: Robert A. Heinlein, "Preface," in Heinlein, *The Man Who Sold the Moon*, p. 15.   **378** "'Who makes: Robert A. Heinlein, "The Roads Must Roll," in Heinlein, *The Past Through Tomorrow*, p. 30. **378** "'Put down: Robert A. Heinlein, "Blowups Happen," in ibid, p. 60. **378** "'Whose spells: Robert A. Heinlein, "Magic, Inc.," in Heinlein, *Waldo and Magic, Inc.* (Garden City, N.Y.: Doubleday, 1951), p. 123.   **378** "'Various of: Ibid.   **378** "the arcane: Ibid, p. 190.   **379** "'We all: Ibid, p. 177.   **379** "the Half-World": Ibid, p. 127.   **381** "The trouble: John W. Campbell, quoted in Frederik Pohl, *The Way the Future Was* (New York: Del Rey Books, 1978), p. 87. **381** "was just: Robert A. Heinlein, *Expanded Universe*, p. 92.   **382** "They were: Robert A. Heinlein, "Blowups Happen," in Heinlein, *The Past Through Tomorrow*, p. 63.   **382** "He had: Robert A. Heinlein, "The Roads Must Roll," in Heinlein, *The Past Through Tomorrow*, p. 43.   **382** "'ridey-ridey home: Ibid, p. 33.   **384** "I promptly: Robert A. Heinlein, *Expanded Universe*, p. 94.   **385** "the Mañana: Ibid, p. 92.   **385** "the Galactic: Edward E. Smith, Ph.D., "The Epic of Space," in Lloyd Arthur Eshbach, ed., *Of Worlds Beyond* (Reading, Pa.: Fantasy Press, 1947), pp. 82-83.   **387** "The 'FALSE: Robert Heinlein, chart in "Brass Tacks," *Astounding*, May 1941, pp. 124-125. **387** "for many: Robert Heinlein, "If This Goes On—," in *Astounding*, March 1940, p. 141.   **388** "'What can: Robert A. Heinlein, "Logic of Empire," in Heinlein, *The Past Through Tomorrow*, p. 340.   **389** "Foreign Policy": Robert A. Heinlein, note in File No. 22, "Solution Unsatisfactory," in the Robert Heinlein Special Collection, University of California at Santa Cruz. **389** "'representatives of: Robert A. Heinlein, "'—We Also Walk Dogs,'" in Heinlein, *The Past Through Tomorrow*, p. 263.   **390** "'I'd like: John W. Campbell, "In Times to Come," *Astounding*, February 1941, p. 67.   **390** "Mapping out: John W. Campbell, "Editor's Page," *Astounding*, June 1940, p. 6. **391** "Fundamentally, science-fiction: John W. Campbell, "Editor's Page: History to Come," *Astounding*, May 1941, p. 5.   **392** "Stories-to-be-told": Robert Heinlein, chart in "Brass Tacks," *Astounding*, May 1941, pp. 124-125. **393** "Shadow of: Robert A. Heinlein, note in File No. 24, *Methuselah's Children*, in the Robert Heinlein Special Collection, University of California at Santa Cruz. **393** "Peril in: Ibid.   **393** "the Rapport: Ibid.   **393** "the dog: Ibid. **393** "'I was: Robert A. Heinlein, *Methuselah's Children*, in Heinlein, *The Past*

Through Tomorrow, p. 543.　**394** "'If there: Ibid, p. 539.　**394** "'It is: Ibid, p. 561.　**395** "'Here's my: Ibid, p. 628.　**395** "The hegira: Ibid, p. 646.　**396** "It lacked: Ibid, p. 648.　**396** *"California here*: Robert Heinlein, *Methuselah's Children*, in *Astounding*, September 1941, p. 162. (In the serial, but not the book version, the first word of the song lyric is omitted.)　**396** "When Lazarus: Robert A. Heinlein, *Methuselah's Children*, in Heinlein, *The Past Through Tomorrow*, p. 540.　**396** "'Bud, you: Ibid, p. 556.　**398** "superior ability: Ibid, p. 563.　**398** "horror-stricken eyes": Ibid, p. 627.　**398** "'Those creatures: Robert Heinlein, *Methuselah's Children*, in *Astounding*, September 1941, p. 142.　**398** "'They weren't: Robert A. Heinlein, *Methuselah's Children*, in Heinlein, *The Past Through Tomorrow*, p. 666.　**398** "'Of course: Ibid.　**399** "I probably: Robert A. Heinlein, "Concerning Stories Never Written," in Heinlein, *Revolt in 2100* (Chicago: Shasta, 1954), p. 19.　**399** "the High: Robert A. Heinlein, "By His Bootstraps," in Heinlein, *The Menace from Earth* (Hicksville, N.Y.: Gnome Press, 1959), p. 59.　**400** "He felt: Ibid, p. 106.　**400** "He was: Ibid, p. 109.　**400** "He knew: Ibid, p. 113.　**400** "'There is: Ibid, p. 115.　**400** "A great: Ibid.　**401** "an oceanographer: Robert A. Heinlein, "Goldfish Bowl," in Heinlein, *The Menace from Earth*, p. 179.　**401** "We've had: Ibid, p. 207.　**401** "They were: Ibid, p. 209.　**401** "BEWARE—CREATION: Ibid, p. 211.　**403** "I do: Robert A. Heinlein, "Heinlein on Science Fiction," in *Vertex*, April 1973, p. 48.　**403** "Atomic War: Robert A. Heinlein, *Beyond This Horizon* (Reading, Pa.: Fantasy Press, 1948) p. 34.　**403** "the Empire: Ibid, p. 35.　**403** "The outcome: Ibid, p. 34.　**403** "They tailored: Ibid, p. 36.　**403** "The Empire: Ibid, p. 37.　**404** "Infants born: Ibid, p. 54.　**404** "the Adirondack: Ibid, p. 62.　**404** "'silly games: Ibid, p. 32.　**404** "an encyclopedic: Ibid, p. 43.　**404** "make it: Robert A. Heinlein, "Heinlein on Science Fiction," in *Vertex*, April 1973, p. 96.　**404** "so far: Ibid, p. 97.　**405** "All the: Robert A. Heinlein, *Beyond This Horizon*, p. 43.　**405** "'You can: Ibid, p. 45.　**405** "Great Research": Ibid, p. 181.　**405** "control natural": Ibid, pp. 177-178.　**405** "If there: Ibid, p. 188.　**407** "the Sons: Robert A. Heinlein, "The Unpleasant Profession of Jonathan Hoag," in Heinlein, *The Unpleasant Profession of Jonathan Hoag* (Hicksville, N.Y.: Gnome Press, 1959), p. 49.　**407** "art critic": Ibid, p. 141.

CHAPTER 15

CONSCIOUSNESS AND REALITY

410 "All the: Werner Heisenberg, "The Debate Between Plato and Democritus," in Ken Wilber, ed., *Quantum Questions* (Boulder, Colorado and London: New Science Library/Shambala, 1984), p. 50.　**411** "Something unknown: A.S. Eddington, quoted on the cover of Ken Wilber, ed., *Quantum Questions*.　**411** "Copenhagen interpretation": We do not know who was responsible for coining this commonly-used phrase, but it is employed and discussed in Heinz R. Pagels, *The Cosmic Code: Quantum Physics as the Language of Nature* (New York: Bantam, 1983), p. 69.　**412** "To put: A.S. Eddington, "Mind-Stuff," in Ken Wilber, ed., *Quantum Questions*, p. 184.　**412** "The mind-stuff: Ibid, p. 185.　**412** "Is there: A. Merritt, *The Metal Monster* (New York: Avon, 1966), p. 116.　**413** "I think: Rene Descartes, *A Discourse on Method*, in Saxe Cummins and Robert N. Linscott, eds., *Man and the Universe: The*

Philosophers of Science (New York: Random House, 1947), p. 182. **413** "I . . . concluded: Ibid, pp. 182-183. **414** "Psychology, as: John B. Watson, quoted in Floyd W. Matson, *The Broken Image* (Garden City, N.Y.: Doubleday/Anchor, 1966), p. 38. **423** "'know more: John W. Campbell, "The Elder Gods," in Campbell, *The Moon Is Hell* (Reading, Pa.: Fantasy Press, 1951), p. 158. **423** "'absolutes of: Ibid, p. 188. **425** "Almost any: John W. Campbell, letter to J.B. Rhine dated November 23, 1953, in Perry A. Chapdelaine, Sr., Tony Chapdelaine and George Hay, eds., *The John W. Campbell Letters, Vol. 1* (Franklin, Tennessee: A.C. Projects, 1985), p. 223. **425** "Your group: Ibid. **425** "Many of: John W. Campbell, "The Scientist," in Harry Harrison, ed., *John W. Campbell: Collected Editorials from Analog* (Garden City, N.Y.: Doubleday, 1966), pp. 69-70. **426** "The engineer: John W. Campbell, letter to J.B. Rhine dated November 23, 1953, in *The John W. Campbell Letters, Vol. 1*, p. 226. **427** "'Look you: Fletcher Pratt and L. Sprague de Camp, *Land of Unreason* (New York: Henry Holt, 1942), p. 41. **427** "'What does: Ibid, pp. 208-209. **428** "'The question: L. Sprague de Camp and Fletcher Pratt, *The Incomplete Enchanter* (Philadelphia: Prime Press, 1950), p. 160. **428** "'That puts: L. Sprague de Camp and Fletcher Pratt, *The Castle of Iron*, in *Unknown*, April 1941, p. 13. **429** "As in: John W. Campbell, "Editor's Page: Mercury," in *Astounding Stories*, February 1938, p. 97. **430** "Robopsychology": Isaac Asimov, "Liar!" in Asimov, *I, Robot* (Garden City, N.Y.: Doubleday, n.d.), p. 108. **430** So persistently that Chip Delany: Samuel R. Delany, "The Necessity of Tomorrows," in Delany, *Starboard Wine* (Pleasantville, N.Y.: Dragon Press, 1984), pp. 28-29. **431** "That would: L. Ron Hubbard, "Typewriter in the Sky," in Hubbard, *Typewriter in the Sky/Fear* (New York: Gnome Press, 1951), p. 33. **432** "Up there: Ibid, p. 134. **433** "growing willingness: Jack Williamson, *Wonder's Child: My Life in Science Fiction* (New York: Bluejay Books, 1984), p. 125. **434** "'a Black: Jack Williamson, *Darker Than You Think* (Reading, Pa.: Fantasy Press, 1948), p. 34. **435** "Probability—he: Ibid, p. 97. **435** "The direct: Ibid. **435** "'I don't: Ibid, pp. 111-112. **438** "the deKalbs": Robert A. Heinlein, "Waldo," in Heinlein, *Waldo and Magic, Inc.* (Garden City, N.Y.: Doubleday, 1951), p. 18 et passim. **439** "Back in: Robert A. Heinlein, "Science Fiction: Its Nature, Faults and Virtues," in Basil Davenport, et. al., *The Science Fiction Novel: Imagination and Social Criticism* (Chicago: Advent, 1959), p. 33. **439** "To Rambeau: Robert A. Heinlein, "Waldo," in Heinlein, *Waldo and Magic, Inc.*, p. 59. **440** "'I've learned: Ibid, pp. 63-64. **440** "Waldo was: Ibid, p. 67. **441** "'One of: Ibid, pp. 78-79. **441** "'I think: Ibid, p. 92. **442** "Waldo was: Ibid, pp. 100-101. **443** "'a thing: Ibid, p. 102. **443** "The world: Ibid. **444** "'As for: Ibid, p. 118.

CHAPTER 16
A NEW MORAL ORDER

447 "an extrovert: A.E. van Vogt, "My Life Was My Best Science Fiction Story," in Martin H. Greenberg, ed., *Fantastic Lives: Autobiographical Essays by Notable Science Fiction Writers* (Carbondale and Edwardsville, Illinois: Southern Illinois University Press, 1981), p. 187. **448** "Childhood was: A.E. van Vogt, quoted in Sam Moskowitz, *Seekers of Tomorrow* (Cleveland and New York: World, 1966), p. 215. **448** "in the: A.E. van Vogt, *Reflections of A.E.*

van Vogt (Lakemont, Georgia: Fictioneer Books, 1975), p. 29. **449** "Reading science: A.E. van Vogt, *The Best of A.E. van Vogt* (New York: Pocket Books, 1976), p. 255. **449** "ESP; trans-light: A.E. van Vogt, letter to Alexei and Cory Panshin, October 10, 1985. **451** "We are: Alfred North Whitehead, *Science and the Modern World* (New York: Free Press/Macmillan, 1967), p. 76. **451** "Is it: Ibid, p. 84. **451** "a system: Ibid, p. 75. **451** "The materialistic: Ibid, p. 152. **452** "My theory: Ibid, p. 91. **452** "If organisms: Ibid, p. 109. **452** "Successful organisms: Ibid, p. 205. **453** "ballistic calculator": Robert A. Heinlein, "Misfit," in Heinlein, *The Past Through Tomorrow* (New York: Putnam, 1967), p. 523. **455** "Mr. System": A.E. van Vogt, letter to Alexei and Cory Panshin, April 22, 1985. **457** "I feel: A.E. van Vogt, *Reflections of A.E. van Vogt*, p. 47. **458** "The creature: A.E. van Vogt, "Vault of the Beast," in van Vogt, *Away and Beyond* (New York: Avon, 1953), p. 7. The text here is van Vogt's original version. The revised text, as it was published in *Astounding*, may be found in John W. Campbell, Jr., ed., *The Astounding Science Fiction Anthology* (New York: Simon and Schuster, 1952). **458** "robot": Ibid, p. 25. **458** "android": Ibid. **458** "great and: Ibid, p. 7. **458** "'Our purpose: Ibid, p. 31. **459** "'I didn't: Ibid, p. 32. **460** "'ultimate prime: A.E. van Vogt, "Vault of the Beast," p. 15. **460** "'ultimate metal'": Ibid. **460** "In a: A.E. van Vogt, letter to Alexei and Cory Panshin, October 10, 1985. **461** "Alfred Vogt": John W. Campbell, unpublished letter to [A.E. van Vogt], January 17, 1939. **461** "On and: A.E. van Vogt, "Black Destroyer," in Raymond J. Healy and J. Francis McComas, eds., *Famous Science-Fiction Stories: Adventures in Time and Space* (New York: Modern Library, 1957), p. 177. **463** "the all-necessary: Ibid, p. 178. **463** "'We're going: Ibid, p. 198. **464** "The sense: Ibid, p. 181. **464** "He whirled: Ibid, p. 182. **464** "It was: Ibid, p. 193. **464** "For just: Ibid. **464** "'In fact: Ibid, p. 202. **465** "'the electronic: Ibid, p. 200. **465** "'We have: Ibid, p. 202. **465** "they found: Ibid, p. 205. **466** "You've done: John W. Campbell, unpublished letter to [A.E. van Vogt], January 17, 1939. **466** "If this: Ibid. **467** "'a race: A.E. van Vogt, "Discord in Scarlet," *Astounding*, December 1939, p. 18. **468** "a devastating: Ibid, p. 32. **468** "'After all: Ibid, p. 34. **468** "'You assume: Ibid. **468** "I have: A.E. van Vogt, *Reflections of A.E. van Vogt*, pp. 78-79. **468** "Generally, either: Ibid, p. 79. **469** "I have tried: Ibid. **469** "'Remember this: A.E. van Vogt, "Repetition," as "The Gryb," in van Vogt, *The Proxy Intelligence and Other Mind Benders* (New York: Paperback Library, 1971), p. 43. **469** "'I have: Ibid, p. 159. **470** "'fix-up' novel": A.E. van Vogt, *Reflections of A.E. van Vogt*, p. 132. **471** "encyclopedic synthesist": Robert A. Heinlein, *Beyond This Horizon* (Reading, Pa.: Fantasy Press, 1948), p. 43. **471** "He was: A.E. van Vogt, *The Voyage of the Space Beagle* (New York: Macfadden Books, 1968), p. 7. **471** "the problems: Ibid, pp. 191-192. **472** "I pointed: John W. Campbell, letter to E.E. Smith, Ph.D., dated May 26, 1959, in Perry A. Chapdelaine, Sr., Tony Chapdelaine and George Hay, eds., *The John W. Campbell Letters, Vol. 1* (Franklin, Tennessee: AC Projects, 1985), p. 368. **472** "The super-*man*: John W. Campbell, letter to Clifford D. Simak, dated June 18, 1953, in *The John W. Campbell Letters, Vol. 1*, p. 178. **474** "the great: A.E. van Vogt, in an unpublished manuscript entitled "Systematic Thought Number Two: The Fictional Sentence," p. 5. **475** "The human-like: A.E. van Vogt, quoted in van Vogt, "My Life Was My Best Science Fiction Story," p. 192. **475** "The writer: A.E. van Vogt, in an unpublished manuscript entitled "Systematic Thought Number Three: Getting Ideas Through

Dreaming," p. 7.   475 "People do: A.E. van Vogt, "The Development of a Science Fiction Writer: III," in *Foundation: The Review of Science Fiction*, No. 3, March 1973, p. 28.   475 "I mean: A.E. van Vogt, *Reflections of A.E. van Vogt*, p. 79.   477 "Checks from: Ibid, p. 62.   478 "sixty electro: A.E. van Vogt, *Slan, Astounding*, September 1940, p. 12.   478 "'Don't forget: Ibid, p. 11.   478 "ten-point steel": A.E. van Vogt, *Slan, Astounding*, November 1940, p. 145.   478 "hypnotism crystals": A.E. van Vogt, *Slan, Astounding*, December 1940, p. 129.   478 "tendrilless slans": A.E. van Vogt, *Slan, Astounding*, September 1940, p. 40, et passim.   478 "'a damned: Ibid. 478 "'Madam, in: A.E. van Vogt, *Slan, Astounding*, November 1940, p. 137. 479 "And she: Ibid, p. 153.   479 "Inside the: A.E. van Vogt, *Slan, Astounding*, December 1940, p. 145.   480 "From a: A.E. van Vogt, letter to the membership of the Science Fiction Writers of America, dated March 1977 (actually 1978).   480 "Kier Gray: A.E. van Vogt, *Slan, Astounding*, December 1940, p. 155.   480 "'Man, man: Ibid, p. 157.   480 "'What is: Ibid, pp. 155-156. 480 "'the mutation-after-man.'": Ibid, p. 157.   481 "'make a: Ibid, p. 160. 481 "It was: Ibid, p. 162.   484 "That son: John W. Campbell, letter to Harry Harrison, dated April 4, 1954, in *The John W. Campbell Letters, Vol. 1*, p. 234. 486 "For years: A.E. van Vogt, *The Best of A.E. van Vogt*, p. 146.   487 "Details penetrated: A.E. van Vogt, *Slan, Astounding*, December 1940, p. 123.   487 "the leader: Damon Knight, *In Search of Wonder* (Chicago: Advent:Publishers, 1967), p. 61.   487 "utter and: Ibid, p. 60.   488 "I had: A.E. van Vogt, *Reflections of A.E. van Vogt*, p. 84.   490 "Slan Shack": See Harry Warner, Jr., *All Our Yesterdays* (Chicago: Advent:Publishers, 1969), p. 33.   490 "Tendril Towers": Ibid, p. 250.   490 "Man is: Claude Degler, in *Cosmic Digest*, Spring 1943, quoted in Warner, *All Our Yesterdays*, p. 186.   490 "the Cosmic: See Warner, op. cit., p. 185.   490 "Fans are: Ibid, p. 42.   491 "Being a: A.E. van Vogt, letter to the membership of the Science Fiction Writers of America, dated March 1977 (actually 1978).   491 "FINE WEAPONS: A.E. van Vogt, "The Seesaw," in Isaac Asimov and Martin H. Greenberg, eds., *Isaac Asimov Presents the Great SF Stories, Vol. 3, 1941* (New York: DAW Books, 1980), p. 212.   492 "THE FINEST: Ibid.   492 "'eighty-four of: Ibid, p. 217.   492 "'trillions and: Ibid, p. 219.   492 "You are: Ibid, p. 224. 493 "Quite suddenly: Ibid, p. 230.   495 "Every unfolding: A.E. van Vogt, "Recruiting Station," in Groff Conklin, ed., *Omnibus of Science Fiction* (New York: Crown, 1952), p. 366.   495 "By April: A.E. van Vogt, "My Life Was My Best Science Fiction Story," p. 189.   496 "I write: A.E. van Vogt, *Reflections of A.E. van Vogt*, p. 92.   496 "I was: Ibid, p. 97.   497 "In order: Ibid, p. 65.   498 "the singleness: A.E. van Vogt, "Secret Unattainable," in van Vogt, *Away and Beyond*, p. 82.   498 "all the: Ibid.   499 "'My invention: Ibid, p. 113.   499 "'Here is: Ibid, pp. 117-118.   499 "'reality of: Ibid, p. 117.   502 "Poor, unsuspecting: A.E. van Vogt, "Recruiting Station," in Groff Conklin, ed., *Omnibus of Science Fiction*, p. 419.   502 "the glorious: A.E. van Vogt, "The Weapon Shop," in Robert Silverberg, ed., *Science Fiction Hall of Fame, Volume One* (Garden City, N.Y.: Doubleday, 1970), p. 144. 503 "'Information Center'": Ibid, p. 170.   503 "'the brilliant: Ibid, p. 176. 503 "'It is: Ibid.   504 "'Weapon Shop': John W. Campbell, letter to A.E. van Vogt, dated June 12, 1942, quoted in van Vogt, "My Life Was My Best Science Fiction Story," pp. 190-191.   508 "Possessor Kingston: A.E. van Vogt, "The Search," in van Vogt, *Destination: Universe* (New York: New American Library, 1952), p. 145, et passim.   509 "probability worlds: Ibid, p. 145. 509 "the time: Ibid, p. 146.   509 "the Palace: Ibid, p. 145.   510 "'When

I: Ibid, p. 152.   **511** "*They're* in: Ibid, p. 153.   **511** "His memory: Ibid, p. 155.   **511** "Science fiction: A.E. van Vogt, "Postscript," *Destination: Universe*, p. 158.   **514** "meteorite": A.E. van Vogt, "Asylum," in van Vogt, *Away and Beyond*, p. 231.   **514** "the first: Ibid, p. 202.   **514** "'life force'": Ibid, p. 203.   **515** "'Its rays: Ibid, p. 246.   **515** "*ultra*": Ibid, p. 198.   **515** "'It is: Ibid.   **515** "Great Galactic": Ibid, p. 249.   **516** "On all: Ibid, p. 242.   **517** "'Return to: Ibid, p. 250.   **518** "'If altruism: A.E. van Vogt, "The Proxy Intelligence," in *The Proxy Intelligence and Other Mind Benders*, p. 63.   **518** "The problem: A.E. van Vogt, *Reflections of A.E. van Vogt*, p. 81.   **518** "That was: Ibid.   **518** "Amazingly, then: A.E. van Vogt, "Asylum," in van Vogt, *Away and Beyond*, p. 252.

CHAPTER 17

AN EMPIRE OF MIND

522 "On the: Isaac Asimov, *In Memory Yet Green* (Garden City, N.Y.: Doubleday, 1979), p. 311.   **523** "Never, I: Isaac Asimov, in Asimov, ed., *Before the Golden Age* (Garden City, N.Y.: Doubleday, 1974), p. 910.   **523** "'mad geniuses'": Isaac Asimov, "Homo Sol," in Asimov, *The Early Asimov, Book One* (Greenwich, Connecticut: Fawcett Crest, 1974), p. 215.   **524** "'his guarded: Jack Williamson, "After World's End," in Williamson, *The Legion of Time* (New York: Pyramid, 1967), p. 182.   **524** "Rhine's famous: Ibid, p. 116.   **525** "Men multiplied: Ibid, pp. 118-119.   **525** "hundred-times-told": Isaac Asimov, *The Rest of the Robots* (Garden City, N.Y.: Doubleday, 1964), p. xii.   **528** "I was: Isaac Asimov, *In Memory Yet Green*, p. 311.   **530** "It's a: blurb for Asimov's "Foundation," *Astounding Science-Fiction*, May 1942, p. 38.   **531** "got longer: Isaac Asimov, *In Memory Yet Green*, p. 312.   **532** "I started: Ibid.   **532** "'And after: Isaac Asimov, "Foundation," *Astounding*, May 1942, pp. 52-53.   The book version says "*thirty* thousand years": Isaac Asimov, *Foundation*, p. 28, in Asimov, *The Foundation Trilogy* (Garden City, N.Y.: Doubleday, n.d.).   **533** "'We have: Isaac Asimov, "Foundation," *Astounding*, May 1942, p. 38.   **533** "the multi-intelligence: Isaac Asimov, *In Memory Yet Green*, p. 405.   **534** "It was: Ibid.   **535** "Psycho-history dealt: Isaac Asimov, *Foundation and Empire*, p. v, in Asimov, *The Foundation Trilogy*.   **535** "I'm sure: Isaac Asimov, letter to Alexei Panshin, dated February 17, 1987.   **536** "'the definitive: Isaac Asimov, *Foundation*, p. 41, in Asimov, *The Foundation Trilogy*.   **536** "'a psychological: Ibid, p. 56.   **536** "'You give: Ibid, p. 64.   **536** "'The Encyclopedia: Ibid, p. 73.   **538** "'To that: Ibid, pp. 73-75.   **539** "'The solution: Ibid, p. 75.   **540** "The idea: Isaac Asimov, *In Memory Yet Green*, p. 314.   **540** "'At present: John W. Campbell, letter to Jack Williamson, October 7, 1941, quoted in Williamson, *Wonder's Child: My Life in Science Fiction* (New York: Bluejay Books, 1984), p. 133.   **541** "Bob has: Jack Williamson, *Wonder's Child*, p. 134.   **542** "'The old: Jack Williamson: "Breakdown," in Williamson, *People Machines* (New York: Ace, 1971), p. 159.   **543** "'the chronological: John W. Campbell, letter to Jack Williamson, date unstated, quoted in Williamson, *Wonder's Child*, p. 135.   **543** "'A robot: Isaac Asimov, "Runaround," in Asimov, *I, Robot* (Garden City, N.Y.: Doubleday, 1950), p. 51.   **544** "'What I: Isaac Asimov, *Foundation*, p. 85.   **545** "'Violence is: Ibid, p. 84.   **545** "'I want: John W. Campbell, quoted in Asimov, *In Memory Yet Green*, p. 318.   **546** "'they could: Isaac Asimov, *Foundation*, p. 93.

547 "'Force the: Ibid, p. 94. **547** "'You have: Ibid, p. 73. **548** "'Let the: Ibid, p. 122. **548** "'In the: Ibid, p. 124. **549** "'With his: Ibid. **549** "'A man: Ibid, p. 129. **549** "'My figures: Ibid, p. 131. **550** "'According to: Ibid. **551** "'flubdub and: Robert A. Heinlein, *Sixth Column* (New York: Gnome Press, 1949), p. 121. **551** "'You were: Isaac Asimov, *Foundation*, p. 86. **552** "'He believes: Ibid, p. 103. **553** "'I started: Ibid, p. 86. **556** "one whose: Ibid, p. 113. **559** "'And never: Ibid, p. 132. **563** "'To-gether we: Isaac Asimov, *Foundation*, p. 104. **563** "'He's the: Ibid, p. 91.

CHAPTER 18

MAN TRANSCENDING

578 "We will: John Campbell, "Editor's Page: Too Good At Guessing," *Astounding*, April 1942, p. 6. **578** So Campbell wrote back to say: this account is based upon George O. Smith, *Worlds of George O.* (New York: Bantam, 1982), p. 3. **579** "Fundamentally, I: John W. Campbell, letter to Jack Williamson, dated October 7, 1941, quoted in Williamson, *Wonder's Child* (New York: Bluejay Books, 1984), p. 134. **579** "Looking for: Williamson, *Wonder's Child*, p. 135. **580** "The seetee: Ibid. **580** "the so-called: George O. Smith, op. cit., p. 4. **581** "Hoping...not: Ibid. **581** "Sixa" and "Seilla" and "Ynamre": Cleve Cartmill, "Deadline," in Groff Conklin, ed., *The Best of Science Fiction* (New York: Crown, 1946), pp. 68, 71, et passim. **582** "I told: Will F. Jenkins, in Dick Eney, ed., *The Proceedings; Discon* (Chicago: Advent, 1965), p. 75. **583** "infinity drive": A.E. van Vogt, *The Weapon Makers*, *Astounding*, March 1943, p. 114. **584** "'restless and: A.E. van Vogt, *The Weapon Makers*, *Astounding*, February 1943, p. 19. **584** "an independent: Ibid, p. 13. **584** "No-man": Ibid, p. 10, et passim. **584** "striking appearance: Ibid, p. 20. **585** "he is: A.E. van Vogt, in the synopses of *The Weapon Makers*, *Astounding*, March 1943, p. 96, and April 1943, p. 94. **585** "'a stabilizing: A.E. van Vogt, *The Weapon Makers*, *Astounding*, April 1943, p. 109. **585** "'I am: Ibid. **585** "'Everything the: Ibid, p. 110. **586** "'All of: Ibid, p. 126. **586** "'Intelligence type: Ibid, p. 101. **586** "'This much: Ibid, p. 130. **586** "village of: According to the entry "Sevagram" in *The New Encyclopaedia Britannica, Micropaedia*, Vol. 10 (Chicago: Encyclopaedia Britannica, 1987), p. 664. **587** Henry Kuttner was born: No adequate account of the life of Henry Kuttner exists. The best to date is in Sam Moskowitz, *Seekers of Tomorrow* (Cleveland and New York: World, 1966). **587** "rotten start": John W. Campbell, letter to Isaac Asimov, dated April 6, 1958, in Perry A. Chapdelaine, Sr., Tony Chapdelaine and George Hay, eds., *The John W. Campbell Letters*, Vol. 1 (Franklin, Tennessee: AC Projects, 1985), p. 338. **588** "the terrible: Ibid. **588** "Hank's basic: C.L. Moore, "Introduction," in Henry Kuttner, *Fury* (New York: Lancer, n.d.), pp. 5-6. **588** "'The most treacherous: Ibid, p. 5. **590** "We collab-orated: Ibid, p. 6. **590** "They worked: George O. Smith, op. cit., p. 31. The story was "Vintage Season" by Lawrence O'Donnell, *Astounding*, September 1946. **591** "After we'd: C.L. Moore, op. cit., p. 6. **592** "'indestructible'": Henry Kuttner, "Deadlock," in Kuttner, *Ahead of Time* (New York: Ballantine, 1953), p. 163, et passim. **592** "the sort: Ibid, p. 167. **592** "The gadget: Ibid, p. 173. **593** "his job: Henry Kuttner, "The Twonky," in *The Best of Henry Kuttner* (New York: Ballantine, 1975), p. 168. **593** "'Great Snell!'": Ibid, p. 169. **594** "Subject basically: Ibid, p. 188. **594** "There was:

Lewis Padgett, "Time Locker," in Raymond J. Healy and J. Francis McComas, eds., *Famous Science-Fiction Stories: Adventures in Time and Space* (New York: Modern Library, 1957), p. 286.   **595** "He could: Ibid.   **595** "'I think: Ibid, p. 287.   **595** "spiky sort: Ibid, p. 290.   **595** "'I suppose: Ibid.   **595** "the shape: Ibid, p. 298.   **595** "A grotesque: Ibid.   **596** "'I guess: Ibid, p. 307.   **597** "Flames licked: Henry Kuttner, "Mimsy Were the Borogoves," in *The Best of Henry Kuttner*, p. 4.   **597** "a maze: Ibid, p. 17.   **597** "a tesseract": Ibid, p. 8.   **597** "'I did: Ibid, p. 9.   **597** "'Let's suppose: Ibid, p. 20.   **597** "'This is: Ibid, p. 31.   **598** "The children: Ibid, p. 33.   **598** "ghastly"..."dead": Ibid, pp. 34-35.   **599** "There's no: Ibid, p. 1.   **599** "some of: Ibid.   **599** "The song: Ibid, p. 32.   **601** "Sometimes he'd: Lewis Padgett, "The Proud Robot," in Padgett, *Robots Have No Tails* (New York: Gnome Press, 1952), p. 7.   **601** "It did: Ibid, p. 22.   **601** "'A positron: Lewis Padgett, "Gallegher Plus," in Padgett, *Robots Have No Tails*, p. 65.   **602** "'Truth will: Lewis Padgett, "The Proud Robot," in Padgett, *Robots Have No Tails*, pp. 34-35.   **603** "'The Lybllas: Lewis Padgett, "The World Is Mine," in Padgett, *Robots Have No Tails*, p. 148-149.   **604** "'What's vastened?': Lewis Padgett, "The Proud Robot," in Padgett, *Robots Have No Tails*, p. 29.   **604** "'You were: Ibid, p. 48.   **606** "This was: Albert Hofmann, *LSD, My Problem Child: Reflections on Sacred Drugs, Mysticism, and Science* (Los Angeles: Tarcher, 1983), p. 14.   **607** "All my: A.E. van Vogt, "My Life Was My Best Science Fiction Story," in Martin H. Greenberg, ed., *Fantastic Lives: Autobiographical Essays by Notable Science Fiction Writers* (Carbondale and Edwardsville, Illinois: Southern Illinois University Press, 1981), p. 199.   **607** "That night: Ibid.   **610** "Science-fiction stories: Fredric Brown, "Introduction," in Brown, *Space On My Hands* (New York: Bantam, 1953), pp. 1-2.   **610** "'I'm an: Fredric Brown, "Paradox Lost," in Brown, *Paradox Lost* (New York: Berkley, 1974), pp. 19-20   **610** "'Yow!' said: Ibid, p. 20.   **611** "'We always: Ibid, p. 21.   **611** "'Huh? Oh,: Ibid, pp. 22-23.   **611** "'Is this: Ibid, p. 25.   **612** "'A struthiomimus!': Ibid, pp. 25-26.   **612** "He looked: Ibid, p. 27.   **613** "'a throwback: Fritz Leiber, Jr., "Sanity," in Groff Conklin, ed., *Big Book of Science Fiction* (New York: Crown, 1950), p. 523.   **613** "'the training: Ibid, p. 525.   **614** "'For instance: Ibid, p. 527.   **614** "'it went: Ibid, p. 528.   **614** "'One hundred,': Ibid, p. 530.   **614** "'As if: Ibid.   **614** "'For ten: Ibid, p. 531.   **615** "'You interested: Ibid, p. 532.   **616** "Outwardly, Jack: Lester del Rey, "Kindness," in Sam Moskowitz, ed., *Modern Masterpieces of Science Fiction* (New York and Cleveland: World, 1965), p. 232.   **616** "Homo intelligens: Ibid, pp. 231-232.   **616** "'I wonder: Ibid, p. 247.   **617** "The first: Murray Leinster, "First Contact," in John W. Campbell, Jr., ed., *The Astounding Science Fiction Anthology* (New York: Simon & Schuster, 1952), p. 223.   **618** "'There was: Ibid, p. 246.   **618** the Lesser Magellanic Cloud: in the book version of these stories, *The Mixed Men* (New York: Gnome, 1952), this is changed to the Greater Magellanic Cloud.   **619** "'cold and: A.E. van Vogt, "The Storm," in Isaac Asimov and Martin H. Greenberg, eds., *Isaac Asimov Presents the Great SF Stories, Vol. 5, 1943* (New York: DAW Books, 1981), p. 250.   **619** "'Excellency, we: Ibid, p. 243.   **620** "pantropy": this word would not be used in "Sunken Universe," but would appear in a collection of stories that was united by this idea, and included this story: James Blish, *The Seedling Stars* (New York: Gnome Press, 1957), p. 8, et passim.   **621** "Lopers": Clifford D. Simak, "Desertion," in Groff Conklin, ed., *Big Book of Science Fiction*, p. 416, et passim.   **621** "thought symbols: Ibid,

p. 420.   **621** "He, Fowler: Ibid, p. 422.   **621** "'It's our: Ibid, p. 421.
622 "'We're still: Ibid.   **622** "'I can't: Ibid, p. 423.   **622** "They were:
Chester S. Geier, "Environment," in Groff Conklin, ed., *Omnibus of Science
Fiction* (New York: Crown, 1952), p. 329.   **622** "Watching, Gaynor: Ibid,
p. 331.   **623** "The machines: Ibid, p. 338.   **623** "'The Third: Ibid.
624 "impedimenta of: Ibid, p. 340.   **625** "Despite all: A.E. van Vogt,
The Weapon Makers, Astounding, March 1943, p. 97.   **625** "--God made:
A.E. van Vogt, in an unpublished manuscript entitled "Systematic Thought
Number Three: Getting Ideas Through Dreaming," pp. 10-11. The original order
of the last two paragraphs is reversed for narrative coherence.   **628** "There
simply: A.E. van Vogt, *World of Null-A, Astounding*, August 1945, p. 174.
628 "*unintegrated* men": A.E. van Vogt, *World of Null-A, Astounding*,
October 1945, p. 157.   **628** "'Haven't you: Ibid, p. 171.   **628** "Analogically,
this: A.E. van Vogt, "Author's Introduction," in van Vogt, *The World of Null-A*
(New York: Berkley, 1970), p. 9.   **628** "go-sane": Ibid, p. 11.   **628** "extra-
brain": A.E. van Vogt, *World of Null-A, Astounding*, September 1945, p. 89,
et passim in the October installment.   **628** "'The evidence: Ibid, September
1945, p. 28.   **629** "He died: Ibid, p. 30.   **629** "'like a: Ibid, p. 25.
629 "'I nourished: A.E. van Vogt, *World of Null-A, Astounding*, October 1945,
p. 178.   **629** "'I was: A.E. van Vogt, *The World of Null-A* (New York:
Berkley, 1970), p. 189.   **632** "'Is there: Isaac Asimov, *In Memory Yet
Green* (Garden City, N.Y.: Doubleday, 1979), p. 394.   **632** "'That will:
Robert Heinlein, quoted in ibid.   **632** "Since Bob: Asimov, ibid.   **632** "Some-
one new: Ibid.   **632** "'Gentlemen, I: Ibid.   **634** "'The Empire: Isaac
Asimov, *Foundation*, p. 224, in Asimov, *The Foundation Trilogy* (Garden City,
N.Y.: Doubleday, n.d.).   **634** "'Siwenna, yes.: Ibid, p. 189.   **634** "'You
see: Ibid, p. 204.   **634** "'And time: Ibid.   **634** "'The whole: Ibid, p. 224.
637 "'You tried: Isaac Asimov, *Foundation and Empire*, pp. 76-77, in Asimov,
The Foundation Trilogy.   **637** "'What keeps: Ibid, p. 77.   **638** "As I:
Isaac Asimov, *In Memory Yet Green*, p. 400.   **638** "I was: Ibid, p. 415.
639 "'Consolidated's machines: Isaac Asimov, "Escape!" in Asimov, *I, Robot*
(Garden City, N.Y.: Doubleday, n.d.), p. 149.   **639** "slyly": Ibid, p. 156.
639 "'Strictly speaking: Ibid, pp. 167-168.   **641** "an excellent: Isaac
Asimov, *Foundation and Empire*, p. 94, in Asimov, *The Foundation Trilogy*.
641 "'Every vice: Ibid, p. 88.   **642** "'Let us: Ibid, p. 149.   **643** "'A
mutant: Ibid, pp. 158-159.   **643** "'Its significance: Ibid, pp. 209-210.
644 "'Foundation Number: Ibid, p. 213.   **644** "'I am: Ibid, p. 216.
645 "'Visi-Sonor'": Ibid, p. 138, et passim. On page 148 given as "Sono-Visor."
645 "'We have: Ibid, p. 226.

AFTERWORD

648 "'Oh, my: John Campbell, quoted in George O. Smith, *Worlds of George O.*
(New York: Bantam, 1982), p. 66.

SUPPLEMENTAL BIBLIOGRAPHY

Campbell, Joseph. *The Hero With a Thousand Faces* (Cleveland, Ohio: Meridian, 1956).

————. *The Masks of God*, 4 vols. (New York: Viking, 1959, 1962, 1964, 1968).

Corbin, Henry. *Creative Imagination in the Sufism of Ibn 'Arabi* (Princeton, N.J.: Princeton University Press, 1969).

Day, Donald B. *Index to the Science-Fiction Magazines 1926-1950* (Portland, Oregon: Perri Press, 1952).

Ibn 'Arabi, Muhyiddin. "The Earth Which Was Created From What Remained of the Clay of Adam," in Henry Corbin, *Spiritual Body and Celestial Earth: From Mazdean Iran to Shi'ite Iran* (Princeton, N.J.: Princeton University Press, 1977).

Panshin, Alexei and Cory. "Science Fiction and the Dimension of Myth," in *Extrapolation*, Summer 1981, Vol. 22, No. 2.

————. *SF in Dimension: A Book of Explorations*, 2nd ed. (Chicago: Advent, 1980).

Tuck, Donald H. *The Encyclopedia of Science Fiction and Fantasy through 1968*, 3 vols. (Chicago: Advent, 1974, 1978, 1982).